KALE AKTE,
THE FAIR PROMONTORY

UNIVERSITY OF BRITISH COLUMBIA
STUDIES IN THE ANCIENT WORLD
VOLUME 3

KALE AKTE, THE FAIR PROMONTORY

Settlement, Trade and Production on the Nebrodi coast of Sicily, 500 BC – AD 500

ADAM LINDHAGEN

With a Foreword by R. J. A. Wilson
and an Appendix by Anders Lindahl

OXBOW | books
Oxford & Philadelphia

for the Department of Classical, Near Eastern and Religious Studies
University of British Columbia

UBC Studies in the Ancient World: Volume 3
Series editor: R. J. A. Wilson

Published in the United Kingdom in 2020 by
OXBOW BOOKS
The Old Music Hall, 106–108 Cowley Road, Oxford OX4 1JE

and in the United States by
OXBOW BOOKS
1950 Lawrence Road, Havertown, PA 19083

Published by Oxbow Books on behalf of the Department of
Classical, Near Eastern and Religious Studies
University of British Columbia, Vancouver BC, Canada

Hardback edition: 978-1-78925-250-7
Digital Edition: 978-1-78925-251-4
A CIP record for this book is available from the British Library

Library of Congress Control Number: 2020938929

Designed and typeset by Charlotte Westbrook Wilson
Printed in the United Kingdom by CLOC Ltd

For a complete list of Oxbow titles, please contact:

UNITED KINGDOM
Oxbow Books
Telephone (01865) 241249
Email: oxbow@oxbowbooks.com
www.oxbowbooks.com

UNITED STATES OF AMERICA
Oxbow Books
Telephone (610) 853-9131
Fax (610) 853-9146
Email: queries@casemateacademic.com
www.casemateacademic.com/oxbow

Oxbow Books is part of the Casemate Group

Contents

Foreword, *by R. J. A. Wilson* vii
Preface and acknowledgements ix

1 The settlements 1
2 The territory: resources and communications 29
3 Archaeological research at Caronía and Marina di Caronía 42
4 The material evidence 65
5 Patterns of production and supply 106
6 Trading mechanisms: market and state 125
7 From trading post to rural village 144

Riassunto italiano 152

Appendix 1 Methodological problems and quantification of finds 160
Appendix 2 Thin-section analyses of selected amphorae, *by Anders Lindahl* 168
Appendix 3 Catalogue of amphora fabrics 177
Appendix 4 Catalogue of finds 180

Notes 203
Bibliography 228
List of illustrations 242
Index 247

Foreword

by R. J. A. Wilson

The notion of the Greek *polis* in Sicily immediately conjures up images of the great urban centres, such as Syracuse, Agrigento and Selinunte, with their magnificent temples and their powerful defences. There were, of course, many other Greek colonies in Sicily which have left physical traces that are less well preserved, but in time, as the indigenous hill-top settlements of the interior began to take on both the trappings and the physical appearance of Greek cities, a process completed during the Hellenistic period, the term *polis* came to be applied to many more urban centres which had not in origin been Greek *apoikiai*. Kale Akte, the subject of this book, is one of the smaller examples of such towns. It was also a unique one, in that when Greek settlers arrived under Ducetius in the middle of the fifth century BC, in what had been up to then a wholly native Sikel centre, it became a unique experiment of a formalised hybrid settlement of Greeks and natives living together. By placing this small hill-top settlement and its accompanying harbour village under such an intense microscope, Adam Lindhagen has provided us with a detailed study of a Greek *polis* of the small-scale variety, a welcome corrective to the emphasis for so long placed, understandably, on the major ancient cities of the island. By following the story through to the threshold of the Byzantine age, he has provided us with a vivid insight into the trials and tribulations, the ups and downs, of this modest settlement on the north Sicilian shore over the course of nearly a thousand years.

When I first visited the site of Kale Akte in 1973, there was nothing ancient to see apart from the remains of a Roman cistern (colour plates 13–14). The first edition of Moses Finley's *Ancient Sicily* had been published just five years before, and he had championed Adamesteanu's view that Kale Akte was to be sought not under the modern hill-town of Caronía, but on an adjacent site in the countryside immediately to the east; so I did not then linger long in Caronía itself. How things have changed nearly fifty years on! Excavations conducted by the Soprintendenza dei Beni Culturali of Messina, first directed by Maria Costanza Lentini and then later by Carmela Bonanno, both at Caronía and at Marina di Caronía, together with the observations of a local *appassionato*, Francesco Collura, have dramatically revolutionised our knowledge of the site. Not only is Kale Akte now known to lie underneath the medieval and modern hill-top town, but much more has also been learnt, thanks largely to a major excavation in *contrada* Pantano, of the coastal village which lay close to a small natural harbour. This book provides a detailed account of all these excavations and what they tell us about the history of the settlement in antiquity.

But it is also much more than that. The author played a major part in the excavations led by Dr Lentini, and the book is therefore written with first-hand knowledge of the site and its material. While most Sicilian excavation reports now include a selection of finds to accommodate the publication of the structures found, such works usually comprise, with a few notable exceptions, only a very small selection of what was actually found. Adam Lindhagen, by contrast, has examined every fragment found in the excavations at which he was present; he knows, as every good archaeologist knows, that even the smallest and most unremarkable body-sherd of pottery has potentially a story to tell. He also possesses the rare skill to recognize the form and fabric of different classes of pottery, and above all to distinguish the myriad different sorts of amphorae that are present at Kale Akte, as they are at most archaeological sites. Unfortunately, it is the very rarity of pottery specialists with this sort of expertise, across the whole of the Mediterranean, that leaves all too often detailed examination of excavated material languishing unstudied, unloved and sometimes even unwashed in archaeological store-rooms. Not all the different fabrics can be assigned an *origo* from visual inspection alone, and this book contains a series of microphotographs of polished thin-sections, as well as a detailed laboratory analysis, in order to distinguish what are likely to be the locally made amphorae from the imported ones.

While such thin-sectioning has become more common in some recent Sicilian archaeological publications, one other aspect of the present book has not. Nearly twenty years ago, John Davies wrote about Hellenistic amphorae as follows: 'My overall impression is that the potential yield of valuable information is enormous, but that the data are far from having been worked over enough for them to be usable in the short run by the non-specialist economic historian' (in Archibald et al. 2001, 20). During the late sixties and seventies of the last century, quantitative analysis was all the rage, especially on large and well-funded excavations, but funding cuts and shortage of expertise has seen less emphasis on it in recent decades. Kale Akte is, therefore, fortunate in having an expert in Adam Lindhagen who had the patience as well as the skill to conduct a quantitative analysis of the material excavated. Of course, one would always like a larger sample to ensure the greater reliability of the conclusions reached, but the author has been able to verify his overall assumptions by close examination also of the material excavated during the later enlargement of one of the same excavation areas (in 2003–05). What has emerged from this painstaking work has been an awareness of the comparative importance of the presence of one type of amphora over another at any one given period, and the ability therefore to provide an outline sketch of the economic history of Kale Akte over a period of many centuries. Let us hope that other excavations in Sicily and elsewhere can mobilise the skills and the funding necessary for others to follow in the footsteps of the author of this book, and to write further comparable and no doubt varied contributions to the economic history of ancient Sicily.

R. J. A. Wilson
Centre for the Study of Ancient Sicily,
University of British Columbia, Vancouver
May 2020

Preface and acknowledgements

Many people have contributed to the present work, which is a revised and greatly extended version of my PhD dissertation, successfully defended at Lund University in 2006.

For the publication of the present work, first and foremost, I am deeply indebted to the series editor, Roger Wilson, Director of the Centre for the Study of Ancient Sicily at the University of British Columbia, Vancouver, and the undisputed authority on Roman Sicily. He was the external examiner of my dissertation, and encouraged me to publish a revised version of it. I am truly honoured and grateful for his kind support, and for helping me to publish the dissertation in his series 'UBC Studies in the Ancient World' with Oxbow Books, for his valuable comments and suggestions, and for his hard work in editing and improving both text and illustrations. Warm thanks also to Charlotte Westbrook Wilson for her diligent and patient work on the elegant layout. I am very grateful for generous contributions from Åke Wibergs stiftelse and the University of Stockholm's Birgitta Bergquists stipendiefond, without which this publication would not have been possible. I am indebted to Ilia Marraffa for improving the Italian summaries of each chapter, and to Bjørn-Håkon Eketuft Rygh and Stian Finmark for some of the plans and drawings. Ingvild Tinglum Bøckman contributed towards editing the illustrations of Appendix Four. Francesco Collura, a native *caronese*, through his passion for local archaeology and his impressive knowledge of the territory, has also made a valued input to the present work, and I thank him for his generosity and friendship. Our excursions around the beautiful landscape of the Nebrodi has greatly improved my knowledge of the territory.

This book would, of course, never have been possible to write at all if it were not for the excavations on which it is based. I am above all indebted to Maria Costanza Lentini, formerly of the Soprintendenza dei Beni Culturali e Ambientali di Messina, director of the Museo archeologico di Naxos, and later director of the Polo Museale at Catania, who generously gave me permission to study the material from Caronia, and as the initiator of the excavations at Caronia therefore made this study possible. It was also thanks to her forethought that the material was transferred to the Museo archeologico at Giardini Naxos, where it was possible to study it under very privileged conditions, both from a professional and a personal point of view.

In connection with the original PhD dissertation, which constitutes the basis for the present work, I am deeply indebted to my tutor, Professor Emerita Eva Rystedt, for her generous help and support, to Anders Lindahl, who generously offered me his help in the ceramic laboratory, and who made an important contribution to this book with his thin-section analysis of the amphorae which appears here as Appendix Two. Warm thanks are also due also to Salvatore ('Totó') Serio, Salvatore Artino, Rossella Pace, Kristian Göransson, Lars Karlsson, Anne-Marie Leander-Touati, Paola Pelagatti, Concetta Marano, Shelley Stone, Malcolm Bell, Carmela Bonanno, Archer Martin, Gloria Olcese, Fabrizio Sudano, Arja Karivieri, Carole Gillis, Karen Slej, Paavo Roos, Bengt Pettersson, Dominic Ingemark and Håkon Roland, all of whom contributed in different ways to the original thesis.

The Swedish Institute in Rome played a fundamental role in my doctoral research. Apart from arranging my first contacts with Sicily, it has always been a warm and welcoming oasis in Rome, almost a second home. I spent a whole year there as a holder of a full scholarship in 2002–03, in addition to innumerable shorter stays; access to the library and its wealth of books were crucial for the preparation and completion of the thesis. My warmest thanks go to the entire staff of the Institute for their help and assistance through the years.

The following funds generously made contributions to enable the PhD dissertation to be completed: Helge Ax:son-Johnsons stiftelse; Torsten och Ingrid Gihls stiftelse; Enboms donationsfond; Svenska Rominstitutets vänner; Stiftelsen Bokelunds resestipendiefond; Uno Otterstedts fond; Nilsson-Aschans släktstipendium; Ryttmästare J. L. Aschans släktfond; Gunvor och Josef Anérs stiftelse.

My mother, Anne Rifbjerg Lindhagen, has offered her constant support during the ups and downs of this work. I am especially indebted to my late father, Nils Lindhagen, who, although he never lived to follow my university studies, always inspired me with his energy and passion for the humanities and the past.

Finally, I want to thank my wife Marina Prusac Lindhagen. Only her assistance made the completion of the dissertation possible. Apart from helping to organise a distracted mind, she created most of the drawings, assisted me in my work in the shadow of Mount Etna and among the lemon groves of Naxos, and generously shared her knowledge on everything from Roman portraits to oil lamps. Furthermore, she has had to put up with this book for far longer than she deserves. I dedicate it to her and to our little miracle, Emanuel, who gives his parents such happiness and joy every single day.

Adam Lindhagen
Askim, Norway
April 2020

NOTE TO READER
The name of the settlement which is the subject of this study went through many changes over the centuries, and its spelling varies widely in modern research: Kale Akte, Kalè Akté, Kaleakte, Kaleakté, Caleacte, Calacte, Kalacte, Calacta. The question becomes even more confusing because of the fact that in mid- and late Imperial times, the maritime settlement inherited the name of the former polis *situated on the hill-top, but with a slight change in spelling (the last four alternatives listed above). I have consequently chosen the original Greek form, Kale Akte, for the reason of simplicity without accents, both for the hill-top urban centre, but also for the site in a general sense, over time. However, for the maritime settlement, the* statio, *which continued after the abandonment of the hill-top from about the second to the fifth centuries AD, I have generally used the name Calacte, following that given to it in the Antonine Itinerary of the third and fourth century AD, and by later itineraries. I sometimes for variety use the modern name Caronía to refer to the hill-town or to both hill-town and maritime settlement together, but Marina di Caronía is reserved exclusively for the latter.*

1

The settlements

The identification of Kale Akte

The modern town of Caronía on the north coast of Sicily is usually identified as the site of the ancient town Kale Akte, founded according to literary sources by the exiled former Sikel leader Ducetius in 446 BC. Caronía enjoys a very advantageous, strategic position on a steeply sloping hill *c.* 304 m above sea level (Fig. 1.1). Thanks to its location, the hill-site controlled the ancient major route connecting urban centres along the north coast of the island, and so also enjoyed direct links stretching from Capo Peloro, at the south-eastern tip of Sicily, all the way to Lilybaeum (modern Marsala) on the west coast (Figs 1.2–3). There have been several different opinions about the exact location of the city supposedly founded by Ducetius. The historian Fazello already in the sixteenth century mentioned ruins at the site of Marina di Caronía *ad aedem Annunciatae circa Caroniae littora*, but identified the site with the ancient Halaesa.[1] At the beginning of the seventeenth century, however, the German geographer Phillip Klüver became the first to identify Marina di Caronía, the maritime counterpart to Caronía, with Kale Akte.[2] Since then both Caronía and Marina di Caronía have remained the firm focus of scholars interested in the location of Kale Akte. Dinu Adamesteanu investigated a high plateau (*contrada* Trapiessi) immediately to the east of Caronía in 1961, identifying through aerial photography what he interpreted as the remains of fortifications. This led him to formulate the hypothesis that this hill-top was the actual site of Ducetius' Kale Akte.[3] Adamesteanu's hypothesis has, however, been shown to be false.[4] In 1982 a short rescue excavation was carried out at Marina di Caronía, uncovering the badly preserved walls of a building.[5] Only from the early 1990s has attention been paid in earnest to Caronía and Kale Akte, witnessed by a series of excavation campaigns conducted by the Soprintendenza per i Beni Culturali di Messina.[6] The campaigns in 1993–

Fig. 1.1. The hill-town Caronía, ancient Kale Akte, seen from the west

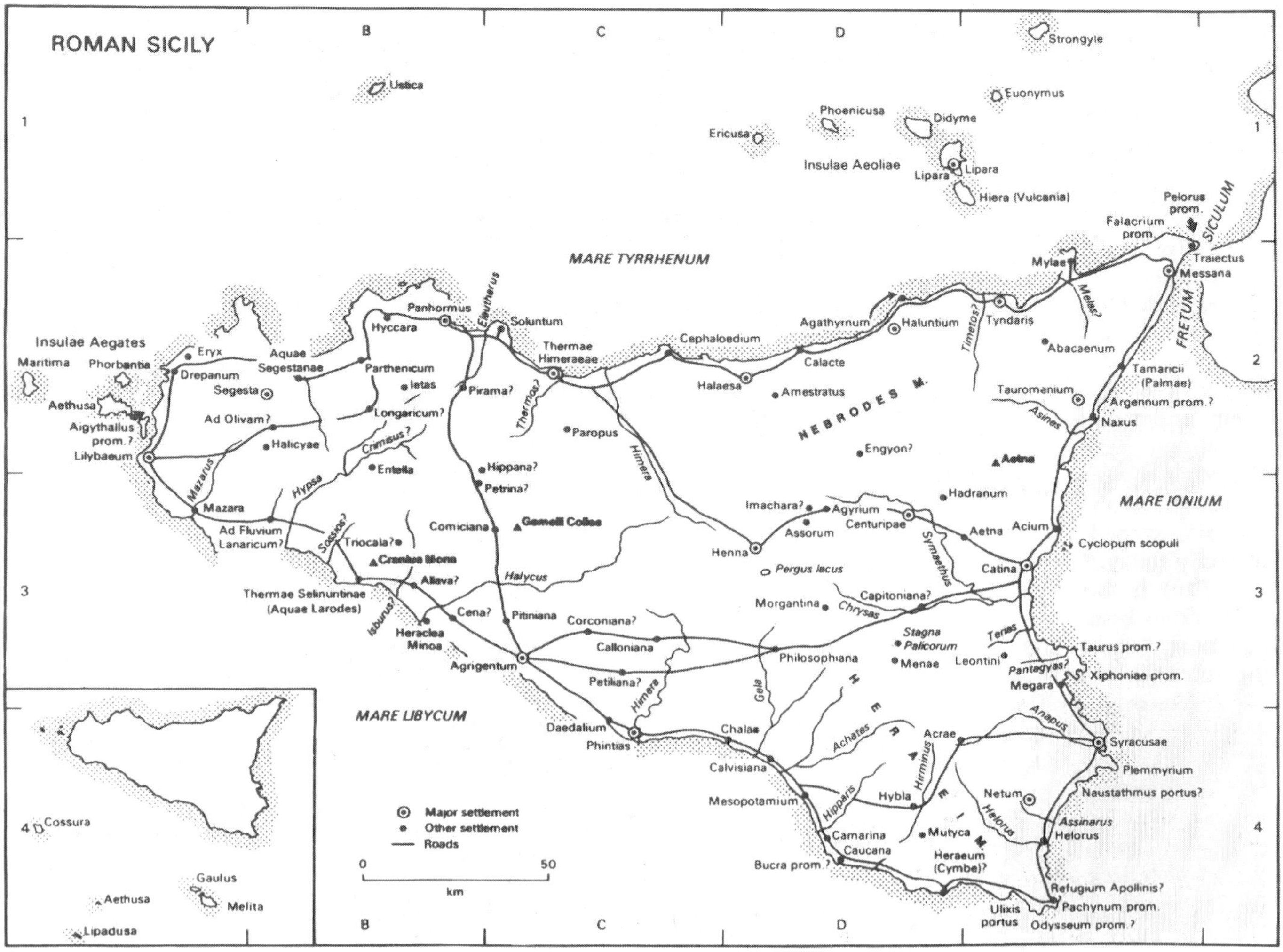

Fig. 1.2 Map of ancient Sicily

Fig. 1.3. The north coast of Sicily as seen from a satellite, indicating the locations of ancient towns

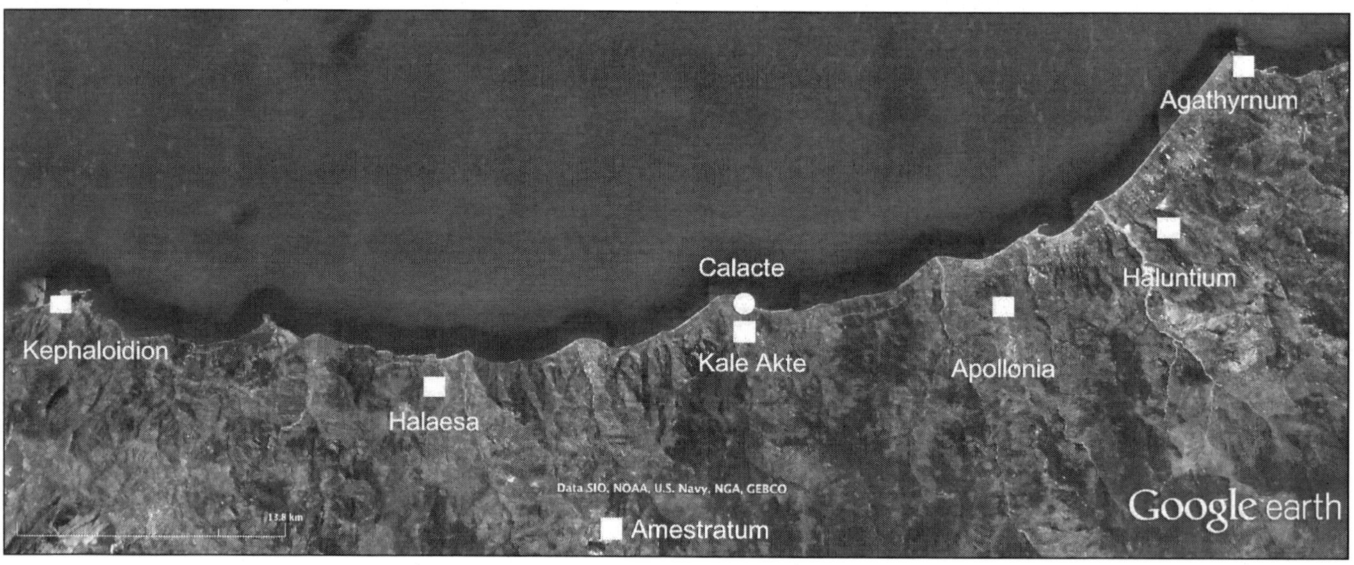

1999 and 2005 in *contrade* Telegrafo and Sotto San Francesco resulted in the discovery of an urban settlement on the hill-top of Caronía dating from the fourth century BC to the first century AD, when several Hellenistic terrace walls and cisterns were uncovered. The latest, and also the most extensive, excavations (in both 1999 and 2005) have concentrated on the ancient maritime settlement at Marina di Caronía.[7]

With the archaeological material available to us today from excavation and field survey, it is possible to confirm finally that the identification of the settlement founded by Ducetius in 446 BC with the hill-town of Caronía is correct. The most important evidence is probably that based on numismatic finds. Coins from the mint of Kale Akte (22 finds) constitute more than a quarter of the identified Hellenistic coins found at Marina di Caronía and Caronía, and all five series known to have been issued by the Kale Akte mint are represented in the excavated material.[8] Other *poleis* are represented only by one or two coins each except, of course, for the prolific mint of Syracuse, which is represented by 19 coins. In addition, two brick-stamps bearing letters which have been interpreted as an abbreviation of the name of the town have been found, one at Marina di Caronía, another in the territory of Caronía.[9] This clear numismatic and epigraphic evidence can be added to the testimony of the Roman road handbooks: the road distances given by the latter fit well with the identification of Caronía as Kale Akte.[10]

The Samos and Miletos joint settlement project[11]

Herodotus mentions an invitation in 494 BC by the city of Zancle to fugitive Ionians to settle at a place on the north coast of Sicily, known as 'Fair Coast' or 'Fair Promontory'.[12] The Samians and Miletians accepted the invitation and left the coast of Asia Minor for Sicily. However, when they had reached Lokri, they were persuaded by the tyrant of Rhegion, Anaxilaos, to found instead a new settlement at Zancle, while his enemies, the Zancleans, were away busy besieging a Sicilian town elsewhere. The Samians and Miletians, therefore, abandoned the project to sail on to Kale Akte but instead took control of Zancle. It is uncertain whether Herodotus, in mentioning Kale Akte, is referring to a general stretch of coastline or is using a precise toponym of a particular site. The Miletians would not have accepted the proposal to found a settlement so far from the motherland unless a secure location had already been chosen by the Zancleans, who would have had, of course, good knowledge of the north coast of Sicily. The finds from Marina di Caronía (*contrada* Pantano) leave little doubt that this site must have hosted a harbour already by the second half of the sixth century BC, and trading activity can possibly be traced even further back, to the end of the seventh century.[13] The daughter foundation of Zancle, Himera, was founded according to tradition in 649 BC, but this lies some 170 km from Zancle. The cove at Marina di Caronía (in antiquity there was possibly also a protected harbour for ships with an artificial quay) is the most sheltered available along the whole stretch of north coast between Zancle's satellite settlement of Mylai (Milazzo) to the east, and Cefalù to the west. More or less halfway between Zancle and Himera, Caronía would have been a perfect port of call for the Greek ships on this (probably very busy) route for seaborne commerce. The Zanclean messengers sent to Ionia would certainly have had detailed information about this small port on the Sicilian north coast, because they knew it well, had trading contacts with it, and would already have found the Sikel inhabitants there friendly and welcoming. The only other possibility for shelter between Milazzo and Cefalù was at Tindari (Tyndaris), but the latter provided no more than a number of very small bays capable of accommodating only a few ships.

Today's settlement of Marina di Caronía is clustered around a shallow bay (Figs 1.4–5; colour Pl. 4). The shore-line here seems to be the same as that in antiquity, but it was probably not the location of the principal port. The deepest part of the bay, which would have been the natural choice for sheltered mooring, was in Hellenistic times occupied by a necropolis,[14] and no buildings associated with a harbour have been found there. Rather, this area must have represented the easternmost outskirts of the settlement, since in antiquity cemeteries were always situated outside the limits of the inhabited area. The area of *contrada* Di Noto, which has not so far been explored archaeologically, has plentiful surface pottery dating back at least to the late Classical period,[15] and there are further finds of Archaic and Classical date in *contrada* Pantano. These suggest that ships would have anchored not only on the eastern, sheltered, side of the promontory, but also in an inlet that probably existed in antiquity in the area of today's *contrada* Pantano (Fig. 1.4). If there had not been a suitable anchorage in the *contrada* Di Noto area, protected on the west from currents, the choice of site for a coastal settlement would be puzzling. We should thus imagine some kind of sheltered basin for ships lying to the west of the excavated ancient buildings at *contrada* Pantano. Marina di Caronía is today the best harbour in terms of its position on this stretch of coastline,[16] dominated by an easily defendable hill. The promontory with shelter for ships on both sides would have made it a perfect choice for a

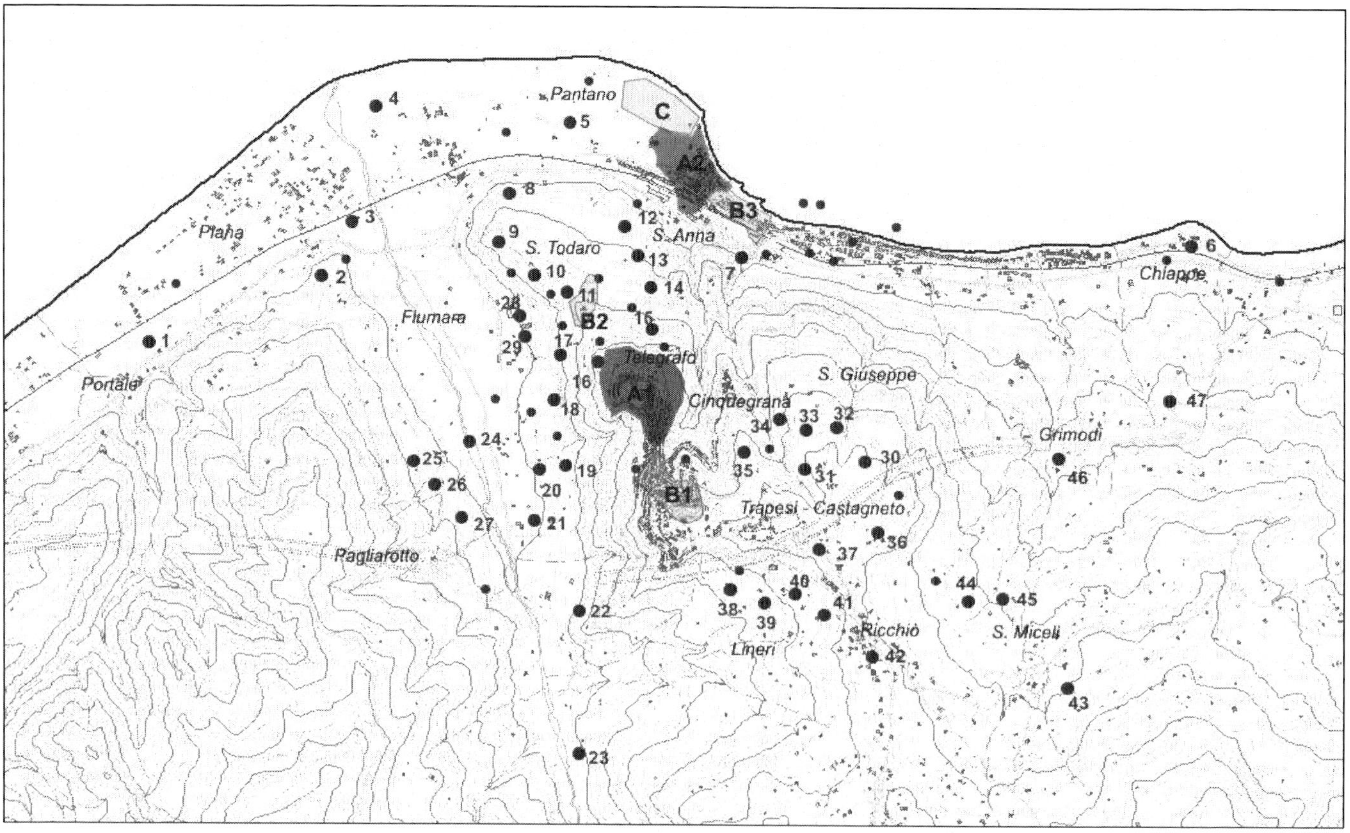

Fig. 1.4. Caronía and Marina di Caronía, map of rural settlements and archaeological discoveries

settlement already before the arrival of the Greeks. As mentioned above, there are signs of a trading post at Marina di Caronía already by the second half of the sixth century BC and possibly earlier, and perhaps by the same date also on the hill-top which dominated the harbour. The later hypothesis is based on unpublished finds from a late Archaic and Classical necropolis in the area of the modern *municipio*, which include a few examples of Sikel pottery of that date.[17] The Zancleans would, of course, not have suggested to the Ionians a site that lacked a decent harbour, and, with the identification of an Archaic trading post at Marina di Caronía, it seems almost certain that Kale Akte referred to a particular place and not the coastline in general here.[18] We do not know if the Sikel population would have been included in this planned settlement. In any case, controlling the wealthy town of Zancle, a vital crossroads of the Mediterranean, was of course much more inviting to the Miletians and Samians than the occupation of a small Sikel settlement, set in a wild landscape a long way from other Greek settlements.

The most straightforward translation of Kale Akte is 'Fair' or 'Beautiful Shore', or 'Fair' or 'Beautiful Coast', in Italian *Bella Costa*, and this has also been the most common interpretation in the scholarly literature.[19] However, a translation of Kale Akte as 'Fair Promontory' or 'Fair Point' is equally possible or even preferable, the primary meaning of ἀκτή meaning 'promontory' or 'point where the waves break'.[20] That would have indicated a precise site, compared with the much more general 'Fair Coast'. The 'Point' would presumably have been the promontory to the west of Marina di Caronía, with its harbour and the plateau (*contrada* San Todaro / Pianu dei Pupiddi), as well as the hill-top occupied by modern Caronía above it. This promontory with its hill must have been an obvious landmark for Greek sailors, just as it still is today (Figs 1.6–7). The nearby settlement of Kephaloidion to the west is an example of how a promontory gave the city its name. There the prominent landmark to sailors was seen as having the shape of a 'head' (in Greek *kefalé*). The example serves to strengthen the hypothesis that the name Kale Akte would also have been derived from a specific and geographically striking natural headland. The name would presumably already have been current in the sixth century BC among Greek merchants, trading with the maritime settlement at Marina di Caronía, long before the invitation was issued to Samians and Miletians to come and settle there. Since no buildings have yet been found which can be identified as part of a settlement of Archaic date,[21] it is not possible to speculate as to whether the harbour was merely a *scalo* (a landing-place) for smaller ships, or whether it also included buildings suitable for permanent habitation.

The hill-top of Caronía above this harbour must surely have had a Sikel settlement. The location was excellent, with a view over a vast part of the north coast and the Aeolian islands; both hill and coastal strip had been settled already in the Bronze Age.[22] Although there is at present no archaeological evidence for a Sikel settlement at the hill-town of Caronía (evidence for it would be deeply sealed beneath the multiple archaeological layers of the late Classical, Hellenistic and early Roman imperial Kale Akte, as well as medieval and modern Caronía), the hill-top represents the typical choice of site for a Sikel settlement. The recently discovered late Archaic/early Classical Sikel *phrourion* at Pizzo Cilona, 2 km south of Caronía, must have been a defensive outpost, of the main nucleus of population at Caronía, designed to protect the hinterland to the south. The harbour at Marina di Caronía, already as we have seen active in the sixth century BC, would not have made sense without a nearby larger settlement controlling it. The notion that Marina di Caronía was in origin a Greek *emporion* can be excluded: the area was in all probability controlled by Sikels. Pizzo Cilona, lacking a good view of the coast, was useless as a protection for this harbour. The hill of Caronía on the other hand is the obvious natural site for a settlement, just as the Classical cities of Haluntium (San Marco d'Alunzio) and Agathyrnon also developed from Sikel settlements in the Iron Age. There is a perfect sight-line between Pizzo Cilona and the hill of Caronía, a point which strengthens the idea that the former was a *phrourion*, probably established soon after the first nucleus of Sikel settlers arrived on the hill of Caronía.[23] No doubt the latter was situated on the uppermost plateau of the hill where the Norman castle stands today (Fig. 1.18, colour Plate 1, and back cover). It is no wonder that no trace of it has yet come to light.

A permanent settlement cannot have existed at an unprotected Marina di Caronía, exposed to perils from both the sea and the land during an insecure age of constant warfare. All Sikel settlements were built on hills. The one at Caronía was easy to defend and

Fig. 1.5. Marina di Caronía, view looking north-westwards

Fig. 1.6. Caronía (left of centre, on the hill) and Marina di Caronía, together with the adjacent coastline, seen from the north-east

enjoyed a perfect view for miles around; an eye could be kept on ships moored below, well in advance of potential trouble. The inhabitants would already have become accustomed to Greek culture by the time of Ducetius in the mid-fifth century, because fifty years previously they had been prepared to welcome Greek settlers, and they had enjoyed imported objects of Greek material culture for a further century before that. We know that an inland Sikel settlement such as Morgantina was already strongly marked by Greek culture by the beginning of the fifth century, and a coastal settlement with a port would naturally have been even more exposed to it. That first the people of Zancle and then later Ducetius chose Kale Akte as a site worth controlling shows that both fully appreciated its advantageous geographical position.

The Samians and Miletians lived in *poleis* which were situated on plains, not hills. It seems probable that the Zancleans had in mind the plateau of the *contrada* of San Todaro (Pianu dei Pupiddi) for the site of the planned settlement, half-way between the sea and the hill of Caronía. The area would have been easy to defend and has easy access to the harbour and a relatively large flat area well-adapted for the lay-out of a regular city plan of Greek type (Figs 1.8–9). Greek settlements in Sicily as well as elsewhere were always planned with a harbour as the main priority (to enable good maritime connections), not a defensive position, which was usually reinforced with strong city walls.

Ducetius by contrast would not have had the same area in mind for his settlement as that intended for the Ionians half a century earlier. He was content with settling on the hill, and in this way creating the *polis* known to us through archaeological finds. If we are to believe the information from Diodorus Siculus, that Ducetius settled Kale Akte between 446 and 440 BC, with a large number of settlers, archaeological traces of such activity should be evident in an area without modern settlement, such as that in *contrada* San Todaro. Investigations have in fact ruled out the presence of any ancient urban centre there.[24] It is therefore very probable that the companions of Ducetius chose to settle on the site of the Sikel village on the hill-top, probably in a redesigned town with a regular, orthogonal street-grid of Greek type;[25] the latter in any case is unlikely to have been present in the Sikel village on the site which preceded Ducetius' activities in the fifth century BC.

Settlements founded by Ducetius prior to Kale Akte

Both Caronía and its maritime settlement, Marina di Caronía, have traditionally been regarded as possible locations of Ducetius' Kale Akte. Archaeological investigations carried out at the beginning of this millennium clearly suggest that the hill-town of Caronía was the site of a Hellenistic *polis*, which (as noted above) we know from coinage and stamps bore the name of Kale Akte. Of urban or quasi-urban settlement preceding the period of Ducetius, however, there are very few traces. This could be explained simply by the fact that the site is overlain by millennia of urban construction, and has so far been explored archaeologically only to a very limited extent. But we must also ask: is Caronía the type of site which would have been attractive for Ducetius' settlement, and how far does its topographical position match other previous settlements founded by him? Diodorus informs us about two possible foundations by Ducetius prior to that of Kale Akte. The first was at Menai, his native town. Since Ducetius originated from there, a settlement must already have existed, as corroborated by archaeological investigations.[26] Nothing has, however, been discovered of a new urban layout at Menai that can be ascribed to the fifth century BC. After the re-foundation of Menai, Cittadella, the predecessor of Morgantina, was seized by the Sikel leader. Some scholars have hypothesised that he would have founded a new city here too, although Diodorus does not mention it. The Morgantina excavators currently think that that city was founded around 450 BC, not by Ducetius, but rather by a mixture of Sikels and Greek settlers.[27] The Sikel sanctuary of Paliké has remains of a settlement on the summit of the hill, which also have been attributed to Ducetius. However, the site has recently been excavated and shown to be a military settlement or fort founded by Dionysius I in the early fourth century BC.[28] This suggests that Ducetius concentrated his efforts on the sanctuary of Paliké, and that he never founded an urban settlement there.[29] The sanctuary was laid out on a series of terraces. Judging

Fig. 1.7. A view of the coast looking eastwards towards Caronía (centre)

Fig. 1.8. The plateau of contrada *San Todaro, presumed site for the intended Ionian settlement in 494 BC*

both by the archaeological evidence and by the description given by Diodorus, it was profoundly Greek in its architecture and lay-out.[30]

Menai was situated on a hill with good strategic and defensive qualities, in accordance with the Sikel tradition. This was also a natural consideration at a time when the Sikels were at war with the Greeks. We know that Ducetius was a Hellenised leader, and he acted in many ways as a Greek tyrant, moving settlements and populations, and founding new cities.[31] It is probable that his 'foundations' in fact were not complete cities established *ex novo*, but consisted of an entirely new influx of people being settled at already inhabited sites, to which fortifications and/or other buildings were added. At Paliké, most attention would have been paid to the sanctuary, which was monumentalised at this period. This was also the political and religious heart of the Sikels, and accordingly would probably have been the focus of the most high-level investment at any of Ducetius's projects. Its construction was also carried out, it should be added, at a time when the Sikel leader was at the height of his power and so would have had large funds at his disposal.

The foundation of Kale Akte and the return of Ducetius

After defeat at the hands of the joint armies of Syracuse and Akragas at Nomai in 451 BC, the Sikel leader escaped to Syracuse where he sought asylum. The city council decided to send him into exile at Corinth.[32] However, only a few years later, Ducetius returned to Sicily to found a settlement on the north coast. The foundation of Kale Akte in 446 BC is mentioned by Diodorus Siculus as being a joint venture between Sikels and Corinthians, guided by the exiled leader in collaboration with the Sikel tyrant of Herbita, Archonides, and legitimised by an oracular response. Having placed a number of new settlers at Kale Akte, Ducetius suddenly died, in 440 BC.[33]

A reply from 'the oracle' to found a settlement 'at the Fair Promontory' (τὴν Καλὴν Ἀκτὴν) was supposedly given as a kind of pretext for the breaking of the agreement between Syracuse and Akragas, which stated that Ducetius was to remain in exile. It has usually been taken for granted that 'the oracle' was that of Apollo at Delphi, but a recent hypothesis has suggested instead that it may have been that of Zeus at

Dodona in Epirus.[34] There has been fierce debate over the problem as to whether Ducetius acted with the consent of Syracuse or rather on his own. Those who have chosen to see the foundation of the new settlement as marking a break with Syracuse underline the phrase in Diodorus that he 'broke the agreement' (τας ὁμολογίας ἔλυσε). The verb λύω can be translated either as its stronger meaning, i.e. 'break', or else as the less strong 'undo' or 'dissolve'. If the latter, then it would imply only that the former agreement was declared null and void, probably with the consent of Syracuse.[35] That the return of Ducetius and the founding of Kale Akte was a delicate political issue is shown by the fact that, immediately afterwards, war broke out between the island's two great powers, Syracuse and Akragas, the latter accusing Syracuse of having allowed their common enemy to return to Sicily from Corinth.[36]

One of the first advocates of the view that Ducetius actively 'broke the agreement', against the wishes of Syracuse, was D. Adamesteanu.[37] He regarded the foundation of Kale Akte and the alliance between Ducetius and Archonides, the latter probably father or grandfather of the founder of the city of Halaesa, as part of a policy against further Greek expansion westwards. Adamesteanu argued that the distance from the Greek cities was one of the main reasons for the location of the new settlement. Here, on the Sikel-dominated northern coast of Sicily, far away from the Greek cities, Ducetius would have been completely undisturbed by Syracusan or Akragantine political influence, with the mountain range of the Nebrodi as a barrier against the Greek-dominated area. Adamesteanu concluded that Ducetius' aim must have been to unite what was left of the Sikel nation, abandoning the eastern parts, since they were by then under strong Syracusan hegemony.[38]

However, as several scholars have noted,[39] it is not very likely that Syracuse would have allowed the exiled Sikel leader to return to Sicily and found a new anti-Syracusan stronghold, especially one located on the strategically important north coast. Two strong arguments can be given in support of a co-operation between Ducetius and Syracuse. Firstly, the fact that war broke out immediately after the return of Ducetius shows that Akragas was clearly infuriated with Syracuse at the turn of events. The fact that Akragas went to war against Syracuse because of the founding of Kale Akte shows clearly that the latter must have had a strong interest in its foundation. The settlement could be interpreted as a means for Syracuse to get an indirect foothold on the north coast, without having to found a daughter settlement of its own – which would have been too great a provocation against Akragas and the Sikel population of the area.[40]

Fig. 1.9. The plateau of contrada *San Todaro, as seen from the site of the ancient harbour*

Through the Sikel leader, Syracuse could appease the Sikel population in the area indirectly, and make it accept the new settlers coming from her own mother city, Corinth.[41] No doubt the Corinthian settlers would have had little interest in living permanently in completely Sikel-dominated territory, under the guidance of a former enemy to their daughter city and to other Greek cities in Sicily, unless the project had been blessed beforehand by Syracuse.

Furthermore, there is no doubt that Ducetius was a very Hellenised Sikel, using Greek policy and being essentially a Greek in his way of acting. He was probably a pragmatic individual rather than a stout idealist in his dealings with the Syracusan aristocracy, as shown by his successful attempt to seek asylum after his defeat. The foundation of Kale Akte provides a very clear example of just how 'Greek' his behaviour was: the Sikel leader uses an oracle (whether at Dodona or Delphi is, as we have seen, uncertain) to legitimise his founding of a new town on the north coast of Sicily, some of whose settlers were to be Greeks. Ducetius had in fact already from the beginning been acting in accordance with Greek tradition, wanting to present himself as an *oikistes*, a founder of new settlements.[42]

The fact that after the death of Ducetius, Kale Akte is not mentioned by the ancient sources until the Late Republican period is a clear indication that the place had little political importance, especially by comparison with its neighbouring towns, which are all mentioned in the sources. Since Ducetius was allowed to return to Sicily thanks to the good will of Syracuse, the Sikel leader could hardly have had much room for political manoeuvre. Rather, he seems to have had Syracuse's interests at heart, controlling Sikel sentiment and hindering the Sikels from taking any action against Syracuse. It is significant that hostility broke out between Syracuse and the Sikels around Paliké only after the death of Ducetius.[43] Obviously, Syracuse would not have allowed the foundation of any settlement that could be conceived as posing a threat. Thus, Kale Akte was founded by the sea, although strategically well situated on a steep hill. It was not as protected as Apollonia and Haluntium to the east, which were formidable strongholds, inaccessible and somewhat back from the coast. The hill on which the settlement of Kale Akte was founded was considerably smaller than that chosen by Ducetius for his previous foundation; it was quite easily accessible from the south, and it was not surrounded by vast fields of rich agricultural lands, as Menai and Paliké were. When Halaesa was founded, around forty years later, a larger hill for the settlement was chosen, with a larger *chora* controlling a more extended plain watered by the Halaisos River. The foundation of Halaesa by itself helps to confirm that Kale Akte did not fully fulfil the criteria for establishing a strong and credible power-base. Archonides must have exercised some control over Kale Akte after the death of Ducetius, since he or his son[44] assisted in its foundation. It is probable in fact that Kale Akte's failure to become an important political actor in the area was a consequence of Ducetius' lack of power after his surrender to the Syracusans. This is perhaps also the main reason why the idea that Ducetius took the lead once more of the Sikel nation after his return to Sicily is unlikely to be correct. He was isolated, and far away from Paliké and the Sikel heartlands where the rebellion against Syracuse began. He controlled a small *polis* which hardly could have been regarded as a viable stronghold, with its unprotected harbour, exposed to the sea and to the potential dangers of the powerful Syracusan fleet. In contrast to Ducetius, Archonides of Herbita, ruler of the most important town in the interior south of the Nebrodi chain, was a strong and autonomous ruler, capable of defying even Syracuse, and could accordingly act without any restrictions: as noted above, he had a hand in the foundation of a city, Halaesa, which in time was to become the most important on the whole of the north coast of Sicily.

The location of the settlement

The choice of the hill of Caronía as the site for his new settlement seems to have been consistent with Ducetius' earlier foundation at Menai. It was also like Menai already inhabited prior to the foundation, and we can thus consider it another 're-foundation', where he probably had to adapt to an already existing inhabited nucleus. How then are we to imagine the first layout of Kale Akte? The foundation of a settlement with a regular city plan would have needed a strong political and economic power. It is probable, however, that Syracuse assisted that financially, since some of the first settlers were Corinthians, from her own mother city. The profoundly Greek character of the sanctuary at Paliké indicates that the city layout of Kale Akte is also likely to have had a predominantly Greek character, probably with a regular street grid. It is impossible to understand, however, how much was achieved over the course of six years, and whether the project even continued after Ducetius' death. Diodorus says that in 440 BC Ducetius 'founded the native city of the Calactians', although he earlier had described the events of the foundation as having taken place in 446 BC.[45] He also adds that when he (Ducetius) had established many colonists there, he laid claim to the leadership of the Sikels, but that he died shortly thereafter, apparently unexpectedly.[46] It is difficult to know what we should make of this passage. It seems somewhat surprising that Ducetius, having been pardoned by Syracuse and allowed to found his own settlement, would once again have taken up arms against Syracuse. Certainly, it is inconceivable that the Corinthian settlers would have had any interest in combining with Sikels in order to wage war together against the Corinthians' own powerful daughter city, Syracuse. We are told that Syracuse controlled all the Sikel towns, except Trinakie (probably identical with Paliké), which was razed to the ground. Kale Akte is not mentioned, something which would certainly not have been the case if it had played a leading role in the rebellion: being the base of Ducetius, it would have been punished harshly by Syracuse. At any rate, it seems certain that the settlement never grew to any significant scale. After the death of Ducetius and the subsequent crushing of the Sikel revolt in eastern Sicily, there can hardly have been any political will at Syracuse to continue with or invest in the project of Kale Akte. The foundation was completely dependent on political cooperation between Sikels and Greeks; when that cooperation broke down, a significant reduction in the strategic importance of the settlement must have followed.

The only way to understand the physical extent of Ducetius' settlement would be to sink deep trenches in the area immediately below the castle and on the uppermost, flat area of the hill of Caronía, which corresponds to the medieval part of the town (colour Pl. 6). Finding traces of fifth-century settlement would obviously be extremely difficult, if not impossible, since above the Archaic and then the Classical deposits are thick layers of, in turn, Hellenistic, early and late Roman, medieval and modern buildings. The small number of finds of fifth-century date from surface survey and from excavations in the harbour area at Marina di Caronía, however, and the total absence of Kale Akte from the ancient sources describing events in the fourth and third centuries BC (especially by comparison with Halaesa), clearly argue against Kale Akte having been a centre of political importance. It is inconceivable that Halaesa would have grown so quickly to become a significant urban centre if Kale Akte, only 17 km away, was still strong, economically and politically. It is even less likely that by the fourth century BC Apollonia, just a few km away to the south-east, would have been established in such a strong position despite its closeness to Kale Akte, if the latter still had influence in the region. Its lower status than Haluntium, even in the late Republican period, suggests that Kale Akte was smaller and also politically less important. If Kale Akte had been an important urban centre by the mid-fifth century BC, before any other urbanisation in the area began, it would surely have played a more important role in the events on the north coast, and have been leading rather than lagging behind other towns in terms of its degree of urbanisation and the size of its population. There is also no doubt, if the amount of archaeological material from the harbour area is an accurate guide, that the population of the late Republican/early Imperial hill-town of Kale Akte considerably exceeded that of the earlier period.

The hypothesis that the absence of any mention of Kale Akte in the sources for late Classical and Hellenistic Sicily indicates a lack of its political strength is not just an argument *ex silentio*. There are several different types of evidence supporting this view. Coinage is one. Haluntium seems to have issued coins already by the first half of the fourth century BC as well as in the Timoleontic period, although on a very restricted scale.[47] Halaesa minted bronze coins by the middle of the fourth century BC, which reflects its connection with the *symmachia* of Timoleon. Kale Akte begins minting coins only in the second century BC as part of the 'Roman' currencies which were introduced then, but issues were, it seems, never in the same quantities as those at Halaesa. Apollonia (until 307 BC), Halaesa and Haluntium are all mentioned in connection with sieges and military campaigns in the area, but not Kale Akte. The constrained area of the hill-top also indicates that the number of inhabitants must have been quite limited. The area of the medieval centre of Caronía, adding the slopes on the east and north, i.e. the area of the town's major expansion in the early Imperial period, measures *c.* 15 ha. R. J. A. Wilson has calculated that in Roman times a normal *insula* on flat ground would measure *c.* 1 ha, and that each *insula* could house 100 individuals, or maybe a few more.[48] Using a higher figure of 150 inhabitants per *insula* for Kale Akte, we would arrive at a maximum population of 2,250 inhabitants.[49] The settlement of Ducetius, which certainly did not expand onto the eastern and northern slopes (in contrast to the late Hellenistic town), must have had a considerably lower population. The upper plateau, identical to the area occupied by the medieval town, measures about half that of its late Hellenistic predecessor, about 8 ha, and thus would have had a maximum population of *c.* 1,200 inhabitants. The true figures were in all probability lower, since not all the urban area was occupied by dwellings: the figures above take no account of space for civic and religious buildings. It seems fair to presume that Kale Akte of the late fifth century BC would have had a population of fewer than 1,000.

Literary and epigraphic sources for the history of Kale Akte

All the known ancient and early medieval literary and epigraphic sources for the settlement and history of Kale Akte are collected below.[50]

446 BC According to Diodorus (12.8.2), the founding of Kale Akte was a joint venture by Ducetius and Archonides of Herbita with Sikel and Corinthian settlers.

440 BC According to a second passage of Diodorus (12.29.1), the founding of Kale Akte was begun only this year, and 'many settlers were established there'. This date seems, however, to be too long after the exiling of Ducetius to Corinth, and does in any case not fit well with the date of the war between Syracuse and Akragas, which broke out in 446 BC supposedly as a consequence of Ducetius' return to Sicily.

440 BC Death of Ducetius (Diod. 12.29.1).

Late third/ early second century BC Honorary inscription from Caronía mentioning an individual, son of Epandros, a benefactor of the *polis*, whose deeds were honoured by the popular assembly (*syngkletos*) and the city council (*boulà*) through a bronze table which was to be deposited in the sanctuary of Apollo. The inscription also mentions an eponymous magistrate, son of Apollodoros (Manganaro 2009; Arena 2016).

Mid-third century BC? The historian Silenos, *ho kallatianos*, 'the one from Kaleacte', author of a history of the Second Punic War and in the service of Hannibal, was born at Kale Akte (Ath. 12.542; Nep. *Hann*. 13.3).

Second half of the second century BC (?) Kale Akte begins minting bronze coins. The mint had ceased to operate by the time of Augustus.

Late second/first century BC Kale Akte is mentioned, together with Halaesa, Herbita and Amestratum, in an inscription from the *agora* of Halaesa, commemorating a naval victory by the allied towns, possibly against pirates (Scibona 1971a, 5–11; Prag and Tigano 2017, 35–8, no. 8).

First century BC Caecilius Calactensis, author of a history of the Sicilian slave wars of the second century BC, was born at Kale Akte. He had a school for rhetoricians in Rome at the time of Augustus, and might possibly be identical with the freed Jewish slave, called Archagathos, mentioned by Plutarch (Ath. 6.272f; 11.466a).

70 BC Contemporary notices by Cicero after his visit to Kale Akte. He tells us about the crimes of Verres, *propraetor* in Sicily, who, when invited to the house of the Calactinian Eupolemos, is said to have stripped off the embossed work on two silver cups put on the table, specially for the occasion (Cic. *Verr.* 2.4.22.49). Kale Akte is mentioned as a *civitas decumana* (Cic. *Verr.* 2.3.43.101).

Mid-first century BC A citizen of Kale Akte, a certain Hippias, the son of Cicero's good friend Philoxenos, and the hospitality at his house, are mentioned in a letter to the family (Cic. *ad Fam*. 13.37).

First century AD Pliny the Elder, in his list of *civitates stipendiariae* in Sicily, records Galacteni (Plin. *HN* 3.91). He was writing around the middle of the first century AD, but his source material is likely in part to date from the Augustan period.

Second century AD Ptolemy lists *Kalakta* together with the cities on the north coast of Sicily in his *Geographia* (Ptol. *Geog*. 3.4.3).

3rd–4th century AD *Calacta* is mentioned as one of the stops along the *via Valeria* in both the *Itinerarium Antonini* and the *Tabula Peutingeriana* (*It. Ant*. 92.4–5; *Tab. Peut*. 7.1; for the latter see here Fig. 2.4). This is the last mention that we have of the place-name which maintains a clear link to the original appellation of Kale Akte.

Early seventh century AD A farm (*massa*) beside the Torrente Furiano, near Caronía, is mentioned in a letter from Pope Gregory the Great, one of 850 he wrote between AD 590 and 604, as the property of the Roman Church. A certain Ianuaria is said to have constructed an *oratorio* there (*Sancti Gregorii Magni Papae Primi Operum Tomus VII*, Rome 1591, 270, n. 85).

Eighth/twelfth century AD A distorted form of the original name, *Calao*, appears in the anonymous author from Ravenna; it was later distorted still further to *Colan* by the twelfth-century geographer Guido (*Ann. Rav.* 5.23.16; Guido 59.4). These geographers based their work on the pre-existing ancient *itineraria* mentioned above, and cannot be regarded as evidence for the existence of Kale Akte at this period.

The Classical period (*c.* 500–320 BC: period A)

Urban settlements

From the promontory of Marina di Caronía one has a splendid view of the area stretching from Capo d'Orlando (Agathyrnum) to the east all the way to Tusa (Halaesa) and the promontory of Cephaloedium (Cefalù) to the west. It is natural that the whole of this area, within sight of Kale Akte, was in many respects very like it in terms of its material culture, having similar if not identical political systems and common traditions. The area around Kale Akte, its 'micro-region', constitutes a natural framework for the understanding of its economic history. All the towns in this region have common geographical features which gave them similar assets and economic bases. The Nebrodi mountain range and its forests constituted an important source of wealth, and also created a barrier towards the interior in times of trouble. The coast, on the other hand, was the uniting factor: the sea was the 'highway' on which goods, ideas and people were transported between networked urban centres in a kind of microcosmos. To the east, this micro-region was dominated by the thoroughly Greek city of Tyndaris. In the west, first Himera, and from the fourth century Cephaloedium, created a similar border, although here it was also cultural, since Cephaloedium was in the hands of the Carthaginians for much of the period before the Roman takeover, and was not part of the Sikel cultural sphere. This was the eastern extremity of the western part of the island, with its Punic heritage, settled and inhabited by Phoenicians and Carthaginians for centuries. The only exception was the Greek city of Himera, which had, however, already been destroyed in 409 BC by the Carthaginians. The Nebrodi area that Kale Akte belonged to was thus a border zone between Greek and Carthaginian influence – an important point to remember in understanding the history of urban settlement in the Nebrodi region.[51]

In the period of the foundation of Kale Akte, i.e., in the second half of the fifth century BC, the area was inhabited by Sikel tribes, controlled by the *dynastes* of Herbita,[52] Archonides. The north coast had to a great extent been ignored by the Greeks, who had taken over the entire eastern and southern shores of the island in settling their new foundations. On the north coast, only Mylai (Milazzo) and to the west Himera, the furthest 'frontier' town, had been founded by Zancle. Off the coast, Lipara had been founded by Cnidian settlers. It has been argued that the exiguous indications of settlement of any sort on the northern coast between Milazzo and Himera could have been due partly to the threat of Etruscan pirates.[53] However, such a scenario seems less likely from the evidence that we now have of a trading post at Kale Akte already in the sixth century BC. It seems more likely that the Greeks were in fact interested in the rich natural resources of the north coast, and traded with the Sikel inhabitants, but that the hilly topography with little arable land and above all absence of good harbours made it a less attractive region for them to colonise. The western part of the north coast was in the hands of the Carthaginians, and the area from east of Cephaloedium as far as Mylai was still inhabited only by Sikels. This was the most rugged and wild part of any of the Sicilian coasts, with endless forests and mountains, limited areas of fertile soil, and only a few good natural harbours. It was no coincidence that this was the last part of Sicily to become Hellenised, and then only indirectly, since none of the towns in the area was a purely Greek settlement.

Less than forty years after the death of Ducetius, in 403 BC, Halaesa was founded by the Sikel leader, Archonides, *c.* 17 km west of Kale Akte, as a direct consequence of the war between Dionysius I and the Carthaginians. The foundation of Halaesa was probably the result of a policy much the same as that promoted by Ducetius before his defeat. It reflects Sikel resistance to Syracusan political and economic dominance in this period. Originally, Halaesa was a settlement for mercenaries who wanted land, and the foundation had from the beginning more political weight than Kale Akte, since it was headed by a leader with a strong power base in the area. The mercenaries' hunger for land also forced the founders to choose a site which controlled a vast and fertile area. The *chora* of Halaesa was larger than that of Kale Akte, and gave better opportunities for growth and future economic and political importance.

The name Halaisa/Halaesa derives from the Greek verb *aleomai*, 'devious fleeing', and gives a clue to the city's function as an asylum for those elements of the population that had been opposed to Syracuse. It was founded on a hill similar to that of Caronía, but more gently sloping towards the east, *c.* 204 m above sea level (Fig. 1.10; colour Pl. 7). Halaesa soon became more important than its declining mother-city, and was

Fig. 1.10. Halaesa, the archaeological site, view from the south

Fig. 1.11. The town of San Marco d'Alunzio (ancient Haluntium), view from the west

Fig. 1.12 The hill of Monte Vecchio di San Fratello, site of ancient Apollonia, seen from the north

joined in a *symmachia* with Timoleon, attested on its coin issues from the middle of the fourth century BC.[54] This league most probably developed as a consequence of the Timoleontic policy to establish alliances with the Sikels in eastern Sicily, so as to unite Greeks and Sikels against the Carthaginians. It is very probable that Kale Akte was part of this *symmachia*, considering the close ties between the two Sikel foundations. As Bernabò Brea and Calciati have pointed out, it is probable that the four centres, of Halaesa, Herbita, Kale Akte and Amestratum, all close to one another, were also united in a smaller, local league or *symmachia*.[55] It seems that in it Halaesa was *primus inter pares* as the dominant urban centre of the micro-region. The political alliance between Kale Akte and Halaesa is important to keep in mind, since both may have had similar political policies and probably also shared economic goals.

The desire for independence from Syracuse is a continuous thread running through the history of Halaesa. As mentioned above, the city was meant to be a Sikel outpost on the Tyrrhenian Sea and a refuge for Sikels and mercenaries, *mistophoroi*, hostile to Syracuse. The hostility of Halaesa towards Syracuse is best shown by the fact that the Halaesinians were the first among all the Sicilian cities to surrender freely to the Romans in 264/3 BC, preferring a subordinate but privileged position under Rome, rather than being subject to imperialistic Syracuse.

Haluntium, located on the hill-top of modern San Marco d'Alunzio, *c.* 20 km to the east of Kale Akte, also began as a Sikel nucleus, but developed urban settlement is only certain from the fourth century BC (Fig. 1.11; colour Pl. 9).[56] From recent excavations, it is now certain that the hill had been inhabited since at least the Archaic period and probably continuously from the Bronze Age.[57] Relatively imposing remains of a city wall can be dated to the fourth century BC,[58] whereas other remains at the ancient site date to the Hellenistic or early Roman imperial periods.[59] According to P. Castrizio, Haluntium belonged to the Timoleontic *symmachia* and was among those cities which struck coins (*c.* 344/39 BC), probably for the financing of the war against Carthage.[60] If correct, it seems that the town had some political weight already by the middle of the fourth century BC.

Apollonia lay between Kale Akte and Haluntium, about 10 km west of Haluntium and west also of S. Agata di Militello. It was situated on the top of Monte Vecchio (near modern San Fratello) (Figs 1.12–13).[61] The hill was probably settled already by the Bronze and/or Iron Ages.[62] Excavations have revealed some parts of the urban settlement which belongs to the Hellenistic

Fig. 1.13. Monte Vecchio (in the centre of the photograph), site of ancient Apollonia, view from the west

period.[63] Some kind of small harbour must also have existed, probably at modern Acquedolci, in a tiny indentation of the otherwise very straight coastline here, and at the foot of the mountain on which Apollonia stands. Diodorus says that Apollonia was controlled by the tyrant Leptines of Engyon at the time of Timoleon: Leptines was exiled to the Peloponnese after the fall of Engyon, and the autonomy of Apollonia was restored.[64] As to the location of Engyon, all evidence points towards Troina in the interior of the island as its site. We have here a parallel to the relationship between Herbita and Halaesa, with a strong Sikel centre in the interior controlling a politically weaker town near the coast. All settlements in the area were situated on hill-tops, in line with Sikel tradition. Kale Akte, as we have seen, is somewhat different from the others, as it was founded on a hill-top but one with a more direct command of the shore and the sea.

Finally, the smallest and most insignificant of the urban centres in our region was Amestratum, today's Mistretta, situated in the interior between Kale Akte and Halaesa. The earliest known remains here date to the fourth century BC, but the settlement never gained any great importance. It was dominated politically by Halaesa and was probably in close contact with Kale Akte as well.[65]

At the beginning of the fourth century BC, after a war between Herbita and Dionysius I, the settlement of Tyndaris was founded east of Haluntium by the tyrant of Syracuse. Tyndaris was an important Hellenising centre: it was a thoroughly Greek urban centre, located not far from Kale Akte.[66] By now, the whole area had come under the domination of Dionysius I of Syracuse, although such peripheral areas, so far from Syracuse must in reality have been difficult to control. By the fourth century BC, all Sikel centres in the area had become completely Hellenised.

The topographical setting

Settlements have always been founded on sites in the landscape which enjoy particular topographical advantages, of importance to the population. In the context of landscape as a contributor to the 'enabling and constraining framework', it is necessary to take a closer look at what were the topographical characteristics of urban settlements in the Nebrodi in order to reach a better understanding of their economic history. Caronía, the site of ancient Kale Akte, is, as we have seen, different from the other urban centres in having very direct control of the seashore, as well as possessing a harbour, a rarity on this coastline. Kale Akte was throughout its life a settlement orientated towards the sea: trade was an important reason for its existence. It was thus more an 'organic' town than a typical 'colonial' one: from humble beginnings, it grew over time as a direct consequence of its advantageous topographical situation. A settlement of 'colonial' type is usually supported by a strong political power, something which Kale Akte was for only the first few years of its existence.

Halaesa is a less obvious choice for settlement for someone arriving from the sea. It is a site situated some way south of the coast, one more adapted for communicating with the hinterland rather than with the sea. Halaesa is a typical case of a 'colony'. In contrast to Kale Akte, Apollonia and Haluntium, it has no signs of settlement prior to the colonial foundation, despite being the most thoroughly investigated site (in contrast to other centres in central northern Sicily, it did not survive into the early medieval period, and so is largely unencumbered by buildings of that date or later). The hill was less suitable from a defensive point of view than the others in our region. It relied therefore on its strong fortifications, which could only have been constructed when a relatively strong political power had the money and inclination to build them.

The reasons for the foundation of Halaesa emerge very clearly from examining the location of the settlement. Lying on a slope towards the Halaisos river valley, it controlled the most important communication artery from the sea towards the interior, where its mother city, Herbita, was located. The Halaisos river valley enters an area of open plains around modern Gangi. This fact makes Monte Alburchia near Gangi the most probable candidate for the site of ancient Herbita. The fertile Halaisos valley would also have been where most of the settlers of 403 BC received their plots of land to farm.[67] Thus, the location of the city reflects quite well the intentions behind its settlement. Halaesa was a settlement in the interior, it controlled the communications route between sea and interior, but it also clearly had the intention of exploiting its position near the sea by means of a small but protected harbour beside the estuary of the river Halaisos, near Castel di Tusa. The harbour's importance in the choice of the site is, however, less than it was in the case of Kale Akte. It can thus be concluded that Kale Akte was more dependent on its maritime connections than Halaesa, while Halaesa to a greater degree was connected with the interior of the island. As long as the latter continued to be of importance, the economic success of Halaesa was almost guaranteed. When the Roman tax system collapsed in the fifth century AD, however, the grain route to the coast, which passed by Halaesa, also fell into disuse. Without any strong political power supporting it in times of trouble, the topographical situation of Halaesa, by then a very small settlement with its fortifications in ruins, was not enough to guarantee its continued existence.

Apollonia and Haluntium, the remaining coastal towns of the region, are quite different in character. These are more hidden away, less accessible from the coast than either Caronía or Halaesa. They command a vast view of the coastline, but have no harbours in their immediate vicinity, the coast here being especially empty of suitable sites. Being Sikel settlements, and not the products of single 'foundation events', they were typical 'organic' ones, coming into existence gradually: both hills had probably been inhabited without interruption since the Bronze Age. The earliest clearly documented finds, however, date to the fourth century BC, by which stage, it seems, both had already grown into urban settlements. Apollonia and Haluntium were first and foremost strongholds, well adapted to resisting a siege, and their choice of situation reflects insecure and troubled times. Since they so obviously lie on strategic positions close to the coast, this would have been important, but neither site was chosen with a suitable harbour as their main concern. The large plateau of Apollonia was in addition topographically appropriate for settlement, and would have been able to accommodate quite a large city. It was no doubt its strategic position that made the tyrant Leptines of Engyon so determined in his attempts to control the town; in the end Agathocles destroyed it, since it had had the temerity to oppose him.

All four of these settlements, however, show a very clear tendency towards an increased strategic and economic importance in the late fifth/fourth century BC, and a gradual development of urbanisation independent of direct Greek intervention. No doubt the new urban centres reflect increasing trading activity on the north coast which had already begun in the sixth century BC because of Greek settlement. In the course of the fifth century BC, commercial exchange increased in intensity because of the ambitions of the rapidly expanding major cities elsewhere on the north and east coasts. For Syracuse, it became increasingly important to control the north coast in order to fulfil its dream of supremacy over the entire island. During the fourth century BC, this central area of the north coast had become an integrated part of Syracuse's sphere of interest; by the end of that century, it had come under the control of the tyrant Agathocles, probably leading to an intensification of urbanisation as well as more regular contact with the east coast. In addition, the scale of international trade grew considerably in the Mediterranean. As we move into the third century, for Sicily of the greatest significance were the emerging super-powers of Rome and Carthage, whose spheres of interest converged on Sicily. Generally increasing

Fig. 1.14 (above) *Pizzo Cilona, view from the north-east*

Fig. 1.15 (left) *Pizzo Cilona, aerial view showing the location of the principal archaeological features*

trade and wealth at this time led to increased population levels and a higher demand for an increasing number of commodities. To meet this demand a number of smaller urban centres grew up.

Rural settlements

In the early history of the towns discussed above, rural settlements seem to have been confined to the immediate *chora* around each town, with small farmsteads cultivating probably wheat, barley, olives and vines. Recently, more information about rural settlement of the Classical period (fifth / fourth centuries BC), hitherto virtually non-existent, has been forthcoming. Preliminary research shows that in the *chora* of Kale Akte only three rural sites date to the late Archaic period, and five to the Classical, all located to the west of the town (in *contrade* Arìa, l'Urmo and Fiumara). The number of such Classical sites are only a quarter of those attested in the Hellenistic period.[68] Insecurity due to the presence of pirates and political instability (such as the wars between Herbita and Syracuse, and between Greeks and Carthaginians) probably did not encourage permanent rural settlements for much of this time.

The richest rural evidence comes from *contrada* Arìa, in the hills overlooking the coast a few kilometres west of Caronía.[69] Here a necropolis dating between the late Archaic and early fourth century BC was found; a red-figure *krater*, a *hydria*, oil lamps, cups, plates, and a silver coin of the type depicting Dionysus and a Silenus, issued by the *polis* of Sicilian Naxos, were among the finds.[70] They show that the Sikel aristocracy in the area was by now strongly influenced by the Greek *symposion* culture, something which is well attested elsewhere in Sikel territory, for example at Morgantina.

Although little work on rural settlements has been done, it is obvious that the number of Classical rural settlements is very much lower than in the Hellenistic and Roman periods, and suggests that farming was small-scale, and reflects also the still very modest size of the neighbouring urban settlement. The data from the recent Halaesa survey also confirm a moderate number of rural settlements prior to, and in the early years of, the city's existence.[71] Herding would have played an important additional role to agriculture in the economy. Apart from in the narrow coastal plain and the gentle hills near the sea, the mountainous landscape was better suited to herding than to agriculture. It has been noted that *komai*, Greek villages, are absent from the literary record of Sicily and other areas of Greek settlement.[72] This may imply that Sicilian farms were scattered around in small units, probably very dependent on urban markets; at any rate, unsurprisingly, they were never of sufficient importance to attract the attention of ancient writers.

Last but not least, the site of Pizzo Cilona deserves inclusion among the rural sites of Kale Akte (Figs 1.14–15).[73] Situated some 2 km south of Caronía, it has been identified through field survey. It was a fortified settlement, in existence from the late sixth to the early / mid-fourth centuries BC. It was thus founded prior to Kale Akte and attests a significant Sikel presence in the area. It could possibly be regarded as a frontier post or *phrourion* of the late Archaic / early Classical Sikel settlement at Caronía; if so, it would presumably have lost its *raison d'être* after the foundation of a *polis* at Kale Akte.

The Early Hellenistic period (c. 320–200 BC: period B)

Urban settlements

Except for the recently found honorary inscription confirming Kale Akte's status as a *polis* in this period,[74] we have no epigraphic or historical data concerning Kale Akte; we have therefore to rely on general historical information of relevance to the wider context of north-central Sicily. With the rise of Agathocles, the direct interest of Syracuse in this area becomes noticeable for the first time. As a result of his campaigns, the autonomy of the urban centres of the region came to an end. In 317 BC, rebel forces against Agathocles gathered in the vicinity of Herbita, apparently still a politically and militarily important stronghold.[75] Ten years later, Apollonia was besieged by Agathocles and sacked; according to Diodorus, most of the inhabitants were killed.[76] This confirms what can already be inferred from its character as a key stronghold – that Apollonia was a *polis* of strategic importance, and that, since it dared oppose Syracuse, it had to be destroyed. At the hill-top settlement of Caronía there are several archaeological contexts which may include evidence for destruction at the very end of the fourth century BC, and of a subsequent re-building phase *c.* 300 BC.[77] Whether this activity had any connection with the Agathoclean campaign in the area, is impossible to say, since much more high-quality archaeological information is needed before any firm conclusions can be drawn. With this military campaign and the expansionist policy of Agathocles, it does seem that the area came under direct Syracusan control. Caccamo Caltabiano has hypothesised that the towns issuing coins in this period, among them Halaesa and Haluntium, were military strongholds, and formed a key part in an Agathoclean policy to protect the north and east coasts. This was especially necessary around the Straits of Messina, which were of course of crucial strategic importance. Haluntium, Cephaloedium and Tyndaris on the north coast would, according to this view, have been military strongholds under the control of Syracuse.[78]

With the intervention of Pyrrhus in Sicily and the ensuing war between the Mamertines and Hieron II, our region once more became a theatre of war. Halaesa and all towns to the east of it were under Mamertine domination in the 280/270s, and probably paid a tribute to Messana.[79] Halaesa gave its *deditio* (surrender) without a struggle to Hieron of Syracuse in 269 BC, and became part of the *symmachia* formed by Hieron after the battle of the Longanos River; in all probability, Kale Akte became part of the *symmachia* too.[80] Once within the hegemony of Hieron, the towns were obliged to pay a tithe according to the *Lex Hieronica*. Halaesa and Haluntium were the towns with the strongest political ambition during this period, probably sometimes in opposition to the rule of Syracuse. With the advent of the Romans in 263 BC, the wounded pride of Halaesa was revenged. The Romans outside the gates of Centuripae were met by a council of the Halaesinians, who offered their allegiance and *amicitia* to the Roman Senate.[81] That turned out to be a fortunate decision, since Rome after 241 BC rewarded the loyalty of Halaesa towards Rome with an exemption from the *decuma* or tithe, a very important privilege, which laid the foundation for the city's future prosperity. The other towns in the region, Haluntium, Apollonia and Kale Akte, became *civitates decumanae*, obliged to pay a tithe of grain to Rome every year. However, this was not a completely new arrangement, since the tithe had supposedly been paid earlier to Hieron II, at the very beginning of his long reign.

Rural settlements

The pattern of rural settlements probably changed little in the early Hellenistic period, but wine production might have become more important. The first half of the third century was dominated by wars between Greeks and Carthaginians, Greeks and Mamertines, and of course the First Punic War between Rome and Carthage, which probably also affected our area more or less directly, even if the ancient sources do not mention any military activities here. One of the most important naval battles took place off the coast of Tyndaris in 257 BC,[82] when it is possible that Halaesa, an important Roman ally, supplied Rome with timber and/or naval equipment.[83]

Precious evidence of rural organisation in the area comes from the so-called *Tabulae Halaesinae*.[84] These fragments of an inscription dating from somewhere between the mid-third and mid-second century BC[85] certainly give us a good indication of rural patterns of settlement in the area during the Hellenistic period. They suggest that small-holdings were the dominant form of land-ownership. The inscription illustrates in detail the division of territory around the *polis* and how it was used. The borders of the plots of land – natural and artificial – are described, consisting of moats, stone blocks, trees, forests, water streams, sacred areas and city walls.[86] The information we have from the *Tabulae Halaesinae* most likely concerns those farmers owning the land which lay closest to the city. At Kale Akte we can expect a similar system with properties scattered around the countryside close to the city, and also in the narrow strip of fertile land along the coast; others are likely to lie along the Torrente Caronía, since access to water was indispensable.[87] From the information available on the Halaesa inscriptions, it is clear that the land was divided in lots and let, the plots not being very large. The limits of the terrain would have been demarcated by the *polis'* markers indicated on poles, small terrace walls, and even on olive trees.[88] It must be supposed that the *chora* of Kale Akte was organised in much the same way.

The Halaesa survey has produced clear evidence for this period. The late fourth and the first half of the third century BC shows little intensification compared to the Classical period. The great watershed comes after the middle of the third century, when the number of settlements increases significantly.[89] This was certainly a consequence of the more settled conditions following the victory of Rome, as well as the increasing economic opportunities that followed. The area was no longer an arena of war for Syracuse, Messana and Carthage, but was instead part of the powerful Roman empire with its strong naval forces, the presence of which would have made maritime trade considerably safer. The evidence for rural settlement around Caronía is sketchy. About fifteen sites can be dated to the Hellenistic period in general, in *contrade* S. Giovanni, Giumentaro, Todaro, Fiumara, Giardino murato, Lineri, Trapesi-Castagneto, S. Miceli, and S. Anna.[90] Judging by the data from Halaesa, it seems probable that the majority of these sites can be dated from the mid-third century BC onwards. What seems certain is that all were situated close to the city itself.[91]

The Late Hellenistic period (*c.* 200–30 BC: period C)

Urban settlements

It is hardly a coincidence that Kale Akte, not mentioned by ancient authors in connection with important political events in the area, began to flourish at the beginning of Roman rule. Other towns on the north coast seem to enjoy increased prosperity, especially from the second century BC: at Tyndaris, Halaesa, Thermae, Soluntum and Monte Iato, building activity was intensive, especially when it came to embellishing the public areas of the city, such as the *agora*.[92] In addition, many private buildings are known from this period, in contrast to the third century. Even though the area investigated at Caronía is quite limited, a third- and second-century flourishing appears to be present here. As a member of the *symmachia* led by Halaesa and with a harbour, important for export to Rome, Kale Akte's economic potential was undoubtedly realised by Rome. It has been claimed that some cities may have started minting coins as early as c. 215 BC, cities in areas with a strong Roman military presence; their coinage has been considered 'occupation money'.[93] However, it seems highly unlikely that Rome would have encouraged the minting of bronze coins, several of which are of very low value, for such a purpose. Money minted for warfare is almost exclusively of silver and therefore of high value. The beginning of civic coinage in the north Sicilian cities may have been granted by Rome to those centres thought to have a certain economic importance, to encourage their trading activity. The date of establishment of the mint at Kale Akte and those of most other Sicilian towns which began minting after the Roman conquest is much debated. It now seems certain that these issues began much later, only when the Roman province was well established and so long after the fall of the Syracusan kingdom.[94] The date of inception for the mint of Kale Akte was dated by Caroccio to the years immediately after 210 BC, and by Mannino on stylistic grounds to the beginning of the second century BC, but it now seems certain that it occurred at some point in the second half of the second century BC rather than earlier.[95] From being marginal towns in the periphery of the dominion of Syracuse, the urban centres in our region become important exporters to the huge, ever-growing urban market of Rome. It is evident that building activity at Kale Akte and intense trading activity, reflected by the rich amphora material from Marina di Caronía beginning in the second century BC,[97] are a direct consequence of Roman policy, in which the northern coast was especially privileged.

The economic boom for Halaesa must have had consequences also for the surrounding towns. From the first half of the second century BC, intense trading activity is noted at Kale Akte. It is certain that beginning after the Second Punic War, and probably already after the First Punic War, proximity to the sea became increasingly essential for cities in order to accumulate wealth. Herbita, earlier the political and probably also the economic centre of the region, with control over vast agricultural lands in the interior, had been a strong city, as it was easily defensible and protected in the interior of the island. Now it was left hopelessly behind by its daughter settlement Halaesa, the latter prospering from maritime trade despite only having a small harbour. Kale Akte and Haluntium also increased their wealth and importance by comparison with Herbita in the last centuries BC. The latter was certainly in decline by the early Imperial period, and appears to have been gradually abandoned.[98] Another town, Apollonia, was also in a state of decline after its destruction at the hands of Agathocles in 307 BC. From recent excavations at the site of Monte Vecchio, it is now known that the settlement in the second/first centuries BC was restricted to the former acropolis of the *polis*.[99] Judging by its small series of very poor bronze coins, it must have belonged to one of the smallest *poleis* of the island. It is known that it furnished just a single ship for the Sicilian fleet under Verres.[100] Nothing is heard of it in the Imperial period; it too seems to have been abandoned, beginning in the late first century BC.[101]

In the civil war between Octavian and Sextus Pompey, which lasted from 43 to 36 BC, the north-eastern part of the island between Capo Peloro and Tyndaris was seriously affected, but we do not know to what extent the coastal stretch to the west of Tyndaris also suffered the same fate. There is no doubt, however, that the ports of the north coast were of great importance to Sextus Pompey for military and strategic reasons. From here it was possible to launch sudden attacks on enemy vessels and on the grain ships from Africa trying to make their way to Rome. Certainly the towns in our area were obliged to supply men for Sextus Pompey's army and materials for the ships in his fleet, since they were situated so close to the strategically important north-eastern corner of the island, where the decisive naval battle off Naulochus was fought in 36 BC. Most *poleis* on the island quite actively supported Sextus Pompey against Octavian, and saw his rule as a last chance to preserve their ancient, at least nominal, independence.[102]

The picture given us by the archaeological material suggests that several towns on the north coast as well as elsewhere on the island were punished for their loyalty to Sextus Pompey, or at any rate they were deeply caught up in the chaos that followed in the aftermath of the war.[103] We know that this was certainly true for Tyndaris, where destruction is well documented and where the new *colonia* planted by Augustus has been clearly identified by archaeological research: new walling of that date was built over the cisterns of the preceding Hellenistic settlement.[104] Several towns had shared the same fate as Tyndaris, among them Tauromenium.[105] At Halaesa traces of violent destruction outside the city walls accompanied

Fig. 1.16. Halaesa, an inscription dedicated 'to all the gods', from the agora; *the Kalaktinoi are named in line 5*

by many finds of sling-bolts have been securely dated to the very end of the late Republican period (certainly no fragments of Italian *terra sigillata* were present).[106] From the study of the finds and of archaeological contexts in Caronía, it is now also possible to suggest a violent destruction there at the same time.[107] The archaeological material from Monte Vecchio also suggests its abandonment by the end of the Late Republican period: again the virtual absence of fragments of Italian *terra sigillata* at the site suggests that occupation there had already ceased around the very beginning of the Augustan period.[108]

The arrival of the Romans did not cause local and regional identity to disappear completely, however. An inscription from the forum of Halaesa, thanking the gods for a naval victory won by the cities of Halaesa, Kale Akte, Herbita and Amestratum,[109] presumably against pirates, is clear proof of the existence still of a *symmachia* at the beginning of the first century BC (Fig. 1.16). The symbols depicted on the coins of Halaesa and Kale Akte issued during the last centuries BC are very similar: the type with Dionysus and a bunch of grapes, and that showing Hermes and the *caduceus*, continued to be favourite motifs (Figs 4.38–40; colour Pl. 15).[110] The principal mints in the Hellenistic period were those of Halaesa, Kale Akte and Haluntium, economically the most important centres of the micro-region.

Rural settlements

With the Roman takeover and institution of the *annona*, the yearly tax in kind on grain, destined for the inhabitants of Rome, grain production is likely to have increased significantly during the last centuries BC. This would have had major implications for a harbour town such as Kale Akte, since large quantities of grain, not only from the *chora* but also from its wider hinterland, now had to be shipped from here. Not surprisingly, therefore, the number of identified rural settlements in the area is much greater than those of earlier periods. The number of rural sites dating to the whole of the Hellenistic period (21) is second only to those known in the Roman Imperial period (38), and it is far larger than that registered for rural settlement in both the Classical and the Byzantine periods (5 and 3 respectively).[111] The substantial number of sites from the *chora* of Kale Akte identified through surface survey can be supplemented by the very rich record from Halaesa, where the late Hellenistic period is the period richest in rural settlement, and reflects the general prosperity of the city during this period.[112] The time following the First Punic War was also for all of Sicily an age of fast-growing prosperity, encouraged by both flourishing trade and the very presence of the *pax romana*. Only five of the 21 Hellenistic rural sites in the *chora* of Kale Akte can be dated specifically to the late Hellenistic period, but this is no doubt due to the difficulty of dating most surface finds precisely, and the preliminary nature of the data so far available. It is hardly surprising that rural sites at Kale Akte, like those of Halaesa, multiplied as a consequence of more stable and peaceful conditions after the Roman takeover in the mid-third century BC. One of the few excavated Hellenistic farmsteads in the area is that excavated near San Marco d'Alunzio.[113] Judging from its remains, it seems to have been of at least medium size, and farms of this type, like those mentioned by Cicero at Herbita, may have become more common in the second and first century BC.[114] It is from Herbita that we have our best information about the size of rural settlements at this period. The evidence suggests that small- and middle-sized farmsteads were the norm at Herbita, where the inland plains, which yielded a rich harvest of wheat in the time of Cicero, would have been well suited for intensive farming. The small-holder appears to have been the norm here by the time of Cicero (although he of course may not be reflecting the full picture), and it is probable that this was also the case at Kale Akte.

Even if parts of Sicily were still troubled by wars, like that between Rome and Syracuse on the eastern coast in the last phase of the Second Punic War, or the terrible slave wars in the late second century BC which particularly affected central Sicily, these events probably did not seriously affect the area on the northern slopes of the Nebrodi mountain chain. Settled conditions would have encouraged the establishment of stable settlements in the countryside, particularly evident in the *chora* of Halaesa.[115]

The Imperial period (*c.* 30 BC – AD 400: periods D and E)

Urban settlement

After the war between Octavian and Sextus Pompey, a major reorganisation of the province took place under Augustus. Our main source for this is the account of Pliny in his *Naturalis Historia*. He probably used two different sources: a *periplous* source from around 200 BC and the list of Italian communities from the time of Augustus, possibly drawn up in 21 BC.[116] There are certainly errors in this account, and the status of the different towns at the time of Augustus is often by no means clear, since two different sources were mingled in Pliny's account. The urban communities mentioned in our area are the Halaesini and Galateni (Calactini), both being *civitates stipendiariae*, and Haluntium and Agathyrnum, which are called *oppida*. The picture is complicated by other evidence: inscriptions, for example, have been found which describe Halaesa and Haluntium as *municipia*.[117] Wilson argues that the two towns were granted this status sometime between *c.* 14 BC and AD 14, and thus only after the date of Pliny's source, which explains why this higher status is not mentioned there.[118] The very fact that that Halaesa and Haluntium had been given municipal status confirms their continued importance at the time of Augustus. Kale Akte clearly remained a tax-paying community, and there is nothing to suggest that paying the *stipendia* would have been any different from paying the *decuma* in an earlier age. Since very little excavation has been conducted in the hill-town, and no inscriptions have been found which date to the Roman period, we cannot completely rule out the possibility that Kale Akte itself might also have been made a *municipium*. However, even allowing for the coastal settlement at Marina di Caronía, which was larger and more important than Haluntium's small *scalo* at Terranova, it is above all the comparatively small size of Kale Akte that probably meant that promotion to a higher municipal rank was never considered. The safe harbour below Kale Akte lent to it a certain economic importance, and some of the imports to and

Fig. 1.17, Torrenova (foreground) and Capo d'Orlando (ancient Agathyrnum), view from the west

exports from Haluntium may well have been handled by the better located and better equipped port facilities at Marina di Caronía.

About Agathyrnum we know next to nothing. Its description as an *oppidum* in Pliny gives us no indication of its precise legal status. It was probably little more than a stronghold, possibly one situated on the hill above modern Capo d'Orlando (Fig 1.17).[119] Most hill settlements were abandoned in early Imperial times, but a coastal village here may have inherited the same name: an inscription to Tiberius has been recorded there. Much later, in the third / fourth centuries AD, a bath-building was erected at S. Gregorio, just east of Capo d'Orlando; but this almost certainly belongs to a villa, and does not throw light on the urban situation of Agathyrnum at the time.[120]

After the Augustan reforms, the importance of the *poleis* in the area seems to have decreased. Halaesa, which was flourishing at the time of Cicero,[121] did not keep its tax exemption privileges after the Augustus reforms.[122] Though having the status of *municipium*, it declined after the mid-imperial period, and was never to regain its former economic significance. Haluntium, in the Hellenistic period a town of some importance, and an Augustan *municipium* like Halaesa, was more inaccessible than the latter and seems to have been in decline after Augustan times. The coast below the hill is not suited for a port, although archaeological finds at Marina di Torrenova do testify to some sort of settlement there.[123] Its communications network and accessibility were certainly less than those at Kale Akte. It rates no mention in the third-century *Itinerarium Antonini*, as it is situated off the main artery, the *via Valeria*. However, it does seem likely that the local *rosso fiorito* breccia was still being quarried in the Roman imperial period, but that could have flourished independently of the town. No inscriptions are known from the Imperial period, whereas there are some from the Late Republican period. A working hypothesis is that most of the population moved to the coastal settlements at Torrenova and San Gregorio and that the hill site was gradually abandoned. We must, however, be very careful in drawing any firm conclusions regarding a complete abandonment of Haluntium in the Middle and Late Imperial periods, since the archaeological strata are sealed deep below the medieval and modern village of San Marco d'Alunzio. The problem is therefore very much the same as at

Caronía, where little is known about the urban layout and its various phases. The finds from Marina di Caronía show us how dangerous it is to draw conclusions about a general economic decline of any area based on the evidence of the hill-top sites alone. As can be seen clearly elsewhere in imperial Sicily, there was not so much a decline in population as such but a transfer of settlement from the hill-top to new settlements in the valleys and coastal plains.

The hill settlement at Caronía may well have declined from the early second century AD onwards, or thereabouts, but its coastal counterpart ensured the survival of Kale Akte as a name, although in a new form. This is suggested by the finds that indicate intense economic activity in the settlement by the sea at Marina di Caronía. It seems clear that after the gradual movement of population away from the hill-town and down to the settlement on the coast, no dramatic changes took place; indeed the location of the main centre of population (*vicus*) along the main north-coast road by the sea meant that the new Kale Akte benefitted from better communications than in the days of the *polis*. Halaesa, Kale Akte and Agathyrnum are all mentioned in the late Roman road handbooks, but in all cases these names probably refer to coastal settlements which were successors of the old hill-towns; Apollonia on the other hand is not included, and it had ceased to exist as a *polis* by the late first century BC.[124] Its decline must be explained by the small size of the late Republican settlement, but more importantly by its remote location and its difficulty of access.

At Tindari, the evidence for urban decline beginning in the second half of the second century AD has recently become evident, suggested by the failure of the civic authorities to keep the drainage system working.[125] A possible economic crisis now and in the third century AD seems to have led to the definitive abandonment of some buildings.[126] On the other hand houses close to the city centre continued to be occupied into the later fourth century. Halaesa, already considered a small town (*polichnion*) by the time of Strabo, also declined from the middle of the second century AD onwards, and increasingly in the third.[127] Contraction is also reflected in the diminishing number of rural settlements in its *chora* at the same period.[128] However, Halaesa to some extent retained its urban character until the mid-fourth century AD, the only one of the hill-settlements of the area to do so. Tyndaris suffered badly in an earthquake *c.* AD 400, and never recovered; after that, apart from a short-lived attempt at urban renewal, the community became ruralized, with scattered pockets of inhabited areas, one of them set in the middle of a former street.[129] Evidence from nearby Lipari is more ambiguous: its low-lying parts may have suffered from the effects of a tsunami in AD 365.[130]

Although the urban hill-top of Kale Akte had been abandoned (probably) by the early second century AD, the maritime settlement inherited a variant version of the same name, now Latinised as Calacte (colour Pl. 5). Continuing to preserve its function as a vital port community, the settlement by the sea seems to have flourished in the third and fourth centuries, and perhaps also, although to a lesser extent, in the fifth century too. Excavations at Marina di Caronía have shown as much. Little late antique material is known from either excavation or surface survey at the upper town of Caronía, and the Hellenistic/early imperial expansion, which had extended down the sides of the steep slopes, did not continue to be occupied. It is beyond doubt that the late Imperial hill-settlement, if it existed at all, was a fraction of the size of its Hellenistic predecessor;[131] most of its inhabitants had long before drifted down to the coast at Marina di Caronía.

Towards the second half of the fourth century AD, the semi-urban character of the village or *vicus* of Calacte seems to have gradually declined, part of a general contraction of urban or quasi-urban life in this part of northern Sicily. It is well illustrated by the fate of the two major cities of the Nebrodi area, Tyndaris and Halaesa. Tyndaris lost its urban character during the fifth century AD, as mentioned above.[132] Halaesa, in contrast to Kale Akte, seemed to have continued life into the first half of the fourth century but not much beyond that.[133] Both Tyndaris and Halaesa have been regarded as 'failed cities', in the sense that they did not have medieval and modern successors, despite both of them becoming bishoprics in late Roman and early Byzantine period. The fact that these settlements administered territories does not imply a high quality of life in the urban centre itself.[134] Cefalù, on the other hand, thanks to its decent harbour, may have enjoyed a certain continuity, although there is very little firm evidence.[135] For the more important cities of the island, all situated by the sea and furnished with good harbours, there was generally a continuity in urban life between late Antiquity and the Middle Ages.[136]

Settlement evidence from around the Strait of Messina and archaeological data from Marina di Caronía both suggest that village-like production centres by the sea, which had taken on the role of quasi-urban nuclei from neighbouring abandoned hill-towns, were themselves in decline by the later fourth century. They still existed in the fifth century, but probably with a more pronounced rural character, and production to an increasing degree seems to have been moved to the countryside and to private estates there. Only the main cities like Syracuse, Catina, Messana and

Panhormus had the means to thrive and for urban life to continue. This was a general trend, and is intimately intertwined with the gradual decline of Mediterranean trade, which in turn resulted from the increasing insecurity and instability after the fall of the Western Roman Empire. Whatever the reason for the destruction around AD 100 in both hill-town and harbour, and later in the second half of the fourth century in the *vicus* at Marina di Caronía, the outcome was very different on each occasion. The destruction of the late Hellenistic/early Imperial settlement at Caronía in the early second century AD was followed by the likely abandonment of large parts of the hill-top settlement and signalled the end of its urban character.

Rural settlements

The absence of urban life did not mean that economic activity ceased also in the surrounding countryside. Production was now centred on rural villages, farms and villas without any need for a local urban market. Around Kale Akte, suburban or maritime villas for leisure may well be found in the future, judging from the beautiful position of much of the coast in the region of Caronía. A mosaic floor discovered a few kilometres west of Caronía, probably belonging to a villa of the Imperial period, gives a hint of the presence of such *villae*.[137] Near Halaesa, at Lancine/Piano Fontane, one of the very few villas that we know of from this entire area of the north coast is indicated by a series of polychrome mosaics dating to the third century AD, discovered in 1912.[138]

Many rural settlements from the Imperial or late Roman periods have been identified in the *chora* of Kale Akte, and the Halaesa survey suggests that there too a flourishing rural production continued at this time, and especially in late antiquity. At Kale Akte, a preliminary mapping of rural sites shows a significant increase of sites from of Roman Imperial date, almost the double number (38) compared with those occupied in Hellenistic times (21).[139] Five of these sites can be dated specifically to the late Imperial period (in *contrade* L'Urmo, La Pernice, Sugherita, Lineri and Chiappe). In addition, three sites carry on into the early Byzantine period (in *contrade* L'Urmo, La Pernice and Chiappe). While several sites that date to the Roman Imperial period also had a late Imperial and early Byzantine phase, the evidence to date is simply not detailed enough to allow more precision. At Halaesa, where the

Fig. 1.18. Caronía, the Norman castle and presumed site of the acropolis of Kale Akte, view from the south

picture is more detailed than at Caronía, a significant decline is detectable in rural settlement in the second/third centuries AD, judging by the absence of African red slip pottery of that date. This might have been a consequence of the decline of the hill-top *polis* at the same time, perhaps more keenly felt at Halaesa than elsewhere since it was the most important town in the region and had enjoyed great prosperity in the late Hellenistic period.

Whether the same is true for Calacte and its territory needs to be tested against the evidence. Such information as there is of local amphora production suggests that it flourished in the first century AD, producing both Dressel 2/4 (wine) and Dressel 21/22 (salted fish) amphorae. In the late third/early fourth century, production of wine amphorae begins again, on an even larger scale; but, for the second and much of the third century, local production seems to have ceased. From the last third of that century onwards, the export of wine from the region continued uninterrupted until the early sixth century. The entire area seems to have profited significantly from the shipping of grain and wine to Rome throughout this period, although, as we have seen, such prosperity does not seem to be reflected in the health of the settlement, in late antiquity at least, at Marina di Caronía itself.

Several of the rural settlements in the *chora* to the south of Kale Akte are close to the line of the ancient *trazzere* which led from Kale Akte towards Capitium (Capizzi) and the interior. During the late Empire rural sites tend to be situated further away from the original urban centre of Kale Akte, no doubt because of the increasing irrelevance of the former *polis* and the greater self-sufficiency of the rural estates. The most obvious sign of this phenomenon is the creation of larger nuclei of rural settlements, such as that in *contrada* Chiappe.

The movement of population from the hill-towns to the countryside in the Imperial period, towards the coast, and, further inland, to well-watered valleys, is a well-documented phenomenon elsewhere in Sicily – a direct consequence of the *pax Romana*. Probably we must imagine a gradual de-urbanization process, happening in some places faster than others, whereby large portions of the population over time moved to the countryside. Large numbers of farmsteads, farms and villas of various size and significance, as well as village settlements, spread out across the territory. The simple consideration that won out in the end was that life on a hill-top was just much less convenient than one on the coast or in a well-watered lowland site, with easier access to communications. In the late Empire, from around AD 325, it is likely that the production and export of grain increased, since Sicily once more became the granary of Rome; a good portion of the grain from Egypt and North Africa was now needed for the new capital of Constantinople.[140] Evidence from many places in Sicily suggests that agricultural production was flourishing from the fourth century until the later fifth or the beginning of the sixth century AD. The Gothic kingdom regarded Sicily as the *nutrix Getarum* according to Jordanes.[141] Yet the evidence from the neighbouring Halaesa suggests a steep decline in rural settlements during the sixth and seventh centuries AD, when hardly any sites have been identified.[142] The territory of Kale Akte may have equally been in decline at the same time.

Continuity in the Arab and Norman periods

Although the toponym Calacte was lost after Late Antiquity, probably with the abandonment of the maritime village, there was clearly some kind of continuity of settlement in Marina di Caronía and around the ancient harbour. Only one coin minted in Byzantine Sicily, possibly from the sixth century, has been found at Caronía,[143] not enough to suggest significant activity. Muslim tombs were found in Building 1 in *contrada* Pantano, dating to somewhere between the ninth and the twelfth century.[144] Caronía may have followed the general pattern of population growth detected elsewhere in Sicily at this time. From the eleventh century, and with the Norman conquest, the hill becomes more densely inhabited, judging by the pottery found on the slopes of Caronía.[145] The small town now called Caronía existed here from then onwards, growing in size in the fourteenth and especially the fifteenth centuries. The Norman castle on the hill-top of Caronía, around which the new town developed, was probably erected between 1131 and 1141 (Fig. 1.18; colour Pls. 1 and 2).[146] A few decades later we have the testimony of Al-Idrisi that the fortress was *di nuova costruzione*:

> *Alla distanza di dodici miglia s'incontra Caronia con cui ha inizio il territorio di Val Demone; è un antica roccaforte, in essa sorge una fortezza di nuova costruzione. Caronía possiede giardini, acque, viti, alberi ed è anche dotata di un porto: qui si tendono le reti per la pesca dei grandi tonni. Tale rocca dista un miglia circa dal mare.*[147]

> At a distance of twelve miles one reaches Caronía, where the territory of the Val Demone begins; it is an ancient stronghold, and on it rises a castle recently built. Caronía possesses gardens, water, vines, and trees, and is also equipped with a harbour. Here they look after the nets for fishing large tuna. The rock lies about a mile from the sea.

The Arab geographer was aware that the castle was built literally on the ruins of a former settlement. No doubt, crumbled parts of the ancient town remained still visible in the twelfth century before the Norman re-occupation. Al-Idrisi elsewhere mentions at Caronía *le camere subacquee per la mattanza del tonno*, 'the underwater chambers for the slaughter of the tuna fish'. Caronía therefore, as well as possessing many vineyards, was also the centre of a tuna-fishing industry. The continuity with what we know of the economy of the town in antiquity is striking: viticulture and tuna fishing were its main staples then, just as they still were a full millennium later. Maybe there never had been a complete rupture in settlement in the area near the cove and the harbour, even if it became extremely reduced during troubled times in the later Byzantine and Arab periods. Equally, at the same time, for reasons of its greater security, some inhabitants began to return once more to the hill-top. Only future research and excavation can throw more light on this period of transition, but the reoccupation of long-deserted hill-tops at this time is a widespread phenomenon all over Sicily.

2

The territory: resources and communications

The geographical framework

The landscape plays the most important part in any discussion of settlement over a long period of time, Braudel´s *longue durée*. The *longue durée* matches the rhythms of landscape and nature, which change very slowly and almost imperceptibly. The natural resources on which the inhabitants of Kale Akte and its territory relied in antiquity were essentially the same as they were well into the last century, although more recently, in the last few decades, pastoralism and agriculture have now all but vanished. The resources exploited did not vary much from the prehistoric period down to modern times, with some variations of course. These variations equate with the conjectured changes that Braudel suggests, which are much shorter than the *longue durée* and can be counted in hundreds of years rather than in millennia. The changes suggested are intimately connected with man-made historical events, the *histoire événementielle*, which shapes the lives of the next few successive generations. This chapter, therefore, will concentrate on the landscape and resources of Kale Akte, and of the Nebrodi area in general, which provided the framework for human activity in this region.

Communications

Many roads can be considered an enduring part of the landscape, since many *tracées* had existed in the landscape since prehistoric times. For example, the *via Valeria*, the Roman trunk route named after the consul M. Valerius Laevinus in 210 BC, represented an upgrading of an already existing road. Maritime connections in a general sense had existed for millennia prior to antiquity, and had probably linked the prehistoric settlements around Caronía with their surrounding world. Maritime connectivity to an important degree depended on geographical features such as currents, winds and the depth of sea-bottoms, the existence of natural harbours, etc. However, to a greater extent than roads, which are constrained by the surrounding geography, maritime routes also changed over time depending on economic, political and cultural circumstances.

(a) Roads

The most important land route passing Kale Akte was the north coast road known as the *via Valeria* in Roman times. Since Greek civilization had already existed in Sicily for centuries before the arrival of the Romans, a well functioning network of communications had already developed. The roads of ancient Sicily are clearly the result of a gradually developing system of roads, following essentially the natural formations of the landscape like coasts, valleys, rivers and plains. The north-coast road would have become of particular importance after the Roman re-organisation of the island after the Second Punic War, when the route was improved in order to function as an efficient communication between key settlements on the east coast (Messana, Catina and Syracusae) and on the west (especially Lilybaeum).[1] The road was also part of a strategy to control the cities on the north coast. Some scholars have hypothesised that a new highway was never constructed in the traditional Roman manner. According to this view, Roman authorities in Sicily never bothered to construct new roads, but were content with overseeing, and when necessary repairing, already existing routes.[2] Furthermore, Sicily lost some of its strategic importance after the Roman conquest and the Second Punic War; and it lost it altogether after the civil wars of the Late Republic, when it ceded its monopoly as Rome's supplier of grain: North Africa and Egypt now produced for the Roman market vastly greater quantities. Sicily lay at the centre of a completely pacified *Mare Nostrum*. Since Roman roads were built initially for military purposes, in order to transport troops rapidly to different theatres of war, the roads of Sicily may have fallen, some claim, into neglect, until a general reorganisation and restoration of the road network after *c.* AD 325. This was due, it has been suggested, to the renewed interest at the time that Rome showed once more in Sicily when it became once again a major supplier of grain to Italy: Egyptian grain in particular was now earmarked for the new foundation of Constantinople.[3]

Kale Akte was founded, as were other towns in the area, on a hill controlling the east-west line of communications (the *via Valeria*) and the sea – the latter with its opportunities for connectivity, but also with its perils, most notably from pirates. The town must have had connections with the interior from its very foundation, since contact with the stronghold of Herbita and its ruler Archonides (with whom Ducetius had collaborated) must have been vital for the new settlers. Further south in the interior lay important Sikel strongholds such as Enna and Morgantina, and the richest grain-producing area of Sicily. The clearest evidence for contact dates to the Republican period and comes from distant Morgantina, where many coins from the mints of Halaesa and Kale Akte as well as Haluntium demonstrate how far inland the coinages of these northern cities penetrated.[4]

It is probable that the road from Kale Akte into the interior followed the eastern ridge along the valley of the Torrente Caronía. This is indicated by the existence of a small *phrourion* identified at the top of Pizzo Cilona, halfway between Caronía and Feudo Samperi, controlling the road and the narrow valley below. The *phrourion* seems to have been constructed in the late sixth century and was in continuous use until its abandonment in the first half of the fourth century BC.[5] In the valley, shortly before the Torrente Caronía discharges into the sea, and somewhat inland (*c.* 1.6 km) from the coast, is the so-called *Ponte Romano*. No elements in this bridge can be said today with confidence to be Roman: the earliest parts date to the late sixteenth century (Figs 2.1 and 2.2; and colour Pl. 3).[6] Visible remains of a pavement beneath the bridge may belong to remains of an ancient road, whether Roman or medieval is uncertain.[7] The paving pre-dates the bridge as it passes below it, and may point to a ford existing here before the sixteenth century. Since the *torrenti* of Sicily carried much more water in pre-modern times, such a road crossing must have been in use only during the summer, when the torrent had mostly dried up. This may have been the point where the Roman *via Valeria* crossed the *torrente*, and a Roman bridge can be conjectured in approximately the same position. Perhaps the ford, if correctly identified, dates to the medieval period.

Just like the modern SS 117, but with a rather different course, the road towards the interior would have passed Capizzi, the ancient Capitium, mentioned by Cicero.[8] Pais also mentions a road that would have connected Kale Akte with Catania.[9] This is unlikely to have been a fully-fledged, engineered road that led directly to Catania but rather *trazzere* (simple mountain paths) over the Nebrodi, which connected Kale Akte with Capitium, and thence with Engyon (Troina). The route then must have continued around the foot of Mount Etna to Catina (Catania) and Tauromenium (Taormina) on the east coast. These mountain paths also must have joined the Catina–Thermae Himeraeae highway somewhere in the region of Assorum or Agyrium. The *trazzere*, which were still being used in the early twentieth century, were above all paths for transhumance: every year in summer, cattle and other livestock were led up in the cooler mountains for fresher pastures, and then in autumn were taken down again to the lowlands when the climate got colder. Several parallels can be seen in the area. Halaesa would have been connected with its mother city, Herbita, via a route mentioned by the eighth-century anonymous writer of Ravenna.[10] The track from Halaesa towards Herbita will have followed the river Halaisos, one of the main arteries leading into the interior (Fig. 2.3).

Fig. 2.1. Part of the so-called Roman bridge ('Ponte romano'), crossing the Torrente Caronía to the west of Caronia, looking south

Fig. 2.2. A detail of the 'Ponte romano'

The physical links between coast and hinterland were not only economically important, but also militarily. The Sikel settlement which must have pre-dated Kale Akte had, as we have seen (p. 5), a *phrourion* a few kilometres to the south at Pizzo Cilona, controlling the river valley and the road towards the interior.[11] Its position is thus likely to represent important evidence for where exactly the road passed on its way towards the interior. Recently, another *phrourion* has been discovered on the top of Monte Trefinaidi, just west of Pizzo Cilona.[12] Being the highest mountain in the area, it was able to control, in addition to the coast, both the valley of the Torrente Caronía and that of the Torrente Santo Stefano. This fortress was occupied from the end of the fourth century and during the first half of the third century BC. Its position suggests that it lay on the border between the territories of Kale Akte and Amestratus (Mistretta). However, in the third century, it seems unlikely to have been controlled by any of these *poleis*, but rather first by the Mamertines, later by Syracuse, and then by Rome. It has been suggested that it was in fact built by the Mamertines to check enemy movement from the interior towards the coast;[13] but since it already existed in the fourth century BC, it seems more likely that it was constructed initially by Syracuse as part of its defence of the strategically important north coast. There is good evidence of military combat here, presumably between the Mamertines and the Syracusans, around the mid-third century BC, after which it was abandoned. The fortress would clearly have lost any strategic importance as a consequence of the Roman conquest in the mid-third century BC.

Amestratus was also linked via the Halaisos valley to the interior, as well as with Kale Akte. Amestratus in turn was connected with the area of Herbita via a large *trazzera*, the course of which is followed by a considerable portion of the modern road, the Strada Statale 117 Centrale Sicula.[14] Amestratus, situated in the 'cornland' of the interior, will have needed good connections with the coast. It was also linked with the sea via Kale Akte and Halaesa.[15] Another neighbouring town, Apollonia, was controlled by the tyrant of Engyon (Troina). The latter lies on the other side of the Nebrodi chain further south. This is another case where a *trazzera* surely connected the two towns. Engyon could more easily have imported its sea-borne goods from the east coast, via the Troina, Salso and Simeto river valleys and the plain of Catania, rather than from the north via Apollonia. The roads crossing the Nebrodi chain, little more than paths, would surely have been impossible for carts to use. Nevertheless, Engyon, just like Herbita, is likely to have had continuing interests during the late fourth century BC in the north coast,

Fig. 2.3. The valley of the Halaisos, looking south from Halaesa

whether political or economic or both, since Apollonia was under its control.

The connections of the coastal cities of Halaesa and Kale Akte with the interior were economically important primarily because of the grain which needed to be transported to a harbour for shipment to Italy. One of the most important east–west routes passed south of the Nebrodi, connecting Catina on the east coast with Thermae Himeraeae in the north-west. This road passed close to Agyrium, a town which was linked to Capitium, and, further north again, with Amestratus, Kale Akte and Halaesa. The land around Enna, Assorum and Agyrium was very fertile, and made a major contribution to the *annona*, the grain as tax-in-kind destined for Rome. Since Enna was located just above the Catina–Thermae highway, one would have expected its grain to be transported to one or other of these two harbours. Cicero, however, claims that grain was transported from Enna to Halaesa.[16] Such a route must clearly have existed, for south of Halaesa lies the only easily penetrable route through the Nebrodi mountains. Nevertheless, one would expect the road between Catina and Thermae to have been of better quality and safer by comparison with one through wild mountains. A not unimportant factor was the size of the necessary facilities, surely very minor by comparison with those at major port cities such as Catina and Thermae Himeraeae .

The evidence for roads derived from the physical geography is supported by a number of documents which attest to the existence of land itineraries. One, recorded on an inscription at Delphi as early as the third or the beginning of the second century BC possibly contains a reference to Kale Akte, although that is not certain.[17] It provides a list of all the places in Sicily visited by the *theoroi* at some point before 175 BC, in order to invite the cities to attend the Pythian games.[18] Manni suggested that the initial K in the list stands for Kephaloidion rather than Kale Akte, supporting the notion that the latter was still at this period a place of little significance.[19] A recent alternative hypothesis suggests that the K stands for Kapition, in the mountains south of Kale Akte.[20] In that case, the route followed by the *theoroi* would have been either Assoros – Kapition – Kale Akte – Halaesa, or else Assoros – Kapition – Herbita – Halaesa. It is certain that Herbita possessed an important cult of Apollo, and there is clear evidence for a cult of the same god also at Kale Akte.[21] However, if the small and insignificant Kapition was included in the itinerary, it must have been only a halt on the way to the coast, which lay only some 20 km to the north. If the journey of the *theoroi* took place around 198/7 BC, Kale Akte would have been a considerably more important centre than Herbita, then in decline. It could also be argued that Halaesa had inherited the previous role played by

Herbita as an important centre for the cult. Kale Akte, the oldest and, together with Halaesa, the only city which had a partly Greek origin, had a Greek name, a foundation with the blessing of a Greek oracle (possibly even that of Delphic Apollo) and with partly Greek settlers, would certainly have been a more natural halt for the Delphic *theoroi* than the old Sikel stronghold in the interior, Herbita. The latter can hardly have been very 'Greek' in appearance. To sum up, a case can certainly be made to interpret the K of the Delphic list as standing for Kale Akte, in which case the Delphic *theoroi* will have visited it on their journey in the early second century BC.

The so-called *Itinerarium Antonini* represents a road list of the Roman Empire from the time of Caracalla (the emperor of its title) revised around the middle of the fourth century AD: it therefore provides information about the road networks in Sicily at the latter period.[22] It lists Sicily's principal main routes as the three coastal roads – the *via Valeria* on the north between Messana and Lilybaeum; the *via Pompeia* on the east between Messana and Syracuse; and the *via Selinuntina* on the south coast between Syracuse and Lilybaeum. The list of places in Ptolemy's *Geography*, of the second century AD, and in the *Tabula Peutingeriana*, which in origin dates to the middle of the fourth century AD, are quite similar to each other but provide less detail than the *Itinerarium Antonini*. Halaesa, Kale Akte and Agathyrnum are mentioned as road stations in all these itineraries (Fig. 2.4). As noted above, it is no surprise that only coastal towns or towns with a closely linked settlement on the coast are mentioned. The two ancient strongholds of Apollonia, probably by then abandoned, and Haluntium, are ignored by the Roman roads which bypassed these hill-top towns. The communication network in the province appears to have been upgraded and improved from the first quarter of the fourth century AD, as suggested by the term in the *Itinerarium Antonini* of *mansionibus nunc institutis*, 'rest-stations newly established'. Giovanni Uggeri has suggested that their foundation was a consequence of the new *annona*, with Sicilian grain receiving renewed political attention at this time.[23] Under the new organisation new road stations were apparently built with *mansiones*, where it was possible to change horses and where accommodation was offered.

In the *Itinerarium*, a *diverticulum* of the *via Valeria* is mentioned at Kale Akte, leading inland to the unknown village of Solusapre, nine Roman miles to the south. This *diverticulum* is not present in the other itineraries.[24] There has been some discussion about the course of this route.[25] In my opinion, it was probably the same one conjectured above as leading towards the interior, following the hills along the river valley.[26] Solusapre

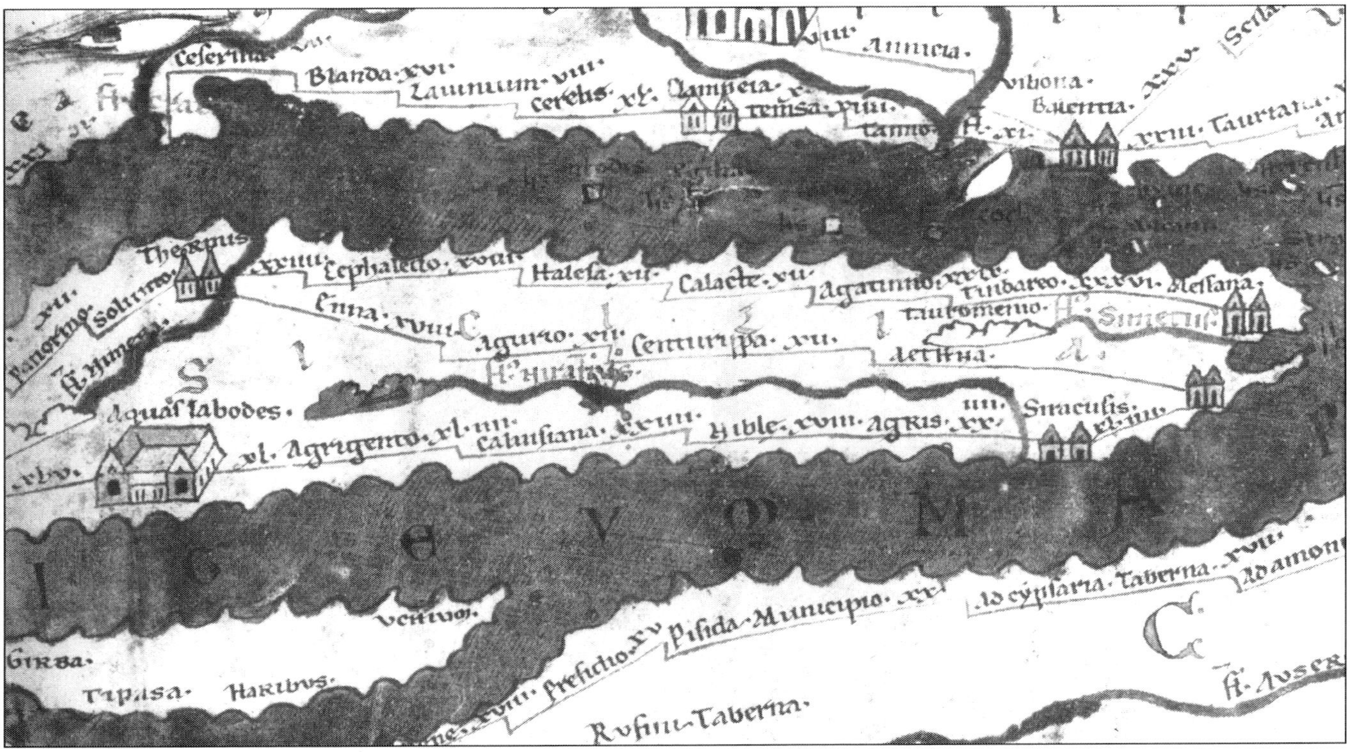

Fig. 2.4. Tabula Peutingeriana, *detail showing Sicily, with Kale Akte included as* Calacte *near the centre of the north coast*

presumably refers to an agricultural community, some 15 km from the coast, perhaps to be identified with a Roman agricultural settlement in *contrada* Samperi.[27]

(b) Maritime routes

Shipping lanes are by their nature not constrained by geography in the same way that roads are. Obviously, Sicily's central Mediterranean position between Italy and North Africa ensured that maritime connection with these areas was an ever-present factor in antiquity. The intensity of these communications depended on the economic and political situation at any one time. Contacts with Italy, especially its southern and Tyrrhenian parts – geographically and culturally the closest – were of course especially strong, and were already so in prehistoric times. Contacts existed with the Aegean area in the Bronze and Iron Ages, and became intensive during the Greek 'colonisation' period and in the following centuries.

Most goods doubtless arrived at Kale Akte by sea. As noted above, the fact that the settlement was founded close to the coast was hardly a coincidence: the town depended on maritime connections from the beginning of its existence. Even if the site was situated on the main communications artery of the north Sicilian coast, which probably existed already in primitive form by the time of Ducetius, transport by sea was superior in many respects to that by land. Ships could carry the goods much faster and in larger quantities than if transported by land. The price edict of Diocletian of AD 301 gives us an idea of how much cheaper it was to carry goods by sea than by land. The north coast of Sicily was also the most privileged part of the island for trade with Rome. It was possible to transport goods cheaper and faster from Kale Akte and other towns on the north Sicilian coast to Rome than it was from parts of inland Etruria or from the Adriatic coast of Italy.[28]

At Kale Akte, we have no specific literary evidence for a port, but one is implied by the fact that grain from Amestratum was transported to the city.[29] Archaeological evidence for a harbour settlement has now come from the excavations at Marina di Caronía.[30] That Halaesa also had a harbour is clear from Diodorus, who claims that the city had a prosperous maritime trade;[31] the presumed river-harbour at Castel di Tusa is only *c.*1.5 km (8 stadia) away. The city dominates this port, just as the hill of Caronía dominates Marina di Caronía. We have no knowledge at present of the size of the harbour, but at least in the Late Republic it may have been of some importance, since it seems likely that large amounts of grain from the interior were shipped from here. Apollonia too must have had a small harbour, at Acquedolci (p. 16), at least until the Early Empire, when the hill-town was given up; whether or not the coastal site continued to flourish later is unknown. Apollonia in the late Republic (as noted above: p. 21) provided a single ship for the Sicilian fleet.[32]

Haluntium is the town situated furthest inland of the coastal towns in our area, more than double the distance as that between Halaesa and the sea; it is also higher, at 540 m above sea level. The coast near Haluntium is not at all inviting for ships seeking haven; but a small trading post can be hypothesised, as we have seen (p. 24) at Marina di Torrenova, and possibly also at Sant' Agata di Militello, judging by the finds from the latter. Perhaps both functioned as outlets of goods from Haluntium, which included its local stone, a *rosso fiorito*, and also a well-known wine.[33] Scramuzza[34] suggested that Haluntium must have had port facilities since it furnished the Roman fleet with timber, but this argument is not by itself conclusive, as towns of the interior like Amestratus and Herbita also furnished ships, even though they did not have harbours. The concept of hill town and maritime town being in close proximity was a model common in Roman Sicily, and still is today. Haluntium, like Apollonia, seems to have suffered in Imperial times from its inaccessibility from the sea, at a time when possession of a good harbour was an important asset to trade during the *Pax Romana*. Another coastal site nearby is Capo d'Orlando, usually identified as ancient Agathyrnum (p. 24).[35]

One of the busiest harbours in the whole of Sicily was Messana, at the crossroads between east and west, north and south: it enjoyed direct contacts with the Aegean, Asia Minor, Alexandria in Egypt, Libya, Carthage, Spain, southern Gaul, as well of course with Italy, especially Puteoli and Ostia. This must have been the port of call from which Kale Akte received many of its imports, at least those arriving from the east, supplied by local shipping after initial warehousing in Messana. Tyndaris might have been a further call along the route, for further sorting of goods and redistribution. Lipari was another highly important commercial centre. Here large ships from Puteoli and Ostia, but also from Gallia Narbonensis, unloaded parts of their cargo. In the other direction, ships from North Africa, carrying especially olive oil and fish preserves, offloaded some of their cargo at Lipari. Lipari may have been an important centre for regional trade and exchange, situated conveniently close to the north Sicilian coast. In the Roman Imperial period ships from southern Spain, with cargoes of oil and *garum,* skirted at least the western part of the north coast, before heading further east.[36] Ships from Italy, North Africa and Spain will also have offloaded parts of their cargoes in other major Sicilian ports, such as Panhormus and Lilybaeum.[37]

Most of the long-distance sea routes will have by-passed places such as Kale Akte. For its port and other small ones on the central north Sicilian coast, small-scale local and sub-regional trade was probably by far the most common type of activity seen there. Horden and Purcell's *The Corrupting Sea* emphasizes that there would have been no Mediterranean commerce without small entrepreneurs, who made shorter voyages along the coast, away from the main shipping routes.[38] The *caboteurs* were the backbone of Mediterranean trade, continuing commercial activity even at seasons of low trading intensity. No doubt most of the ships anchoring at the harbour of Kale Akte were therefore *caboteurs*, carrying produce from the local area, for example from Halaesa, Kephaloidion, Tyndaris or Messana, or else carrying redistributed goods imported from more distant lands, such as North Africa, Italy, southern France and Spain.

Economic resources

Arable and grazing land

(a) Production of grain

From the early Greek period, Sicily was famous for its fertility and for its rich fields of grain. Its importance is attested by the ubiquitous cults to Demeter and Kore, deities omnipresent on the Greek city coinage of Sicily. Barley had been cultivated in Sicily since the Neolithic, and wheat since at least the Bronze Age.[39] Most grain came in antiquity from the inland plains and hills of the island, to which Herbita in our region belonged. The so-called *Lex Hieronica* dating from the reign of Hieron II (*c.* 275–215 BC) forced the subjects of the vast kingdom of Syracuse to pay a tithe, 10%, of their annual harvests, to the king, and this system was taken over by the Romans, who called it the *decuma* (the 'one-tenth'); they applied it to the entire province.[40] Sicily was 'the Republic's storehouse, the nurse at whose breast the Roman people is fed',[41] and it continued to be so until Octavian's conquest of Egypt in 31 BC. Later, in addition to the tithe, all towns were obliged to sell to Rome an additional quantity of wheat almost equal to it. This happened for the first time in 191 BC, but was fixed as a law only in 73 BC with the *lex frumentaria (Terentia et Cassia)*.[42]

Most middle-sized or small towns in Sicily were *civitates decumanae* during the Roman Republic, including Kale Akte, Herbita and Amestratus, but not Halaesa, which was exempt from the *decuma*.[43] Halaesa, among the wealthiest cities on the island, had the largest territory and yielded the biggest harvest of all the cities of our region. Cicero singled it out: 'you will find none more abundant in its resources' (*nullam enim reperietis . . . copiis locupletiorem*).[44] We do not, however, have any exact figures for its annual yield. Verres demanded a contribution of 60,000 *modii* from the city and pocketed the proceeds for himself (the real point of Cicero's mention of the place), but we do not of course know what fraction of the annual yield this represented.[45] Large parts of the harvest were probably sold to Rome, since the city was exempted from the *decuma,* and income from it no doubt constituted one of the city's principal sources of revenue. It has been thought that the economic importance of Halaesa diminished decisively after the reforms of Augustus, when it became initially a *civitas stipendiaria,* but only temporarily, for it was soon raised to the rank of *municipium,* before the end of Augustus' reign,[46] and there seems to have been no dramatic decline in its economic importance during the Early Empire.[47] Grain production was probably even more important at Herbita, since the *decuma* of the city was estimated in 71 BC at 7,500 *medimnoi,* a figure not much lower than that at Enna, a larger city and one of the most important grain producers in the inland (8,200 *medimnoi*), or the important city of Thermae Himeraeae (8,000 *medimnoi*).[48] In addition to many small landowners, most *chorai* in this part of central northern Sicily were probably cultivated by medium-sized landowners. At Herbita, in 73 BC at any rate, it has been calculated that 6,412 *iugera* of wheat were cultivated by 252 farmers, if Cicero's figures are to be believed; the 'average' farm might have consisted of around 155 *iugera* (about 96 acres).[49] Amestratus, with a much smaller and less fertile territory, paid only 800 *medimnoi*.[50] Kale Akte would have been placed somewhere in between; although it did not command a large *chora*, the cultivation of grain may have been possible in parts of the coastal area.[51] Grain from the fertile inland plains was transported to the harbours on the north coast; that from Enna was apparently transported to Halaesa, as we have seen (p. 32), and so probably also that from Herbita.[52]

(b) Viticulture

The cultivation of the vine in Sicily already existed before the arrival of Greek settlers in the island: Tamar Hodos rightly questions the notion that the Greeks were the pioneers who introduced it.[53] The *vitis vinifera* originated in forest regions where the land was not particularly fertile,[54] but it thrives in moist conditions. The coastal strip of Kale Akte must have been suitable for vine growing, as well as the hills around – the area enjoys a mild and moist Tyrrhenian climate – but the vine was grown more or less everywhere around the Mediterranean basin.[55] An indication, however, of its importance to Kale Akte's economy is probably to be found in the city's coinage in the second century BC.

Many of the numismatic motifs there (and on Halaesa's coinage) are derived from the *symmachia* issues of Halaesa/Herbita in the second half of the fourth century BC. The motif with a bunch of grapes, for example, is found on the reverse of the Apollo Archagetas coins, the god who accompanied the settlers. The grapes appear alongside the thunderbolt of Zeus, protector of the *symmachia*. Later in this series, in the second century BC, came a coin with the head of Dionysus on the obverse, and a bunch of grapes alone on the obverse. This is the issue that was copied later by an issue of Kale Akte, and it seems unlikely that this choice would have been made if the grape had little or no relevance to the community.

The interpretation of symbols that on one hand stand as attributes of gods and on the other hand indicate local produce is complex. Are they only indications of certain cults, or do they also constitute an important source for our knowledge of local economies? Beginning with the issues of the *symmachia*, the ears of grain and of Sikelia crowned with ears of grain are common motifs.[56] These are of course symbolic of the rich grain fields of Sicily, the main pillar of the island's wealth. The second most important agricultural produce of the island were without doubt grapes and the wine produced from them. Olive oil was also of importance, but as far as we know it never enjoyed an export market, as wine certainly did, in large quantities. The selection of both divinities and motifs was surely dictated by the relevance of each to the individual cities themselves, when they in turn came to coin. So an issue featuring a head of Dionysus on one side and a bunch of grapes on the other is likely to have been popular among grape-growing *poleis*, who naturally worshipped Dionysus to ensure their continued good fortune.[56] It is perhaps rather odd, therefore, that the appearance of grapes is mostly restricted to the coinage issued by communities in the north-eastern part of the island – Halaesa, Kale Akte, Haluntium, Tyndaris, Lipara, Tauromenium and Katane. Grapes were clearly grown in other parts of Sicily, but apart from Enna in the centre of the island, the only places elsewhere minting an issue depicting a bunch of grapes were Entella and Iaitas (Monte Iato), both in the interior of western Sicily.[57]

According to Vandermersch,[58] it is possible to assign vine cultivation to a given city only if a representation with connotations of wine on a coin or an amphora stamp (for example, Dionysian motifs or a representation of an amphora) is attested along with one of two other categories of evidence: either an ancient literary source mentioning viticulture at the same period, or else its continuing practice today. Local production of wine amphorae is a further criterion. From a survey of the sources for wine production in cities which mint coins with Dionysian motifs, such correlations in most cases exist. The issues of Taormina, for example, depict Apollo with laurel wreath, facing left on the obverse and a bunch of grapes on the reverse, or else Apollo on the obverse, and on the reverse a lyre, above which is a small bunch of grapes. The choice of motif is no coincidence: Tauromenium was the heir to the famous wine-producing city Naxos.[59] Another city minting coins featuring a bunch of grapes was Haluntium,[60] where a famous wine was produced in the Late Republican/Early Imperial periods.[61] Catania was also doubtless a wine-producing city, as it lies on the lower slopes of mount Etna, today one of the most important wine-producing districts in Sicily.[62] Lipara was another town minting coins depicting a bunch of grapes: this is one of many places in the central Mediterranean where the wine amphora of shape

City	Archaeological indications	Literary indications	Known modern production
Halaesa	x		
Kale Akte	x		
Haluntium		x	
Lipara	x		x
Tyndaris			
Tauromenium	x	x	x
Naxos	x	x	x
Catane		x	x
Entella		x	x
Iaitas	x		

Table 2.1. Table showing cities minting coins which depict bunches of grapes among their motifs listed on the left, compared with archaeological evidence (column 1) and literary evidence (column 2) for wine production in antiquity, and places with notable grape and/or wine production today (column 3)

Dressel 2/4 was being produced in the Augustan period.[63] Lipari with its fertile volcanic soil had very good potential for vine growing, and it still does today, when it is known above all for its *Malvasia delle Lipari*. Entella, which also issued coins with a bunch of grapes, does satisfy Vandermersch's conditions, since its wine is mentioned in an ancient source;[64] it is also situated close to the vine-growing lands where Marsala wine is produced today.[65] By contrast, at Iaitas, Tyndaris[66] and Halaesa, the remaining three cities, we have no information concerning local wine production in antiquity beyond that suggested by the coin issues themselves (Table 2.1). At the Kale Akte mint, the issue depicting Dionysus on the obverse and a bunch of grapes on the reverse is the most frequently occurring type and presumably the most popular (Fig. 4.38; colour Pl. 15). The other local issues all reflect divinities and their attributes – Athena, Apollo, Hermes and Herakles – but none with relevance to the local economy (Figs 4.37–40). There are indications of wine production at Kale Akte between the fourth and the first centuries BC, including locally produced transport amphorae destined for wine, and large quantities of red-gloss resin-lined jugs.[67]

In addition to north-eastern Sicily, Bruttium in the toe of Italy (modern Calabria) was also a wine-producing area: their cities too minted coins with Dionysian motifs.[68] In Sicily, the reputation of wines from the Etna area and from Haluntium has been referred to above; but still in the late Roman and Byzantine period, wine from north-eastern Sicily was continuing to reach western Mediterranean markets as far away as Spain, France and Germany.[69] One of the production centres is now thought to have been at Kale Akte (Marina di Caronía) itself, and this variety, known elsewhere in Sicily further west on the north coast at Capo d'Orlando and Termini Imerese, has been identified through thin-section analysis at Marseilles.[70]

The use of wooden barrels for storing wine is known from Catania, and the use of such containers cannot be excluded in a region with great forests such as ours, especially for short-distance transport. However, it is evident from the finds of probably locally produced amphorae[71] that for long-distance transport ceramic containers were preferred. Recently a late Roman wine amphora with a distinctly Catanian fabric (in the form of volcanic inclusions) has been identified as a distinctive type.[72]

(c) Oleiculture

The cultivation of olives in Sicily has its roots in prehistory, and ever since it has been one of the mainstays of the Sicilian food production. Olives were an important part of the diet, and the oil made from pressing olives was used at *gymnasia*, as a fuel in lamps, and in the kitchen for cooking. Since olives and olive oil were such basic dietary commodities, virtually all towns in Sicily were probably surrounded by olive groves, at least in Classical and Hellenistic times; indeed they played a central part in Greek culture and society.

Olive groves remain a very conspicuous feature in the Sicilian landscape today, and modern Caronía is even called the *Città dell'olio*, showing that high-quality oil is still being produced nearby. For antiquity, however, the fullest evidence we have for oleiculture in the region comes not from Kale Akte but from Halaesa, in a Hellenistic inscription which makes clear its importance to that city's local economy.[73] Whether it played an important role at Kale Akte as well is hard to gauge.[74] Halaesa also struck coins featuring olive wreaths, as did Tyndaris and Haluntium, and Holm thought that this was sufficient evidence to denote oil production at the former; Wilson has concluded the same for the latter.[75] The absence of any identified Sicilian-produced oil amphorae is, however, striking, a conclusion confirmed by the now quite consistent material from Caronía; and the same situation is matched everywhere else in Sicily, both in Hellenistic and Roman Imperial times. This suggests that Kale Akte, along with most of Sicily in the Hellenistic period and later, probably consumed locally- or regionally-produced olive oil, and it was apparently not transported in amphorae. It is also still uncertain how far Sicilian oleiculture was affected by the arrival of high-quality olive oil from the Iberian peninsula after the mid-first century AD, but the low numbers of Spanish oil amphorae so far identified in early imperial contexts in Sicily suggest that the quantity of Spanish imports was quite modest. A more significant impact is likely to have been made by the massive increase in oil production and export in *Africa Byzacena* and *Tripolitana* from the later second century AD onwards, documented by the huge numbers of African amphorae arriving at Ostia; they are ubiquitous too all over Sicily. Although published quantified deposits are few, these imports are likely to have seriously affected Sicilian oil production, and led to a decrease in its relative importance.

The forests

The area of the Nebrodi mountain range is still comparatively rich in forests today, but they were much more extensive in antiquity. Silius Italicus talks about this range as being 'as rich in shade as any mountain in Sicily'.[76] The dense forests in Kale Akte's immediate hinterland were obviously, therefore, one of its main natural resources.

(a) Ship-building

The *Bosco di Caronía* is today a protected fragment of forest, until recently the largest in Sicily but now much reduced; it has a museum dedicated to it in Caronía itself. It consists largely of oak (excellent for shipbuilding) and of beech. In antiquity this formed only a small part of the great forests of the Nebrodi Mountains, the most important source in Sicily of shipbuilding timber, as many literary sources attest.[77] The area stretching from Etna in the east to Agrigento in the south to Himera in the north-west and Messana in the north-east was densely covered in forests at least down to the Imperial period.[78] It was from this region that Gelon planned to get the timber for the 300 ships he needed to give Athens and the Greek city-states in their war against Xerxes.[79] Shipbuilding can be assumed to have been an important branch of economy in a timber-rich area like that of Kale Akte. Cicero relates how Verres gave the command of a fleet to a certain Cleomenes of Syracuse: led by a quadrireme from Centuripae, and including six ships supplied by Segesta, Tyndaris, Herbita, Herakleia, Apollonia and Haluntium, it was 'a fine fleet to look at'.[80] Amestratus was also apparently involved in this fleet, as it was one of the towns from which Verres took payment for exempting rowers and sailors from duty.[81] Herbita and Amestratus, despite being inland *poleis*, furnished ships for this fleet, helped no doubt by ready access to plentiful oak-timber in their territories. Kale Akte, on the coast and with a harbour, is surely likely to have had a ship-building industry. Access to timber sources close to the sea helped reduce costs, as land transport was expensive. That Kale Akte and Halaesa indeed constructed warships is also indicated by the inscription that was found in the *agora* of Halaesa, commemorating a naval victory (maybe against pirates) by the combined cities of Halaesa, Kale Akte, Herbita and Amestratus (Fig. 1.16).[82] The inscription, which has been dated to the late second or the early first century BC, provides evidence that a *symmachia* was capable of building and furnishing a fleet of its own. Timber was also of course exported as a commodity in its own right for use elsewhere: much later, for example, in the Price Edict of the Emperor Diocletian (dated to AD 301), 14 ells of oak timber is assessed as being worth 250 denarii, the same price as for beech.[83]

Under the regime of Sextus Pompey, Sicily had to produce military and naval material on a very large scale in order to put its defenses on a war footing, and Sextus struck gold, silver and bronze coins to pay for it.[84] Kale Akte and the neighbouring coastal cities may well have had to provide substantial quantities of timber for Sextus Pompey's fleet; no doubt their ship wharves were alive with activity at the time.

(b) Livestock and pastoralism

The hilly areas of Kale Akte with its forests provided a good environment for cattle- and livestock-breeding. Pastoralism had existed in Sicily for millennia before the arrival of the Greeks: it was a natural economic activity in a marginal area like that of the Nebrodi, which lacks abundant fertile arable land. Pastoralism probably played an important part in the economy of Kale Akte from the very founding of the settlement. Loom weights have been found in large numbers at Caronía, Marina di Caronía and Apollonia, indicating textile activity in the area (Figs 2.5 a–c).[85] Mountainous areas have always been considered marginal, and impenetrable to communication. Mountain micro-ecologies are almost always part of a larger ecological network. Closeness to markets was and is crucial for the pastoralist,[86] and Kale Akte provided one such market for those feeding their flocks and herds in neighbouring parts of the Nebrodi. Diodorus mentions Damophilos, a rich owner at Enna of 'vast herds of cattle'.[87] Cattle bones are common in prehistoric and Roman contexts in Sicily,[88] and literary sources mention the export to Rome of cattle hides during the Social War.[89] Seasonal movement of animals was the norm (p. 30). The most common system in use was that which Horden and Purcell have called 'vertical' transhumance, with herds of moderate size moving to upland pastures in summer.[90] In the Appennines, sheep- and cattle-rearing seems to have expanded in the Roman period, when Strabo says that *ager publicus* was leased out as pasture.[91] It is possible that underdeveloped regions like the Nebrodi Mountains were retained as part of official policy as marginal lands specifically for pasture.[92] We do not know if Sicily's reduced importance as a grain producer after the conquest of Egypt in 31 BC led to less grain being cultivated, or merely whether it represented a decline in the island's relative importance as a grain-producer in the wider Roman economy; certainly there is no evidence to suggest that pastoralism expanded at the expense of cereal cultivation. In the case of Kale Akte, its economic strategy throughout antiquity must have focused on the flexibility of mixed farming.[93]

Sheep were the most common of all animals in Sicily. Their economic importance was huge; they provided meat, wool, milk, and cheese, and not surprisingly it is the most commonly represented animal in both prehistoric and late Roman bone assemblages in Sicily (Fig. 2.6).[94] Wool was the biggest potential money spinner;[95] it seems therefore probable that a harbour town with a mountainous hinterland (such as Kale Akte) would have included the shipment of wool for export among its activities. A dyeing industry is known from the *Tabulae Halaesinae* to have existed at Halaesa.[96]

Fig. 2.5. Loom weights: (a) *with swastika and* (b) *with circle decoration, both from the* phrourion *at Pizzo Cilona, fifth century BC;* (c) *with an image of Medusa, from Caronía, surface find during field survey*

Sicily was noted in antiquity for its horse breeding. Other than for riding, horses were also used as draft animals, and they were also in demand as racehorses in Roman circuses.[97] At Halaesa a certain Dio raised *greges nobilissimarum equarum* ('herds of the finest steeds') in the first century BC;[98] he was the target of a million-sesterces extortion racket perpetrated by the notorious Verres, or so Cicero claims.[99] Sicilian horses continued to have a high reputation in late antiquity,[100] and to this day the famous *Sanfratellani* horses, which are of Norman descent, are still being raised at the small town of San Fratello, near ancient Apollonia, just a few kilometres from Caronía (Fig. 2.7). The mule and (for less onerous tasks) the donkey were other important animals in Sicily (Fig. 2.8). Mules, for example, were used as pack-animals for transporting grain and other agricultural produce from the inland plains to the coastal harbours. Along the *trazzere* which led from the hills of Herbita, as well as from Capitium and Amestratum across the Nebrodi mountain chain to Kale Akte and Halaesa, mule trains must have been a common sight, since carts were hardly usable there in the steep mountainous terrain.

Pork was an important part of the diet of the Romans. The Sicilian forests, such as those of the Nebrodi, offered vast quantities of large acorns, and so a free food-supply for pigs.[101] Pig bones are very common in the archaeological deposits at Marina di Caronía. Studies of animal bones in Sicily from both prehistoric and late Roman contexts have indicated that pig was generally the second most important domesticated animal after sheep/goats.[102]

(c) Hunting

Sicilian forests abounded in game; the name Nebrodi derives from the Greek word *nebrodos*, meaning deer. In antiquity deer (today extinct) roamed the forests of Sicily and were systematically hunted.[103] Red, roe and fallow deer all had the island as its habitat, and at the late Roman rural site at Campanaio in southern Sicily, deer bones were second only to sheep/goats.[104] The find of a deer antler in the excavations at Caronía in 1999 suggests that the situation was not much different there: the large forests of the Nebrodi constituted a perfect habitat for them. In addition to providing meat and important protein, the skin of deer was also prized: in Diocletian's price edict of AD 301, its price was set at 100 *denarii*.[105]

Products of the sea

The sea is, of course, a tremendous natural resource for any harbour city, and Kale Akte was no exception. The poet Silius Italicus extols the *litus piscosa Calacta* ('the Kale Akte shore that abounds in fish'),[106] and Athenaeus ranks Sicilian tuna-fish as 'next in merit only to those caught at Cadiz'.[107] An Egyptian papyrus notes that in the Hellenistic period fish from the island even reached Palestine.[108] Athenaeus mentions that 10,000 amphorae containing salted Sicilian fish reached Alexandria – a conveniently round number, but an indication of Sicily's potential for the export of fish products.[109]

There is up to now no evidence for fish-salting at Kale Akte. Ancient sources mention Cetaria, Tyndaris, Cephaloedium and Soluntum for their fish,[110] and archaeological research has identified fish-salting

Fig. 2.6. Sheep grazing in contrade *Mastrostefano and Impallaccionata on the edge of the Nebrodi forests*

Fig. 2.7. Spirited horses of the San Fratello breed

Fig. 2.8. Mules in a field near Pizzo Cilona, south of Caronía

establishments at S. Vito Lo Capo, Solunto, and Isola delle Femmine, as well as on the Egadi islands off the west coast.[111] Most of these appear to have continued into late antiquity.[112] Salted fish and fish sauces, such as *garum*, *muria* and *allec*,[113] were important ingredients in the Roman kitchen, used as a seasoning in place of salt, and constituting of course an important source of protein in the diet.

Tuna fishing seems especially to have been practised on the north coast: Athenaeus mentions Cephaloedium and Tyndaris as being especially famous.[114] A well-known fourth-century BC red-figured krater from Lipari shows a fish vendor: the fish he is preparing for his customer is usually thought to be tuna, in view of its considerable size (see colour Pl. 16). Obviously, Kale Akte would have had the same opportunities for fish exploitation, and bones of tuna have been found in archaeological contexts there, especially from excavations at *contrada* Pantano.[115] Silius Italicus might have been thinking of tuna when he referred to Kale Akte as *litus piscosa*, and if so the tuna was presumably salted and exported, because otherwise he was unlikely to have even heard of it; but we cannot be absolutely certain about the exact fish species, or indeed perhaps multiple species, for which Kale Akte had gained its special reputation.[116] Tuna fishing is certainly still attested here in medieval times, since the twelfth-century Arab geographer, Al-Idrisi, cites the poet Kadì Ibn-Qâlâqî's verses about the nets of tunny that were tossed into the sea at Caronía.[117] Still in the early twentieth century there was a *tonnara* at Marina di Caronía; its remains are still visible today. So it looks as though there has been a tradition of tuna fishing in the Caronía area for centuries, one likely to have gone back at least as far as the Roman period and possibly to Hellenistic times as well. Fish-sauce (*garum*) was sometimes produced only in small quantities, for local markets.[118] Certainly it would not be a surprise if an ancient fish-preserving complex, whether large or small, were one day to be found at Caronía.[119]

3

Archaeological research at Caronía and Marina di Caronía

Caronía

Excavations at the hill-town of Caronía were first conducted in 1992–1993 by the Superintendency of Messina, directed by Dr Carmela Bonanno, and were followed by two shorter campaigns in 1999 and 2005, directed by Dr Maria Costanza Lentini.[1]

It is today very difficult to reconstruct the original urban layout of Classical-period Kale Akte as nothing of it has been revealed: it lies beneath the multiple archaeological layers of Hellenistic and Roman Kale Akte, and of medieval and modern Caronía. However, it is possible to hypothesize about the extent of the earliest settlement from the topography and from the archaeological data currently available, which have increased significantly since the 1990s. The combined evidence of a late Archaic trading post at Marina di Caronía, finds of pottery from the late fifth century BC at the hill-town, the large proportion of coins found coming from the mint of Kale Akte, brick stamps with the abbreviated letters of the town's name,[2] and the testimony of the Roman itineraries,[3] all leave no doubt at all that Caronía is the site of Kale Akte, and that its harbour lay on the coast below, at Marina di Caronía.

The maritime settlement at the latter was certainly not anything like a Greek *apoikia*: rather the main settlement was founded on a strategic hill, in accordance with Sikel custom. This, with an area suitable for settlement of about 3 hectares (5 hectares if we include the acropolis), was presumably where the town was laid out: it is smaller than Ducetius' foundation at Mineo (Menai) (*c.* 8 hectares). However, the ancient town at Caronía occupied only about half the area of the ridge that today is urbanized in its entirety (an area of almost 10 hectares). A Sikel settlement probably predated Ducetius' foundation at Caronía, of no doubt modest dimensions. As we have seen (p. 10), nothing is heard of Kale Akte for several centuries after the death of Ducetius in 440 BC, in contrast to other towns in the area, such as Halaesa, Haluntium and Apollonia, which are mentioned in the sources. One is left with the impression that the potential political importance of the site evaporated with the death of Ducetius in 440 BC.

On the basis of what we know about the Hellenistic town, the Kale Akte of Ducetius had more similarities with Sikel towns in its choice of site than any Greek one. Its hill-top situation close to the sea is very similar to the Sikel foundations of Halaesa and Haluntium. If the Classical urban layout was not markedly different from the Hellenistic one, the town from its beginning would have had a regular street-grid with its main orientation north–south. The medieval town is dominated by the Norman castle, situated on what is a perfect site for an acropolis. *Spolia* of Roman columns decorate the courtyard of the castle,[4] which certainly, like the many square Hellenistic bricks reused there, come from ancient buildings. The most important sanctuary of Halaesa was situated at the highest point of its hill,[5] and it seems probable that this was also the case at Kale Akte, obliterated by the Norman castle. The southern limit of the upper town probably lay in the area of present-day Porta Torre. Such was the steepness of the rock on which Kale Akte was founded that an entire circuit of fortifications may not have been necessary; but walls were needed in the area where the southern medieval city defences at Porta Torre ('Arco saraceno') were later built, at the weakest part of the approach to the top: an attacker could otherwise have easily climbed the low hills to the east in *contrada* Trapesi and followed a ridge all the way to the south entrance of the town.

Very recently, a small glimpse of the earliest phase of urban life of Kale Akte was revealed after a landslide behind (west of) the so-called Case Popolari in *contrada* Sotto San Francesco, on the eastern slope of Caronía (Fig. 3.1).[6] Two rooms had been carved out of the rock, with walls above constructed of mud bricks. The ceramic material was dated to the end of the fifth century BC. It seems that the structures of this first phase were destroyed around 330/325 BC – whether from a natural phenomenon like a landslip or through human agency is unknown. The earliest wall so far found in excavation was dated by Bonanno to the mid-fourth century BC, on the basis of a Pagenstecher-type *lekythos* found embedded in the wall.[7] Pagenstecher *lekythoi* date from between the mid-fourth century and the early third century BC; so this wall may well have belonged to a general re-building of the city, if the destruction mentioned above at this date is detected frequently elsewhere in the town.

The excavations undertaken at Caronía in 1992–93, 1999 and 2005 have demonstrated that the late Classical/Hellenistic settlement was built on a series of terraces, with well-built retaining walls, sometimes strengthened by brick buttresses (*contrafforti*) (Fig. 3.2).

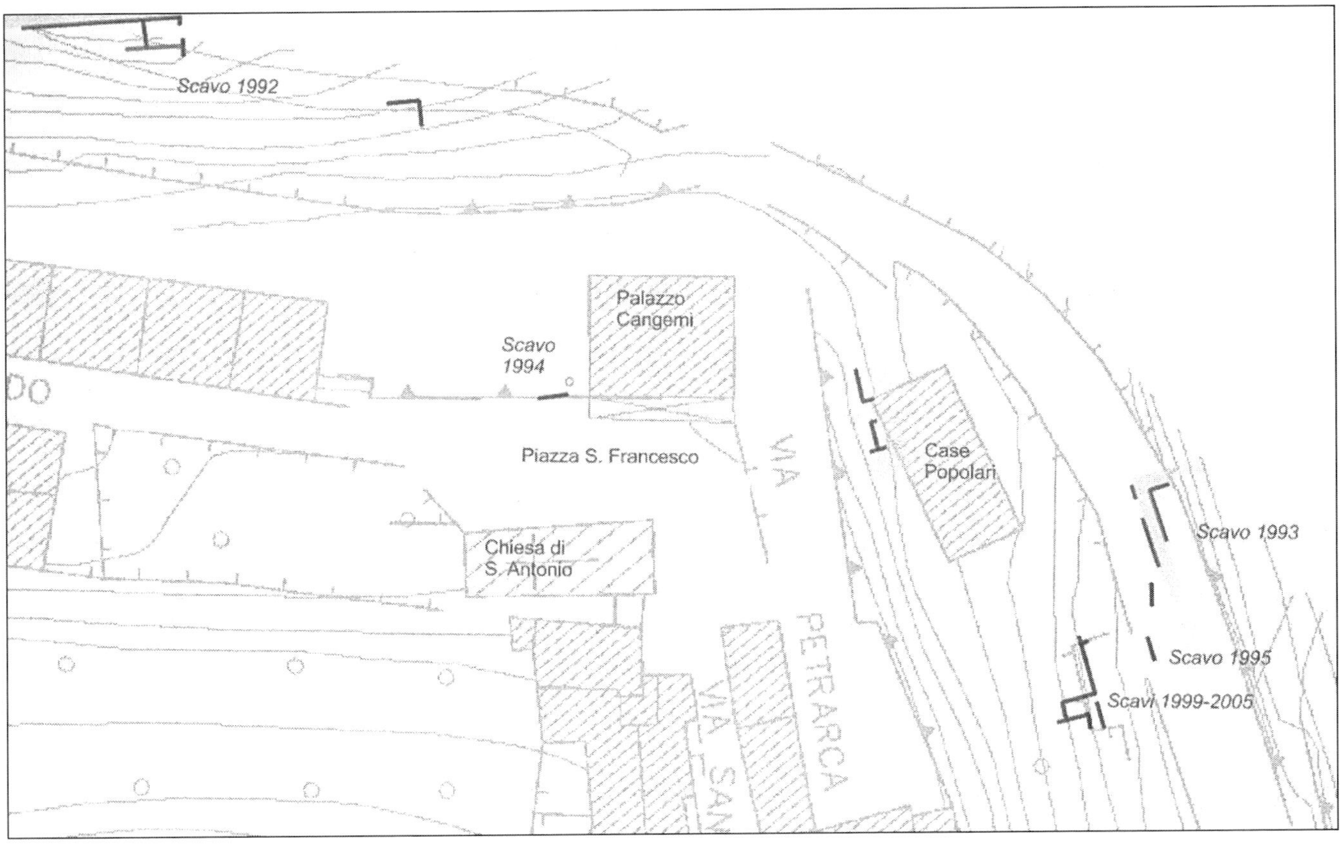

Fig. 3.1 Caronía, plan showing the location of archaeological excavations in contrada *Sotto San Francesco between 1992 and 2005.* Contrada *Telegrafo lies on the north side of the hill in the area of 'Scavo 1992' (top left).*

Due to the difficult, steeply-sloping terrain, the only area where it has been possible to excavate a continuous portion of buildings is in *contrada* Sotto San Francesco ('Scavi 1999–2005' on Fig. 3.1).[8] Here, a well-preserved wall was revealed, built in dressed limestone with a central section made of brickwork, a technique found commonly at Caronía (Fig. 3.3).[9] It may have been constructed in this way to withstand earthquakes more effectively, since the technique gives the wall both stability and flexibility. Outside it a complete *pithos* was found. The wall, presumably dating to the first century BC, had been partly built over a bell-shaped cistern. Judging from the oldest ceramic material found in it (not necessarily a good indication of construction date), the latter can probably be dated to the end of the fourth/early third century BC. This cistern is one of at least nine encountered on the hill-top of Caronía.[10]

The urban settlement clearly stretched out on terraces down the northern and eastern slopes of the hill, on which houses were built. On the north slope, the urban settlement continued more than half-way down to the plain of *contrada* Todaro. Only a few small alleyways have been found, surfaced by a beaten layer of broken tiles and pebbles.

A surprising aspect of the urban plan of Kale Akte is that no trace of fortifications have so far been detected, in contrast to the neighbouring cities of Halaesa, Apollonia and Haluntium – something that is almost without parallel in Sicily.[11] As mentioned above, however (p. 00), parts of the hill which were the most easily approachable demanded some kind of defence, in antiquity as in medieval times. Theoretically, at any rate, the uppermost plateau of the hill may originally have been surrounded by a wall in the town's earliest days, prior to its later expansion down the slopes.[12] However, since we now know that the earliest settlement already expanded on the upper part of the eastern slope in the area known as the Case Popolari (Fig. 3.1), such a hypothesis seems not to be tenable. There is unlikely to have been a city wall surrounding Kale Akte on the east, north or west sides; the terrain is simply too steep there. The southern part of the town, on the other hand, was much more accessible; not protected by steep slopes, it seems likely (as noted above) that some kind of fortification must have existed there.[13] When the town was originally laid out, in the mid/late fifth century BC, the steep slopes elsewhere were probably regarded as sufficient in themselves for

Fig. 3.2 Detail of a terrace wall with a supporting pillar of locally-made bricks, found during excavations in contrada *Telegrafo, 1992–93*

Fig. 3.3 Terrace wall of stonework with a middle section (left) made of brickwork (probably in the first century BC), found during excavations in contrada *Sotto San Francesco, 1999*

defence. If Ducetius had been allowed to return with the consent of Syracuse (p. 9), it would not have been in the interest of the latter for him to create a stronghold at Kale Akte: rather the foundation was primarily intended to serve as an outpost harbour community. From the very beginning, therefore, its character probably differed from neighbouring Sikel settlements, which arose out of local claims for territorial power.

The layout of the settlement differs from that of an *apoikia* of the classic Greek type. It was situated on a hilltop, built on terraces and with relatively narrow streets (*stenopoi*). It seems improbable that this layout changed significantly in antiquity after the time of Ducetius. Halaesa, founded as a joint settlement by Sikels and Greek mercenaries, was built in a very similar manner, on terraces in a sloping, hilly setting (colour Pl. 7), as is also the more extensively excavated Hellenistic town of Soluntum, between Cephaloedium (Cefalù) and Panhormus (Palermo). The street layout in an orthogonal grid can be regarded as typically Greek, but the hill-top location is, as we have seen, not: Kale Akte should be regarded as a Sikel-Greek hybrid. Its urban characteristics were shaped above all by two factors: the demands of natural topography, and the political and military capabilities of the *polis*. For a small *polis*, it was simply necessary to choose the most advantageous site from a defensive point of view, since it would have had restricted financial means to construct any major fortifications. The hybrid settlement of Ducetius had to respond to the challenge of the hilly topography, and, curbing ambitions, had to be built on a relatively small scale. The 'colonisation movement' would have consisted of new settlers being placed in an already existing Sikel community, who helped adapt its layout to a more regular plan – something which probably also happened at Menai.[14] This *modus operandi* seems to have been the norm in Ducetius' foundations.[15] Diodorus claims that the project of Kale Akte was on a fairly important scale, involving a large number of settlers.[16] This seems improbable, judging by the very modest structures and the scarcity of finds from the fifth century BC, in both hill-town and the harbour area, and also by the quite limited size of the later Hellenistic settlement, surely itself larger than its Classical predecessor. Diodorus, writing some 400 years after the event, had a tendency out of patriotism (as he was himself Sicilian) to exaggerate the significance of the Sikel leader's achievements.

The Hellenistic urban layout

We know little in detail of Kale Akte's urban layout in the Hellenistic period. The best evidence concerns the construction of houses (which made up the *insulae*) on the steep terraced slopes of the hill on the east and north sides. The earliest known wall can, as we have seen (p. 42), be dated to the last quarter or the very end of the fourth century BC; it shows that at least by this date the concept of an urban centre already existed.[17] An abandonment context in the earliest house found at Caronía may, however, indicate destruction almost immediately afterwards: the earliest ceramic material in a cistern excavated in 1999 was dated *c.* 300 BC, so it is possible that the cistern was part of a new layout of the town in the last quarter of the fourth century BC. It is of course impossible to say what caused this destruction shortly before 300 BC. We know that Agathocles besieged and sacked Kale Akte's close neighbour and probable ally, Apollonia, in 317 BC, and it may be that Kale Akte was also destroyed by him at the same time, as a punishment for having sided with Apollonia. The sources, however, are silent, and such a hypothesis remains pure speculation until future excavation and research can provide more detailed evidence about the scale of destruction at this date.

Most walling excavated at Kale Akte dates to the later Hellenistic period, mainly in the second and first centuries BC. Of the street-grid, the principal thoroughfare of the town (the *plateia*), probably followed the same course as today's Via Ducezio/Via Calacta, and was thus orientated north–south (colour Pl. 6).[18] The plateau of the hill was clearly too narrow to allow for more than one *plateia*.[19] The *stenopoi* would therefore have run east–west, and this has been confirmed by both excavation and surface survey. Both *plateia* and *stenopoi* continued down the slopes of the hill. Only small stretches of three *stenopoi* have been identified: in *contrada* Sotto San Francesco (the eastern slope), beneath the Palazzo Cangemi (Fig. 3.1), and in *contrada* Telegrafo on the north slope of the hill.[20] One is about 1.50 m wide; another has a breadth of 1.80 m and is bordered on one side by a terrace wall.[21] The *stenopoi* have a surface of rounded river-worn pebbles or other small stones, and in some cases additional fragments of brick are included. A short stretch of one of them was revealed, accidentally, by a recent landslide in *contrada* Telegrafo. Because of the sloping terrain, the streets are provided with steps, as are the *stenopoi* on similar terrain at Halaesa.[22]

One portion of a regular urban plan at Hellenistic Apollonia, near Kale Akte, dating to the early third century BC, has recently been partly revealed through excavation;[23] but in contrast to Kale Akte, where the town was partly constructed on steep slopes, at Apollonia it was built on a flat plateau. We know nothing about the earlier town at Apollonia sacked and burnt by Agathocles in 317 BC, but the third-century one probably followed the same plan, even if smaller than its predecessor. The plateau was divided into regular plots measuring *c.* 93 m square.[24] Since the area included was large (around 40 hectares), most of these probably represent agricultural land-divisions rather than urban *insulae*.

Although we possess no information about the plans of houses in the hill-town at Kale Akte, partial excavation has demonstrated that their interior walls were usually covered by painted plaster with simple decorative schemes, for example red on white. The cornices below the roofs were often of painted terracotta. That some houses were quite opulent is shown by the finds of mosaic floors and of different types of marble for the decoration of the walls.[25] Open spaces such as courtyards were paved with the locally-produced square bricks of Hellenistic type (Fig. 3.4). There seem to have been water channels running beneath the streets, covered with the same type of square bricks.[26] Water provision was always a problem on a hill-top where ground-water was inaccessible. Instead, a series of rain-water cisterns were dug out of

Fig. 3.4 Part of a courtyard paved with locally-made bricks, contrada *Telegrafo, 1992–93*

the rock; as noted above, nine have been identified on the hill.[27] They are all bell-shaped and have walls covered with lime. Water was, however not only provided by rainwater from cisterns. In the Hellenistic period, probably in the third century BC, an aqueduct was constructed, bringing water from springs in the hinterland to the town.[28] It was of a much simpler type than famous later Roman ones, consisting of a simple pipeline of terracotta, either U-shaped and covered with tiles, or tubular, the different lengths of which fitted into one another. Both types were probably set in trenches dug below the surface and then covered, so that they would have been invisible on the ground. From Kale Akte itself only a few fragments are known, but the course of a similar aqueduct at Halaesa has been well studied and much of its course reconstructed.[29] The Kale Akte one probably ran from the natural sources of springs at Piano Piraino, Pizzo Castellano and Piano della Chiesa, towards Serra Lisi and Acqua Ramusa.[30] There are some indications that Haluntium was also provided with water in the same way.[31] Judging from the stamped bricks and the flourishing of urban culture in the Nebrodi during the third century BC, it may be that the construction of all three of these aqueducts should be placed around the same time; but once again more fieldwork and dating evidence is required before this can be claimed with confidence.

The agora/*forum*

The whereabouts of the *agora* of Kale Akte is not certain, but it is logical to assume that it would have been situated somewhere on the plateau of the hill. It has recently been suggested by Francesco Collura that it lay on the flat area beneath the Norman castle, to the north of the Chiesa Madre.[32] Such a location fits well with the conjectural course of the *plateia* (the principal street artery of a town), which would have passed by here, and it also corresponds to the area where many rich finds have been made, especially on the slope below to the east. They include a Greek inscription in marble (a material rarely used in Sicilian Hellenisrtic epigraphy) which records the benefaction of a city magistrate (Fig. 3.5), a well-preserved sundial (Fig. 3.6) and part of a terracotta statue, all recently discovered.[33] The size of the foot of the last of these finds certainly suggests that it belonged to a monumental, over life-sized statue (Fig. 3.7). The footwear indicates that it depicted not a deity, who were usually shown bare-footed, but rather a civic magistrate, erected in the *agora* sometime in the Hellenistic period, probably between the third and first centuries BC. Sundials would also have been a feature typically seen in an *agora*/forum. In addition, a standing marble male statue, a *togatus*, unfortunately headless, found long ago on the northern slope of the hill, presumably also once stood in the public area of

Fig. 3.5 (top left) *Honorary inscription in Greek from the east slope of Caronía (late third/early second century BC)*

Fig. 3.6 (top right) *Sundial of limestone, a surface find from the east slope of Caronía; height: 23 cm; width: 26 cm (perhaps late first century BC or early first century AD?)*

Fig. 3.7 (above) *Terracotta foot, perhaps from a life-size statue, a surface find at Caronía*

Fig. 3.8 (right) *Headless statue of a* togatus, *marble, from Caronía (Tindari, Antiquarium)*

the *agora* / forum (Fig. 3.8).[34] The man portrayed must have been a prominent citizen of Kale Akte, probably in the first century AD. That there was an élite of well-connected, wealthy men here already by the early first century BC can be deduced from the evidence of Cicero, who mentions the Kalaktinian Eupolemos, the owner it is claimed, of fine, silver-plated cups. The latter was an 'intimate friend of the Luculli', and served in the army of Lucius Lucullus at the time of his Eastern war against Mithradates.[35]

Necropolises

The necropolises of Kale Akte have never been the subject of scientific excavation: all excavation of tombs has been conducted either as the result of clandestine activity in the post-war period, or through poorly documented work conducted more recently. A survey of what can be gleaned from the available information has been made by Francesco Collura.[36] The hill-town of Kale Akte possessed two, a southern one and a northern one (for the position of the former, see colour Pl. 6). The southern was by far the larger, extending immediately outside the presumed south gate of the ancient town, from the area of the modern Municipio at Piazza Porta Torre, as far as *contrade* Pozzarello and Trappeto.[37] The burials here are mostly inhumations *in cassa*, i.e. tombs made up of stone blocks along the sides and ends, and a cover of either slabs or square bricks; these can be dated to between the end of the fifth century BC and the late Hellenistic period. This area was almost completely free of urban building before the 1950s; during the Medieval period it lay immediately outside the southern limits of the town. Piazza Municipio constitutes a small 'valley' between the upward slope of the urban area, and the similarly upward slope towards the south. There can be no doubt that the road leading from the town to the interior would have passed right through here, since cemeteries were always clustered along the roads leading to and from ancient cities. The most common finds in these burials are black-gloss vases such as *lekanai, pelikai, alabastra*, cups, black-gloss or plain oil-lamps and bronze coins; more unusual was the discovery of a bronze mirror in one tomb, and another burial was of *enchytrismos* type within an amphora.

The northern necropolis is much smaller, and seems to have been only sporadically in use. It was situated beneath the north slope of the hill-town, just above the point where the descent levels out, at the start of *contrada* San Todaro. It can be dated generally to the Hellenistic period. Due to extensive clandestine activity during the last century, it is highly likely that many burials have been destroyed without record. Terracotta figurines (locally produced?) were common finds in the tombs here, as the plain of *contrada* San Todaro is known in local dialect today as Chianu dei Pupiddi (Plain of the Puppets).

A purely academic question concerns the whereabouts of the last resting place of Ducetius, the famous Sikel leader. As *oikistes* of the city, he would presumably have been buried in accordance with Greek custom in the *agora*, believed (as we have seen) to have been located in the area of the modern Chiesa Madre (near a street which now bears his name). His ashes may, however, have been transferred to his native city of Menai (Mineo), or else to the Sikel sanctuary of Palikè, like Kale Akte founded by Ducetius. On the other hand, Syracuse might have regarded the proposed burial of the former Sikel leader in one of these two symbolic places in the Sikel heartland as provocative, and could have vetoed it, making remote Kale Akte his more likely resting place. Since the Classical and later Hellenistic and Roman *agorai* are today overlain by at least a millennium of continuous and dense urban activity, the riddle of the site of Ducetius' grave, if it really was at Kale Akte, is unlikely ever to be solved.

Cults and sanctuaries

Apollo

The recently found honorary inscription from Caronía, dating to the third/second century BC, mentions a sanctuary to Apollo, and provides a confirmation of the existence of a cult of this god suggested also by other sources. The remains of Roman-style columns in the courtyard of the Norman castle suggest that some kind of monumental sanctuary existed on the summit of the hill (clearly the town's acropolis). While we cannot, of course, know the identity of the deity worshipped there, one of the more probable candidates is Apollo. Neighbouring Halaesa had an important cult of Apollo too, inherited from its mother *polis*, Herbita.[38] The cult was popular elsewhere on the north coast, as witnessed for example by the name of the town of Apollonia and the frequent appearance of the god on coin issues. For example, Apollo features on the coinage of both Kale Akte (Fig. 4.39) and at Halaesa: either the deity himself or one of his attributes are the most common motifs.[39] The sculptured torso of a nude male standing figure, drawn by Houel during his short stay at Caronía in the eighteenth century but now lost, may also have represented the god (Fig. 3.9).[40] It could possibly have served as the cult statue in one of the late Republican or early Imperial sanctuaries of the *polis*.

Artemis

Wherever there was an important cult of Apollo, one of his sister Artemis would normally also have been present. At Halaesa its existence may be witnessed by a late Hellenistic marble torso from the area of Temple A, if this was indeed part of a cult statue.[41] In addition, the town struck coins with Artemis wearing a *stephane*; her bow and quiver feature on the reverse.[42] Amestratus was another north-coast city with coin issues depicting Artemis.[43] In a rugged and wild environment with mountains and forests, which the Nebrodi certainly is, worship of the goddess of the hunt would have been entirely appropriate; so a cult of Artemis also at Kale Akte might be expected.

Fig. 3.9 Headless marble statue from Caronía, possibly of Apollo, now lost, known from an eighteenth-century drawing by Jean Houel

Dionysus
Dionysus features on the most common coin issue of Kale Akte, and archaeological finds show beyond any doubt that the town was an important producer of wine; so a cult of Dionysus is also likely.[44] It was important also at Halaesa, where a bunch of grapes appeared already on the early SYMMACHIA coin issues, while in the Roman Republican period a coin of Halaesa featured Dionysus on the obverse and a standing warrior on the reverse.[45] Additional indications of the popularity of Dionysus and his followers in both cities include the terracotta head of a silenus from Caronía, and a marble statuette from Halaesa possibly showing a silenus with the infant Dionysus.[46] The father of a famous historian of Hannibal who hailed from Kale Akte may have been a devotee; at any rate he named his son Silenos after the god's companion.[47]

Hermes
Hermes was for obvious reasons revered in any town with strong commercial interests, and his cult was apparently common in the towns of north-eastern Sicily, judging by the many coin issues depicting Hermes or his *caduceus* – Katane, Kephaloidion, Henna, Halaesa, Halontion, Menainon, Tyndaris.[48]

Athena
A cult of Athena might be deduced from the Kale Akte coin issues depicting Athena on the obverse and an owl sitting on amphora on the reverse, but in this case the motif may have been borrowed from Athenian coinage just to convey the notion of a flourishing commercial centre. Halaesa also struck coins with Athena (a very small series),[49] and a head of Athena was found in excavations of Temple A,[50] so a cult probably existed there (and perhaps also at Kale Akte). Maybe it was a local cult of Athena in combination with a desire to express its commercial ambitions which prompted Kale Akte to imitate the famous coins of Athens (Fig. 4.37).[51]

Heracles
The cult of Heracles was very popular in Sicily, not least on the north coast, and he featured on the coinage of Haluntium,[52] Halaesa (a Timoleontic issue) and Kephaloidion, in addition to that of Kale Akte, suggesting the presence of a cult of Heracles at each of these places. Since the coin issues were an important means of expressing the *polis'* cultural identity, reflecting also the surrounding landscape and economic conditions, the popularity of a cult of Heracles on the north coast is not surprising. He was the protector of herders and their cattle, and the pastoral economy was clearly, as we have seen, of great importance in the mountainous, forested area of the Nebrodi.

Demeter and Kore/Persephone
This rural cult of fertility was ubiquitous in Sicily. At Halaesa a cult of the goddesses is deduced from coins (the torch between two ears of grain appears on one of the Timoleon-period issues). In addition, there is a marble statue of Ceres from the forum, as well as statuettes representing one or other of these goddesses.[53] Kale Akte, as dependent on the produce of the land as any other Sicilian *polis,* also very likely paid homage to the chthonic deities. A figurine found at

Caronía may portray one of them (not in itself evidence of religious worship, of course), but there is no direct proof of such a cult.[54]

Other attested cults in the area

Other cults in the area are attested at Halaesa, but they did not necessarily feature also at Kale Akte. That of Zeus Eleutherios was probably linked with a particular historical phenomenon, the *symmachia* of Timoleon's time,[55] but that the cult continued later is supported by the appearance of Zeus (with an eagle on the reverse) on the coinage of the Roman Republican period there. His absence on the coinage of Kale Akte suggests that the cult did not have the same importance there. The unusual cults of Zeus Meilichios and of Adranon were probably peculiar to Halaesa alone and did not feature in other north-coast towns. The Imperial cult, also attested at Halaesa, was often only practised in the major centres which enjoyed privileged ties with Rome; Kale Akte was not one of them.

Destruction in the late first century BC – a consequence of the Civil War?

The excavations of the many cisterns and terrace-walls in the hill-town of Caronía have given irrefutable proof that some kind of destruction took place in the latter half of the first century BC. Excavated terrace walls were clearly built afresh immediately after that period, i.e. in the late first century BC or the first century AD.[56] One partly founded on top of a cistern might have been part of a rebuilding programme after destruction around 36 BC, since the latest material can be dated to the first two-thirds of the first century BC; but no Italian *terra sigillata* (which started production c. 30 BC) is present.[57] Although it is always dangerous to link archaeological finds with historical events, many towns in Sicily do seem to have destruction layers dating from exactly this period. Shelley Stone has convincingly linked these to the aftermath of the Civil War between Sextus Pompey and Octavian.[58] In fact at Caronía a spear-head and a lead sling-bolt have been found in connection with the destroyed terrace walls of this period, suggesting a possible military context for the destruction.[59] It remains impossible to determine whether such deeds of war took place out of revenge, as Octavian punished cities which had supported Sextus, or as a consequence of the general chaos in the island in the aftermath of the war.[60] That Kale Akte sided with Sextus Pompey might be suggested by the central importance of Lipara in his defence of Sicily, and of its loyalty to him; that island was severely punished by Octavian as a result.[61] Lipara is situated only a few miles from Kale Akte; the two are inter-visible. The propinquity of Kale Akte to Lipara and the former's access to the Nebrodi forests, rich in timber for ship-building, would have made Kale Akte and neighbouring north-coast towns natural collaborators and supporters of Sextus Pompey. As a punishment for opposing him, Octavian had the inhabitants of Lipara deported to Neapolis (Naples).[62] Although a small town like Kale Akte was probably not as harshly treated, it may well have been attacked and sacked by Octavian's troops for having sided with Sextus Pompey.

Destruction in the late first/early second century AD

The settlement of the hill-town suffered a further significant destruction during the early Empire, witnessed by tilted terrace walls and ubiquitous traces of fire. This event, thanks to excavations in the hill-town in 1992–93 and 1999, can now be dated with confidence to the end of the first century AD. More than a thousand fragments of Italian *terra sigillata* found on the eastern slope of Caronía lends further support to this hypothesis. The fragments discovered here from surface survey show that Italian *terra sigillata* is about nine times more common than African red slip pottery, of which only the earliest forms are present. This suggests a date of abandonment for the hill town either late in the first or early in the second century AD. The only 'event' in the historical sources that we have reported from Sicily in the later first century AD is an earthquake, mentioned by Pliny the Elder, when half of Tyndaris fell into the sea; this must have happened before Pliny's death in AD 79.[63] However, one fragment of African red slip on the surface of a *stenopos*,[64] not earlier than *c.* AD 80/90, seems apparently too late for the date of Pliny's earthquake, if Kale Akte was affected by the same seismic event which struck Tyndaris. This does not, however, rule out another earthquake as a possible contributing factor in its decline: there are so few literary sources referring to the history of Sicily at this period, and not all Sicilian earthquakes are documented in the pages of history. At any rate, the hill-settlement was abandoned by the very end of the first century or during the first few decades of the second century AD. It is probable that the abandonment was caused or at least hastened by an earthquake, based on the indications that we have of destruction at Marina di Caronìa at approximately the same period.

Marina di Caronía

The *statio/vicus* at Marina di Caronía

We know little of the layout of the settlement by the sea at Marina di Caronía. It was not at any stage an urban settlement, a *polis*, like that on the hill-top, with an *agora* and civic administration (Fig. 3.10 shows the

Fig. 3.10 The hill of Caronía, as seen from the settlement of Marina di Caronía below (at the excavation site in contrada *Pantano). The house in the foreground is the site of the cistern of the later first or second century AD* (proprietà *Barna).*

latter as seen from the former). In the late Classical and Hellenistic period it functioned, as we have seen, as the harbour of the town, with its warehouses, deposits and industries, situated more or less directly on the important north-coast road artery, known in Roman times as the *via Valeria.* The settlement at Marina di Caronía, recorded in the road handbooks by the Romanized form of Kale Akte, viz. Calacte, seems to have begun prospering in the early Hellenistic period, and continued to do so down through the late Hellenistic and Imperial periods into the second half of the fourth century AD. It would have had the character of a *vicus,* a roadside settlement specialising in the production of different goods and offering storage facilities around the harbour. In the imperial period, villas would probably have been scattered along the coastal plain. Their owners would no doubt have been the sort of *viri nobilissimi* mentioned by Cicero (the urban élite who will also have had their rural estates with villas, like Sthenius at Thermae Himeraeae); the standing *togatus* (missing his head) found on the northern slope of the hill, and which probably once stood in the *agora*/forum of the hill-town, may have been one of them (Fig. 3.8).[65]

A certain level of prosperity in the early Imperial period is indicated by a fragment of marble column, found during the rebuilding of the Annunziata church at Marina di Caronía after the Second World War (Fig. 3.11).[66] Its precise provenance is unknown. It might have come from a bath-building, the presence of which is to be expected in a Roman road station like Calacte, or it might have belonged to an opulent rural villa, although none with the level of wealth indicated by the presence of marble columns is known in the immediate vicinity of the settlement. It is unlikely to have belonged to a public building such as a temple or forum, since a *statio* or *vicus* did not normally possess such grand civic structures. If the find-spot reflects its original position, its location at the very centre of the ancient settlement would support the idea that it belonged to a bath building. Judging from what we know from archaeological evidence about the settlement's history and marble building elsewhere, the column (and the building to which it belonged) is not likely to be before the second century AD; it could well be later.[67]

Something of the infrastructure provided in the maritime settlement is illustrated by the large water cistern (colour Pls 13–14) which still exists in *contrada* Palme, and another in *contrada* Pantano (in proprietà Barna). Their exact chronology is uncertain, but construction technique suggests neither predates the first century AD; both may belong to the second century.[68]

The coastline seems to have altered only slightly since antiquity. Bonanno thought that the excavated area of *contrada* Pantano had been flooded at least once in antiquity, something that would be impossible today due to a substantial difference in levels between land and sea. However, the evidence of flooding is far from conclusive. Collura suggested that a series of underwater structures extending to the north of the promontory may be remains of what was once dry land with remains of moles – structures that are also visible in satellite photos; but these observations have yet to be confirmed by scientific investigation. In fact, evidence from ancient harbour sites elsewhere in Sicily suggests that the coastline has in general extended outwards towards the sea since antiquity. At Naxos, it has grown by some hundred metres, at Himera the same. At Solunto, the ancient coves of the harbour area have completely silted up, while at Tindari's ancient port site, Oliveri, the coastal strip has grown wider by several hundred metres. At no known site has the coast line receded since antiquity. Marina di Caronía is probably no different: the shoreline is unlikely to have changed dramatically in the last 1500 years. The coastal promontory has probably in fact grown over time rather than retreated, helped by deposits of silt from the Torrente di Caronía which discharges into the sea immediately to its west.

Fig. 3.11 Fragment of a Roman marble column with spiral fluting, now kept near the altar in the Church of the Annunziata at Marina di Caronía (second century AD or later)

As noted above,[69] there is much to support the idea that an inlet of the sea, a harbour basin (now silted up) existed in the area of *contrada* Pantano in antiquity. Judging from what we know of the extent of the ancient settlement at Marina di Caronía, it seems that the innermost part of the bay was not at the centre of the settlement, as it is today, but lay to the west (in the present-day outskirts of the settlement). There are many surface finds from *contrada* di Noto, and they extend all the way to *contrada* Sugherita at the mouth of the Torrente Caronía.[70] Phillip Clüver ('Cluverius') stated in the early seventeenth century that ancient ruins were visible at Marina di Caronía for 2,000 *passi*,[71] i.e. over a distance of about 1.5 km. This is more or less the same as that which separates the area of the eastern necropolis from that in *contrada* Sugherita in the west.

Why the promontory was more attractive for settlement in antiquity than it is today is probably due to reasons of topography. The principal difference today by comparison with earlier centuries is that a marshland (*pantano*) formerly existed here until it was drained in the 1920s and filled in with rounded beach pebbles (Fig. 3.12). Even today, despite the great cordon of stones which protects it from the sea, the depression fills with water during the rainy season, showing that the underlying subsoil is not able to absorb water.[72] The contour of the marsh can easily be traced from the stones that cover the area and also from the row of eucalyptus trees that was planted along the southern border of the *pantano*. Interestingly, this east-west line is perfectly aligned with the east/west alignment of the ancient buildings excavated in *contrada* Pantano. It seems highly probable that this now swampy low-lying area once formed the harbour basin of ancient Kale Akte/Calacte. Whether it was artificial or natural is now difficult to determine. The digging of a large, completely artificial harbour basin from scratch at a small site like Kale Akte seems a rather unlikely investment in infrastructure, but it is not impossible that an already existing, natural inlet of the sea may have been enlarged in Roman times. The area is quite extensive, measuring some 350 by 70 metres, and would suggest

Fig. 3.12 The drained marshland in contrada *Pantano, now filled with stones, probably the site of the ancient harbour basin*

a port of a certain importance. Its entrance is probably to be sought at its eastern extremity, immediately north of where there is today a boat-house, less than 150 metres north of the excavation area in *proprietà* Barna.[73] The basin must have silted up at some stage in early medieval times. In the former harbour basin, the standing water would have become marshland, the *Pantano*, from which this area has received its modern name.

The discovery of this harbour basin has important implications for our understanding of the history of Kale Akte. Its presumed size, together with other indications of commercial activity over a wide area, gives the impression that Kale Akte had a port much larger than a *polis* (and later coastal settlement) of modest size would actually have needed. Kale Akte was not, like Halaesa, a major outlet for the export of grain from the inland plains. Instead, if a large port was needed, we have to presume that the town had generated its own exports for shipment overseas, and may have served other neighbouring communities like Apollonia and Haluntium.

Pottery dating to between the fourth century BC and the Roman Imperial period has been found on the surface of the vast *contrada* di Noto, which extends south and west of the ancient harbour basin. Immediately south of the latter, the remains of several ancient north/south walls, built of concrete and dressed stones, are probably of Roman Imperial date.[74] They end approximately where the harbour begins, and possibly indicate structures directly connected with it. Some 230 m north-west of the so-called Case Salomone is a very overgrown structure, several meters deep and filled with water. Skeletons have reportedly been found inside.[75] The structure may be a cistern, like the other two at Marina di Caronía mentioned above (pp. 51–2). The one in *contrada* Pantano was certainly reused for burials during the Byzantine period.

Limited excavation took place at Marina di Caronía for the first time in 1982–83. This was conducted by the Archaeological Superintendency of Syracuse. At *contrada* Nunziatella (Villetta Comunale) near the church, wall structures thought to have belonged to storage buildings which date to the Imperial and Late Imperial periods were found, but these have never been properly published.[76] In 1996, four tombs belonging to a necropolis of Byzantine date were excavated in front of the Annunziata church.[77] Otherwise the only scientific archaeological excavations of the settlement are those conducted in *contrada* Pantano between 1999 and 2005, and to these we must now turn.

Excavations at *contrada* Pantano

From October 1999 to February 2000 and then again between July and August 2001, the Soprintendenza dei Beni Culturali of Messina conducted two campaigns of excavation in *contrada* Pantano (*proprietà* Barna), directed by Dr Maria Costanza Lentini (Fig. 3.13). A large structure, identified as a storage building,

Fig. 3.13 Plan of the structures at contrada *Pantano (proprietà Barna) at Marina di Caronía at the close of the first excavation campaign, Febrary 2000*

and another which in its first phase may have served as a *thermopolium* (a snack-bar), in addition to several other, smaller buildings, were partially uncovered. They date between Hellenistic times and the Late Imperial period.[78]

The excavation was later continued under the direction of Dr Carmela Bonanno of the Messina Superintendency, between 2003 and 2005.[79] The area now excavated was much larger than in previous campaigns, covering some 1,500 m^2 in all (Fig. 3.14). This allowed for a major part of the structures to be uncovered, and the work also identified other buildings both earlier and later than the principal phase of development.[80] This second excavation was published in 2009, with a detailed discussion of the structures, although the finds were only published in preliminary form. This publication does, however, contain a number of errors, especially in the reconstruction of the building phases and in their dating. Since the excavations of 1999–2001 have not so far been published *in extenso*, the following account will try and reconstruct the entire building history of the site through a combination of

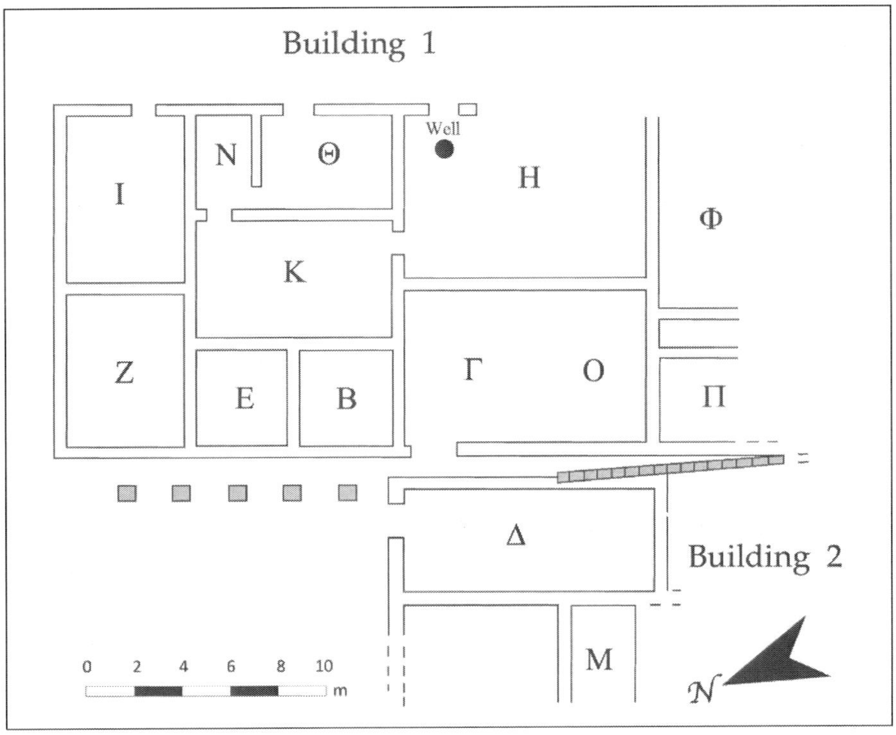

Fig. 3.14 Marina di Caronía, contrada *Pantano, schematic plan of Buildings 1 and 2, phases 2a (white) and 2b (grey)*

the excavation evidence of 1999–2001 (some of it hitherto unpublished) with that from the 2003–05 campaigns.

One important difference between these two excavations must be stressed at the outset. At the time of Dr Lentini's work, although it was more modest in extent, the archaeological contexts were still largely undisturbed. By 2001, however, large parts of the area had been deep-ploughed by the land-owner, so compromising the archaeology. As a result, the Bonanno excavations had to rely on very few undisturbed contexts for dating. Furthermore, Bonanno's publication did not take into account the site records of the Lentini excavations.

Phase 1 (late fifth–c. *150/100 BC)*

Excavation revealed scattered traces of at least two small buildings, the more substantial at the north-west corner of the excavation (not marked on Fig. 3.14, but visible in the uppermost part of Fig. 3.26),[81] constructed at the end of the fifth or the beginning of the fourth century BC.[82] The vicinity of these buildings to the sea and their relative modesty suggest that they were associated with commercial activity at the harbour; they may also have been concerned with production.[83] Although the precise chronology is uncertain due to the limited extent of deep excavation conducted to explore this early phase, the discoveries are closely matched by the remains of a building of similar date near the railway station of Marina di Caronía.[84] Together they seem to indicate that organised harbour facilities were present by *c.* 400 BC, a direct consequence of the founding of the settlement on the hill by Ducetius a generation or so earlier.

These early structures had been for the most part destroyed by later buildings. Some fragments of walling were generally orientated N–S and E–W, but the one to the north-west has a slightly different orientation to the rest, perhaps because the coast changed direction at this point.[85] These buildings were constructed with accuracy and care, with a facing of dressed blocks and a fill of smaller river-worn stones.[86]

Phase 2a (c. *150/100–36 BC)*

According to Bonanno and Sudano, these buildings were destroyed by flooding, witnessed by a thick layer of beach pebbles.[87] The date of this flood was originally placed in the second half of the third century BC, but later Building 1 (Fig. 3.14), which post-dates the flood layer, was ascribed by Bonanno to no later than the early third century BC, suggesting that the flood had happened *c.* 300 BC.[88] This chronology is, however, very debatable, as we shall see.

Building 1, square in layout, consists of several larger rooms arranged around a central courtyard (K); the latter had a pavement of *opus signinum.* Area H contained a well in its north-eastern corner (Figs 3.15–18),[89] which was filled with material dating to the first and second centuries AD.[90] These finds provide a *terminus ante quem non* for the destruction of the building, and for the subsequent changes in its original function and layout. Immediately to the south of the courtyard were two open spaces (H and Γ/O), the former communicating with the courtyard (K).[91] The building technique of the walls is markedly different from that of the Phase-1 structures: Phase-2 walls were accurately built with squared limestone blocks, sometimes using small sections of brickwork. On top of this foundation the upper part of the walls were presumably constructed of mud-bricks or *pisé* (rammed earth).

The building was probably constructed in the second half of the second centruy BC, as suggested above all by coins. One from the mint of Kale Akte was virtually embedded in the layer of beach pebbles, giving the building a *terminus post quem* date of *c.* 120 BC, the time when the mint was established and the first local coins produced.[92] A Mamertine coin dating to 220/200 BC was found near the foundation level of the walls, but this may be residual and cannot be used to date the construction of Building 1.[93] It is possible that work on it was started slightly earlier in the second century and that the coin in the pebbles is a later intrusion; at any rate, judging from the number of coins of the local mint found, the building was flourishing in the last quarter of the second century and into the first century BC. The dating of Building 1 by Bonanno and Sudano, to the end of the fourth or the beginning of the third century BC is, therefore, undoubtedly too early.[94] Quite apart from the numismatic evidence, the use of short sections of small, locally-made bricks, as in the walls of Building 1, is not compatible with such an early date. The large size of the structure also fits better with a date after the Roman conquest, and the expansion of commercial activity that resulted, especially in the second half of the second century BC, than with the still relatively modest scale of trade and commerce around 300 BC. Building 1 was thus not built before the middle decades of the second century BC or a little later.

Its precise function remains unclear, but it must have been connected with commercial activity in an area where goods were redistributed. The character of the finds (dominated by amphora and coarse pottery fragments, with fine ware and lamps in much smaller quantities), the sheer size of the building complex, and at the same time its simple character, together with its location on the sea, all point to the building having a storage function (i.e. it was a *horreum*). The building was obviously part of a larger settlement, of which other structures further south at the Scuola Materna formed a part; a water channel at the latter seems to have been heading towards the large Roman cistern which lies only *c.* 50 meters further south again.[95] That cistern is built of brickwork (*opus testaceum*) with a vaulted roof, and although it has been ascribed to the

Fig. 3.15 The northern part of Building 1, seen from the west, excavations of 2003–05

Fig. 3.16 The southern part of Building 1, seen from the north-west, excavations of 2003–05

Fig. 3.17 View of Building 1 during the excavations of 1999–2000, seen from the north

first century BC, this type of construction does not appear in Sicily until the early imperial period.[96]

Immediately to the south-west of Building 1, another building was uncovered (Building 2) (Figs 3.19–20; for the plan, see Fig. 3.14). A limited test-pit inside the entrance to Building 2 showed a layer of burnt soil with finds of the first century BC. This probably corresponds to that detected by Bonanno inside Building 1, and suggests that Building 2 was also destroyed by fire.[97] The layer of pebbles was also found inside and under the entrance to Building 2. The material immediately above it clearly belongs to the first century BC (it contains, for example, Campana C pottery), and since the material is exclusively of that date, Building 2 was probably constructed sometime in that century, perhaps soon after 100 BC. However, future excavation needs to clarify if Building 2 is indeed later than Building 1 or is contemporary with it. It rests on top of earlier activity, such as a deposit of animal bones and charcoal found immediately below the pebble layer; whether or not this can be associated with an earlier phase of the same building on the same site remains to be determined.

Building 2 had a simple beaten earth floor. Occupation layers contained plentiful amounts of animal bones and charcoal, indicating that eating took place here; the discovery of a spoon supports that interpretation (Fig. 3.21). Two *styli* (or one *stylus* and a possible eraser) for use in writing were also found (Fig. 3.22). The building may have been a *taberna* or *thermopolium*, common near market-places and harbours in antiquity. Interpretation

Fig. 3.18 View of Building 1 during the excavations of 1999–2000, seen from the south

Fig. 3.19 Building 2 (Phase 2) seen from the west, with room Δ at the centre and room M and Λ *to the right, during excavations in 2004. The south wall of Building 2 with its entrance was destroyed prior to the start of these excavations, and so is not visible (right). The Phase-3 water drain marked by the row of square bricks can be seen at top left.*

Fig. 3.20 Building 2 viewed from the west, during excavation in 2001

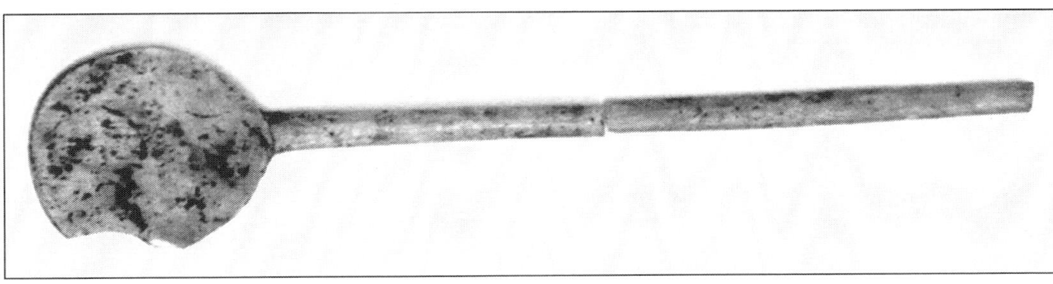

Fig. 3.21 Bone spoon from Building 2 (first century BC or first century AD); length: 9.5 cm

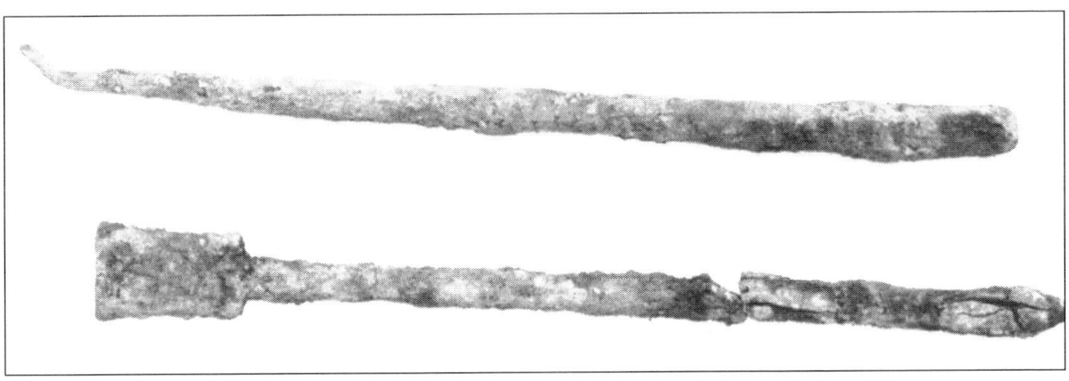

Fig. 3.22 Stylus (upper) *and* (lower) *possible eraser (?) from Building 2, found in 2001 (first century BC or first century AD); lengths: 9.4 cm* (upper) *and 7.0 cm* (lower)

of it as a private house is not likely in view of its proximity to the large public building, with which it was closely connected via an open space. A coin from the mint of Sextus Pompey in near-mint condition (Fig. 4.36), and the complete absence of *terra sigillata* in this context, suggests a destruction date during or immediately after the time of Sextus Pompey's regime in Sicily. Asses issued by Sextus Pompey are very common in destruction levels of this date elsewhere in Sicily, and so, as noted above (p. 22), the hill-town Kale Akte and its associated harbour settlement are both likely to have been at least partly destroyed in the aftermath of the war between Octavian and Sextus. An attack would have come from the sea, where the defenceless harbour settlement at Marina di Caronía would have been an easy target.

Phase 2b (c. 36 BC–AD 100)

In a second phase, Building 1 was provided with a portico of five brick columns constructed on its west

Fig. 3.23 Roof-tile collapse and a fallen brick pillar (left) in Room B of Building 1, 2004

side, at a level slightly above that of the foundations of the original building (Fig. 3.14, marked in grey). This reconstruction may have taken place shortly after the defeat of Sextus Pompey at Naulochus in 36 BC. A broad *ambitus* (alley-way), 1 m wide, between Buildings 1 and 2, and a U-shaped water conduit covered with square bricks (Fig. 3.19, top left) were probably constructed during this building phase.[98] If the conduit was supplying water from the cistern located a few metres to the south (in *proprietà* Barna), it was probably not added until the first century AD at the earliest. The oldest fragments of pottery found inside the cistern are of locally produced Republican red-gloss pottery and the ubiquitous local red-slip jugs, but these belong to deposits which were clearly dumped there much later, after the cistern ceased to function, and cannot be used to date the structure.[99] It is not certain quite when the destruction of Building 1 took place. The Bonanno excavations dated it to the first half of the second century AD, on the basis of a Sicilian-made lamp from the workshop of Proclus Agyrios found in the tile-fall.[100] These lamps were probably, however, already in production during the late first century AD (as suggested by the volute type at the wick hole). In view of what we know about the date of destruction in the hill-town, and the likelihood that the region was hit by an earthquake at this period, it is logical to think that the harbour settlement was damaged at the same time, perhaps in the 80s or 90s of the first century AD. Nor is the suggestion of Bonanno and Sudano that Building 1 was simply abandoned at all convincing. This area was the focus of commercial activity for a millennium, and a very large building like this is unlikely to have been simply given up at a time when (in the early Empire) the local economic climate was flourishing. Not only the falls of roof-tile but also the collapse of brick piers indicate a sudden destruction, when the entire building fell (Fig. 3.23). There was no trace of fire damage, so an earthquake must remain the likely cause of the destruction. Building 2, where excavation has been much more limited, was probably also in use until towards the end of the first century AD.

Phase 3 (c. *AD 100*–c. *360*)

The southern half of Building 1 was clearly reused after its destruction. The ground level was raised and new paving was laid with second-hand square bricks. Several partition walls were built, the function of which remains uncertain. It seems certain that the area was now open to the sky.[101] The complex seems to have been used for some kind of industrial process, possibly textile production, which is presumed in the previous phase here to have been conducted on these premises, but the rest of Building 1 was abandoned.

Building 2 by contrast continued life during this period.[102] New walls were constructed on top of the old ones in its northern part, less carefully than before, using river-worn rounded stones or beach pebbles. In addition, the original entrance on the north was closed off (Fig. 3.24). The phase-2 wall beneath was only partly encountered at the entrance; we do not know at present whether it continues towards the west, as do two other walls further south. The corner of a later building runs obliquely, immediately outside its north-west corner. It is possible that the north wall was deliberately interrupted here to leave space for a new building. The layout seems awkward, with a long room protruding towards the north, while the remaining building extends mainly in an east–west direction; but only further excavation can clarify details of its plan. It no longer served as a *taberna* or *thermopolium* after the first century AD, but quite what its new function was is unclear. The second destruction layer, with well-preserved roof-tile falls, can be dated to the second half of the fourth century AD.

Other than the reconstruction of Building 2 and the south part of Building 1, Phase 3 is characterised by the erection of a number of small buildings which completely ignored the layout of the earlier Building 1. One of them, for example (building Y on Fig. 3.25), was constructed in the middle of the earlier building, destroying one of the latter's internal walls. Its floor was composed of both square and circular bricks.[103] The huge number of wine amphorae around building Y, mostly local but also including imports from North Africa, together with a concentration of amphora stoppers inside the building, suggests it was used for storage; it may well have contained consignments of the local wine, destined for export. This hypothesis is supported by further finds in another building (Σ on

Fig. 3.24 The entrance to Building 2, later blocked, excavated in 1999–2000

Fig. 3.25), constructed in a rather haphazard and untidy technique to the west of the now ruined portico. Inside it was a small *dolium* found *in situ*, and outside it the lower half of an amphora of type Keay 27 (*c.* mid-fourth to fifth centuries AD), which might suggest that it too functioned as a storage building.[104] It seems that the southern half of Building 1, now open to the sky, co-existed with these smaller storage units. All, together with Building 2, were destroyed simultaneously, in the second half of the fourth century AD.

The material from the later part of phase 3 suggests intense economic activity within a less organised settlement, perhaps a consequence of a diminished level of civic pride. The settlement at Marina di Caronía was no longer the harbour settlement belonging to a political and urban unit, the *polis* of Kale Akte, but an independent maritime village, with the harbour as its focus.

*Phase 4 (*c. *fifth–seventh centuries AD)*

Buildings A and possibly Ξ, which belonged to this last phase, were set at an oblique angle to Buildings 1 and 2 of phase 2a, for reasons unknown; but structures S and Y in phase 3 had also been of irregular plan (Figs 3.25–26). The new structures are later than the buildings destroyed in the second half of the fourth century, but their remains are too fragmentary to understand their purpose. Certainly the area continued to be used for activities connected with the harbour throughout the fifth century AD; but the large buildings of an earlier age were now completely abandoned.

The construction techniques used through the centuries can give us some idea about the evolving nature of different building styles in the settlement over time. Walls during the fourth and third centuries BC were built in a somewhat rudimentary style, using rounded blocks taken from the sea and inserting smaller pebbles in the interstices. By *c.* 150/100 BC this tecnique was replaced by a much more elegant style of walling, made up of neat, regularly-cut and squared blocks, now with the use of bricks to fill the gaps in between. At this stage, the large building (A) was flanked by Building 2 on the same alignment, which together form a unified, planned layout around an open space to the west and another to the north, to which was added a portico sometime in the late first century BC. The scale of investment suggests increasing wealth in the settlement during the second half of the second century BC, at a time when the maritime settlement was probably growing considerably in size. After their destruction towards the end of the first century AD, new buildings of smaller size were constructed in neat and accurate coursed walling, with the absence of any brick insertions. Structures in and after the second century

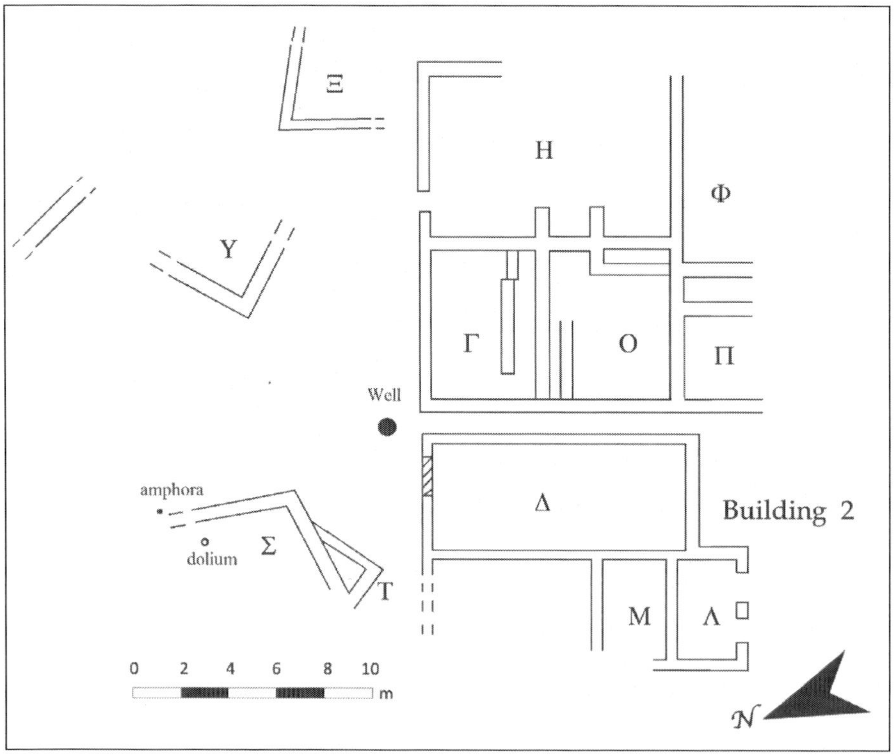

Fig. 3.25 Schematic plan of Buildings 1 (Η–Φ) and 2 (Δ, Λ and Μ) as well as newly-built structures (Τ, Σ, Ξ and Υ). The plan shows buildings in use during Phase 3 destroyed in the mid-fourth century, except for Ξ which possibly belongs to Phase 4

Fig. 3.26 Remains of parts of four storage-buildings from three different phases, as excavated in 2004; north is at the top. On the extreme right is the west wall of Building 1 (Phase 2a, second century BC), with the portico added later (Phase 2b, probably late first century BC or early first century AD). The three walls in the centre of the photograph are, from bottom upwards, T, Σ and A, of which the first two belong to successive periods in Phase 3, and the last (which is not indicated on Fig. 3.25) to Phase 4 (fifth century AD). The wall in the uppermost part of the photograph belongs to phase 1 (end of fifth/early fourth century BC).

AD are smaller and irregularly built, using recycled building materials robbed from earlier, now demolished, structures. Since ceramic evidence shows that the export trade from the *vicus* was flourishing in the fourth century AD, a fall-off in building standards does not necessarily indicate economic decay. Decline probably accelerated only after the destruction of many buildings in the mid-fourth century. Nevertheless, a nucleated settlement around the port, which also served as a road station (*statio*) on the *via Valeria*, with buildings still involved in storage and trade, did not disappear altogether until sometime during the sixth century AD.

The destruction of the fourth century and the earthquake of the AD 360s

The destruction of the late antique buildings at Marina di Caronía can be dated to the second half of the fourth century AD, on the basis of the complete absence of African red slip pottery forms characteristic of the later fourth century, and of any coins after AD 361.[105] Interestingly, St Jerome mentions in connection with the death of the Emperor Julian in AD 363 a very violent earthquake, as a result of which "all the large cities of Sicily lie in ruins." An earthquake around this date has been postulated elsewhere in Sicily, for example at the villa near Piazza Armerina.[106] Messina might also have been affected by an earthquake around the middle of the fourth century AD, and contraction has been detected in the number and size of settlements in north-east Sicily and southern Italy after then.[107] It may also be argued that even a major earthquake would not cause destruction on such a widespread scale, far away from any hypothetical epicentre. So not all the destruction ascribed to the 360s in Sicily need have been due to a single earthquake, but perhaps rather to a series of devastating earthquakes, possibly triggered by a major seismic event elsewhere, in somewhere like the Straits of Messina. Certainly settlement decline in the north-east is unlikely to have been caused by general economic factors, since this was on the whole a very peaceful and prosperous period for Sicily.[108]

The destruction at Marina di Caronía, which has left such clear traces, must be due to some kind of disaster, of which, in the absence of fire damage, an earthquake seems the most plausible explanation. The hard evidence, however, is slight: one wall of poor construction (building Σ on Figs 3.25–26) was tilted on an awkwardly leaning angle. In room Λ, a complete amphora of local type was found lying on the floor. Bonanno has suggested that this room was a later addition to the building because of differences in its construction technique, and because it lay on a higher level than the rest of the building; she concluded that the amphora was 'Byzantine'.[109] There is, however, no doubt that it is identical to fourth-century-AD examples of type Termini Imerese 151/354, and the higher level of the room is explicable because the building is located on elevated terrain.[110] This and other evidence suggests that it may have served as a depot for amphorae and other goods at the time of its destruction, just after the middle of the fourth century AD.

The possibility of an earthquake at Marina di Caronía was rather prematurely dismissed by Bonanno.[111] Inspection by a geological expert took place in the beginning of the 2003/5 campaigns when fallen roof-tile deposits had not been fully exposed, nor were the structures excavated in 1999–2000 inspected in their original state of conservation.[112] Furthermore the walls are only about 0.50 m in height, the superstructure above being presumably of mud brick, *pisé* and/or wood. Registering earthquake damage of such low walls is difficult, and in any case after such an event most of the evidence would have been taken away to allow occupation of the site to continue and for fresh structures to be built. Over an occupation time-span of more than half a millennium, it is perfectly plausible that this seismically active area would have been struck by at least two major earthquakes. Earthquake damage in antiquity may well have been more serious than it is today when seismic events occur of the same magnitude, since buildings were so much less solidly constructed sixteen hundred years ago.

After the destruction of the *vicus* at Marina di Caronía in or around the 360s, it seems that the settlement contracted, with production perhaps dispersed to rural suburbs or farmsteads dotted around the countryside. The evidence from the *chora* of Kale Akte for this increase in late Roman rural settlement has emerged from recent fieldwork.[113] The location of a fifth-century amphora kiln in *contrada* Chiappe, some 2 km to the east (no. 6 on Fig. 1.4, p. 4), is an example of this; by that time the nucleated settlement at Marina di Caronía had become much reduced.

To what extent Vandal raids in the middle of the fifth century AD affected Calacte is difficult to assess. Lipari seems to have survived the period without major problems, and indeed prospered in the later fifth and early sixth centuries. However, a large coin hoard there from the 460s or 470s hints at some insecurity, and we know that other places on the north coast, such as Termini Imerese and Soluntum, received a tax remission from Valentinian III in compensation for Vandal raids, which clearly did not only affect the south and east coasts.[114] An unprotected harbour village with a prospering wine industry may have been an easy target for Vandal raiders, although whether it was large enough or important enough to attract such attention is a moot point. Whether Calacte's wine export survived into the sixth century is uncertain on the basis of current data, but at present it seems doubtful that Vandal raids had any lasting effects on production and trade in the area.

By the late sixth century AD, however, it seems certain that the *statio* no longer existed. No buildings are known from the harbour area in this period (on the contrary, tombs started to invade the former habitation areas), and the countryside also shows signs of serious decline at the same time.[115] Only a very small community, perhaps dependent largely on fishing, and living in patched-up, partly-ruined buildings, with tombs not far away, is attested at this period (Fig. 3.27).[116]

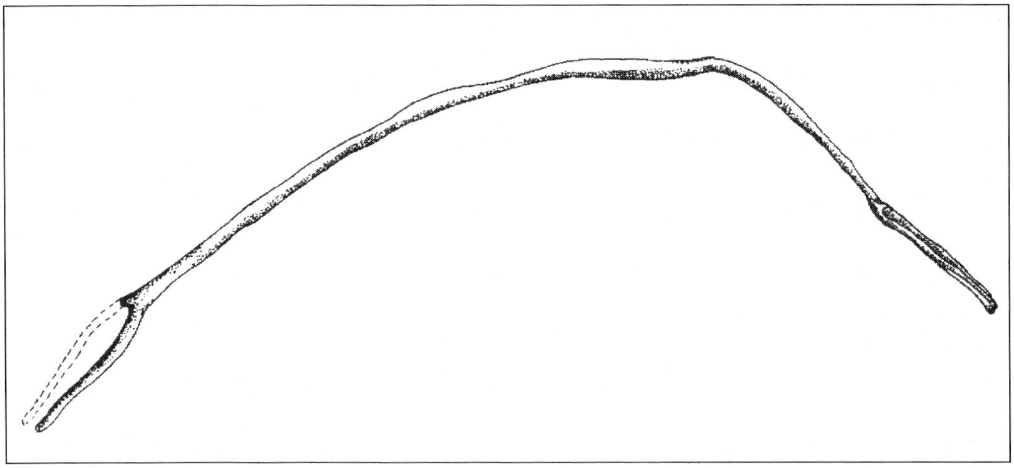

Fig. 3.27 (left) *Copper alloy tool for mending fishing nets, from the excavations; length: 17 cm*

Fig. 3.28 (below) *Funerary monument of Q. Caecilius, probably from* contrada *S. Anna at Marina di Caronía (late first century BC or first century AD; Palermo, Museo Archeologico Regionale)*

The necropolises of Marina di Caronía

The main cemetery at Marina di Caronía lay in the area immediately east of the Piazza Nunziatella and the railway station; it stretches at least as far as the former Agip petrol station (colour Pl. 5).[117] The burials are mostly Hellenistic, but Late Roman tombs have also been found.[118] The tombs are quite scattered, giving the impression that we are dealing with a small community rather than with large organized cemeteries. The absence of Classical burials reinforces the idea that no significant maritime settlement existed in the fifth or fourth centuries BC, even if some harbour infrastructure of that date has been discovered. This area today forms the centre of modern Marina di Caronía, but, as noted above, it represents the eastern periphery of the ancient settlement. The core of that, with its attendant harbour, lay further west.

The site of the necropolis in use during the Roman Empire has not been located with certainty, but it may have been on the northern slope of the Pianu dei Puppiddi, on the border between *contrada* San Todaro and *contrada* Sant'Anna (i.e. immediately south of the western part of Marina di Caronía). Apart from some actual burials, funerary monuments including one honouring a certain Quintus Caecilius in Latin are known from here (Fig. 3.28).[119] Since Kale Akte had ceased to function as a *civitas* by AD 100, this inscription, if it recorded an inhabitant of the upper town, must surely date no later than the first century AD.

4

The material evidence

Introduction

Amphorae

The largest category of material from the Marina di Caronía excavations comprises transport amphorae, also the most important key to our understanding of the local economy and of trading connections between this small Sicilian coastal settlement and elsewhere. Amphorae constitute a direct form of evidence for ancient economic history. To a great extent, through study of their shape and the fabric of their clay, assisted by petrographic (thin-section) analysis, the likely areas where amphorae were produced can be determined; sometimes even, when kilns are found, the exact location of their origin is known. The fact that amphorae were never transported empty as goods *per se*, as, for example, fine-quality table pottery or lamps were, but functioned only as containers for the valuable goods they carried (such as wine, olive oil, or fish sauce) makes them direct indicators of trade in certain commodities. Establishing therefore what these basic foodstuffs were, represented by the amphora remains, is very important for our understanding of the economy of any ancient site. Furthermore, in the case of Marina di Caronía, the possibility of studying this material from a single place over the *longue durée* makes it possible to gauge important fluctuations in the supply of individual categories of foodstuffs over time.

Presentation of the material below is divided into five discrete periods: (1) the Classical (*c.* 500–320 BC); (2) the early Hellenistic (*c.* 320–200 BC): (3) the late Hellenistic (*c.* 200–30 BC); (4) the early Imperial (*c.* 30 BC–AD 200); and (5) the mid / late Imperial (*c.* AD 200–500). Discussion of amphorae, which are present in quantities many times larger than that of other material, is divided according to geographic origin and content, rather than by amphora type as such. In this way the aim is dwell less on technical aspects of amphora study but instead focus on the most important and interesting data that they yield, viz. the likely contents of these containers and their wider economic importance. In order to help the reader, most but not all of the amphorae discussed here are illustrated by more or less complete examples of their type, so that the overall shapes of these multifarious containers, and the differences between them, can be more readily appreciated. It is important to remember, however, that these illustrations are intended to serve as a generic guide only, since there are many minor variants and sub-groups within each amphora type. Fabric numbers in the text of this Chapter refer to the Catalogue of Fabrics listed in Appendix 3, object numbers to the Catalogue in Appendix 4 (pp. 178–202).

Up until recently Sicilian publications of amphorae and other ceramic material have concentrated on limited time spans, often without systematic, statistical and quantitative analysis of the finds.[1] Lipari is one of the few sites where amphorae from both the Greek and Roman periods have been published, although the amount of Late Republican and Imperial material included is slight.[2] Two studies of the distribution of Roman-period amphorae in Sicily were published by Massimo Denaro in 1995 and Daniele Malfitana in 2008,[3] indicating important patterns of distribution of the different amphora types; but such maps can be misleading in that they reflect information only from the few sites that have been published rather than the likely real distribution pattern, had it been possible to include all excavated but unpublished material. There is, in short, much work to be done.

The study of Roman amphorae in Sicily is no longer in its infancy (as Wilson considered it in 1990),[4] but it is still in a backwater, since vast amounts of material, especially Roman, from excavations all over Sicily have never been identified, studied in detail or properly published. The old-fashioned view that the Greek period in Sicily was a sublime period of vitality, invention and creativity, never surpassed before or since, and that Sicilian 'greatness' vanished with the arrival of the Romans, has left its mark on the study of Roman Sicily. Whereas it could be said in 2006 that the most thorough recent studies on Sicilian amphorae, including thin-section analyses, had been made on material of the Archaic and Classical Greek periods only,[5] this is no longer true: several such studies for Roman material have appeared in recent years. Roman Sicily in general has experienced a renaissance after the important *magnum opus* on the imperial period published by Roger Wilson in 1990,[6] and especially during the last two decades. Since an interest in general in the study of amphorae really only began anywhere in the late 1960s and early 1970s,[7] and in Sicily not until the 1990s, the study of Roman amphorae in the island is still comparatively young. The recent research of Carmela Franco, and in particular her forthcoming book, is likely to mark a major breakthrough in our study of this material in Sicily.[8]

Fine wares

Fine wares often travelled as complementary cargo on amphorae ships,[9] and they can help to date more precisely when a specific amphora type began to be imported, since the chronology of pottery is better established than that of amphorae. This is, however, not always the case, and differing patterns of supply between amphorae on the one hand and fine wares on the other are interesting in themselves. Such differences might suggest that certain kinds of pottery commonly associated with a certain amphora type did not always travel with it, or reflect different patterns of production at source; alternatively, consumption patterns on the site under study might have been different from elsewhere, curtailing the need for certain pottery types there.[10] The necessity of studying amphorae in close association with fine wares has been stressed, among others, by the expert on Campanian fine wares, Jean-Paul Morel.[11] Of particular importance is the comparison of local/regional (Sicilian) productions of fine ware with those of amphorae. The coarser and cruder transport amphorae were not subject to changes in fashion and style to the same extent that fine ware and lamps were.

The amount of fine ware present at Marina di Caronía is in general much lower than the quantity of amphorae, although the contrary is true for material from the early Hellenistic cistern. The publication of fine wares has been much more extensive than that of amphorae, due to the attraction of the former category for art-historical reasons. The publications from the Lipari excavations, once again, are the best corpus that we have of Classical and Hellenistic fine wares from Sicily, thanks to the immense research carried out over decades by Madeleine Cavalier and the late Luigi Bernabò Brea.[12] For the Roman period, the study by Shelley Stone of Hellenistic and early Imperial Sicilian fine ware from Morgantina is of fundamental importance,[13] and also of great value are the publications by the Swiss team of black gloss wares and *terra sigillata* from Monte Iato.[14]

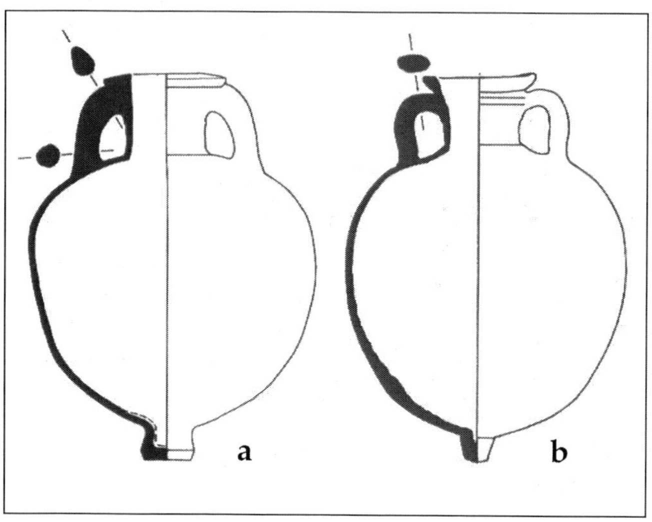

Fig. 4.1 Amphora types 1: (a) *Corinthian A, 64 cm high;* (b) *Corinthian B, 51 cm high; both mid-fifth century BC*

The Classical period (*c.* 500–320 BC)

Imports from Greece

Olive oil

The type of amphora known as Corinthian A (Fig. 4.1a) was imported to Lipari, Himera and other Greek settlements on the north coast throughout the sixth and fifth centuries BC. At Lipari in the fifth century BC they are never as common as those of the the Western Greek type known as MGS II ('pseudo-Chian').[15] Judging from the evidence of the Portinenti necropolis there, where it is absent, Corinthian A was no longer common in the fourth century, although a few examples have been found in levels of that date at Tindari.[16] According to Koehler, the Corinthian A amphora carried olive oil, and was the principal container for transporting this commodity to Greek colonies and elsewhere in the western Mediterranean during the sixth and fifth centuries BC.[17]

Just one piece of a Corinthian A amphora was found in the excavations at Marina di Caronía (Cat. no. 1), and another in a reddish fabric, as well as a fragment of a variant (Corinthian A') was found during surface survey in *contrada* Pantano.[18] Two of these finds predate by about half a century the traditional foundation of Kale Akte in 446 BC. A type with slanting handles can be dated to the last quarter of the sixth or the beginning of the fifth century BC, as it was found in destruction layers at Athens from the Persian sack there in 480 BC.[19] The fragments confirm the presence of Corinthian oil amphorae at Marina di Caronía (they are known also elsewhere on the north coast) at the beginning of the fifth century BC.

Wine

Corinthian B amphorae (Fig. 4.1b), produced at the Corinthian settlement of Kerkyra (Corfu) and carrying that island's wine,[20] are relatively common at Kale Akte, as they are elsewhere in Sicily as well as at Lipari,[21] although they are of course vastly outnumbered by contemporary containers of Sicilian and South Italian origin. Sporadic surface finds of Corinthian B vessels have been found near the railway station of Caronía (at Marina di Caronía) in remains of a building that was probably used for storage. Their shape suggests that they belong to the late fifth or early fourth century BC, and this is also the date of the archaeological context where they were found.[22]

Fig. 4.2 (left) *Fragment of an Attic black-figured column*-krater, *surface find,* contrada *Pantano; c. 500 BC*
Fig. 4.3 (centre) *Fragment of the neck of an Attic black-figured column* krater, *surface find,* contrada *Pantano;* c. *500 BC*
Fig. 4.4 (right) *Fragment of the base of a Corinthian* kotyle, *surface find,* contrada *Pantano;* c. *500 BC*

Attic black-gloss pottery

Attic pottery dominates imported fine ware in Sicily during the fifth century BC. The plentiful material, especially from Lipari but also from Himera, shows us that trading contacts between these Greek cities on the northern Sicilian coast and the mainland Greek world were intense. The import of Attic pottery was seriously disturbed by the hostile relations between Athens and Syracuse after 415 BC, and many scholars believe that this explains why imports of Attic pottery to Sicily had drastically declined by *c.* 400 BC. The absence of Attic pottery at this period opened up market possibilities for imitations of Attic crafted by Sicilian potters. The new Sicilian pottery industry, however, may have been an independent phenomenon, part of the expansionist policy of Dionysius I already in train by the end of the fifth century BC.[23]

Finds of black-figured pottery from *contrada* Trapiessi suggest that Attic wares, like Corinthian A amphorae, were already being imported to Marina di Caronía before the foundation of Kale Akte.[24] The proximity of Lipari, and the traffic between Himera to the west and Greek colonies in eastern Sicily, together with the fact that Attic pottery is common on Sikel sites in the interior, make it likely that by the second half of the fifth century BC Greek pottery was readily available to the Sikel population, especially those living close to the coast.

Few finds of Attic pottery have been made at Marina di Caronía (or at Caronía itself), principally because few deep *sondages* have been dug to explore early levels. However, unstratified finds made during survey work in *contrada* Pantano[25] demonstrate that Attic pottery was already reaching the site by the late sixth and early fifth century BC. Two pieces of column-*krater*, one with a palmette on the shoulder, the other with a frieze of lotus buds (Figs 4.2–3; lengths: 5.6 and 4.6 cm), can be dated to the late sixth or early fifth centuries BC. The finds suggest that a harbour and associated settlement must have existed here prior to Ducetius' foundation of Kale Akte. Furthermore, *skyphoi* of typical Attic fifth-century production have also been found, including a rim with stamped owls which is difficult to parallel; it may belong to the fourth century BC.[26] A bowl with out-turned rim from the Marina di Caronía excavations, dated to *c.* 400 BC, might also be an Attic product.[27]

Corinthian pottery

A fragment of a Corinthian *kotyle* with rays around the base (Fig. 4.4; diam. 6.2 cm), possibly dating to *c.* 525/475 BC,[28] was found in *contrada* Pantano, together with the other late Archaic material described above. There is also one tiny fragment decorated in Late Corinthian style which dates to the late sixth century BC.[29]

Oil-lamps

A sporadic fragment of an oil-lamp of Athenian Agora type 12 (late sixth/first half of the fifth century BC) may rather be a Corinthian import, since its fabric shows the typically Corinthian buff clay.[30] Oil-lamps sometimes accompanied (in 'piggy-back' fashion) shipments from Corinth in which the principal constituents were oil amphorae and table wares.

Imports from Sicily and Southern Italy

Wine

The second half of the fifth and the first half of the fourth centuries BC witnessed an important production of wine transported in the so-called 'pseudo-Chian' amphorae, dubbed MGS (Magna Graecia and Sicily) II by Vandermersch (Fig. 4.5a).[31] The type is widespread all over the island, even on indigenous inland sites. It was probably the most common wine amphora in Sicily during the fifth and fourth centuries BC.[32] These amphorae are often found with red-figure and black-gloss Italian or Sicilian pottery.[33] The most important centre of production for MGS II amphorae was probably Lokri Epizephyrii (Locri) in the toe of Calabria; such is the source proposed, for example, for the finds from Lipari.[34] Shipwrecks at Porticello and Marzamemi H

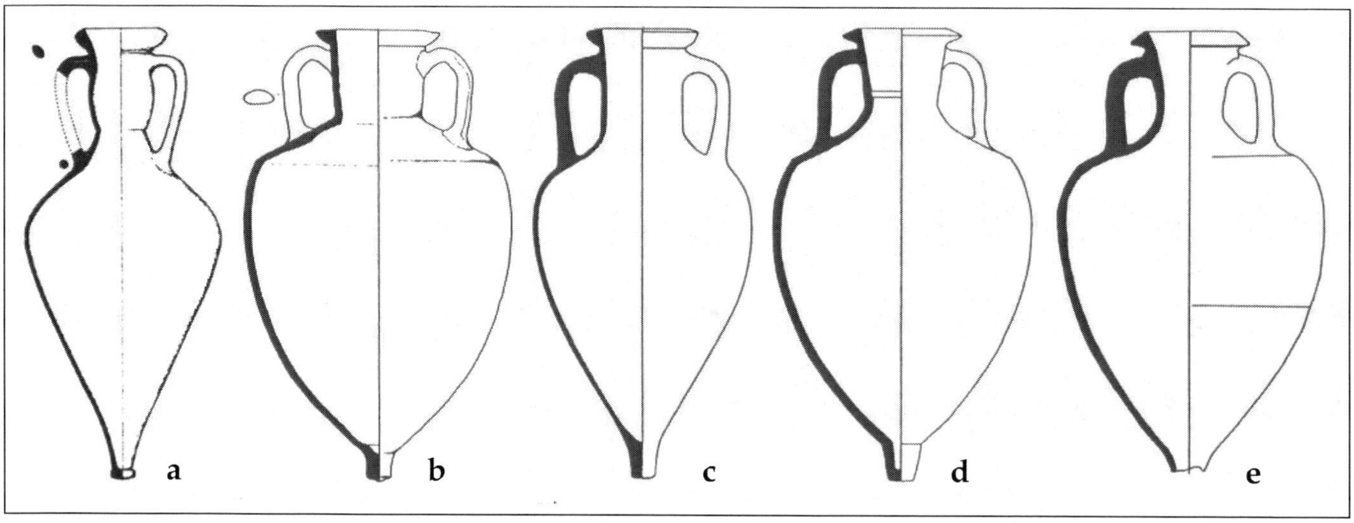

Fig. 4.5 Amphora types 2: (a) *MGS II;* (b) *MGS III;* (c) *MGS IV* (d) *MGS V;* (e) *MGS VI (not to scale; as an example, the MGS VI* [e] *is 64 cm high)*

also carried MGS II amphorae, possibly also produced at Locri.[35] The Locri amphorae have a characteristic buff fabric and are easily recognisable. The second most important production, in a reddish fabric with a whitish-buff slip, is common at Lipari, but its production centre is unknown.[36]

The situation at Caronía reflects that of other sites along the north coast. A few finds of MGS II amphorae were made during excavation in *contrada* Pantano, but a significant number has also been found during surface survey nearby, as well as in an excavation near the railway station at Marina di Caronía.[37] Fragments of the second fabric type listed below (Fabric 3, p. 178), quite similar to that of some later amphora production, have been identified at Caronía itself. It was probably made somewhere in the region, either in northern Sicily or on the Tyrrhenian coast of southern Italy. Finds in the typical Locrian fabric of an early type of MGS II (with a 'cushion' rim) have been made in Caronía itself (these date as early as 500 BC),[38] while another belongs to a later phase of production (*c.* 300 BC) (Fabric 4).

Sicilian drinking cups

Among the earliest finds of fine ware at Caronía are fragments of the late Archaic Iato K 480 cup.[39] These colonially produced cups[40] can be dated to between the last third of the sixth century and the early decades of the fifth century BC.[41] They were probably produced at the Greek settlement of Himera, on the north coast not very far to the west of Kale Akte.[42] They are especially common at Colle Madore in the hinterland of Himera as well as at Monte Iato, but they spread in addition to many indigenous centres in both the western and the central parts of Sicily.[43]

Sicilian red-figured pottery

From the very end of the fifth and during the whole of the fourth century BC, red-figure Sicilian pottery was produced at Gela, in the area around Etna and at Lipari in particular.[44] At the same period similar imitations of Attic red-figure pottery were produced in Campania and elsewhere in Magna Graecia. The first productions were influenced strongly by the Attic style; it has even been suggested that potters from Attica itself were active in Sicily.[45] At the beginning of the fourth century BC, it seems that production was limited.[46] Red-figure pottery was also traded from southern Italy: towards the middle of the century, for example, Italian *kraters* made in various centres there including Paestum were imported to Lipari.[47] These, however, were undoubtedly luxury goods, and arrived only in limited quantity. At a well-studied site such as Morgantina, for example, not a single find of Apulian red-figure pottery has been made.[48] It seems that in the course of the fourth century BC the production of Sicilian pottery managed to exclude Attic pottery completely from the Sicilian market, as finds from all over the island strongly suggest. In the Nebrodi area, at San Marco d'Alunzio and at Troina, as well as at Cefalù, fourth-century-BC graves with Sicilian *skyphoi, aryballoi* and *lekanai* are common.[49] Sicilian red-figure pottery also reached further west, for example Monte Iato, Entella, Segesta and Marsala, although it is less frequent in the very far west.[50] So in the fourth century BC the whole of Sicily became a *koiné* of Sicilian red-figure pottery, especially in the Greek-dominated eastern part of the island.

The Sicilian red-figure pottery found in excavations at Caronía is not abundant, but domestic contexts of early Hellenistic date are few; by contrast field survey

Fig. 4.6 Sicilian red-figured lekythos *with a female head wearing a* sakkos *(a hair covering made of cloth), from the south necropolis of Kale Akte in* contrada *Trappeto at Caronía; late fourth century BC (private collection)*

of the slopes of Caronía have yielded numerous fragments, especially of *lekanai*. In addition, the material from the necropolis of Kale Akte shows the ubiquity of red-figured Sicilian pottery. Pottery of the Manfria-Lentini groups as well as the Etna group centred in Centuripe was widespread all over the island, and was certainly present at Caronía also. Most finds have parallels in the material from Lipari, where *lekanai* are also very common. *Lekanai* and *lekythoi* in the Sicilian red-figure tradition are widespread in the funerary material from the necropolis of Kale Akte, in the south part of modern Caronía, of which a well-preserved example from *contrada* Trapetto featuring a woman's head is illustrated here (Fig. 4.6).[51] On a fragment of a *lekanis* lid, from an excavation context, the *sakkos* (cloth hair-covering) of a female figure can be seen, in a style that can be attributed to the NYN painter and his school (Cat. no. 148). Trendall hypothesized that this painter originally had his workshop in Sicily, before moving northwards to Campania.[52] The NYN painter's workshop is represented by finds at Cumae, Paestum and Laos in southern Italy,[53] and at Lipari and elsewhere in Sicily,[54] including now Caronía, a distribution which supports the idea that production was first located somewhere in Sicily. Another Caronía find, the neck of an *olpe* decorated with vine leaves similar to works by the ZA painter of the Etna group, dates to the last quarter of the fourth century BC (Cat. no. 150).[55] Also noteworthy is a fragment of a *krater* with a meander frieze; this is not a shape very common in the Sicilian tradition.

Three Pagenstecher *lekythoi*, one found in the excavations in *contrada* Telegrafo in 1992–93, and two in the south necropolis of Kale Akte, are of exactly the same type as those from Lipari and other sites in Sicily (Fig. 4.7).[56] It has been thought that the Pagenstecher *lekythoi* had a Campanian origin, but the frequency of this type in Sicily, and the not very high quality of the painting, brings this judgment into question. I would argue that it is rather a Sicilian product.[57]

Fig. 4.7 Pagenstecher lekythos *with a painted bird, from the south necropolis in* contrada *Trappeto; height: 11.7 cm; late fourth/early third century BC (private collection)*

Oil-lamps

As noted above, almost no contexts of Classical date have been excavated at Caronía and Marina di Caronía, although sporadic surface finds from a soil dump in *contrada* Pantano contained a few lamp fragments, of Athenian Agora type 22a, belonging to the end of the sixth or the first half of the fifth century BC.[58] They are of an open type, without handle, and the quality of their black-gloss slip is variable. It is impossible from these two finds to say if these are Athenian products or not, since not all Attic goods had high-quality gloss. The finds of Agora 22a-type lamps probably belong to one of the many 'colonial' Sicilian-Greek productions imitating mainland models, since the black-gloss is of low quality and sometimes applied only to the shoulders or the interior of the lamp. It can be argued that Kale Akte followed the general pattern of other settlements (for example, Lipari or Himera) in having contacts with major Greek settlements, and so was able to import 'colonial' products. Lamps were already being made in Sicily during the fifth century BC, often imitating the Attic shapes and indeed their glossy appearance.[59] These Sicilian lamps were widely available at markets in Kale Akte, but so too were much smaller numbers of Attic lamps, which presumably arrived with the Attic pottery that we know was imported to the area.

Sicilian Punic imports

Fish products

No finds of Punic amphorae of Classical date were made during excavation, but four fragments from soil dumps in *contrada* Pantano all seem to belong to a type which belongs to the early part of the sixth century BC.[60] I have not been able to study these finds, and in any case it would be hard to determine their origin from visual inspection alone. It would seem, however, that the type was common in this part of the island, produced presumably in one of the Punic centres further west on the north coast. It seems reasonable to assume that such amphorae were imported from early on, although surely in much smaller quantities than amphorae produced in the Greek centres. Punic containers, both North African- and Sicilian-made, are well attested already in the Archaic period at Greek sites in eastern Sicily, such as Milazzo, Naxos, Syracuse, Gela and especially Camarina.[61] A Punic centre such as Solunto seems to have produced itself such large quantities of amphorae that imports there from other Punic areas (North Africa, Spain or Sardinia) were limited.[62]

Local production

Kale Akte already in the fourth century BC seems to have produced wine for export which was transported in locally produced MGS II amphorae (cf. Fig. 4.5a). Only one find has so far been made, from surface survey, so the scale of this trade at the time may have been inconsequential. The rim is large and bulbous, with an edge running below.[63] The fabric is quite characteristic, being very coarse-grained and in colour orange, with a grey core. The suggestion that it is indeed a local product is confirmed by finds of *pithoi* from the Pizzo Cilona site, in the hinterland of Caronía,which are in an identical fabric. Huge *pithoi* are always thought to have been produced locally, since they were so heavy and bulky as to make long-distance transport (at least at this period) difficult.

The Early Hellenistic Period (*c.* 320–200 BC)

Finds from the early Hellenistic period in the excavations at Caronía are not plentiful. Most have come from domestic contexts or were surface finds in the upper town, whereas the number of contexts of this date excavated at Marina di Caronía is limited. However, the large amount of early Hellenistic pottery discovered through field survey at Caronía in recent years show that the relative dearth of finds from this period is due to the fact that only very few contexts of this date have so far seen systematic excavation. The vast majority of finds from the latter are those that come from *contrada* Pantano, where the priority has been to reveal major buildings which (as it happened) dated only from the late Hellenistic period and later; levels below were hardly touched. Further excavation in the urban area of Caronía will no doubt in the future yield rich finds of early Hellenistic pottery, and indeed in the harbour area as well, where the imported goods would have arrived. Nevertheless, judging from the few early Hellenistic contexts which have so far been excavated in *contrada* Pantano, there seems to have been a marked difference in the relative numbers of finds belonging to the early as opposed to the late Hellenistic period in the harbour area. This probably indicates an important increase in the size of the settlement and the scale of its trading activity during the latter period.

South Italian imports

Wine

MGS III amphorae (MGS, as noted above, stands for Magna Graecia and Sicily) contained wine, and belong mainly to the second half of the fourth and the beginning of the third century BC. Some fragments from Caronía are in a coarse orange fabric, without doubt a Sicilian, and probably a local, production. Among the more common fabrics is one which is dark brownish or red, with volcanic inclusions, probably of Campanian origin; it has been found in large quantities at Lipari and Tindari.[64] Present also among material of this date is a rim which seems to be of Locrian manufacture

(Fabric 4), probably part of a small amphora. In the Nebrodi area, MGS III amphorae have been found apart from Caronía, at Apollonia, Halaesa, San Marco d'Alunzio and Capo d'Orlando, as well as further afield, at Lipari, Tindari and Solunto.[65] They were probably produced also in Bruttium (modern Calabria), especially at Locri, as well as in Lucania.[66] The small to medium size points to a limited production, and the type was probably not distributed further than the north and north-eastern Sicilian coastal area and the Tyrrhenian shore of Calabria; at any rate they have not been recorded outside this region.[67]

MGS III amphorae also have a sub-group, the so-called *anfore ad orlo echino* ('rim in the shape of an *echinus*', the 'cushion' part of the Doric capital), which have the same basic form except for the rim, which is almond-shaped. It occurs quite frequently in *contrada* Portinenti at Lipari, and was clearly one of the more common containers in Sicily and South Italy in this period, although not as common as the standard MGS III type. At Caronía, several examples have been found through surface survey, one of which is illustrated below (p. 182, no. 9).[68] Some belong to the typical production of Locri mentioned above (Fabric 4), while others were produced locally (see below).

The somewhat later MGS V, or 'ancient' Greco-Italic amphorae, are distinguished by a triangular rim, ovoid handles and a pear-shaped body (Fig. 4.5d). 'Greco-Italic' is the collective name for several different amphora forms, all originating in the Greek areas of southern Italy and Sicily; they began in the fourth century BC and continued production right down to almost the end of the second century BC. The earliest types were stamped with Greek names, and the later ones with Latin ones. Vandermersch has shown that they carried wine.[69] Elizabeth Lyding Will was the first to create a typology of them, in 1982, which was tied very closely just to the shape of the vessels. Vandermersch later, in 1994, inserted Greco-Italic into the more general typology of MGS amphorae, treating them as merely the latest forms of a continuous development of western Greek wine amphorae. The MGS V containers and their prototype, MGS IV (Fig. 4.5c), obviously had close links with their predecessor MGS III, and were indeed often manufactured in the same fabrics. It is established beyond reasonable doubt that MGS IV/V amphorae also carried wine.[70] They are clearly linked with the transport of red-figure and black gloss Italian and Sicilian table pottery, as most obviously suggested by the Filicudi F wreck which dates to *c.* 300/250 BC; this, found not so very far from Kale Akte, contains both pottery and amphorae in the same cargo.[71] The very high number of MGS IV amphora fragments in the deposit from the sanctuary in *proprietà* Maggiore at Lipari suggests that the type was reaching there in good numbers.[72]

The MGS V amphora is a later variant of MGS IV, the only difference being in the shape of the triangular rim, which is slightly sloping. The MGS V type was manufactured in many places on the southern Tyrrhenian coasts: Vandermersch lists sixteen known production sites, dispersed throughout Etruria, Latium, Campania, Bruttium, Lucania and Sicily.[73] Intense discussion about the origin of the most common products, several of which contain volcanic inclusions, has been going on for decades. The interest has usually been concentrated on the area around Vesuvius in Campania, or around Etna in Sicily.[74] Recent work by Gloria Olcese, however, has convincingly shown that the typical fabric of volcanic origin was produced at Ischia in the Bay of Naples.[75] This study shows that the amphorae from the well-known shipwrecks of Secca di Capistello, Filicudi F and Roghi (Panarea) were produced in this very fabric, and this is true also for the most common fabric of MGS IV and V amphorae from Lipari.[76] These shipwreck cargoes were considered by some previous scholars as Sicilian, and the amphorae as originating from the area around Etna,[77] but now there is enough evidence to indicate that Campanian MGS V amphorae were exported in large quantities to Sicily.[78] A handle with the stamp Q.ANTR from Morgantina, for example, is of probable Campanian production,[79] while at Gela also, and maybe at Camarina too, both important wine producers in their own right in the third century BC, amphora stamps have been identified which are considered by Olcese to be Campanian.[80] In addition to Campania, the MGS V amphora was also produced in eastern Sicily, in Bruttium (at Hipponion) and on the Tyrrhenian coast of Lucania.[81] Probable production sites in Sicily are Gela, Camarina, the area around Etna (Naxos/Tauromenium), and possibly Lipari.

MGS V amphorae are found all over Sicily in great quantities and in varying fabrics. It seems that these vessels indicate the beginning of a more intensive economic activity at Caronía, since it is the earliest Hellenistic amphora type that is found in significant numbers. This ties in well with the information given to us by the Halaesa survey, which shows a consistent increase in number of rural settlements from the beginning of the First Punic War onwards.[82] The dominating fabric at Caronía is the typical Ischian/Campanian one, a coarse fabric containing shiny black volcanic inclusions (Fabric 5a–b). The amphorae frequently have a cream-coloured wash. The fabric is not the same as the Campanian so-called 'black sand' fabric present in the later Greco-Italic and Dressel 1 amphorae of the second and first centuries BC, but is somewhat similar.[83] The fabrics show some variations in colour and in the number and type of inclusions, but all can be interpreted as belonging to the same general category. It is uncertain whether a stamped handle with the name ΙΩΛΙΟ, in a reddish fabric with volcanic inclusions, belongs to a Campanian MGS V form or to MGS VI (Fig. 4.5e).[84] In addition to these finds, a number of body-sherds were also retrieved. The fabric of these is identical to that of amphora handles from Morgantina stamped Q. ANTR, ΠΥΘ(Ε), ΜΑΚ, ΕΛΩ, ΕΥΩΝΥΜΟΥ and ΠΑΣΙΩΝ.[85] The last three have been recorded earlier in Sicily, and have been considered as Sicilian,[86] but they are probably best regarded as Campanian. The finds from Caronía attest to the importation, therefore, of Campanian wine at least from the first third of the third century BC. MGS V amphorae of presumed Campanian origin have been found also at Lipari, Tindari and Termini Imerese.[87] At the first two sites, they constitute, as at Caronía, the dominant fabric-type among Greco-Italic amphorae.[88]

North African imports

Fish-sauce

The Punic amphora Ramòn 7.1.2.1 is represented by several finds. It was produced in the area of modern Tunisia around Carthage as well as in western Sicily, in the second half of the fourth and the first quarter of the third century BC.[89] The finds all have the same characteristic – a fine, orange or yellowish-buff fabric, sometimes with a pink core (Fabric 10).[90] The type has been found in the western Sicily, at Palermo, San Vito lo Capo, Erice and Mozia, and also further east at Gela, as well as at Roccagloriosa in Calabria.[91]

Few pre-Roman Punic amphorae have been published from Sicily outside the Punic area of the western part of the island:[92] they were rare, for example, at the necropolis of Portinenti on Lipari.[93] However, they are also found east of Caronía, for example at Milazzo, which seems to indicate that the centres on the north coast were an integrated part of the Punic trading network.[94] The contents of Punic amphorae are thought to have varied, because of their very many different shapes. Known commodities from North Africa were wheat, olives, oil and *garum*.[95] Empereur and Hesnard suggested that *garum* and/or other fish products were transported in them, referring to one specimen with a *titulus pictus* in support of this view.[96] That Punic amphorae commonly carried fish-based commodities is also indicated by the find of one in the agora of Morgantina containing fish-scales.[97] Punic amphorae of type Bartoloni D (produced in Sardinia) certainly contained fish,[98] and Punic amphorae are commonly found on fish-salting sites in western Sicily,[99] which strengthens the hypothesis that these vessels carried fish or fish-related products. At the sites of S. Vito lo Capo near Palermo and Tonnara del Cofano, close to Trapani on the west coast of Sicily, large amounts of sherds of Punic amphorae were found in the immediate vicinity of the basins.[100] Alternatively, as in the case of Africana 1 and 2 forms, they may have contained some other product sold together with the local fish products.[101] The production of Punic amphorae also in western Sicily is now well documented by work at Marsala and elsewhere, and that further supports the view that fish preserves were its principal contents, not least because the island was famous for its fish and had a productive fishing industry.[102]

Sicilian imports

Wine

A rim of reduced size in non-Campanian fabric, found in the 2003–05 excavations at Marina di Caronía, is in all probability of Sicilian origin. The thin-section analysis showed inclusions of sandstone and basalt, which might indicate an origin in the Etna area, or else in the Aeolian islands where basalt is also found (Fabric 7).[103] However, basalt is also present in the tuff sandstones in the area around Tusa (Halaesa) and in the Nebrodi, in the hinterland of Caronía itself. Halaesa must be considered the most probable candidate, being situated close to the sea. I would therefore suggest, on the basis of thin-section analysis, that this amphora had an origin either at Lipari or in the *chora* of Halaesa, i.e. not far from Kale Akte. An origin in the Etna area can of course not be excluded, but the small sample size, implying a trade of limited geographical range, and the fact that the places mentioned above were all wine-producing *poleis* in this period, make a north Sicilian or a Lipari origin more probable.

Sicilian black-gloss pottery

The Greek colonies in Sicily had already started producing black-gloss pottery by the fifth century BC, initially as imitations of Attic black-gloss pottery.[104] Campanian pottery seems not to have been common in Sicily in the fourth/third centuries BC, and even at Lipari, very few finds have been made of the refined Campana A ware of that date.[105] The high-quality black-gloss found in the Secca di Capistello wreck off Lipari, from *c.* 310/280 BC, was first attributed to workshops in Punic Sicily or Carthage, but most scholars think that the best parallels are in Campanian ware from Ischia,[106] a conclusion further confirmed by recent studies: the accompanying amphorae were probably produced on that island, on the basis of both their stamps and their style of manufacture.[107] The apparent lack of finds of Campanian pottery at Lipari, as well as at Apollonia and Caronía, raises the question as to whether most of the black-gloss ware on board the Secca di Capistello ship was intended for market at Carthage or somewhere in western Sicily, and not Lipari or anywhere in eastern Sicily at all. Morel claims that central Italian black-gloss ware *à petites éstampilles* is completely absent from Greek Sicily in the third century BC, but it certainly appears in settlements of Punic origin, such as Solunto.[108] It is uncommon at Morgantina and was not produced there.[109] The large body of stamped black-gloss wares from Monte Iato is generally considered by Caflisch to be of regional origin.[110] Thus it seems reasonable to assume that any export of Campanian black-gloss to eastern Sicily, and indeed to Sicily in general, was on a very limited scale, mostly hampered by the flourishing existence of a black-gloss pottery industry within Sicily itself during the third century BC. Certainly the very rich and varied material in this ware found at both Caronía and Apollonia was a regional production, in a workshop located either on the Sicilian mainland or else on the offshore island of Lipari.

Platters, especially the series Morel 1534 and 1312 (= Lamboglia 36), which date from the end of the fourth and throughout the whole of the third century BC, seem to have been common in the area.[111] Very frequent are *paterae* of the series Morel 1510 (forms 1514 and 1534). Their fabric varies in colour between brick red and light red, usually with a matt rather than a shiny gloss. The bottoms of *paterae* often have purple tondos.[112]

Cups after *paterae* are the next most common form, especially the series Morel 2600, 3200 and 4200.[113] Type 2621, which has a matt gloss of poor quality, has numerous parallels from Sicily and Calabria, suggesting a regional production that can be dated to between the end of the fourth and middle of the third centuries BC.[114] The same is true for type Morel 4262.[115] Morel 3211 with a 'profiled foot' is very common, probably produced in the so-called *officine dello Stretto* around the Strait of Messina.[116] This shape, which dates to the first half of the third century BC, is common at Monte Iato and at Lipari.[117] The only closed form at this period is a *pelike* of type Morel 3681, of the fourth century BC.[118]

Skyphoi and cups are of course common and of Sicilian production, some of which were probably also made locally. Cups or bowls with a rosette stamp in the floor are not uncommon at Caronía (Cat. no. 167).[119] Similar stamps have been found at Monte Iato and Morgantina, and have been compared with those from the *atelier des petites éstampilles* based in central Italy.[120] The many finds from Sicilian sites, especially at Monte Iato, and the often mediocre quality of the gloss, rules out in my opinion a central Italian origin. The rosette bowls are, rather, Sicilian products made in the same tradition as those of the *atelier des petites éstampilles*.

Cruciform stamps on the black-gloss regional wares are common at Caronía,[121] and a Sicilian production of these is indicated by the quantity of finds from Monte Iato and Lipari.[122] The floor of a cup with flower and palmette stamps (and very bad-quality gloss), has an exact parallel from Halaesa, and similar examples are found at Monte Iato and Lipari.[123] The cup can be dated to the third century BC, and is certainly of Sicilian production. Published finds of stamped third-century-BC black-gloss platters from the area include two *paterae* of the early third century from the *tomba del kottabos* at San Marco d'Alunzio: these have four palmettes arranged in a cross, surrounded by two concentric circles.[124] Other black-gloss *paterae* with stamped palmettes are known from Halaesa.[125]

Another Sicilian product, so-called Gnathian ware (after the site at Egnazia in Apulia), typical of the late fourth/early third century BC, is very common at Caronía as elsewhere in Sicily (Fig. 4.8). This has a shiny black-gloss slip and has painted white (and sometimes red and blue) floral motifs, often using incised decoration. The abundance of the finds here, as well as in Sicily more generally, and the fact that vessels are sometimes misfired (and so as 'seconds' would not have travelled far) clearly suggests a Sicilian production.

Black-glossed cups decorated with relief ornamentation, known as 'medallion ware', were produced in various places in eastern Sicily, including Morgantina, and can be dated to *c.* 275/175 BC.[126] The products were clearly inspired by silver vessels with similar relief decoration. One example was a surface find on the eastern slope of Caronía.[127] The medallion shows a sitting Nike/Victoria writing on a shield, a motif that is not uncommon in Hellenistic and Roman visual culture. It appears most famously on Trajan's Column in Rome, but it also occurs on private objects such as gems and intaglios. Our Caronía example has no precise parallel. The style is not as refined as that of the Morgantina cups, and it may have come from a production site somewhere on the north coast, or elswhere in eastern Sicily (Fig. 4.9).[128]

A stemmed cup with iridescent black gloss found at Caronía has a painted flower with twelve petals in brown and purple colour at the centre (colour Pl. 11).[129] The decoration was certainly inspired by 'medallion cups' mentioned above,[130] and the very iridescent gloss shows how this kind of vessel was designed as a deliberate imitation of the originals in silver. Good examples are in the Morgantina treasure of the third century BC, where a similar type of twelve-petalled flower occurs.[131] The find from Caronía is probably a North Sicilian product, since it is a poor imitation of the more sophisticated and better-quality mould-made medallion bowls made elsewhere in eastern Sicily.

Fig. 4.8 Fragments of Gnathian ware (the largest measures 6 x 8 cm), found during surface survey at Caronía; third century BC

Appliqué ware C

An appliqué head from a black-gloss vessel, probably of the third century BC, was found on the slopes of Caronía (Fig. 4.10). The headgear suggests that it may represent Heracles with his lion-skin, a type common at Morgantina among black-gloss appliqués which were certainly produced in Sicily.[132]

Sporadic finds have been made at both Caronía and Marina di Caronía of a cup (type Morel 2132b1) with three moulded clam-shells as feet, dating from sometime in the third or second centuries BC. The type was produced at Morgantina and is found, for example, at Lipari and Monte Iato.[133]

Black-gloss lamps

The earliest lamps from excavations at both Caronía and Marina di Caronía belong to the early third century BC, and are doubtless of Sicilian production. Black-gloss lamps imitating Greek mainland forms dominated the Sicilian market from the fourth to the first centuries BC, but distinctive Sicilian shapes were also produced, usually with a round chamber containing the oil and a long nozzle. The most common type in third-century-BC Sicily seems to have been the so-called *Flachschulterlampe* (Agora type IV), present also at Caronía in both domestic and funerary contexts.[134] Another find (of the first half of the third century) comes from a necropolis at San Marco d'Alunzio.[135] Finds have been made also at Lipari.[136] The huge numbers found at Monte Iato suggest that the type was produced on the island.[137] Lamps circulating in the South Tyrrhenian area, with either a shiny or a matt black gloss, and certainly of regional production, are well known from the Lipari publications.[138]

Local production

Wine

A few fragments of the type of amphora of the variant known as *ad orlo di echino* (see p. 71 for the explanation), a subgroup of MGS III, have been found at Caronía in the course of surface survey. The fabric is similar to that of later locally-made containers, with a brownish-red wash (Fabric 36). A rim and a toe belonging to a small-size variant of the MGS III type, from excavated contexts, probably also belong to the local Kale Akte production at this period, in the second half of the fourth and in the early third centuries BC, when the hinterland of the *polis* was producing a surplus of wine for export.

Another local product may have been the MGS V amphora (Fig. 4.5d). The second-most common MGS V fabric identified at Caronía is easily distinguishable. It is usually orange in colour with quartz and feldspar inclusions, as well as reddish-orange *chamotte* (a grog of calcined clay with high silica content), and is sometimes fired black. Some variants are particularly distinctive, showing poor levigation of the clay (Fabric 6). It is clearly a North Sicilian production, and a local one in all probability. An important distinctive feature is its buff surface-wash, common in later amphora production at Kale Akte. The fabric type fits well with that of both earlier and later Caronía containers. Kale Akte's coins from the late second century BC onwards feature the image of Dionysus with a bunch of grapes and demonstrate the importance of wine to the town. A local production of these amphorae seems likely. They were apparently exported in some numbers, since examples in the same fabric have also been recorded at Morgantina.[139] A small-scale variant is also known.

Fig. 4.9 Black-gloss medallion bowl, moulded figure depicting Nike sitting on a pile of shields, and writing on another of them; width: 6.6 cm; c. *275/175 BC*

Fig. 4.10 Moulded appliqué from a black-gloss vessel, head possibly of Herakles, found during surface survey at Caronía; c. 5 cm high; third century BC

Bricks and tiles

Bricks and tiles were produced locally in Hellenistic times, as commonly in many Sicilian urban settlements. Early in the period, as we shall see (Fig. 4.11), brick-making was under the control of the *polis*, but at some stage during the late Republican period, local manufacture of bricks seems to have become decentralised, when it began to take place in the larger rural estates. A kiln of this type, producing both circular bricks and square ones, has been identified in *contrada* Giumentaro, a few kilometres to the south of the town.[140] Square bricks are ubiquitous in excavated contexts at Caronía and Marina di Caronía, and robbed examples were later re-used in the vaults (and for polychrome effect) in the Norman castle built in the twelfth century, situated on what is taken to have been the one-time acropolis of Kale Akte. The largest bricks measure 50 x 25.5 x 8.5 cm, while smaller examples have the same or a similar width and thickness, but have a shorter length of either 36 or 23 cm.[141] Some excavated in *contrada* Pantano measure 32 or 34 cm square, but are only 3.5 or 4 cm thick. That Kale Akte had an important production of bricks and tiles is not surprising: there were good supplies of timber for fuel from the Nebrodi, and of clay from the river bed locally, which helped ceramic production of all sorts to thrive in Marina di Caronía and nearby in both Hellenistic and Roman Imperial times. Hellenistic production is witnessed by several brick-stamps in Greek attested at both Caronía and Halaesa.[142] Halaesa, however, had its own separate production, as a stamp with the letters ΠΑ on a square brick shows (it is likely to be an abbreviation of ΠΟΛΙΣ ΑΛΑΙΣΙΝΩΝ, 'the city of the people of Halaisa').[143] Another brick-stamp, found in the hinterland of Kale Akte, has been interpreted as (κέραμος) ΔΑΜΟΣΙΟΣ ΚΑΛΑΚΤΙΝΩΝ ΙΕΡΟΣ – '(brick) of the people of Kale Akte; sacred' (Fig. 4.11).[144] An identical stamp was found at *contrada* Pantano on a square brick of Hellenistic type.[145] A state-production of pottery as well is suggested by a sherd stamped Δ for Δ(αμόσιος) ('belonging to the people') within a square (Fig. 4.12). Whatever vessel this sherd once belonged to was presumably produced for and used by state officials of the *polis*. Both flat pantiles (*tegulae*) and curved cover tiles (*imbrices*) have been found in *contrada* Pantano, the roofing system typical of Hellenistic Sicily.

The many bricks of Hellenistic type found everywhere at Caronía, in the upper town on the hillsides and reused in many buildings at Caronía, were ubiquitous in excavated walling of this period, and attest to an abundant local production of bricks as well as roof-tiles. Comparison between the fabrics of the tiles and the locally-produced amphorae indicates a local production for the former as well. The late Hellenistic building technique most prevalent employed bricks as

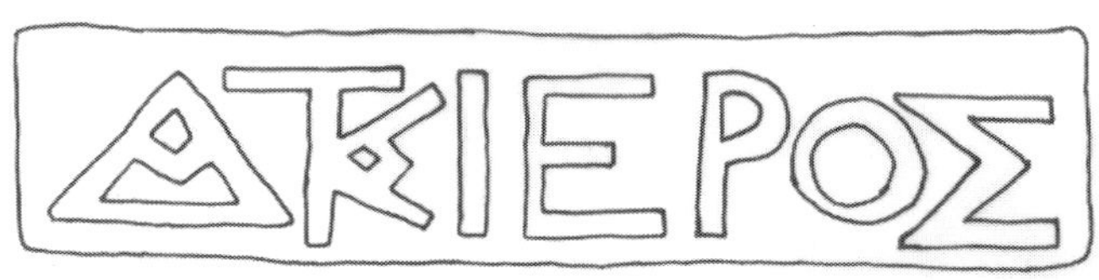

Fig. 4.11 Brick-stamp from Caronía with an abbreviated reference to the polis *of Kale Akte;* c. *third/first century BC*

Fig. 4.12 Sherd of locally-produced pottery with the stamp Δ, standing for demosion *('of the people'); maximum width 15.0 cm;* c. *third/first century BC*

a complement to dressed limestone (e.g. Fig. 3.3 on p. 44),[146] a construction style also attested at Halaesa. Both cities produced square bricks; for example, the forum at the latter is paved with them.[147] Bricks were also used to pave courtyards, noted at Caronía in both domestic buildings in the hill-town of Caronía (e.g. Fig. 3.4 on p. 46) as well as in Building 1 at Marina di Caronía.[148] Floors of this type are attested at Morgantina by the mid-third century BC,[149] and there are direct parallels also in the courtyards of houses at, for example, Tindari and Solunto.

Local terracotta production

The manufacture of Hellenistic terracotta figurines at Kale Akte is witnessed by the discovery in a cistern at Caronía of a third-century-BC mould of a male head (apparently wearing a laurel wreath: Fig. 4.13a–b). The mould implies local coroplastic production. The head closely resembles the features of late Hellenistic ruler portraits, for example the wrinkles around the eyes and above all the presence of a wreath / diadem, which rules out identification with a deity. A non-religious figure produced in late Hellenistic Kale Akte must have shown a Roman, and a possible candidate is Agrippa, the victor at Naulochus in 36 BC.[150] The quantity of terracotta figurines present in *contrada* San Todaro has given rise to the local name for the area,which is *Chianu dei Pupiddi* (Plain of the Puppets).[151] Several female terracotta figurines of Hellenistic date have been found at Caronía, especially in the upper town (Figs 4.14a–d). Other discoveries include a small appliqué mask of a bearded silenus (Fig. 4.15) and another appliqué mask portraying a slave from the New Comedy; and there are also coarser products, such as another appliqué in the shape of a silenus head, and several depicting animals, including one *protome* in the shape of a lion's head.[152] All these, given the observations made above, are probably of local production, with a likely *floruit* in the third century BC, continuing into the second. If a place like Calacte had a local coroplastic industry, it seems likely that many small urban centres in Sicily with access to clay would have had them, imitating the larger production centres such as at Lipari and Morgantina.

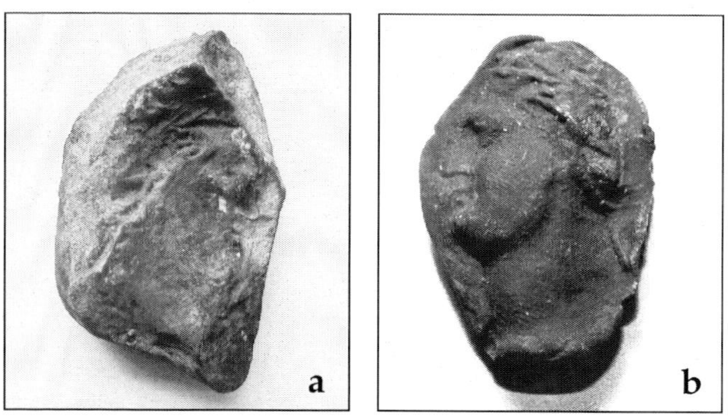

Fig. 4.13 a–b *Terracotta mould for the head of a male figurine* (a)*, and a modern impression taken from it* (b)*, from the cistern in* contrada *Sotto San Francesco, Caronía, excavated in 1999; height: 3.6 cm; first century BC*

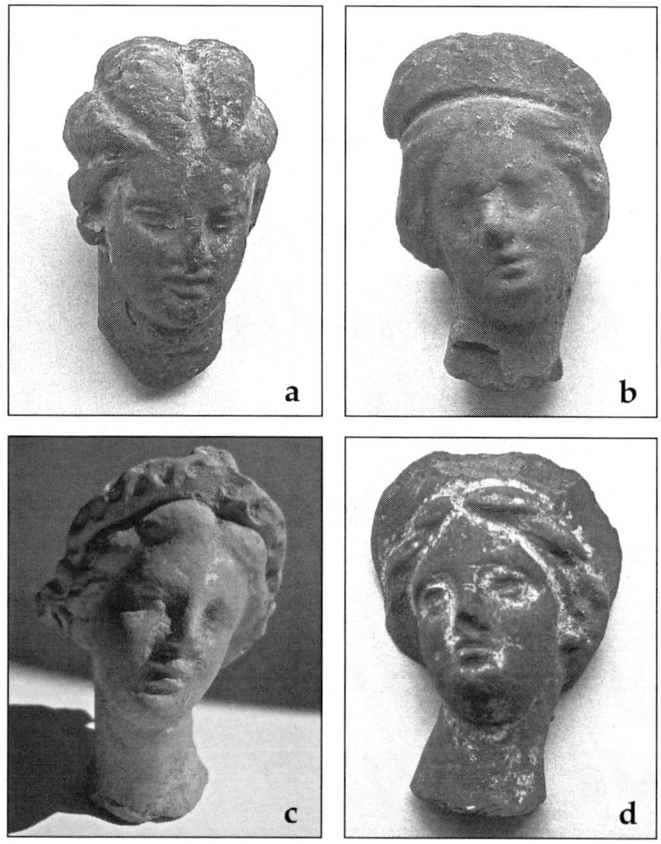

Fig. 4.14 a–d *Heads of female terracotta figurines, found during surface survey at Caronía; third/second century BC*

Fig. 4.15 (left) *Terracotta head of a silenus, local production, found during surface survey at Caronía (height: 6 cm)*

Fig. 4.16 (right) *Fragmentary handle of a Campanian MGS VI amphora stamped* ΑΝΔΡΩΝΟ[Σ *in retrograde, found unstratified at Marina di Caronía (length: 3.9 cm); third century BC*

The Late Hellenistic period (*c.* 200–30 BC)

Italian imports

Wine

I have included in this section both the MGS VI of Vandermersch (belonging to the second half of the third century BC (Fig. 4.5e) and the later forms of Will's classification (which date to the first two thirds of the second century BC), which are the dominant amphora types in the western Mediterranean at this period. The two forms are essentially the same, but those of Will's series are taller, more slender, and have a rim which slopes more steeply downwards, a development which ends in the Dressel 1A amphora form described below. The best-known shipwreck of this date off the north coast is the Filicudi A wreck of around 160/140 BC.[153] An even more massive export of amphorae from Campania in the direction of Sicily began in the aftermath of the Second Punic War, at the very beginning of the second century BC, stimulated no doubt by the building of a *portorium* at Puteoli in 199 BC, and the foundation of the *colonia* there five years later.[154]

In the cistern in *contrada* Sotto San Francesco at Caronía were found an amphora rim and a handle marked with an A, the initial letter of a stamp. A nearly complete stamp with ΑΝΔΡΩΝΟ[Σ], in retrograde on the top of a handle, which is of exactly the same type and fabric as the fragmentary stamp at Caronía, was found unstratified in *contrada* Pantano (Fig. 4.16; Cat. no. 20); the two might very well have been from the same producer. The find-spot distribution of this stamp is concentrated in Sicily and Magna Graecia; it probably belongs to the last decades of the third century BC.[155] The possible finding of two stamps of this producer at the same site is interesting, and perhaps indicates that he was one of the more important producers exporting to the area. Apart from these stamps, a few fragments of Campanian MGS VI and Will D–E were found at Caronía (Fabric 8), a very common type which must have been available in the region in large numbers.[156]

The Dressel 1 amphora shape is tall and cylindrical with a massive spike, a long, cylindrical neck, and lengthy, broad, oval handles. The first variant is the Dressel 1A, which has a triangular rim, very similar to, and often indistinguishable from, the late Greco-Italic amphorae from which it evolved (Fig. 4.17a). Dressel 1A amphorae appear around 140/130 BC and are common until around 75 BC, when they were replaced by the Dressel 1B form (Fig. 4.17b).[157] This is larger and coarser, with broader handles and a greater capacity than the 1A shape. The rim is higher, around 4/5 cm, vertical and collar-formed, and sometimes somewhat concave. The type seems to have been manufactured at the same sites as Dressel 1A amphorae. Yet another variant of the form is Dressel 1C, first produced towards the end of the second century and continuing into the first century BC. It also has a high collar rim, around 6 cm tall, but is more slender overall, with a short spike, and with very broad, ribbed handles. Both Dressel 1B and 1C continue until the end of the first century BC.[158] The Dressel 1 is the most common and widespread of all amphorae in the Late Republican period in the central Mediterranean. Its origin is clearly to be placed on the central Tyrrhenian coast of Italy, mainly in Campania, Latium and Etruria.[159] The common version in 'black sand' fabric is consistent with an origin from the area around Pompeii and

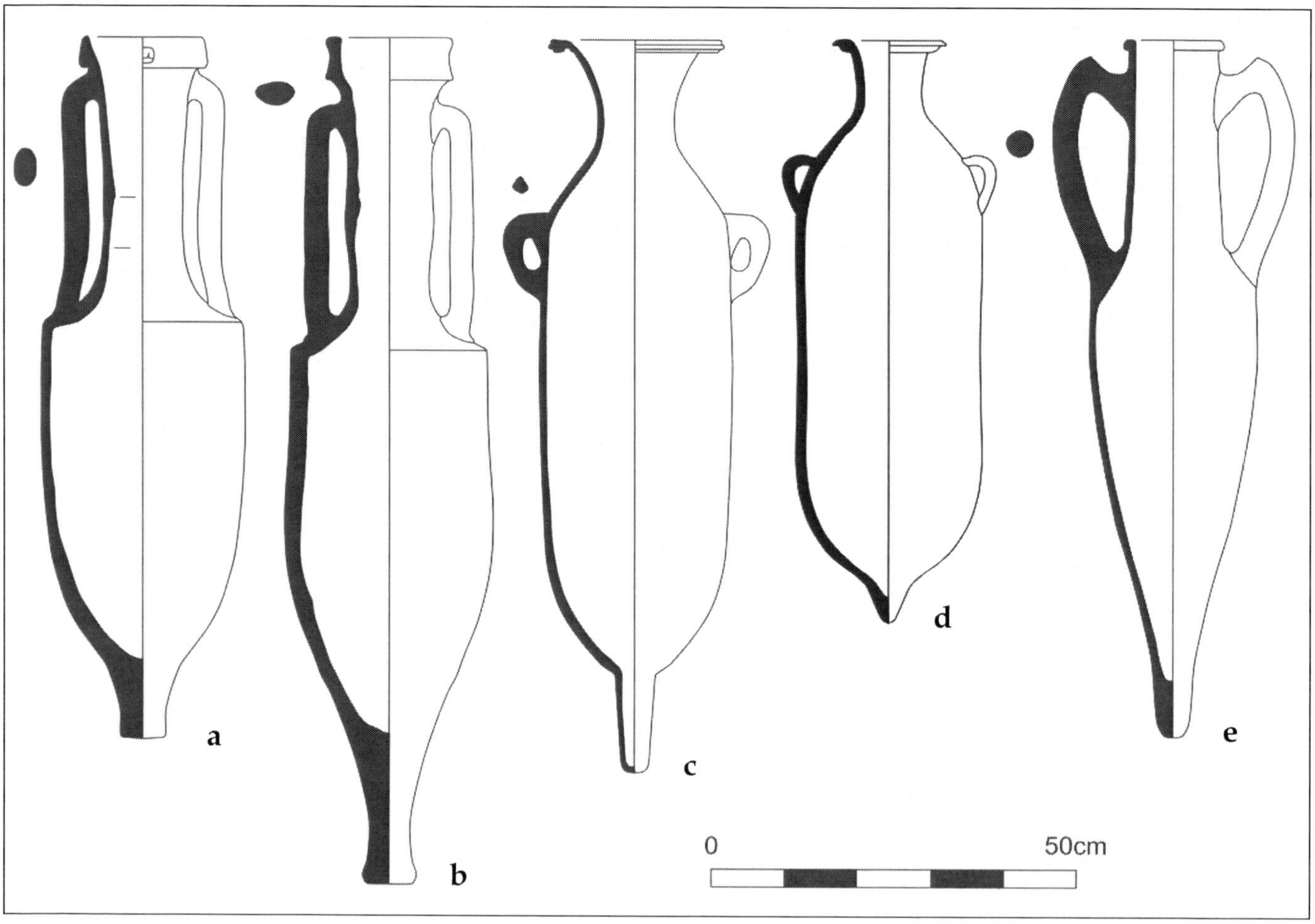

Fig. 4.17 Amphora types 3: (a) *Dressel 1A;* (b) *Dressel 1B;* (c) *van der Werff 1/Ramón 7.4.3.3/Maña C2B;* (d) *van der Werff 2/Ramón 7.5/Maña C2C;* (e) *Rhodian*

Herculaneum, and shows that the Dressel 1 form was the inheritor of the latest Greco-Italic type. Dressel 1 amphorae carried most probably the famous Campanian wines from Falernum and Caecuba.[160] Its shape is known to have been imitated outside Campania, Latium and Etruria, for example in southern Gaul and in Spain.[161] In Sicily, too, the form seems to have been imitated: the Naxos kilns, for example, produced a variant of Dressel 1.[162] Many shipwrecks off the north coast of the island, and indeed around other Sicilian coasts as well, attest to a very intensive trade in wine transported in (especially the Campanian) Dressel 1 amphorae.[163]

At Caronía, more than 50% of the Late Republican amphorae belong to the Dressel 1 group, with Dressel 1A being the more common variant at both Caronía and Marina di Caronía.[164] The dominance of Dressel 1 and especially Dressel 1A is also illustrated by the very large numbers found in the latest excavations at Marina di Caronía.[165] Examples in Campanian 'black sand' fabric dominate, an impressive 87% of the total; a similar situation is attested also at Apollonia.[166] The Campanian Dressel 1 amphorae attested in Carthage may have reached there via Sicily.[167]

Olive oil

There are very few indications that olive oil was imported at this period. The most common contemporary container for oil was the so-called Brindisi amphorae from Apulia, where kilns producing this type are known at Apani and Giancola.[168] They seem to have been produced from the late second to the late first centuries BC.[169] Only one handle from Caronía may possibly belong to this type, but even this is very uncertain, since the fabric is not very characteristic of Apulian production. The handle has a fine, orange fabric with a few white inclusions (Fabric 9). Some Apulian oil, however, was imported into the area, since a well-preserved example of the type has been found at Apollonia.[170] No shipwrecks with a cargo of Brindisi amphorae are known from the waters off Sicily. The very meagre finds show that Apulian olive oil reached Sicily in only very modest quantity despite the relative geographical vicinity of Apulia to Sicily.

Campana B pottery

Campana B ware is characterised by its pale-coloured fabric (caused by the presence of limestone in the clay), and by the metallic sheen of its black-gloss surface.[171] It was produced in Etruria and Campania during the second and the first centuries BC. Considered common in Sicily by Caflisch, it occurs infrequently in eastern Sicily according to Stone, probably because many of the same shapes were available also in the regionally-produced Campana C ware (made at Syracuse and elsewhere).[172] At Monte Iato Campana B first becomes common towards the end of the second and during the first century BC, when it replaces Campana A pottery which had dominated there during the second century.[173] One shipwreck with Campana B ware on board is known off Sicily, the Capo Graziano (Roghi) wreck at Filicudi.[174]

From Marina di Caronía, only a single fragment is known of Campana B, a platter of high quality and shiny gloss, with rouletting. The fact that Campana B was available in Sicily in the first century BC, but is not present at Caronía, is probably due to the availability (as at Morgantina, for example) of local or regional productions of east Sicilian Campana C ware. The impression is that Campana B was relatively uncommon in eastern Sicily. More was found in the 2003–05 campaigns, but several of these were what Caflish calls 'B-ish' type, not true B ware,[175] probably to be placed in the category of 'miscellaneous other black-gloss wares', which are of Sicilian, not Italian, origin.

Black/red-gloss lamps

From around 70 BC, the first non-Sicilian import of lamps since Attic examples in the fifth century BC began with the *Warzenlampen*, which were produced in central Italy and continued into the Augustan period.[176] They are among the first ever mould-made lamps, and the earliest to be mass-produced and exported over the entire Western Mediterranean. Following in their wake, all major types of lamps circulating in the Imperial period were mould-made. The *Warzenlampen* were first produced with a black-gloss surface, but switched to red-gloss when this became fashionable from the mid-first century BC.[177] *Warzenlampen* are present at Marina di Caronía, but only in the the form of a few fragments. The low number of finds suggests a still-dominant regional production of lamps at this period.

Sicilian imports

Wine

A local production of MGS VI (Fig. 4.5e) is attested by a rim of the same characteristic fabric in which the small-sized MGS V amphorae were made (Fabric 6),[178] from Caronía, and it indicates a continuing production of local wine for distribution to places elsewhere in the island during the second century BC.

Fish-sauce

In the recent excavations at Apollonia, a number of so-called 'tubular amphorae' were found, related to the Maña C type (van der Werff 1 and 2: Fig. 4.17c–d), and mostly found in the eastern Mediterranean.[179] On the basis of thin-sections it seems that the fabric is Sicilian,[180] as is that of identical vessels from a shipwreck off the coast at Solunto. The characteristic ringed toes of these amphorae have a parallel in a fragment from Marina di Caronía in a fabric very similar to that of the local / regional Dressel 21/22 (Cat. no. 37). The tubular shape and hollow toe are suggestive of amphorae intended for fish products. That such an amphora type, undoubtedly influenced by Punic shapes, developed in Sicily where the Punic heritage was strong is hardly surprising.

Black-gloss pottery

Different productions of black-gloss ware under the denomination 'Campana ware' amount at Caronía to almost 20% of the total fine-ware assemblage. The term Campana ware was coined by Nino Lamboglia, who divided the material into three classes, A, B and C.[181] The original Campana A was made in Ischia and around the Bay of Naples, in workshops active from the third to the middle of the first century BC. It is characterised by a reddish fabric colour, and the black-gloss has a bluish, sometimes greyish, metallic sheen.[182] Campana B was probably produced mainly in Etruria and Campania in the second to mid-first centuries BC, but its production centre or centres have not been identified with the same certainty as those of Campana A. Campana C ware is characterised by its greyish fabric, with a black-gloss surface which often peels off easily.

Its production was centred on Syracuse and other east Sicilian workshops, of which Morgantina is one.[183] It is widespread from the mid-second century BC onwards, especially in eastern Sicily, but a west Sicilian site such as Monte Iato also has it in abundance, demonstrating its vast diffusion over much of the island. It peters out together with the other Campana wares at the beginning of the Augustan period.[184] In his great work on Italian black-gloss ware, *La céramique campanienne*, Morel underlined the complexity of so-called Campanian ware, saying that many different production centres outside Campania existed, especially in Latium and Etruria, especially for A and B wares. Only the C category was with certainty produced only in eastern Sicily. Black-gloss Campanian wares went completely out of fashion with the production of new red *sigillata* wares in northern Italy from the early Augustan period onwards.

Sicilian black-gloss pottery

After 198 BC, with the founding of the *portorium* and *colonia* of Puteoli, Campana A pottery (Morel's 'Campana A moyenne') became exported initially on a huge scale, diminishing gradually in the course of first century BC.[185] It seems not to have been abundant in eastern Sicily, where local Campana C was produced.[186] Shelley Stone has suggested that the latter impeded Campana A imports there.[187] On the north coast, the same might also have been true because of Sicilian regional production of Campana A,[188] at Lipari, at centres in western Sicily, and in many places all over the western Mediterranean.[189] No shipwrecked cargoes of Campana A dating to the second/first centuries BC have been found in the waters off Sicily.

Campana A pottery of probable north Sicilian production is frequent at Caronía in contexts of the second and first centuries BC, and dominates (together with Campana C) the fine ware assemblages from this period.[190] This frequency can only be explained in terms of the existence of a local or regional production. At Halaesa, contexts from the second and first centuries BC have a much higher percentage of Campana A than Campana C,[191] so the latter did not dominate there as much as it did in the eastern part of the island. The strong presence of Campana A at Caronía, especially open forms, was confirmed by the excavations of 2003–05, but it seems that Campana C ware is slightly more common there.[192] Forms Morel 1314 and 1315 (second/first centuries BC) are very common both there and at nearby Apollonia.[193] A second-century *patera* is another form widespread throughout southern Italy and Sicily.[194]

The fabric of the regional productions is reddish yellow (5 YR 5/6-6/6), very similar to those of probable Sicilian origin in the fourth and third centuries BC. Some items have a gloss with metallic or silvery sheen, which are good imitations of genuine Campana A. Among these is a fragment of a *skyphos* with painted white decoration from the first half of the second century BC.[195] The Lamboglia form 36 platter of the second century BC is by far the most dominant shape present at Caronía, and is also presumed to have been a local production.[196]

Campana C ware was first produced in the second half of the second century BC.[197] On the basis of the considerable quantity of black-gloss which came from the excavations of 2003–05, it seems to have been the most important category of the Campana wares present;[198] but some 15 km further west, at Halaesa, as already noted, Campana C is less common than Campana A.[199] Campana C did not totally dominate the north-coast markets, therefore, as it did those of eastern Sicily. At Caronía, in contexts from the late second and first century BC, it is the second most common category of pottery found. Among the most frequently found types is a platter with rouletting, Morel's form 2284 d1 (Cat. no. 173), while another very large platter/*patera*, probably of the late second century BC, has a shinier gloss of better quality (Cat. no. 175). A number of other *paterae*[200] and plates/*paterae* with rouletting[201] are also present in these deposits. A small group of second/first century BC black-gloss fabrics which do not correspond to any of the Campana A, B or C wares can probably be attributed to a regional workshop or workshops. One example is a bowl in a fine, buff fabric which comes close to descriptions of Campana B, but the gloss is matt, and the centre of the interior (with a purple circle) is not properly fired.[202]

Megarian bowls

'Megarian bowls' is the common name for the classic Hellenistic pottery decorated with mould-made reliefs. They began their production in the late third century BC, most importantly on the coast of Asia Minor and in Athens, and continued at least into the Augustan period.[203] Megarian bowls were made also in Sicily at Tyndaris, a little before the Augustan period, and a mould for one has been found at Morgantina.[204] Examples of probable Sicilian production are known also from Monte Iato.[205] The type is not especially common at Caronía, only a few fragments having been identified; they too may have been Sicilian-made.[206]

Lamps

The regional production of wheel-made black-gloss lamps continued in Sicily during the second and first centuries BC, but little attention has so far been paid to their many different production centres. At Marina di Caronía, several examples of second/first-century black-gloss lamps have been found, of which one type has a very distinctive north-coast distribution, with only occasional examples elsewhere.[207] In the first century BC, the first mould-made lamps appear, including a fine example found during surface survey, which was probably a Sicilian product imitating Greek prototypes (Fig. 4.18).[208]

The Sicilian variant, in a bright orange fabric, of the wheel-made Corinthian type known as Broneer XVI is characterised by its simple nozzle with pointed angles; its slip varies from reddish brown to grey (Fig. 4.19). Most seem to have been manufactured between the late first century BC and first half of the first century AD.[209] This is the most common type at Caronía then as it is

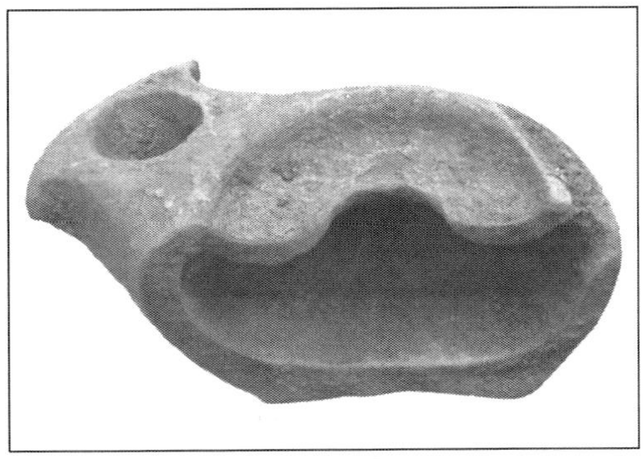

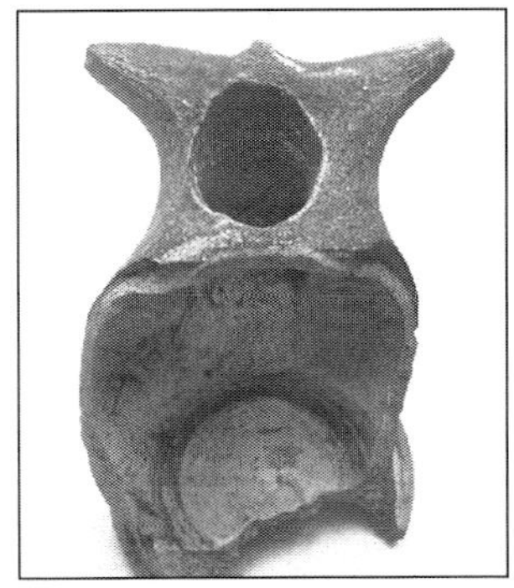

Fig. 4.18 (left) *Late Hellenistic mould-made oil-lamp, found during surface survey at Caronía; length 10.4 cm; late second/first century BC*

Fig. 4.19 (centre) *Fragmentary oil-lamp of type Corinth XVI, found during surface survey at Caronía*

Fig. 4.20 (right) *Fragmentary oil-lamp made in a Sicilian workshop, found during surface survey at Caronía; length: 9.2 cm; late first century BC*

elsewhere in Sicily. Production was clearly large, since in volume it comes close to the common Italian-made volute picture-lamps of the first century AD. The variety most commonly found at Caronía often also has a pointed projection at the centre of the nozzle; the lamps are sometimes referred to as *di lumaca* ('snail-shaped') or *becco d'incudine* ('anvil-nozzle') (Fig. 4.20). Collura thought from its frequency that it must have been a local product,[210] but more evidence is needed before this can be regarded as certain: the type is very common as well elsewhere in Sicily.

Local production

Wine

Imitations of Dressel 1 containers were, as we have seen (p. 78), produced in Sicily, but at Caronía only a few fragments of non-Campanian manufacture were found. Thin-sectioning for analysis of one rim of a Dressel 1A amphora (Fig. 4.17a) did suggest a local origin (Fabric 37).[211] The coarse fabric of another rim, this time of a Dressel 1B amphora (Fig. 4.17b), reddish orange in colour with quartz and limestone inclusions and red spots, is also very similar to local amphora fabrics. It was not possible to take a thin-section of this, but since we have evidence of a probable local production of Dressel 1A amphorae, I consider a regional, north Sicilian (and possibly a local) origin for the Dressel 1B type as also highly likely (Fabric 38). Another Dressel 1B rim at Marina di Caronía bears the Greek stamp ΑΗΛΥΘ.[212] Since Italian-made Dressel 1 amphorae were never stamped in Greek, a Sicilian (or south Italian) origin for this too seems probable.

Republican red-gloss ware

This ware, recently dubbed 'Republican red-gloss' by Shelley Stone to replace the older somewhat misleading term 'pre-*sigillata*', was produced in Italy and Sicily in the first century BC,[213] when experiments were being made with red-gloss pottery-production in Sicily, inspired by Eastern *terra sigillata* A.[214] Many fragments of it were found at Marina di Caronía, including cups with profiled base, *paterae* and bowls.[215] It may well have been produced at Kale Akte, since large amounts of it were found in the 1992 excavations in *contrada* Telegrafo at Caronía.[216] Republican red-gloss pottery was produced at Morgantina (and no doubt elsewhere) and is not uncommon at Tindari and Centuripe.[217]

Wine-jugs

Many well-preserved jugs with a coral-reddish slip were found in the 1992–93 excavations in a cistern in *contrada* Telegrafo.[218] Fragments of this jug-type are abundant at both Caronía and Marina di Caronía in contexts of the first century BC and the early first century AD.[219] They were probably used for pouring wine, since they were lined with resin on the interior. The sheer quantity of finds suggests that the jugs were produced by a local workshop;[220] perhaps the implication is that the wine they contained was also local.

Louteria

Local production also of *louteria* can be presumed from a fragment found in *contrada* Sotto San Francesco (Fig. 4.21).[221] The moulded decoration on the rim shows a winged *putto* and two running hounds. The fabric seems to be the typical local one, with a dark purple wash on the surface. Another *louterion* rim from Caronía can probably also be taken as of local production.[222] The stamped decoration of vine-leaves on the rim is perhaps a hint that it was intended to hold the local wine.

North African imports

Fish-sauce

Late Republican Punic amphorae were studied by Mañá in 1951 and more extensively by van der Werff in

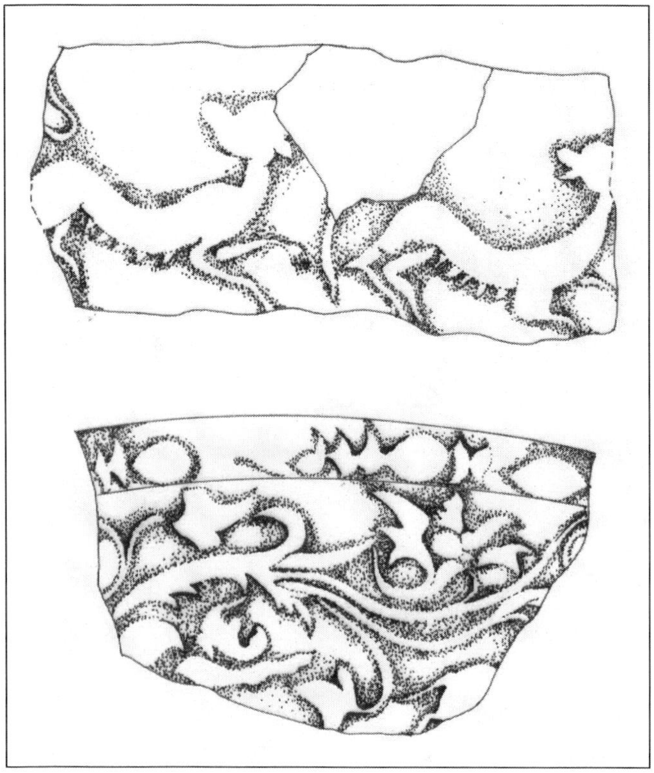

Fig. 4.21 Rim of a louterion *with moulded scenes of running hounds and floral decoration (the lower is 8.4 x 3.7 cm); excavated in* contrada *Sotto San Francesco, 1999*

1978.[223] Their typologies were further refined by Ramón in 1995.[224] That proposed by van der Werff, as pointed out by Empereur and Hesnard, is not completely convincing, and I have here used it only with reference to earlier finds identified by this classification (Fig. 4.17e–d).[225] The neo-Punic types have their origins in Tunisia, Morocco and Libya. The majority of fragments among our material displays the typical Tunisian fabric (van der Werff A).[226] As for contents, much of what has been noted above about earlier Punic amphorae (p. 72) is true also for the more recent ones. North Africa was celebrated for its sweet wine (*passum*) by Pliny,[227] but otherwise wine was not produced on a significant scale, nor was it exported in huge quantity. Shape is perhaps the most important key to the contents of these amphorae. Spanish *garum* containers share the same basic characteristics – an everted rim, a broad neck and a hollow toe – and it seems likely that the examples found in Sicily also carried fish products.[228] Maybe olive oil could sometimes have been transported in them, but at present there is no strong evidence for considering that likely. All the finds from Caronía belong to types with hollow toes, and I would argue that such amphorae contained fish products, as did the earlier Punic amphorae.

Van der Werff's distribution maps show that neo-Punic amphorae were exported to all parts of the western Mediterranean.[229] In production during the second and first centuries BC, they probably also continued into the first century AD, at least for a short period.[230] At Caronía they are relatively common.[231]

One type (the Maña C2; van der Werff 1; Ramón 7.4.3.3: Fig. 4.17c), the most characteristic form of all Late Republican Punic amphorae, has a wide, flaring mouth with characteristic profile, and a long cylindrical body with handles attached to it; at the base is a hollow toe. Rarely reported from Sicily, the type is attested by only a few published finds from the western tip of the island, at Lilybaeum (Marsala).[232] This, however, almost certainly reflects the low level of interest in the study and publication of Roman amphorae, rather than its true distribution in Sicily. The type is represented by several fragments from Marina di Caronía, all sharing the same typical red Tunisian fabric, together with plentiful white calcite inclusions and their reaction rings (Fabric 11).

Another Punic type (Ramón 7.5.2.1; van der Werff 2: Fig. 4.17d), produced in the Sahel region of Tunisia sometime during the second century BC, has an everted rim, and a cylindrical body with handles attached to it; there is a hollow toe, sometimes ringed.[233] Two unstratified fragments of this type were found at Marina di Caronía. The fabric is reddish, made of finely levigated clay, with the remnants of a fine, light wash on the surface (Fabric 12). It is very similar to other Punic fabrics. A small rim, belonging probably to a reduced-size amphora of the same type, can also be added to this group.

A third type (Ramón 7.6.1.1), produced in Tunisia from the late second to at least the middle of the first century BC, has a flaring mouth with a rounded lip, and a slender, cylindrical body with small handles attached to the body; there is again a hollow toe.[234] No finds are known from Sicily, and it is poorly attested in the western Mediterranean.[235] It was produced in an orange, powdery fabric, rather untypical but still definitely Tunisian (Fabric 13).

Olive oil

There are very few indications of imports of olive oil at this period. The only amphora type from Caronía which more or less certainly carried this liquid is the Dressel 26, with a wide mouth, vertical rim, and handles attached to the short cylindrical neck and the body. The shape of the lower half is unknown. The Dressel 26 was once thought to have been of Italian origin,[236] but it has been recognised as North African by Martin-Kilcher.[237] It dates to the first century BC or the early first century AD.[238] The shape of the rim is similar to

Ramón type 7.2.1.1 as well as to examples published by van der Werff,[239] but the Dressel 26 has a much longer neck. The bulbous shape recalls various oil containers of the first century AD, including Tripolitanian 1.

Aegean imports

Wine

Rhodian amphorae are characterised by their egg-shaped body, cylindrical neck, short, beaded rim, and especially from the first century BC, their pointed, high-arched handles (Fig. 4.17e). They were often stamped with the names of eponymous archons or of their makers in the late third and the second centuries BC. The presence of Rhodian wine in our area is further confirmed by several stamped handles found at Halaesa, dating to the later third and the first half of the second centuries BC.[240] A distribution map of find-spots of Rhodian amphorae in Sicily shows that they were widespread all over the island.[241] Messana, a major port on the route between the eastern and western Mediterranean, was probably one of the main stops for this traffic.[242] From here, Rhodian wine was probably distributed to smaller Sicilian ports such as Kale Akte. The late third and first half of the second centuries BC seem to have been the *floruit* for the export of Rhodian wine to the western Mediterranean.[243] The popularity of its sweet wine, *passum*, seems to have been due more to its low price than any superior quality.[244]

Rhodian amphorae are relatively common in the excavation material, and surface survey at Caronía shows that in the Hellenistic period they are second in quantity only to Greco-Italic amphorae.[245] The fabric of the Caronía finds is the typical Rhodian one, a well-levigated creamish-buff, sometimes with a pink core (Fabric 16). At least five Rhodian handles have been found in *contrada* Pantano, all stamped with the *caduceus*, and probably dating to around the middle of the second century BC.[246] In addition four stamps have been found through surface survey in *contrade* Sotto San Francesco and Telegrafo.[247] One stamp has the legend ΜΑΡΣ[ΥΑ]/ΠΑΝΑΜΟΥ, referring to a producer Marsyas (active in the 170/160s BC) and a production in the Rhodian month of Panamos (Fig. 4.22). Another stamp, only partially preserved, reads . . .]ΛΚΙΑ/. . .]ΕΥΣ ΠΕΔΑΓΕΙΤΝΥΟΥ' (Fig. 4.23), referring to both a priest and a producer as well as to the Rhodian month of production, Pedageitnos. The stamp cannot be dated, but it no doubt belongs, along with the majority of Rhodian imports to Sicily, to the end of the third or sometime in the course of the second century BC. The massive presence of high-quality Campanian wines on the western markets, which began in the late second century BC, led to a restriction of Rhodian exports, as suggested for example by the finds from Apollonia, where Rhodian amphorae occur less frequently than the Dressel 1 and Lamboglia 2 types.[248]

Koan amphorae, which are found at Caronía in some quantity, are characterised by their large body, slender, cylindrical neck with ring-shaped rim, and especially the arched, bifid handles. The most common fabric is a fine reddish-brown, usually with a whitish-buff wash (Fabric 17). Two fragments from Marina di Caronía have a separate fabric (Fabric 21). The similarity of this to Baetican fabrics led it to being erroneously identified as coming from a Baetican Dressel 2/4 amphora, but in fact the fabric is identical to Bezeczky's Koan fabric F, identified at Ephesus[249] – yellowish buff, burnt greenish on the surface, with small red spots. Thin-section analysis revealed grains of basalt in the matrix.[250] Similar to Rhodian, Koan wine was not of the finest quality, but its special taste – it was mixed with sea-water – made it clearly very popular.[251] They continued

Fig. 4.22 (left) *Stamp of a Rhodian amphora, of the producer Marsyas, in the Rhodian month of Panamos, found during surface survey at Caronía;* c. *170/160 BC*

Fig. 4.23 (right) *Stamp of a Rhodian amphora, produced in the Rhodian month of Pedageitnos, found during surface survey at Caronía; late third/second century BC*

to be exported into the first century AD.[252] Never common in the western Mediterranean, as indicated by their absence in shipwrecks from the waters off Sicily, they have only recently been recognised in Sicily.[253]

Between the first half of the third century and the first century BC, Koan amphorae were often stamped.[254] One handle from a context of *c.* 100 BC at Marina di Caronía, with a stamp that looks like IAΩNOC written in retrograde, should probably be read as IACONOC. A Rhodian maker with the name Iason is known,[255] but Koan stamps have been little studied, and I know of no parallels (Cat. no. 43).

In addition to Rhodian and Koan wine, somewhat smaller quantities of Knidian wine seem to have been imported to Kale Akte, on the basis of a handle of the second or first century BC that is supposedly of Knidian origin. Similar in shape to the Rhodian, Knidian amphorae have a more slender body and a characteristic ring around the toe; handles are oval in cross-section. They are not well attested in Sicily. Our handle has a high arch, which dates it to the 'Roman' period according to Grace (after 146 BC).[256] The fabric is brownish and very soft, with small inclusions of limestone (Fabric 18). Since the specimen is unstratified, from a disturbed context on the slopes of Caronía, it can only generally be dated to the Late Hellenistic period.

Central Adriatic imports

Wine

The Lamboglia 2 amphora has a thick-walled, bag-shaped body with a pointed or stub toe and a triangular or squarish rim (Fig. 4.24a).[257] The Caronía finds belong to the dominant Lamboglia 2 fabric-group as described by Peacock and Williams, Riley and Martin-Kilcher.[258] The typical fabric[259] is finely levigated and rather powdery; it is easily recognisable, buff in colour, with a large red, reddish-brown or brownish *chamotte* (grog) (Fabric 19). Since the identification of the form by Lamboglia in 1950, the type is thought to have originated in Apulia or on the Adriatic coast of Italy,[260] but I have recently argued that it began on the central coast of Dalmatia (modern Croatia), especially on the island of Vis (Issa) and at the later Roman colony of Narona.[261] A handle of the same fabric as the Caronía finds has been found at Morgantina, with the stamp SARAPI. Lamboglia 2 amphorae have also been reported from Apollonia in the Nebrodi, elsewhere in Sicily at Syracuse, Segesta, Erice and elsewhere, and also in wrecks off the coasts of Marsala and Lipari.[262] As Peacock and Williams pointed out, it is very important to distinguish locally-made amphorae from intrusive material which occurs on any amphora production site but was not actually manufactured there.[263] In fact, Empereur and Hesnard emphasised that there is little evidence that many of the forms published from the production site of Apani near Brindisi were actually manufactured there. That Lamboglia 2 amphorae were ever produced in southern Apulia has never been conclusively proved: the hypothesis that they were has been reached only by considering superficial similarities in fabric, stamps and distribution patterns between the Brindisi type and the Lamboglia 2 containers.[264] Further north along the central Adriatic coast of Italy, several more kiln sites known to have been producing Lamboglia 2 amphorae have recently been identified; a full programme of thin-section analysis is necessary to determine the relative importance of these various different productions.[265]

There has been much discussion about the contents of the Lamboglia 2 containers. For a long time the *opinio communis* was that it was olive oil, but this changed when Tchernia and Hesnard proved, by examination of examples from the Madrague de Giens shipwreck, that the containers were resin-lined and so contained wine.[266] Denaro, on the other hand, ignoring this discussion completely, simply refers to the Lamboglia 2 type as olive-oil containers in his survey of amphorae in Sicily.[267] In favour of the wine hypothesis is the sometimes triangular-shaped rim, very reminiscent of Greco-Italic types that certainly contained wine. Vineyards on the central coast of Dalmatia were already known in the fourth century BC,[268] judging from local amphorae of that date and coins depicting Dionysus, *kantharoi* and bunches of grapes.[269] In the early Augustan period, around 25 BC, the Lamboglia 2 type evolved into the Dressel 6A form (see below).[270]

Doubts have been expressed as to whether Lamboglia 2 amphorae were exported to Sicily in any great numbers. Several stamps belonging to this type have, however, been found in the island,[271] and its alleged absence there is likely to reflect the scant interest shown for many years in Roman amphorae in general rather than the true state of affairs. Several shipwrecks with Lamboglia 2 cargoes have been identified off the island's coasts.[272] At Marina di Caronía the Lamboglia 2 amphora is the second most common type after the Dressel 1 containers recorded in Late Hellenistic contexts in *contrada* Pantano. The excavations at Apollonia have also yielded some finds, including one complete amphora of this type.[273]

Several indicators point to a production of Lamboglia 2 amphorae on the Central Dalmatian coast. Narona was the most important city and port of trade in Dalmatia in the Late Republican period. Italic *negotiatores* are known there from the second century BC, and an inscription from a village close to Vid mentions two *fratres*, M. Papius Kanus, who probably belong to the same *gens* that features on stamps of Lamboglia 2 amphorae,[274] celebrating Octavian's vic-

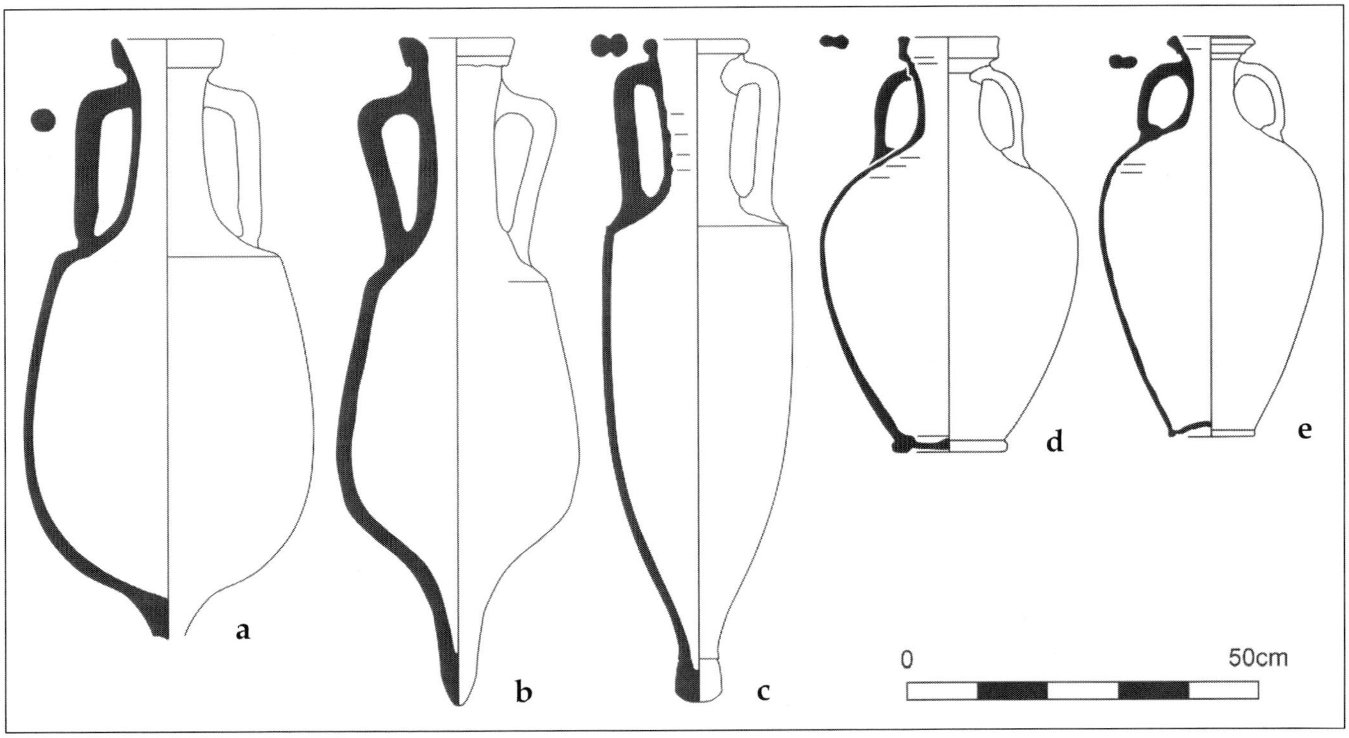

Fig. 4.24 Amphora types 4: (a) *Lamboglia 2;* (b) *Dressel 6A;* (c) *Dressel 2/4;* (d) *Gauloise 2;* (e) *Gauloise 3*

tory over Sextus Pompey in 36 BC.[275] The end of the war in Sicily was understandably welcomed by *negotiatores*, because it freed up once more the Straits of Messina – the gateway to Rome and to the entire western Mediterranean for any ship coming from the Adriatic.

Dressel 6A amphorae began, as noted above, around 25 BC and continued until the Claudian period in the mid-first century AD. It is very similar in shape to its predecessor, but always has a squarish rim, and is rather more thick-walled by comparison with the Lamboglia 2 type (Fig. 4.24b). Like the latter it probably contained wine.[276] Identification of it has frequently been confused with that of Lamboglia 2, since only the shape of the body is different. There are no Sicilian shipwrecks with cargoes of Dressel 6A amphorae (and just three with a cargo Lamboglia 2), and hardly any published finds.[277] We know that Dressel 6A had the same beige or yellowish clay with red spots, just like that of Lamboglia 2:[278] the form is in effect just the first-century-AD version of the Lamboglia 2 amphora, produced in the same *officinae*, and also carrying wine.

No certain examples of Dressel 6A amphorae have been made at Caronía. In the preliminary publication of the finds from the 2003–05 campaign, Bonanno mentions finds of Dressel 6A type but none of Lamboglia 2. This is probably another example of confusion between the two types,[279] the 'Dressel 6A' here in fact being Lamboglia 2 amphorae. Nevertheless the small numbers of Dressel 6A fragments in Sicily in general suggest that Adriatic exports to Sicily diminished at the beginning of the first century AD, and that these new amphorae did not have the same vast market that the Lamboglia 2 containers had previously enjoyed in the island.[280] Rather the distribution pattern of Dressel 6A amphorae shows clearly that it concentrated on northern Italy and on the Eastern Mediterranean.[281] The only cities in the west outside the Adriatic which imported large numbers were Rome and Carthage. Its rarity in Sicily, despite the fact that large shiploads would have passed its shores on the way to Rome and Carthage, seems to indicate that the island now had a strong wine production of its own, which it lacked prior to the Augustan period. Dressel 6B, produced in Istria and intended to carry oil, is completely absent and did not reach Sicily at all.[282]

Spanish imports

Iberian kalathoi

So-called Iberian pottery dates to the second and first centuries BC, and has been attested only in small quantity and in scattered locations in Sicily, all of them coastal (Tindari, Marsala, Lipari, Eraclea Minoa and Taormina).[283] The preferred form is the cylindrical *kalathos* with a flat base, and it probably contained the famous Iberian honey. A few finds have been made at Caronía during surface survey (Fig. 4.25).[284]

Fig. 4.25 A fragment of Iberian kalathos, *found during surface survey at Caronía; width 12.2 cm; first century BC*

The Early Imperial period (30 BC–AD 200)

Local production

Wine

A local production at Marina di Caronía of the standard early imperial wine container, the Dressel 2/4 amphora (Fig. 24c), was identified by comparing fragments of it with local versions of Termini 151/354 amphora fabrics (on which see below, pp. 96–7), and through careful thin-section analysis.[285] The reddish brown or orange fabric is commonly characterised by quartz inclusions, sometimes coarse, as well as limestone and red spots of grog, but there are large variations: sometimes, for example, well levigated clays were also employed (Fabrics 39–40). The surface is occasionally covered with a cream-coloured or brownish wash. One group of suspected local Dressel 2/4 amphorae is characterised by a clay lacking any sand temper, which results in a yellowish surface colour. The absence of temper means that this sub-group cannot be tied to any other local production through thin-section analysis.[286] Its frequency, however, supported by the characteristics of its clay (iron-rich and calciferous), suggests a local origin for this too. Examples of identical fabric were found in Marina di Caronía, including finds from the 2003–05 excavations there, as well as a few in Caronía itself (where they are not likely to be later than the first century AD). Since the fabric, which occurs in almost 70% of the Dressel 2/4 containers found, does not belong to any of the large production centres of this amphora in Campania, central Italy, Spain or Gaul, a local production seems highly probable, starting sometime in the first century AD.[287] In stark contrast, it was imported late Greco-Italic and Dressel 1 amphorae from Campania that had completely dominated assemblages at Caronía during the second and first centuries BC.

There is no indication of any other locally-produced amphora, serving as a link between the Dressel 2/4 imitation and the Late Roman Termini 151/354 type (pp. 95–9). Production of flat-bottomed wine amphorae had already begun elsewhere in Sicily in the first century AD, and it is unlikely that the local imitations of Dressel 2/4 would have continued production much after AD 100. Why the local export of wine seems to have stopped at Kale Akte after the first century AD is difficult to explain. Settlement data from the territory of Halaesa suggests a decline in rural settlements between the second and the third centuries AD. It is difficult to prove that this was the consequence of a natural catastrophe like a major earthquake, which may have ravaged the area at the end of the first century AD. Kale Akte as a *polis*, however, disappeared during this period, and if the export of wine had been organised by the *polis*, that might explain why wine exports ended and the trade remained dormant for nearly two hundred years.

Local production of Dressel 2/4 containers is known elsewhere in northern Sicily, for example at Lipari during the Augustan period, at Naxos/Taormina, near Alcamo and probably also at Tindari, at all of which evidence has been discovered in recent years.[288] A well-preserved example of a Dressel 2/4 amphora of local production (possibly at Kale Akte itself) has also been found at Apollonia.[289] In Calabria and Apulia too, production of Dressel 2/4 containers has also now been identified.[290] The discovery of local production of Dressel 2/4 amphorae at a place as small as Caronía makes it probable that many Sicilian urban centres that produced wine at this period transported it in locally-made versions of Dressel 2/4 amphorae, something suspected in the past but not well documented until recently. As with the Calabrian and Apulian amphorae, the main market for the Sicilian Dressel 2/4 containers is presumed to have been Rome.[291]

Two fragments of a local variety of the Gauloise 2/3 wine amphora (Fig. 4.24d and e) were also identified at Marina di Caronía in a fabric identical to that of the local Dressel 2/4 and Dressel 21/22 fabrics (Fabric 44) and different from that of the Gaulish containers.[292] Sicilian production of Gaulish-type amphorae is known from Naxos,[293] and it is presumed that such amphorae held wine. It is, however, somewhat odd that they were imitated at all in Sicily, since Gaulish originals (which initially needed to be present to make the imitation) do not occur very frequently in the island; perhaps they were present in greater numbers than is currently recognised.[294] The Gauloise 2/3 has a small rim with a groove in it. The handles, either flat or also with a groove, are attached to a short cylindrical neck and to the shoulders of an ovoid body; there is a large flat base with a foot ring. This type is the pre-cursor of the more common and widespread Gauloise 4/Pélichet 47, which came originally from the lower Rhône valley in southern Gaul and is datable mainly to the first century AD (see below, pp. 93–4). No shipwrecks with cargo of Gauloise 2 and 3 amphorae have ever been encountered in the waters off Sicily, nor has the type ever been recorded on the island itself.

Fish products

The Dressel 21/22 container has a very wide mouth, a concave rim with a lower 'step', and a broad, cylindrical body ending in a solid spike; the handles are oval, sometimes with a ridge (Fig. 4.26a). The type has long been considered as an exclusive production of Campania, and *tituli picti* suggested that it contained fruit. Now, however, its production has also been confirmed in southern Spain, as well as at Alcamo Marina and at Termini Imerese in Sicily.[295] The origins of the type are now most likely to be sought in southern Spain. Belo (*Bolonia*) and nearby El Rinconcillo (Algeciras) are both candidates for identification as production sites, the former probable,[296] the latter certain.[297] Both of these were important manufacturing centres of *garum* and salted fish both for local consumption and for export.[298] Fragments of Dressel 21/22 from here date to the first century BC somewhat earlier than the traditional dating of the Campanian Dressel 21/22, which are thought belong to the first century AD.[299] The type is reminiscent of the shape of Punic amphorae produced in the same area in southern Spain from the fourth to the beginning of the first centuries BC.[300] Already Loeschcke, nearly eighty years ago, attempted to trace the origin of the Roman *cadus* (any large container for liquid foodstuffs) back to Punic prototypes with wide rims.[301] The validity of such a conclusion was queried by Zevi, who argued that the large mouth was created for purely functional reasons.[302]

Several years ago I suggested that Dressel 21/22 amphorae were likely to have been designed to carry salted tuna or *garum* of tuna.[303] This hypothesis has now been confirmed by Emanuel Botte, whose studies of *tituli picti* on these containers at Pompeii show that the letters CE, interpreted by Dressel as meaning *cerasa* (cherries), instead should be interpreted as an abbreviation of *cetus*, indicating a large fish such as tuna.[304] Apart from the *tituli picti* – which are not always certain indicators of original content, since in some cases they were added only when the containers were reused – a number of other indications point to the same conclusion. Production sites in southern Spain and western Sicily are in areas with a long tradition of producing fish preserves, and the amphora shape, with its wide mouth and neck essential for packing and unpacking non-liquid goods such as salted fish, is also significant, as are the obvious comparisons with the shape of Punic amphorae which are also predominantly containers of fish preserves.[305] Stamps on one type of Punic vessel depict not only the tuna fish itself, but even the process of packing tuna inside the amphora.[306]

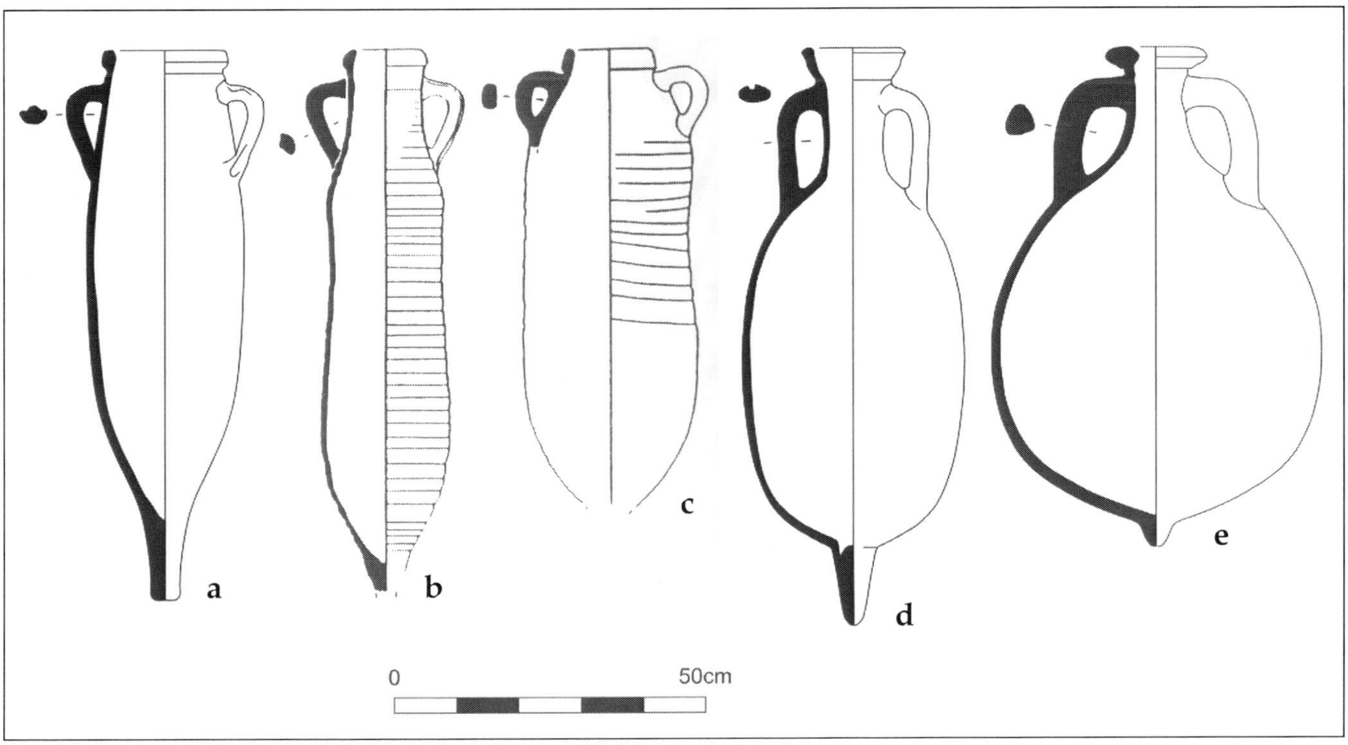

Fig. 4.26 Amphora types 5: (a) *Dressel 21/22;* (b) *Richborough 527, type 1;* (c) *Richborough 527, type 2;* (d) *Haltern 70;* (e) *Dressel 20*

Fragments of amphorae of the same type as those found at Marina di Caronía, only recently recognised as a variant of the Dressel 21/22 classification, are often present at fish-processing sites in western Sicily.[307] Two *tituli picti* on Dressel 21/22 amphorae from Campania mention *garum* as the commodity within.[308] One amphora of exactly the same shape and fabric as the Caronía examples has been found at Pompeii (colour Pl. 12).[309] At the *officium* of the Umbricii there, where *garum* was produced, the majority of amphorae were Dressel 21/22 types. They were once thought to be containers which had been acquired second-hand, to be reused for transporting fish-sauce, like various Dressel 2/4 amphorae also in the same *officium*.[310] Other finds along the south coast of France also appear to be identical to the examples at Caronía. This suggests a considerable north Sicilian export of fish products to Italy, Rome and southern Gaul.

Very interesting in this context is that Dressel 21/22 amphorae are now known also to have been produced at a kiln site near Alcamo Marina in north-western Sicily, an area with a centuries-old tradition of fish salting; significantly, the kilns are located close to a modern *tonnara*, a tuna-fishing centre.[311] A distribution map of Dressel 21/22 containers shows them mainly in the western part of the island, with numerous finds from Alcamo Marina, Termini Imerese, Solunto, Palermo, Segesta and Entella, as well as from Vendicari in south-eastern Sicily.[312] The examples excavated at Termini Imerese were interepreted as wine-carriers, produced to compete in the market with Campanian and central Italian Dressel 1s and 2/4s,[313] but the broad width of both body and mouth does not support such a hypothesis. Very large quantities of Dressel 21/22 have also been found at Monte Iato;[314] one is stamped *Ceioni Maximi*.[315] Casual surface finds from Solunto have erroneously been dated to the sixth century AD:[316] but examples from Termini Imerese and Monte Iato come securely from contexts of the first century AD.[317] One of only two Sicilian shipwrecks containing them has been located off the coast at Solunto (the other is off Panarea).[318] The type was also produced in Calabria, and likewise there interpreted as being carriers for fish products.[319] We know for certain that Sicilian *garum* and the fish industry in general were still prospering in the first century AD, whereas there is no indication of any significant commerce at that time in conserved fruit. Salted tuna cuts had been transported from the island for centuries; allegedly 'ten thousand jars of Sicilian salt fish' were to be found on a ship of Hieron II destined for Alexandria, if Athenaeus is to be believed.[320]

The richness of the coast of Kale Akte is mentioned by Silius Italicus, who exults in the *litus piscosa Calacta*, 'Kale Akte whose strand abounds with fish'.[321] He was writing when the local production of Dressel 21/22 amphorae was in full swing, and his specific naming of this small north Sicilian town implies that Kale Akte's reputation as a supplier of fish and fish products must, by the later first century AD, have extended as far as Rome. Its importance as a fish production centre resumed in more recent times, as the remains of an old *tonnara* at Marina di Caronía still testify.

A local or north Sicilian origin for the amphora fragments from Caronía and Marina di Caronía is indicated mainly by the large quantity found, constituting approximately a third of all Early Imperial containers.[322] Most come from Marina di Caronía, but several are known from rural settlements in the surrounding *chora*. There are further examples from Caronía, the hill-town, mostly from disturbed contexts, but some are known from a secure context datable to the first century AD. Two main fabric groups can be discerned. The more common (group 1) is reddish orange, and usually tempered with quartz, calcite, sandstone and feldspar; there are sparse reddish or black inclusions, probably iron ore or grog (Fabric 42); but some are very pure, almost lacking inclusions. The second group is similar to Tunisian fabrics, with plenty of limestone 'reaction rings' and frequent 'brush-strokes' on the surface, and with a surface burnt to a dark, greyish colour (Fabric 43). An almost complete Dressel 21/22 found in excavation at Apollonia is certainly of north Sicilian production,[323] with the same type of rim, handles and groove on the belly right beneath the handles as the one at Pompeii in the same fabric mentioned above.[324] Both groups can be clearly differentiated even by eye; the identification is confirmed by thin-section analysis.[325] Fabric 43 is tempered only with a little quartz; sandstone and feldspar are lacking, whereas these are recurring components in the local clay of western Sicily used to produce Termini 151/354 and Dressel 2/4 amphorae (pp. 86 and 97).[326] Both fabrics (42 and 43) are likely to represent a local production: they share the same basic clay characteristics (rich in iron and calciferous), and similar colour ranges. Occasional examples of both have greyish or blackish surfaces due to over-firing, as do roof-tiles of local production (which are particularly close to Fabric 43). The frequent use of a cream-coloured skin in fabrics 42 and 43 and on over-fired tiles (a greyish or blackish 'skin', sometimes with 'brush-strokes'), links local Dressel 21/22 amphora production with that of contemporary Dressel 2/4 containers. The very slight fabric differences between the two may possibly be due to different production sites with different clay sources, a distinction also observed on amphorae at Termini Imerese and Solunto.[327] The actual production site or sites have not been found, but they must lie in the immediate territory of Kale Akte or in its micro-region. Differences in both shape and fabric indicate that this is a quite separate production from those of similar containers at Termini Imerese and Alcamo.

Bricks and tiles

The general picture is that in the Imperial period there are no imported bricks or tiles at Kale Akte.[328] Roof-tiles seem to be without exception of local manufacture. Square bricks, so abundant in the Hellenistic and possibly also in the early Imperial period, continued to be produced into late Antiquity. Bricks in early imperial times were produced at at least two rural sites immediately south of the town.[329] In late antiquity, a kiln producing exclusively bricks is known to the west of the *statio* of Marina di Caronía, at the mouth of the *torrente* Caronía (colour Pl. 5, left; Fig. 1.4, no. 4).[330]

Italian imports

Wine

The Dressel 2/4 container, with a ring-shaped rim and characteristic bifid handles, is quite thin-walled; its slender body ends in a solid toe or 'spike' (Fig. 4.24c). This was the most important and most widely distributed wine-carrying amphora of the late first century BC and the first century AD, an imitation of similar containers, also holding wine, from the Greek island of Kos, which likewise has bifid handles.[331] They represent a continuation of the tradition initiated by late Greco-Italic and Dressel 1 containers, but now in a lighter and more manageable form. The main production area was the Tyrrhenian coast, especially Campania, and also Tarraconensis (Catalonia) in Spain, but this amphora shape was also imitated at kiln-sites around the shores of the Adriatic, and, as we have seen, in Sicily (and no doubt elsewhere) as well.

The type is abundant in all Roman contexts from the late first century BC onwards and throughout the first century AD, but less so in the second century, although new evidence suggests that Campanian Dressel 2/4 containers continued to be exported to Sicily then, probably in greater quantities than has been hitherto assumed. At Ostia, its numbers decline after the first century AD, but it continued to circulate at least until the middle of the second century.[332] Fragments of Campanian Dressel 2/4 containers have also been found in third-century contexts at Monte Testaccio in Rome, showing that they were still being produced even then.[333] Its export to Sicily as late as the third century seems unlikely, as Campanian production was then much reduced, and Sicilian wine production was enjoying a revival.[334] That the type was manufactured in several different regions is clear from the number of fabrics, principally four of them, present at Caronía. It constitutes one of the largest groups of material at the site, for amphorae second only after the local version of Termini 151/354 containers. A few examples of reduced size are also present.[335]

Campanian versions represent 18% of the total of Dressel 2/4 numbers at Marina di Caronía, and so is the second most common group of this amphora shape at the site. The fabric is the typical Campanian 'black sand' type, in which Dressel 1 containers were also made (Fabric 8). It transported the same famous Campanian wines previously carried in Dressel 1 and Greco-Italic amphorae. None of the Caronía examples could be closely dated, so it is impossible to know if they were still being imported in the second century. By then, as noted above, Kale Akte was producing its own Dressel 2/4 amphorae, making continued imports from Campania unlikely.

A smaller group of Dressel 2/4 fabrics of probable central Italian origin was also identified, in a buff fabric with coarse inclusions of quartz and felspar, spots of reddish brown and black colour, and occasional large surface flakes of golden mica (Fabric 22), identical to Bezeczky's Italian Fabric B.[336] Thin-section analysis showed that it also contained plagioclase feldspar.[337] It was previously identified as Baetican, erroneously, because of its similarity to Dressel 20 fabrics.

Terra sigillata

Italian *terra sigillata* began to be produced at Arezzo in Tuscany around 40 BC, and was made on a huge scale until the end of the first century AD. The *sigillata* of the later period, the so-called *tardo-italica*, was produced mainly in other areas, such as the Po Valley and the area around Pisa. In quality it represents the peak of the red-glossed pottery tradition, and is abundant on all sites throughout the Mediterranean region during the late first century BC and the first century AD, with a distribution range unrivalled by any earlier fine-ware production.

Terra sigillata from Italy seems not to have arrived in any quantity in Sicily prior to the arrival of Roman settlers in the *coloniae* in the last two decades BC; early Augustan forms are rare. According to Stone it was widely disseminated in the island only after *c.* 10 BC.[338] The dominance of Italian *sigillata*, from its first appearance until the destruction of buildings at both Caronía and Marina di Caronía in the late first or early second century AD, is overwhelming, representing 20% of the total fine-ware assemblage, and 65% of the material from Phase 2b.[339] At Halaesa considerable quantities of Italian *sigillata* have been reported, but little has been published. It was once argued that relatively low number of finds in Sicily by comparison with other provinces suggested that *terra sigillata* imports were limited;[340] but that conclusion needs revision in the light of the abundant finds from Monte Iato,[341] Morgantina[342] and other sites, and indeed from the wide range of forms present in the assemblage from Caronía.[343] That variety is matched also at Tindari:[344] the north coast no doubt benefitted from easy access to shipments of these wares direct from Italy.

At Marina di Caronía relatively modest quantities were found in the excavations in *contrada* Pantano, where amphorae and coarse wares dominate. The most important finds of *terra sigillata* have been recovered through surface survey of the eastern slope of Caronía hill: as many as 1300 fragments have found.[345] Most, as at Halaesa, are from undecorated forms, but several have mould-made decoration. All seem to belong from mid-Augustan to Flavian times (and the majority are Augustan or Julio-Claudian). Italian *terra sigillata* is the third most common category of fine ware at Caronía after Campana A and C and the local red-gloss pottery. It is almost ten times more common than African red slip ware at the hill-town, which is an important indicator for the likely date of abandonment of that settlement.

The recorded *terra sigillata* stamps are as follows:

P.COR/ ANTHVS (within square), Arezzo, late first century BC
AT(EI) RVF, Ateius Rufus, from Pisa, around AD 15
L.R.P (*in planta pedis*), Lucius Rasinius Pisanus, Flavian (?), two finds
L.R.PIS (*in planta pedis*), Pisa, AD 50/120
C.H. ( ) FES ( ), Pisa ?), AD 50 or later
SEX. M. C(L), *c.* AD 80 or later
C.P.P., second half of first century AD
C. AVILI, *c.* AD 50
DVM, complete platter, A-production from the Bay of Naples, Augustan
L. TI.TI (*in planta pedis*), Lucius Titius, Arezzo, first half of first century AD

The most common forms are plates and cups.[346] The decorated sherds include products of P. Cornelius, M. Perennius Bargathes and M. Perennius Tigrates. Plates, often with rouletting, represent almost half of the fragments, the earliest large-size varieties dating from the early to mid-Augustan period.[347] Later forms of Tiberian to Claudian date are represented by platters with concave or upright vertical rims, the latter being especially common (Cat. nos 189–92), as they were throughout in the Roman Empire in the middle years of the first century AD.[348] Next in frequency are cups, such as the small hemispherical shape with a vertical rim, a pronounced flange and *in planta pedis* stamps; this form is common in Sicily, for example on or near the north coast, at Halaesa, Solunto, Monte Iato and Lipari.[349] Another cup with an *in planta pedis* stamp, LRPIS, standing for the potter Lucius Rasinius Pisanus, is also very similar to this form (Cat. no. 187).

Only four stamps were found in controlled excavation at *contrada* Pantano:

L.R.PIS (*in planta pedis*) Lucius Rasinius Pisanus, Pisa, AD 50/120
S. M. P., Sextus Murrius Pisanus (?), Pisa, AD 60/150[350]
C SENT FIRM, C. Sentius Firmus, unknown production site, AD 1+ [351]
OPTATVS (in two lines, within a square), Central Italy, AD 1–20

The stamps found at Caronía, Halaesa and San Marco d'Alunzio give a clue to possible ancient trading routes. The potter Lucius Rasinius Pisanus exported in large numbers to Sicily, including Halaesa[352] and Marina di Caronía.[353] Pisa was well situated for exports especially to the north coast of Sicily.[354] Stamps from Halaesa indicate a prevalence of pottery made in central Italy and in Campania, another area equally well situated for export to Sicily.[355] A few stamps have also been reported from San Marco d'Alunzio.[356]

Some scraps of so-called 'Tripolitanian' *sigillata* were also identified. This, produced in an orange, micaceous ware, was once believed to have been produced in what is now western Libya,[357] but subsequent discoveries have demonstrated that it was made exclusively in Campania, near Cales, and on the Bay of Naples at and near Pozzuoli.[358] It is not uncommon at Monte Iato.[359]

Mould-made lamps

The earliest volute lamps date to the Augustan period, probably from the last two decades of the first century BC, and the latest type continued into the early Trajanic period, being the dominant lamp shape of the first century AD in Italy and the Western Mediterranean. Several finds have been published from Tindari.[360]

Volute lamps are common at Caronía,[361] especially in the second half of the first century AD. All are likely to have come from central Italy. Two examples preserved entire, together with a decorative ornament above the pierced handle, were found during the 1995 excavation of a cistern at Caronía.[362] Another volute lamp with handle decoration, consisting of palmette and volutes, from Halaesa, was made *c.* AD 25/75, probably in Campania.[363] Among fragments of discus decoration from Caronía, one probably shows Bacchus, facing left and standing in front of a vine. In his left hand he holds a *thyrsus*, in his right a *cantharus*. It can be dated to the late first century BC/early first century AD.[364] Another discus shows a dolphin, datable on stylistic grounds to around AD 50/75.[365]

Another lamp-type of the second half of the first century AD is the 'ear-lamp', of probable Italian production,[366] of which an example is known from Lipari.[367] Just one fragment of this uncommon lamp was found in Marina di Caronía. Manufactured certainly in central Italy, in the last decades of the Republic and during the first century AD, are so-called *Vogelkopf* lamps, of which a few have been found at Caronía, and some also at Apollonia.[368]

The earliest variety of the so-called 'fat lamps' started production in Italy in the mid-first century AD and the type continued until the mid-third century, but North African workshops had also begun to make them from the late first century AD.[369] Fat lamps represent more than 25% of the total lamp assemblage at Marina di Caronía, by far the largest category. Their frequency from the second century and the first half of the third centuries provides the clearest evidence for a continuity of activity at Marina di Caronía after the destruction of Building 1. Some of the fat lamps, with a beige-pink fabric, can be attributed to a central Italian workshop.

Lipari imports

Alum

Richborough 527 amphorae contained the very precious mineral alum, produced at Lipari between the first and early third centuries AD.[370] It was used in medicine as an antiseptic, but it was also in demand especially for dyeing and preparing skins. The material is rare in the Mediterranean, and Lipari was famous for it.[371] The container made on the island to transport it has a large, thick, rounded rim with short, chunky, ridged handles, and a cylindrical body with horizontal ribbing; its bottom ends in a small spike (Type 2: Fig. 4.26c). There is also a smaller version with a thinner more elongated body (Type 1: Fig. 4.26b). It was exported mainly to Italy, especially Campania (Puteoli), as well as to Gaul, Spain and even as far as Britain.[372] It is not frequently found on the island of Sicily itself, however, despite the latter's proximity to Lipari – or rather its presence has not hitherto been recognised.[373]

Its very coarse and distinctive fabric with large volcanic inclusions should, however, make it easily recognizable; a few fragments were identified at Caronía and Marina di Caronía (Fabric 28).[374] As we have seen (p. 38), textile and leather industries were supposedly active at Kale Akte.[375] The presence of this amphora reflects commercial contacts with Lipari, presumably directly in view of the latter's proximity. Our finds at least show that Richborough 527 amphorae did reach Sicily itself, or at least its northern coast, but probably only in modest quantities; with the growing interest in amphora studies, more examples surely await discovery elsewhere in the island.

Sicilian imports

Thin-walled ware

Thin-walled ware was made during the first century BC and the first century AD, mostly in central Italy, but also in some provinces, including Sicily, where a production centre is known at Syracuse; others are likely elsewhere.[376] At Marina di Caronía it constitutes the most important group, after Italian *sigillata*, in the late first century BC and the first century AD. Some of Augustan date can be attributed a central Italian origin.[377] One almost complete cup discovered in Caronía, with prominent sand particles which give the surface a rough feel to the touch, is very similar to one found in 1992.[378] Fabrics vary in colour between buff, greyish and orange, but very little came from the 2003–05 excavations at Marina di Caronía,[379] probably due to the commercial character of the buildings there; thin-walled ware, as a fine-quality product, is more usually associated with domestic contexts.

Sicilian terra sigillata

This category is attested by one chance find from Caronía, a small cup decorated on the inside of the base with a circular stamp showing a female figure holding a sceptre (?), and around her the signature CN DOMITI. The piece has been tentatively assigned a Sicilian origin,[380] a hypothesis supported by the poor quality of its gloss slip.

Sicilian/Pergamene appliqué ware

A fragment of a *skyphos*, decorated with a bunch of ivy leaves and clusters of berries, was found at Marina di Caronía (Cat. no. 186). Datable to the late first century AD, it belongs to a class of very refined appliqué wares produced in western Asia Minor, and especially Pergamon, which date from the second half of the first century BC onwards.[381] It is however known to have been imitated regionally at Morgantina,[382] and our fragment may have been produced there (or at some other Sicilian centre) rather than at Pergamon. Another fragment, in buff fabric with traces of a black slip, also has a moulded appliqué, possibly showing Aphrodite tying her hair (Cat. no. 197), but its relative crudeness probably rules out the possibility that it ts an import from Asia Minor; in all likelihood it was made in Sicily.

Lamps

The workshop of the manufacturer Proklos Agyrios is perhaps to be located at the Sicilian inland town Agyrion, south of the Nebrodi massif.[383] An east Sicilian origin is suggested by the dense distribution of these lamps there, although they are found in lesser numbers all over the island; one example even reached Carthage.[384] The dating of these lamps to the first half and the middle years of the second century AD has now been firmly established through grave goods. A lamp of this type was found in a tomb at Butera with a North African CIVNDRAC lamp as well as a coin of the younger Faustina (AD 147/75), while in a necropolis at Sambuco east of Caltanissetta another was associated with coins of Hadrian (AD 117/138) and Antoninus Pius (AD 138/161).[385] The stylistic similarities with volute lamps which they imitate also make a general date in the first half of the second century probable. The beginning of production might even be stretched back to the late first century AD: finds from central Sicily of lamps identical to later ones signed AGY are dated in the first century AD.[386] It would also seem probable that a type with volutes would have its origins in the period when volute lamps were at the height of their popularity, i.e. in the late first rather than in the second century.

Many examples of this lamp-type have been found at Kale Akte.[387] Some are stamped ΑΓΥ or ΑΓΥΡΙ, or else have the leaf- or heart-shaped handle decoration characteristic of these lamps.[388] They occur in a ratio of about 1:4 compared with the 'fat' lamps, but since several of the latter lamps continue in the second half of the second century, a rather higher share of the market might be suggested for Proklos Agyrios lamps during the first half of the second century. They are also present at Halaesa.[389] They seem to have competed successfully with the increasing influx of North African lamps during the first half of the second century AD, and were much more widespread at least on the eastern part of the north coast than has previously been realized.[390]

Spanish imports

Wine

The Haltern 70 container has an everted collar rim with oval handles on which is a deep vertical groove; its cylindrical body ends in a solid toe (Fig. 4.26d). They carried boiled wine-must, *defrutum*, sometimes with olives in it, and were produced in Baetica in southern Spain from early Augustan times to the middle of the first century AD.[391] The fabric is the same as that of the Dressel 20 oil amphorae from the same region (see the next section; it is Fabric 23). Small amounts of Baetican wine seem to have reached Sicily, as these amphorae have been noted both in eastern (Taormina, Ragusa) and western Sicily (Monte Iato, Palermo and Erice).[392] Two Haltern 70 amphorae were found aboard the Terrasini A wreck off the western north coast of Sicily, but the main cargo of that was Baetican Dressel 8 and 9 containers; on that ship at least, Haltern 70 was not the main cargo.[393] At Kale Akte Haltern 70 amphorae are represented by just two handles.

Olive oil

The Dressel 20 has a characteristic, globular body with thick handles, often with an internally concave rim and a small basal knob (Fig. 4.26e).[394] It was one of the largest amphora productions in the Roman world, and contained *annona* oil from southern Spain destined for Rome from the first to the third century AD, but especially down to AD 200. Most of the rest of the output was sent to the north-western provinces of the Empire,[395] and finds from Sicily are few; on the north coast they have been recognised at Tindari, and shipwrecks with Dressel 20 cargoes in the waters off Cefalù and Lipari also attest their presence.[396]

Dressel 20 fragments from Caronía amount to just two rims, one dating to around AD 100, the other a third-century form.[397] It has been doubted if Baetican oil reached Sicily in any significant quantity, especially if there was a plentiful local production of olive oil. Spanish cargoes clearly passed the island, however, on their way to places like the Adriatic, where Dressel 20 amphorae are attested along the Croatian coast.[398] Future publications of amphorae will likely indicate the presence of Dressel 20 containers in eastern Sicily also. In the third century AD, that trade came to a halt when massive North African oil exports took over and dominated the market completely. Not even at the height of its popularity was Baetican oil imported into Sicily on anything like the scale that North African oil was later to be, during the third and fourth centuries, as is clear not only from the Caronía material but also from everywhere else in Sicily. Perhaps the Sicilian olive oil industry was still strong enough in the first and early second centuries to resist any serious competition from high-quality oil of the type produced in Spain. Hardly any imported oil amphorae are known from the first century BC, indicating a strong local or regional production then. The much larger quantity of Dressel 20 amphorae in Croatia, despite its distance from Spain, may be connected with the low quality of local Dalmatian oil.[399]

Fish-sauce

The Dressel 7/11 was the Spanish fish sauce carrier *par excellence*, and was widely distributed in the western Mediterranean, especially in the first and second centuries AD (Fig. 4.27a). There is no doubt that it contained the famous *garum* or *muria* from Baetica.[400] There are few published finds of Dressel 7/11 from eastern Sicily, but the type might possibly be more common in the western part of the island: for example at Monte Iato, it is one of the most common types in the first century AD.[401] Two shipwrecks with Dressel 7/11 amphorae off Sicily are known – Terrasini A, where the main cargo of about 200 examples were of this type, and Capo Graziano C off Filicudi, where only one Dressel

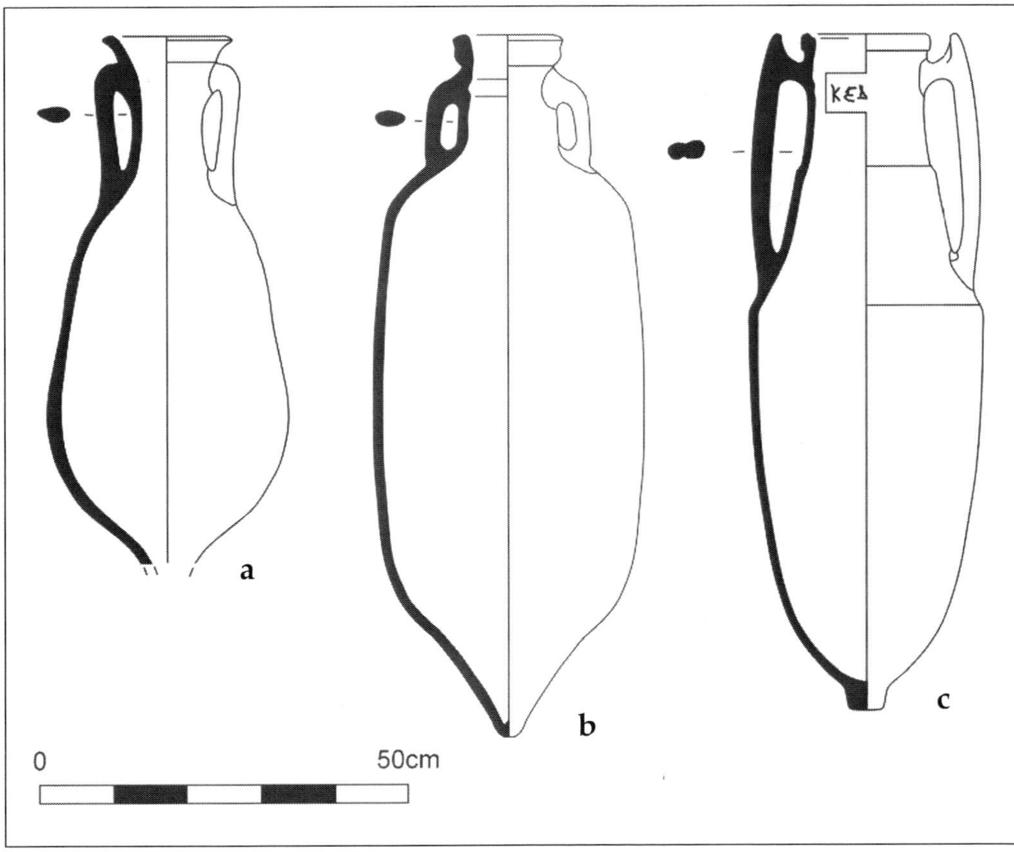

Fig. 4.27 Amphora types 6: (a) *Dressel 7/11;* (b) *Tripolitanian 1;* (c) *Schöne-Mau 13/ Agora G198/Pompeii 13*

7/11 container accompanied the main cargo of Dressel 20 amphorae. Both wrecks can be dated to the first half of the first century AD.[402] These Baetican *garum* cargoes may have been heading for the city of Carthage, where these containers are recorded in some quantity.[403]

From Caronía 9% of Early Imperial amphorae has been identified as Dressel 7/11, suggesting there was a moderate but perhaps regular Sicilian import of fish sauce from Baetica in southern Spain.[404] The fabric is typically buff sometimes with a greenish surface, in line with standard Dressel 7/11 amphorae from Baetica (Fabric 24).

Gaulish imports

Wine

Two fragments of handles at Marina di Caronía were identified as coming from Gauloise 2 or 3 amphorae, in a light brown fabric with a pink core (Fig. 4.24d–e: Fabric 25).[405] Since production of this type ceased around the middle of the first century AD, Gaulish wine must have already reached Sicily in Augustan and Julio-Claudian times, but no finds of this form have been reported elsewhere in the island.

The Gauloise 4 type (also known as Pélichet 47) has a thick, rounded rim and short, flat handles with a groove in the middle, attached to a short neck and broad shoulder; a thin-walled tapering body ends in a flat base with a foot-ring (Fig. 4.28a). This, the most commonly exported Gaulish amphora, was also a wine carrier, as witnessed both by *tituli picti* and the resin lining of some examples.[406] Production started in the second half of the first century AD, and by the second century it was at the zenith of its popularity, when it became the principal wine container at Ostia.[407] It was still being exported in large numbers to the western Mediterranean in the third century, but became gradually less common then.[408] Other than the Rome market export was principally aimed at central and northern Europe.[409] Individual finds of Pélichet 47 have been reported from five Sicilian sites,[410] but no shipwrecks with cargoes of this type have been found off the coasts of Sicily, leading Wilson to suppose that Sicily had no regular or large-volume import need for Gaulish wine.[411]

A surprisingly high figure of Pélichet 47 amphorae was found at Caronía, amounting to almost 12% of the imported containers from Periods D and E.[412] The dominant fabric is light buff, using a well levigated clay, identical with the most typical Gaulish fabric found at Augst and made in a number of different sites in the province of Narbonensis in southern France (Fabric 26).[413] A few fragments are of a different, red fabric, with a yellow wash, also encountered at Augst and believed to have been made in the Rhône valley.[414] Imports to Kale Akte are attested from the second half of the first to the third century AD, since types from this entire time span are represented.

The finds of this amphora from a small site such as Caronía suggests that its apparent rarity elsewhere in Sicily is due once again to a chronic lack of recognition and so of published examples. After the main stop at Rome, ships with cargoes including Pélichet 47 amphorae are likely to have headed south for Tunisia, no doubt putting into Sicilian harbours en route. This is suggested by the few recorded finds of this amphora shape which happen to be all in western Sicily, although such a hypothesis may be premature.[415] The very high quality of Gaulish wine would surely have attracted some demand from Sicilian customers elsewhere, and many more of the containers that carried it no doubt remain to be identified and published in the island.

Gaulish terra sigillata

Gaulish *sigillata*, or so-called Samian ware, was produced in southern Gaul and exported to Italy and Rome from the Claudian to the Flavian period. South Gaulish *terra sigillata* has been identified in Sicily before, for example at Lipari, Tindari, and Troina in the Nebrodi area,[416] as well as from the shipwreck of Panarea (Alberti) (one fragment), but it has never been found in large quantity.[417]

From Marina di Caronía, the base of a cup with the *in planta pedis* stamp ARDACI can be attributed to the south Gaulish potter Ardacius, active in Tiberian and Claudian times. Other finds include a bowl of type Dragendorff 36 and a cup with floral decoration.[418] Such material is present, however, only in paltry amounts when set beside the dominant quantities of Italian *sigillata* at this period.[419] Nevertheless, the finds do suggest that Gaulish ceramic imports might have been more regular in the first and second centuries AD than previously thought, and certainly the surprisingly numerous finds at Kale Akte of different Gaulish amphora types demonstrate strong trading contacts at that time with southern Gaul.[420]

Tripolitanian imports

Olive oil

The Tripolitanian 1 container has a thick rim (concave on the outside), a cylindrical neck, and small handles joining neck and body; the latter is also cylindrical, and there is a hollow conical spike at the bottom (Fig. 4.27b). It carried olive oil from Tripolitana, the western part of modern Libya.[421] First imported to Rome in the first century AD, it constitutes at Monte Testaccio in the second century some 35 % of all North African amphorae.[422] It is represented by just a single fragment at Caronía, in the standard pinkish-red Tripolitanian clay (Fabric 27),[423] and by a handful of additional fragments from the 2003–05 excavations [424] African oil was not much imported here in the first and early second centuries, in contrast to the abundant evidence of oil imports from the mid-second to the fourth centuries AD. This was presumably because Sicilian olive oil was, as noted above (p. 92), widely available in the first and early second centuries.

Tunisian imports

African Red Slip pottery

African Red Slip (ARS), the reddish-orange slipped pottery made in Africa Proconsularis, was exported to the entire western Mediterranean from the last decades of the first century AD, and dominated the entire Mediterranean market between the second and the fifth centuries. The earliest variety, so-called A ware (*c.* AD 80/200), has a shiny gloss reminiscent of the best Italian and Gaulish *terra sigillata*, but it is never of the same high quality as the latter. African by its orange colour is easily distinguishable from Gaulish *sigillata*. Starting in the late second century, the A version of the ware was superseded by other versions (C and D ware), which dominate the third and fourth centuries AD.[425] Well documented at Halaesa,[426] the pottery flooded the market for fine tableware into the fifth and sixth centuries all over the island.[427]

African red slip ware occurs at Marina di Caronía in significant quantities, alongside Italian *sigillata*. In the 1999 excavation in the hill-town of Caronía, it was absent, although surface finds from *contrada* Sotto San Francesco and *contrada* Telegrafo indicate small-scale resettlement of the hill in mid- or late Imperial times after its previous abandonment *c.* AD 100.[428] The most common form from Marina di Caronía is Hayes 8A, ubiquitous all over Sicily,[429] but other finds of A ware include form 3C[430] and a fragment with stamped concentric circles.[431] These can all be dated between the Flavian period and the mid- or later second century. The 2003–05 material has yielded abundant amounts, including Hayes' types 2, 3, 5, 6, 7, 8 and 9,[432] and, among the many finds from field survey at Caronía, Hayes forms 2 and 8A are especially common.[433]

Aegean imports

Wine

The amphora type Schöne-Mau 13/Agora 198, also known as Pompeii 13, has a wide mouth with a ring-shaped rim and a large, cylindrical body with curved, pointed, bifid handles (Fig. 4.27c). Probably produced on the southern coast of Asia Minor, mainly in the late first and second centuries AD, it certainly contained wine.[434] A single handle of this type was found at Marina di Caronía, so at least a small amount of this wine reached Kale Akte. The fabric is light reddish brown with white grits and red spots (Fabric 29).

Syrian imports
Eastern terra sigillata
This pottery was manufactured somewhere in western Syria and / or Palestine, and it first reached the western Mediterranean in the first half of the first century BC, where it started the new fashion of red-gloss wares, culminating in first Italian and then later African *sigillata* production in the Imperial period. Most finds of eastern *sigillata* from Sicily can be dated to the first century BC, and so predate Italian *sigillata*, but small amounts may have continued to reach the island also in the first and early second centuries AD.[435] It has been documented at Halaesa, Tindari and Lipari on or near the north coast, and at Monte Iato and Morgantina elsewhere in Sicily.[436] The modest amount of this *sigillata* at Kale Akte, [437] from its distant Eastern Mediterranean or Levantine source, includes one fragment of a cup from Caronía with stamped decoration of palmettes set around two circles.[438]

Mid to Late Imperial period (*c.* AD 200–500)
Local production
Wine
The locally produced flat-bottomed amphorae from this period carrying wine are difficult to place within a precise category. There is no doubt that they belong to the same type as the amphorae produced at Termini Imerese and Capo d'Orlando referred to as Termini Imerese 151 / 354 (Fig. 4.28b). This is small flat-bottomed container with a triangular or ring-shaped mouth (sometimes flaring), a cylindrical neck, round or oval handles and a pear-shaped body. The Termini 151 / 354 amphora is often labelled more generally as belonging to form Keay 52, but the latter should be reserved for the somewhat different type with triangular rim and high neck produced in Calabria and at Naxos in eastern Sicily (Fig. 4.28c).[439]. The shape was first identified by Panella at Ostia.[440] Current evidence points to a secure fourth-century date for this form, continuing with small alterations of shape into the fifth and sixth centuries AD,[441] although at Ostia, a fragment shows that an early version was already being made as early as the mid-third century.[442]

The Keay 52 and Termini 151 / 354 amphorae were first considered to be an eastern Mediterranean container.[443] Paul Arthur in 1989 then suggested that the former was made in Calabria, and more recent excavations have corroborated this, showing that they were produced at a number of sites in both Calabria and Sicily, the latter especially the north-eastern part of the island.[444] The type may also have been produced at Syracuse; at any rate large quantities of fragmentary amphorae of this type have been found in the harbour there.[445] For a long time, production was thought to have centred in the area around the Strait of Messina, but in the last decade kilns have been discovered, in addition to Naxos, at Campanaio near Heraclea Minoa in southern Sicily, at Agrigento, and near Acireale (perhaps the ancient Acium), north of Catania.[446] Local production has also been assumed at Capo d'Orlando (Agathyrnum) and Halaesa in our micro-region, and at

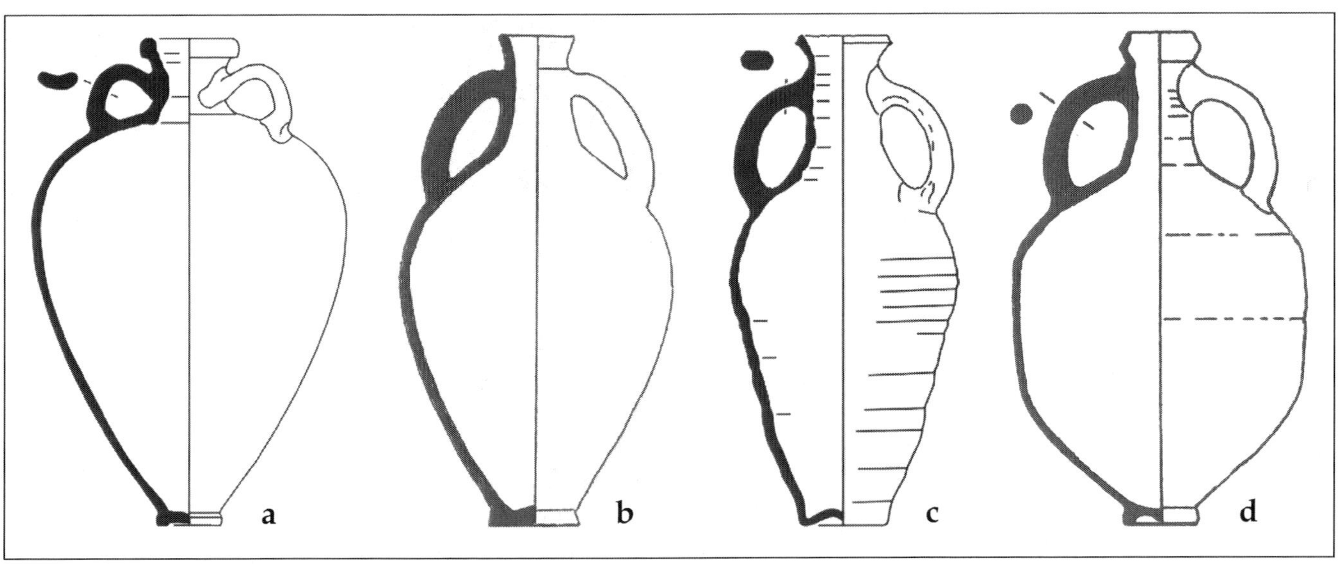

Fig. 4.28 Amphora types 7: (a) *Gauloise 4;* (b) *Termini Imerese 151/354 (from Marina di Caronía);* (c) *Keay 52;* (d) *Middle Roman 1 (not to scale: their heights are respectively 63 cm [a], 56 cm [b], 50 cm [c] and 47 cm [d])*

Furnari (Tonnarella) and Termini Imerese, on the north coast well to the west of Caronía.[447]

The Termini 151/354 amphorae produced at Termini Imerese belong to the late fourth and early fifth centuries AD, and can be divided into two main categories.[448] The finds from Capo d'Orlando are more or less contemporary, although early variants were already being produced in the last decades of the third century AD.[449] Significant quantities of this type, from a number of different production centres, reached Rome between the beginning of the fourth century AD and the early sixth.[450]

The type is the descendent of Italian flat-bottomed containers such as the Forlimpopoli and Mid-Roman types, which increased production in the second century AD when (as has been well documented) the Dressel 2/4 amphorae gradually disappeared.[451] Sicilian Naxos was one of the main producers of this earlier type (Mid-Roman 1: Fig. 4.28d), which shows that in some parts of the island Sicilian wine production was accompanied by its own distinctive locally-produced containers. Panella has suggested that the smaller size of such amphorae from the mid-Roman imperial period and later was dictated by a desire on the part of consumers to have a wine which did not turn easily to vinegar, a problem with the earlier, large-capacity containers.[452] The smaller, flat-bottomed amphora was the result, of which the Termini 151/354 shape is a late Roman variant, continuing the same tradition.

The Calabrian specimens have been analysed; the were all lined with resin and so, in all probability, were wine containers. This is strongly suggested by the fact that a well-known Sicilian producer of wine, Naxos, produced both Keay 52 and forms similar to the Termini 151/354 type.[453] Panella has underlined the importance of the *canon vinarius* imposed on Bruttium and Sicily by the *titulus canonicus vinarius* in the fourth century AD.[454] Earlier, around AD 270, the emperor Aurelian had already decided to secure for the State the wine supplies of this region.[455] The Keay 52 amphorae of Calabria must surely have carried the Calabrian wine mentioned by late ancient sources, but which wine did the Sicilian amphorae carry? We know very little from literary sources about Sicilian wine production in late antiquity. A variant of the early imperial wine *Aminaeum* is known to have been produced in the island, although Galen distinguished two types, one good for the stomach, transported in *lagynoi* (flagons), and one of lesser quality which was transported in *keramìa*, i.e. larger ceramic vessels such as amphorae.[456] Peña has studied the wines mentioned in Diocletian's price edict of AD 301, and identified the *Aminnei* mentioned there as wine exported from Sicily.[457] The *Aminaeum* may have been that produced on the slopes of Etna mentioned in the *Expositio Totius Mundi et Gentium*, and was carried in the amphorae known to have been made at Naxos and Acium.[458]

This production would have been at its height in the second half of the fourth and during the fifth centuries. In addition to Rome, the wine travelled mainly to the north-western Mediterranean, to the Ligurian and Provençal coast (including Marseille) and up the Rhône.[459] Numerous finds have been made at Salona, Dalmatia (where it was used as a fill in the city walls); so the distribution of this Sicilian wine also embraced the Adriatic. The containers from Salona date to the first half of the fifth century (the reign of Theodosius II) or to the early sixth century.[460] Some of these Sicilian containers also reached Carthage and elsewhere in Africa Proconsularis:[461] trade connections between Sicily and Africa Byzacena were strong at this time, with almost all imported amphorae (95%) from Caronía in the third and fourth centuries AD coming from there or Tripolitania. Locally produced wine would have been exchanged for the olive oil and fish preserve imported from North Africa.[462] The main destination of Calabrian and Sicilian wines in late antiquity is, however, likely to have been Rome.

The excavations in Marina di Caronía produced a huge number of fragments of this wine amphora, comprising almost 40% of the entire assemblage, and 64% of all amphorae in the period between AD 100 and 500. From numbers alone a local production could be assumed. An amphora kiln at Punta Chiappe, two kilometres east of the centre of Marina di Caronía (Fig. 1.4, no. 6) was identified by Giacomo Scibona as having produced 'Dressel 35' amphorae,[463] but on-site inspection identified a huge dump of partly mis-fired local variants of the Termini 151/354 type, some of them close to the Crypta Balbi 2 form of the mid-fifth century AD (Fig. 4.29; cf. Fig. 4.28b).[464] A small amphora of this type displayed in the Halaesa antiquarium may come from the same source (Fig. 4.30).[465] The kiln site produced only late variants, with a short neck and handles crudely attached, often just below the rim; the latter is pronounced and sometimes folded over, sometimes rounded or ring-shaped, sometimes again distinctly triangular. Some have handles which are flat on the top with a pronounced oval shape, typical of the late fifth century. This late amphora type was seldom found in the excavation area in *contrada* Pantano; activity there had by then virtually petered out. Judging by the shape of amphora necks and rims, the kiln and the surrounding rural buildings belong to the fifth or even perhaps the early sixth century AD. Although most necks are short, some are tall, taller than many of the fourth-century finds from *contrada* Pantano. The height of the neck, however, cannot be used as a safe

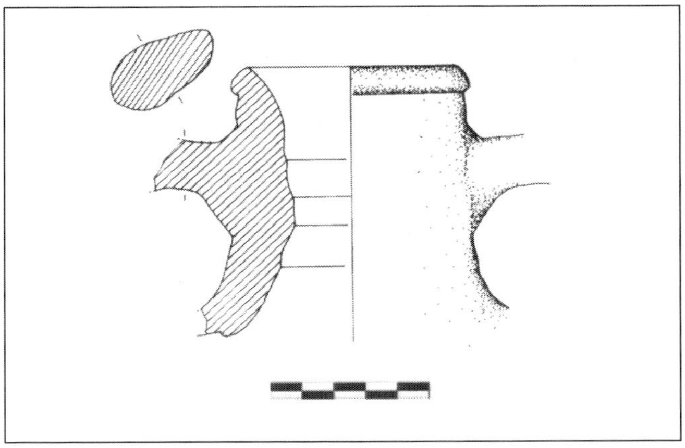

Fig. 4.29 Drawing of the neck of a Termini 151/354 amphora from the kiln in contrada *Chiappe at Marina di Caronía; scale: 5 cm;* c. *fifth/early sixth century AD*

chronological indicator, even if short necks become increasingly common in fifth-century versions of this amphora. One fragment with a tall neck and a well-defined rim might belong to an earlier production of the kiln in the late fourth or early fifth century AD, or early variants were produced somewhere else in the near vicinity. The kiln site has only been briefly noted and is not excavated; chronology remains uncertain.

In the absence at this kiln site of the early/mid fourth-century variant of these Termini 151/354 amphorae, another production site may have been located elsewhere, perhaps closer to the *vicus* at Marina di Caronía. That also this earlier type was produced locally is beyond any doubt, not only from the sheer number of fragments, several misfired, from the *contrada* Pantano excavations, but also by thin-section analysis, which has shown the fabric to contain minerals that are completely compatible with a local origin.[466] There is a wide variety of fabric colours, most commonly reddish-yellow, but ranging from buff to red, depending on firing temperature; there are also small variations in shape (Fabric 45).

It is difficult to date the beginning of production precisely. The type found in *contrada* Pantano most commonly has a poorly defined rim, often slightly flaring. The height of the cylindrical neck varies from quite tall (*c.* 10 cm) to very short, and the round handles are attached either midway down the neck or immediately below the rim. A small minority of them have a 'ridge' attached to the shoulders of the ovoid body; the latter ends in a flat base with an *omphalos* at its centre. There are very obvious wheel-marks both inside and out. The surface is frequently smoothed and given a thin brownish or reddish-brown wash. A complete amphora of this form was found inside a room in Building 2 (here Fig. 4.28b).[467]

Fig. 4.30 A local amphora of type Crypta Balbi 2, from the necropolis at Halaesa; height: 48 cm; fourth/fifth century

Dating evidence for this type is scarce, and comes mostly from Termini Imerese itself, where the fragments date to the end of the fourth or to the fifth century. Those examples generally have a shorter neck than the Caronía examples, and during the fifth century (especially from the mid-fifth) the rim is triangular.[468] Parallels found in Rome reflect this typological development,[469] as do also examples from Lipari.[470] A few fragments from *contrada* Pantano are of this later, fifth-century type.

In addition to amphorae, many finds of ceramic stoppers have been made. Judging by their size, they were mainly intended for the Termini 151/354 type

(Fig. 4.24). They are usually cut from body sherds of North African amphorae, another indicator of just how plentiful the latter were at Kale Akte at this period.

Several amphora finds of exactly the same type as those found at Caronía, and so probably of the fourth century, came from the Nordic excavations of the Temple of Castor and Pollux in the Forum Romanum in Rome.[471] The technique employed in making them, especially the crude way in which the handles are attached to the neck, is identical. Thin-section analysis of one sample proved that the fabric is indeed identical to that of the local Caronía Termini 151/354 containers of the third and fourth centuries AD (Fig. 4.32),[472] so demonstrating that wine from Kale Akte was exported to Rome at that time. Others of the same north Sicilian Termini 151/354 type have recently been found elsewhere in Rome, in an excavation on the Palatine; they too belong to the early fourth century AD.[473] Furthermore, the Termini 151/354 type produced at Marina di Caronía is now known from recent research to have travelled westwards as far as southern Gaul and southwards to Lepcis Magna in Tripolitania.[474] The fact that these amphorae travelled such distances and reached such varied markets, in addition to Rome, suggests that a private enterprise was active alongside state-supported wine exports to Rome in the late imperial period.

Since Kale Akte's wine production had apparently been dormant for almost two centuries, its sudden rebirth in the late third or early fourth century needs explanation. It is possibly connected with an offer of state subsidies for production. At Sicilian Naxos, amphora production is also known from both the early and the late Empire, but not much during mid-imperial

Fig. 4.31 Ceramic amphora stoppers found in excavations at contrada *Pantano (the central one cut from a lamp stamped CIVNDRAC); late third/fourth century AD*

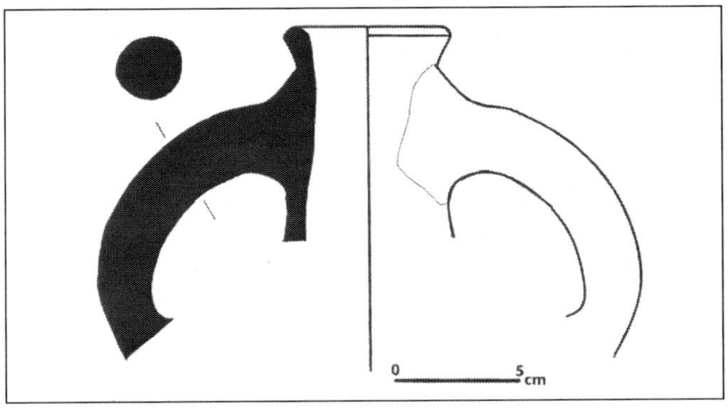

Fig. 4.32 An amphora of Termini 151/354 type from the Boni excavations of the Temple of Castor and Pollux at the Forum Romanum, Rome, of identical fabric to that of Fig. 4.29

times in between.[475] Why production ended after the first century at Marina di Caronía is hard to understand. To say that competition had become too intense is probably not correct, because in Augustan times and during the first century AD, Sicilian wine had successfully competed with massive imports from Campania, a competition which would have been even more intense than that from southern Gaul.

As for the type of wine produced at Calacte, it is impossible to prove that it was the *Aminaeum* type discussed above, especially since that refers to a grape variety rather than to an identifiable wine from a specific region. On the other hand, the same type of amphora produced at Calacte was used also in the Etna area, and that exported Sicilian wines were known to the ancient sources as *Aminaei*, as mentioned above; so it is possible that our north-east Sicilian wine also counted among the *Aminaei*. The produce transported in the local Termini 151/354 amphorae was perhaps of mediocre quality, as mass-market wines often are.

At *contrada* Pantano very few fragments can be dated to the period after the destruction of the buildings, probably in the 360s AD. It has been claimed that Sicilian production came to an end around the middle of the fifth century, perhaps a direct result of Vandal incursions which started in AD 440 (although these are unlikely to have affected the north coast).[476] Products from the amphora kiln near Marina di Caronía, are likely, as we have seen, to date from the fifth century (Figs 4.29–30).[477] The Termini Imerese finds of the same type are found in levels throughout the fifth century AD, while those produced at Capo d'Orlando may have continued into the sixth century AD.[478] It is present throughout the fifth and early sixth centuries at a site on the Palatine in Rome.[479] So Sicilian wine continued to be exported to Rome into the early sixth century AD, in containers of type Termini 151/354 and its later variants. Whether that trade included amphorae made at Calacte as late as that date, present evidence does not allow us to say; but it would not be surprising if it did, especially considering the settlement's favourable position for exports to Rome and Italy.

That however presupposes continuing use of the harbour: evidence seems to indicate it was in gradual decline around then. The location of a kiln 2 km east of Calacte perhaps hints that amphora production had lost its connection with the *vicus*, and was now located in a rural suburb on or near the estates which produced the wine. A rural economy, reflected perhaps in falling production standards (crudely attached handles?), had now taken control.[480]

Pantellerian imports

Kitchen ware

From the island of Pantelleria, strategically situated between Sicily and North Africa, Calacte imported some of its kitchen ware. Although considerable quantities of this ware circulated for 500 years over a wide area of the central Mediterranean, it is generally more plentiful on the southern coasts of Sicily than it is on the north. At Calacte its presence is limited; among imports, North African cookware is preferred.[481] A significant local/regional output in addition took a sizable share of the cooking-ware market, so there was little opportunity for Pantellerian ware to make much of an impact.

Tunisian imports

Olive oil

The Africana 1 ('Piccola') amphora has a thickened, everted rim, convex on the outside and concave on the inside, with a short, straight neck, and small, sharply bent handles; the body is long and cylindrical, and ends in a short spike (Fig. 4.33a). Numerous shipwrecks of its cargoes have been identified off Sicilian coasts.[482] It was designed to carry olive oil;[483] indeed its rim form is very similar to that of Dressel 20 oil-bearing amphorae (Fig. 4.26e). Sometimes, however, it seems to have been used, or rather reused, to carry fish preserves, as in the Grado shipwreck, and perhaps their presence at fish-salting establishments on the Sicilian coasts can be explained in this way.[484] It first appears at Ostia in the Antonine period,[485] and by then Sicilian oil production was already being rapidly outmanoeuvred by large-scale imports of olive oil from Africa Byzacena, which became even more widely available in the third century. From the time of Septimius Severus (AD 193–211), when an *annona olearia* was imposed on Africa Byzacena and Tripolitana,[486] and throughout the third and fourth centuries, North African oil flooded into Sicily in huge quantities.

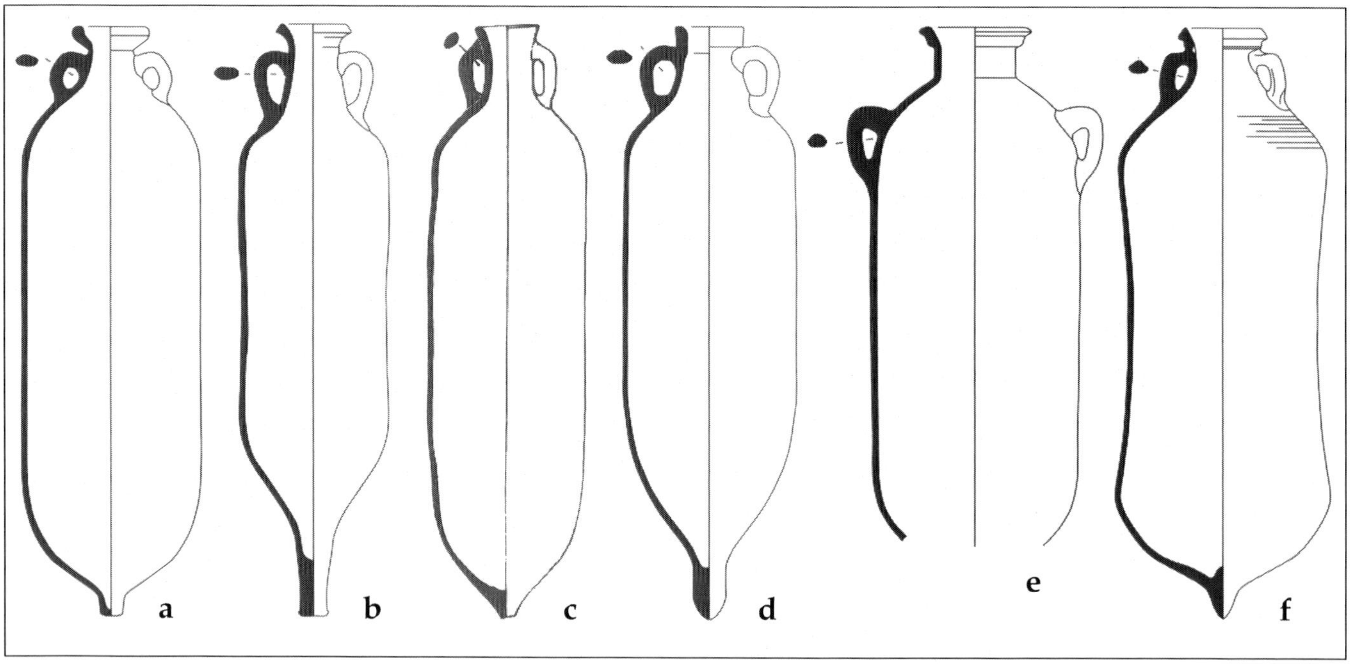

Fig. 4.33 Amphora types 8: (a) *Africana 1;* (b) *Keay 25/Africana 3;* (c) *Keay 27;* (d) *Africana 2;* (e) *Tripolitanian 2;* (f) *Tripolitanian 3 (not precisely to scale, but all the amphorae here vary between 1.0 m [a and b] and 1.15 m [c])*

At Marina di Caronía, the Africana 1 container is by far the most common type, accounting for almost half the imported amphorae in the period AD 100/500 (and 17% of all amphorae, including local ones).[487] The fabric is typically Tunisian, orange to red in colour, with a hackly fracture, and with grey or orange quartz inclusions and rare specks of mica (Fabric 30).[488] No stamps were found, but the letter C (a counter-mark?), impressed on a body sherd of Tunisian fabric, probably comes from an Africana 1 container (cat. no. 109).[489] The large number of finds from Caronía includes several Africana 1 rims which appear to be of second-century shape: olive oil from Africa Byzacena probably began to reach Sicily around the same time that the first shipments went to Rome.

The Keay 25 amphora is represented by only a few sherds at Caronía,[490] which belong to the second half of the fourth century AD; [491] but variants of it (Keay 25C) are known from the territory of Halaesa.[492] The fabric is of the typical Tunisian type (Fabric 30).[493] This form has a cylindrical body with a cone-shaped neck and a rounded, lip-flange rim (Fig. 4.33b).[494] Finds from shipwrecks contained fish products, but Keay thought that the primary contents would have been olive oil, in view of the colossal importance of this commodity in North Africa at the time (the fourth and early fifth centuries).[495] The small numbers of Keay 25 at *contrada* Pantano probably date from the time when export of this shape was at its height, in the late fourth century AD.[496]

The Keay 13A amphora, with a short, squat neck and concave sides, a triangular rim and thin handles, was produced in Spain and Tunisia and probably also contained olive oil.[497] It can be broadly dated to the fourth and fifth centuries AD.[498] It has to my knowledge not been recognised on any Sicilian site before. The few *contrada* Pantano finds, which date to the fourth century, were probably made in central Tunisia (Fabric 31),[499] supporting Keay's hypothesis that this amphora was made in Tunisia as well as in Spain.[500]

The lower half of an amphora found standing outside the line of the wall of building Σ seems to belong to the Keay 27 type, common in the second half of the fourth and the fifth century AD (Fig. 4.33c).[501] The fabric is over-fired, but thin-section analysis showed a considerable difference in the temper compared to that of local amphorae, although it contains some of the same minerals (Fabric 41).[502] If the destruction of the building is correctly dated, this would mean that the amphora is not later than *c.* AD 360.

Fish-sauce

Amphora form Africana 2 ('Grande'), widespread in the Mediterranean in the third and fourth centuries, is the second most common in mid- and Late Imperial deposits at Calacte, comprising 25% of all imported amphorae.[503] The Africana 2 has been divided chronologically into four sub-types (A, B, C and D), all of which are all present at Marina di Caronía, representing imports which stretch from the second century to the end of the fourth. The fabric is typically Tunisian (Fabric 30). The amphora has a thickened, vertical or slightly rounded rim with a short, upright neck, and small, sharply bent handles. The long cylindrical body ends in a solid spike. It appears along with the Africana 1 type in the Antonine period at Ostia.[504] In the overwhelming majority of cases where the contents are preserved, the Africana 2 containers have been found to carry fish products.[505] However, this is an amphora which cannot be considered absolutely commodity-specific: the North African cylindrical containers of the late fourth and fifth centuries AD probably mostly carried olive oil, but they are also known to have transported fish sauces and pitch.[506] In the publication of the amphorae from Augusta Raurica (Augst in Switzerland), the authors conclude that this container was not used exclusively for fish-sauce.[507] It is present in the Capo Graziano M and Ognina shipwrecks, but in both cases it forms a lower percentage of the cargo than the Africana 1 which accompanies it.[508] Like the Africana 1, it is very common in Sicily.[509]

African Red Slip pottery

The fine ware assemblage of the middle and late Imperial periods at Marina di Caronía is completely dominated by African red slip ware. Several different vessel-types have been found, all of them common on the north Sicilian coast, including Hayes forms 17, 23, 32, 45B, 50, 52, 58, 61, 72, 76 and 80.[510] There are very few finds of ARS D ware, which was introduced in the late Constantinian period; apart from a few examples of Hayes form 61, there are just occasional platters with stamped decoration from the fifth century AD.[511] Of great interest is the almost complete absence at Caronía of this pottery after *c.* AD 400:[512] only two vessels belong later than the early fifth century, and none can be dated to the sixth. This evidence points unequivocally to the beginning of a decline in activity at *contrada* Pantano from the late fourth century AD, and to the complete abandonment of this area as a commercial centre by *c.* AD 500. Elsewhere at Marina di Caronía, just below the Annunziata church, an African platter with stamped palm branches has been reported; this dates to the second half of the fourth or the beginning of the fifth century AD.[513] Finds at other places on the north coast, however, for example from the Conventazzo at Torrenova, on the coast below San Marco d'Alunzio, as well as at Tindari, show that African red slip ware continued to reach this part of Sicily in quantity throughout the fifth and sixth centuries.[514]

Lamps

Most second-century lamps from *contrada* Pantano seem to have been made in North Africa, on the basis of their decoration, shape and fabric. Two fragments stamped CIVNDRAC, for example, come from the workshop of C. Iunius Draco in Carthage *c.* AD 120/200 (see also Fig. 4.31, centre).[515] They are among the most common in the western Mediterranean, and large numbers have been found at Lipari and in many other places in Sicily.[516] Among further lamp finds from Marina di Caronía, a discus fragment with a rosette dates to *c.* AD 150/200,[517] and another depicts a running animal, perhaps a lion;[518] animals are in general one of the most popular motifs decorating Roman lamps.[519] A heart-shaped nozzle with an ovolo on the shoulder is also probably North African;[520] 'fat' lamps with rays decorating the shoulder certainly were.[521] In the second century AD examples stamped LASCIVI were imported to Halaesa.[522] A 'fat' lamp of Tunisian origin at Marina di Caronía might also be from this or another North African manufacturer; it is decorated with an olive wreath on the shoulder and has a heart-shaped nozzle.[523] The fat lamps were circulating above all during the later second century and the first quarter of the third. Only partly preserved was a lamp base with an illegible signature, very similar to other North African name-stamps in the second and third centuries AD.[524] The frequency of this 'fat' type was conspicuous among lamp finds from the 2003–05 excavations at Marina di Caronía.[525] Some from Halaesa stamped EX OFFICINA are further evidence of the popularity of North African lamps in Sicilian markets from *c.* AD 200 onwards.[526]

Globular lamps, dated from the middle of the third to the end of the fourth centuries, were made both in Italy and in North Africa. Around the middle of the fourth century AD, their market share was challenged by a completely new type of North African lamp produced by the same centres that made African Red Slip ware and in the same tradition.[527] There are no signs of a Sicilian regional production of lamps at this period, although in time (during the fifth century) Sicilian copies of African lamps start appearing. African lamps are plentiful in contexts of the late fourth and fifth centuries everywhere in Sicily: Calacte is no exception.[528] Examples from the slopes of the hill-town indicate renewed settlement there in late antiquity, and a good number have been found at Marina di Caronía. They mostly have floral or geometric patterns on the shoulder; common types include Atlante X from the late fourth/fifth century AD[529] and the Atlante VIIIA from the mid-fourth to the late fifth centuries AD.[530] The absence of any lamps of later date supports evidence discussed above that the excavated area at *contrada* Pantano was abandoned during the course of the fifth century. Another lamp is reported from *contrada* Nunziatella, some two hundred metres east of *contrada* Pantano, which confirms activity there at this period.[531]

Kitchen wares

Among the substantial quantities of coarse wares found in Marina di Caronía,[532] North African cooking pots account for approximately a third – a significant if hardly surprising import, given the huge amount of other African goods reaching Sicily at the time of the middle and late Empire.

Tripolitanian imports

Olive oil

The Tripolitanian 2 and 3 types are characterised by a rim with two 'steps', and two small handles joining the tall cylindrical neck to the shoulders (Fig. 4.33 e–f). The long, cylindrical body ends in a short, conical toe. The type began to be exported to Rome at the same time as Africana 1 and 2 amphorae in the mid/late second century AD, and increasingly so from the early third century.[533] Tripolitanian amphorae are to be found, for example, together with Africana, on the Capo Plaia wreck of *c.* AD 200/275.[534] The type is common all over the island.[535] Several scholars think that these Tripolitanian amphorae in the third and fourth centuries carried state *annona* oil from Tripolitana.[536] Fragments were found in large numbers at Marina di Caronía.[537] The surface colour varies between grey and orange with a thin white or beige skin. The fabric colour varies from orange to dark brown and brick red (Fabric 32).

Mauretanian imports

Wine

The Keay 1B/Dressel 30 type has a collar-shaped and rather elongated rim, as well as two curved handles (with a broad groove in the middle) which join the short neck with the broad shoulders; the ovoid body ends in a small, flat base or toe, either solid or hollow (Fig. 4.34a). The type is reminiscent of the Gauloise 4 amphora, of which it is obviously a later imitation. Both the shape and *tituli picti* suggest that it was intended to carry wine.[538] Keay 1B amphorae were produced in Mauretania Caesariensis (modern Algeria), and were common in the western Mediterranean throughout the third and fourth centuries.[539] In Sicily, however, few have hitherto been reported.[540] At Caronía, the type represents a consistent group at this period, although it is present in much smaller quantity than Africana 1 and 2 and Tripolitanian containers.[541] Almost all fragments are hard-fired, and brownish to dark purple in colour (Fabric 33).

Aegean imports

Corinthian relief bowls

These moulded bowls with flat base and figured scenes in relief on the exterior were produced at Corinth from the mid- or late second century to *c.* AD 300.[542] The paltry distribution of these in Sicily is confined to the eastern half of the island and is mostly coastal; along the north coast, examples are known from Messina, Milazzo and Capo d'Orlando, as well as a pair in Lipari.[543] The clay is the typical Corinthian – yellowish buff, with sometimes a more greyish, sometimes a reddish fabric.[544] A few fragments of this ware have been found at Marina di Caronía, evidence for trading contacts with Greece at this period, but the small number of finds in general in the island indicates that this pottery occupied only a very small share of the Sicilian fine-ware market.[545]

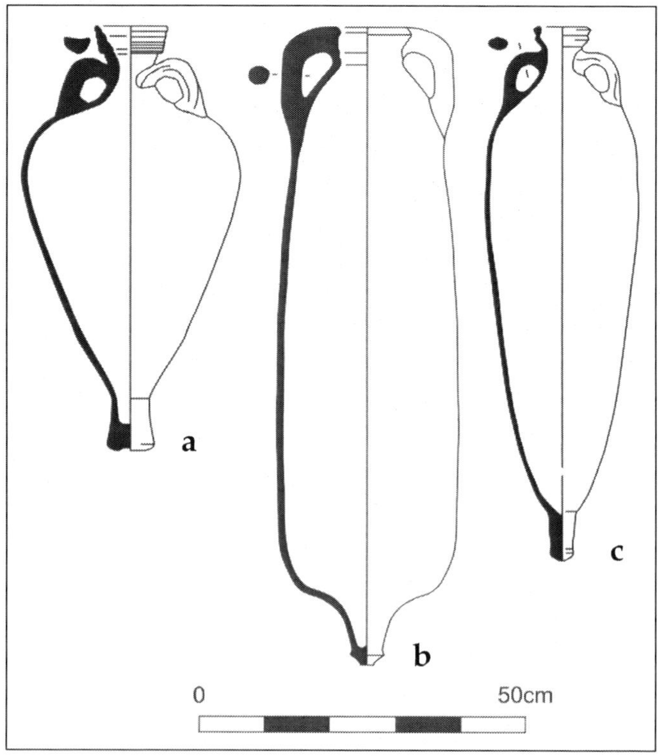

Fig. 4.34 Amphora types 9: (a) *Keay 1B/Dressel 30;* (b) *Almagro 50;* (c) *Almagro 51*

Lamps

A single lamp at Marina di Caronía can probably be attributed to a Greek workshop in Patras, with moulded decoration of vines and grapes on the shoulder, and rays on the discus (Cat. no. 224). It can be dated to the middle of the third century AD. These lamps, only recently recognised in Sicily, reached also the Adriatic and peninsular Italy. Greek-made lamps in general reached Sicily in mid- and late imperial times only in very small quantities.

Lusitanian imports

Fish-sauce

The Almagro 50/51 amphora has a small, pronounced rim (sometimes thick), with handles affixed on or just below the rim; the long, cylindrical body ends in a short, characteristic hollow spike (Fig. 4.34b–c). The type, which circulated from the early fourth to the fifth century, originated in Lusitania, on the Algarve coast of what is now southern Portugal. Fish products were the principal commodity carried in this container; the area was renowned for its fish.[546] A ship wrecked near Randello, close to Camarina on the south coast of Sicily, was loaded with Almagro 50 amphorae; they were full of sardines.[547]

A few fragments of this type were found at Marina di Caronía, belonging to two different fabrics – one the buff clay usual for Almagro 50 and 51 amphorae,[548] and the other a fine pinkish one (Fabrics 34–35). They represent a continued import of fish products from the Iberian peninsula to Sicily during the fourth century, but the numbers were much lower than those of the Africana 2 containers from Tunisia at the same period, which also, as we have seen, are likely to have been mainly fish-carriers.

The numismatic evidence

A total of 262 coins were found in the excavations at Caronía (Fig. 4.32), which together with plentiful numismatic evidence from the neighbouring cities of Apollonia and Halaesa, gives us a good overall picture of coin circulation in the area. With a few exceptions, all coins are of bronze, the left-overs of daily, small-scale trade among the inhabitants of the town. Of the coins found in excavation, the lion's share comes from the harbour area at Marina di Caronía, hardly surprising in view of the area's commercial character.

The Classical and Hellenistic periods

The earliest coins date from the end of the fifth or the early fourth century BC. The Nebrodi towns would by then, like all other Sicilian urban settlements, have been part of an economy which to a great extent was monetarised, using small change in bronze. The coin assemblage, together with that from Apollonia[549] and Halaesa,[550] shows that the bronze coins circulating on the north coast during the Hellenistic period were almost exclusively of Sicilian or south Italian origin. The only exception to that, at Kale Akte, are two coins found during surface survey in *contrada* Telegrafo at Caronía: one *denarius* issued by C. Scipio Asiaticus (106 BC), and a bronze coin from the mint of Erythrai in Asia Minor of the second or first century BC.[551] Of other non-local mints, coins struck by Syracuse are not surprisingly the most common, especially the issue of Hieron II featuring the head of Poseidon on the obverse and a trident on the reverse, sometimes split into two halves (Fig. 4.35a and b). Another Syracusan issue found at Kale Akte is one with the head of Kore on the

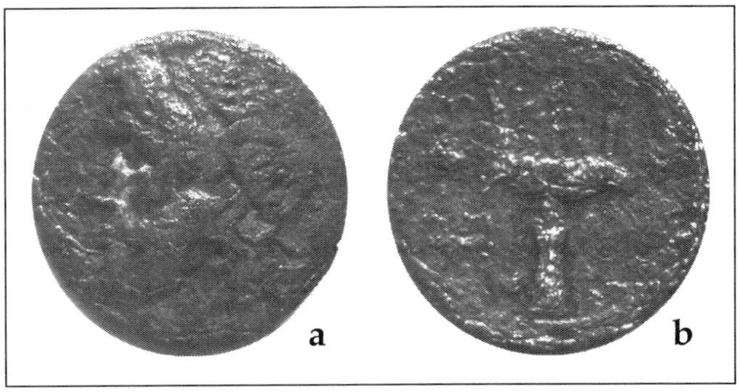

Fig. 4.35 Bronze coin from the mint of Syracuse with (a) *the head of Poseidon on the obverse and* (b) *his trident on the reverse, surface find, in* contrada *Telegrafo at Caronía; issued by Hieron II, 263/212 BC*

obverse and a prancing bull on the reverse.[552] After Syracusan coins, Mamertine issues from Messana are the most numerous, followed by coins from the mints of Tauromenion and Katane. Plentiful numismatic evidence at all three sites (Kale Akte, Apollonia and Halaesa) show that very large amounts of bronze coinage must have been circulating in Sicily in the third and second centuries BC. This is suggested by the small number of Roman coins that can be dated between the second century BC and the first century AD. Between 43 and 36 BC, new local coinage issued by Sextus Pompey during his control of the island are common, as shown also by several coins of his at Caronía and Halaesa, and these too may have continued in circulation into the first century AD.

The date of establishment of the mint at Kale Akte, and those of most other Sicilian towns after the establishment of the Roman province in 241 BC, has been much debated. The issues depict the following motifs: a helmeted Athena / owl sitting on a Panathenaic amphora, Dionysus / bunch of grapes, Apollo / lyre, Hermes / *caduceus*, Herakles / club (Figs 4.36–40; for the reverse of Fig. 36 see colour Pl. 15), of which those featuring Athena and owl, and especially that showing Dionysus with a bunch of grapes seem to be the most common.[553] One view is that they began after 210 BC, when Rome took control of the whole of Sicily for the first time, and that they can be seen as part of a desire by the Sicilian *poleis* to match the newly-circulating Roman currency. Carroccio has suggested that all were minted within a very short time-frame, from *c.* 210 to 190 BC, and he agrees with Caccamo Caltabiano that they represent a kind of 'occupation currency'.[554] A second view has been put forward by Mannino, that the mint was not established until the beginning of the second century BC, on stylistic grounds.[555] I think it a mistake to regard these issues as limited to such an

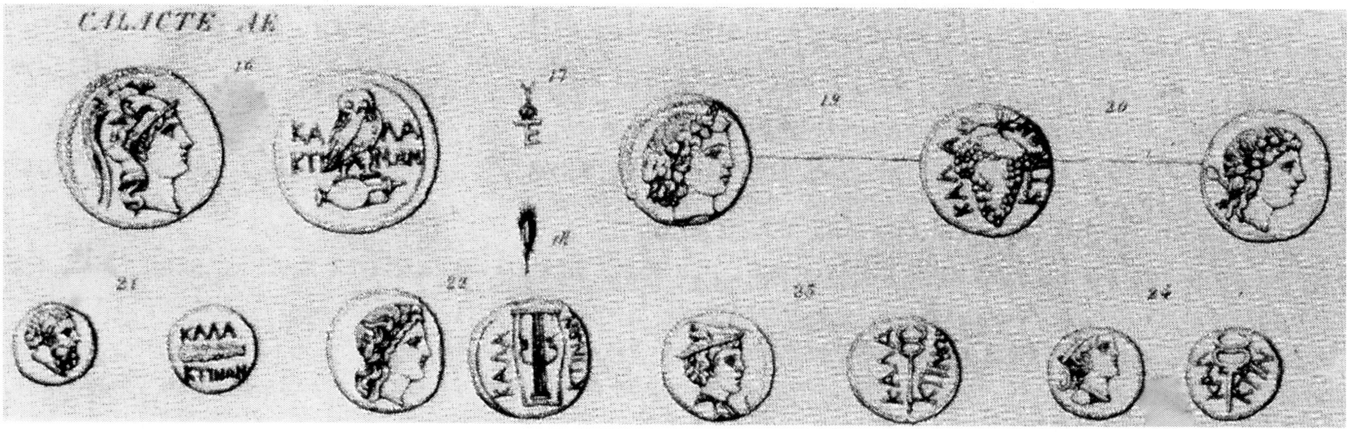

Fig. 4.36 (above) *The coin series minted by Kale Akte, as recorded by Antonino Salinas in 1876*

Fig. 4.37 (left) *Bronze coin from the mint of Kale Akte with* (a) *head of Athena on the obverse and* (b) *an owl sitting on amphora on the reverse; late second century BC (Coin Cabinet, Museum of Cultural History, University of Oslo)*

early period as the late third / early second centuries BC. That the north Sicilian towns and most other *poleis* in Sicily issued money in the second and first centuries BC is a general trend, and the most reasonable explanation would be that Kale Akte, like these other *poleis*, issued coins throughout much of this time period. Now a third opinion has been put forward by Frey-Kupper, on the basis of the abundant numismatic material from Monte Iato, that the phenomenon of Sicilian civic coinage in late Hellenistic Sicily only came about towards the end of the second century, after the first Slave War, and can be seen as a replacement for the Romano-Sicilian issues which ceased around 120 BC: the establishment of a civic coinage seems to represent an attempt to give Sicilian communities more autonomy in the hope of quelling further unrest.[556] If that view is right, then the coinage of Kale Akte is not earlier than the late second century BC. The material from Caronía, and indeed that from Apollonia and Halaesa, show that coins minted at Rome were indeed not very common throughout this period, and that 'small change' currency was dominated by Sicilian civic issues.[557]

Fig. 4.38 Bronze coin from the mint of Kale Akte with the head of Dionysus on the obverse (for the reverse image see colour Pl. 15); late second century BC (private collection)

At Apollonia only a single coin from the town's own mint was found in excavations, by comparison with over a dozen struck by the Kale Akte mint; the coinage of Haluntium, Apollonia's near neighbour, is represented by just three issues. This appears to suggest that Apollonia was only a very small *polis* in later Hellenistic times, Kale Akte later taking over as the more important commercial centre in the area. Kale Akte's port enabled it to supply goods with ease to the two *oppida* of Apollonia and Haluntium, which themselves had only small *scali* rather than proper harbours.

Very few bronze coins minted in Sicily travelled outside the island. The finds therefore of coins of the

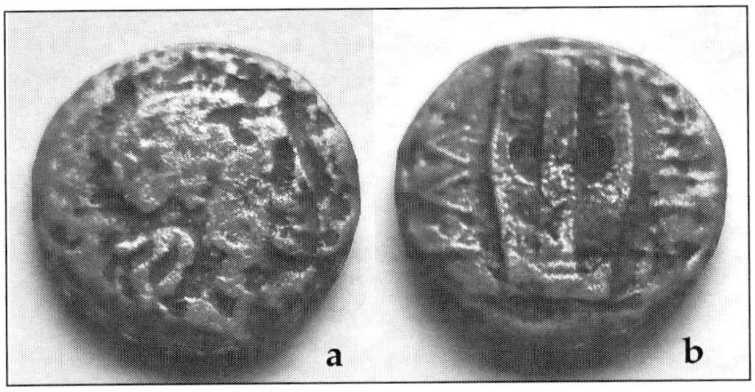

Fig. 4.39 Bronze coin from the mint of Kale Akte showing (a) *the head of Apollo on the obverse and* (b) *his lyre on the reverse; late second century BC (private collection)*

mint of Halaesa at the Dalmatian island of Vis (Issa), and even further up the Adriatic at Ancona, are all the more surprising.[558] Together with several other Sicilian coins, the finds probably indicate the close contacts enjoyed between Sicily and the wine-producing island of Issa, which exported Lamboglia 2 amphorae to Kale Akte and other Sicilian sites (p. 84).

The Roman Imperial period

Provincial mints came to an end after the reign of Augustus, and all later coins issued from the Roman state mints; as everywhere else, they provide an important chronological help in dating settlement at Marina di Caronía. A striking feature is how low the numbers of Roman imperial coins are in the first century AD: either the local economy was not much monetarized then, or else earlier Sicilian local coinage was still in circulation for much of this century.[559]

Fig. 4.40 Bronze coin from the mint of Kale Akte showing (a) *the head of Hermes on the obverse and* (b) *his* caduceus *on the reverse; late second century BC (private collection)*

Among the many mid- and late imperial coins are two 'barbarous radiates' of Tetricus (AD 271–3), a poor-quality imitation of the *antoniniani* issued by the Gallic usurper of that name, which are surprisingly common in Sicily. No coin later than AD 361 came from the *contrada* Pantano excavations, a further indication of the area's decline after the mid-fourth century (Fig. 4.41). Halaesa offers a similar picture of decline now: none of the hundred or so published coins there date later than AD 360, except for one of the fifth/sixth century AD and a few Byzantine coins of uncertain date.[560] It is possible that the abandonment or at least the decline of settlements might well have been a consequence of an earthquake in the 360s AD, which resulted in definitive end of normal civic life in Halaesa, as well as marking the beginning of the end of the *statio* of Calacte.

Fig. 4.41 Antoninianus *minted by Quintillus, AD 270, from the excavations in* contrada *Pantano, 1999/2000 (diameter 2.2 cm)*

5

Patterns of production and supply

Introduction

In the previous chapter, the remains of production and exchange at Kale Akte in antiquity were analysed in detail: this is the economic 'hard evidence' that the site has produced. In the present chapter, we will go into more detail and analyse the trends in production and supply at Kale Akte/Calacte over time, and set them in the context of the situation elsewhere in Sicily. The import of wine, olive oil, fish sauces, table wares and lamps, as well as local production of vessels to contain some of these products for export, followed their own individual patterns and trends over time. How far do these patterns reflect the Sicilian picture as a whole? Economic trends were taken by Braudel as examples of typical *conjonctures*, which he envisaged as being somewhere in between the *longue durée* and individual historical 'events' (*événements*). The trends discussed below should not be confused with short economic *conjonctures* lasting only a couple of years.[1] The production and export on a certain scale of a certain commodity could last for any time between considerably less than a century and two centuries or even more. In turn, these 'production cycles' were part of a larger process or 'bundles of processes' which were connected with the life of city states and empires. The cycles of production and export are partly made up of many interrelated events of political history, but in a long-term perspective they are dependent on the longer *conjoncture* of a political entity, such as a state or region. A good example is the export of *terra sigillata* from Italy. This was partly caused by the increasingly central role that Italy acquired as a consequence of the accumulation of historical events during the rapid expansion of the Roman empire, and resulted in Italy becoming the economic centre of this empire for a very long period. With a shift in economic focus from Italy to especially North Africa towards the end of the second century AD, export from Italy dwindled and it soon ceased altogether. In the Imperial period, economic *conjonctures* were not as dependent on dramatic historical events, as the rise of Italy to economic primacy had been, since the provinces were all part of the same political entity. Italy reached economic supremacy in the western Mediterranean as a consequence of conquest and warfare, but the provinces during the *pax Romana* achieved their success through peaceful economic competition in a vast and open market. During the imperial period, the shifts in *conjonctures* were mostly dependant on production capacity, supply and demand, and advantages or disadvantages in geographical links with Rome and Italy. Towards the end of the imperial period, however, the economic *conjonctures* are clearly again inter-related with historical events, which led to the fall of the western Roman Empire, and that in turn soon had dramatic consequences for trade and production in northern Sicily.

Goods and commodities

In what follows, I will summarise the archaeological evidence at Caronía for different imports and local products presented in detail in the previous chapter (Figs 5.1–2). I have classified them according to origin, whether local, regional or extra-regional.[2] This has been done in order to understand the varying patterns of production and supply over time. These patterns will constitute the basis for Chapter 6, which will discuss what the implications of these results are for their impact on private trade and state-directed trade. The patterns illustrated in the accompanying diagrams are of course necessarily schematic. The periods have been chosen to correspond in general with those already defined in Chapter 1, namely:

Period A (Classical period) *c.* 500–320 BC
Period B: (Early Hellenistic period) *c.* 320–200 BC
Period C: (Late Hellenistic period) *c.* 200–30 BC
Period D: (Early Imperial period) *c.* 30 BC–AD 100
Period E: (Mid/Late Imperial period) *c.* AD 100–500

It has not been possible, however, to avoid in some cases discussing a type of amphora or fine ware that overlaps the periods chosen. An example is the Pélichet 47/Gauloise 4 wine amphora, which is most common in Period D but continues into Period E. With these the typological development is sufficiently well understood, however, to be able to distinguish approximately between forms that should be attributed to period D and those that belong in period E. In the case of the local Dressel 2/4 amphorae, this is unfortunately impossible, and I have thus extended Period D to include the whole of the second century AD in the diagrams where this container is shown (Figs 5.1–3). The aim of these diagrams is to illustrate important general trends over

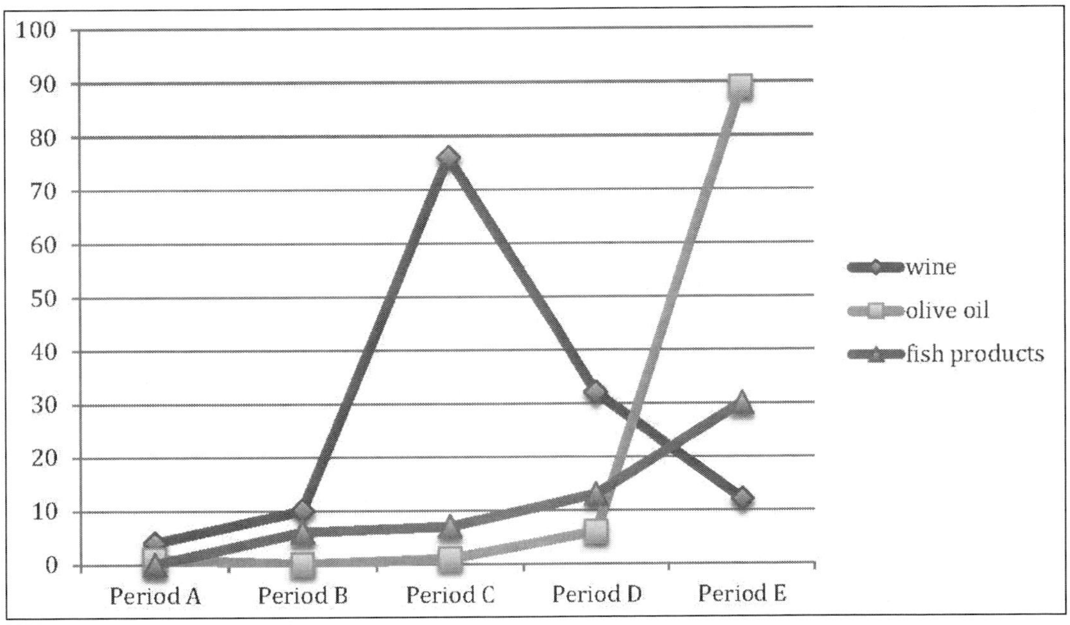

Fig. 5.1 Imported foodstuffs transported in amphorae which have been found at Caronía, and Marina di Caronía, separated according to content. The numbers here (and in Figs 5.2–6) are based on the estimated minimum number of vessels (amphorae) present

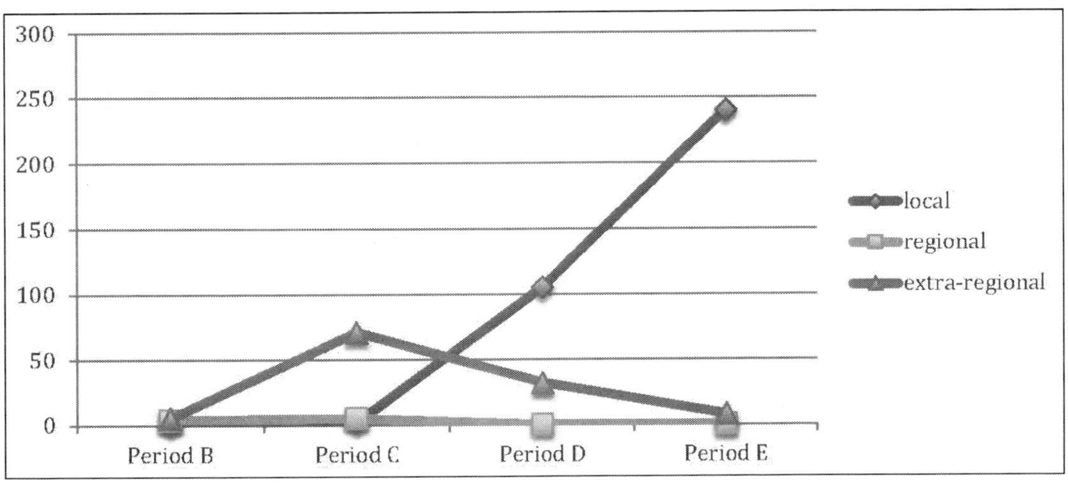

Fig. 5.2 Foodstuffs transported in amphorae found at Caronía (all types of contents), both locally made and imported

time; only the most significant fluctuations are considered, since much of the material cannot be dated in precise detail. Period A has been excluded from the discussion since finds are not sufficiently numerous to provide a reliable statistical basis for analysis. Period B is significantly richer in finds, but periods C–E are clearly the periods where statistical reliability is at its highest.

Wine

Wine is without doubt the principal trading commodity at Caronía, and had the greatest economic importance throughout all periods, accounting for almost 70% of the total number of amphorae (Fig. 5.1). It is also unrivalled as the most important locally produced amphora-borne commodity; this is especially true in Period E (Figs 5.2 and 5.3). While the settlement of Kale Akte and other settlements in its micro-region were too insignificant in size to have a wine production of importance in the fifth century BC, there is now evidence that some wine was being produced and exported as early as the fourth century BC.[3]

Local productions

The first production of wine for export in the Nebrodi area appears to have begun in the fourth century BC. The proportion of imported wine containers at this period is much greater then of course than that of local ones, but the finds are statistically too low in number to make calculations about the relative quantities of local and non-local wines meaningful.

It is, however, possible to trace a local production of wine at Kale Akte throughout the Hellenistic period, although it was never, it seems, on a large scale. Local production aimed at a larger, extra-regional, market can be presumed only from period D onwards, when

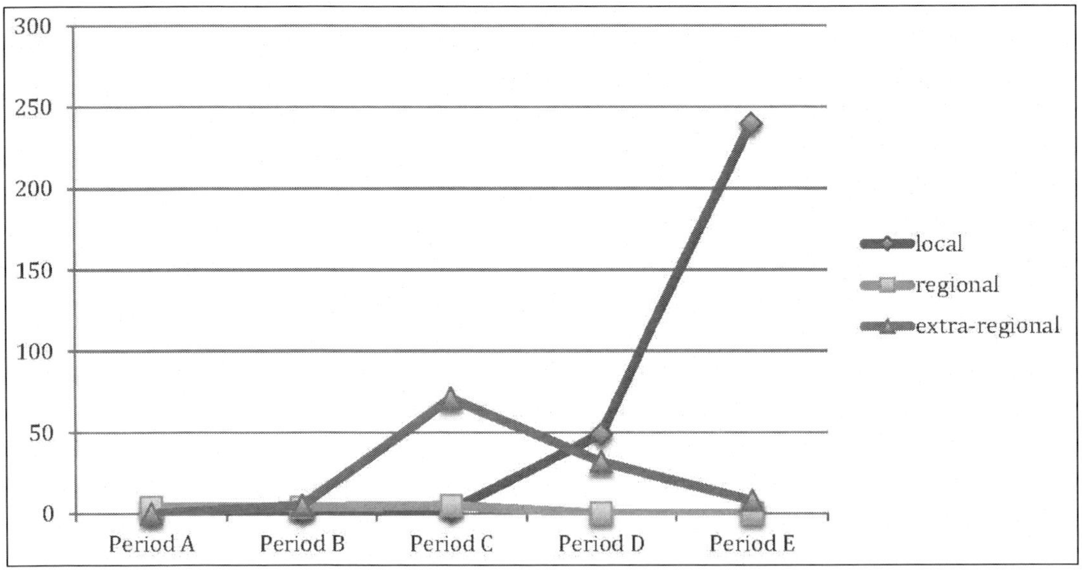

Fig. 5.3 Wine amphorae at Caronía, showing the likely sources of each type. Period D in this diagram covers the period from c. *30 BC–* c. *AD 200,* i.e. *a century later than usual, because of the difficulty of distributing Dressel 2/4 containers between the first and second centuries.*

local versions of Dressel 2/4 amphorae in the first century AD were produced in large numbers for the first time, comprising up to 60% of the total number for this type in deposits of that date. It is, however, currently impossible to date these containers more precisely within the first and second centuries. Production began in the Augustan period, but how long it continued is uncertain. It is tempting to think that it continued throughout the second into the mid-third century, a time when imports of wine to Calacte were quite modest, but evidence for a local production as late as that is lacking. The alternative, that our site transported its wine in wooden barrels or skins at this period, is a hypothesis that can certainly be ruled out.[4]

Wine produced locally for an overseas market can be postulated with absolute certainty from period E, beginning in the late third century AD, and important surpluses were produced from then until the fifth century, possibly even until the sixth century AD. It was transported in the small flat-bottomed amphora known as type *Ostia* 1, 455/456, or Termini 151/354 (with later versions called Crypta Balbi 2: see Fig. 4.30), and it was probably intended especially for the Roman and Italian market, as a part of the *canon vinarius* in the fourth century AD. Since many towns in north-eastern Sicily seem to have produced wine at this period, circulation elsewhere in Sicily was probably limited. That a local production, aiming at large-scale export, had begun to dominate the local market too then is also clear from the fact that imports to Calacte (to use its Roman name) of both regional and extra-regional wine diminish drastically in the Late Roman period, comprising a mere 5% of the wine amphorae there in Period E (Fig. 5.3).

Imports

The wine imported to Kale Akte in period A was probably mainly of regional origin; the MGS II container, of which the largest production was at Locri in Calabria, is the only securely attested wine-carrier in a period (the fifth and fourth centuries BC) for which we possess very little material. In general, it can be said that the great majority of amphorae circulating in the Mediterranean until the early first century AD carried wine, especially those from Greece and Italy. The MGS V container is the first type present in significant numbers at Caronía in both hill-town and harbour, including some vessels of reduced size (Appendix 1, Table A1.1). Judging from the fabrics of this amphora type, they were produced in the area or at least in the general region. MGS VI containers were also regional, and from the same production centres that also made Dressel 1A amphorae, since fragments of the latter belonging to the same fabric group as that of MGS VI have been found. Between them they represent a continuous regional wine production (Sicilian and Calabrian) stretching from at least the early third to the first century BC, and constitute an important parallel production alongside local amphorae of the same shapes. Imports of Sicilian wine from outside Calacte are completely absent in periods D and E (Fig. 5.3).

Imported wine from Campania arrived in Lipari and Sicily in general from the beginning of the third century BC at least, and probably even earlier.[5] This is also evident from the many finds of Campanian-produced MGS V amphorae at Caronía. The imports continued throughout periods B and C in containers of types MGS VI, Will D/E and Dressel 1, the last being the Late Republican wine amphora-shape *par excellence*. Beginning in period C, extra-regional wine was imported to Kale Akte in very large amounts by comparison with Sicilian products. The typical Campanian fabric is the principal one for both the Will D and Dressel 1 amphorae represented at our site, taking up almost 80% of the total number of containers present. The share of Sicilian wine from elsewhere in the island (i.e. apart from that produced at Caronía) becomes more or less non-existent in Period D, and the extra-regional imports diminish in quantity consistently over time due to a steep increase in local production at that time (Fig. 5.3).

Apart this huge import of wines from Italy, Greek vintages were imported on a smaller scale from the second century BC until the first century AD. The dominant group among these is that of Rhodian amphorae, which probably arrived in earnest on the Sicilian market in the last third of the third century BC. Koan containers are second in importance, followed by Knidian amphorae, but these last are only very infrequently attested (Appendix 1, Table A1.1). There is no doubt whatsoever concerning the content of all three: the famous wines described by ancient authors. These amphora types were, however, less common at Kale Akte than Italian and probably even Adriatic wines. The Lamboglia 2 amphorae transported the latter from the island of Issa, and later also from the territory of the Roman city of Narona, from the third century BC until the early Augustan period, as well as probably from elsewhee in the central Adriatic. There are no certain finds at Caronía of Dressel 6A amphorae, the successor of the Lamboglia 2 type, and it is possible that from Augustan times Adriatic wine could no longer compete with Italian, Spanish, Gaulish and Sicilian wines on the Sicilian market. Aegean wine containers from the first century AD are also only very marginally attested, and seem to have disappeared completely by AD 100 (Appendix 1, Table A1.1).

During the first century AD, the production of wine expanded exponentially in the provinces of the Roman world. Campanian wines in Dressel 2/4 containers, which began in the late first century BC, were now joined at Calacte by Gaulish wines in the Gauloise 2 and 3 amphorae and then especially, in the second half of the first century AD, by the Pélichet 47/Gauloise 4 containers. These finds can all be dated between the first and the third centuries AD, but in the later part of the third century, Gaulish wine production gradually petered out. For most of the second century AD, however, Gaulish wine was the only extra-regional wine imported to Calacte.

In the third century, some wine from Mauretania, although only representing 3% of the total number of amphorae from Period E, was imported in Dressel 30/Keay 1B containers. As noted above (p. 102), they clearly imitate the Gaulish Pélichet 47 type, and so were wine-carriers, a conclusion strengthened by relevant *tituli picti*. However, the vessels are small by comparison with the Dressel 2/4 containers, and the share of extra-regional wine is exiguous compared with the situation in the first century AD: extra-regional wines fall dramatically in their market share at Calacte from about 40% in period D (the early Empire) to only 5% in Period E (the mid- and late Empire: Fig. 5.3). When comparing the volumes of these small wine-carriers (about 20 litres) with those of the olive-oil and fish-sauce carriers (60/70 litres), we find that the real amount of imported wine is even lower, perhaps only around 2% of total imports in Period E (Fig. 5.4; Appendix 1, Tables A1.1–3). After the third century, local wine completely dominated the market, and

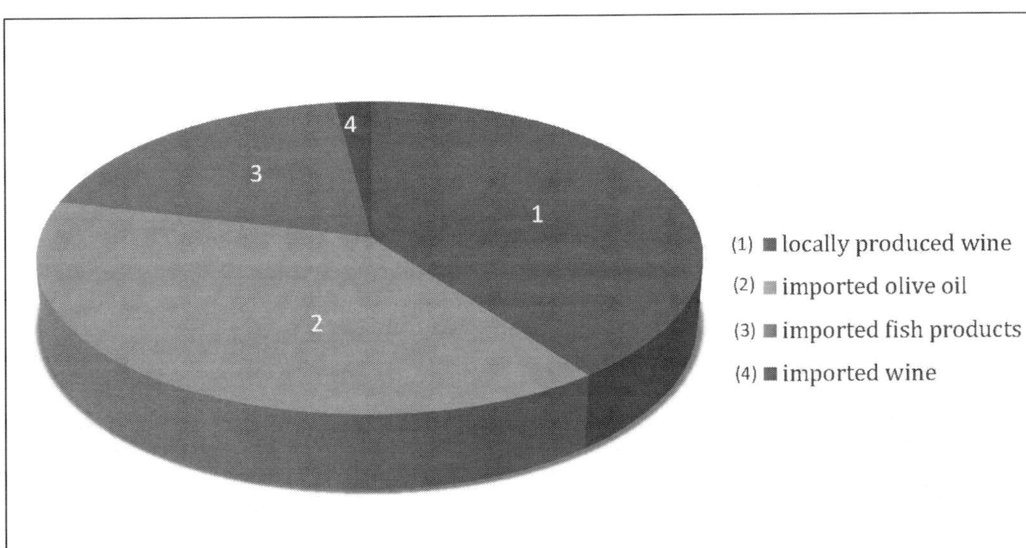

Fig. 5.4 Estimated amounts of commodities at Caronía for Period E (here AD 200–500), in litres

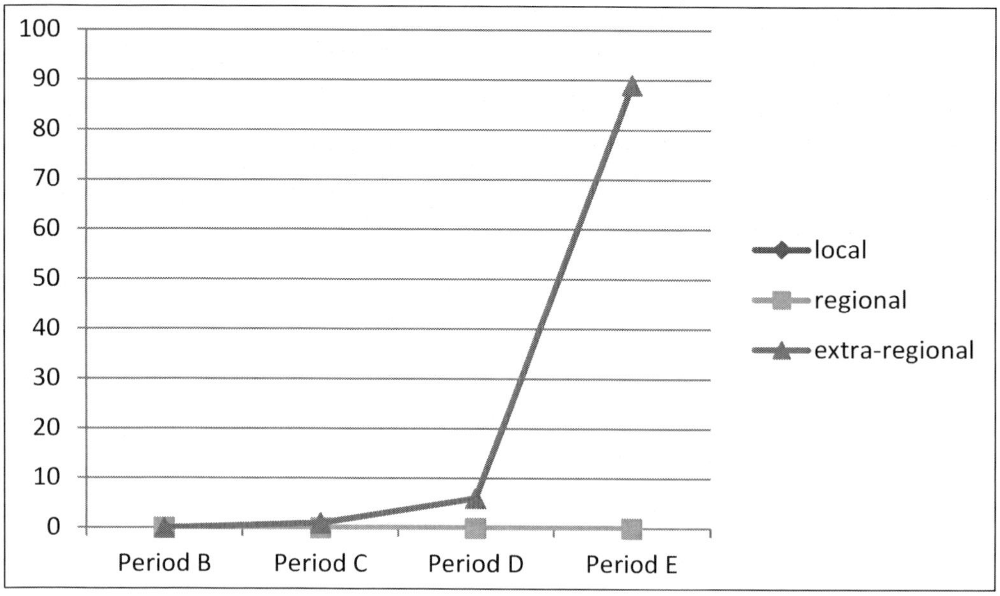

Fig. 5.5 Olive oil amphorae at Caronía, showing the likely sources

no overseas imports of wine can be discerned at all. As at Termini Imerese, there is no trace of the Aegean wine-carriers Kapitän I and II, which are widespread elsewhere in Sicily – another indication of Calacte's self-sufficiency in wine in Late Roman times.

Olive oil

Olive oil was the third most important commodity traded at Caronía, not far behind that of fish products (Fig. 5.1). If only non-local amphorae are counted, however, oil is the second most imported commodity after wine. Oil from outside was needed for a relatively short period at the very beginning of the settlement's history and, more importantly, from the first and second centuries AD onwards. Between the seventh and fifth centuries BC, Corinth was the most important exporter of oil to the newly-established Greek colonies in Sicily, but this trade ceased in the course of the third century BC. The identification of amphorae that certainly carried oil are curiously lacking in the Mediterranean area for the most of the third and second centuries BC. Only in the first century BC does that change, when oil from Brindisi and North Africa began to be more widely exported, but is containers always occur at Caronía in much smaller numbers than wine amphorae. There is no evidence at all of amphorae carrying local or even Sicilian regional oil at any period. Perhaps this was transported, where necessary, in skins or wooden barrels.[6] Olive oil, like grain, was a staple commodity, together with grain a basic necessity for daily life and survival. By contrast wine and fish products were of secondary importance – in some cases even extravagant delicacies – although wine was considered by many also to be a staple commodity.[7]

Imports

Prior to the arrival of Ducetius, and probably throughout the fifth century BC, olive oil from Corinth was imported to Kale Akte, since local production had yet to begin, as in much of Sicily. Many basic foodstuffs were commonly imported from the Greek motherland in the early stages of Greek colonisation.[8] It is probable that local and regional productions of olive oil in the course of the fourth and third centuries BC gradually made imported Corinthian oil superfluous. Concerning Caronía, this can only be speculation, since few amphorae are known from the fifth and fourth centuries BC, but such a conclusion is in accordance with a well-established pattern of a diminishing quantity of imported goods from the Aegean to Sicily in the course of the fourth century BC. In Periods B–D, a vast chronological span of four centuries (320 BC–AD 100), only a very small proportion of amphorae can be considered as certain oil containers: what few there are come from Africa Proconsularis, Hispania Baetica, Tripolitania and Apulia, and date from the end of the first century BC to the early second century AD (Appendix 1, Table A1.2). If olive oil had been transported in the Mediterranean in any significant quantity during the third and second centuries BC, it would be surprising if the containers transporting it have not yet been identified. I exclude here neo-Punic amphorae as potential oil containers; in any case, those found at Caronía, all types with hollow toes, most probably contained fish products. Nevertheless, there are small quantities of non-diagnostic fragments from this period, of unknown origin and function; even if some of these do turn out in future to be identifiable as oil containers, they would still be numerically insignificant.

From the fourth to the first centuries BC, therefore, and still during the first century AD, Kale Akte must have been primarily dependent on local and/or regional production of olive oil. Only during the first century AD did Tripolitanian and Baetican amphorae begin to make an impact, albeit still a relatively modest one, on the markets of Calacte (Appendix 1, Table 2; Fig. 5.5).

This picture was dramatically altered at the end of the second century AD, when large amounts of olive oil from Africa Proconsularis and Tripolitania began to be imported, in Africana 1A and Tripolitana 3 amphorae, for the first time. At Caronía, from a mere 1% of the total assemblage in period D, the percentage of olive oil amphorae reaches an impressive 70% of the total number of imported containers (Figs 5.1 and 5.5). The real amount of olive oil imported cannot, however, be reckoned by means of a simple calculation of the minimum number of vessels present or from the total of fragments recovered. North African oil amphorae had a much higher capacity than earlier containers, between 60 and 70 litres compared with about 25/30 litres for most earlier amphorae.[9] These African containers must also be compared with the contemporary, local and much smaller containers known as Termini 151/354, which at half the height clearly contained less volume than the earlier standard cylindrical amphorae. This means that estimates of the total amount of oil transported in Africana 1 and Tripolitana 1 and 3 amphorae can be almost doubled: in terms of quantity of oil delivered they represent a truly impressive import (Appendix 1, Tables A1.1– 2; Fig. 5.4). Baetican oil was still available in the third century at Calacte, but in very modest quantities compared to that from North Africa.

Fish products

Second in importance among the commodities transported in amphorae, on the basis of total fragment counts, are fish products (Fig. 5.6). If we exclude the locally produced (north Sicilian) Dressel 21/22 containers from this total, however, fish products are third in importance after wine and olive oil. In periods B and C at Caronía (between the fourth and the first century BC) North African (Punic) imports dominate: fish-sauces and salted fish were an essential part of Greek culture, and like wine were distinguished by different types according to taste, character and quality. This encouraged a range of alternative 'brands', which competed with each other for market share.[10] Fish-sauce amphorae, however, represent a low percentage of total containers, since those carrying wine far outstripped the rest (Appendix 1, Tables A1.3 and 5). A site like Calacte, known for its fish in antiquity and for tuna fishing in medieval and modern times (pp. 27–8 and 39–41), probably relied to a great extent on local resources, like other north-coast harbour settlements.

Local/north Sicilian production

Local production of Dressel 21/22 amphorae in or near Calacte can be determined from the excavated material, on the basis of fabric and on the high number of fragments present. Production possibly began in the first century BC, but was at its height in the first century AD. The Dressel 21/22 form with a wide mouth may well

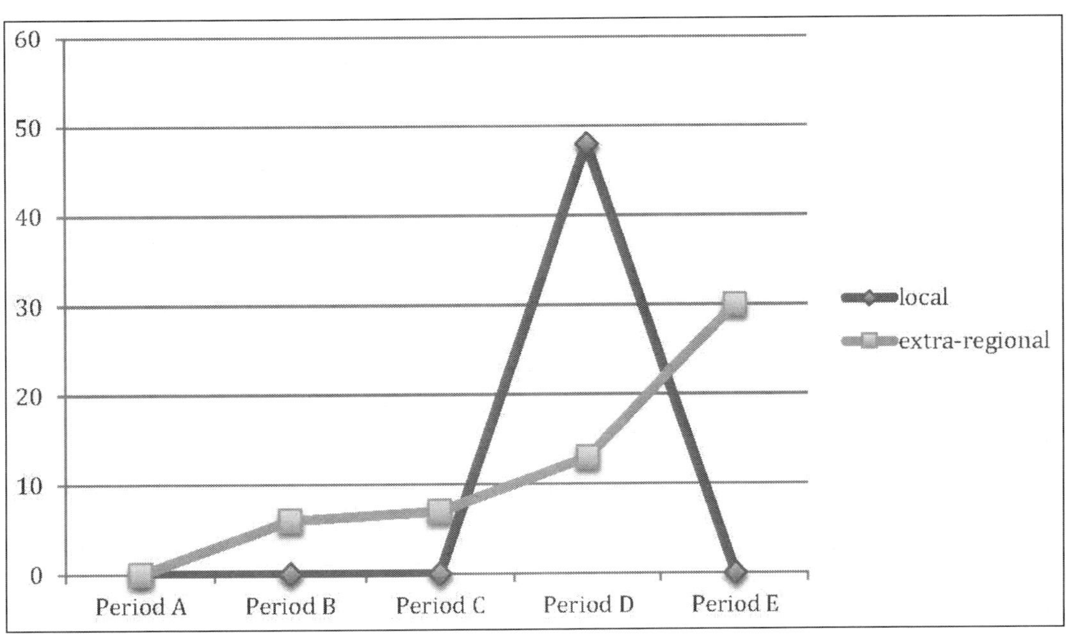

Fig. 5.6 Amphorae at Caronía carrying fish and fish products, showing the likely sources

have been modelled on the shapes of earlier Punic amphorae. The produce that they in all likelihood contained, mostly salted tuna or *tarichós*, may well have reached the Italian market and Rome: certainly fresh fish from Sicily in general is mentioned by the sources as having been reached there.[11] Local or micro-regional large-scale production of fish products in the first century AD explains in part the relatively low numbers of Spanish *garum* amphorae present at that time: the Dressel 21/22 containers represent about 80% of the total numbers presumed to have carried fish products (Appendix 1, Table A1.2).

Imports

From earliest times in Kale Akte's history (Period A, in the fifth and fourth centuries BC), fish-sauce from the Punic-controlled areas of western Sicily was surely available, although no evidence has so far been identified by excavation. All the signs point to Punic amphorae in general containing salted fish.[12] Those from period B (late fourth and third centuries BC) are certainly regional, i.e. Sicilian-made, but in period C and in the early part of period D (200 BC to Augustan times), North African amphorae take over (Appendix 1, Table A1.3). These seem to have contained (for the most part at least) fish-products such as *garum*, *muria* and *allec* prepared at North African coastal sites. These imports ceased, however, when Baetican *garum* appeared on the western Mediterranean market at the beginning of the first century AD (in containers which incidentally are a further pointer to the Punic amphora-type being used as a container for *garum* and/or salted fish, a conclusion which has sometimes been disputed). The imports of Spanish *garum* in the first century AD are small by comparison with the quantity of North African fish-sauce brought later from Africa Byzacena to Calacte in period E (second/fifth centuries AD): Africana 2 amphorae, for example, are attested in assemblages during that period five times more often than Spanish Dressel 7/11 containers (Appendix 1, Table 3). Although the Africana 2 type sometimes contained olive oil, it is principally regarded as a *garum* carrier.[13] No other *garum* amphorae of the second/fourth centuries have been identified in the Calacte material, except for a few Almagro 50/51 amphorae from Lusitania, which also carried fish products (Appendix 1, Table A1.3).[14] Their small numbers compared to the Africana 2 containers reflect the North African dominance not only in the oil market, but also in the trade in fish.

Alum

Imports

This very important material was used, as noted above (p. 91), for many purposes – as an antiseptic, for dyeing, and in the dressing of hides. All amphorae carrying alum (known as the Richborough 527 type, after a site in Kent in south-east England where one of the two varieties was first recognised) originated on the island of Lipari, where dumps close to the production site on the south side of the town were located in the 1990s. Lipari virtually had a monopoly of this commodity in the Roman worl (Appendix 1, Table A1.5). The small number of finds from Caronía shows that alum was not imported there at any time on a scale comparable with the main foodstuffs, even at the height of the alum exports to western Europe during the first and second centuries AD.

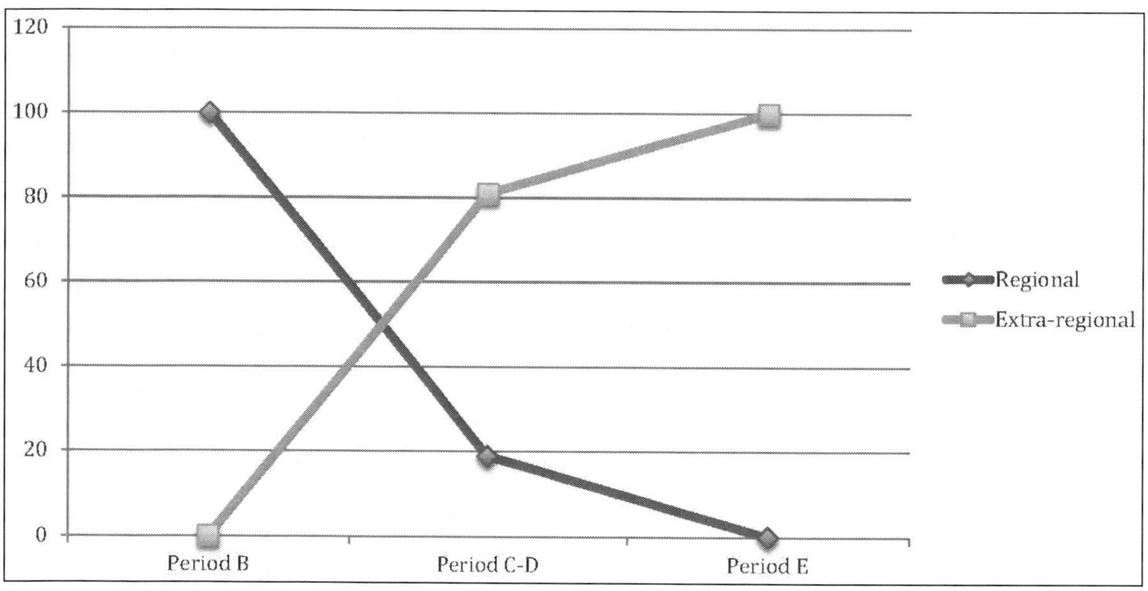

Fig. 5.7 Sources of fine wares found at Caronía. The numbers here (and on Fig. 5.8) represent the percentages of total finds.

Fine wares

Imports

The majority of the table-ware pottery (so-called 'fine wares') at Kale Akte (Fig. 5.7), as at other sites in Sicily, was produced at a number of different places on the island throughout the Classical and Hellenistic periods, with only a small quantity representing imported wares. In Period A, no calculations about the proportion of regional to extra-regional finds can be made on the basis of the very few excavated sherds of that date (the fifth and early fourth centuries BC). During the fourth century BC, red-figure and black-gloss pottery as well as lamps were being produced regionally in large quantities, with Lipari and Centuripe important centres of manufacture, neither very far from Kale Akte. This pattern continues until Augustan times: all production of black-gloss pottery and lamps at Caronía is either local or from somewhere else in Sicily, the latter comprising some 80% of the finds (Fig. 5.7). I have counted finds of Sicilian red-gloss as 'Sicilian' (i.e. non-local) products, although several sherds point to the possibility of a local production of this as well, although more evidence and more fabric analysis are necessary to confirm this. Campana C pottery, the last major Sicilian production of fine ware, was made in and around Syracuse from sometime in the second half of the second century BC until the arrival of Italian *sigillata* in early Augustan times. Regional thin-walled ware reached Calacte until well into the first century AD,[15] but no regional fine ware pottery is known after that.

The first extra-regional (overseas) imports to arrive at Caronía in the fifth century BC consisted mainly of Attic pottery, but soon after the beginning of the fourth century, increasing competition from Sicilian-made red-figure and black-gloss pottery effectively closed down the market completely for Attic wares. Not until Italian *sigillata* came in the late first century BC did any substantial amounts of extra-regional fine ware reach Kale Akte again. Very small quantities of Campana B, imported from central Italy in the second century BC, and of Eastern *sigillata* from the province of Syria which first reached Sicily *c.* 75 BC, are the only other fine wares attested at period.

Terra sigillata from Italy starts to appear at both Caronía and Marina di Caronía, as elsewhere in Sicily, after *c.* 20 BC. That was by far the largest category of fine pottery on the market between *c.* 20 BC and the end of the first century AD (Period D), comprising some 80% of the fine ware then in circulation. Thin-walled pottery, mostly from Italy, makes up another 10%. The remaining 10% consists of Eastern *sigillata* A, a few scraps of south Gaulish *sigillata* (which is very scarce), and insignificant numbers of Megarian bowls and Pergamene pottery. Then,from the Flavian period in the late first century down into the fifth century, North Africa becomes to all intents and purposes the exclusive provider of fine wares to the Sicilian market, and eventually to many parts of the Mediterranean, in the form of its distinctively orange African Red Slip wares.

Lamps

Imports

Lamps made before the first century BC are all Sicilian products. They are generally black-gloss or plain wheel-turned lamps, but from the first century BC these were replaced by the most common form, a Sicilian copy of the 'Corinth XVI'-type lamps, which remained in widespread circulation until the middle of the first century AD. The first imports of Italian *Warzenlampen* began in the first century BC, and later and more consistently volute lamps with figured designs on the discus arrived in Sicily, which signalled the beginning of a decline in the Sicilian lamp industry. Nevertheless, Sicilian-made lamps account for almost half the total lamp assemblage in periods C and D when considered as a whole (i.e. the three hundred years between 200 BC and AD 100: Fig. 5.8). One Sicilian survival in lamp production was the workshop of Proclus Agyrios, turning out its own version of imitation 'Corinth XVI' lamps. This may have started already in the second half of the first century AD and continued into the second century; if so, there was no significant interruption in Sicilian lamp production during the first century. Proclus Agyrios lamps account for up to a third of the 'fat' lamps at Caronía during the apex of their production from the late first century AD until the middle of the second century when, it seems, competition from a new source of supply, North Africa, became too strong. It may not be coincidental that the Proclus Agyrios production was at its height precisely between the time when the trade in Italian lamps began to fade out, and when the North African workshops began their massive export drive. This market takeover ended more than 650 years of almost uninterrupted lamp production in Sicily, and it did not resume again until the late Roman and Byzantine periods. African lamps comprise 80% of all those at Calacte in the third and fourth centuries, but fell slightly in the fifth century when Sicilian lamp production revived (Fig. 5.8). It started with poor-quality copies of African red slip lamps in the fifth and sixth centuries, presumably designed to provide cheaper alternatives to their high-quality models, but when the latter ceased production in the seventh century, Sicilian lamps on their own had perforce to serve local markets once more. Eastern lamps are rare at Calacte after the first century AD: just a single lamp, for example, is known there from a Greek workshop, active at Corinth *c.* AD 200.

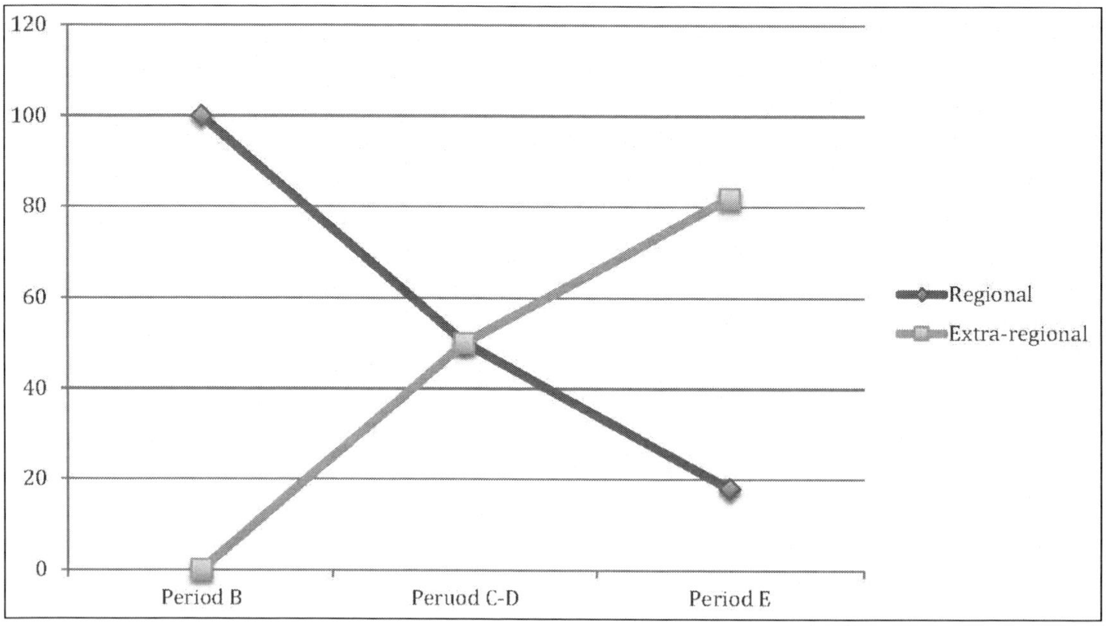

Fig. 5.8 Sources of lamps found at Caronía

Patterns of production and supply: Kale Akte in context

How does the pattern of trade and connectivity at Kale Akte compare, firstly with that of its micro-region (i.e. other settlements on the Sicilian north coast), and secondly with that of the wider region (i.e. Sicily as a whole)? Such comparisons help to fill lacunae in the Caronía material, especially in Periods A and B which are represented by only a handful of finds. Some of the evidence comes from sites on or close to the north coast, such as Lipari or Himera/Termini Imerese, at other times it comes from sites spread over the whole of Sicily. How far does the Sicilian pattern overall look by comparison with the north Sicilian one? Does evidence from Caronía fit into either of these frameworks?

The Classical period (*c.* 500–320 BC)

Evidence for the earliest period (Fig. 5.9) of economic life at Kale Akte is, as we have seen, exiguous. Other sites by contrast give us a good idea of the commodities circulating in or near the shores of the south Tyrrhenian Sea, in particular about the key component, amphorae, in the late Archaic and Classical period, these being well published from sites such as Camarina, Naxos, Gela, Himera, Entella, Colle Madore, Monte Polizzo, Montagna di Ramacca and Morgantina.[16] Lipari and Monte Iato are further major type-sites for the archaeological material of this period.[17] The first wines to arrive in Sicily come from the eastern Aegean.[18] From the second half of the sixth century onwards, however, wine consumed in Sicily was to a very large extent provided by regional sources from different Sicilian and south Italian centres. The wine was carried in the so-called 'Ionian-Massaliote', 'pseudo-Chian' or MGS II amphorae,[19] and later the MGS III type. Lokri Epizephyri was one of the most important producers of wine in the region, and a major *polis* in Magna Graecia during the sixth and fifth centuries BC. The finds at Caronía of MGS II containers from Locri which are also common at Lipari suggest that both Sicilian settlements were importing the same Calabrian wine. Second in quantity after Calabrian at Lipari was Etruscan, but this is not attested at Caronía.[20] A third type of wine which is present at Kale Akte was carried in Corinthian B amphorae in the Kerkyra (Corfu) fabric, matched by many similar finds elsewhere in Sicily.[21] They illustrate contact between Sicily and the wine-producing Corinthian settlement of Kerkyra, but wine from there and the eastern Aegean arrived in much smaller quantity in Sicily than that carried in the regional western Greek products in MGS amphorae mentioned above.[22]

In the fifth century BC, Corinth was the major supplier of oil to Sicily, transported in Corinthian A (and A') amphorae, and a few finds of these types have been made at Caronía; but in the fourth century BC these drop off at the same time as Attic pottery does, which followed the same trade route – probably because by then Sicily was producing wine, oil and red-figured and black-gloss pottery of its own. The number of Corinthian A oil amphorae reaching Sicily falls still further in the third century.[23] As we have seen, however, locally-made oil containers from the early third and for the whole of the second century BC are invisible at Caronía, or, for that matter, anywhere else in Sicily or indeed in other parts of the western Mediterranean. Oil must largely have come from local and/or regional

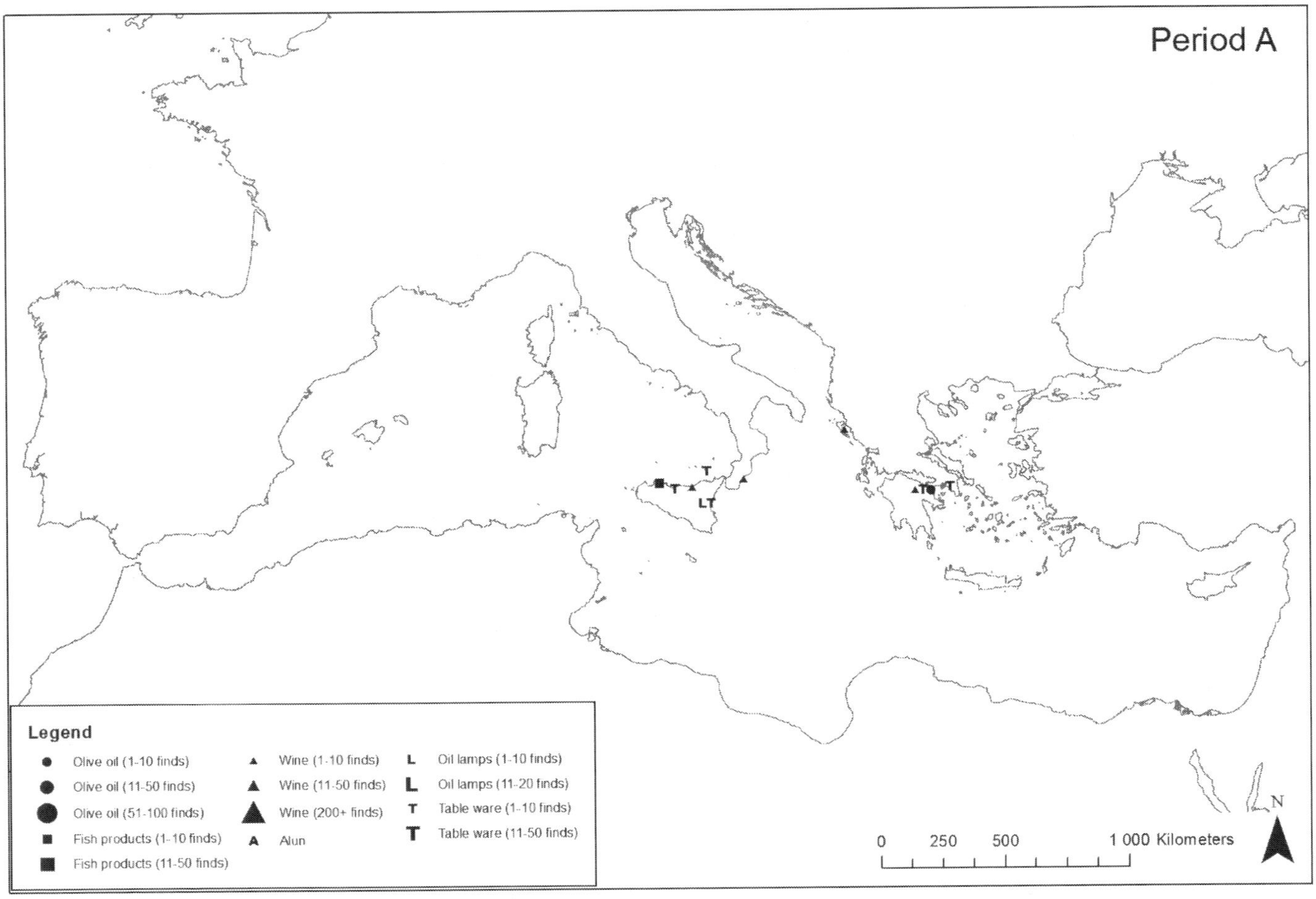

Fig. 5.9 Map illustrating the sources of imported goods, Period A (c. *500–320 BC). This and the following maps (Figs 5.10–13) are based on the estimated minimum number of finds.*

sources at that period. Conversely, at the same time, Punic amphorae carrying fish products from North Africa, southern Spain and western (Punic) Sicily are very common, especially on west Sicilian sites, where a local production of such amphorae is attested at Solunto and Mozia.[24] Punic containers are also present on late Archaic and Classical sites in eastern Sicily, but always in modest numbers by comparison with Greek amphorae.[25] Most 'Punic' containers of the Classical period found in Sicily are in fact likely to have been Sicilian-made, although this needs to be verified by more extensive clay analysis. Only a single Punic-type amphora of this period has been found at Caronía, but they are known to have circulated elsewhere on the north coast in large quantities (although always fewer than Western Greek containers), and many more are likely to have reached Kale Akte, as future excavation of contexts of the right date will no doubt prove. However, there are also indications that Sikel populations were especially fond of Greek wine and oil, but only moderately interested in Punic fish-products.[26]

Attic black-figured and red-figured as well as plain black-gloss pottery are ubiquitous in Sicily in the late sixth and fifth centuries BC, but they decrease during the latter century, and cease altogether in the first half of the fourth.[27] That Attic pottery was imported to Kale Akte in the fifth century BC is shown by sporadic finds from Marina di Caronía. More test-trenches and deep excavations of Classical contexts are needed at Caronía itself in order to get a better view of the situation at the hill-top *polis* at the same time. The fact that Sicily now produced its own red-figured and black-gloss pottery was a natural step towards a self-sufficiency that had already existed in wine and oil for more than a century, and the same was true also of lamps: no Attic lamps were imported after the fifth century BC, when regional Sicilian production took over.[28]

Present archaeological evidence indicates significant imports of Aegean products at the beginning of this period, which were substituted to an increasing degree by South Italian and Sicilian products in the fifth and fourth centuries BC. Medium-range regional trade

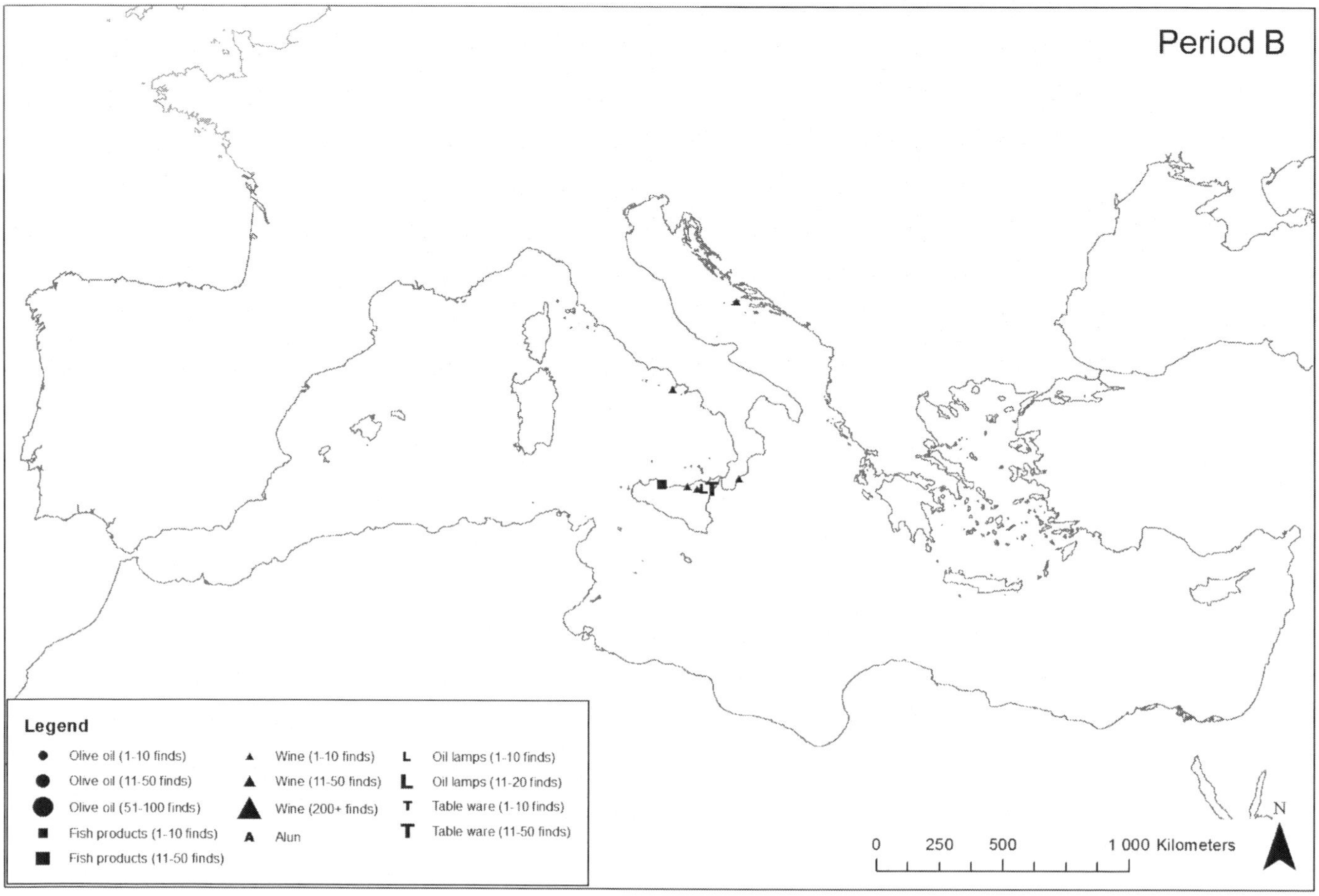

Fig. 5.10 Map illustrating the sources of imported goods, Period B (c. *320–200 BC*)

dominated, especially from the late fifth and fourth centuries BC.

The Caronía finds (Corinthian A and B amphorae, Attic and Corinthian pottery) indicate that there were still commercial links with Greece in the fifth century, in line with the general situation in many others parts of Sicily. Strong contacts with the south Tyrrhenian area, witnessed especially by imports of regional wine-carriers (such as the MGS II containers from Locri), are closely mirrored by a similar situation at Lipari. In general amphorae from Magna Graecia and Sicily (the MGS range) are very common in fourth-century contexts at all well-studied sites in Sicily and the south Tyrrhenian area.[29] In fine pottery, the late Archaic/early Classical Iato K 480 cups belong to a group (perhaps made at Himera) which seems to have been circulated quite widely in central and eastern Sicily as well as in the western half of the island.

The Early Hellenistic period (*c.* 320–200 BC)

The most important general comparisons for Caronía at this period (Fig. 5.10) can be made with Lipari and Monte Iato, but for amphorae only the material from Entella has been extensively published.[30] The early Hellenistic is a period when Sicily had become to a very large extent self-sufficient: it produced its own wine, olive oil, black-gloss and Gnathian pottery, lamps, and of these products the wine at least was exported overseas. Imports of Punic fish products from North Africa continue to be numerically significant, with Punic amphorae common on Sicilian sites in the third century BC (of which Caronía is one) as well as on the Italian mainland, as for example at Roccagloriosa in Bruttium (Calabria).[31] Another indication of the increasing extra-regional contacts is the presence of Rhodian wine amphorae, which are ubiquitous in the island in the second century BC.[32] Again, Kale Akte is no exception.

With the Roman takeover in the mid-third century BC, trade with Campania and central Italy is likely to have increased, but that had started already by at least 300 BC with the arrival of MGS V amphorae. In recent years these have been found in significant numbers at Lipari, and are also present at Termini Imerese; in addition, many of the amphora stamps in a deposit at Erice in the far west of the island are now considered to be Campanian. The finds from Caronía support the

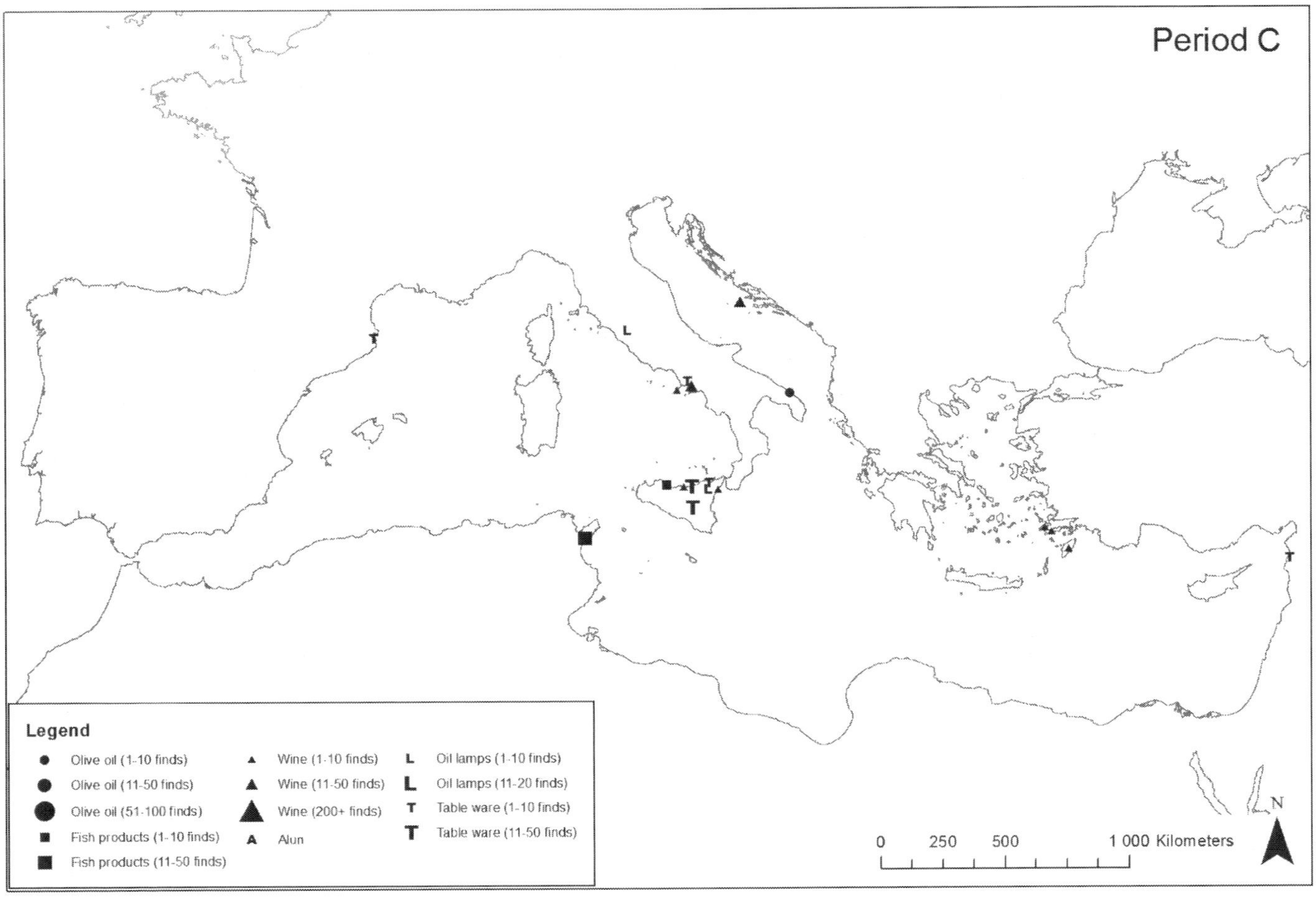

*Fig. 5.11 Map illustrating the sources of imported goods, Period C (*c. *200–30 BC)*

view that Campanian MGS V containers were the largest category of imported amphorae at this period. The trade in Italian fine wares comes later: little Campanian or central Italian pottery (from the *atelier des petites éstampilles*) is attested in Sicily (including Lipari) before the second century BC.[33] The fine wares which dominate the market throughout the third century, in Caronía as elsewhere in Sicily, is regional black-gloss pottery, made in a number of different centres in the island.[34] Maybe a little Campana A *ancienne* and pottery of the *atelier des petites éstampilles* reached the north coast in the third century together with Campanian amphorae, but if they did it was not in any quantity.[35] The most characteristic feature of the third century is the increasingly large scale of imports from beyond Sicily, including now those from non-Greek areas – a sign of what might be called the growing 'internationalization' of trade.

Caronía's pattern in this century, with Campanian and Punic amphorae making up the lion's share of the amphorae present, but with Sicilian-made products being preferred for black-gloss pottery and lamps, is precisely mirrored at most other Sicilian sites at this time. Wine from Kerkyra in Corinthian B amphorae reached Lipari and Kale Akte, but, as elsewhere in Sicily, not in significant numbers; Kerkyran wine was, as we have seen, less popular than Campanian. Again, imports of Rhodian amphorae at Caronía follow a similar pattern to their circulation elsewhere in Sicily, as shown for example by a comparison of Rhodian stamped handles at Halaesa with those at Kale Akte (they are very similar).[36] Most of those found in the 2003–05 excavations at Marina di Caronía date to the period *c.* 225/150 BC, again as elsewhere in Sicily.[37]

Finds at Caronía of the early Hellenistic period (*c.* 320–200 BC) are more numerous than those in the Classical, but are still numerically limited by comparison with later periods. This is especially so for amphorae. Oil cannot be detected, as already noted, as a product carried in amphorae. Among imported commodities, wine was dominant, mostly from Campania, but partly also from elsewhere in Sicily, leaving North African fish products a poor second. Fine-ware pottery is without exception regionally produced until the second century, lamps too until the beginning of the first century BC. The phenomenon of strong regional production of these items was probably stimulated by local production of wine in numerous centres, initially distributed to satisfy local markets. Import patterns fluctuated. It was apparently difficult for Italian fine-ware pottery to conquer the Sicilian market during the third century despite the huge demand for Italian wine – possibly a tribute to the high quality of Sicilian pottery at the time (contented customers have no need to look elsewhere). The local economy seems to have been flourishing, despite the Punic Wars, with local kilns producing amphorae, local kitchen ware, and figurines at a number of different centres.

The Late Hellenistic period (*c.* 200–30 BC)

Commercial activity in Sicily after the Second Punic War is relatively scarcely documented compared with that of earlier periods (Fig. 5.11). Amphora studies of this date are of limited scope. Along the north coast, Termini Imerese is one of the important points of reference,[38] and some late Hellenistic material has also been published from Lipari.[39] For the fine ware, the picture is detailed because of excellent studies now of material at two sites, Monte Iato and Morgantina.[40]

With Sicily now unified as a province, the 'international' network of trade, of which our micro-region was already a part, grew intensively in the last two centuries BC. Wine was now imported in great quantity from central Tyrrhenian Italy,[41] as elsewhere in Sicily, probably for the most part from Campania; to a lesser extent wine from Rhodes also continued to reach the island. At Caronía, the vast majority (c. 80%) of imported amphora-borne commodities comprises wine, and most of that is extra-regional (Campanian, Adriatic, Rhodian and Koan) and only a little comes from Sicilian sources. The imports of Italian and Rhodian wines are well known, but the extent of wine from Dalmatia has not until recently been realised. Some Campana A and B pottery from Campania might have followed in the wake of the massive wine exported from that region to Sicily, but it had stopped by the beginning of the first century BC, when east Sicilian Campana C was the preferred table pottery. That is certainly so at Tindari,[42] but it is not the same everywhere on the north coast. No Campana C reached Termini Imerese, it seems, although its presence is not insignificant at Monte Iato, suggesting that this Syracuse-made table-ware was in fact reaching western Sicily as well. The discovery, however, of local and north Sicilian productions of black gloss fine wares at Caronía suggests that circulation patterns of fine wares in Sicily at this period is more complicated than has hitherto been realised. The data from Caronía shows that Campana C and A is present in almost equal numbers, but the 'Campana A' is not Italian but local: Campanian-produced Campana A imports in the second and first centuries BC took only a small share of the market. The same is true also at Halaesa.[43] A local or at any rate north Sicilian production of Campana A continued in the first century BC.[44]

For the Late Hellenistic period (*c.* 200–30 BC), a very large majority (80%) of the commodities imported in containers consists of wine, predominantly coming from outside the region (Campanian, Adriatic, Rhodian or Koan), together with a little regional (Sicilian) wine; the remaining 20% is represented by Sicilian fish-sauce amphorae, containing *garum* / pickled fish or, much less probably, for olive oil (Fig. 5.1). Perhaps oil in particular, a basic commodity in the Roman diet, was produced locally and / or regionally, and perhaps transported in skins.[45] Very few amphorae intended to carry oil could be identified, just some Dressel 26 and Brindisi containers in the first century BC. Towards the end of the second and throughout the first century BC, Campania becomes the major exporter of wine from Italy, in the West rivalled only by that from the central Adriatic. Pickled fish and *garum* was initially imported from North Africa, but already towards the end of the first century BC, Sicilian Dressel 21 / 22 containers began to be produced, a reflection of a growing north Sicilian fish industry, which seems to have had a significant output, continuing through the first century AD. The dominance of wine-carriers in the assemblages in the Late Republic has been widely attested, and underlines the importance of wine at this period (Fig. 5.1). The first century BC represents the apex of Kale Akte's dependence on extra-regional wine imports, when few local or Sicilian varieties seem to have been available (Fig. 5.3). In sharp contrast, for fine table-wares, our site, like most of Sicily, was independent of extra-regional supplies. Lamps in general needed minimum organisation and investment to produce, and most of those at Kale Akte were made on the island; few Italian lamps reached our site during this period.

Early Imperial period

Relatively little archaeological material has been published in Sicily which dates to the early Imperial period (Fig. 5.12): the best comes from Termini Imerese and Lipari (in general), and from Segesta for amphorae and from Monte Iato and Morgantina for fine ware. The last two publications cover only the Augustan and Julio-Claudian periods, because both towns were either abandoned or in severe decline by *c.* AD 50. From the first century AD, we find evidence for more or less the same products everywhere in Sicily: they came from Italy (wine, thin-walled ware and lamps), North Africa (oil, fish products, lamps), the Iberian peninsula (fish

Plate 1. *View from the south of the Norman castle at Caronía, presumed site of the acropolis of Kale Akte*

Plate 2. *Caronía at sunset*

Plate 3. Caronía, the site of Kale Akte, perched on its rocky hill-top 302 m high, as seen from the west. The remains of the so-called Ponte Romano, of late sixteenth-century date, cross the Fiume di Caronía in the foreground.

Plate 4. Marina di Caronía, aerial view looking north-west

Plate 5 (right). *Marina di Caronía, aerial view showing the position of the ancient settlement (excavation site arrowed) (red); cisterns (blue); the site of the necropolis; and an area of scattered suburban activity (yellow)*

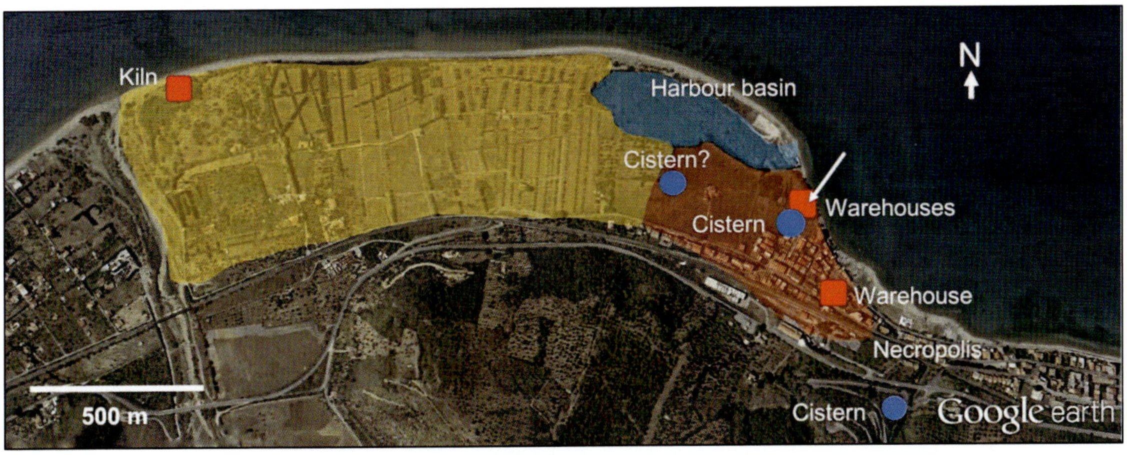

Plate 6 (right). *Caronía, aerial photograph of the modern town, with overlays showing the approximate extent of the ancient town of Kale Akte, the suggested street layout and the site of the* agora *(all in red) and of the necropolis (in yellow)*

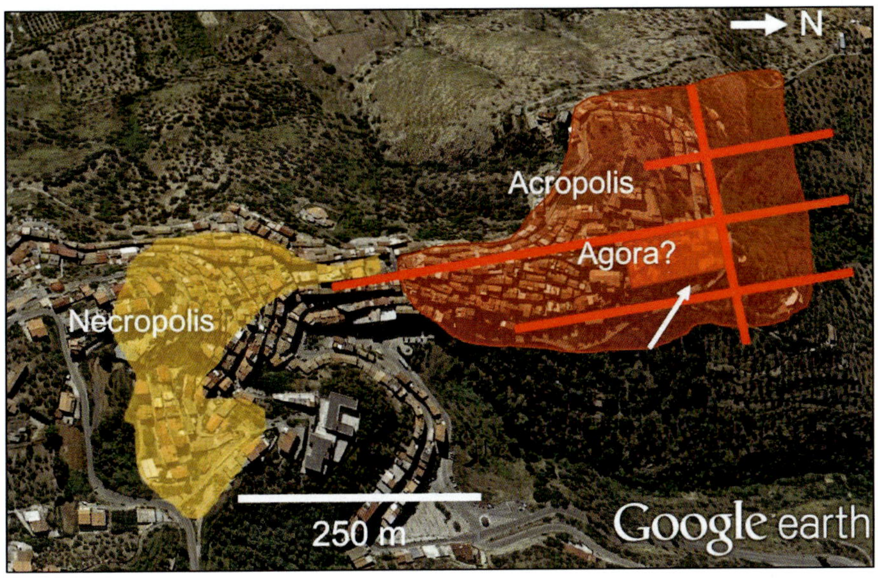

Plate 7 (below). *Halaesa, site of the ancient city from the south-east, with the line of the defensive walls in the immediate foreground and the remains of the* stoa *bordering the* agora *at the centre (under the red roof). The island of Alicudi in the Isole Eolie is visible in the distance.*

Plate 8 (left). *San Marco d'Alunzio, the so-called Temple of Hercules, a small Hellenistic temple (the steps and west wall on the left are original) turned into the church of S. Marco in the high Middle Ages*

Plate 9 (below). *San Marco d'Alunzio, 548 m high, from the north. The summit was crowned by a castle built in 1061, but less remains of it than of its counterpart at Caronía.*

Plate 10 (right). *Caronía, sherds of red-figure Sicilian pottery from a cistern deposit, excavated in 1999; last quarter of the fourth century BC*

Plate 11 (below left). *Caronía, surface find, black-gloss imitation of a medallion bowl, with painted rosette; width 14.4 cm; third century BC*

Plate 12 (below right). *Pompeii, House of Caecilius Iucundus, example of a Dressel 21/22 amphora, of North Sicilian production, found in a shop attached to this property; late first century BC/first century AD*

Plate 13 (left). *Marina di Caronía, Roman cistern, showing the central dividing wall in a double-aisled structure; probably second century AD. Its location is indicated by the southern-most blue circle on Plate 5. Scale: 6 ft.*

Plate 14 (below left). *Marina di Caronía, Roman cistern, the other face of the same structure illustrated in plate 13, showing the use of brick-faced concrete for the walls; the beginning of the barrel-vaulted roof is also visible. Scale: 6 ft.*

Plate 15 (bottom left). *Coin from the mint of Kale Akte depicting a bunch of grapes; late second century BC*

Plate 16 (bottom right). *A tuna-fish vendor, detail of a red-figure bell krater made in Sicily in the early fourth century BC, found in 1864 in a necropolis at Lipari (Cefalù, Museo Mandralisca)*

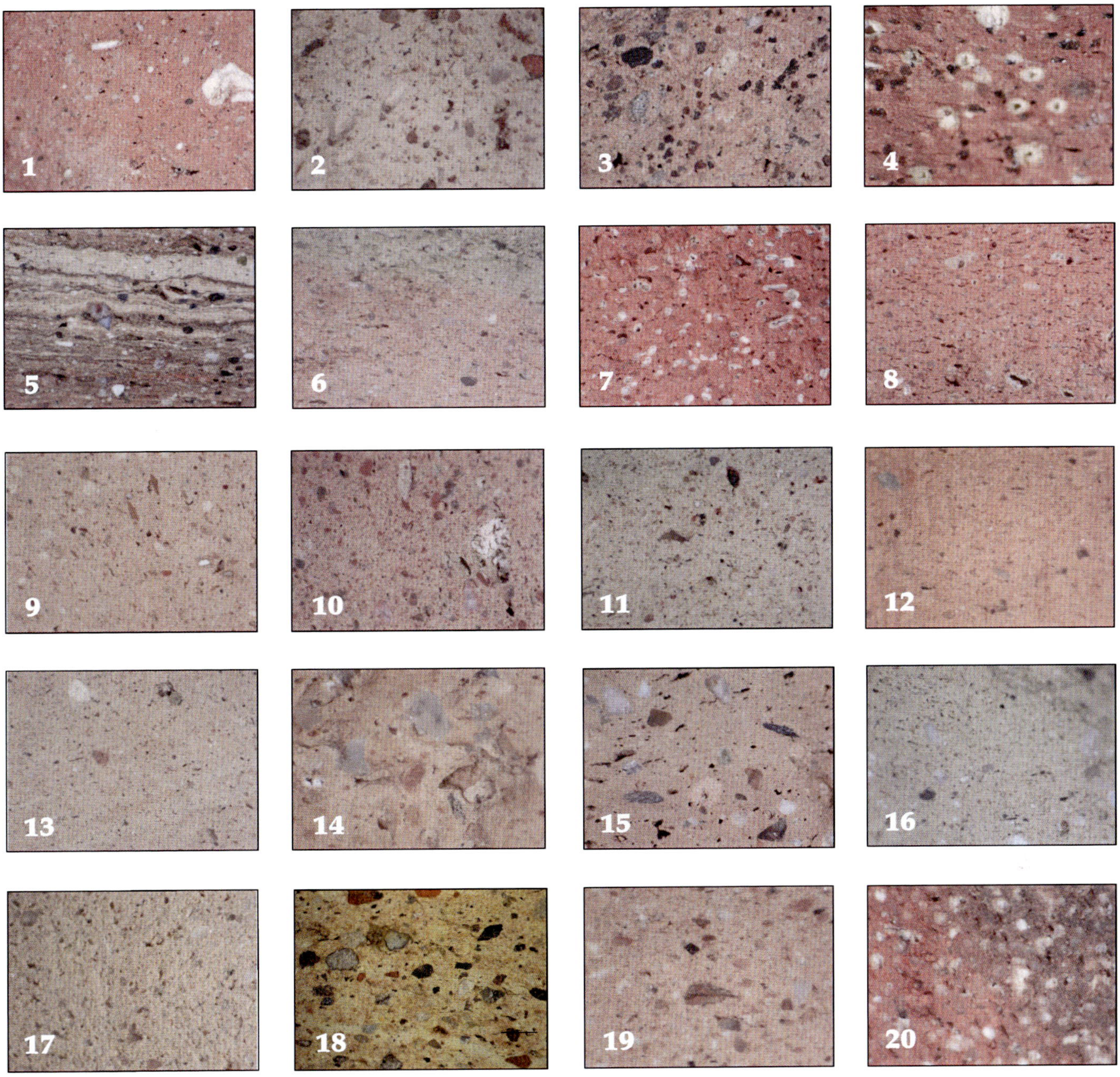

Plate 17, part 1. Amphora fabrics:

1. *MGS II (northern Sicily), fabric catalogue no. 2*
2. *MGS II, MGS III (Locri, Calabria), fabric catalogue no. 3*
3. *MGS V (Ischia, Campania), fabric catalogue no. 4a*
4. *MGS V (Ischia, Campania), fabric catalogue no. 4b*
5. *MGS V–VI (northern Sicily), fabric catalogue no. 5*
6. *Ramón 7.1.2.1 (north-west Sicily?), fabric catalogue no. 9*
7. *Ramón 7.4.2.1-7.4.3.3 / Maña C (Tunisia), fabric catalogue no. 10*
8. *Ramón 7.5.2.1 (Tunisia), fabric catalogue no. 11*
9. *Rhodian (Rhodes), fabric catalogue no. 14*
10. *Koan (Kos), fabric catalogue no. 15*
11. *Koan 2 (Kos), fabric catalogue no. 18*
12. *Knidian (Knidos), fabric catalogue no. 16*
13. *Lamboglia 2 (Vis, Dalmatia), fabric catalogue no. 17*
14. *Dressel 2/4 (central Italy), fabric catalogue no. 19*
15. *Baetican Dressel 20; Haltern 70 (Guadalquivir Valley, Andalucia) fabric catalogue no. 20*
16. *Baetican Dressel 7/11 (Cadiz, Andalucia), fabric catalogue no. 21*
17. *Pélichet 47/Gauloise 4 (Narbonne, southern France), fabric catalogue no. 23*
18. *Richborough 527 (Lipari), fabric catalogue no. 25*
19. *Schöne-Mau 13/Agora G198/ Pompeii 13 (Cilicia/ south-east Turkey?), fabric catalogue no. 26*
20. *Tripolitanian 2/3 (western Libya), fabric catalogue no. 29*

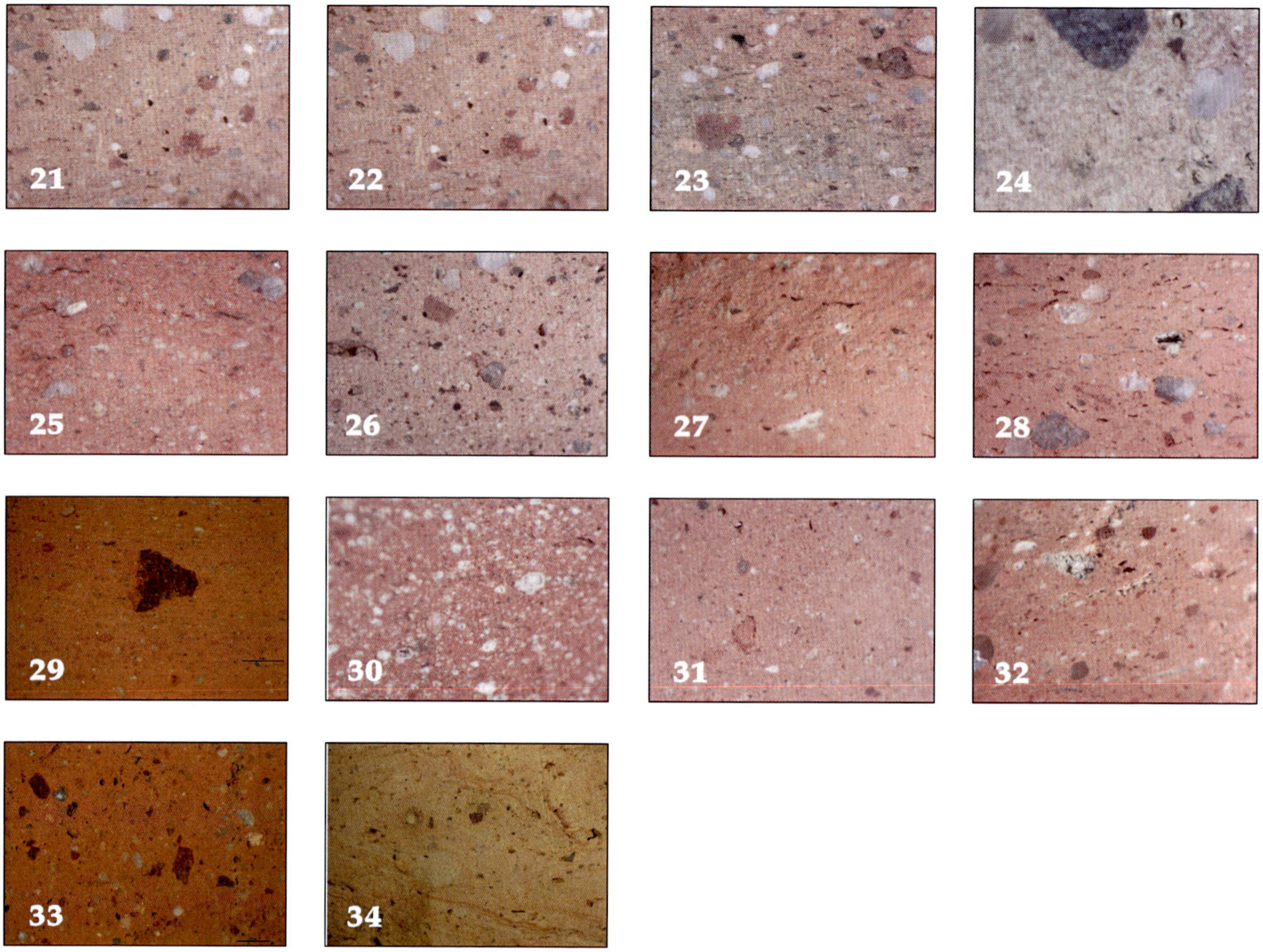

Plate 17, part 2. Amphora and brick fabrics:

21. *MGS III (local), fabric catalogue no. 33*
22. *MGS V–VI (local/northern Sicily), fabric catalogue no. 6*
23. *MGS V–VI (local/northern Sicily)*
24. *Dressel 1A (local), fabric catalogue no. 34*
25. *Dressel 1B (local), fabric catalogue no. 35*
26. *Dressel 2/4 (local, coarse), fabric catalogue no. 37*
27. *Dressel 2/4 (local, fine), fabric catalogue no. 36*
28. *Dressel 21/22 (local/north-western Sicily), fabric catalogue no. 39*
29. *Dressel 21/22 (local/north-western Sicily), fabric catalogue no. 39*
30. *Dressel 21/22 (local/north-western Sicily), fabric catalogue no. 40*
31. *Gauloise 2/3 (local), fabric catalogue no. 41*
32. *Termini Imerese151/354 (local), fabric catalogue no. 42*
33. *Brick (local), fabric catalogue no. 43*
34. *Brick (local), fabric catalogue no. 44*

NOTE: a full description of the above thin-section photographs can be found in the Fabric Catalogue in Appendix 3 (pp. 177–9)

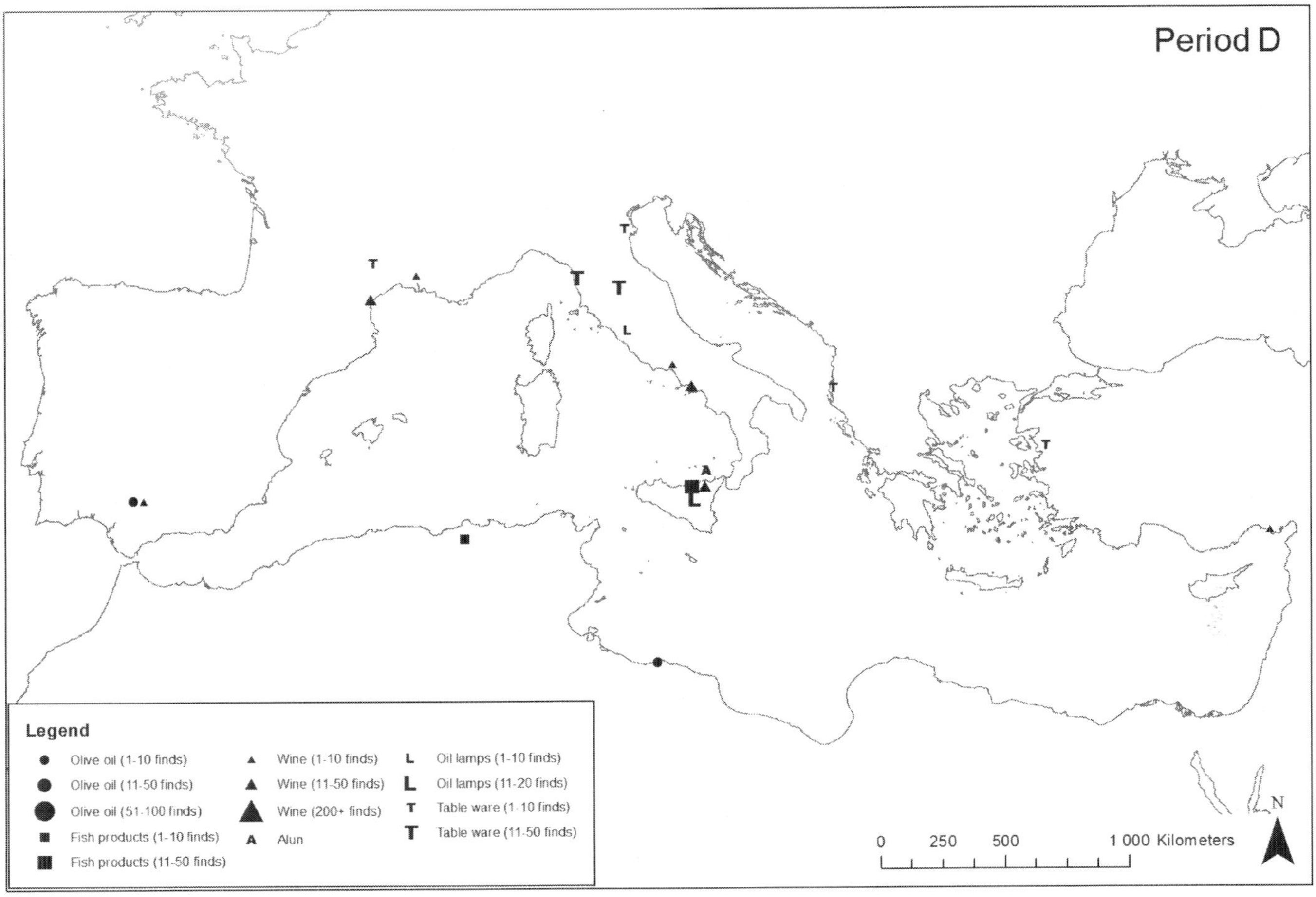

Fig. 5.12 Map illustrating the sources of imported goods, Period D (c. *30 BC–AD 100*)

products, oil, wine), Gaul (wine, *terra sigillata*), the Greek islands (wine), and Syria (*terra sigillata*).

A local wine industry together with the manufacture of containers to carry it was also developing, especially in the north-eastern part of the island. Similar shapes were used everywhere. Sicilian wine in the first and second centuries AD, transported in local versions of Dressel 2/4 amphorae, is known at Lipari and Naxos, and flat-bottomed early Roman amphorae were produced at Naxos. Local production seems to be a phenomenon now in many parts of the island. Dressel 21/22 amphorae, probably containing salted tuna, were manufactured in north-west Sicily, in places such as Alcamo Marina, Termini Imerese and Solunto. A major shift in the supply pattern of lamps (in the opposite direction) comes around the middle of the first century AD, with an increasing market share taken by imported products. The first century AD also represents a major watershed in the supply of fine wares, since from *c.* AD 50 these were, almost without exception, bought in from outside the island. Generally speaking, imports to Sicily were becoming even more uniform than they had been in Period C (the Late Hellenistic), and they came from more diverse and more distant locations than ever before. Sicily was now part of a pan-Mediterranean pattern of trade. From the last decades of the first century BC and throughout the early Imperial period, Empire-wide trade intensified, and products from all over the Mediterranean flood the market. The evidence from Caronía matches this pattern perfectly – wine from Italy, southern Gaul, Spain and the Aegean is present, oil from Tripolitania and Spain (but only in small quantities), fish sauce from Spain in moderate quantity, *terra sigillata*, thin-walled ware and lamps in considerable numbers from Italy, and very small amounts of *terra sigillata* from southern Gaul and Syria. The Caronía material also gives further, more specific information: oil imported from North Africa and Spain, even though in small quantities, has not been much recognised else-where in the island, and we can also confirm a significant local production of wine in imitation Dressel 2/4 amphorae, as well as an industry putting salted tuna in Dressel 21/22 containers, made either at Calacte itself or somewhere else on the north coast not far away. They can be identified as 'local' on grounds of fabric, and represent about a third of all

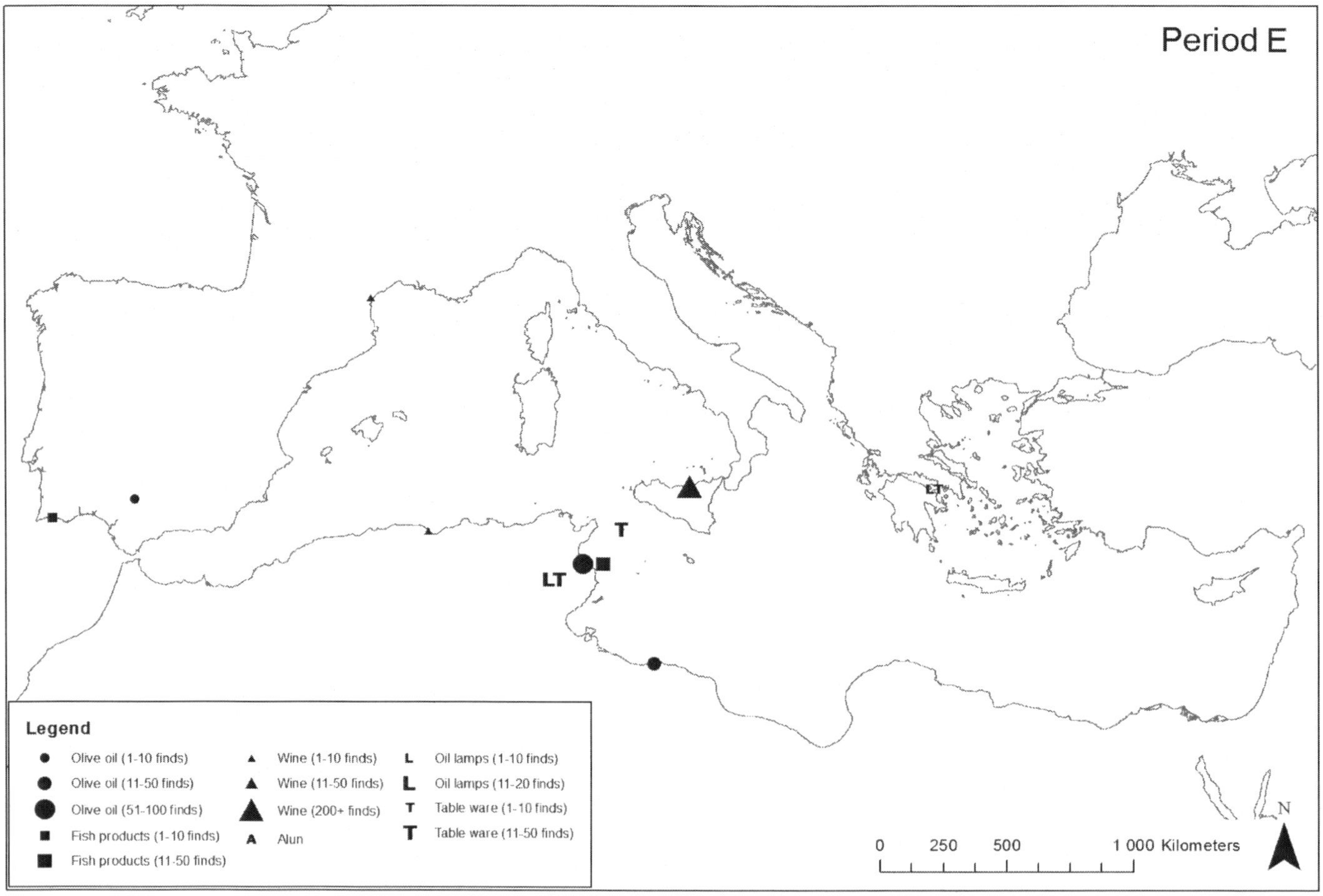

Fig. 5.13 Map illustrating the sources of imported goods, Period E (c. AD 100–500)

early Imperial amphorae. Wine is still the largest category, accounting for almost 60% of the total at this period; an important part of that is made up of local containers, production of which stepped up a gear now. The proportion of fish-sauce arriving from overseas, carried in Spanish amphorae, remains more or less constant. Most oil needs are assumed to have been met from local olive trees, but small amounts of high-quality oil, from Spain, Apulia, and Africa Proconsularis and Tripolitana was also available. Collectively, however, this accounts for a mere 3% of the amphora assemblage.

Mid- and Late Imperial periods

During the time of the middle and late Empire (Fig. 5.13), the market in every corner of the island was completely dominated by North African products, be it in oil, fish products, table pottery or lamps. For the amphorae of this period, little work has been done in Sicily, but the survey by Denaro shows widespread distribution of North African containers all over the island.[46] The publication of urban excavations at Termini Imerese provides the clearest account of the containers in circulation. On lamps, Lipari is well studied, and the necropolis of Sambuco near Caltanissetta is another important source of information. On both these sites North African lamps and the Sicilian Proclus Agyrios type are strongly represented. For wine in the mid-Roman and late Roman period, Sicilians had plentiful sources to choose from in the island itself, and the evidence is growing for production at a number of places of the small and distinctive flat-bottomed container known as the Termini 151/354 type which carried it. Apart from Caronía itself, production of these and closely similar types of amphorae are attested at Termini Imerese (where the 'name-type' comes from, of course), Capo d'Orlando, Furnari and Lipari on the north coast, Naxos, Aci and probably Syracuse on the east coast, and Agrigento and Campanaio (near Heraclea Minoa) on the south coast. More production sites no doubt remain to be found. The type was produced from the end of the third to the fifth or even until the early years of the sixth century AD; it may have been designed to contain the *canon vinarius* for Rome.[47]

The finds from Caronía accord perfectly with the Sicilian picture as a whole. The local production of wine in their own versions of the Termini 151/354 amphorae is further testimony to the huge economic importance of the Sicilian wine industry at this period. The most important contribution of the Caronía material is the quantification of the finds, which indicates both the colossal scale of North African oil import, as well as conversely the very low number of wine imports by comparison with the figures from the early Empire down to *c.* AD 100. The mid- and late Empire shows the most dramatic change (Fig. 5.1). Extra-regional import of oil, in North African Africana 1 and Tripolitana 2 and 3 containers, rises from 3% to an astonishing 71% of the total imports, while that of imported wine drops from about 60% to less than 5%. Gaulish wine probably arrived in modest amounts throughout the second century, and even into the third; most of this trade dates to the first century AD. In all probability, the market share of Campanian Dressel 2/4 amphorae was already in decline by the start of the second century: at Ostia, for example, these containers constitute only some 15% of the total *c.* AD 100/120.[48] During the third century, wine from Mauretania arrives in Keay 1B/Dressel 30 amphorae, but only in small quantities, especially by comparison with other North African imports (Appendix 1, Tables A1.1 and 6). When production of local/north Sicilian salted tuna stopped, imports of extra-regional fish products clearly increased to fill the gap, and account for about 20% of imported mid- and late Roman amphorae.

This period is also characterised by the almost total dependence on African fine ware and lamps (Figs 5.7–8), but for foodstuffs the picture is more mixed. When wine supplies from Italy ceased, local wine production became increasingly important up until the fourth century AD, to the extent that no wine was being imported from elsewhere any more. Local (and Sicilian) oil and fish-sauce production became marginalised, replaced by huge supplies of both from North African sources (Appendix 1, Tables A1.2–3 and 6).

Caronía and the Sicilian shipwreck evidence

Shipwrecks and their cargoes encountered off the shores of Sicily can give us important information on ancient trade routes and the types of goods that were the most commonly transported along them. Equally importantly, they hint at fluctuations in the scale of trade between one period and another. Of course, one must not assume that all cargoes which went down off Sicily's coastline were also intended for a Sicilian market, but in this section I compare amphora types from Caronía with those found on shipwrecks in Sicilian waters, precisely in order to see whether there is a correlation or not between the evidence from the latter and contemporary finds made on dry land (Figs 5.14–15).

The containers most commonly found in Sicilian waters, according to A. J. Parker's comprehensive survey,[49] were the early and later Greco-Italic types (MGS V/VI), Dressel 1A and B, Corinthian A, Lamboglia 2, the North African Africana 1 and Africana 2 forms, and Dressel 2/4 and Aegean Kapitän I and II containers (Fig. 5.14).[50] The Greco-Italic and Dressel 1 amphorae constitute by far the most important category, with twelve cargoes of each in total. A further twenty additional cargoes contained amphorae of either one or both of these types. This corresponds well with the Caronía finds, where these two types are among the most commonly attested imported amphorae. That the Dressel 1C container is much less common than the 1A

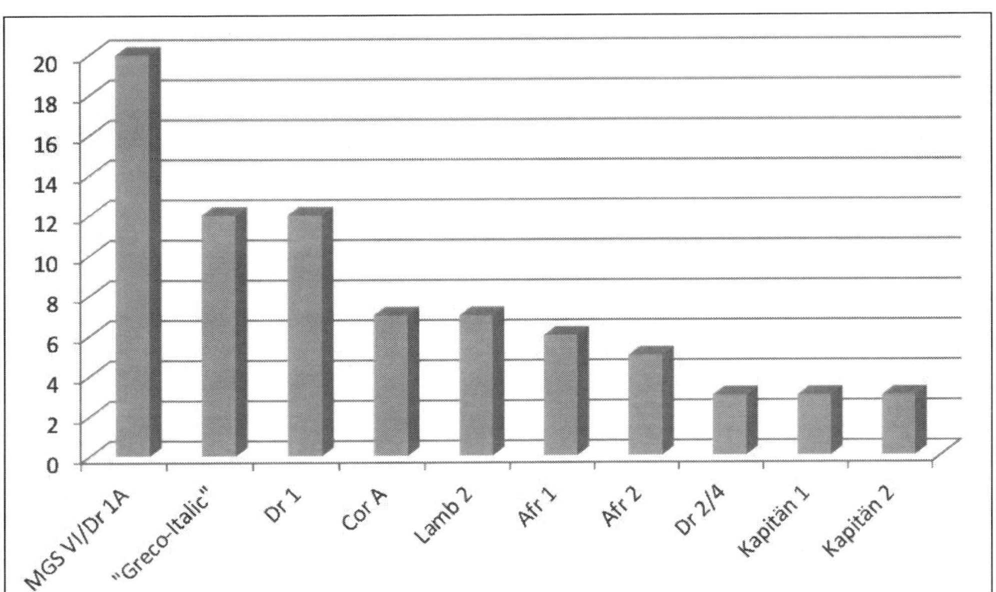

Fig. 5.14 Number of shipwrecks in Sicilian waters with principal cargoes of a specific amphora type

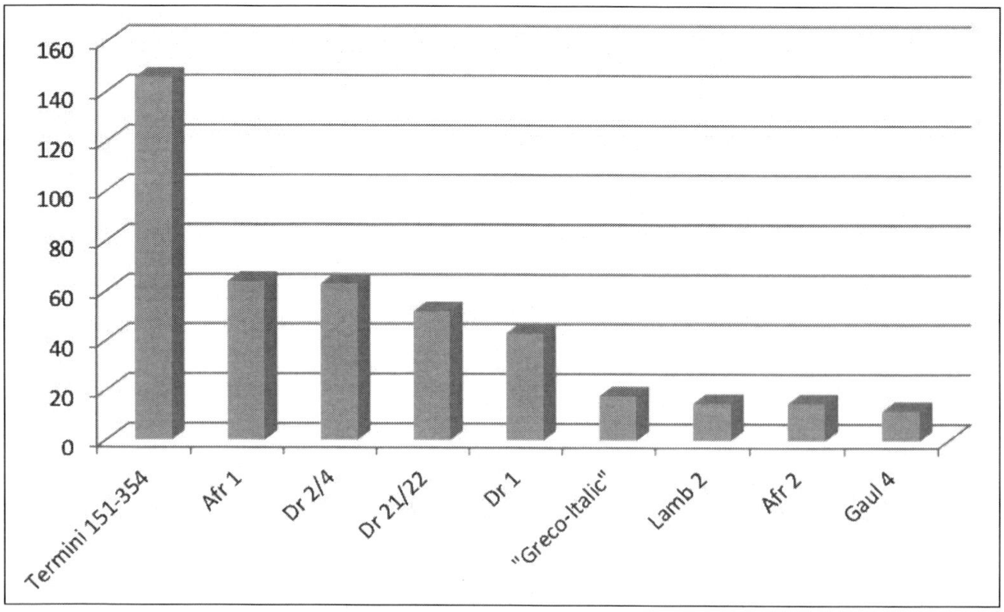

Fig. 5.15 Most common amphora types at Caronía and Marina di Caronía based on the number of finds

and 1B forms can be seen both at Caronía and from the shipwreck record. The Corinthian A and B types were produced for more than 300 years, whereas Lamboglia 2 amphorae, which occur in the same number of wrecks as Corinthian, were circulating for barely 150 years: so a crude count of wrecks containing any one particular amphora has to be considered alongside the longevity of the production-span of each type. Dressel 1 containers are found in even larger quantities than Lamboglia 2 over a similar period of time (a century and a half). If we make an exception for Corinthian A and B types, which are barely represented in our material because of material from the fifth and fourth centuries BC, the overall pattern represented by the shipwreck evidence is comparable with that of the Caronía finds.

The only important group which is poorly represented in shipwreck cargoes by contrast with the Caronía evidence is the Dressel 2/4 type, which appears in only three wrecks: one of these probably carried a Spanish-made version of this form, but they constitute only a small part of a cargo mainly consisting of Dressel 20 oil amphorae (and just one wreck with Campanian Dressel 2/4 containers also on board).[51] The large number of Dressel 2/4 at Caronía is divided into several different productions, most of which were locally made: the Campanian export of Dressel 2/4 to this north Sicilian port was, it seems, not as big as the influx of Dressel 1 containers had been in pre-Augustan times. The low number of Dressel 2/4 wrecks (three) against twelve containing Dressel 1 amphorae may, however, be entirely due to coincidence, in view of the comparatively small statistical sample (126 wrecks). The high share of Lamboglia 2 amphorae among the Late Republican types at Caronía is matched by the high number of shipwrecks carrying these containers. Earlier speculation that Lamboglia 2 amphorae had no market in Sicily[52] can now be decisively rejected on the basis of the finds from Caronía. The large numbers of MGS V and VI (partly or even mostly produced in Sicily), Dressel 1, Africana 1 and Africana 2 were already known from other sites in the island, and their presence at Caronía is not surprising.

There is, however, less agreement on some of the types. Among the categories at Caronía with a moderate percentage of market share is the Gaulish Pélichet 47/Gauloise 4 type. We have no recorded finds of this container in Sicilian shipwrecks, but it is well represented off the Tyrrhenian coast of Italy, and of course along the shores of southern France. The many finds in both areas clearly point to the principal trade route as being between the production centres in southern Gaul and the main consumer, Rome. As witnessed by our finds at Caronía and by those from Carthage, the Gauloise 4 were exported to Sicily and Africa Proconsularis on a regular basis, primarily in the second half of the first and during the second century AD, but also in smaller numbers during the third century AD too.

Tripolitanian amphorae are also poorly attested, with only a single cargo among the Sicilian shipwreck evidence, but they are well represented by many finds at Caronía. The number of wrecks with these cargoes off Sicily and in the Mediterranean in general is much lower than that for ships carrying the Africana 1 and 2 containers,[53] whereas the Caronía figures suggest that Tripolitanian amphorae were the third most plentiful type there, not very far behind Africana 2. That the export of Tripolitanian amphorae north-westwards was commonplace, especially after the beginning of the second century AD, is clear from research conducted at Monte Testaccio in Rome. The apparent scarcity of Tripolitanian amphorae in the shipwreck record is probably the result of the rudimentary knowledge of amphora types when these wrecks were first discovered and published, in the 1960s and 1970s, when large numbers were noted merely as having 'cylindrical amphorae' on board, without further precision.[54]

The most glaring discrepancy between the Sicilian shipwreck record and the results on land is the very large number of Dressel 21/22 amphorae present at Caronía. This is another indication, confirmed by thin-section analyses, that these containers must have been manufactured locally, or if not locally then somewhere else not far away on the north cost of the island.[55] Only two wrecks with this type of amphora is known in the entire Mediterranean, and there is also only two isolated underwater examples elsewhere, both of which lack a certain provenance.[56] The only amphora categories reasonably well represented in Sicilian shipwrecks that are not matched by finds at Caronía are the Kapitän 1 and 2 mid-imperial wine containers from the Aegean. This is all the more remarkable, since amphora material of the second and third century AD is abundant at Caronía, and Kapitän 2 amphorae are widespread all over the western Mediterranean as well as in Sicily, especially on the east coast. The only explanation for their absence at Caronía must be the strong local wine production there in the third century AD, which was of good enough quality to see off the competition of Aegean wines in the local market. A similar situation can be deduced from the finds at Termini Imerese, which also indicate a local production of wine and a complete absence of Kapitän 1 and 2 amphorae.[57]

The few other amphora types which are found in Sicilian shipwrecks but are not represented at Caronía do not add significant fresh information. The few examples of Rhodian horn-handled and Camulodunum 186 wine-carriers from shipwrecks of the first century AD are compatible with the conclusion reached above that Aegean imports to Sicily were limited then, and the Spanish *garum* amphorae (types Beltran 2B and 68) in the first and second centuries AD carried the same products, and came from the same areas, as the Spanish Dressel 7/11 amphorae which are present at Caronía. That an excavation of comparatively limited size, like that at Caronía, cannot give an exhaustive picture of all the amphora types circulating in the Mediterranean over several centuries is obvious, and current lacunae may well be filled by further excavation elsewhere at Marina di Caronía. However, the material studied here is large enough for a good understanding of the frequency of types and the foodstuffs present on the site.

Summary

Production and transportation of goods

Dependence on overseas imports at Kale Akte/Calacte was in general far greater for foodstuffs than for economically less important goods, such as fine pottery or lamps. This was already so by the Early Hellenistic period, when extra-regional wine and fish-sauce had an important role to play in supplying Kale Akte at a time when fine pottery and lamps were being made entirely by regional (Sicilian) workshops. Olive oil must also have been supplied locally. Wine was the most important imported commodity, and many different varieties and qualities were available. Punic fish products were also apparently in high demand.

A connection between the production and export of wine and that of fine table pottery can be seen first in the fourth century BC in Sicily and southern Italy, when there was a parallel Sicilian production of wine (represented by MGS V/VI amphorae) and of red-figure/black-gloss vessels for drinking that wine. In the second century BC these amphorae were replaced by containers imported from Italy, the Campanian, late Greco-Italic and Dressel-1 types, and they in turn were directly linked with imports of Campana B pottery as well as of Central Italian lamps, which were the first Italian products of their type to arrive in Sicily (in the first century BC). Later, in the early Empire, the massive production of Italian red-gloss *terra sigillata* and lamps with highly decorative scenes on the discus, both produced in massive quantities in a number of different Italian centres, is also closely linked with contemporary exports of wine from Campania and central Italy which reached Sicily at the same time. Then, around the beginning of the second century AD, all these Italian products disappear in Sicily at roughly the same moment. A similar fate befell Gaulish *terra sigillata* and the then recently started wine industry of southern Gaul, both of which had a limited impact in Sicily during the first century AD but had disappeared completely from the Sicilian market by the start of the second. The next important wave of imported goods to arrive in the island starts around AD 200, and this saw olive oil, fine wares and lamps arriving from North Africa in colossal quantities, a phenomenon that continues right down into late antiquity.

This clear pattern of ebb and flow between using local or imported goods emerges clearly at Kale Akte throughout the period studied. Of course, sometimes the occurrence of a particular amphora type in a deposit does not automatically imply the presence also of the fine ware that normally (elsewhere) accompanied it. For example, while Campanian wine was imported, Campana A pottery from Ischia was not – not even in the second century BC when wine imports from this region were at their peak. The availability of good-quality Sicilian imitations of Campana A, and of the distinctively Sicilian Campana C pottery, clearly shut out the Campanian pottery from the islands' markets. So the fortunes of the trade in wine and other foodstuffs and of fine-ware production in a particular region were not as intertwined as they were later to become, for example, in the case of North African products between the second and the sixth centuries AD. It can be argued that a successful production and export of wine or other key foodstuffs create an excellent opportunity for other exports, such as fine-ware pottery or lamps, to 'piggy-back' on them, but this depends very much on the level of competition from contemporary locally-made products, and their capacity to create new fashions and new markets for themselves. Scale and quality are the key words here. The scale of production of Italian *terra sigillata* and later of Tunisian-made African Red Slip pottery was vastly greater than that of Campanian black gloss ware, even if at the time the latter was a large industry compared with its contemporary competitors. Apart from scale, the quality of these table wares was also far superior to anything that smaller Sicilian enterprises could produce. The vast output of high-quality pottery from Italy and later North Africa during the imperial period was made possible both by the superior nature of the products and their ability to capture a market which was truly Empire-wide.

Main trends of production and supply

From the many different aspects of production and supply at Kale Akte outlined in this chapter, some key patterns of interest are worth stressing. One of these is the local production of wine, which constitutes a more or less continuous theme from the fourth century BC to at least AD 500, a period of over 800 years. The most intensive production took place between the first and the late fifth centuries AD, when large-scale export overseas is attested. Hand-in-hand with this naturally goes ceramic production, since there was a need for locally-made amphorae to carry the surplus wine and create the export opportunity. The only surplus commodity other than wine, as far as it is visible in the archaeological record, were fish products, which were exported for a period of not more than a century in local versions of the Dressel 21/22 container.

The extra-regional imports, sometimes large-scale and especially of foodstuffs, constitute another long-lasting trend, continuous throughout the entire period studied. The general availability of extra-regional goods and commodities can probably be considered typical for the entire Roman period, but this was not of course the case in the period before or after it. The scale of trade diminished considerably during and after the fifth century AD, as indicated not only by the Caronía finds, but also by a decline at that time in the number of Mediterranean shipwrecks. The high water-mark of life at Kale Akte, at first as an urban settlement and later as a specialised production centre with its own harbour, coincides with the most flourishing period of trade in the Mediterranean. Decreasing trade in late antiquity meant fewer imports, but more significantly the end of surplus wine production at Calacte in the early sixth century AD would have to have led to less cash being available to pay for such imports. The possible silting up of Calacte's harbour at this time may have been a further contributory factor to decline.

Noteworthy trends over shorter periods of time include the change from importing substantial quantities of wine and limited amounts of oil in Period D (*c.* 30 BC–AD 100) to almost no imports of wine but very significant amounts of oil in Period E (AD 100–500). In general, during both periods, there was increasing emphasis on using locally-produced commodities, with the import of goods from elsewhere, even from within Sicily, coming virtuallyto a halt.

The changing patterns outlined here for Kale Akte are very similar to those that emerge from other sites in Sicily and which recur also in what can be gleaned from the shipwreck evidence. Both the north Sicilian micro-region as well as the island as a whole were bound together, already by the fifth century BC, as participants in the same commercial network, connected above all by the sea: the same types of imported and regionally-produced amphorae and pottery are found everywhere. The study of imports, exports and local production at Kale Akte, therefore, reflects to a great extent a similar economy both in the wider micro-region as well as in Sicily as a whole, all sharing similar economic and political conditions, especially after the third century BC. The quantitative analysis from Calacte gives us a valuable insight both into trading links between the north Sicilian coast and elsewhere,and also into central Mediterranean trade as a whole, in which northern Sicily played a small but indispensable part.

6

Trading mechanisms: market and state

In the previous chapter, I discussed patterns of production and supply at Kale Akte in particular and Sicily in general over the period of nearly a thousand years. The account illustrated the fluctuations of change from a dependence in late Hellenistic times on amphora-carried foodstuffs entirely from either elsewhere in Sicily or overseas, to one in the Imperial period which relied on locally made as well as overseas products. In this chapter I turn to the larger economic situation in which that exchange took place, not only in Sicily, but also in the western Mediterranean – and more specifically in the south Tyrrhenian Sea, which connected both Kale Akte and north Sicily on the one hand, and the economically important region of North Africa on the other, with the city of Rome, as well as with Italy and other areas further to the north-west. Only by understanding this wider framework can we begin to appreciate the mechanisms behind economic activity at Kale Akte. The main themes here are the market or markets and the role of the State (or in the imperial period the Empire), and the ways in which, and the extent to which, they interacted and motivated production and exchange – at Kale Akte itself, at other places in Sicily, and in the wider western Mediterranean. The influence of states and empires can be regarded as rhythms in history (Braudel's *conjonctures*), rising and falling, but how can the influence of market behaviour be characterised – was it constant, or did it depend on political forces?

Market behaviour

The debate on the role of the market

Can we speak of a market economy in the Classical and Hellenistic periods? Whereas there is little which contradicts Peter Temin's hypothesis that the early Roman Empire was essentially a market economy,[1] this issue has not been discussed very much when it comes to the economies of the Classical and early Hellenistic Greek periods, and has been overshadowed for far too long by the 'Finley debate'. Finley's *The ancient economy* has been a battleground for nearly fifty years, mainly focussing on the character of the economy, its 'primitiveness' or its modernity. Mikhail Rostovtzeff (1870–1952) based his studies on a wide range of archaeological, textual and epigraphic sources, and viewed the character of the Roman economy as comparable to the modern one, based on industrialism and market economy dominated by a 'bourgeoisie'.[2] This modernistic view also considered long-distance trade as an important characteristic in the Roman economy. This 'old orthodoxy' was replaced in the seventies and eighties of the twentieth century by the 'new orthodoxy', represented by the primitivist school of Moses I. Finley (1912–1986). Finley based his research exclusively on textual sources, and was sceptical about archaeological material as a source for economic history. He viewed the Classical Greek and Roman economies as one – *The ancient economy* – having in common the low level of technology, the dominance of self-subsistence, and the absence of market trade.[3] Finley based his studies on the sociological theories of Max Weber, and inherited much from the work of Karl Bücher, Johannes Hasebroek and certain aspects of Karl Marx.[4]

The main problem with this debate was that it focussed on the question of whether the ancient economy, or rather economies, were similar or different from our own industrialised and capitalistic economy. This debate has naturally been closely tied to the question of the degree to which ancient trade was controlled by the state or was a result of private initiative. Many scholars following in Finley's footsteps have argued that no 'real' market economy existed in the Graeco-Roman world, and any large-scale economic actions can be explained by the preoccupation of the state in securing staple supplies.[5] 'The ghost of Finley is everywhere', lamented Jeremy Paterson in 1998.[6] Archaeology has now more or less buried the ghost forever with the huge amounts of material that have been forthcoming from excavations over the past fifty years, attesting without a shadow of doubt the vast scale and reach of ancient trade, at least during the Roman period. The different sides have now taken up more moderate positions in the modern debate, and they can be divided between the formalists and the substantivists, where the formalists view the ancient economy as a sphere of activity separated from society, and the substantivists regard it as embedded, both socially and politically. The difference between the two streams has been excellently described as being between 'those for whom the modern science of economics is the key to understanding ancient economics, and those for whom the key is anthropology'.[7]

Finley and his followers based their work partly on anthropological ideas, expressed most importantly by Karl Polanyi, that 'models' of pre-modern societies could be made, in which production, distribution and consumption were accomplished only through familial or political relationships. No economic activity could occur that did not have a social basis: the economy was 'embedded' in society.[8] Polanyi divided economic history into three stages.[9] The first, and most primitive, one is represented by the reciprocal economy, which is characterised by gift exchange;[10] the second is the redistributive level, which includes some form of taxation, or a collection of resources brought to a central point. The last and most developed stage, typical for the industrialised, modern age, is the market economy.[11] This framework was later modified by Pryor.[12] He distinguished between exchange and transfer, where the former stands for a system in which goods changed hands in return for others of equal value. Transfers, on the other hand, are one-way transactions, where no return is expected. These systems, of course, correspond respectively to a market economy and to Polanyi's redistributive economy.[13] It must be stressed that all market economies contain both command (the characteristic for a redistribution level, with taxation and allocation of goods by the state) and market behaviour.[14] Concerning the Roman economy, which is usually regarded as showing the characteristics of market behaviour, the question is therefore not whether it had either a 'market' or a 'command' character, but rather determining the nature of the relationship between the two, and the proportion of each in that relationship.

In what follows below, I argue that exchange at Kale Akte took place from the very beginning within the framework of a supply-and-demand-based market economy. I have based my arguments partly on the material from Caronía in particular and from Sicily in general, as discussed in the previous chapters, and partly on general research on the ancient economy. My position will be close to the 'formalist' stand, which acknowledges that the economy was separated from society to a certain degree. I will not discuss here the evidence for a market economy in the early Roman Empire, which has been done very convincingly by Temin.[15] Nor do I see any point in questioning the continued existence of a market economy in the later Roman Empire.[16]

Evidence for market behaviour and exchange in the Classical and Early Hellenistic periods

An area in the study of the ancient Greek economy which has been neglected until recently is the division of labour and its importance for social development and the growth of markets, which for a long time was a central topic for most major economic historians. The influential sociologist Max Weber also considered the specialisation of labour as an important indicator of a market economy.[17] The study of the organisation of labour is of prime importance when trying to understand the differing scales of export and production. Edward M. Harris has collected the evidence for the occupations of individuals in Classical Athens, finding that as many as 170 different ones are mentioned in the sources.[18] This is clearly an indication that Athenian society had extensive 'specification of function', to use a term coined by Weber.[19] Among the occupations, we find those directly linked to commodities and goods produced and imported to Kale Akte: the *amphoreaphoros* (amphora-carrier), the *amphoreapoios* (amphora-maker), the *heduoinoi* (sellers of sweet wines), the *luchnopoles* (lamp-seller), the *oinopoles* (wine-seller) and the *tarichopoles* (seller of salted fish), for example. Also mentioned in the sources are the *arguramoibos* (money-changer) and the *trapezites* (banker).[20]

The specialisation of labour, Weber's 'specification of function', was considered by him typical of medieval cities by contrast with ancient cities, which according to him would have had an economy built on the non-specialised labour of the *oikos*.[21] 'Specification of function' means that one item is produced by the same worker, independent of the different technical stages of production, and stands in contrast to 'specialisation of function', which implies that many different skills or work-roles are involved in the preparation of a product.[22] It seems that specialisation of labour was a common phenomenon already in the Classical period, since Plato clearly offered insights into the relationship between it and the growth of the market.[23] It can be argued from the evidence that we possess, both textual and archaeological, that Greek and Roman economies had a considerable degree of 'specification of function'. Due to a low technological level in antiquity, however, 'specialisation of function' (also called 'vertical' specialisation) was low by comparison with modern society. This does not mean that it did not exist: many products, pottery for example, were the result of the work of specialists.

The commodities transported by amphorae (wine, oil and fish products) represented the final stage of a long process consisting of many steps. If we take wine as an example, it was the final product of the planting, cultivating, picking, pressing, and fermenting of the grapes, which was then poured into amphorae specifically made for it by specialised potters. This production was, however, achieved by quite simple means within the *oikos*. For the production of wine, all that was needed was a rack for drying the grapes, basins or *pithoi* for the fermentation, and a press.[24] Wine could therefore be easily produced by just one person, without the involvement of specialised labour. Olive-oil production would have been similar,[25] as also fish-salting; fishing itself was an activity which could be and was done on an *oikos* level.[26] At the moment, however, when the final product was to be packed into amphorae and sold, a higher form of organisation was necessary, which involved potters and *negotiatores*. The selling of commodities in amphorae presupposed specialised occupations like those listed above. The production of amphorae and pottery and the sale of these commodities are difficult to imagine outside a society which had very considerable specialised labour.

A central concept in any discussion concerning the motivating forces behind trade is profit, in Greek *kerdos*.[27] This word is known in several contexts from the Archaic period onwards, and constitutes an important indication that the late Archaic economy was not foreign to individual commercial enterprise.[28] Aristotle wrote of *allagé*, 'commercial exchange', and considered that the new 'moneyed mode of acquisition' was due to the businessmen who were motivated by considerations of profit.[29] Cohen has no doubt that Aristotle described a system where production, distribution and consumption were controlled by a supply-and-demand pricing mechanism.[30] The writings of Xenophon also constitute an important witness of the outspoken strife among Greek *emporoi* to achieve profit.[31] The most obvious way to satisfy the desire for *kerdos* was to sell off agricultural surplus on a market.[32] The primitivist view, that the *oikos* and the self-sufficient farmer were the norm in antiquity, has dominated for a long time, but it seems increasingly clear that farmers of small- and middle-sized estates were also dependent on the markets both for certain commodities that they needed, and in order to sell their surplus.[33] By the Hellenistic period, Italian farmers were certainly dependent on the market. Its importance is well illustrated by the writings of Cato, who reported sample contracts for the sale of olives, grapes and wine by the mid-second century BC.[34] Temin has argued that Cato acted in order to earn money within a market economy; his behaviour was not 'command' or 'customary'.[35] It is clear that the aristocracy and the merchant class combined their interests in commerce, contrary to a long-held view that aristocrats did not engage in trade.[36] This can be inferred from the *Lex Claudia* of 217 BC, which did not allow any senator, or his son, to own a ship that could carry more than 300 amphorae.[37] Senatorial economic activity in large-scale trade is above all confirmed by amphora stamps bearing the names of famous Roman *gentes*.[38]

That the Sicilian economy was one possessing market behaviour already by the time of the Roman conquest of the island in the third century BC can be argued also from what we know of the taxation system, the *decuma*. The right to collect the *decuma* was auctioned off every year in Syracuse, and the collector would buy the *decuma* from a certain city, hoping that he could negotiate a good price in order to make a profit.[39] A clearer allusion to an economy based on pricing is difficult to find, and since the *decuma* itself went back at least to the time of King Hieron,[40] this way of organising its collection may also have gone back to that period.

Exchange can be achieved by means of barter, money or credit, of which barter can be considered the original and most ancient form.[41] There is little doubt that money was introduced as a means to measure and compare values more easily, something acknowledged by Aristotle.[42] One of the most crucial characteristics of a market economy is its monetarisation.[43] This is a difficult notion, the meaning of which has rarely been defined precisely by scholars who deal with ancient Greek and Roman economies.[44] This is not the place to discuss the matter; I have here simply considered a monetarised economy as an economy where coins can be supposed to have been used to a high degree in daily exchange. Henry Kim has argued that the Greek economy was monetarised to a certain extent already from the birth of coinage in the Archaic period, since small denominations for day-to-day exchange were minted from the beginning.[45] It has been pointed out that the Agora, the market place of Greek cities, developed at the same time as, or shortly after, the adoption of coinage.[46] The Greek world was certainly monetarised to some degree already by *c.* 400 BC, and with the start of bronze coinage in the late fifth century, small-scale retail trade was given a formidable boost. We do not, of course, expect rural exchange to have been monetarised to any significant extent, but at a coastal town like Kale Akte, it is reasonable to assume that coins were used to some extent in daily exchange by the fourth century BC. That bronze coins were in use in large quantities in the late Classical period in Sicily is not in doubt, and of the nearby towns Halaesa was minting its own bronze coinage from around 340 BC.[47] These were clearly not used for extra-regional transactions, since they hardly ever travelled outside Sicily.

In addition, lending of money from banks or individuals for commercial enterprises is another criterion of a market economy, and a further development of a monetarised economy.[48] Edward Cohen has made a thorough analysis of money-lending in Classical Athens, concluding that bankers did lend money at interest.[49] It seems increasingly clear that loans were productive and were taken to achieve commercial goals, since already in the late Classical period there is plenty of evidence for loans being made to finance ship cargoes.[50]

That therefore an economy with market 'behaviour' existed in the Greek world during the Classical and Early Hellenistic periods is based on four considerations, that there existed:

Specialisation in and division of labour

Profit as a driving force behind trade (as attested by literary evidence)

The existence of an economy built on pricing

The use of money and the existence of banking and credits for commercial enterprises

The late Archaic trading post at Kale Akte

Although late Classical Athens certainly had the prerequisites for an economy with market behaviour, it is a far cry in the fifth and fourth centuries BC from the metropolis Athens to the small settlement of Kale Akte. Hardly any coastal Sikel settlements or market places are known in Sicily in the fifth century BC: harbours had usually been already occupied by Greeks (and in the west by Carthaginians).[51] The site at Marina di Caronía might have functioned in the first half of the fifth century BC, in the words of Polanyi, as a 'port of trade',[52] a 'gateway community' or, to borrow a phrase from anthropology, a 'middle ground'.[53] The last implies a place where different cultures and influences met and merged, and where it becomes impossible to place a convenient label such as 'Greek' or 'Sikel', since the character of the settlement was something different, a hybrid. As a 'gateway community' or 'middle ground', the small trading post at Marina di Caronía would have introduced Greek goods, ideas and customs to the Sikel communities which were (supposedly) located on the hill of Caronía, as well, a little further inland, at Pizzo Cilona. In this bilateral exchange, economic interests were more important than the cultural differences between Sikels and Greeks: it marked the beginning of a profound Hellenising process in the area.[54]

This trading post has recently been characterised as an *emporion*,[55] and I myself used this term in my 2006 dissertation. It is, however, a term often used with little or no attempt at defining what it means. An *emporion*, in the classical Greek meaning of the word, was a trading community founded by Greeks and exclusively Greek in character. It usually had defensive walls, both to protect it from a potentially hostile indigenous population nearby, and as a status symbol to underline the exclusiveness of the settlement. It seems highly unlikely that the pre-Ducetius port com-munity at Marina di Caronía was exclusively Greek. It was certainly without defences and must have been very small. This part of the north coast was wild and mountainous, inhabited only by Sikels. It is inconceivable that those living here would have lacked any interest in commerce and trade, and it seems equally unlikely, therefore, that Greek merchants would have been able to construct a community of their own at such a strategically important site without any fortifications to shield them from potential attack. But Greek merchants could probably have traded with Sikel inhabitants here and even lived alongside them without having to found an *emporion*. If we suppose that it was mainly merchants from Zancle (Messina) who were the first to come here, we can compare Kale Akte with the formal settlements founded by Zancle – at Mylai (Milazzo) well to the east, and at Himera much further to the west – both of which were founded at highly strategic locations. The foundation of an *emporion* would only have been in the interest of Greek merchants if the area possessed resources which were particularly important from a commercial point of view. The forests and their timber would have been our area's greatest asset, but it would have been easy to procure timber also from the *chorai* of, for example, Mylai and Himera. Rather, it would have been in the interest of Greek merchants to trade with the Sikels on relatively neutral terms in a port community, like that at Marina di Caronía, which was probably a kind of small-scale 'gateway community'.[56]

A substantial settlement at Marina di Caronía in late Archaic and Classical times can surely be ruled out, although some modest infrastructure would have been necessary to provide port facilities and support its activities. Lacking fortifications, it would not have been a safe place for habitation until settled conditions were established after the Roman conquest, and in particular after the Second Punic War. Then began a period of *pax Romana* which lasted for some seven centuries.

It was, therefore, the probable character of a 'neutral' trading environment and peaceful commercial exchange here which attracted Ionian Greek settlers in the early fifth century BC, and later the ethnically mixed settlement of Ducetius. If Greek settlers early on had tried to impose themselves by force and founded an exclusively Greek-style *emporion*, good will would have been in short supply among the Sikels already living in the area.

Kale Akte was situated at the intersection between the natural east–west road corridor along the north coast, and one of the few river valleys that pierced through imposing mountains and provided limited access to the interior. Precipitous mule tracks also provided routes through and across the Nebrodi (see p. 39). It was in short an ideal position for a 'gateway community'.[57]

It seems likely that Greek *emporoi* (traders) regularly frequented the port at Marina di Caronía from the sixth century BC onwards, if not earlier. It could have been these pioneer merchants who furnished the Samians and Miletians with information about Kale Akte as a suitable site for a settlement. The mere idea of a *synteleia* (a joining together of communities) here must have been only possibly if the territory had already become quite Hellenised. If some people from Corinth had settled at Kale Akte, there may have been direct contacts for a time with that major trading city. However, even if such privileged links had not been established, large quantities of Aegean goods would have arrived anyway, as it had for already half a century in other parts of Sicily, as we have seen. Kale Akte was, with or without the Corinthians, part of a wider Greek trade network, with both city-states and much smaller settlements interconnected through market exchange. This was a result of the close connections between colonies and the Greek motherland. In the words of Horden and Purcell, 'the Mediterranean colony is a direct manifestation of the maritime *koine*: it is always part of a seaborne network, a bridgehead of the easily navigable world in a different social medium, or a gateway settlement where two societies – and their economies – come face-to-face'.[58]

Kale Akte would have been a redistribution point for Attic pottery and other Aegean imports into the Nebrodi area in the fifth century, since it was the only settlement on the sea in the entire micro-region; in addition, from the time of Ducetius' foundation onwards, it also had a partly Greek population. As we have seen earlier, historical event and the wider trend cannot be separated; the historical event, the settling of Kale Akte, was significant because within a short time it became the focal centre of the micro-region with increased levels of trading activity, a natural consequence of the phenomenon of the so-called 'Greek colonisation' movement in Archaic and Classical times. Even without the foundation of Ducetius, Kale Akte might well have developed with time into some sort of trading centre because of its favourable location – growing gradually with a series of minor settlement 'events' when new groups arrived and inhabited the site, rather than through one big foundation event enacted by an *oikistes*.

The trade between Greeks and the first Sikels at Marina di Caronía was one between two different socio-political structures.[59] We know very little of the structure of Sikel communities, other than that, by the end of the sixth century BC, they were exposed to Greek artefacts, foodstuffs and customs; presumably the tastes of the Sikel aristocracy would have been an important stimulus in this trade.[60] To the Sikels, Greek products had the character of exotica, at the start only available to wealthy élites, who were keen on absorbing the Hellenic life-style;[61] but with increased availability they became accessible to a broad cross-section of society, at least by the late sixth century BC. Tamar Hodos has suggested that the new custom of wine drinking in Iron-Age communities, for example, was a short-cut for ambitious individuals to win a more influential and powerful position in society.[62] How can this trade be characterised? We are certainly not dealing with a transfer economy, since tributes or taxes would imply Greek political control of Kale Akte and the north Sikel settlements – something which is neither plausible nor suggested by the sources. The presence of Greek imports is the clearest evidence against such a hypothesis, since the definition of this category is that it is a one-way transfer without return (the latter meaning, in this case, the Sikels transferring taxes or paying tribute to the Greeks). A gift-exchange system can also be excluded, since the Greek economy did not work in that way, and in any case it was one that presupposed, as its name suggests, some kind of reciprocity.[63] We have considered Marina di Caronía in the Archaic and early Classical period as a small 'gateway community', implying some sort of exchange between two quite different societies in a relatively neutral environment.[64]

The harbour at *contrada* Pantano to the west of the Archaic centre of Marina di Caronía was not a traditional Sikel-type settlement; Sikels normally lived on hill-tops. The shore-side village was by contrast open to the sea and undefended. A neutral area excludes any forms of customary economic behaviour, and the law of supply and demand is the most likely to predominate, since the latter is independent of social and cultural customs. That Greek goods reached the Sikels illustrates the fact that both ethnic groups turned outwards, beyond the *oikos*, in search of goods and commodities. Like the Athenian citizen who went to the Agora, the Greek *emporos* or Sikel merchant at Marina di Caronía left the informal rules of *philia* (their customary behaviour) at home and entered the world of the market where their main preoccupation was *kerdos* – getting a bargain and making a profit.[65] The scale of relatively low-value imports to indigenous sites that were more difficult to reach, such as Monte Iato (25 km inland), also points to the impossibility of a gift-exchange economy. The character of trade at Kale Akte, and of its trading contacts during the Classical period, can probably best be compared with that of well-explored indigenous sites such as Monte Iato[66] and Montagna di Ramacca,[67] but Marina di Caronía was much better situated for trade in being located on the sea.[68] Considering the large scale of Greek imports even at the more isolated Sikel inland sites, it is clear that a coastal trading post such as Kale Akte with its good communications would have been an important point of entry and transmission for such imports.

How then did exchange take place at Kale Akte? It is obvious that barter must have been the means by which the first exchanges happened in the sixth century BC, and gradually money would have become part of that exchange after Greeks settled at Kale Akte as part of Ducetius' foundation in 446 BC. As mentioned above, it seems that the initial use of coinage in the Greek world was intimately connected with the birth of a market place. The items offered by the Sikels of Kale Akte in exchange for Greek manufactured goods are impossible to determine from the archaeological data that we possess, but it is generally assumed to have been raw materials.[69] A look at Kale Akte's natural resources gives some indication of them, most obviously forests and livestock.[70] Timber for shipbuilding was easily transported from the hillsides to the sea, and animal hides and wool were in high demand among the Greeks.[71]

The position of Kale Akte as a 'gateway community' between Greeks and Sikels, therefore, is of crucial importance for the understanding of the nature of the earliest exchanges that took place there. Gift-exchange, normally practised within closely related societies, can, as we have seen, be excluded. A state-directed transfer economy is also ruled out because the Greeks did not have political control of the Sikels in the area. Using the terminology discussed by Polanyi and Pryor, we can thus suggest (by means of exclusion) that it was the supply-and-demand model that was the principal factor shaping trade at Kale Akte in the earliest period. The law of supply and demand is present in all societies which have reached a certain basic level of economic development. The urge to 'make a bargain' or to gain the best possible material advantage would have been the reason why both Greek and Sikel traders were attracted to the trading post at Kale Akte. This 'economic' mentality is part of human nature. It had always existed side by side with the gift economy in Bronze Age and Iron Age societies. Such an enduring mentality, which does not alter over millennia, can be regarded as part of the *longue durée*, since it is not affected by changing trends or historical events. Increasing wealth in the late Archaic period probably intensified the search for economic gain. There can be no doubt that, throughout the period studied, which stretches over a millennium, economic gain for individuals was the driving force in most of the trading transactions which took place at Kale Akte.

Production, consumption and demand

The organisation of production is, as we have seen above, a crucial key to the understanding of an economy. What can the scale of production and its variations over time tell us about the scope of that production? The patterns presented in Chapter 5 show with clarity the development from a dependency on small- to medium-sized regional (i.e. Sicilian) production in the Hellenistic period, to an increasing amount of large-scale extra-regional (i.e. overseas) products beginning with the Roman takeover of the island, and ending with the complete domination of such produce (some of them now also locally made) in the Imperial period. Local production at Kale Akte can be divided into two main stages – the first, small in scale, and the later, considerably larger, especially in the late Imperial period. Beginning in the fourth century BC, it is certain that the manufacture of wine amphorae, and later in the third century BC of bricks, kitchen ware and figurines, is evidence of a specialised production, at least by the late Classical and early Hellenistic periods. The production of wine and pottery in Hellenistic Kale Akte, and probably elsewhere on the north coast, was certainly on a rather limited scale, aimed first at micro-regional customers and then by extension at the wider Sicilian market. The small scale of the production of amphorae and pottery could have been limited to a few urban *maison-ateliers,* but might also have been practised in independent rural establishments in te neighborhood; if the latter, they were doubtless sited not far from the urban area, in other words with good connections to the sea and the harbour.[72] These workshops also produced bricks, roof-tiles, kitchen wares and other pottery for local consumption.[73]

This beginning of specialisation in the production and export of wine at Kale Akte can be connected with the increasing scale of trade in the Tyrrhenian area, and the growing importance of the north coast's part in this during the late fifth and fourth century BC. The availability of more and more different kinds of goods and commodities led to the creation of urban settlements, which in their turn increased demand. That same growth created a need for specialization to an increasing degree. The perfect opportunities available on the Sicilian north coast for both grape growing and the manufacture of pottery made the choice of produce in which to specialise easy: wine. In the Hellenistic and Late Republican period, there are signs that Sicilian production was often organised on a *polis*-level, although not directed as such by the State.[74] The stamps found occasionally on tiles and amphorae are interesting documents for our knowledge of the organisation of production. Those on bricks and tiles from both Kale Akte and Halaesa clearly indicate an organisation of ceramic production by the *polis* at this time.[75] Some *ateliers* may have had kilns for amphorae, roof tiles and pottery in the same establishment (since different kilns are normally needed for each product), and it is probable that this production was also organised within the framework of the *polis*.[76] However, although a few Sicilian and south Italian amphora stamps bore the name of the *polis*,[77] none in the West show any of the 'official' character that those of Rhodes and other important Aegean wine-producing centres display. The names on stamps in Sicily are mainly ordinary Greek ones, probably that of the producer of the amphora, the owner of the *officina*, or the owner of the estate where the wine was produced.[78] None of the stamps on wine amphorae belonging to the period between the fourth and first centuries BC implies anything official or state-related. As a matter of fact, few of the Greco-Italic MGS IV, V and VI amphorae produced in Sicily seem to have been stamped at all, since most name-stamps on Greco-Italic containers are now known to be Campanian.[79]

It has been proposed that the occurrence of stamps on amphorae might indicate a higher level of organisation.[80] When discussing the involvement of the *polis* in production, it is difficult not to say a few words about the role of the 'producer-city'. The example of Kale Akte shows how difficult it is to divide city from countryside. Even though the hill-top at Caronía was occupied by an urban settlement in the Hellenistic and very early Imperial periods, production most probably took place at Marina di Caronía, close to the road system and the sea – part of the *polis/civitas*, but in character more like a *vicus* than a *civitas*, and physically separated from the latter.[81] Nevertheless Kale Akte is an example of how even the smallest *polis* or *civitas* was involved in production of a surplus aimed for export.

Vandermersch has stressed that the expansion of viticulture in Sicily and in Magna Graecia in the fourth and third centuries BC was not a result of expanding estates or increasing wealth, but rather of a larger number of people getting access to land.[82] We know that in Sicily during the Classical and Hellenistic periods – and certainly this is true of the forested and rugged Nebrodi area – the small- to medium-sized farm was the norm in rural settlement.[83] Large estates based on slave labour were a not common phenomenon in all parts of Sicily during the early Hellenistic period, and there is nothing to suggest that production at Kale Akte then would have involved slave labour. These indications suggest a limited produce output that is unlikely to have reached outside the region. The availability of local wine was not in itself sufficient, in either quality or quantity, to satisfy the needs of the inhabitants (other wines were being imported at the same time), a further indication that local production was not on any considerable scale. This stands in marked contrast with the later Imperial period, when only small amounts of wine (or even at times none) was imported.[84]

In the larger cities of Hellenistic Sicily with good conditions for growing vines, a larger scale of wine production can be expected, but it need not have been organised very differently. The distribution of Sicilian pottery outside the island, albeit in modest amounts, might suggest that some of the more important of the island's wines in the fourth and early third centuries BC were being exported outside Sicily and that pottery was accompanying it. If that is correct, it was not on anywhere near the scale of the Campanian producers, because imported containers from there dominate the Sicilian wine market at this time.[85] Some of the most important producers of surplus wine between the fifth and third centuries BC were Gela, Kamarina, Naxos and Messana, all of which produced their own amphorae.[86] Although several Sicilian wines were famous, like the *Mamertinum*, *Tauromenium*, *Naxios* and *Murgantinum*, and are mentioned in the ancient sources, we still have surprisingly little clear evidence of the type of amphorae that was carrying this and other wine outside Sicily during the fourth and third centuries BC.[87] On the whole Sicily at that time seems to a large extent to have been focused in and on itself, economically speaking, and this is not contradicted by the evidence from Caronía.[88]

The size of the *polis* and its *chora* determined to a large extent the scale of the output. Kale Akte can be seen to be among the smallest towns, towards the bottom on the scale of production, with larger *poleis* in the middle, and even larger civic entities, controlling huge territories, at the top. All producers had a single goal: they were all trying to sell surplus goods on the market, to make a profit and generate more wealth.

Taking production of amphorae as an indicator of market behaviour means that we must consider the law of supply and demand when trying to understand the driving forces behind production. To what demands and consumption habits were producers reacting?[89] The most important wine-making cities were powerful *poleis* with vast *chorai*, located by the sea and well placed for overseas export. The initial production of wine at Kale Akte and Halaesa in the late fifth and fourth centuries BC must have been the result of a need to supply the inhabitants of growing towns with good-quality *oinos*: their inhabitants were now eager to display a deeply Hellenised life-style, but also had an interest in selling their produce for profit. From this very period, there are multiple signs of an intensification in wine-drinking,[90] which shows that this activity was becoming increasingly popular, one that was no longer restricted to the aristocracy alone. This trend is intimately linked with what Vandermersch called *mouvements démocratiques*, i.e. the distribution of land and extension of civic rights to large groups of people.[91]

In the years around 300 BC, an increase in demand is one explanation for the rapid development of Campania. It is precisely in this period also that Rome's population increased greatly. It is thought to have doubled from around 30,000 in the middle of the fourth century BC to 60,000 around 300 BC, and to have exceeded 90,000 by the time of the war with Pyrrhus (280–75 BC)[92] – in other words a three-fold expansion in the very short period of seventy-five years. The consequent massive increase in the Roman market base, and the prospects of trade for any region with the capacity and the capability to tap into it, was an important reason why Campanian wine, principally directed towards Rome, also arrived in some quantity at Kale Akte and Sicily already during the reign of Agathocles, before, that is, the First Punic war.[93] This development is intimately connected with the same phenomenon of the 'democratisation' of wine-drinking throughout southern Italy and Sicily, which was becoming part of an increasingly uniform cultural *koine* across the whole of the Greek West.[94]

The shift from an economy based on small- to middle-sized production to a villa economy based on slave labour had clearly by the later second century BC become established in some parts of Sicily, but this process had taken place earlier in Campania and elsewhere in the Italian peninsula.[95] Wealthy patricians with substantial estates and large-scale production were certainly present in Sicily by the end of the third century BC,[96] no doubt specialising mainly in grain. From the ancient sources we know of the importance of Sicilian grain to Rome at this period, but there is scarce evidence for large-scale contemporary wine production. In Campania a dramatically increasing population and increasing wealth, stimulated by demands for its produce from outside Campania, saw not only massive exports of wine, but the creation especially in the second century of large estates which were well on their way to becoming the type of large-scale production centres exemplified by the *villa catonienne*.[97] The Roman villa phenomenon has been compared with modern colonial 'plantations' of the eighteenth and nineteenth centuries, and it is clear from the ancient sources that they were expected to be highly profitable, partly through the exploitation of slave labour.[98] As Carandini has put it, villa agriculture was inconceivable without slave labour and the context where slaves were able to achieve their full economic potential.[99] The most important implication of the 'slave mode of production' was the intensive, large-scale production for a market, and so an obvious indication of 'market behaviour'. In the Nebrodi area, large villa estates certainly did not exist at any stage during the Hellenistic period – and even in the Imperial period they seem to have been the very rare exception rather than the rule.[100] The increased production of wine at Kale Akte in the first century AD and later in the fourth and fifth centuries AD was probably generated by an increasing number of medium-sized estates rather than by the creation of a few huge ones.

Large-scale production of wine at Kale Akte, and probably at other centres along the north coast, as well as at Lipari (from the first century AD), must however be seen in the framework of the increasing number of farms and villas in Sicily in the Late Republican and early Imperial periods.[101] It formed part of a production of agricultural surplus, and of amphorae and pottery, that started to change at Kale Akte by the beginning of the Imperial period.

Not all surplus production for export was organised within the framework of the 'villa' economy, however. The fishing industry, for example, was a more specialised one than that of wine and oil, products derived from plants and trees which normally were inter-cultivated with other crops (often grain).[102] The salting installations investigated on the Sicilian north coast do not seem anywhere to have been directly connected with villas.[103] However, many fish-salting installations elsewhere in the Mediterranean were connected with maritime villas.[104] This need not imply an aristocratic involvement in that business, however, as it was socially frowned upon, and Robert Curtis pictures the owners of fish-salting installations as normally freedmen (or occasionally free-born), who could achieve moderate, even considerable wealth from such business activities – sometimes enough to allow their sons to become members of the municipal élite.[105] The fish-salting production at Kale Akte and its micro-region was probably therefore organised by private individuals from non-aristocratic levels of society. The fact that fish products did not derive from an aristocratic *fundus*, together with the ready availability and the relatively low cost of these fish products,[106] obviously contradicts the argument proposed by Tchernia and Manacorda, in which commerce during the Republic was entirely built up around networks of *amicitia* and clients, entirely controlled by and for aristocratic *domini* to their own economic advantage.[107] Even if not organised within the villa economy, the more important fish-salting industries were nevertheless comparable in size with those of wine and oil.

The beginning of large-scale production at Kale Akte in the Imperial period, aiming at an extra-regional market, needs, like earlier production, to be viewed in context.[108] The huge size of the production of (especially) olive oil, and also of fish-sauce, is suggested above all by the large *figlinae* on the Tunisian coast, where amphora production on an industrial scale, with an output of hundreds of thousands of amphorae each year, has been documented.[109] The enormous amount of oil imported to Rome from Spain in the early Imperial period is witnessed by the huge man-made 'hill' of amphora sherds at Monte Testaccio, which demonstrates eloquently just how huge a market Rome represented.[110]

The increased production of oil around the Mediterranean can probably be regarded as a response to the growing Roman and Italian market during the Augustan age and the early Imperial period. Kale Akte, and by extension Sicily as a whole, in view of its favourable geographical position, must also have been stimulated by the existence of a thriving market in the *Urbs* to specialise and produce on a larger scale.[111] The increasing provincial wine production must have been in response to growing demand, something that changed patterns of land use. Economic theory suggests that such increased demand raises the probability that farmers acquire more land in order to maximise yields. Inevitably the increasing prosperity of some must have caused a loss of land and the impoverishment of others.[112]

The Roman economy can be regarded as a 'substitution economy', meaning that the presence of increasing numbers of one given product on the market leads to the decrease of another.[113] The decline of large-scale wine production in Italy towards the end of the first century AD can be explained by the increasing competition from the wines of the provinces, of which Kale Akte was a minor player out of hundreds.[114] On a more local level, in line with this view, the intensified production of wine would have implied the decrease of another crop. In the case of Kale Akte (and perhaps of Sicily as a whole), this could have had an increasingly negative impact on the olive-oil industry, a development which was probably accelerated by the start of large-scale exports of African oil from the middle of the second century AD. The hypothesis that the huge North African exports had a decisive (negative) impact on Sicilian oil production is further strengthened by the fact that Sicilian lamp production also ends at this period, probably due to the increasing availability of high-quality products from North Africa. *Ateliers* mass-producing lamps had existed continuously in Sicily since Classical times, more than 600 years before (see p. 113); but now they disappeared completely for over two hundred years. In an increasingly 'global' economy, it is obvious that Sicily had to increase specialisation in order to compete. Since it was impossible to match the output volume of North Africa and Spain in the oil and fish-produce market, wine was the obvious alternative. Low-value goods such as pottery and lamps were simply no longer competitive any more.

From the discussion above it can be concluded that the scale and mode of production that oscillated over time at Kale Akte can be considered as responses to changing levels of demand throughout the period under study. Entirely dependent on economic and political conditions was the increasing scale of production and the changes in organisation which accompanied it during the imperial period: they were closely related to the needs of the city Rome and of other markets in Italy and the wider Roman Empire.

Modes of distribution and market behaviour

Already in late Archaic times Greek and eastern Mediterranean commodities repeatedly changed hands before reaching their final destination. This practice has been called 'redistribution' by Horden and Purcell, changing the meaning of this traditionally theoretically-charged term.[115] Shipwrecks give us explicit evidence: mixed cargoes were the norm already in the Archaic period, and continued to be so throughout antiquity.[116] Mixed cargoes indicate that the goods and commodities were unloaded in different ports several times, from larger 'hubs' in the web of trade, and then to smaller 'nodes', and in turn to yet smaller centres, connected with those nodes. This system lasted throughout antiquity, and could be regarded as a long-term phenomenon, lasting more than a millennium and approaching the time-span of the *longue durée*.

Most evidence indicates that trade in north Sicily was on a mainly regional level in the fifth and fourth centuries BC, based on small-scale cabotage traffic (see p. 145). Small-scale trade is in itself a contradiction of the command economy, which should be large in scale. We have distinguished a number of local and regional products which were circulated in a capillary manner in Sicily, i.e. they reached many parts of the island by 'trickle-down' distribution. An example of this is the production of Greco-Italic amphorae, made both locally at Kale Akte and in other areas of Sicily and south Italy, with a solely regional distribution. This trade on a regional level, even on a considerable scale, ignored the borders of political territories, and was, needless to say, incompatible with any form of the command economy.

The differing patterns of distribution between Campana B and C pottery on the Sicilian north coast in the second and first centuries BC are a further indication of the workings of regional trading networks: different products compete for a share of different regional markets.[117] These patterns of distribution constitute clear evidence in favour of the dominance of a free market. Moreover, the patterns of regional and extra-regional distribution indicate the existence of different markets, operating on different levels. This is compatible with the model of regional *loci* or hubs for economic activity, which functioned as 'gateways' – in Sicily ports such as Messana, Syracuse or Lilybaeum – and which had direct access to the extra-regional (overseas) markets. The local centres would also have had their own markets, but they were to become more closely linked with major regional centres in periods of intensified economic activity.[118] The veracity of this model is confirmed by the presence at Caronía of both local, regional and extra-regional products throughout the period studied.

We would expect a 'centric transfer' to be characterised by a concentration of finds at specific key-sites, rather than widespread diffusion.[119] The gradual 'trickle-down' distribution of a commodity is in itself an indication of interconnected markets. This phenomenon existed already at the beginning of the period under study, with a widespread distribution of products from Greece and the Greek colonies in the West to sites that lay outside the Greek cultural sphere, such as Caronía, Montagna di Ramacca and Monte Iato. Likewise, the long-distance, inter-regional trade in wine and fish products between Punic and Greek areas was clearly not part of a command economy, since we are dealing with two completely different political and cultural spheres.[120] The patterns of distribution of all extra-regionally produced amphorae and table ware found at Caronía show that these products were distributed to most corners of the western Mediterranean from the Classical period to late Antiquity. The ubiquitous presence of wine amphorae on sites all over the Mediterranean in the Hellenistic period indicates that this commodity was not directed only to specific major metropolises. The distribution of Lamboglia 2 amphorae, well attested at Caronía, constitutes a good example of a large-scale production, which is then transported as far and wide as possible through private initiative.[121] The almost identical pattern of extra-regional imports at Caronía with that at other north Sicilian centres, including Lipari, is striking; it also demonstrates that even small towns like Kale Akte were able to import the same types of mass-produced products as other, more important urban centres did. The widespread distribution of the same range of goods and commodities in Sicily in the early fifth century BC is consistent with Robin Osborne's hypothesis that the Mediterranean already in the Archaic period was a web of interdependent markets.[122]

Contacts with the Aegean might under certain, short-lived, historical circumstances have been direct, possibly in connection with the Samian and Miletian attempt to colonise Kale Akte in 494 BC, and later in connection with the project of Ducetius. The Sikels of the north coast under Archonides were explicitly philo-Athenian in the conflict between Athens and Syracuse between 415 and 413 BC, and it is possible that direct trade connections with Athens intensified in this short period.[123] These were, however, exceptions to the rule. The earliest arrival of Greek commodities and pottery did not begin all of a sudden with the arrival of colonists at Kale Akte: Greek goods had by then already been imported more or less regularly for more than a century, as a consequence of the small-scale cabotage trade discussed below (p. 145).

We have so far discussed patterns of distribution as an indication of market exchange. But, do we have more concrete evidence about who supplied the goods – information which could tell us something of the nature of the trade? There is very little evidence for the modes of product distribution before the Imperial period, but in the Classical and Hellenistic periods wine was certainly supplied through *emporoi* acting in a framework of private initiative.[124] Even for the Imperial period, a time when state initiatives would have been more frequent, most scholars agree that the demand for wine was satisfied mainly by private business arrangements, prior to the first interventions by the state in AD 270.[125]

We do have some information about the trade of fish products in the first or second century AD in Rome, when we hear of a *negotians salsarius* who was chief officer of the *corpus* of traders from Malaca in southern Spain.[126] This would suggest that this commodity, at least in the Roman imperial period, was supplied through private initiative. Fish products were not a staple necessary for survival, and they were probably fourth in importance among the bulk commodities traded in antiquity, after grain, oil and wine.[127] State involvement in this business is also, therefore, highly unlikely before the Imperial period.

In antiquity pottery was generally of little economic importance; only Attic might have had a higher intrinsic value.[128] Table ware therefore always constituted a minor part of a ship's cargo, the bulk of which was represented by more valuable commodities, such as grain, wine, oil, fish products, metals, etc.[129] Consequently the sale of pottery was of no interest to the State. Evidence for specialised traders in pottery in the Imperial period is scarce, with only a single reference to a *negotiator cretarii*, in a northern province.[130] Peña has hypothesised that *navicularii* bought African Red Slip pottery at the ports of embarkation, transported it to Italy along with other cargo, and then sold it to wholesalers at Ostia or Portus. The second alternative is that itinerant sellers purchased pottery, accompanied it aboard merchant vessels and then sold the pottery to middlemen at Ostia, Portus or Rome.[131] There is no evidence prior to the Imperial period for the organisation of the pottery trade, but the fact that ships' cargoes had mostly the same relative proportions between 'valuable' goods (foodstuffs) and pottery (the latter always a tiny minority) suggests that the mode of organisation changed little in the long time-span between the Classical and late Imperial times.

The evidence discussed above suggests four main indications of market behaviour throughout the period studied:

The 'capillary' distribution of regional and imported products within Sicily

The 'capillary' distribution to large parts of the Mediterranean, including Kale Akte, of the same, mass-produced products

The participation of private traders, in response to private market demands

The large-scale sale of simple, low-cost goods (pottery, lamps), mainly for private consumption, of no interest to the state

This short survey of evidence for modes of supply for a number of non-staple goods shows that trade in such commodities was usually privately run by individuals or corporations of traders. Individually-based entrepreneurship of course dominates, which is in fact the foundation for all trade. Such individual enterprises were all motivated by a striving for profit. In the late Imperial period economic problems forced the wine trade to become State-directed, but wine was only a late comer to this situation: the principal staple foodstuffs had already been for long under State control, and that will be the focus of the next section.

State-directed trade and taxation

Kale Akte and taxation under the *basileia* of Syracuse

During its history, Kale Akte was subject to taxation by two different states at different times: the *basileia* of Syracuse, and the Roman Empire. The sources indicate that Kale Akte was under Syracuse's dominion under Agathocles between 304 and 289 BC, and again from from *c.* 269/265–263 BC in Hieron's reign: during that time a tithe would have been paid to Syracuse. Possibly a tribute was demanded by Messana during the short intermediate period of Mamertine rule.[132] A tithe on all agricultural produce was the most important regular tax in Greek Sicily at this time. According to Sebastiana Consolo Langher, and other scholars before her, such as Jerôme Carcopino, it had already been in place since the time of Gelon and Dionysius I.[133] It would have become better organised by the time of Agathocles, and was an institution under Hieron II, who established the regulations cited in Roman times as the *Lex Hieronica*.[134] The tithe was collected on grain, but probably also on wine, oil and vegetables.[135]

We have no direct evidence from Caronía as to which commodities were affected by the tithe. We know nothing about one on olive oil, since no Sicilian oil amphorae from this period are known. The grain tithe was certainly the principal one, and must have been shipped where possible by sea to Syracuse. Fish products, not being agricultural produce, were presumably exempt. Were the locally produced amphorae, datable to the period *c.* 320–270/60 BC, intended to contain tithe wine for Syracuse? We simply do not know. Perhaps a much larger share of local amphorae might have been expected if this had been the case, and not a majority of imported wine amphorae (in the absence to cash to buy the latter), but that is of course speculation. Wine production will obviously have been carried on here before the Agathoclean era.[136] By the Hellenistic period, over much of Sicily, it was abundant, and stockpiling was unnecessary. Syracuse, a city of not more than 100,000 inhabitants, would easily have been able to cover its needs from its surrounding territories and through imports from other parts of Sicily. One might also argue that if there was no tax on oil, there would surely not have been one on wine.

Kale Akte and taxation under the Roman Empire

There has been much discussion concerning whether, under the Empire, tax in the form of the *annona* was an essential prerequisite to mass production and the commercial success of other produce from the same territory. Does the data from Caronía and, more widely, from elsewhere in Sicily during the Late Republic, shed light on this problem?

Kale Akte came under the control of Rome around 263 BC. The 10% tithe, known as the *decuma,* was copied by the Romans from the kingdom of Syracuse and levied throughout the Late Republican period.[137] The tithe proper concerned grain, while other products such as oil, wine and *fruges minutae*, albeit part of the *decuma,* were taxed at the reduced level of 5%.[138] The right to collect the tithes were auctioned off every year, according to the regulations of the *Lex Hieronica*.[139] The *decuma* was part of the *annona* – it was a demand of the city of Rome. Kale Akte had to play by the rules, and its economy was very much affected by it. In particular it was the grain *annona* that played far and away the most significant role.[140]

Taxation on grain

Annona grain at least during the Imperial period was transported on ships subsidised by the State.[141] Several scholars have underlined the importance of state subsidies for the growth of trade: different products of a province were able to 'piggy-back' on cheap shipments of the corn dole.[142] Along the same lines it has also been argued that the exploitation of Spanish oil was initiated because of an already flourishing trade in metals and minerals between Spain and Rome.[143] How important was the *annona* for the intensification of overseas trade at Kale Akte and elsewhere in the western Mediterranean in the Republican period? Initially it was a time when there was 'an ad hoc atmosphere to the arrangements with insufficient understanding on either side as to who was committed and for how long to making sure that corn commensurate to Rome's needs was being brought to the city.'[144] As there was no merchant marine owned by the State, tithes from Sicily had to be transported privately.[145] Although ships were not yet subsidised by the State, the marginal costs would already have been covered by the needs of the grain supply.[146] Cheap shipping was not sufficient, however, to make, for example, the export of Campana C pottery a success outside Sicily.[147]

In the second and first centuries BC, wine would have been, after (but a long way after) grain, the product with the highest commercial potential, but no major Sicilian centre seems to have produced anything like the scale of Ischia / Campania wine or that of Issa / central Dalmatia and other sites on the Italian Adriatic coast. Why Sicilian wine in the late Hellenistic period could not compete with these areas despite advantages in cheap and efficient transport was probably due to their incapacity to compete in volume output with the much larger wine production of Campania, central Italy and the central Adriatic. Significantly, it was not in Rome's interest for Sicily to compete with Italy's own important wine production.[148] Roman control of Sicily in Late Republican times probably therefore put a brake on the island's already considerable wine production. The Sicilian economy was not allowed to take advantage of the situation and let its most important product after grain 'piggy-back' on subsidised shiploads.

Africa Proconsularis can be compared to Sicily in having similar transport advantages from the moment it became a Roman province in 146 BC. At this time a levy of grain was imposed on it, although the chief supplier of that commodity was at the time still Sicily.[149] It is probably true that the African Red Slip pottery in the Imperial period had competition advantages from 'piggy-backing' on grain ships, since it was easy to load as an extra cargo.[150] This, on the other hand, is hardly true of Tunisian 'neo-Punic' amphorae, exported to Sicily and the western Mediterranean in the Late Republican period[151] – containers not suited as secondary cargo, due to their bulk and their relatively high value (compared to pottery).

Although, therefore, the grain *annona* may have been essential to the initial success of the export of African pottery and North African lamps in the mid-Empire, neither the Sicilian nor the North African economy seem to have gained any such advantages during the Late Republican period. Subsidised transport cannot explain the sudden increase in scale of the Sicilian export of wine and salted tuna in the first century AD, nor can it explain the flourishing wine trade of Campania and the central Adriatic in Late Republican times, since these regions were not affected by the grain *annona*. Sicily, and probably Kale Akte, began to export its wine to Rome on a larger scale only in the first century AD, after the island had lost its position to North Africa and Egypt as the privileged grain exporter to Rome.[152] It is thus not possible to explain the appearance of high-volume trade simply as a consequence of State-directed grain shipments, even if the latter must have had an encouraging and intensifying effect on the overall volume of trade.

Just how important the province of Sicily was for the Roman grain supply during the Empire has been much debated. Soraci's in-depth study argued for a continued importance of Sicily in this period, but at a reduced level by comparison with that enjoyed during the late Republic.[153] She concluded that Sicily's contribution would have been small in terms of volume compared with that of North Africa, but in certain circumstances it was still essential.[154] Interestingly, she argues that Italy had no need of Sicilian grain between *c.* AD 50 and the reign of Commodus,[155] and only began importing it again when the expansion of the North African economy from *c.* 200 onwards affected Sicily in a positive way.[156] Also debated is how big a role Sicily played in Rome's grain supply after AD 324 when Egyptian grain was redirected to newly-founded Constantinople: many scholars suppose that it was central to Sicily late Roman prosperity, others that Sicily remained only a back-up source.[157] By that time at least some Sicilian grain certainly came from the island's Imperial estates.[158] We cannot dwell on this question here. Suffice it to say that the territory of Kale Akte and the Nebrodi was not ideal for the cultivation of grain on a large scale, and so would not have been greatly impacted by a corn *annona*. Grain from Sicily in the Imperial period must have come from the vast plains of the interior and the eastern parts of the island.

Kale Akte in Imperial times may therefore have been freer than in the late Hellenistic period to specialise in other produce than grain. Sicily's less central role in the corn supply then also implies that its exports could not exploit as much the subsidised transports to Italy, especially if it is right that in the period *c.* 50–200 AD Sicily shipped restricted amounts of grain to Rome.

Taxation on oil

With oil, the situation is different. It was, like grain, a staple commodity, but was surprisingly little traded in the Classical and early Hellenistic period, the notable exception being Corinth's remarkable export success, which is usually seen in the framework of Greek 'colonisation'. Cultivations of olives large enough to sustain the demands of the colonies and the indigenous populations in their hinterland had apparently not yet been developed in the Archaic and early Classical periods. Oil continued to be imported to Sicily in the Hellenistic period, but only in small amounts from Corinth in the third century BC and from Apulia in the late second/first centuries BC. As we have seen, oil was part of the tax on agricultural produce from early on. A late Republican taxation on Sicilian oil is, however, difficult to reconcile with the fact that no oil amphorae are known from that period, which is equally true for the reign of Agathocles, as we have seen (p. 110). It is hardly conceivable that oil was transported overseas from Sicily to Rome in skins, considering the enormous output of transport amphorae for other foodstuffs in this period. A solution to this problem might be that the 5% tax on oil and wine was consumed not in Rome, but in Sicily, as a part of the provisions for the governor and his staff.[159] Oil extorted by Verres, for example, might have been intended for his household.[160] This suggestion is supported by Cicero's mention of *fruges minutae*, minor crops, as being subject to the tithe together with wine and oil. It is hardly conceivable that crops such as vegetables were transported as tax to Rome.

Oil became a commodity traded on a large scale inter-regionally by the beginning of the first century AD, when Spanish and Tripolitanian oil was sent to Rome.[161] It remains unclear how strongly involved the Roman State was in the early stages of this trade, but it was certainly at least partly involved from the middle of the first century AD.[162] The first more obvious traces of State involvement, however, date to the middle of the second century, when a *praefectus annonae* is mentioned as having surveyed oil imports from Baetica and Africa.[163] From the reign of Septimius Severus, a program for the distribution of free oil to the populace of Rome was instituted,[164] and thus the State from now on could control the oil trade more directly. State distributions of oil continued at least until the 430s.[165]

While oil arrived in Rome in great quantity during the first century and the first half of the second century AD, this does not seem to have been the case at Kale Akte/Calacte. Tunisian oil in Africana 1A amphorae arrived at Caronía more or less at the same time as the first imports of these same amphorae to Rome around the middle of the second century.[166] The numbers of Dressel 20 and Tripolitana 1 amphorae in the first or early second century are very limited by comparison with the huge amounts of Africana 1A amphorae in the second half of the second and the third century. The implications are, firstly, that Tripolitanian and Baetican oil was imported before *c*. AD 150 but in moderate amounts, and, secondly, that both Sicily as a whole and Kale Akte in particular became dependant on African oil only when trade in oil became State-directed with the institution of the *canon olei* in the early third century AD. Thus dependence on African oil from the middle of the second century AD would seem to have been due partly to its greatly increased availability in Sicilian ports. According to the law of supply and demand, it would have been increasingly difficult to compete with African prices, subsidised as they were by the State. Especially with the expanding demand for Sicilian wine in mind, it would have been an obvious choice for local farmers to concentrate on producing wine rather than oil, with the possibility of much higher profits. Since Kale Akte was obviously not a stop for larger ships carrying African oil to Rome, the big quantities of African oil at Caronía must indicate a trade independent of the state,[167] where its arrival must have been due to a pattern of redistribution from the main harbours of Sicily to smaller ports through Sicilian *negotiatores*.

The massive imports of African oil to Sicily in late antiquity have been noted and discussed for some years. Wilson posed the question of whether Sicilian oil production decreased as a consequence of increasing imports of oil, or whether the expanding wealth of the island simply allowed the inhabitants to pay for better quality oil.[168] Elizabeth Fentress and her colleagues have viewed these imports as a sign of the generally low productivity of Sicily at this period,[169] but they were writing before the new evidence of recent years, especially of Sicilian wine production in Late Antiquity. It is instructive to compare Sicily with Dalmatia, where despite abundant archaeological evidence for olive oil production in the Roman period, Spanish and North African oil, perhaps because of its superior quality, was still being imported.[170] Although we have no such evidence for comparison in late Roman Sicily, local production of low-quality cheap oil at a certain level was presumably available alongside the imports. There might be some truth, therefore, in the notion of greater wealth providing the purchasing power for increased amounts of imported oil, but more important was the ready availability of such imports and the obvious disadvantages in competitiveness when faced with such a large-scale North African production.

Taxation on wine

According to the ancient sources, Sicilian wine was as much a part of the Late Republican tithe as was oil.[171]

The exiguous evidence of wine amphorae produced at Kale Akte (or Sicily in general) in the late third to first centuries BC suggests that few communities would have been liable for taxation in wine. As mentioned above (p. 137), both wine and oil tithes may have consumed on the island by the Roman authorities, and would never have reached Rome. Theodore Peña has, however, hypothesised a tax on wine from Sicily (and Asia Minor) at least from the first century AD, based on the important numbers of Sicilian amphorae which were imported to Rome at this period.[172] However, as well as Sicily, Bruttium, southern Gaul, Hispania Tarraconensis and Baetica also began producing wine for the Roman market in the first century AD.

It is hard to understand why Sicily would have been subjected to a tax on wine, when the major part of the wine supply arrived at Rome through private initiative. A flourishing wine trade in the Mediterranean in the first century AD hardly made taxation necessary. It is only from the later third century AD that we can speak of direct State involvement in the wine industry, when it became crucial to secure supplies for Rome as the free market shrank. Why even at this time a tax on wine was considered necessary is not completely clear, but it may have been connected with the breakdown of the monetary system and the interruption of important trade routes during political unrest during the Roman Empire in the second half of the third century, with a decline in trading activity and volume as a consequence.[173] The already flourishing wine production in Sicily and Bruttium must have been the reason why State requisitions began in the late third century AD, and was followed in the fourth century by the *canon vinarius*. Sicilian wine could now travel along the already busy maritime 'highway' between Carthage and Rome (a major grain-supply route). The large production of wine in addition to grain must clearly have been the most important factor in the prosperity of Sicily during the fourth, but also still in the fifth and early sixth centuries AD.[174] In the fourth century, and especially after the middle of it, the *Ostia* 1, 455–6 flat-bottomed amphora, now recognized principally as a Sicilian type, became increasingly common in Rome. Also relevant here are the edicts of Valentinian and Gratian, which condemned the turning of the wine tribute into money.[175] Pacetti thinks that these may indicate that the Roman State received more wine than it could consume.[176]

The trade in staples, therefore, was controlled for long periods by the Roman State. In the Republican period, the *decuma* on agricultural produce, with the exception of grain, must be considered as an instrument of provincial government, not of the Senate in Rome. Grain production was controlled by the State during almost the entire period studied, with the exception of the earliest, when Kale Akte lay outside the control of Syracuse. The grain tithe was not, however, the initial force behind increased exchange at Kale Akte, in Sicily and the South Tyrrhenian. It is clear that trade developed independently of the grain *annona*, and that even State grain and oil were supplied partly through private *negotiatores*.

The impact of Empire and 'the consumer city'

The key issue here is to ask what the impact on Kale Akte's economy was when it was absorbed along with the whole of northern Sicily into a larger political unit. We have already discussed the more direct forms of involvement by the State in the Sicilian economy. But what were the repercussions at a more abstract, less formal, level on local economic development as a result of the political dominance of first Syracuse and then Rome? The development of the urban metropolis was a direct consequence of an expanding empire.

The ancient city and its economic character were widely discussed throughout much of the twentieth century. The so-called 'consumption-city model' is constructed on an image of the city or metropolis as a centre for consumption rather than production. Its most important creator, Max Weber, was influenced by the ideas of Werner Sombart and Karl Bücher, who regarded consumer cities as non-productive parasites, mainly having a negative influence on their hinterlands.[177] Weber compared the ancient *polis* with the medieval town, and concluded that capitalism, with its independent class of entrepreneurs as one of its main hallmarks, was unable to exist in the ancient city, since the latter was indivisible from the countryside.[178] His ideas were later adopted by Moses Finley.[179] The idea that the major ancient cities were non-productive is rooted in a linear view of history, most fervently advocated by Karl Marx. From his standpoint, capitalism was non-existent in any pre-modern society; since it had not always existed in the past, it would not continue to exist forever in the future.[180] These ideas inspired the comparison of different 'stages' in economic history, such as the one in between the ancient and the medieval city.

More recently, interest in the consumption-city model has experienced a renaissance, but it has now inspired research in quite different directions. In last twenty years one of the most influential interpreters of the consumption-city model, and the relationship between city and hinterland, is Neville Morley, who in his book *Metropolis and hinterland* argued that in the Roman Empire some economic growth was possible within the limits of a pre-industrial economy and that 'the growth of the city of Rome was an important stimulus to such growth'.[181] The development of a huge urban market is central to this model of metropolitan influence, where the demands of the metropolis led to an important stimulation of the economy of the hinterland.

The regional power of Syracuse

From at least the late fourth century until *c.* 263 BC (with the interval of Mamertine rule *c.* 289–70 BC), Kale Akte was part of the Syracusan kingdom, and thus would have been influenced mainly by this metropolis – as it had been already earlier, but less directly. The growth at Kale Akte of urban settlement and harbour activity between the end of the fifth and the beginning of the third century BC coincides with three important developments:

The foundation of Halaesa by Archonides of Herbita (403 BC) and of Tyndaris by Syracuse (396 BC)

The inclusion of Kale Akte and its micro-region in the *basileia* of Agathocles (304–289 BC)

The increasing importance of the south Tyrrhenian trade route between Rome and Carthage

The foundation of Halaesa was a consequence of a new era of professional warfare, in which hired troops (mercenaries) played an essential part. This also brought a hunger for land when peace finally arrived, and the *polis* as a concept was a natural solution to the problem. By 400 BC, with the foundation of Halaesa, the Sikel area on the north coast had embraced a thoroughly Hellenic life-style based on the cultural and political concept of the *polis*. Within a short period of time, the settlements of Haluntium and Apollonia also became *poleis*. The earliest foundation in the area, that of Kale Akte, was itself a consequence of the increased interest of Syracuse in the north coast, a sign of its increasing power and desire for control over the island as a whole. It is with Agathoclean rule that our region, now quite intensely urbanised, became a direct part of the Syracusan empire.[182] The *basileia* of Agathocles was a form of empire which in character was different from earlier ones. The Syracusan empire was now a monarchic, territorial state, the last phase of a development that had been going on since the age of the Deinomenids at the beginning of the fifth century BC.[183] Like the empire of Dionysius the Elder, the shaping of a state had gone hand-in-hand with territorial and economic expansion.[184] The kingdom of Agathocles was a fully developed Hellenistic monarchy with all its normal characteristics: a territorial state, headed by a *basileus* with full powers, expanding its territory with a strong army, and enjoying a large sphere of economic interest. It is obvious that the concentration of power in the hands of large territorial states made production at a higher scale possible, giving those states huge economic assets through taxes, tributes and spoils of war. The kingdom of Syracuse can in many ways be compared to other Hellenistic monarchies in the East, with which it had close ties, but also with Rome.[185] The connection between the construction of a more constant empire in Sicily, with institutions and a *basileus* as its institutionalised ruler, and the intensification in the production and trade of wine in Sicily are obvious. It was in the last third of the fourth century that the MGS IV / V production begins to flood western Mediterranean markets. There are strong indications that the interests of Syracuse in the north Sicilian coast by the end of the fourth century BC had economic, as well as military, reasons. With the mass exports of Campanian wine and pottery and North African fish products, the south Tyrrhenian trade route between Rome and Carthage became from the commercial point of view a critically important one. The destruction of Apollonia in 307 BC is clear evidence for a new interest in ports on the north Sicilian coast and a desire to control them.[186]

The Hellenistic period is characterised by strong economic control by the State, especially in the empires of Alexander's followers. This is true to a certain degree also for Sicily, but the latter differs in many respects and does not share the same political history. How did this affect Kale Akte and its region? The most immediate consequence would have been that a growing number of farms were now obliged to pay a tithe to Syracuse. This was in essence a fair fiscal system, since the amount yielded to the State was related to the size of the harvest. However, the loss of produce might have been a considerable burden, especially for small to middle-sized estates which were the most frequent type in the area of the Nebrodi. An increase in efficiency and labour intensity must, however, have improved the conditions of the single farmer. Since there was an increasing demand for wine due to the population growth in the area (and in Sicily in general: see above), vines would have been the most profitable crop after that of grain. The limited cultivable area and small population, however, made large-scale production in the Nebrodi area impossible. Large-scale Sicilian wine production in the late fourth and third centuries BC took place on the east coast, both on the slopes of Mount Etna, and towards the south-east corner of the island. The taxation model formulated by Keith Hopkins, who saw intensification in trade during the Roman Empire as a consequence of the farmer's need to create surplus in order to pay taxes in cash,[187] isclearly not applicable to Sicily. The tax transferred to Syracuse was a tithe, not one paid in cash. Furthermore, as we have seen, the intensification of trade in the southern Tyrrhenian took place long before 200 BC and the end of the Second Punic War, which was Hopkins' point of departure. We must look elsewhere for the forces behind the intensification of trade at Kale Akte.

Morley has convincingly shown that Augustan Rome with around one million inhabitants had a huge impact on its hinterland and on the provinces, but is it possible to apply the same model to fourth-century-BC Syracuse as a 'consumer city', or was it too small? Syracuse had a population comparable to that of Rome around 300 BC, with a minimum of 100,000 inhabitants,[188] but the island in this period never achieved a level of export of both wine and pottery that is comparable to the volume coming out of Campania. There is no doubt that the explosive growth of the city of Rome in the late fourth and early third centuries BC was one of the main explanations for the huge Campanian output, but it is hardly the only one. The demands of a metropolis like Syracuse must have been as important, comparable in scale to that of Rome at this time, and the significant Sicilian output of wine amphorae and fine ware can be seen as a response to those demands. There is some indication in the early Hellenistic period that the scale of the output did not so much depend on the size of the most important urban market (like Syracuse or Rome) as on the size and resources of its empire. The impact on the economy of Syracuse and Republican Rome cannot, for obvious reasons, be compared in scale with that of Rome under the Empire.

At first glance, the two early 'empires' of Syracuse and Rome had superficial similarities. Sicily and Campania were part of the same Graeco-Italic *koiné* in this period, and the material culture was in many ways identical. The Hellenistic *basileia* of Agathocles and Hieron also had things in common with the Roman Empire in terms of economic and military policy. As William Harris has noted, 'economic gain was to the Romans (and generally in the ancient world) an integral part of successful warfare and the expansion of power. Land, plunder, slaves and revenues were regular and natural results of success'.[189] When we consider the economic dominance of amphora production at Carthage, Corinth and Rhodes, the brutal destruction of these very cities at the hands of the Romans can be seen as an inevitable political outcome. The link between extension of territory and scale of surplus production is obvious already at a much earlier period in the history of Greek *poleis*. The vast territory and the large populations of Locri and Sybaris, for example, in combination with the presence of good-quality vines in their territories, were the prerequisites which made these cities the most important wine producers in the southern Tyrrhenian Sea throughout the Archaic and Classical periods.[190]

There is, however, of course no question that the Empire of Rome was more powerful than the *basileia* of Syracuse already by the beginning of the Hellenistic period. Crucial in the comparison is the large territory controlled by Rome, and also the existence of a very strong army. The Roman *coloniae*, founded and inhabited by Roman citizens, are a key difference between the imperialism of Syracuse and that of Rome. Roman *coloniae* controlled vast areas in an efficient way and were inhabited by Roman citizens whose interests were intertwined with those of the senate in Rome, whereas Greek Sicily, even when part of it was united in a single kingdom, was still very much a culture based on the *polis*. The *basileia* of Syracuse comprised in reality an area of individual *poleis*, each with an identity of its own, with Syracuse acting as *hegemon*, as incomparably the most powerful *polis*. Although the rest of the *poleis* were inferior in importance and subject to Syracuse, their economic and political interests rarely coincided with that of the leading city. Furthermore, the instability of the political system at Syracuse, with innumerable *staseis* and the constant state of flux in the extension and the degree of control of its territory, made long-term political projects difficult. Syracuse could not therefore conduct and maintain a coherent and far-sighted economic policy in the same way that Rome could and did. It was only during the long reign of Hieron that Syracuse became politically more stable, but by then most of Sicily, including Kale Akte, was no longer part of its territory, and the kingdom was considerably reduced in size after the intervention of Rome in 263 BC; it was in effect a 'client-kingdom' of Rome. The indications are, therefore, that Rome was the more important agent behind intensification of trade at Kale Akte before its inclusion within the Roman Empire.

Kale Akte in the Roman province and Empire

After the *foedus aequum* of 326 BC, Roman and Neapolitan interests united in the wine-exporting business of Campania and Ischia. The collaboration between the Greek aristocracy and *emporoi* of Naples on the one hand, and the Roman aristocracy and *negotiatores* on the other, combined with the hugely advantageous conditions for vine growing in the Vesuvian area, created an unusually successful business.[191] This development of Campanian wine production seems to go hand-in-hand with Roman expansion and the building of their empire. The large share taken by Campanian wine in the Sicilian market already before the Roman conquest, evident from finds at Caronía and elsewhere in Sicily, is impressive. Between the mid-third century BC and the Augustan period, amphora production at Kale Akte (as all over Sicily) was limited: Roman economic interests are likely to have restricted the inherent possibilities of Sicily to develop a strong and coordinated wine export of its own. The impact of Rome on the wine market can be illustrated by the example of Rhodes. Rhodian wine flooded onto the Sicilian market between *c.* 230 and 170 BC, but the creation of Delos as a free harbour in 166 BC marked the beginning of the end of a great era for Rhodian wine in the western Mediterranean.[192] The wines imported to Sicily were from now onwards Campanian, in vast quantities, and to a lesser extent Adriatic. Rhodian wine was still being imported to Sicily, at least until the first century AD, but only in very small quantities. The fact that the two major production areas of wine, Campania and the central Adriatic, were tightly controlled by Roman senators shows how closely the economic interests of the wine trade were intertwined with those of the Roman state.

Rome in the Republican period, in short, treated Sicily in typical imperialistic fashion: it needed Sicilian grain and raw materials, and it supplied the island with specialised commodities. That our area was exploited early on by Italian *negotiatores* is clear from the inscription at Halaesa of 193 BC, recording an already formed group of *Italicei*, who were honouring probably the governor of that year, L. Cornelius Scipio.[193] It was merchants like these who imported large amounts of Campanian wine to Sicily which is so well represented in both Caronía and elsewhere in Sicily at this time.[194]

The imperialistic trading interests of Rome are well illustrated by these examples, and by the decline of Sicilian wine exports after the third century BC (as seen above). It is significant that the rise of a Sicilian wine industry coincides with the demise of the wine exports of Campania and central Italy. The potential for success already existed in Sicily during the second and first centuries BC, but her primary role at that period was to deliver grain and not wine: Campania, central Italy and the Adriatic produced enough of that to satisfy demand in Rome.[195]

After the Augustan reforms, Rome no longer had the same vital interest in Sicily as it had in the Republican period; the island had to adapt to her diminished role as a grain-supplier, with the abolishment now of the tithe system and the introduction of a fixed levy, the *stipendium*.[196] Wine had always been ranked second in economic importance after grain in Sicily, and new economic conditions might have provided the impetus for an emerging large-scale wine production at several places in the island during the first century AD. Even though Sicily was obliged to pay its *stipendium* most likely in grain, grain production probably did not have to be of the size that it had been in the Late Republic, since now Egypt and North Africa bore the brunt of the burden. Consequently, land that had been reserved for grain could now be claimed for viticulture. The former main suppliers, Campania and central Italy, were no longer capable of meeting Rome's demand for wine themselves, and important wine producers elsewhere, notably in Spain (Tarraconensis) and southern Gaul, began supplying Rome during the first century AD. The market was therefore opened up to provincial wines, and when Italian wine production began to decline significantly towards the end of the first and the beginning of the second century AD, the impact of provincial wines including Sicilian was at least partly responsible. Not only Sicily, but also its neighbour Bruttium, the ancient *Oinotria*, which geographically and geologically is virtually a continuation of north-eastern Sicily, also started producing wine for export at the same time.[197]

Kale Akte, as we have seen, lay on the north Sicilian coast in a very advantageous position for exports to Rome. It was actually closer to the metropolis than parts of inland Etruria and Umbria, and it is interesting to observe that the major suppliers of goods to Rome (with the exception of the provinces of Baetica and Tarraconensis) are found within the same privileged area that had easy and quick access to the Roman market, such as that other important supplier of wine and *terra sigillata*, namely southern Gaul, as well as Tunisia and other parts of North Africa for red slip pottery, oil and fish-sauce (Fig. 6.1). Following Morley's model, it could be said that Kale Akte's fortunes were very much linked to those of the city of Rome and its Empire. The central importance of the *caput mundi* for the creation of a prospering trading network in the Mediterranean has been further emphasised in recent scholarship.[198] Keith Hopkins suggested that the high degree of urbanization around the Mediterranean was to a great extent caused by economic considerations: towns developed (Hopkins called them 'feeder towns') as a direct consequence of the demands of Rome.[199] This created increasing employment and specialisation, since they were encouraged to export their commodities to Rome, to pay for taxes and rent.[200]

We have seen that Kale Akte along with other settlements in the region in the second half of the fourth century BC became thoroughly urbanised. This was most probably a consequence of increasing trade along the south Tyrrhenian shipping routes between Rome and North Africa and the increasing strategic and economic importance that this gave the north Sicilian centres. The treaty between Rome and Carthage in 348 BC demonstrated that Rome already had by then strong interests in maritime trade.[201] Increased economic activity at Kale Akte towards the end of the fourth century BC seems to be less a consequence of Syracuse's ambitions to control the northern coast than one of

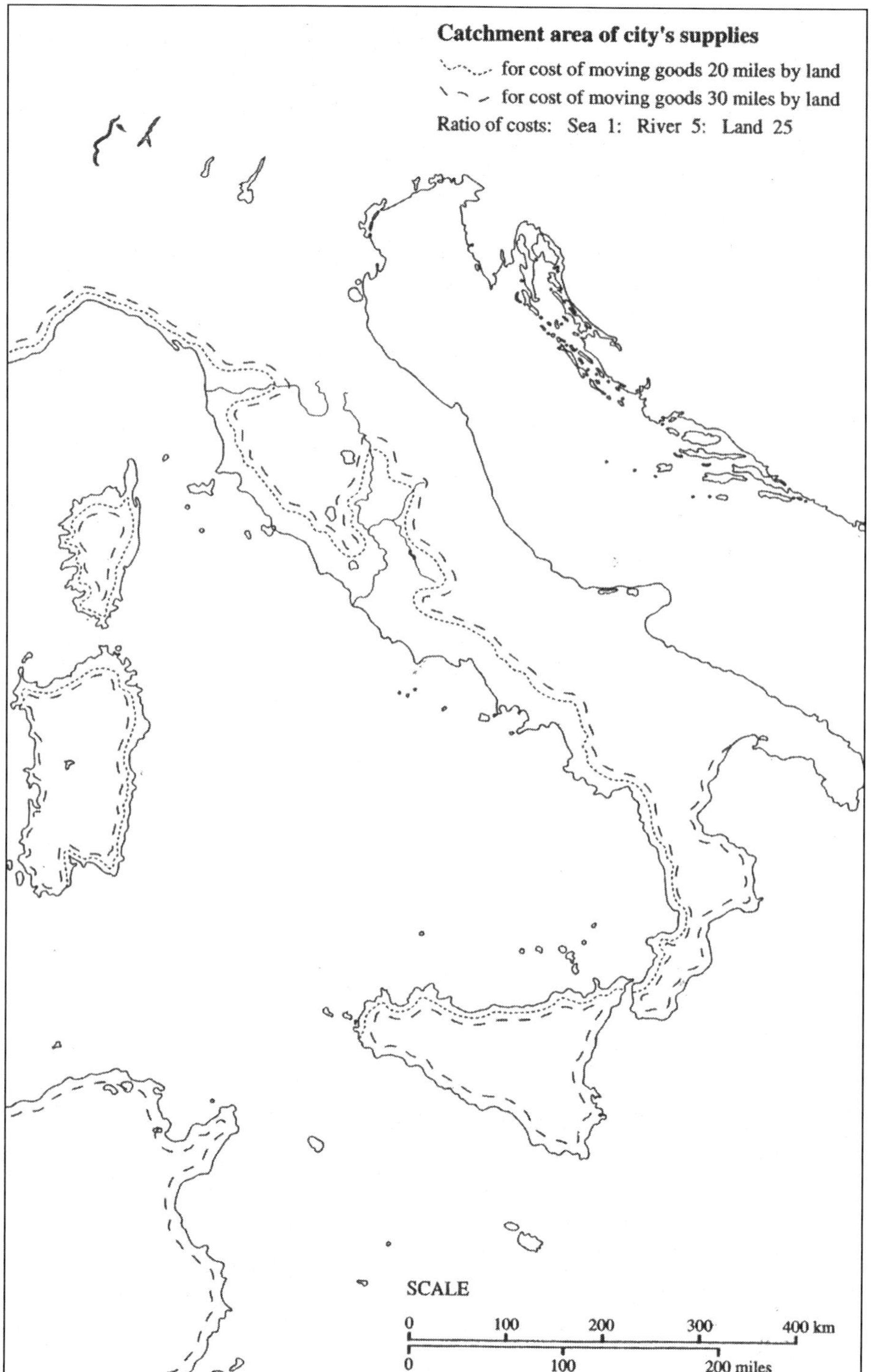

Fig. 6.1 Map showing the catchment area of Rome's supplies, based on the cost of transport. It shows clearly that the north coast of Sicily was within the area of privileged access to Rome, closer, for example, than the inland parts of Etruria and Umbria in the heart of Italy.

increasing possibilities for profit which arrived concomitant with wider commercial exchanges. The growing importance of the Tyrrhenian trade route was something quite new; earlier, the most important Greek settlements had been founded on the eastern and southern seaboards, on the main route between Greece and Magna Graecia on the one hand, and linking Greece with North Africa and Spain on the other. Central Italy and Campania, controlled by Rome, and the Carthaginian empire were agents behind Kale Akte's growing prosperity and possibilities for trade. The early production of a surplus of local wine at Kale Akte could thus be viewed as an outcome of these developments: it was mainly the result of the general expansion of Rome's overseas possessions. The development from the Late Republican period onwards at Kale Akte is clearly more strongly connected than before with the needs of the city of Rome, with grain as the most obvious source of wealth in the Late Republic. The voracious demands of the *Urbs* were the most important single factor behind increased output of wine at Kale Akte (and elsewhere in Sicily), a development which started in the first century AD and peaked in the fourth and fifth centuries. In addition, the important export of fish products in the first century AD can probably also be explained by increased demand in Rome, where Spanish fish-sauces began to be imported in the same period. The intimate connection between the demands of Rome, and the grain and wine exports from Sicily in the late Empire to meet them, is obvious, and is well illustrated by the generally flourishing state of Sicily in this period.

There are no finds from either Caronía or Marina di Caronía datable to later than the beginning of the sixth century AD, and although a continuity of scattered settlement can be considered highly probable, a steep decline in both trade and production must be assumed. The Justinianic reconquest of Sicily and the problems that followed clearly damaged the Italian economy,[202] something which is probably reflected by the dramatic decline in rural settlement in the territory of Halaesa, as well as in that of Calacte itself. The role of Rome as a stimulator of trade and production was now taken over by Constantinople and the Byzantine Empire, and the *annona* from North Africa to Constantinople was clearly an important factor in that.[203]

Mediterranean trade between East and West was relatively stable throughout the sixth century AD, although its scale cannot be compared with that of earlier centuries. The great divide comes in the early seventh century AD, when the Byzantine Empire within a short period of time lost much of its territory and fiscal control. This would have affected the *annona* system, and with its end disappeared also much of the specialised large-scale production in North Africa.[204] Both it and long-distance trade were dependent on the existence of the economic demands of an empire.

The history of Kale Akte as an urban centre began, in the late fourth century BC with the emerging Rome-Carthage overseas trade, connected with the sudden demographic expansion of the city of Rome and its growing sphere of influence, along with the simultaneous rise of Carthage. Kale Akte's prosperity increases significantly with the Roman annexation of Sicily and particularly when both Rome and its Empire were at their peak between the first and fourth centuries AD. Our settlement's decline in both production and overseas trade coincides first with the collapse of the western Roman Empire in the late fifth century AD; it fell still further with the Gothic wars in the sixth century AD, which led to a demographic crisis in Italy and at Rome.[205] The close inter-relationship between the prosperity of Kale Akte and that of the Roman Empire supports the view that Italy, along with its metropolis was the *primus motor* behind increased economic activity on the north coast of Sicily. The empire first of Syracuse, but then of Rome, provided the preconditions for economic growth and wealth at Kale Akte.

7

From trading post to rural village

In this final chapter I attempt to sum up the most important features of the history and archaeology of Kale Akte and its micro-region, as defined in the course of this study. Starting from a Braudellian framework, as discussed at the start of Chapter Five, but setting aside Braudel's view that human agency was unimportant, I have stressed by contrast the vital part played by the latter, and how intimately human activity and initiative are connected with historical processes throughout. Taking as my time-frame the *longue durée* of a thousand years of history, I have tried to throw light on long-term developments, such as the role of geography in shaping settlement patterns, as well as considering the more detailed perspective brought to certain periods by the relevant historical sources.

Structures

Geography and natural resources

The settlements on the 'Fair Coast' and the communication network linking them with each other and with the outside world, together with the micro-region's formidable natural resources, combined to create the essential prerequisites for the growth and economic prosperity of Kale Akte. The absence of large plains and the consequent lack of even moderate stretches of fertile soil was a constraining factor in the cultivation of grain. A narrow river valley, and the restricted area available for the settlement's *chora*, limited not only opportunities for expansion but also the size of the population. No less important, Kale Akte had neighbours very close by – Apollonia only 12 kilometres to the east (as the crow flies), and Halaesa some 15 km to the west – so expansion of the *polis*'s territory in either direction was not an option. If the border between Kale Akte and its neighbours was drawn roughly half-way between these two other communities, it can have controlled a coastline no more than 15 to 20 km long. On the other hand, the hilly nature of the landscape was a necessary prerequisite, or at least provided favourable conditions, for the cultivation of vines. The forests constituted a further asset of great economic importance, furnishing (apart from construction timber) vital fuel for the local ceramic industry, which stands out as an important element in the micro-region's economy throughout the period studied. Its geographical position, at a crossroads of key land- and sea-routes, determined the outward-looking and trade-oriented character of the settlement. The sea gave the opportunity to export locally-produced goods, and to trade with other parts of the region and beyond, throughout the millennium studied. Ships from other small harbour towns along the coast would have had intense communication with Kale Akte's maritime settlement.

Hill-top and maritime settlement

The dichotomy of hill- and maritime settlement and their interdependency are major, long-term features of Kale Akte. Both co-existed during the entire period studied – as indeed they still do – and reflect a continuing dependence on the sea and openness to the outside world presented by the maritime settlement on the one hand, and the closed, protected security provided by the hill-top settlement on the other. The relative importance of the hill-top versus the maritime settlement and vice-versa fluctuated over time, according to a variety of factors – cultural, economic and political.

Exchange, supply and demand, cabotage

The terms 'exchange', 'supply and demand' and 'cabotage' can be considered as different expressions of the *mentalités* of history, and therefore also of long-term *structures*, ever-present factors that shaped the nature of settlement. These fundamental terms, that are basic for most trading activity, were already dominant in the Bronze Age and remained in place of course also after our period. *Kerdos*, the desire for profit, and demand, were the main forces which stimulated trade outside Kale Akte's own small community. From the end of the Archaic period, and probably even from the Bronze Age, Kale Akte was linked with other settlements through exchange contacts based on supply and demand. Private individuals constituted the backbone of this trade – most commodities arrived at Kale Akte thanks to private initiative. State intervention in the economy became an important factor only when the town was included within the kingdom of Syracuse, and later when it was part of a province of Rome. The trading post at Marina di Caronía (Fig. 7.1) from the late Archaic period onwards enjoyed trading connections with other parts of the Mediterranean, a world which already by 400 BC was to a certain extent monetarised and economically showed characteristics of 'market behaviour'. Exchange took place from the very beginning within a framework of supply and demand, which lay at the root of all economic activity at Kale Akte. A successful wine industry, here as elsewhere in the Greek world, was made possible initially because of a local demand which was ever-increasing, and that in turn led to the production of a wealth-creating surplus which could be exported overseas. Exports of grain and wine in part went towards paying tribute and taxes imposed and organised by Rome, but wine was produced over and above for sale on the open market.

Horden and Purcell's view of cabotage or 'coast-hopping' activity as the most important component of Mediterranean trade is corroborated by the material from Caronía and Marina di Caronía, which is very similar to that recorded at other nearby towns, as well as by the composition of cargoes from shipwrecks off Sicilian shores. In other words, the very same goods and commodities that were carried on the main sea routes, with Rome as the most important destination, were also reaching Kale Akte – not because it was a stop for larger ships on the main sea 'highways', but because small-scale traders, who sailed shorter distances, brought such merchandise from the more important commercial harbours. Kale Akte was just one of a host of smaller nodes of connectivity and exchange, which had intense contacts with the large hubs of the region such as Messina – a virtual crossroads of the Mediterranean – but also with places like Lipari, an important stop on the Italy–Sicily–North Africa trading route. Basic, low-cost, goods and commodities circul-ated within and around Sicily and the central Mediterranean, no doubt thanks mainly to small-scale cabotage activity and independent private trade.

The few variations in the patterns of production and supply between different parts of the island (seen, for example, in the arrival of Campana fine wares from Italy) reflect particular local conditions, which have to be taken into consideration for a more nuanced view of the ancient Sicilian economy. Regional patterns could also be identified in the circulation of certain goods: for example, Sicilian wine, olive oil, black-gloss pottery and lamps were traded in considerable quantities in Hellenistic and early Imperial times but hardly any of it went outside the island. Interconnected markets clearly operated on different levels. Most centres on the north coast in fact had very similar natural assets and economic frameworks, and many show closely similar patterns of production, import and export. The north-coast settlements discussed here were primarily markets in which the exchange of goods and commodities took place between each one with its own hinterland on the one hand, and with the outside world on the other, both elsewhere in Sicily and further afield.

Fig. 7.1 The bay of Caronía and the modern village of Marina di Caronía, site of the ancient maritime settlement of Kale Akte/Calacte, seen from the east in contrada *Chiappe*

Conjonctures

Urban and non-urban settlements

Kale Akte had the character and appearance of an urban centre for about half a millennium, from the late fifth century BC until *c.* AD 100, when the hill-top seems to have been largely abandoned. The maritime settlement cannot be regarded as fully urbanised but rather was an economic extension of the *polis*, centred on the port, with a principally storage, redistribution and commercial function. By Roman imperial times, with the hill-top largely deserted, the maritime settlement can be considered a *vicus*, with strong productive capacity and a service centre for traffic on the main north-coast trunk road. There was some sort of settlement here from at least the early fourth century BC, but its main growth and period of economic prosperity as an independent settlement occurred from the first to fourth century AD. Perhaps the population reached its peak in the first century AD, when both the hill-settlement and the maritime settlement prospered. With the abandonment of the hill-top town around AD 100, the size of the maritime village may have expanded to accommodate those who had left their homes on the hill, but what also took place was a ruralisation of the area, with a denser pattern of farms and dwellings in the hinterland. Contraction in the size of the maritime settlement began probably after the earthquake in the 360s and still further after the fifth century AD when commercial activity in the area of *contrada* Pantano gradually petered out after more than a millennium of uninterrupted commercial activity. This coincides with a general decline of urban culture in Sicily around the same time. The villa-based economy seems to have taken shape in the first century AD, while the depopulation of the urban hill-town around AD 100 must be seen also against the backdrop of similar abandonment of hill-top towns across large swathes of Sicily during the late Republic and early Empire. At least from the late third century AD, the rural villa was probably the main economic unit in this large-scale mode of production, although detailed evidence is lacking.

Surplus local production

Surplus production of wine at Kale Akte and in the Nebrodi area can be traced back at least to the fourth century BC, and constitutes a continuous theme for almost its entire existence over the next millennium. As mentioned above, the pottery industry was a long-lived phenomenon at Kale Akte, an enduring *conjoncture*. The amphorae in which the wine was transported overseas have been demonstrated to have been locally made, and the quantification of the finds and the careful study of the fabrics, aided by thin-section analysis, has led to the identification of a range of local products, with an especial concentration in the Imperial period. We can say with absolute certainty that wine-carrying amphorae of forms Dressel 2/4 and Termini 151/354 were manufactured locally at Kale Akte/Calacte, and there is a high degree of probability also that earlier containers, in circulation during the later Hellenistic period (the types known as MGS III, MGS VI or 'late Greco-Italic', and also a local version of Dressel 1), all of them wine containers, were likewise made in kilns at Kale Akte or very close by. In addition, local versions of the MGS II, MGS III, MGS V wine-containers and in particular of the early imperial Dressel 21/22, a Punic-inspired shape that like its predecessors carried fish-sauce, were also manufactured either at Kale Akte itself or somewhere in the Nebrodi coastal region not far away. This production and export of fish extracts on the north Sicilian shore was comparatively short-lived, lasting for much of the first century AD, when Sicilian fish products were able to compete on the Mediterranean market. But this was small-scale production by comparison with the local wine output, which lasted many centuries longer. The thin-section analyses undertaken on the amphora material suggest that there were significant variations in the clays, and especially in the degree of tempering that the potters used, all within a fairly restricted, localised area of production.

Overseas imports

The importing of considerable amounts of overseas produce can also be considered a very enduring aspect (*conjoncture*) of the history of Kale Akte, which can be traced for the entire period between its first emergence as a small trading post, through the establishment of an urban centre, and lastly in the form of a maritime *vicus* specialising in production and export. Imports began when Kale Akte had trading connections with the Aegean already in the late sixth century BC, and as a trading centre did not fade out until sometime in the course of the sixth century AD, when demographic decline is demonstrated above all by the increasing abandonment of rural settlements in its hinterland; this by itself was no doubt due mainly to a fall in the volume of trade. This was a time of uncertainty in the western Mediterranean with growing security concerns, a demographic crisis, shrinking demand, and a collapse of markets. Rome did not need small centres of production like Calacte any more: after the catastrophic Gothic wars its reduced size meant that it could supply itself from its hinterland. This crumbling of empire was accompanied also by a collapse of the economy of Italy and of much of the western Mediterranean.

The ceramic evidence from Caronía and especially Marina di Caronía, above all the amphorae, constitutes the main source for the understanding of the patterns of production and supply – of what commodities were imported, exported and consumed at the site. The material presented constitutes important evidence for trade at Kale Akte and its nearest region. Since Sicily played a central role in ancient Mediterranean trade, in particular between Italy and North Africa but also between east and west, the finds of extra-regional origin also reflect the goods and commodities that reached even places like Kale Akte, one of many small settlements that lay beside a major trading route.

An unusual aspect of the present work is that in addition to the study of fabrics and the attribution of different amphora types to specific geographical sources, is the fact that quantification of finds was also attempted. This has allowed a more exact understanding of the numerical proportions of different amphora types and foodstuffs at any one given period. Although the percentages should be regarded as indicators rather than hard-and-fast 'facts', they still reflect important fluctuations over time, and the tentative conclusions reached will in all probability not be dramatically changed by future research. The same can be said about the patterns of production and supply which emerge from these figures. Some very strong trends can be singled out as especially important: first, the gradual shift from the dominance of regional, Sicilian products in the Hellenistic period (especially in fine wares and lamps, but also in wine), which reflect a productive and flourishing Sicilian economy at the time, to a complete domination of overseas imports and, at the same time, of locally produced goods (wine and fish products) during the Imperial period, the last two exported on a large scale. From a more generalised production of several different commodities on a small to medium scale during the Hellenistic period, there is a change in the imperial period to a very strong concentration on the export of wine, and for a shorter time also on fish products. At the same time Calacte relied almost exclusively on imports from other parts of the Empire for supplying other goods and commodities. At that time there existed a highly integrated market with the same large-scale productions, from a few key centres, dominating finds assemblages not just at small settlements like Calacte but everywhere around the shores of the Mediterranean. The second significant trend is a shift, between the early Imperial period and late antiquity, from a modest to a very considerable importation of olive oil, and a shift too from a dependency on wine from Italy and Gaul in the first century AD, to a comprehensive supply of locally produced wine in the fourth and fifth centuries AD.

Of course imports of different commodities created their own individual patterns. For imported amphorae, the prevalence of Campanian fabrics among the MGS V containers at Kale Akte is a significant discovery, as it demonstrates that Campanian wines reached Sicily over a much longer period than previously recognized, stretching for some 300 years from the late fourth century BC to the first half of the first century AD. There was little overseas import of olive oil at this time, and no sign that North African production in the Hellenistic period ever reached the island; presumably local oil served Sicily's needs, but we lack the details. The late Punic amphorae that did reach Kale Akte and elsewhere in Sicily at that period are more likely to have contained fish products. Our work has also shown that wine amphorae of form Lamboglia 2, previously little recognised in the island, were certainly reaching the north coast from its production centres in central Dalmatia (principally Narona, the island of Issa, and probably also Salona) and probably from other known production sites on the Italian coast of the Adriatic; this container was long thought to have carried oil rather than wine. The discovery of a Dalmatian production also underlines the important role of Roman colonies in the provinces as large-scale producers of wine. The significant number of Gaulish amphorae at Kale Akte was also a surprise, in terms of quantity a larger import than has been generally hitherto assumed for Sicily. In the Late Empire, the massive imports of especially the oil-carrier Africana 1 but also Africana 2 (fish products) and Tripolitana 2 and 3 (oil) are striking, but this African dominance is a pattern repeated in many places throughout Sicily. Among fine wares, while huge quantities of Italian and African *sigillata* occasion no surprise, comparatively small assemblages of Eastern, 'Tripolitanian' (Campanian) and Gaulish *terra sigillata*, as well as Megarian bowls and Pergamene ware, are noteworthy, not least because it suggests that these rarer products are to be expected even on small coastal sites like Calacte and not only in the larger urban centres. The problem, as so often, is the absence of detailed study of ceramics at all but a handful of Sicilian sites during this period.

Taxation

Taxation was an economic fact of life whenever Sicily was intimately connected with a politically dominant empire. State intervention in the economy of Kale Akte became important when the town fell under Syracuse's sway in the fourth century BC, and again later when it formed part of the Roman province. Whereas taxation under the former did not intensify the economy, the Roman grain *annona* from the late third to the late first centuries BC certainly did, directly and indirectly, by stimulating agricultural production of all sorts, by the increased use of established shipping routes to Rome and elsewhere in Italy, and by the increase in regional trade between Sicilian ports. Taxation played a less important role from the late first century BC to the late third century AD, when the likely demise of the local oil industry was directly caused by the availability of imported cheap *annona* oil from North Africa. From the early fourth to the early sixth centuries AD, however, Roman taxes on wine and grain played a crucial role in the Sicilian economy. Taxation therefore (a *conjoncture*) stimulated increased production of particular commodities at particular periods, but in the long run it was subordinate to the law of supply and demand – and it was above all the demands of a growing metropolis that were the targets of production, in Sicily as elsewhere in the Mediterranean, and which the island's geographical location, so comparatively close to the *caput mundi*, presented an ideal opportunity to exploit.

The apparent non-existence of Late Republican Sicilian oil amphorae and the small numbers of Sicilian wine amphorae from the same period at Caronía and other Sicilian sites suggest that these commodities were not shipped overseas to Rome. Contrary to what has been supposed up to now, it seems that the oil and wine *decuma* under Roman control was a tax in kind that was consumed wholly within the island. Only foodstuffs which were considered basic for survival (grain, and from the third century AD also oil) were part of the official *annona* destined for Rome. Because of their huge social and economic importance, it was too dangerous to leave these commodities to the whims of the free market. Fish products never achieved this status as a food staple, but wine apparently did in Late Antiquity, not because of a change of its status as a taxable commodity, but the result of the weakening of market mechanisms after the middle of the third century AD. Wine was not essential for survival, but was such an important feature in everyday life and culture that it was considered crucial to secure supplies of it for the *Urbs* in order to satisfy the *plebs*.

Empires

Kale Akte was of course strongly influenced by the political structures responsible for taxation, *Empires*. Already from the beginning of Kale Akte's history, the city of Syracuse was ever-present in the background, interested in the foundation of a friendly settlement on the north coast. The trading post and the earliest exchanges between Greeks and Sikels at Marina di Caronía were a direct consequence of that larger phenomenon, the Greek 'colonisation' of Sicily. The foundation of the *polis* of Kale Akte by Ducetius can be considered therefore as the tail-end of this phenomenon, when the indigenous inhabitants, increasingly 'Greek' in their behaviour, began to merge with Greeks and establish ethnically mixed communities.

The reason for this endeavour under the aegis of Syracuse was, as we have seen, driven by an interest to 'Hellenise' the non-Hellenic Nebrodi coast. It had not been a very attractive area for Greek colonists, as it lacked really good harbours and in particular large expanses of agricultural land for cultivation. Nevertheless, the Nebrodi were rich in other natural resources and the area was strategically important as a buffer-zone against the Carthaginian *epikrateia* further west. If a Hellenising goal was the main reason for the foundation of Kale Akte, it certainly made an impact. The foundation of a *polis* of Greek character, partly settled by Greeks, would have increased the volume of Greek imports to the Sikel hinterland, and not least brought with them Greek culture and Greek ideas. This was to become a principal mission of Kale Akte during its millennium-long existence: to supply both coast and hinterland with goods, commodities and ideas from the wider world, while simultaneously exporting a surplus to provide cash to enrich its inhabitants.

The power of Rome and its Empire was of course much more durable and on a completely different scale. Its influence on the economy as well as that of the Carthaginian Empire were already being felt in Sicily from the late fourth century BC. The direct political control of Rome determined Kale Akte's local economy to a very large degree: the increasing growth of production and scale of export out at Kale Akte between the Late Republican and the Late Imperial period is a phenomenon impossible to imagine without the impact of Rome and its Empire.

Increased demand is the single most important factor behind the intensification of trade in Classical and Hellenistic times, clearly connected with the political expansion of the *polis*. Increasing demand in the Hellenistic period is also connected directly with the rise of empires, especially Rome's from the second century BC. We have seen the correlation between *poleis* or *empires* with their enormous territories on the one hand, and large-scale amphora production on the other, an illustration of the intimate connection between ithe two. Local products exported northwards from Kale Akte and elsewhere along the north and east Sicilian coasts, from the beginning of the first century AD onwards, can be directly connected with the growth of the city and Empire of Rome.

The economy of the Roman Empire was not a genuinely free 'world economy' in the modern sense, without borders, because it was intimately connected with and related to the needs first of the city of Rome and only secondly elsewhere in its Empire. When Rome lost political control of Sicily, to Byzantium in the sixth century, economic activity at Kale Akte was drastically reduced. Quite simply the vitality of a small trading centre like Kale Akte/Calacte cannot be imagined without both the voracious demand and the magnetism of Rome. It was Rome and the Italian peninsula that first supplied our small Sicilian community with products and commodities when it needed them, but which later also gave Kale Akte the incentive to make a profit through its own productivity, to help meet the insatiable demands of the *caput mundi*. When we speak of a 'free' market economy, it is in the sense that it is not one fundamentally organised by the State: traders are free and independent. However, in Roman times, the framework around which and in which such people lived and worked was the Empire and its interests, just as during the Classical period the economy was dominated by the concerns of the *polis*, although traders acted independently of it. It could be argued that the main difference between the earlier Greek economy and the larger Hellenistic and Imperial ones was one of scale and organisation: the main components of trade and how it functioned remained essentially the same. From the late Archaic period until the Late Roman empire, trade based on private individual enterprise, and cabotage with small ships carrying mixed cargoes, loading and unloading goods in many different ports, was the principal means of commercial exchange, quite separate from the main maritime 'highways' that connected the big urban centres of the Mediterranean.

'Events'

The short-term perspective within the *longue durée* concerns political narrative history and individuals. To what extent can it be argued that historical events which directly and indirectly impacted on the history of Kale Akte were important compared to the long- and middle-term *structures*? Take the supposed foundation of a settlement by Ducetius. A combined hill- and maritime settlement existed here more than a century before this date, so Ducetius was not building anew on a virgin site, nor did it constitute a dramatic break with the past. Rather, an already existing Sikel hill-top settlement, enlarged in 446/440 BC with Sikel and Greek settlers, gradually grew into a small urban centre (*polis*) towards the end of the fifth century BC. Other hill settlements in the micro-region such as Haluntium and Apollonia cannot show any historical foundation events (*ktisteis*), but evolved gradually into urban communities in the course of the late fifth and fourth centuries BC. All this may have been made possible because of increasing interest on the part of Zancle, Syracuse and other powerful Sicilian *poleis* in northern and eastern Sicily. By contrast the only town in our micro-region founded by an *oikistes*, Halaesa, grew very quickly, within the course of only fifty years, to become the most important urban centre of the area.

The inclusion of Kale Akte within territory under Agathocles' control, from 307 to 289 BC, and then Mamertine domination between the 280s and 269 BC, probably impacted negatively on our settlement, if as seems likely they had to pay some kind of grain tax during this time. This may have begun to stimulate farmers and craftsmen to increase production in order to create a surplus to balance the economic hardship caused by taxation. The main 'game-changer', however, was the First Punic War, after which Kale Akte came under Roman rule. The close economic ties with Rome and the grain *annona* would have further stimulated agriculture and local crafts. A crucial consequence of the Second Punic War was that Mediterranean trade increased to new levels, unthinkable before, thanks to the creation of a unified *Mare Nostrum*. The possibilities of enrichment through trade, especially after the inclusion of Africa into the Empire in 146 BC, opened up exponentially for Kale Akte and for harbour towns everywhere in the central Mediterranean, and the island of Sicily at the heart of that sea, and not least its north coast, lay in pole position to take advantage of both north–south and east–west routes that were now to dominate sea-borne commerce for centuries.

In the third quarter of the first century BC, the Nebrodi area and the north-east coast may have supported Sextus Pompey, and so were meted out punishment at the hands of Octavian. Both Kale Akte and Apollonia may have suffered serious damage and looting at this time, the latter fatally. Kale Akte with its harbour was more resilient and bounced back, beginning wine exports for the first time on a large scale in the early Imperial period; at the same time a salted tunny industry, also for export, started up either at either Kale Akte or close by. The Augustan reforms of 22/21 BC had little effect on Kale Akte, but hit wealthier Halaesa harder, since the latter lost the privileged tax-free status that it had enjoyed under the Roman Republic; there are some signs of economic stagnation in its territory soon after. Otherwise, it seems that the settlements in the early Imperial period followed the same general trends as elsewhere in Sicily: hill-towns were gradually depopulated and abandoned, whereas maritime centres prospered. The decline and abandonment of our hill town *c.* AD 100 can be seen, therefore, as part of a general economic change, but it may have been hastened at Kale Akte by some kind of natural disaster, possibly an earthquake. An increase in rural settlement in the second century AD is a likely corollary of this population shift.

Meanwhile life in the maritime settlement, as the excavations in *contrada* Pantano have shown, continued until a general decline in the fifth and especially the sixth centuries AD; but it suffered a major setback before then with a disastrous earthquake in the fourth century, possibly in the 360s AD. The place still had some economic importance because of its harbour, but activity was now on a reduced scale. Much of the population in the area probably now lived in the surrounding countryside. The new economic focal point was no longer the town or the *vicus*, but rather the rural estate.

Events like the incursions of the Vandals in AD 440 have been used often to explain Sicilian economic decline, but it is unlikely that they reached as far north as Calacte, and in any case continued amphora production throughout the fifth century showed no signs of rupture. To be sure, western Mediterranean trade declined significantly in volume during the fifth century, and reduced demand would have been felt economically at Calacte. The short-lived Vandal control of territory in western Sicily in the middle years of the fifth century AD foreshadowed Rome's loss of Sicily (then part of the Ostrogothic kingdom of Italy) to Constantinople in AD 535. With it came the breaking of a centuries-old link binding Sicily, and particularly its north coast, with Rome. The rupture should not, however, be exaggerated: although the Roman Church did not control all of Sicily as a territory, it inherited economic interests there from the emperors, and still owned vast estates in the seventh century AD, as the letters of Gregory the Great show; and those estates may well have still exported wine. However, such a trade was on a completely different scale (a much smaller one) than before, and was now centred on rural estates, not urban or semi-urban centres. In a Mediterranean world where the western part including Italy was in serious economic decline, and an eastern part which still to a large extent prospered, the north coast of Sicily, the one which naturally looked towards the Italian peninsula and Rome, became a shadow of its former self. Just as it once, in Archaic times, had been a backwater when the principal Greek trading routes passed Sicily's east and southern shores, Calacte was now once more a Mediterranean backwater, remote from the main trade routes heading for the east and its great metropolis, Constantinople.

The long-term consequences of any 'catastrophic' event, such as earthquake, warfare, plunder and fire, depend on the extent to which a society, any society, is economically, politically and culturally resilient. If there was an interest and economic capacity to reconstruct what had been destroyed, that would take place. After the early Empire, the *polis* of Kale Akte disappeared, and with it its associated political and economic organization. From now on, from the second century AD onwards, the maritime settlement depended entirely for its very existence on the volume of maritime trade and the demand of the markets in Rome, Italy and elsewhere. Calacte seems to have been at least partially rebuilt after the earthquake of the 360s AD, but it seems likely that there either was no interest or no money to rebuild the larger commercial buildings in the harbour area. Unless new structures were built elsewhere, the decline seems to point, from the second half of the fourth century onwards, to a lower level of business activity connected with production and trade.

Conclusions

Not surprisingly, it is difficult to identify individual short-lived events that left a profound impact on the economic history of Kale Akte, especially if we only consider events brought about by Sicilian agency alone. With the town's inclusion, along with the rest of Sicily, into the framework of the Roman Empire, it became part of a much wider story, where external political forces were the much more powerful agents of economic prosperity and decline. The Second Punic War is one of these major turning points, when human decisions and agency had enormous repurcussions, not least for the north coast of Sicily.

The different *conjonctures* constituted the context for events. However, they are intrinsically part of the same fabric and cannot be divided from each other. Processes are made up of a series of events, each more or less important; each is on a different scale of magnitude, but all are part of a unity. Here, this viewpoint has been adopted to show not only that historical events were part of a much larger whole, but also that processes cannot be viewed as impersonal ones, or 'natural forces', since they are shaped by human agency and human activity. Most trends or processes which have been stressed in this study are of a 'medium-duration' nature. All these different kinds of process – surplus production, imports from overseas, the impetus that led to greater production and exchange – were very largely dependent on long-term geographical processes and attitudes during the *longue durée*. In antiquity, as today, human activity shaped the landscape, and attitudes such as a natural human desire to strive for economic advantage in order not only to survive but to prosper, inevitably fluctuated over the course of a millennium. The nature and intensity of that desire shifted according to varying economic and political conditions. Production and exchange at Kale Akte, as in ancient Greco-Roman economies as a whole, was not brought about merely through interference by a centralising state or empire. The state wanted to secure staple supplies for its metropolis, and did so through the *decuma/annona*, but many other products were also commercialised *en masse* long before such arrangements were put in place; and later private commercial activity ran parallel to, and independently of, state-driven commerce and trade. More fundamental and significant in the wider picture than the interventions by state or empire were the forces of supply and demand, the framework within which the state was also forced to operate. The intensity of those demands was no doubt boosted by the rise of powerful empires, which gave birth to new incentives and new opportunities to acquire and accumulate wealth. Intimately connected with the forces of supply and demand is independent cabotage activity, the 'connectivity' and 'redistribution' of which Horden and Purcell write, primarily motivated by the constant desire for profit. Kale Akte/Calacte was a small settlement intensely involved in both large-scale production and commercial exchange. The results from this study of a small north Sicilian settlement and its micro-region are consistent with the view that the Mediterranean truly was a network of innumerable interdependent, inter-connected, and mostly small-scale, market entities.

Riassunto italiano

Capitolo 1: Gli insediamenti

Il Capitolo 1 tratta innanzitutto la storia della città di Kale Akte (greco) o Calacte (latino), l'odierna Caronía e Marina di Caronía, e anche degli insediamenti vicini di Apollonia (Monte Vecchio), Haluntium (San Marco d'Alunzio) e Halaesa (vicino Tusa). Kale Akte ('Bel promontorio' o 'Bella costa' in greco) fu già menzionata da Erodoto che racconta come i profughi milesi e sami furono invitati dalla città di Zankle a fondare una città presso un sito chiamato Kale Akte nel 494 a.C. Ma quando i profughi Ioni arrivarono a Rhegion furono persuasi ad abbandonare il progetto e ad occupare la città di Zankle i cui cittadini erano occupati in quel momento con l'assedio di un'altra città. Tradizionalmente il nome Kale Akte è stato tradotto come 'Bella costa' non indicando così un sito preciso. Comunque è poco probabile che gli Ioni avessero accettato di intraprendere un viaggio così lungo e pericoloso senza avere un sito preciso e ben definito ove fondare un nuovo insediamento. Optando per la seconda alternativa 'Bel punto' o 'Bel promontorio' avrebbe risolto il problema, il nome indicando così un sito topografico ben preciso. Tale interpretazione è avvalorata anche dai nuovi dati provenienti dai recenti scavi a Caronía e Marina di Caronía, che indicano l'esistenza di un porto già a partire dal VI secolo a. C. Il primo sito di Marina di Caronía fu quindi situato su un promontorio facilmente individuabile dalle navi greche, e potrebbe essere identificato come il 'Bel promontorio', punto di attracco per i marinai e commercianti greci. Il sito esatto dell' insediamento pianificato dagli Ioni rimane sconosciuto, ma è altamente probabile che l'altopiano di contrada San Todaro, che controllava il porto, sia il luogo prescelto. È certo che nè Marina di Caronía, in mancanza di una posizione protetta, nè l'altura di Caronía, limitata in estensione ed inaccessibile con i suoi dirupi scoscesi, fossero adatte per un tradizionale insediamento urbano del tipo greco.

Secondo Diodoro Siculo, nel 446 a. C. il capo siculo Ducezio, di ritorno dall'esilio di Corinto insieme a coloni corinzi e siculi, fondò l'insediamento di Kale Akte. Se si paragona il sito di Caronía con l'altro sito presumibilmente fondato da Ducezio, Menai (Mineo), si evince che i due siti collinari sono topograficamente simili e hanno una posizione topografica simile ad altri siti siculi, tranne per il fatto che Kale Akte fu fondata vicino al mare. Gli scavi recenti non hanno dato informazioni sul suo piano urbano nel V secolo. Questo fatto dipende dai diversi strati di insediamento urbano costruiti dal periodo ellenistico fino ad oggi. Finalmente l'identificazione di Caronía con la Kale Akte di Ducezio è ormai certa, confermata sia da mattoni bollati con il probabile monogramma della città, sia dalla presenza di numerose monete bronzee coniate dalla *polis* in età ellenistica.

Dopo la discussione sulla fondazione di Kale Akte segue un riassunto della storia della città e delle città vicine, dal periodo classico fino alla tarda antichità. Si arriva alla conclusione che la città di Halaesa si distingue dalle altre città poichè fu fondata come insediamento *ex novo* con uno scopo assolutamente strategico da una forza politica radicata nel territorio. Al contrario Kale Akte fu probabilmente fondata in un sito già abitato, non da una forza politica che controllava il territorio stesso, ma da poteri esterni che avevano il solo interesse di fondare una base puramente commerciale su questa costa. Come gli altri insediamenti vicini di Apollonia e Haluntium, anche Kale Akte aveva le caratteristiche di una città che si sviluppava gradualmente e lentamente; le sorti di questa dipendevano dal controllo sul porto e dal suo successo commerciale. Il sito di Halaesa fu scelto invece come centro del potere da una forza politica radicata nel territorio, ed il suo successo dipese dal commercio del grano ed altri prodotti e dal potere acquisito controllando tale commercio.

L'importanza di Kale Akte continua a crescere nel periodo ellenistico. Durante la prima e seconda guerra punica, soprattutto durante quest'ultima, molto probabilmente Kale Akte godeva della miglior posizione per lo sfruttamento del commercio marittimo tra le *poleis* dei Nebrodi. Halaesa e Haluntium rimangono comunque politicamente le città più importanti fino al primo impero, essendo tutte e due *municipia* dal periodo augusteo, mentre Kale Akte rimane *civitas stipendiaria*. Dopo il I secolo d.C. l'insediamento di Marina di Caronía, ormai conosciuta come Calacte, diventa il secondo insediamento in importanza dopo Halaesa grazie al suo porto e alla sua posizione favorevole all'esportazione e al commercio, mentre l'inaccessibile Haluntium, priva di un buon approdo, rimane più o meno abbandonata. L'insediamento di Marina di Caronía fiorisce nei secoli III e IV d. C. insieme a quelli di Halaesa e Capo d'Orlando, centri dediti ad una fiorente produzione e conseguente esportazione del vino locale.

Capitolo 2: Il territorio: risorse e communicazioni

Il Capitolo 2 studia il territorio che circondava Kale Akte e le città limitrofe. Entrambi il territorio e il paesaggio definivano i confini dell'insediamento, dettandone la capacità di sviluppo. Il paesaggio favoriva le comunicazioni e la viabilità, decisive per la crescita dell'insediamento. La valle del Halaisos costituiva un passaggio naturale attraverso i monti dei Nebrodi, segnando la differenza tra Halaesa, una delle città più importanti della Sicilia, e Kale Akte che invece non raggiunse mai un ruolo politico importante. Le vie, probabilmente di origine preistorica, erano spesso poco più che tracce nel paesaggio e seguivano le configurazioni del terreno. È dubbio in che modo la Via Valeria, via primaria della costa settentrionale, sia stata migliorata nel periodo romano. Le comunicazioni con l'interno furono essenziali per l'economia di Kale Akte; non si trattava di vie vere e proprie, ma solo di sentieri di montagna, le cosidette trazzere, che attraversavano i Nebrodi. La via principale verso l'interno seguiva il dorsale ad est della valle del torrente Caronía, dove sono stati segnalati diversi insediamenti rurali. Uno di questi fu probabilmente quello di Solusapre menzionato nell'*Itinerarium Antonini*.

La geografia indubbiamente dettò anche le condizioni per le vie marittime le quali, tuttavia, dipesero più da congiunture economiche e politiche. È importante differenziare le rotte che seguivano le coste e facevano parte del commercio su scala ridotta, dalle 'autostrade' del mare che facevano parte del commercio inter-regionale su grande scala. Le rotte costiere a cabotaggio probabilmente rimasero costanti durante i secoli qui studiati, se paragonate alle rotte del commercio su grande scala che furono più influenzate da circostanze economico-politiche.

Kale Akte come insediamento può essere capito soltanto partendo dalle sue possibilità di comunicazione. La città offriva uno sbocco alle merci provenienti dai Nebrodi; le materie prime più importanti erano probabilmente il legno e la lana. A questi bisogna aggiungere anche prodotti manufatti a Kale Akte come la ceramica, il vino e il tonno salato. Semplici mulattiere, le trazzere, collegavano l'entroterra collinare e montuoso dei Nebrodi alla pianura costiera, a Kale Akte ed al mare.

Si può presupporre che Kale Akte sia stata una tappa del viaggio dei *theoroi* delfici all'inizio del II secolo a.C., ipotesi avvalorata dal fiorente porto commerciale di quell'epoca e dalla presenza del culto di Apollo. Si discute inoltre del cosidetto 'ponte romano' a Caronía, considerato una struttura non anteriore al XVI secolo. È probabile che il ponte sia stato costruito sopra una struttura esistente già nel periodo romano, che permetteva il passaggio attraverso il torrente.

Il territorio collinare e montuoso era adatto alla coltura della vite e al pascolo; invece era chiaramente limitata la sua potenzialità per l'agricultura in generale, se paragonata a quella delle grandi pianure della parte orientale dell'isola o a quelle che circondavano Himera e Palermo ad ovest. L'esistenza di piccole città indipendenti situate in un raggio di breve distanza, nessuna con un particolare vantaggio rispetto alle altre, rese impossibile lo sviluppo di una *polis* di più grandi dimensioni in questo territorio.

Il grano era la risorsa più importante della Sicilia ma la sua importanza nell'economia di Kale Akte fu probabilmente modesta, viste le limitate aree di suolo fertile. La viticoltura, secondo ramo economico per importanza in Sicilia, fu invece il più rilevante a Kale Akte e nei dintorni. Ciò è suggerito da una delle più comuni monete coniate dalla città che rappresenta Dioniso e grappolo d'uva. L'oleocultura era probabilmente praticata ovunque nell'isola e sembra che Kale Akte fosse autosufficiente nel consumo di olio di oliva fino alla tarda antichità, quando l'olio nordafricano a buon mercato potrebbe aver messo in crisi l'oleocultura siciliana.

I boschi dei Nebrodi erano una riserva cruciale di ricchezze naturali. Il legno era di straordinaria importanza usato soprattutto per la costruzione delle navi, le quali avevano un'importanza strategica soprattutto durante il dominio di Sesto Pompeo sull'isola. Le fornaci della ricca produzione di ceramica della città erano alimentate da imponenti quantità di legno provenienti dai boschi. Il pascolo deve aver giocato un ruolo economico per i Nebrodi di non poco conto; i tanti oscilla qui trovati suggeriscono una fiorente economia tessile e probabilmente la lana fu un prodotto di esportazione particolarmente richiesto. Oltre ai boschi e alla viticoltura, il mare costituiva la risorsa principale della città. La produzione di tonno salato fu quasi sicuramente un'attività importante per l'esportazione in periodo tardo-ellenistico e in prima età imperiale.

Capitolo 3: La ricerca archeologica a Caronía e Marina di Caronía

La Soprintendenza di Messina intraprese scavi a Caronía nel 1999 e 2005 e a Marina di Caronía nel 1999–2001 e 2003–05; tali scavi hanno fornito molte informazioni nuove sulla storia dell'insediamento urbano di Kale Akte e della sua frazione marittima Calacte. Le tracce più antiche dell'occupazione urbana risalgono alla fine del V/inizio IV secolo a.C. mentre non si sa praticamente nulla sulle caratteristiche della fondazione di Ducezio. Quello che si può dedurre dalle informazioni pervenute finora è che l'insediamento si estendeva sulla parte settentrionale della collina, dall'area della moderna Porta Torre verso nord e che l'orientamento del piano urbano era organizzato su un'asse nord-sud, est-ovest.

In età ellenistica la città si espandeva su terrazze che davano sui versanti settentrionali e orientali. L'agorà, in base ai ritrovamenti sul versante orientale, può ipoteticamente essere localizzata nell'area pianeggiante sottostante il castello, tra Casa Cangemi e la Chiesa Madre. È probabile che sulla sommità, dove oggi si erge il castello normanno, fosse nell'antichità situato il santuario principale della città, forse quello di Apollo. Un santuario di Apollo è stato menzionato da un'iscrizione greca pubblica trovata a Caronía. In aggiunta si può presumere l'esistenza soprattutto del culto di Dioniso, ma anche quello di Atena, Eracle ed Ermes, divinità tutte presenti sulle monete coniate da Kale Akte. A sud della città antica l'area del municipio moderno e di contrada Pozzarello era destinata alla maggiore necropoli della città, mentre una necropoli più piccola si trovava a nord in contrada San Todaro.

La scoperta di alcuni muri di terrazzamento risalenti alla fine del I secolo a.C., che furono in parte fondati in cisterne preesistenti, suggerisce una ricostruzione almeno parziale della città in questo periodo. Ritrovamenti di punte di lancia e missili di piombo, nonchè tracce di fuoco, indicano che Kale Akte fu saccheggiata verso la fine della guerra tra Ottaviano e Sesto Pompeo, forse come rivendicazione per il supporto dato a quest'ultimo.

I dati archeologici fanno pensare ad una distruzione e ad un repentino abbandono dell'insediamento verso la fine del I secolo d.C. Probabilmente un terremoto ne fu la causa, meno probabili gravi smottamenti del terreno. Anche se la maggior parte degli abitanti abbandonò il sito, vi rimasero sparsi insediamenti rurali in età medio e tardo-imperiale.

A contrada Pantano, Marina di Caronía, gli scavi sono stati decisamente più estesi e possediamo dati molto più dettagliati rispetto a Caronía. Gli edifici più antichi si possono datare alla fine del V secolo a.C. e furono probabilmente usati per lo stoccaggio delle merci nell'area portuale. Ritrovamenti ceramici dalla fine del VI alla prima parte del V secolo a.C. fanno pensare ad un'attività commerciale pre-esistente la fondazione di Ducezio, anche se finora nessun edificio di questa prima fase di sviluppo del porto è stato identificato.

In una seconda fase edilizia datata al II secolo a.C., fu costruito un grande edificio (Edificio 1) con diverse camere intorno a un cortile, che indica una certa prosperità e attività commerciale della *polis*. L'edificio probabilmente era luogo atto a una produzione 'industriale' e funzionava anche come centro per la distribuzione di merci e derrate. Nello stesso periodo fu costruito accanto un altro edificio (Edificio 2) che probabilmente serviva come *taberna* o *thermopolium*. Più tardi fu aggiunto un portico sul lato occidentale dell'Edificio 1, presumibilmente poco dopo la guerra tra Ottaviano e Sesto Pompeo, quando ambedue gli edifici potrebbero aver subito dei danni. Circa un secolo più tardi gli edifici furono distrutti da un terremoto, forse lo stesso che colpì la città collinare verso la fine del I secolo d.C.

Nel periodo seguente la distruzione, l'Edificio 2 fu ricostruito sopra le sue antiche fondamenta ma il canaletto coperto fu bloccato insieme all'entrata settentrionale dell'edificio. Sembra che in questo periodo l'edificio fosse destinato soprattutto allo stoccaggio di derrate, come ad esempio il vino locale. L'Edificio 1 fu riutilizzato solo in parte; soltanto l'area aperta del cortile sembra essere stata riutilizzata ma per quali attività rimane sconosciuto. Piccoli edifici, probabilmente destinati allo stoccaggio, come per esempio il vino locale per esportazione, furono costruiti sopra i resti della parte meridionale dell'Edificio 1 e all'esterno del lato occidentale. Si nota un declino in accuratezza e qualità della tecnica usata per gli edifici medio e tardo-imperiali, cosa che coincide con altri dati pervenuti dalla costa settentrionale, dove si evidenzia un chiaro decadimento della cultura urbana a cominciare dal II secolo d.C.

Dopo la distruzione degli edifici probabilmente causata da uno o più terremoti che colpirono la Sicilia orientale e centrale negli anni intorno al 360 d.C., rimaneva soltanto qualche piccolo edificio per lo stoccaggio nel V e forse nella prima parte del VI secolo d.C. È certo che l'attività commerciale si ridusse ad una scala minore rispetto al periodo antecedente. Nonostante non esista quasi nessuna evidenza archeologica del periodo medievale (soltanto due tombe islamiche) è probabile che a Marina di Caronía ci sia stata una continuità di insediamento; una comunità molto piccola ed isolata era probabilmente presente a partire dall'epoca tardo-imperiale fino al XII secolo e alla costruzione del castello normanno quando il geografo arabo Al-Idrisi fa menzione di un porto a Marina di Caronía.

Capitolo 4: La cultura materiale

Gli scavi a Caronía e Marina di Caronía hanno dato alla luce una grande quantità di materiali ceramici che testimoniano un intenso scambio di merci e di derrate, nonchè l'esportazione di una vasta gamma di prodotti locali. Nei periodi arcaici e classici venivano importati:

ceramica attica, corinzia e più tardi siceliota, vino di Locri e vino della costa settentrionale della Sicilia in anfore MGS II, vino da Kerkyra (Corfù) in anfore Corinzie B e olio di oliva corinzio in anfore Corinzie A e A'; purtroppo esistono soltanto ritrovamenti sporadici di questo periodo. Il vino locale forse veniva esportato in anfore MGS II nel IV secolo a.C.

Nella prima parte del periodo ellenistico il vino era importato in anfore MGS III e MGS V da Ischia/Campania, dalla Sicilia settentrionale (MGS III e V) e da Locri (MGS III); i prodotti ittici, probabilmente della costa settentrionale della Sicilia, forse di Solunto, erano importati in anfore puniche tipo Ramón 7.1.2.1. La ceramica cosiddetta 'Gnathia' a vernice nera, come anche le lucerne, erano in questo periodo fatte esclusivamente in Sicilia.

Nel periodo tardo-ellenistico grandi quantità di vino furono importate dalla Campania (Dressel 1), dalla Dalmazia centrale (Lamboglia 2), da Rodi, Cos e Cnido e dalla Sicilia settentrionale; le conserve di pesce provenivano dalla Tunisia e dalla Sicilia nord-occidentale (in anfore 'tubulari' di tradizione punica) e infine quantità ridotte di olio di oliva dalla Puglia (Brindisi). La ceramica a vernice nera e le lucerne erano importate dalla Sicilia orientale e settentrionale ed alcune lucerne anche dall'Italia centrale. La ceramica a vernice nera e quella cosidetta presigillata (a vernice rossa) era prodotta localmente a Kale Akte. Quantità limitate di ceramica di terra sigillata orientale arrivavano dalla Siria ed i pochi frammenti ritrovati di ceramica iberica indicano un'importazione limitata dalla Spagna nord-orientale.

Durante il primo impero cominciò un'esportazione del vino locale su una scala maggiore (Dressel 2/4), ma si importavano anche i vini della Campania (Dressel 2/4) e della Gallia meridionale (Gauloise 4). Sulla costa settentrionale siciliana sembra che fossero prodotte quantità ingenti di tonno salato, poi esportate in Italia e nel Mediterraneo occidentale (Dressel 21/22). Invece quantità limitate di prodotti ittici arrivavano dalla Hispania Baetica (Dressel 7/11) e altrettanto ridotte quantità di olio di oliva dalla Libia Tripolitania (Tripolitana I) e dalla Hispania Baetica (Dressel 20). Pervenivano anche grandi quantità di terra sigillata dall'Italia, soprattutto da Arezzo e Pisa, in quantità inferiori dalla Campania, e ancora più ridotte dalla Gallia meridionale. La ceramica di tipo pergameno, forse dall'Asia Minore, è attestata dalla presenza di un solo frammento, ma potrebbe anche essere di produzione siciliana. Le lucerne erano importate in questo periodo in grande numero dall'Italia centrale, ma venivano prodotte anche nella Sicilia orientale.

Nel periodo tardo-imperiale il vino prodotto allo *statio* di Calacte era esportato su vasta scala in piccole anfore a fondo piatto (Termini 151/354) che col tempo diventarono il tipo Crypta Balbi 2. Una fornace a contrada Chiappe produceva questi tipi di anfore, probabilmente da dopo la metà del IV secolo fino almeno a tutto il V secolo d.C. Si importava vino in piccole quantità (in contenitori del tipo Gauloise 4 e Keay 1B/Dressel 30), fino a quando la produzione vinicola locale cominciò ad essere esportata su grande scala verso la fine del III secolo d.C. Nello stesso periodo notevoli quantità di olio di oliva arrivavano dalla Tunisia, in numeri più ridotti ma sempre importanti dalla Tripolitania, mentre un solo ritrovamento (Dressel 20) indica un' importazione dalla Spagna meridionale. Il *garum* ed altri prodotti ittici erano importati in grandi quantità dalla Tunisia e soltanto pochi frammenti attestano un'importazione dalla Lusitania (Almagro 50/51). La ceramica fine da tavola, la ceramica da cucina e le lucerne erano importate in questo periodo esclusivamente dalla Tunisia. I conten-itori più comuni provenienti da contrada Pantano sono: Dressel 1 campana, Dressel 2/4 campana, MGS V/VI campana, Dressel 2/4 locale, Termini 151/354 locale, Africana 1, Africana 2, Dressel 21/22 locale/nord-siciliana, Gauloise 4 sud-gallico, Tripolitana 3.

Le categorie di ceramica da tavola più comuni sono: terra sigillata italica, terra sigillata africana, vernice nera siciliana (Campana A e C) e ceramica 'gnathia' di produzione siciliana.

Comuni sono le monete a contrada Pantano e nella città collinare, ne sono state trovate per un numero totale di 262, tutte in bronzo tranne un esemplare. L'alta percentuale di monete coniate a Kale Akte conferma l'identità del sito con l'omonima *polis*. Non si ritiene probabile che le monete di Kale Akte siano state coniate solo per un breve periodo negli ultimi decenni del II secolo a.C.; sembra invece che siano state prodotte per una buona parte del I secolo a.C., come le coniazioni di altre città siciliane. Nessuna delle monete provenienti dal cospicuo materiale ritrovato a contrada Pantano può essere datata dopo il 361 d.C., fatto che dimostra un declino nell'attività commerciale e forse denota che lo *statio* di Calacte e il suo porto stavano perdendo la loro centralità, diventando dopo questa data una comunità rurale più piccola e decentralizzata.

Capitolo 5: Modelli di produzione e fornitura

Questo capitolo analizza il materiale ceramico quantificato e discusso nel capitolo 4 e cerca di individuare le tendenze di maggior portata nella produzione e nello scambio di derrate, di ceramica da tavola e di lucerne.

Dai numeri sembra chiaro che a Kale Akte il vino sia stato il prodotto più commercializzato, seguito da olio e prodotti ittici. Incluse le anfore Dressel 21/22 nord-siciliane, atte a contenere prodotti ittici, tali prodotti sono i più commercializzati localmente dopo il vino. Considerando solamente le merci importate, l'olio prevale sui prodotti ittici, e le tendenze variano sensibilmente a seconda del periodo.

Nel Periodo 'A' il materiale proveniente da Caronía è troppo esiguo per qualsiasi statistica o analisi, ma l'immagine generale fornita dai dati archeologici di tutta la Sicilia suggerisce un'elevata importazione di vino dall'Italia meridionale e da Locri, insieme a quantità più ridotte provenienti da Kerkyra (Corfù). L'olio era una derrata relativamente comune, importata da Corinto; ció era possibile grazie agli stretti contatti tra le *poleis* siceliote e le loro città madri in Grecia. Inoltre le importazioni suggeriscono che l'oleocultura non fosse ancora molto sviluppata in Sicilia, visto che l'isola non riusciva a soddisfare la richiesta interna. Per quel che riguarda le conserve di pesce sappiamo molto poco, soltanto che provenivano soprattutto dalla Sicilia punica occidentale, probabilmente in quantità limitate. La ceramica fine da tavola e le lucerne erano realizzate soprattutto nei centri greci della Sicilia, con un'importazione limitata dalla Grecia.

Questo quadro cambia poco nel Periodo 'B'. La tendenza principale è che la produzione di vino in alcuni centri di produzione (per es. Ischia), comincia a crescere fino a raggiungere una scala notevole. Il vino è senza dubbio il bene più richiesto, mentre le importazioni di olio da Corinto sembrano diminuire gradualmente fino a sparire. La Sicilia continua a fornire più grandi quantità di ceramica fine da tavola e di lucerne.

Il Periodo 'C' vede una sostanziale continuità delle tendenze del Periodo 'B' e sembra chiaro che la Sicilia sia ormai autosufficiente in olio, visto che pochissimi contenitori di olio importato sono stati identificati. I prodotti ittici arrivano dalla Tunisia, ma sempre in quantità inferiori rispetto al vino. La ceramica fine da tavola e le lucerne continuano ad essere realizzate in Sicilia, ma ora iniziano alcune importazioni anche dall'Italia centrale. Come nel Periodo 'B' Kale Akte sembra aver prodotto ed esportato il proprio vino locale, ma sempre su modesta scala. Anche la ceramica fine da tavola viene prodotta localmente, ma non è certo se fosse anche esportata.

Nel Periodo 'D' la produzione locale e l'esportazione vinicola crescono in modo significativo, come anche l'esportazione delle conserve di pesce (tonno) di Kale Akte stessa e della sua micro-regione. Nello stesso tempo le importazioni di olio dalla Spagna (Andalucia) e dal Nord Africa incominciano a crescere anche se in quantità moderate.

Nel Periodo 'E' la produzione del vino locale inizia su scala maggiore dal III al V secolo d.C., mentre le deboli importazioni di vino sud-gallico e mauretano spariscono completamente dopo il III secolo. L'olio diventa la merce più importata, seguito dai prodotti ittici, dalla ceramica fine da tavola e dalle lucerne, tutti provenienti dalla Tunisia.

Capitolo 6: Meccanismi commerciali: il mercato e lo stato

Questo capitolo studia il quadro storico-economico di Kale Akte e della Sicilia e quali furono gli incentivi alla base di questo prospero commercio. Quale ruolo giocarono il regno di Siracusa e l'impero romano nella produzione e nello scambio commerciale a Kale Akte? Quale fu il rapporto tra il commercio diretto dallo stato e il libero commercio regolato sulla domanda e offerta?

Sembra che lo scambio commerciale a Kale Akte si sia svolto fin dall'inizio nel quadro di un libero sistema di domanda e offerta. Tramite la sua posizione di 'gateway community' (comunità di accesso) tra greci e siculi, Kale Akte faceva parte della rete commerciale tra la Grecia e le economie in loco, ed era un luogo dove le leggi di domanda e offerta sostituivano le leggi di *philia* che esistevano in ognuna delle società greche e sicule. Anche dopo il V secolo a.C. e la completa acculturazione dei siculi, Kale Akte conservò il suo carattere di 'gateway community' grazie alla sua attività di città portuale dove si incontravano e mescolavano diverse culture. Inoltre Kale Akte era anche un porto di accesso tra il mare e l'entroterra montuoso dell'isola.

Il motore principale alla base di questo scambio commerciale era una certa mentalità, definita dai Greci come *kerdos*, ossia la ricerca del profitto. Guardando lo sviluppo di Kale Akte in modo diacronico, i vari livelli e modi di produzione possono essere collegati ad altrettante variabili dovute all'intensità della domanda. La distribuzione capillare in Sicilia e nel Mediterraneo delle stesse merci e derrate sottolinea l'esistenza di un commercio su piccola scala oltre a quello su scala maggiore e a lunga distanza. Il fatto che già nel periodo arcaico e durante il periodo qui studiato le navi in tutto il Mediterraneo portassero carichi misti di origini diverse, è una chiara indicazione che i mercanti commerciavano su iniziativa privata e indipendente dallo stato. Kale Akte stessa supporta questa tesi: pur essendo una piccola città vi arrivavano molte delle stesse merci e derrate come nei centri urbani più importanti; ciò evidenzia che l'attività di cabotaggio, ossia il commercio su scala minore e quindi privato, giocasse un ruolo fondamentale. Le varie modalità di distribuzione di certe merci indicano prodotti che competevano con altri in un mercato. L'espansione e la contrazione degli scambi erano suscettibili alla concorrenza e alle variabili condizioni economiche locali. La vendita di merci di scarso valore da parte di privati commercianti, prive di interesse per lo stato, sottolinea il ruolo giocato dal singolo mercante che era in grado di agire indipendentemente dallo stato. Il vino e le conserve di pesce venivano senz'altro venduti su iniziativa privata tranne che nel periodo tardo-antico quando il commercio privato del vino non poteva più soddisfare la domanda e lo stato fu costretto ad intervenire. L'olio, al contrario del vino e delle conserve di pesce era fondamentale e divenne il prodotto principale di smercio. Il commercio dell'olio nei periodi classici ed ellenistici non era diretto dallo stato, ciò avviene soltanto con l'impero, per il bisogno di assicurarne agli abitanti di Roma una fornitura costante. Nel frattempo Kale Akte e la Sicilia divennero gradualmente e poi completamente dipendenti dall'olio nord-africano, fatto dovuto all'elevata disponibilità, all'alta qualità e presumibilmente al prezzo basso di tale olio. Conseguenza naturale del dominio dell'impero romano su questo territorio fu la tassazione imposta a Kale Akte.

La crescità di Roma aumentò enormemente le possibilità di profitto e quindi anche quelle per il commercio, questo vale in particolare per i centri costieri come Kale Akte. Roma e il suo impero sembrano essere di importanza cruciale nello stabilire l'influenza della domanda sulla produzione e sul commercio. La metropoli 'Roma' esisteva già nel II e I secolo a.C. con una popolazione di più di mezzo milione di abitanti, ma la produzione su maggior scala cominciò a Kale Akte soltanto nel periodo augusteo. È ovvio che bisogna cercare in altre motivazioni il perchè della domanda sempre più crescente di derrate non riguardanti la sola metropoli.

Non c'è dubbio che la nuova organizzazione dell'impero, insieme alla Pax Romana, giocassero ruoli importanti in questo contesto. Fondamentale per il successo della vinicoltura siciliana fu anche la stagnazione della produzione vinicola nel resto d'Italia, proprio in un periodo di grande crescita demografica dell'Urbe. La domanda da parte di Roma influì sull'economia di Kale Akte già in età tardo-repubblicana e soprattutto influì sull'economia l'*annona*, la tassa sul grano. Però la domanda non creò a Kale Akte una produzione specializzata in grano di tipo 'villa rustica' a causa del territorio relativamente ristretto e non prettamente adatto alla produzione di grano su larga scala.

Comunque il numero delle fattorie aumentò in modo significativo grazie alla crescita della domanda e alle conseguenti opportunità di profitto. L'annona sul grano probabilmente contribuì a sviluppare la specializzazione anche in altri rami dell'agricultura. A Kale Akte e nel suo territorio le fattorie non sembrano mai aver superato una scala media di produzione, furono piuttosto determinanti nell'incremento della produzione la loro crescita in numero e l'aumentata specializzazione. Di conseguenza nel tardo I secolo a.C. e I secolo d.C., i produttori di merci e beni che non potevano competere in qualità e quantità con il mercato pan-Mediterraneo morirono. I centri urbani lontani dal mare avevano difficoltà a sopravvivere poichè i buoni collegamenti erano indispensabili all'accessibilità dei loro prodotti sui mercati dell'*Urbs* e del *Mare Nostrum*. Le merci prodotte su modesta scala e di conseguenza i loro mercati diventarono in questo periodo marginali per l'economia.

Sembra che il commercio diretto dallo stato divenne importante già sotto il regno di Ierone II di Siracusa. La conseguente tassa sul grano ne avrebbe sollecitato la coltivazione soprattutto nelle aree costiere. Dopo pochi anni Roma conquistò la Sicilia, e da allora in poi, il grano assunse un ruolo sempre più importante nel commercio. Dato che le forniture di grano per Roma erano sussidiate, altri prodotti siciliani potevano facilmente viaggiare insieme al grano senza ulteriori costi. Questo fatto avrà certamente stimolato la produzione di derrate nelle *poleis* siciliane, ma sembra proprio che, eccetto il grano, la maggior parte della produzione sicula fosse destinata al mercato regionale. Comunque con l'inizio del periodo imperiale Kale Akte cominciò ad esportare vino su scala maggiore, probabilmente con destinazione l'Italia e Roma. È impossibile essere certi riguardo le cause di questo aumento di produzione, ma presumibilmente fu una strategia per bilanciare la perdita di reddito dal grano, visto che la Sicilia non era più il fornitore principale dell'Urbe. Alla fine del III secolo d.C. fu imposta anche una tassa sul vino siciliano per poter bilanciare la generale carenza di questa merce. La tassa sul vino avrà un effetto fortemente stimolante sull'industria vinicola siciliana e quindi anche su Calacte, la quale tra la fine del III e la fine del V/inizio VI secolo d.C. produsse ed esportò vino su una scala mai raggiunta prima. Le importazioni di olio in Sicilia sono insignificanti fino al primo impero, ma quando l'olio verrà sussidiato dallo stato romano la richiesta aumenterà considerevolmente. Infatti quando l'olio viene prodotto in scala massiva in Nord-Africa ed in più è sussidiato, il mercato cambia completamente. La Sicilia adesso importa grandi quantità di olio, probabilmente come già accennato, per una combinazione di buona qualità del prodotto, prezzi bassi e disponibilità. Lo stato e i suoi sussidi quindi giocano un ruolo fondamentale dettando le regole della produzione siciliana in dati periodi. Comunque la tassazione e i sussidi furono delle eccezioni alla regola; la maggior parte del commercio si svolgeva grazie alle iniziative private.

Capitolo 7: Da trading post a villaggio rurale

Questo capitolo riassume gli argomenti dei capitoli precedenti e cerca di trarne le conclusioni. In questo lavoro la cronologia è stata importante poichè la panoramica dei vari periodi facilita la comprensione dei molti processi coinvolti e della loro interazione. Si parte da una visione di lungo termine della geologia, della geografica e della storia dell'insediamento, per poi procedere attraverso fenomeni e tendenze di medio termine fino a una più dettagliata visione storico-politica. La costante durante tutto il periodo studiato è lo scambio commerciale che segue l'andamento del mercato ed il principio di domanda e offerta insieme al cabotaggio, ossia il commercio su modesta scala di iniziativa privata. La maggior parte dell'interazione commerciale a Kale Akte fu probabilmente e in gran parte motivata da interessi privati, ma i mercanti agivano in un più ampio contesto, per molti versi soggetto allo stato che ne dettava le regole. Il commercio privato fu costretto ad adattarvisi con relative conseguenze. Kale Akte attirava i mercanti grazie alla sua posizione geografica di accesso tra il mare e l'entroterra montuoso della Sicilia con le sue ricche risorse.

Tra le tendenze o congiunture di medio termine possiamo annoverare varie forme di insediamento: l'emporio, l'insediamento urbano, il villaggio marittimo/*statio* e i processi di urbanizzazione e ruralizzazione. L'insediamento urbano giunge al suo apice nel I secolo a.C. e I secolo d.C., quando ambedue gli insediamenti collinare e marittimo prosperano. La ruralizzazione comincia nel II secolo d.C. con l'abbandono dell'insediamento collinare e si intensifica verso la fine del IV secolo d.C., dopo la distruzione di gran parte dell'insediamento marittimo. Una locale produzione di eccedenza può essere individuata nel corso di tutto il periodo urbano (fine del V secolo a.C./fine I secolo d.C.) e anche nel periodo tardo-antico dello statio di Calacte tra la fine del III secolo e il V secolo d.C. Nel II e III secolo d.C. c'è un periodo di stallo nella produzione di eccedenza causato da vari fattori. Determinanti furono il collasso della *civitas* di Kale Akte e la diminuzione della domanda sia di grano che di vino. Le importazioni extra-regionali continuarono per più di un millennio dal VI secolo a.C. fino al V secolo d.C. La quantificazione dei ritrovamenti ha permesso una miglior comprensione della relazione quantitativa tra merci e derrate. Grazie al materiale ritrovato, si constata il passaggio dalla dipendenza da merci e derrate prodotte in Sicilia o nell'Italia meridionale ad una completa dipendenza da merci e derrate extra-regionali. Un altro cambiamento è lo sviluppo da una predominante produzione locale su scala medio-piccola di vino e ceramica fine da tavola, ad una crescente specializzazione di produzione di massa di vino locale. La tassazione è un altro importante elemento che stimolò a lungo sia la produzione che il commercio. È possibile concludere che a parte il grano, che era d'importanza vitale per Roma e veniva quindi trasportato oltremare, il vino e l'olio, ambedue tassati come parte della *decuma* nel periodo tardo-repubblicano, venivano probabilmente consumati sull'isola dal governo provinciale.

Gli imperi o altri potenti stati giocarono un ruolo importante nello sviluppo economico della città, soprattutto Siracusa e naturalmente Roma. Siracusa ebbe un ruolo decisivo nella fondazione di Kale Akte e poi nell'ellenizzazione della costa settentrionale, con la fondazione di Tindari e l'incorporazione dell'area nebroidea nei regni di Dionigio I e più tardi di Agatocle e Ierone II. La fondazione di una vasta *epikrateia* o stato ha intensificato e stimolato la produzione ed il commercio in Sicilia. La prosperità di Kale Akte dipendeva quasi esclusivamente dal fiorente commercio di Roma, dalla ricchezza e vastità del suo impero. Anche se il commercio in generale non era monopolio di stato, non si può parlare di un 'world economy' senza frontiere.

Tutte le attività si svilupparono entro il contesto politico dell'impero romano. Quando questo iniziò il proprio declino per poi morire, di conseguenza morì anche il commercio.

A livello locale/regionale la fondazione della città da parte di Ducezio è ovviamente di importanza fondamentale ma non può essere separata dal processo di urbanizzazione di tutta l'area nebroidea. Infatti Ducezio non era un potente capo al momento della fondazione della città e non era in grado di influenzare gli eventi politici in modo decisivo. Da quando Kale Akte diventò parte dell'impero romano, si moltiplicarono di conseguenza eventi storico-politici di una certa portata. La Sicilia diventò la mela della discordia durante le prime guerre puniche e più tardi nella guerra civile tra Ottaviano e Sesto Pompeo. Con la prima guerra punica Kale Akte cadde sotto il dominio di Roma e verso la fine della seconda guerra punica cominciò un rapido sviluppo economico, quando Roma decise di investire concretamente sulla costa settentrionale siciliana. La guerra tra Ottaviano e Sesto Pompeo influenzò probabilmente Kale Akte in maniera negativa, ma la sua importanza come porto commerciale le assicurava ad ogni modo una ripresa veloce. Da dopo la guerra civile fino agli attacchi da parte dei Vandali quattro secoli più tardi, nessun evento storico-politico influenzò negativamente il commercio delle coste siciliane. Sembra che i raid dei Vandali abbiano in se avuto un impatto relativamente limitato sulla prosperità della costa settentrionale.

L'insicurezza generale dopo la fine della *Pax Romana* fu sfavorevole alla produzione ed al commercio. Tutto sommato la *raison d'être* di Kale Akte fu il suo mercato, la sua posizione sul mare e il suo porto, e quando la domanda a Roma e in tutta la penisola declinò in modo drammatico nel corso del VI secolo d.C., i prodotti del *vicus* non furono più richiesti. L'esistenza di Kale Akte per più di un mill-ennio dipese dalla vitalità del cabotaggio, dalla capacità del centro di rimanere un importante nodo nella rete commerciale siciliana e romana – con facile accesso alle rotte principali di Messana e Lipara. Il presente studio dimostra come la Sicilia ed il Mediterraneo in genere costituiva un insieme di numerosi mercati intradipendenti, la maggior parte dei quali piccoli, e come insieme giocassero un ruolo fondamentale per il commercio nel mondo ellenistico e romano.

Appendix 1

Methodological problems and quantification of finds

The material which forms the core and statistical basis of this study is derived from the excavations carried out by the Soprintendenza archeologica di Messina at Caronía and Marina di Caronía in 1999/2000 and 2001. These excavations were directed by Dr Maria Costanza Lentini, and supervised in the field by the author.[1] The excavations were carried out partly at *contrada* Sotto San Francesco on the eastern slope of the hill-town of Caronía, and to a larger extent on a site near the coast in *contrada* Pantano at Marina di Caronía.

The archaeological contexts

The stratigraphic contexts in *contrada* Pantano are difficult to distinguish clearly from each other. The soil is very hard, filled with pottery, and difficult to excavate. Only the deeper contexts from the Early Hellenistic period, and the Classical levels below them, could more easily be distinguished, thanks to damper soil conditions and the tendency of these layers to produce far fewer finds. It seems that all are the remains of commercial activity connected with the different buildings encountered during the excavation. Its large extent and a close study of the finds have, however, made it possible to date all the periods during which the uncovered buildings functioned. The earliest contexts can be placed between the early fifth and the late fourth century BC, but the total area excavated to such a depth was very limited. Because of this, but also because the density of finds was lower, material from this early period is very scarse, nor can it be connected to specific structures. Most of the excavated buildings (phase 2a) probably date to the second half of the second century BC (p. 56). After some alterations (phase 2b), a destruction date at the end of the first century AD for this main building phase is probable. A third phase (pp. 60–1) begins probably not very long afterwards, and continues until the second half of the fourth century AD.

The many coins recovered, albeit most of them badly corroded due to the acidic soil, give us important *termini post quem* dates for many of the deposits. Even if not all of them are able to be fixed precisely, the coins do provide good dating evidence for determining the approximate periods when the material was deposited. A considerable part of it, however, derives from ploughsoil. Although disturbed out of archaeological context, it is still worthwhile including this in the investigation. Studies of the mechanisms involved in ploughing have strengthened this conclusion. Material from a field like the area investigated, which is not sloping and has not been intensely cultivated, is usually well preserved and has not been moved to any greater extent from its original position.[2] It is worth reflecting on the uniqueness of the site: contexts from warehouses or buildings with economic function connected with a harbour have rarely been published or adequately studied anywhere in Sicily. The fact that goods arriving at the port were probably stored here, combined with the abundance of amphora finds, the key to understanding patterns of commercial exchange, gives us a unique opportunity to shine a spotlight on trade and economy at one small settlement on the north Sicilian north coast over a chronological spectrum which spans more than 800 years.

The material which is the focus of the present study is therefore one of only a limited number of Roman archaeological assemblages in Sicily from stratified (and unstratified) contexts that have been extensively studied and published. It consists mainly of ceramic sherds, the majority of which are amphorae, but there are also large amounts of kitchen ware, and somewhat less of fine ware and lamps, the last being the least represented category. Other finds include fragments of terracotta figurines and loom-weights. Roof-tiles, both flat and curved, circular bricks for columns, and flat square bricks were also found in abundance. Apart from the bronze coins, there were many metal objects such as nails, needles, *spatulae* and fishing tools. The glass material was limited and for the most part very fragmentary.

Quantification

Quantification of the material from these excavations is presented below in a series of six Tables. In addition, I have included finds from surface survey at Caronía.[3] The purpose of each table, labelled A1.1–6, is explained in the accompanying captions. In the discussion of quantification, I have also made comparisons with the statistics of finds from the excavations at Marina di Caronía, which took place between 2003 and 2005, which I was also able to examine.[4] The publication of those, however, was a preliminary one, with only a small selection of objects being chosen for cataloguing and even fewer for illustration. The published finds from that excavation, therefore (approximately one hundred pieces only) are not, therefore, representative or comprehensive. I have only made general reference to the main types of finds made in these later excavations.

Problems of representativity

All the 1,152 diagnostic amphora fragments from 1999–2001 were catalogued in an Excel database. Since I have been able to compare them with the larger amount of material excavated at Marina di Caronía in 2003–05, I have been able to check the extent to which the assemblage studied here matches the larger body of material recovered later, which due to its size (at least 3,000/4,000 diagnostic fragments, or about 300 *cassette* [boxes] of material)[5] constitutes a very substantial sample from the site. Here the function of the buildings and the ancient use of the area must be emphasised. It is probable that the range of amphora types excavated in a harbour context is more representative of export/import activities than might be found in a normal domestic settlement context. The area excavated in 2003–05 uncovered more of the same buildings initially excavated in 1999–2001, and thus the general nature of the finds as well as the chronology is the same for both. The material excavated in the later seasons comes from an area three or four times larger than that from which the finds studied here came, but it produced merely more examples of the same types: the new material did not, in short, change in any way the general picture provided in this study or the conclusions reached. The abundance in the late deposits excavated in 2003–05 of the locally produced Termini 151/354 containers, for example, was hardly surprising, nor were the important quantities of other local productions (e.g. imitations of Dressel 2/4 amphorae) and local/micro-regional varieties (Dressel 21/22), as well as Campanian Dressel 1, Tunisian Africana 1 and 2, Tripolitanian 2 and 3 amphorae. The considerable presence of Gaulish amphorae noted in 1999–2001 was also confirmed by the later work.

It is quite likely that large differences in the quantities present of the various types – differences of at least 10% – reflect reality, distinguishing the very common amphora categories, which have more than a 10% share of the material (for example, the local productions, Campanian Dressel 1, and Africana 1 containers) from the rare or fairly uncommon ones that represent 1% or less of the total. The relationship between these smaller categories is, however, more difficult to assess. Chance, natural agents, selection choices dependent on different strategies or excavation techniques, and the skill of individual archaeologists, are all factors in deciding what is excavated, preserved, identified and published for posterity. In view of this, and also because of the limited area excavated, categories represented by only a few fragments can nevertheless be said to be representative of a reasonably large number of amphorae of the same type imported to Calacte. As with any excavation, we must always bear in mind the fact that the material extracted and kept constitutes merely a sample, which gives us a good general idea of the situation at a given site, but not of course a completely exhaustive or comprehensive picture. However, the relative quantities of the major types of amphorae published here have in broad terms been confirmed by the published (and unpublished) material of the 2003–05 excavations, as well as by a collection of 125 amphora fragments from surface survey, also included here.[6]

Quantification of amphorae

Quantification of the material is necessary for any economic study. Without a knowledge of the size and composition of individual components which comprise the total assemblage of material, it is impossible to establish the relative frequency of one category of material against another, or indeed to identify types and sub-types within each category and compare those to each other. In the case of a harbour settlement like Kale Akte/Calacte, quantification is especially important to enable an assessment of the nature and extent of commercial exchange, both exports and imports, as represented by the amphorae.

Amphora fragments were quantified on the basis of the number of rims, bases and handles (hereafter referred to by the shorthand RBH). Handles constitute the largest category (552), followed by rims (401), and then toes and bases (88 and 114 respectively). Each toe/spike generally represents one amphora, since they do not break easily. Handles, on the other hand (which are probably over-represented), do break easily into two: one must, therefore, count at least four fragments for each whole amphora. Rims and bases are also easily broken, often themselves into four or more fragments.[7] Counting rims alone normally excludes the problem of whether or not fragments come from the same vessel, since it is usually possible to see whether two fragments belong to the same rim or not. However, the diameter of the rim sometimes varies greatly from type to type, and therefore in the case of some versions with wide mouths (where exact rim diameters are more difficult to measure on the basis of small fragments, and which are likely to break into more fragments), rims tend to be over-represented compared to handles and spikes. For example, the wide-mouthed Dressel 21/22 type would have been reckoned to be by far the most common amphora type at Marina di Caronía, if only rim sherds were counted. One method which has been proposed to solve this problem is the use of estimated vessel equivalents (e.v.e.).[8] This consists of measuring the arc of a rim sherd and calculating the percentage of the total rim present. The sum of these percentages is then added up, and the result gives the equivalent number of rims/whole vessels. However interesting the e.v.e. method is, I considered the information given by handles and toes/bases too important to be excluded. Furthermore, the e.v.e. method would probably give a much lower estimate than the true amount of vessels present in each assemblage.

It has been argued that only the relative proportions between types can be said to be truly indicative, whereas the absolute number of vessels is much harder to establish.[9] In my study, I have however considered it of vital importance to establish a quantitative basis in order to get a rudimentary idea of the volume of imports and exports at any one period. Two methods were used in order to quantify the amphora assemblage:

A. Those RBH that were of the same type and fabric but the find-spots of which were physically separated by more than two metres from each other, I have counted as belonging to two separate vessels. Fragments of the same type and fabric which came from the same context, or from less than two metres apart, could be reckoned to belong to the same vessel, and so were considered as parts of the same one. The probability that diagnostic fragments from different contexts should belong to the same vessel, among the very fragmented material consisting of several thousand fragments, often very mixed if the contexts were disturbed, must be considered extremely low. This method was carried out on all amphora categories except the local *Ostia* 1, 455/456 (Termini Imerese 151/354) amphora type. It seems likely that the number of vessels calculated according to the RBH method corresponds closely to the real number of vessels.

B. The very large number of RBH from the local Termini 151/354 amphorae, ubiquitous in the excavation area in late Roman levels made it impossible to use the method described above on this category. Here the method of counting with four rim fragments or four handle fragments or four base fragments to estimate each whole amphora was applied, in order to reach a figure for the minimum number of vessels (EMN).[10] The total number of RBH was thus divided by four. This figure must be considered as likely to be some way below the true number of containers. The actual number of vessels present lies somewhere between that representing the minimum number of amphorae on the one hand, and on the other the number calculated by a counting method which treated one fragment as equivalent to one vessel, i.e. the figure stands for the maximum possible number of containers present. The wisest solution seems, therefore, to count this medium number between the possible highest and lowest figure as a rough calculation of the total of containers present. Although not ideal, I regarded this method as the only possible solution in this case, and it was applied only to this single category of material (i.e. just one amphora type), which in any case was unique in being present in vastly superior numbers by comparison with other amphorae, whatever method of quantification was used. For various reasons it was not possible to weigh or count the body fragments in order (perhaps) to achieve a statistically more reliable quantification of the material. I decided that the possible advantages of adopting such an approach would not be matched by a corresponding increase in information, given the amount of time and labour necessary for such an enterprise.

Calculating the number of vessels has meant that it was also possible to calculate the relative amounts of individual commodities (wine, oil, fish sauce or pickled fish) that was transported in each container (Table A1.1–3). This gives more reliable information than the mere counting of RBH, since the latter figures do not take the varying capacity of an individual amphora type into consideration. A North African cylindrical amphora represents more than double the amount of liquid (in that case oil) that a Gaulish or a Sicilian container could carry (of wine). Amphorae prior to the second century AD generally did not differ hugely in capacity (although there are exceptions, like the Dressel 1 container), and as far as possible, therefore, I have taken these discrepancies of capacity into account only when discussing containers from the latest period here under consideration (Period E: p. 106).

About one third of the total assemblage could not be identified or attributed with certainty to any of the known amphora forms, due in part to their very fragmentary nature. Most of these consisted of very poorly preserved handles, most of them in the easily recognizable standard Tunisian fabric. The vast majority certainly belong to the common Africana 1 and 2 amphorae, but they could not be attributed to any certain type. Many of the unidentified fragments, therefore, are likely to document further the substantial presence of late Roman Tunisian amphorae carrying olive oil and fish-sauces, already confirmed in the contexts of that date.

Period	Type	Caronía	Caronía Marina
A	MGS II	0	2
B	MGS III	0	3
B	MGS V	3	4
C	MGS VI/Dressel 1A	3	5
C	Dressel 1A	3	7
C	Dressel 1C	0	2
C	Dressel 1B	2	7
C	Dressel 1	2	21
C	Lamboglia 2	1	10
C	Knidian	1	0
C	Koan	0	5
C	Rhodian	1	6
D	Local Dressel 2/4	3	44
D	Local Gauloise 2 and 3	0	2
D	Central Italian 2/4	0	4
D	Campanian Dressel 2/4	1	15
D	Pélichet 47/Gauloise 4	0	9
D	Schöne-Mau 13/Agora 198/Pompeii 13	0	1
D	Haltern 70	0	2
E	Pélichet 47/Gauloise 4	0	5
E	Keay 1B/Dressel 30B	0	8
E	Termini Imerese 151/354	0	>96 (<384) (240 mean value)
	TOTALS	**20**	**>258 (<546)**

Table A1.1. Local and imported wine amphorae found at Caronía and Marina di Caronía

Fabric analysis

Little attention has been paid in Sicilian archaeology to the fabrics of amphorae, and few publications include thin-section analyses made in a laboratory.[11] This has hindered any serious attempt to assign the production sites of these vessels to specific geographical areas. This is especially so for the 'Greco-Italic' types, some of which are suspected to have been produced in Sicily. One of the few sites where amphora thin-sections studies have been undertaken is Sicilian Naxos, where the different local productions have been thoroughly analysed.[12] The present study aims further to underline the importance of thin-section analysis for the serious study of amphorae and their origins. Samples were taken from a chosen range of diagnostic fragments, and then analysed by Professor Anders Lindahl at the Ceramic Laboratory of the Institute of Quarternary Geology, at Lund University in Sweden (see Appendix 2, pp. 168–76, for full details). Interest was directed primarily in samples taken from what were suspected to have been the locally and/or regionally produced amphorae of types MGS V, Dressel 2/4, Dressel 21/22 and Termini 151/354. The main goal was to identify what were assumed to be the various local fabrics, and samples taken from them were compared with each other, with locally produced pottery and tile, and with the known geological make-up of the Kale Akte area (see Table A1.4). Some fragments also of non-local containers in various fabrics were also examined, in the hope of being able to identify the source of each.

Period	Type	Caronía	Caronía Marina
A	Corinthian A	0	1
C	Brindisi	0	1
D	Dressel 26	0	3
D	Dressel 20	0	2
D	Tripolitanian 1	0	1
E	Dressel 20	0	1
E	Tripolitanian 2 and 3	0	20
E	Africana 1	0	64
E	Keay 13A	0	2
E	Keay 25/Africana 3	0	2

Table A1.2. Imported olive-oil amphorae found at Caronía and Marina di Caronía

The most common amphora types of the late Hellenistic period, such as the Greco-Italic, the Dressel 1 and the Dressel 2/4 forms, were produced in a multitude of different centres, and so in diverse fabrics, in Sicily, Italy and the western Mediterranean, and it is

Period	Type	Caronía	Caronía Marina
B	Ramón 7.1.2.1	0	6
C	Ramón 7.4.2.1–3.3 / van der Werff 1 / Maña C2B	0	3
C	Ramón 7.5.2.1 / van der Werff 2 / Maña C2C	1	2
C	Ramón 7.6.1.1	0	1
D	Dressel 21/22	7	41
D	Dressel 7/11	0	13
E	Africana 2	0	30

Table A1.3. Local and imported fish-sauce amphorae found at Caronía and Marina di Caronía

often extremely difficult to come to conclusions about the production area of each by eye alone. The latter is only possible for certain types, such as the characteristic so-called 'black sand' fabric for Campanian amphorae (from the volcanic regions around the Bay of Naples), and for the most distinctive and easily recognisable of the Tunisian and Spanish fabrics.

There are a number of possible relationships between the shape of a ceramic vessel and its fabric, and this is especially true of the amphorae.

1. One shape is equated with a single fabric (e.g. the Richborough 527 containers from Lipari)

2. More than one shape is produced in the same fabric (for example, Campanian 'black sand' amphorae, such as Dressel 1 and 2/4)

3. One shape is produced in several fabrics (for example, Graeco-Italic amphorae)

4. An unknown shape is produced in a known fabric
5. A known shape is produced in an unknown fabric

6. An unknown shape is produced in an unknown fabric

In the last two cases, the mineralogical characteristics can be decisive for the attribution of a shape to a specific geographical area. At Caronía, thin-section analysis was able to give invaluable information, confirming or denying conclusions reached on other grounds concerning the likely area of production and the relationship between different productions. For a detailed catalogue, see Appendix 3 below, and also colour Pl. 17.1–32.

Type	Caronía	Caronía Marina
MGS V	1	0
Dressel 1A	1	0
Dressel 1B	0	1
Dressel 21/22	7	41
Gauloise 2 and 3	0	2
Dressel 2/4	3	44
Termini Imerese 151/354	0	>96 (<384)
Total	**12**	**>184 (<472)**

Table A1.4. Locally produced amphorae (all types) found at Caronía and Marina di Caronía

Reuse of amphorae

The main problem in using amphorae as a source for extrapolating commercial activity lies in their nature as containers: could they have been reused and redistributed, after their original contents had been emptied out?[13] Was the reuse of amphorae common or just an occasional occurrence? In the absence of *tituli picti*, it is impossible to fully avoid the problematic question of reuse: increasing information from maritime archaeology suggests that the practice might have been widespread. Research conducted by T. Peña, for example, has thrown much light on amphora reuse.[14] The main problem concerns what Peña calls Type A Reuse, which means the employment of a container, previously used for wine, oil, fish products, fruit or some other product, for the packaging of a cargo of either the same or some quite different substance.[15] As Peña points out, the evidence suggests that a certain type of amphora shape was generally designed to take a certain standard commodity, referred to as the 'principal content'.[16] It is also clear that amphora types were known by individual names, and therefore could be identified just from their shape by many people in the Roman world as containing a specific variety of wine or oil, for example.[17] If the practice of reuse was widespread, however, it would make such identification hazardous. *Tituli picti* were frequently used to signal content, but only rarely are they preserved in the archaeological record, and even then we cannot be certain that they are always primary. What can be said with some certainty is that amphorae lined with resin were hardly reused for a different substance like oil, since the resin would have dissolved and given the oil an unpleasant smell and taste. Nor were containers designed for carrying fish-produce and oil normally used for other substances, since it was difficult to remove the absorbed residues in the clay walls of the container.[18] So reuse was no doubt most common when refilling a container with the same or a very similar substance to the one that the amphora originally carried. A wine container, however, could have been reused for fish products, since not only did it have a protective lining of resin, but wine also did not leave a strong smell or residues.

In discussing reuse, it is important to differentiate between systematic reuse over long distances, and local *ad hoc* reuse when goods needed delivering only a short distance from the place of consumption of the original contents. The latter is likely to have been a very common practice. That an amphora emptied of its wine at Kale Akte may then have been re-used as, say, a container for a local fish product, and transported to one of the nearby inland settlements such as Kapition or Amestratus, does not make the record of the wine amphora at Kale Akte lose its value, since the towns were so close to one another and had more or less identical patterns of consumption. The wine amphora at Amestratus in any case reflects the import of wine to the micro-region, whether reused or not.

One of the few pieces of evidence for systematic reuse on a large scale and over longer distances is provided by the Grado shipwreck.[19] In general, however, for any operators intending to export large quantities of a commodity such as wine, it made sense for them to invest in making their own amphorae in their own kilns. The thin-section analysis shows that precisely this was going on at Kale Akte itself. Only a small producer with a much lower scale of operation is likely to have considered reusing containers on an occasional or even a regular basis. Even if such producers could not afford to invest in their own kiln, empty amphorae could always be bought according to need from a larger *officina* which had.

When looking at the picture of amphora imports in Sicily as a whole, or for that matter any other region in the Mediterranean, it is clear that patterns do not differ dramatically; for instance, in the Hellenistic period elsewhere in the island, wine containers are by far the most numerous, while oil and fish sauce amphorae are much less common. In the mid/late imperial period, the relation between oil and wine containers is more even, often with an advantage in favour of the oil amphorae (Africana 1), over those carrying fish-products (Africana 2), except in areas where fish-sauce was locally produced. If amphorae really were very widely reused, ignoring the form and original content, the percentages of amphorae containing wine, olive oil and fish products respectively could be expected to vary dramatically from one site to another – something that definitely does not occur. The shape of a vessel was also important – for instance, the Dressel 2/4 imitating the earlier famous Koan wine-carrier – in order to 'signal' clearly that the contents were wine. If reuse was so widespread that a customer could no longer tell with certainty from the form what the content was likely to be, amphora shape would have been of little importance, and consequently one would expect a wide variety of shapes in each single production centre. If an amphora type is considered to be, say, a wine container on the basis of recent research, the probability that it actually contained wine must surely always be considered as high.

Origin	Type	Caronía	Caronía Marina
Locrian	MGS II	1	1
	MGS III	0	3
North Sicilian	MGS II	0	2
	MGS V	0	1
	MGS VI	1	0
Lipari	Richborough 527	1	1
Total		**3**	**8**

Table A1.5. Non-local but Sicilian (or Calabrian) amphorae found at Caronía and Marina di Caronía

In the mid- and late imperial periods there was little opportunity for reuse of the containers reaching Caronía: the large oil- and *garum*-carriers from Tunisia were not suitable for carrying wine, which in this period was transported for preference in smaller containers. The huge local output of small wine amphorae would have limited the reuse there of other carriers. In the early imperial period, containers for wine and fish products were also produced locally at Kale Akte or its micro-region, and this indirectly reflects the large amount consumed of the original content, even if they might sometimes have been reused in a local/micro-regional context. The locally or regionally produced containers of the Hellenistic period point to a vibrant wine economy; organised and widespread reuse seems improbable. The geographical origin of the contents might, however, sometimes be somewhat distorted by reuse; for example, all Spanish amphorae might not have contained only Spanish fish-sauce, as they could theoretically have been reused for Sicilian fish products and sold on to another customer. Shape, however, could have been a deterrent to reuse: for example, the Hellenistic Punic amphorae and the local Dressel 21/22 fish-product containers, without neck and with a wide opening, were not suitable for a liquid like wine or oil.

It is probable that a significant amount of what was imported to Sicily first arrived in a major port or

Origin	Type	Caronía	Caronía Marina
Aegean	Corinthian A	0	1
	Knidian	1	0
	Koan	0	5
	Rhodian	1	5
	Schöne-Mau 13/Agora G198/Pompeii 13	0	1
Total Aegean		**2**	**12**
Campanian	MGS V	2	3
	MGS VI/Dr 1A	3	5
	Dressel 1A	2	5
	Dressel 1B	2	5
	Dressel 1C	0	2
	Dressel 1	2	21
	Dressel 2/4	1	15
Total Campanian		**12**	**57**
Tunisian	Ramón 7.1.2.1	0	6
	Ramón 7.4.3.3/van der Werff 1/Maña C2B	0	3
	Ramón 7.5.2.1/van der Werff 2/Maña C2C	1	2
	Ramón 7.6.1.1	0	1
	Dressel 26	0	3
	Africana 1	0	64
	Keay 13A	0	2
	Keay 25/Africana 3	0	2
	Keay 27	0	1
	Africana 2	0	30
Total Tunisian		**1**	**114**
Libyan	Tripolitanian 1	0	1
	Tripolitanian 2 and 3	0	20
Total Libyan		**0**	**21**
Mauretanian	Keay 1B/Dressel 30B	0	8
Total Mauretanian		**0**	**8**
South Gaulish	Gauloise 2 and 3	0	3
	Gauloise 4/Pélichet 47	0	14
Total South Gaulish		**0**	**17**
Baetican	Dressel 7/11	0	11
	Dressel 20	0	3
	Haltern 70	0	2
Total Baetican		**0**	**16**
Central Adriatic	Lamboglia 2	1	10
Total Central Adriatic		**1**	**10**
Apulian	Brindisi	0	1
Total Apulian		**0**	**1**
Lusitanian	Almagro 50	0	1
	Almagro 51	0	1
Total Lusitanian		**0**	**2**
TOTAL EXTRA-REGIONAL		**17**	**258**

Table A1.6. Extra-regional (overseas) imported amphorae found at Caronía and Marina di Caronía

'transport hub' elsewhere in the island. Smaller harbours such as that of Kale Akte received products which might have changed hands at least a couple of times since their first voyage; so the possibility that some of the containers might have been reused my have been somewhat greater, since the item was now a few stages further away from its original source. Generally, the further away from its origin that the amphora is, the greater is the possibility of reuse.[20]

The question whether the practice of reuse should seriously undermine calculations on food supply based on amphorae is thus closely connected with the question of need. The evidence discussed here suggests that reuse was mainly confined to local and micro-regional, small-scale trade or else within the very community where the amphora was emptied of its original contents. Incontrovertible evidence for systematic reuse is extremely rare. Since amphora-production was widespread in the Mediterranean area during the period discussed here, only minor producers of restricted means are likely to have regularly reused amphorae instead of producing their own containers.

Other ceramic materials

The ceramic categories other than amphorae have received less attention in this study because fine ware and lamps in Sicily from all periods have been studied and published far more extensively in other publications than have amphorae. Kitchen wares were not quantified and have not been discussed in detail, since the study of this large category would have required further specialist knowledge, and constitutes a vast field of research on its own. Finds of this category have been discussed in some detail by Bonanno.[21]

Fine wares

All diagnostic sherds of fine ware were counted for quantification. Here method A described above (p. 162) was employed. The amount of fine ware at Marina di Caronía is much less than that of amphorae, whereas the contrary is true for material from the early Hellenistic cistern at Caronía itself. As noted above (p. 66), the publication in Sicily of fine wares has been much more extensive than that of amphorae,no doubt due to their attractiveness as art-historical material. The publications of the Lipari excavations remain fundamental,[22] and more recently those of the hill-towns of Morgantina and Monte Iato have put for the first time the study of Hellenistic, Late Republican and Early Imperial fine wares in Sicily onto a firm foundation.[23]

Lamps

All fragments of lamps from Caronía were counted and quantified. Lamps have in general been intensively studied, both on art-historical grounds (the designs on the discus) and as reasonably reliable chronological indicators. A survey of Roman lamps published in Sicily is helpful, and those from Lipari are well published, although important information about them, including fabric descriptions and profile drawings, are lacking.[24] The more common Sicilian forms in circulation have been studied by Bailey in his catalogues of Hellenistic and Roman lamps.[25] While Roman lamps are well known both more generally and within Sicily, this is unfortunately not the case with Classical-period and Hellenistic lamps. The many Sicilian-produced lamps in these two time-periods are not well studied or published, and little interest has been shown in the important question of where they were made.

Appendix 2

Thin-section analyses of selected amphorae

Anders Lindahl

Introduction

The amphora was a common container for transportation of goods, and in particular of liquid goods, in the Graeco-Roman world. There are many known production sites of these vessels around the Mediterranean. The shapes of the different amphorae have been amply described and grouped by different scholars.[1] There have also been several works describing the fabric of the vessels as well as attempts to link vessels to clay sources (provenance), based on fabric analyses established by means of the petrographic microscopy of ceramic thin sections.[2]

Of the material found at Kale Akte, Lindhagen made fabric analyses based on polished surfaces of 115 different amphorae. The groupings made by Lindhagen were the basis for the selection of sherds studied by petrographic microscopy.

This report focuses on trying to answer the question about the extent of the information that analysis of ceramic thin-sections can add to the identification of specific workshops and production sites. To achieve this, and to minimize biased conclusions, the analyses were made without any prior knowledge as to type of amphora to which each sample belonged, its find-spot or its assumed production area. However, to get a more accurate picture, the results have to be weighed in relation to the variables mentioned above. It is also important that the results are understood in relation to the probable date of the individual sherds.

The investigations were carried out at the Laboratory for Ceramic Research, Department of Quaternary Geology, Lund University. The aim of the laboratory analysis was to investigate the variation in the production of the containers found at Caronía, with a focus on the choice of raw material.

Samples

Thirteen sherds, from Caronía and Marina di Caronía, were chosen for thin-section analysis. Five of the sampled amphorae are assumed to be of local origin from the immediate environs of Caronía itself (samples 1, 5, 6, 7, 8), three are either local or at any rate North Sicilian (samples 4, 11, 12), two are considered to be Sicilian in general (samples 3 and 9), one is presumably from Central Italy (sample 2), one from Tunisia (sample 10) and one from the island of Kos (sample 13). One of the sherds (sample 5) was found in the Forum Romanum in Rome, and according to Lindhagen has a very similar fabric to that of the local Caronía ware (see Table A2.1 for a summary of the analysis).

Methods

Microscopy

The method used is the study of ceramic thin-sections under a polarising microscope. A ceramic thin-section is a piece of a sherd that has been ground down to a uniform thickness of 0.03 mm. The thin-section is analysed at magnifications ranging from 20 times to 630 times in both parallel and polarised light. This analysis makes it possible to identify different minerals and rock fragments in the silt and sand fractions. Furthermore, remnants of organic matter, diatoms and impurities of the clay are studied. Particular observations of, for example, minerals, rocks and other features of the temper and clay are noted. Measurements and calculations are performed on the coarse fractions in two different grain fractions – grains ≥0.1 mm and grains <0.1≥0.01 mm – at two different magnifications, 20 times and 100 times respectively. The software used for the image analysis is KONTRON KS 300.

The grain-size distribution in ceramics has different ranges, depending on the natural inclusions in the raw clay and any addition of temper by the potter. In raw clay, the grain sizes may vary, depending on the location of the clay deposit but even within the same clay deposit. The latter varies according to the depth at which the clay was quarried. Thus, the calculation of the grain-size variation of samples is a means of distinguishing different occasions of manufacture.

Hydrochloric acid test

In order to estimate the carbonate content, the sherd samples were all tested with a solution of 3% hydrochloric acid (HCl).

Results

Microscopy (Table A2.1)

A majority of the samples have a rich brick-red colour. Thin-section samples 2, 3 and 13 differ in that they are yellowish in colour. The colour of fired clay is

Thin-section no.	Amphora		Added inclusions		Clay		HCl-test	Grains >0.1 mm			Grains in the interval <0.1>0.01 mm		
	Type	*Assumed origin*	*Grog*	*Organic matter*	*Minerals & rock fragments, grains >0.1 mm*		*Reaction to HCl-test (3%)*	*Number of grains, mean value*	*Area of grains mm sq. mean value*	*Area of grains % mean value*	*Number of grains mean value*	*Area of grains mm sq. mean value*	*Area of grains % mean value*
1	Termini 151/354	Local			+q, s, qz, -c, -f	Silty	Weak	62	2.178	7.1	277	0.05418	4.4
2	Dressel 2/4	Central Italy			+q, +f	Fine silty	No	75	2.251	7.3	500	0.05704	4.6
3	MGS VI	Sicily			+c, -q, -f	Fine silty	V. strong	119	1.676	5.5	378	0.05010	4.1
4	Dressel 21/22	Local/N Sicily	?		q, c, s	Fine silty	Strong	82	0.661	2.1	443	0.07277	5.9
5	Termini 151/354	Local, found Rome			+q, s, qz, -c, -f	Silty	Strong	60	2.203	7.2	311	0.06040	4.9
6	Dressel 1A	Local			+q, s, qz, -c, -f	Fine silty	Strong	66	1.632	5.3	497	0.07764	6.3
7	Dressel 2/4	Local			+q, s, qz, -f	Silty	Weak	62	2.585	8.4	237	0.04820	3.9
8	Dressel 2/4	Local	?		q	Fine silty	Weak	54	0.312	1.0	453	0.05230	4.3
9	MGS V	Sicily			+q, f, s, -b	Uns. Coarse	No	164	3.581	11.7	318	0.08063	6.6
10	Keay 27	Tunisia			+q, f	V. coarse silty	No	240	3.065	10.0	169	0.08653	7.0
11	Dressel 21/22	Local/N Sicily			+q, s, -f	Coarse silty	No	100	2.555	8.3	249	0.07058	5.7
12	Dressel 21/22	Local/N Sicily		+	+q	Coarse silty	Weak	100	0.987	3.2	246	0.09064	7.4
13	Koan	Kos			+q, f, -b, m	Coarse silty	No	125	1.552	5.1	202	0.08428	6.9

Table A2.1 Data derived from the microscopic analyses and the HCl test

determined, to a large extent, by the amount and type of iron and calcium carbonate in the clay, together with firing temperature and firing atmosphere. Often if the fired clay has a yellowish colour, this is an indication of a clay rich in calcium carbonate and possibly also with a lower iron content. With one exception (sample 13), the samples are poor or very poor in mica. The silt content varies from fine silty to very coarse silty, although the majority of the samples are considered to be fine silty to silty. In addition, the number of grains of the sand fraction, as well as their size, varies in the material. The sintering temperature is a result of the firing temperature in combination with fluxing agents, substances that help lower the sintering temperature (for example, iron and calcium carbonate).

A varying degree of vitrification is observed in several of the samples. The ware is sintered especially around voids. In these sintered areas, the colour of the ware is greyish-yellow, in contrast to the brick-red of the rest of the sample; as mentioned above, this is an indication of calciferous clay (Fig. A2.1). The choice of clay and the mixing of temper is a deliberate action on the part of the manufacturer, the potter. The potter in most cases is well acquainted with how the clay behaves at all the different stages in the manufacture of the product. For example, the adding of a temper (type, grain size and amount) in order to 'balance' the natural coarse inclusions in the clay is the type of knowledge and experience passed on from a senior potter to his/her apprentice.

Experimentation is therefore not normal in an established workshop. Only if production for some reason fails – the regular type of clay in the old quarry being exhausted, for example, or a fresh demand for a new type of vessel, etc. – will there exist an incentive for experimentation. However, small variations in the amount and size of temper can often be observed in the thin-sections and are considered normal, even among vessels that are produced in the same firing.

Firing is a critical part of the manufacturing process. Several of the samples are fired to a sintering temperature. The sintering interval – the temperature range in which the clay begins to sinter until it melts – is very narrow for the iron-rich clays examined in this investigation. It takes special skills on the part of the potter to reach and not exceed that temperature in a wood-fired kiln, especially in an age without thermometers when heat-levels were judged by experience alone. The danger of losing the whole kiln-load due to over-firing has to be weighed against the advantage of achieving a strong and less permeable ware. Especially in the case of amphorae, often used for the transport of liquids, this advantage was worth the risk.

Thin-section 1

The sample consists of iron-rich, silty clay with an added temper of sand (Fig. A2.2). The mineral and rock composition of the sand fraction is mainly quartz, grains of sandstone and quartzite and few grains of feldspar. There are traces of calcium carbonate around voids in the ware. There are also patches, especially around the voids, where the clay has begun to sinter. The maximum grain size is 1.1 mm. The amount of grains larger than 0.1 mm is calculated as 7% (volume), and the amount of grains smaller than 0.1 mm but larger than 0.01 mm is calculated as 4.4% (volume).

Thin-section 2

The sample consists of fine, silty, calciferous clay with an added temper of sand (Fig. A2.3). The mineral composition of the sand fraction is quartz and feldspar, both alkali feldspar and plagioclase. The clay has begun to sinter, especially around voids in the ware. The maximum grain size is 1.0 mm. The amount of grains larger than 0.1 mm is calculated as 7.3% (volume), and the amount of grains smaller than 0.1 mm but larger than 0.01 mm is calculated as 4.6% (volume).

Thin-section 3

The sample consists of calciferous fine, silty clay, most likely naturally tempered (Fig. A2.4). The majority of the grains of the sand fraction are calcite or limestone, and there are also some grains of quartz and feldspar. The calciferous material is also found in the silt fraction. The maximum grain size is 0.9 mm. The amount of grains larger than 0.1 mm is calculated as 5.5% (volume), and the amount of grains smaller than 0.1 mm but larger than 0.01 mm is calculated as 4.1% (volume).

Thin-section 4

The sample consists of fine, silty, iron-rich clay, with no added temper, possibly with the exception of a few grains that may be grog (Fig. A2.5). The few grains of the sand fraction – quartz, calcite and sandstone – are most likely a natural component of the clay. There are also traces of calcium carbonate around voids in the ware, indicating calciferous clay. The maximum grain size is 0.72 mm. The amount of grains larger than 0.1 mm is calculated as 2.2% (volume), and the amount of grains smaller than 0.1 mm but larger than 0.01 mm is calculated as 5.9% (volume).

Thin-section 5

The sample consists of iron-rich, silty clay tempered with sand (Fig. A2.6). The mineral and rock composition of the sand fraction is mainly quartz, grains of sandstone and quartzite as well as a few grains of feldspar and calcite. Calcium carbonate is also embedded in the clay and traces of calcium carbonate are found around voids in the ware. Around these voids the clay has begun to sinter. The maximum grain size is 0.93 mm. The amount of grains larger than 0.1 mm is calculated as 7.2% (volume), and the amount of grains smaller than 0.1 mm but larger than 0.01 mm is calculated as 4.9% (volume).

Thin-section 6

The sample consists of iron-rich, fine, silty clay tempered with sand (Fig. A2.7). The grains in the sand fraction are mainly quartz, grains of sandstone and quartzite, and a few grains of feldspar and calcite. Around voids in the ware there are traces of calcium carbonate, indicating calciferous clay. The ware is sintered, especially around these voids. The maximum grain size is 2.74 mm. The amount of grains larger than 0.1 mm is calculated as 5.3% (volume) and the amount of grains smaller than 0.1 mm but larger than 0.01 mm is calculated as 6.3% (volume).

Thin-section 7

The sample consists of iron-rich, silty clay with added temper of sand (Fig. A2.8). The mineral and rock composition of the sand fraction is mainly quartz, grains of sandstone and quartzite, and a few grains of feldspar. Although there are no visible grains of calcium carbonate, it is most likely calciferous clay. Indications of this are the small patches, especially around voids in the ware, where the clay is sintered. The maximum grain size is 1.45 mm. The amount of grains larger than 0.1 mm is calculated as 8.4% (volume), and the amount of grains smaller than 0.1 mm but larger than 0.01 mm is calculated as 3.9% (volume).

Thin-section 8

The sample consists of iron-rich, fine, silty clay, with practically no grains of sand. There is no added temper except for a few grains that may be grog (Fig. A2.9). Around voids in the ware the clay has begun to sinter, which may be an indication of calciferous clay. The maximum grain size is 0.33 mm. The amount of grains larger than 0.1 mm is calculated as 1.0% (volume), and the amount of grains smaller than 0.1 mm but larger than 0.01 mm is calculated as 4.3% (volume).

Thin-section 9

The sample consists of iron-rich, coarse, unsorted clay, rendering added temper unnecessary (Fig. A2.10). The grains in the sand fraction are mainly quartz and feldspar, as well as rock fragments of sandstone and basaltic rock. The maximum grain size is 1.75 mm. The amount of grains larger than 0.1 mm is calculated as 11.7% (volume), and the amount of grains smaller than 0.1 mm but larger than 0.01 mm is calculated as 6.6% (volume).

Thin-section 10

The sample consists of iron-rich, very coarse, silty clay, possibly with an added temper of fine sand (Fig. A2.11). The mineral composition of the grains of the sand fraction is mainly quartz. There are some grains of feldspar in the silt fraction. The clay is sintered around voids in the ware, which may be an indication of calcium carbonate content in the clay. The maximum grain size is 0.55 mm. The amount of grains larger than 0.1 mm is calculated as 10.0% (volume), and the amount of grains smaller than 0.1 mm but larger than 0.01 mm is calculated as 7.0% (volume).

Thin-section 11

The sample consists of iron-rich, coarse, silty clay tempered with sand (Fig. A2.12). The mineral and rock composition of the grains of the sand fraction is mainly quartz, some grains of sandstone and a few grains of feldspar. The grains of the silt fraction are mainly quartz and some feldspar. The clay has begun to sinter, especially around voids in the ware, which is an indication of calciferous clay. The maximum grain size is 1.19 mm. The amount of grains larger than 0.1 mm is calculated as 8.3% (volume), and the amount of grains smaller than 0.1 mm but larger than 0.01 mm is calculated as 5.7% (volume).

Thin-section 12

The sample consists of iron-rich, coarse clay, very rich in silt (Fig. A2.13). Although there are no visible grains of calcium carbonate, it is most likely calciferous clay. Indications of this in the clay are patches, especially around voids in the ware, where the clay is sintered. There are few grains in the sand fraction, mainly quartz, and the maximum grain size is 0.5 mm. The amount of grains larger than 0.1 mm is calculated as 3.2% (volume), and the amount of grains smaller than 0.1 mm but larger than 0.01 mm is calculated as 7.4% (volume). There is also an admixture of organic matter in the clay. Except for one possible hull of a grain with cell structure, the rest is very fragmented (Fig. A2.14). At any rate it represents most likely an addition of plant material to the clay.

Thin-section 13

The sample consists of coarse, very silty clay, rich in mica (Fig. A2.15). Although there are no visible grains of calcium carbonate, it is most likely calciferous clay. The clay is sintered, especially around voids in the ware. There are few grains in the sand fraction; maximum grain size is 0.4 mm. The amount of grains

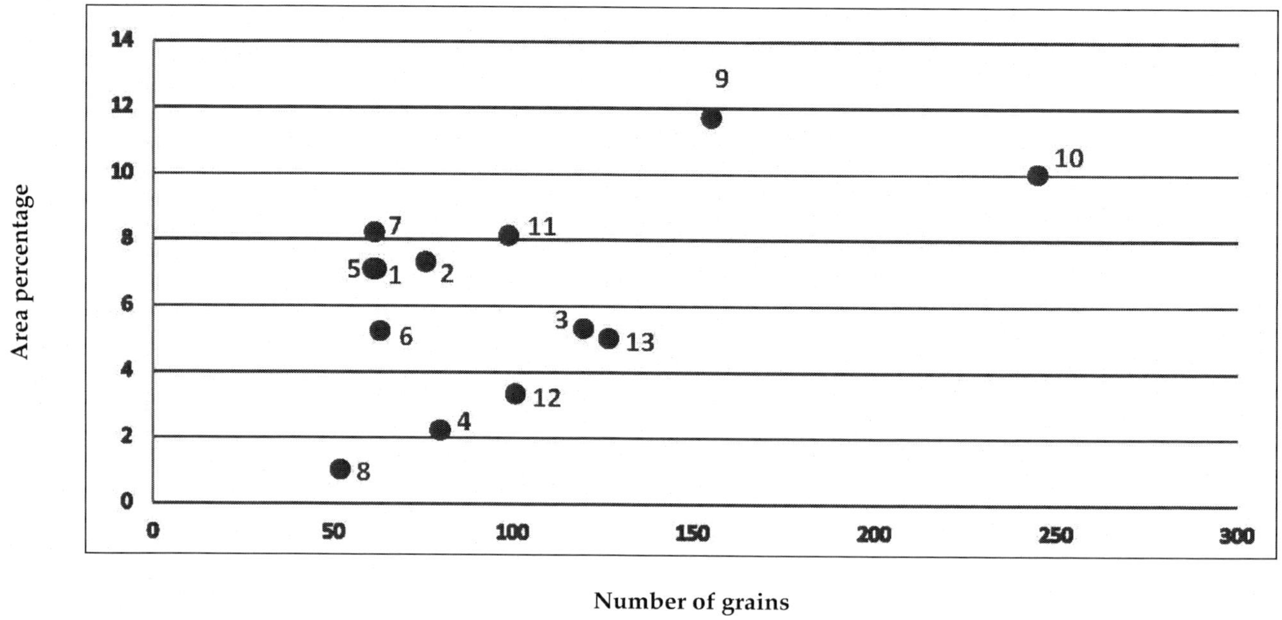

Table A2.2 Scatter-plot diagram of grains greater than 0.1 mm

larger than 0.1 mm is calculated as 5.1% (volume), and the amount of grains smaller than 0.1 mm but larger than 0.01 mm is calculated as 6.9% (volume). The mineral and rock composition is quartz and feldspar. A few grains of basaltic rock occur both in the coarse and fine fraction.

Hydrochloric acid test
The HCl test displays a very strong reaction for calcium carbonate in thin-sample 3, and a strong one in samples 4, 5 and 6. The reaction to the acid is weak in samples 1, 7, 8 and 12. The remaining five samples – 2, 9, 10, 11 and 13 – display no reaction to the test, although they may still have contents of calcium carbonates less than 3%.

Discussion and conclusions

As mentioned above, the majority of the samples have a rich brick-red colour. Thin-section samples 2, 3 and 13 differ. They are yellowish in colour, and therefore are assumed to have lower contents of iron and higher contents of calcium carbonate.

The microscopy of the ceramic thin-sections under a polarized microscope is used to describe the mineralogical composition of the grains of the sand and silt fractions. It also provides a basis for comparing the coarseness of the clays used for the manufacture of the different vessels. There are at least two different ways to make these distinctions:

- Groupings based on the visual impression of the sample (preferably a comparison of photos from different areas of the thin-section)
- Groupings based on grain-size distribution achieved by using an image-analysing system

The former is generally very accurate, but is time-consuming. It also requires an experienced ceramological microscopist. The latter is less biased, since it is based on computer calculation. The sampled sherds from Caronía display a variety, for example in the coarseness of the silt fraction – fine-silty, silty and coarse-silty – as well as in the amount and the size of the grains in the sand fraction. The measurements of grains in two sets of grain fractions – grains ≥0.1 mm and grains <0.1≥0.01 mm – are used to illustrate the variation in the coarseness of the clays.

In Table A2.1, the mean values of the amount of grains, as well as the area of grains (both in mm^2 and in percentage), are presented. One way to illustrate the result of this analysis is to plot the mean values of the number of grains against the percentage values that these grains cover, as seen in the thin section. For the grains ≥0.1 mm the plot is seen in Table A2.2. Thin-section samples 1, 2, 5, and 7 form a group with the same characteristics in this grain size. Samples 6 and 11 could be considered as add-ons to this group. Samples 3 and 13, as well as 4 and 12 – possibly with 8 as an add-on – form two groups. Thin-section samples 9 and 10 differ from all other samples. For the grains in the interval <0.1≥0.01 mm, the plot is seen in Table A2.3. Samples 10, 12 and 13 form one group, samples 1, 5 and 7 a second, and samples 4 and 6 a third. Finally, thin-section samples 2 and 8 constitute a fourth group. Samples 3, 9 and 11 form individual entities.

Neither of these two plots displays the full picture of the samples, i.e. a combination of the two measurements. One way to achieve that is to compare the two plots, and see which samples occur together in both plots. Only three samples – 1, 5 and 7 – are in the same group in both plots. In order to minimize subjective evaluations, the data of the measurements has been statistically evaluated in a Principal Component Analysis (PCA). The data presented in Tables A2.2 and 3 (see also Table A2.1) are treated independently, and the calculated values of the first data set in each PCA analysis are presented in a scatter-plot (Table A2.4). To some extent the result is very similar to what has been concluded on the basis of Tables A2.2 and 3: samples 1, 5 and 7 form a very close group. However, thin-section samples 4 and 6 most likely also belong to this group. Samples 2 and 3 form a second group, and 12 and 13 form a third. The four remaining samples, 8, 9, 10 and 11, form individual entities.

When the mineralogical observations are included in the picture, samples 1, 5, 6, and 7 are still very similar. Sample 4 has a low amount of coarse fraction, but could very well belong to the same group. Samples 2 and 3 differ from each other. Apart from the very rich calcium carbonate content of sample 3, the coarse fraction is most likely a natural component of the clay in it, whereas sample 2 has an added temper of sand. Samples 12 and 13 cannot belong to the same production, because their mineralogical composition is too different – for example, a richness in mica, and the grains of basaltic rock present in sample 13. Furthermore, sample 12 has a low number of grains in the sand fraction, and an added component of organic matter.

The hydrochloric-acid test, and the notations made concerning the calcium carbonate contents of the clay, add yet another variable to the results. Calcium carbonates, in the form of calcite or limestone, may be observed in a thin-section of ceramic if the sample has not been fired to a temperature above 700/800° C. A test on a very calciferous clay from San Giovenale, for example, showed no trace of calcium carbonate when the clay was fired to 825° C. This clay changed colour from yellowish at 650° C to brick-red at 825° C.[3]

Thin-section sample 3 is rich in calcium carbonate and has a yellowish colour, indicating that this amphora had been fired to a temperature that most likely was below 700° C. Samples 4, 5 and 6 have grains of calcium carbonate, and traces of calcium carbonate

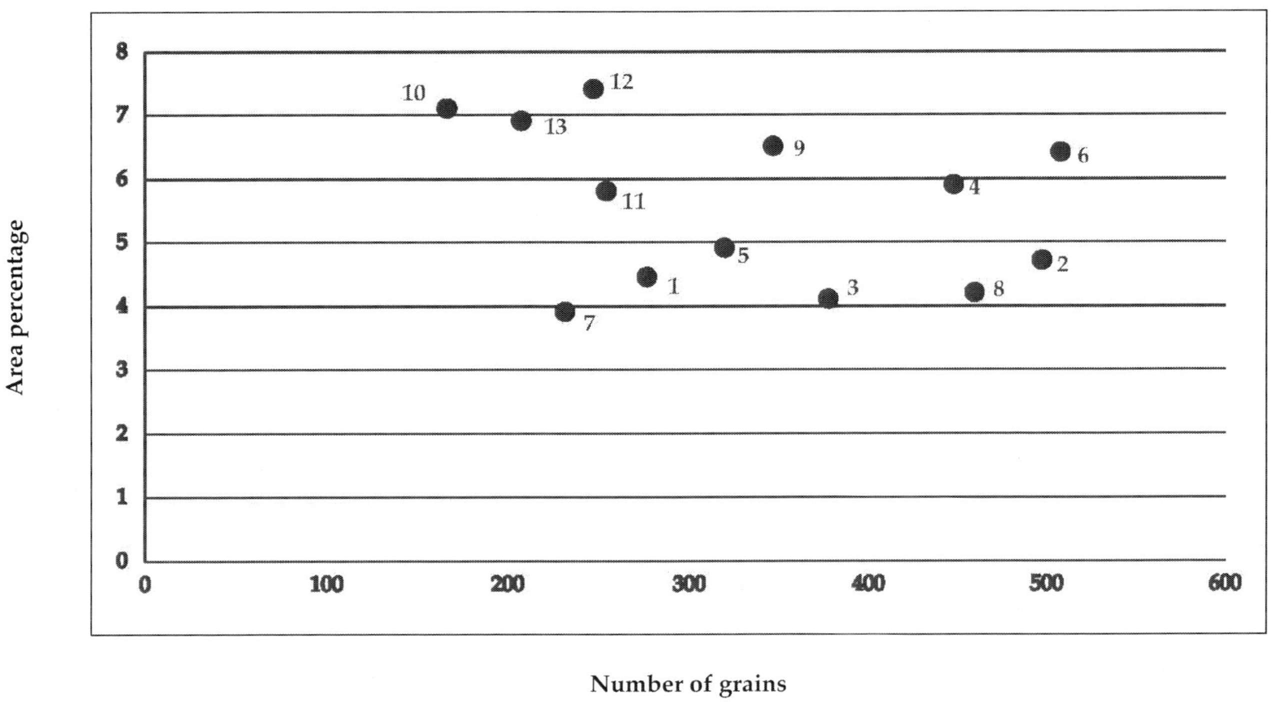

Table A2.3 Scatter-plot diagram of grains less than 0.1 mm and more than 0.01 mm

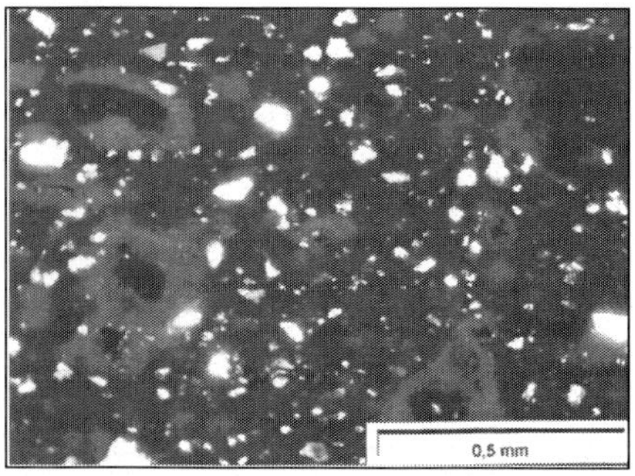

Fig. A2.1

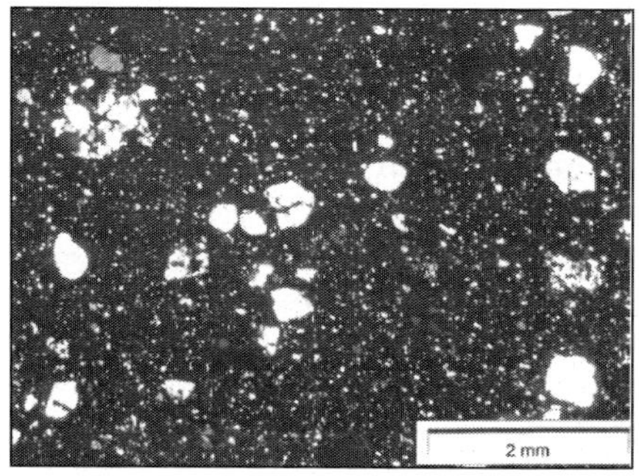

Fig. A2.2

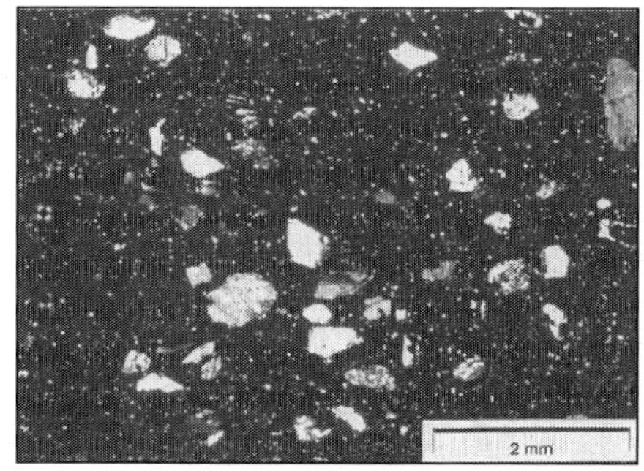

Fig. A2.3

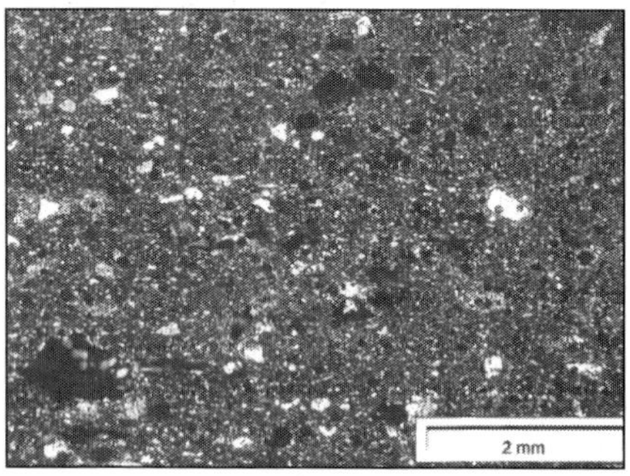

Fig. A2.4

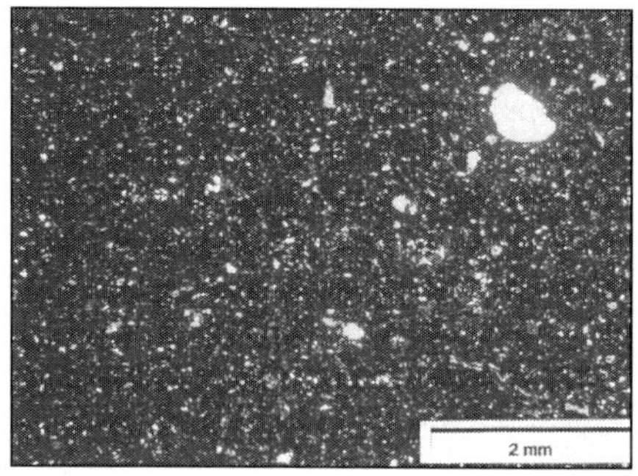

Fig. A2.5

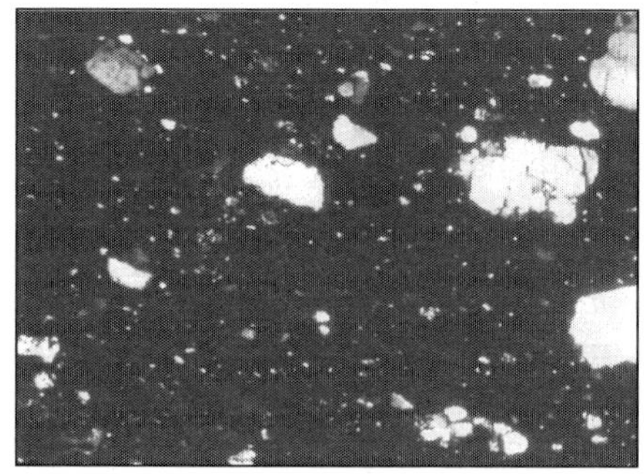

Fig. A2.6

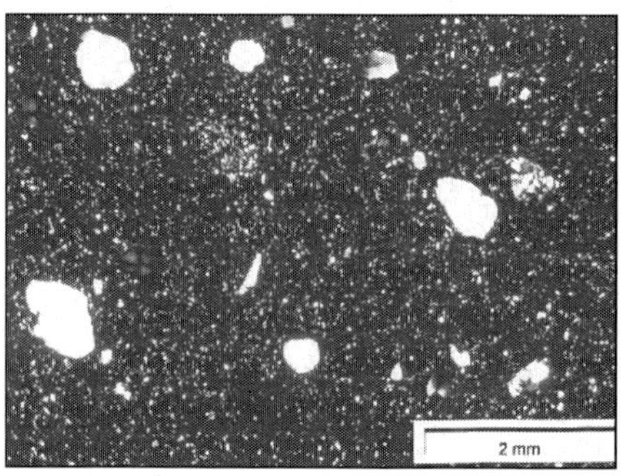

Fig. A2.7

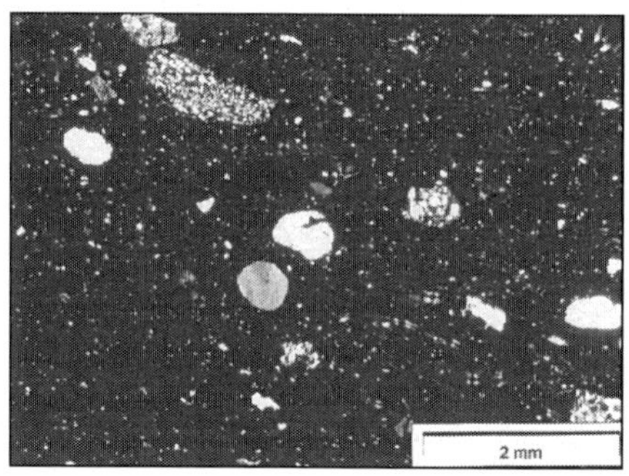

Fig. A2.8

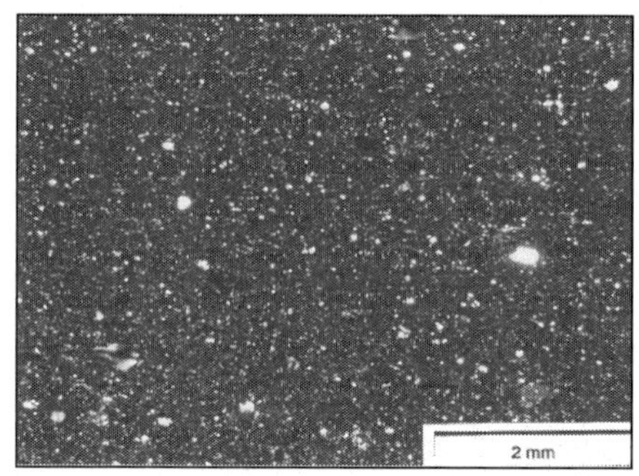

Fig. A2.9

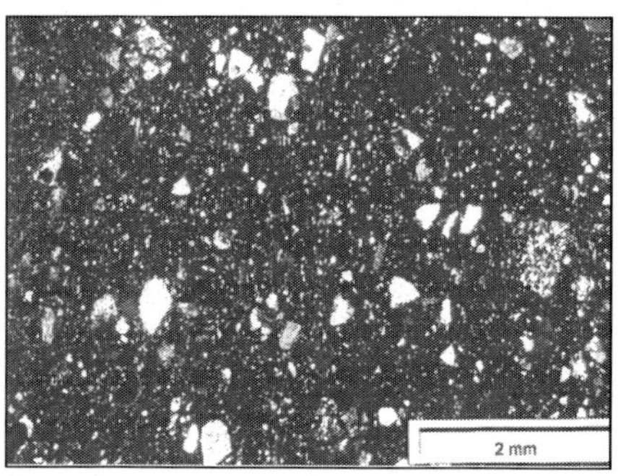

Fig. A2.10

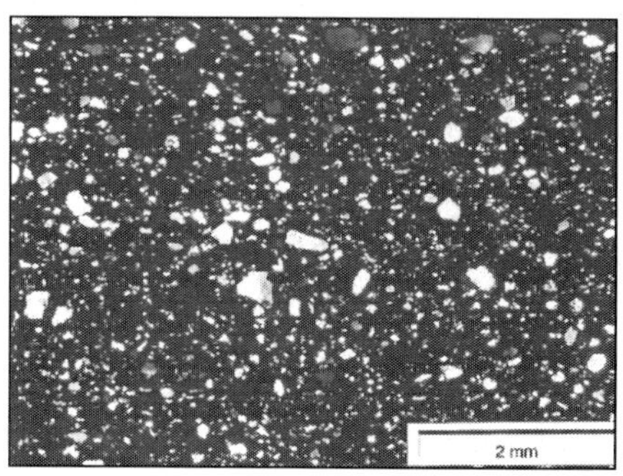

Fig. A2.11

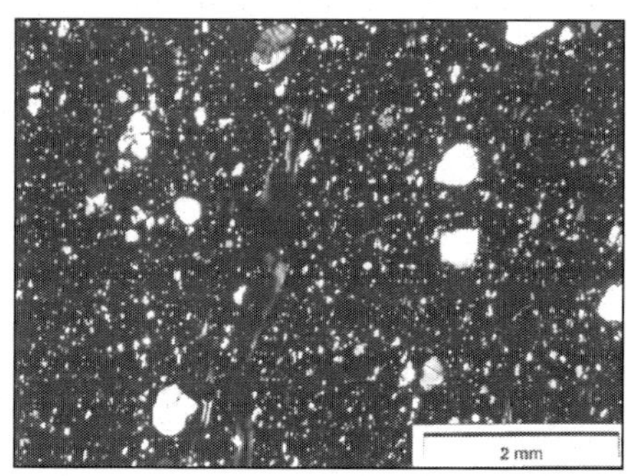

Fig. A2.12

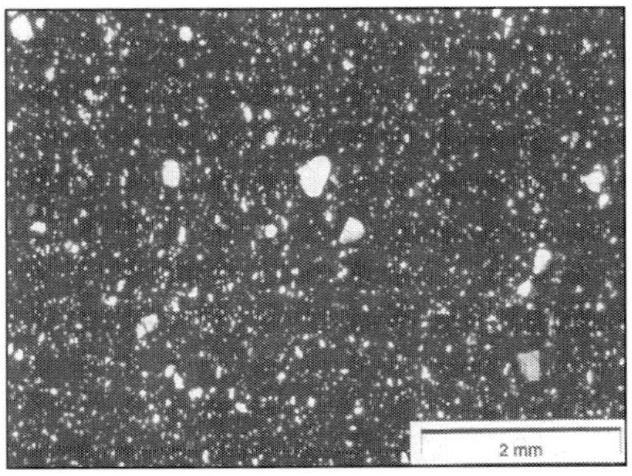

Fig. A2.13

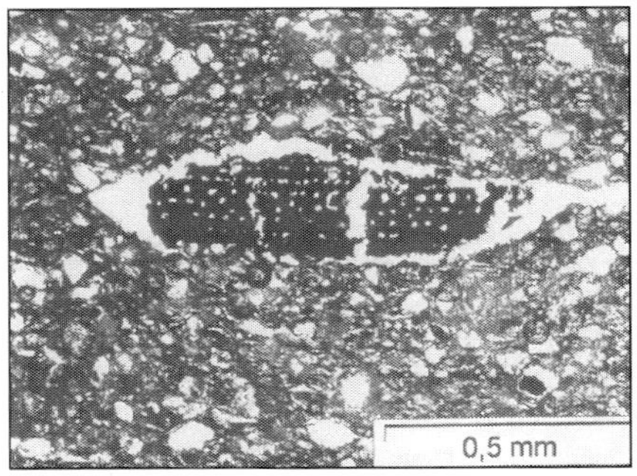

Fig. A2.14

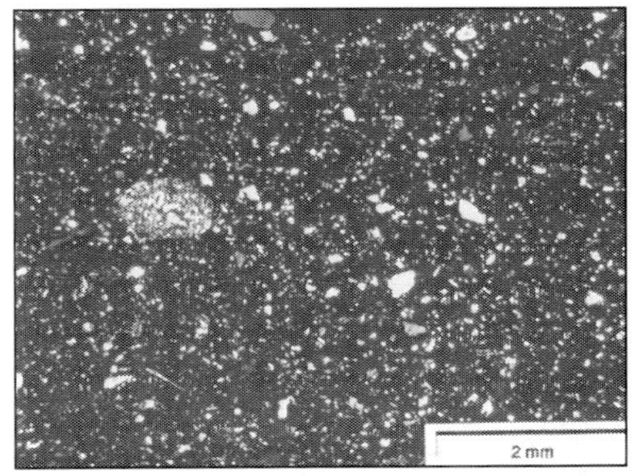

Fig. A2.15

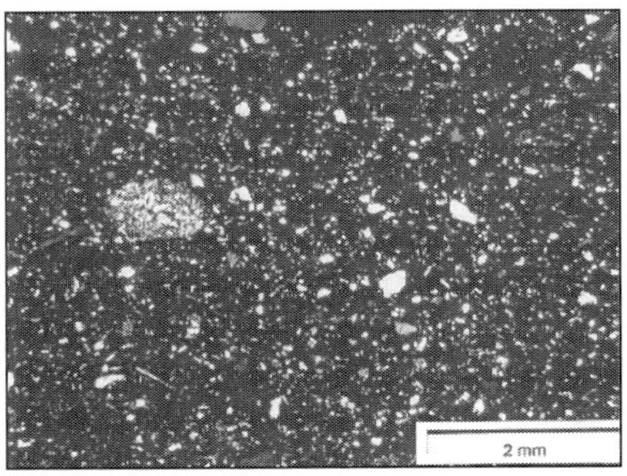

Fig. A2.16

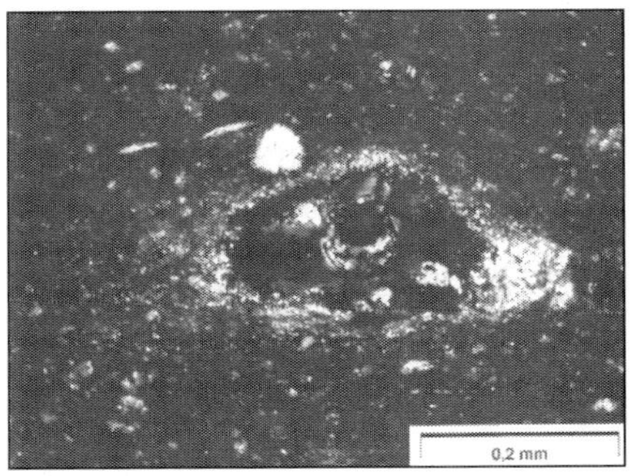

Fig. A2.17

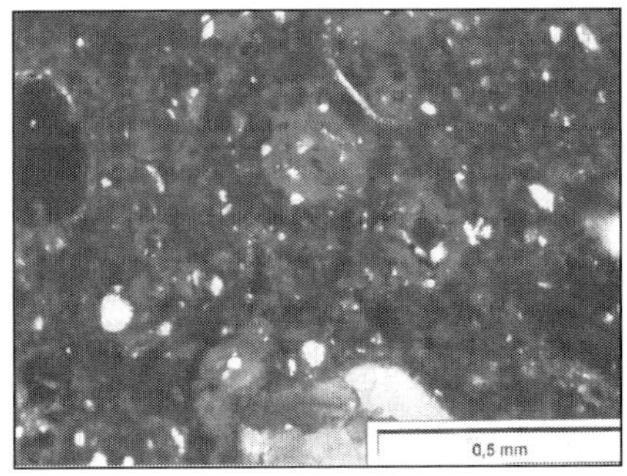

Fig. A2.18

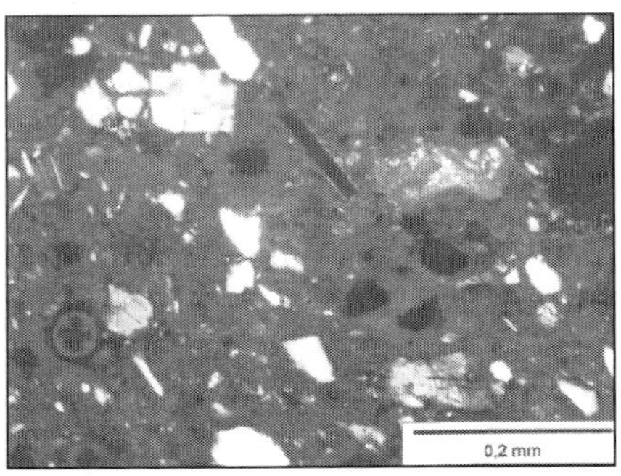

Fig. A2.19

Fig. A2.1 Micrograph in polarized light of sample 12 Dressel 21/22 local

Fig. A2.2 Micrograph in polarized light of sample 1 Termini Imerese 151/354

Fig. A2.3 Micrograph in polarized light of sample 2 Dressel 2/4 central Italy

Fig. A2.4 Micrograph in polarized light of sample 3 MGS VI Sicily

Fig. A2.5 Micrograph in polarized light of sample 4 Dressel 21/22 local?

Fig. A2.6 Micrograph in polarized light of sample 5 Termini Imerese 151/354 (from Rome but local)

Fig. A2.7 Micrograph in polarized light of sample 6 Dressel 1A local

Fig. A2.8 Micrograph in polarized light of sample 7 Dressel 2/4 local

Fig. A2.9 Micrograph in polarized light of sample 8 Dressel 2/4 local?2

Fig. A2.10 Micrograph in polarized light of sample 9 MGS V Sicily

Fig. A2.11 Micrograph in polarized light of sample 10 Keay 27, from Tunisia

Fig. A2.12 Micrograph in polarized light of sample 11 Dressel 21/22 local?

Fig. A2.13 Micrograph in polarized light of sample 12 Dressel 21/22 local?

Fig. A2.14 Micrograph in parallel light of sample 12 Dressel 21/22 local?

Fig. A2.15 Micrograph in polarized light of sample 13 Koan amphora

Fig. A2.16 Micrograph in polarized light (magnified) of sample 4 Dressel 21/22 local?

Fig. A2.17 Micrograph in polarized light (magnified) of sample 5 Termini Imerese 151/354 (from Rome but local)

Fig. A2.18 Micrograph in polarized light (magnified) of sample 7 Dressel 2/4 local

Fig. A2.19 Micrograph in polarized light (magnified) of sample 13 Koan amphora

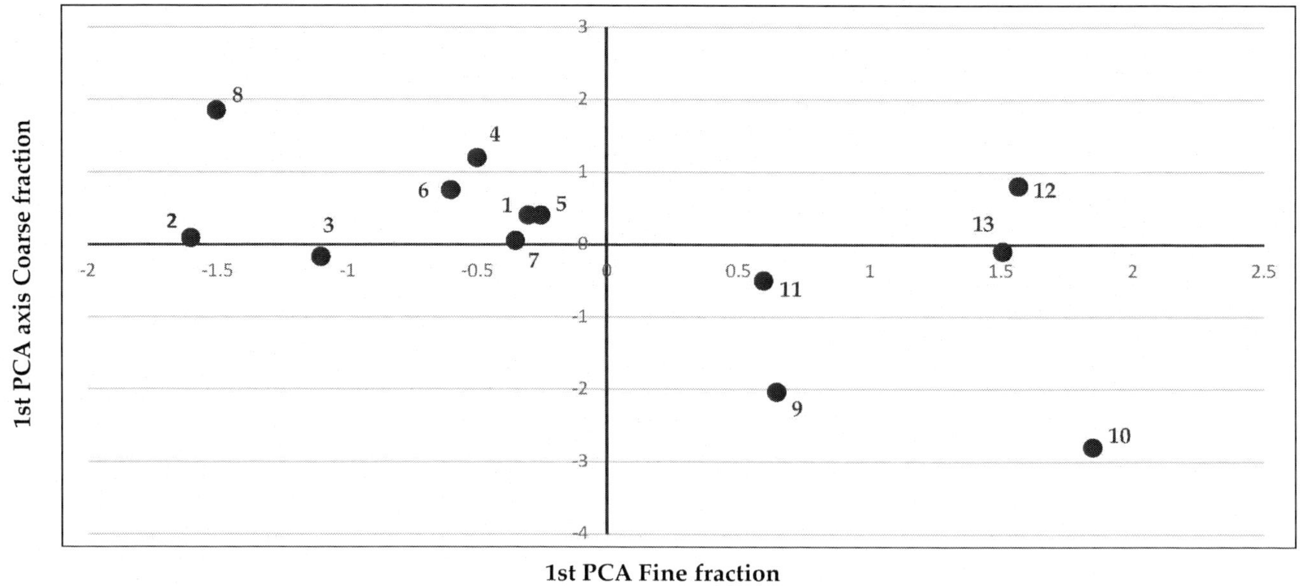

Table A2.4 Scatter-plot diagram of grains evaluated in a Principal Component Analysis (PCA)

around voids in the ware (see Figs A2.16 and 17). These also display a relatively strong reaction to the hydrochloric acid. Sample 4 shows no sign of sintering, whereas samples 5 and 6 have begun to sinter around several of the voids in the ware. This would imply that sample 4 was fired to a lower temperature – perhaps 700/750° C – than samples 5 and 6, which may have been fired to just under 800° C.

Thin-section samples 1, 7, 8 and 12 have no visible traces of calcium carbonate. However, they have a weak reaction to hydrochloric acid, indicating that there is calciferous material in the clay. The ware is also sintered, especially around voids in the ware (Fig. A2.18). The firing temperature for these samples was probably in the range between 800° C and 850° C.

None of the remaining five samples has visible traces of calcium carbonate, nor did they react to hydrochloric acid. Samples 2, 10, 11 and 13 are sintered, and the vitrification is especially strong around voids in the ware (Fig. A2.19). This is an indication that the clay originally had a content of calcium carbonate, but that the vessels have been fired to a rather high temperature – probably exceeding 900° C – and at this temperature all traces of the calcium carbonate has decomposed and disappeared.

The composition of clay may vary to a large extent even within a very limited area and depth in the clay deposit. Clay surveying around the Etruscan settlement at San Giovenale disclosed more than fifteen clays in the immediate vicinity of the ancient site, all very different to one another.[4]

Another element that has to be considered is the time-factor. Although pottery production is reckoned to be a 'conservative' craft, deliberate or accidental changes in the choice of raw material do occur. In the time-span of a hundred, not to say several hundred, years, the chances are quite high that workshops for various reasons might have changed the clay quarries that supplied them, or extracted clay of a slightly different composition in the same quarry; alternatively a clay bed might have become exhausted and an alternatve source nearby used instead. In a hundred years there are at least three generations of potters in a workshop; so it is safe to assume that the manner of mixing clay and temper, and of working the clay, should vary at least slightly in the vessels produced.

According to the analyses of the thin-sections, there is no absolute identity between any of the sampled amphorae. However, there are several similarities that may indicate a common source of raw material, craft tradition and workshop.

Based only on what can be derived from the analyses of both the thin-sections and of the hydrochloric-test samples, thin-sections 1, 4, 5, 6 and 7 may very well have a common source of raw material, and also belong to the same craft tradition.

Appendix 3

Catalogue of amphora fabrics

Key to the catalogue

The entries are divided in four parts:

- Name of amphora type/origin
- General description of surface colour
- General description of fabric colour
- General description of inclusions: colour/type, size, shape, frequency

Bold numbers in square brackets refer to **Colour Plate 17**, where thin-sections of 31 of the 45 fabrics here are illustrated. Colours are from *Munsell Soil Color Charts* (Grand Rapids, MI)

1. Corinthian A (Corinth, Greece)
Surface: 10 YR 7/6 yellow
Fabric: (N7/) dark grey
Inclusions: grey, small-medium, angular, abundant, coarse; golden mica

2. MGS II (northern Sicily)
Surface: pinkish-beige skin (7.5 YR 7/4 pink)
Fabric: 5 YR 6/6 reddish-yellow **[1]**
Inclusions: yellowish-white (calcareous), small/very small, rounded, common; grey crystals (quartz?), medium, round, sparse; glassy crystals, medium, rounded, very sparse; black, very small, round, very sparse

3. MGS II and MGS III (Locri, Calabria, Italy)
Surface: 10 YR 7/3 very pale brown, with flakes of golden mica
Fabric: 10 YR 7/2 light grey, with greyish core (10 YR 5/1 grey) **[2]**
Inclusions: dark grey-blackish, small, rounded, common; voids, small, common; quartz, grey, medium, angular, sparse; golden mica flakes

4a. MGS V (Ischia, Campania, Italy)
Surface: wash (10 YR 7/6 yellow to 10 YR 8/3 very pale brown)
Fabric: 5 YR 5/6 yellowish-red **[3]**
Inclusions: black, sometimes shiny, small/medium, angular, abundant; reddish-brown,small/medium, rounded, very sparse; yellowish-white (calcareous), medium/large, rounded, very sparse; golden mica

4b. MGS V (Ischia, Campania, Italy)
Surface: 10YR 8/4 very pale brown
Fabric: 2.5YR 5/8 light red **[4]**
Inclusions: limestone, small, rounded, abundant; quartzite (glistening flakes): angular, small/medium, abundant

5. MGS V/VI (northern Sicily)
Surface: buff wash
Fabric: 2.5 YR 5/6 red, usually very badly mixed, with stripes of 10 YR 8/4 very pale brown **[5]**
Inclusions: white grits (limestone), small/medium, rounded, abundant; black, small, rounded, common; red/reddish-brown, small/medium, rounded, common; grey (quartz), small/medium, angular, very sparse

6. MGS V/VI (local/northern Sicily)
Surface: 7.5 YR 7/4 pink
Fabric: 5 YR 6/4 light reddish-brown **[22]** and **[23]**
Inclusions: quartz, medium/large, angular, abundant; buff calcite reaction-rings, very small, rounded, abundant; reddish/reddish-brown spots, medium/large, rounded, sparse

7. Late Greco-Italic, Dressel 1, Dressel 2/4 (Pompeii, 'Campanian black sand', Italy)
Surface: 7.5YR 8/6 reddish-yellow; glistening black and gold flakes on the surface, abundant, fine/coarse
Fabric: 2.5YR 5/8 red
Inclusions: black, angular, medium, abundant; white/grey (quartz), moderate, angular, medium; buff (calcite), small/medium, rounded, common

8. Punic tubular amphora (northern Sicily)
Surface: gley 2 6/1 bluish-grey
Fabric: 2.5 YR 5/8 red
Inclusions: yellowish buff limestone reaction-rings, small/medium, rounded, abundant

9. Ramón 7.1.2.1 (north-west Sicily?)
Surface: 2.5 Y 8/2 pale yellow
Fabric: 2.5 Y 8/2 pale yellow with core 2.5 YR 7/4 light reddish-brown **[6]**
Inclusions: greyish (quartz), medium, sub-angular, common; whitish buff, calcite reaction-rings, small, rounded, abundant

10. Ramón 7.4.2.1–7.4.3.3/Maña C (Tunisia)
Surface: 10 YR 8/3 very pale brown
Fabric: 2.5 YR 5/8 red **[7]**
Inclusions: greyish (quartz), medium/small, sub-angular, common; whitish buff, calcite reaction-rings, small, rounded, sparse

11. Ramón 7.5.2.1 (Tunisia)
Surface: 2.5 Y 8/3 pale yellow
Fabric: 2.5 YR 5/8 red **[8]**
Inclusions: whitish grits, calcareous, very small, rounded, common; grey (quartz), small, sub-angular, sparse; black, medium, rounded, very sparse; mica

12. Ramón 7.6.1.1 (Tunisia)
Surface: 7.5 YR 7/6 reddish-yellow, single very large white calcite bits (5 mm) visible
Fabric: 5 YR 6/6 reddish-yellow
Inclusions: whitish (calcite), small/very large, rounded, sparse

13. Dressel 26 (Tunisia)
Surface: 10 YR 7/4 very pale brown
Fabric: 10 YR 7/4 very pale brown
Inclusions: greyish white (quartz), medium/large, sub-angular, abundant; white calcareous, small/medium, rounded, common

14. Rhodian (the island of Rhodes, Greece)
Surface: 10 YR 8/3 very pale brown
Fabric: 7.5 YR 6/4 light brown – 2.5 YR 6/6 light red **[9]**
Inclusions: white, calcareous, small, rounded, sparse/common; light brownish, small, oblong, sparse

15. Koan (Kos, Greece)
Surface: buff wash (5 Y 8/12 pale yellow)
Fabric: 10 YR 7/3 very pale brown **[10]**
Inclusions: whitish-buff calcareous, small, rounded, common; reddish spots, small/medium, rounded, sparse

16. Knidian (Knidos, Turkey)
Surface: 5 YR 6/6 reddish-yellow
Fabric: 5 YR 6/6 reddish-yellow **[12]**
Inclusions: greyish, very small, sub-rounded, very sparse; calcareous, medium/small, sparse; golden mica

17. Lamboglia 2 (Vis, Dalmatia)
Surface: 7.5 YR 7/4 pink
Fabric: 7.5 YR 6/4 light brown **[13]**
Inclusions: reddish, small/large, rounded/oblong, sparse; calcareous, small/large, rounded, sparse; abundant silver mica

18. Koan (Kos, Greece)
Surface: 5Y 8/3–8/4 pale yellow
Fabric: 5Y 8/3–8/4 pale yellow with pink core (7.5 YR 8/4) **[11]**
Inclusions: grey/whitish grey, moderate, angular, medium; voids, rounded, medium, sparse; red, fine/medium, angular, sparse

19. Dressel 2/4 (central Italy)
Surface: 7.5 YR 8/2 pinkish-white – 10 YR 8/6 yellow
Fabric: 10 YR 6/4 light yellowish-brown – 5 YR 6/4 light reddish-brown **[14]**
Inclusions: greyish (quartz), medium/large, angular, common; glassy, rounded, large, sparse; reddish-brown (iron ore?), small/medium, rounded, common; black, small/medium, rounded/oblong, sparse

20. Baetican Dr 20 and Haltern 70 (Guadalquivir valley, Spain)
Surface: 5 YR 7/4 pink
Fabric: 5 YR 5/6 yellowish-red **[15]**
Inclusions: white, round, medium, common; quartz crystals, angular/round, common; blackish, oblong, medium, sparse; greenish, medium, angular, sparse; golden mica

21. Baetican Dr 7/11 (Cadiz, Spain))
Surface: 10 YR 8/2 very pale brown
Fabric: 10 YR 7/4 very pale brown **[16]**
Inclusions: grey (quartz), medium, rounded, common; white grits, small, common; black, medium, rounded, sparse; reddish/reddish-brown, rounded, very sparse

22. Gauloise 2/3; Pélichet 47/Gauloise 4 (Rhône Valley, France)
Surface: 7.5 YR 7/6 reddish-yellow
Fabric: 7.5 YR 7/6 reddish-yellow with pink core
Inclusions: whitish, small, rounded, sparse; greyish, medium/small, sub-rounded, sparse

23. Pélichet 47/Gauloise 4 (Narbonne, south France)
Surface: 7.5 YR 6/6
Fabric: 7.5 YR 6/4 light brown – 2.5 YR 6/6 light red **[17]**
Inclusions: greyish-white, small/medium, rounded, sparse; white, medium, rounded, very sparse; golden mica

24. Tripolitanian 1 (western Libya)
Surface: 2.5 YR 7/6 light red
Fabric: 2.5 YR 6/6 light red
Inclusions: white, calcareous, small, rounded, common

25. Richborough 527 (Lipari)
Surface: 2.5 Y 8/2 pale yellow
Fabric: 2.5 Y 8/2 pale yellow, very coarse **[18]**
Inclusions: reddish brown-black, small/very large, rounded, common; greyish (quartz), large/very large, angular, sparse

26. Schöne-Mau 13/Agora 198/Pompeii 13 (Cilicia/south-east Turkey?)
Surface: 7.5 YR 7/6, with flakes of golden mica
Fabric: 7.5 YR 7/4 **[19]**
Inclusions: yellowish-white grits, small/medium, rounded, common; greyish (quartz), small, angular, sparse; reddish, medium, rounded, sparse; black, medium, rounded, sparse

27. Africana 1–2 (Tunisia)
Surface: reddish-yellow (orange) 5YR 7/6
Fabric: light red 2.5YR 6/8, occasionally with purple-brown core
Inclusions: calcareous, small, rounded, abundant

28. Keay 13 A (Tunisia)
Surface: 10 YR 8/4 very pale brown
Fabric: 2.5 YR 6/6 light red
Inclusions: grey crystals (quartz?), matt, small/medium, rounded, common; white, calcareous, small, rounded, abundant

29. Tripolitanian 2 and 3 (west Libya)
Surface: 7.5 YR 5/1 grey (5 YR 7/6 reddish-yellow on interior)
Fabric: 10 R 5/8 red **[20]**
Inclusions: yellowish-white grits, small/medium, rounded, abundant; limestone reaction-rings, small, rounded, abundant

30. Mauretanian Keay 1B/Dressel 30 (Algeria)
Surface: 10 YR 5/3 brown – 2.5 YR 6/8 light red
Fabric: 7.5 YR 5/3 brown – 2.5 YR 5/6 red
Inclusions: whitish-buff (calcite) grits, small/very small, rounded, abundant

31. Almagro 50 (south Portugal)
Surface: 2.5 YR 7/6 light red
Fabric: 2.5 YR 6/4 light reddish-brown
Inclusions: greyish (quartz), small/medium, sub-angular, common; whitish, small, rounded, sparse

32. Almagro 51 (south Portugal)
Surface: 7.5 YR 7/4 pink
Fabric: 7.5 YR 7/4 pink
Inclusions: whitish grits, small/medium, sub-angular, common

33. MGS III (local)
Surface: 10 R 5/6 red
Fabric: 5 YR 5/6 yellowish-red **[21]**
Inclusions: greyish (quartz), small/medium, sub-angular, common, reddish or blackish spots, very small, rounded, common

34. Dressel 1A (local)
Surface: 10 YR 7/4 very pale brown
Fabric: 2.5 YR 5/4 reddish-brown **[24]**
Inclusions: greyish (quartz), small/medium, sub-angular, common, reddish-blackish spots, very small, rounded, common; buff (limestone), small/medium, rounded, common

35. Dressel 1B (local)
Surface: 7.5YR 6/6 reddish-yellow
Fabric: 5 YR 6/6 reddish-yellow**[25]**

Inclusions: greyish (quartz), small/medium, sub-angular, common, reddish/blackish spots, very small, rounded, common; buff (limestone), medium/very large, rounded, angular, common

36. Dressel 2/4 (local, fine)
Surface: 5 YR 6/8 reddish-yellow
Fabric: 5 YR 6/6 reddish-yellow **[27]**
Inclusions: buff grits (calcareous), small/very small, rounded/oblong, very sparse; greyish (quartz/feldspar), medium, sub-angular, sparse; reddish/blackish spots, very small, rounded, common

37. Dressel 2/4 (local, coarse)
Surface: 5 YR 7/6 reddish-yellow
Fabric: 2.5 YR 5/6 red **[26]**
Inclusions: quartz/feldspar, medium/large, sub-angular, abundant; reddish/blackish spots, medium, rounded, common; calcite reaction-rings, small/very small, rounded, abundant

38. Keay 27 (Tunisia)
Surface: 10 YR 6/3 pale brown
Fabric: gley 2 4/1 dark bluish-grey
Inclusions: quartz/feldspar, greyish, medium, sub-angular, common; buff, small, rounded, common

39. Dressel 21/22 (local/north-west Sicily)
Surface: wash (10 YR 8/4 very pale brown)
Fabric: 2.5 YR 5/6 red **[28]** and **[29]**
Inclusions: greyish (quartz/feldspar), medium, sub-angular, sparse/common; blackish/reddish spots, medium, rounded, common

40. Dressel 21/22 (local/north-west Sicily)
Surface: 5 YR 6/4 light reddish-brown
Fabric: 2.5 YR 4/6 red **[30]**
Inclusions: yellowish-buff (limestone reaction-rings), small/medium, rounded, abundant

41. Gauloise 2/3 (local)
Surface: 5 YR 7/4 pink
Fabric: 2.5 YR 5/6 red **[31]**
Inclusions: greyish (quartz/feldspar), medium, sub-angular, sparse/common; blackish/reddish spots, medium, rounded, common

42. Termini 151/354 (local)
Surface: 5 YR 6/8 reddish-yellow
Fabric: 5 YR 6/6 reddish-yellow **[32]**
Inclusions: buff grits (calcareous), small/very small, rounded/oblong, very sparse; greyish (quartz/feldspar), medium, sub-angular, sparse; reddish/blackish spots, very small, rounded, common

43. Brick (local)
Surface: 5 YR 6/4 light reddish-brown
Fabric: 2.5 YR 4/6 red **[33]**
Inclusions: purple, large/medium, angular, common; purple, medium, rounded, sparse; greyish white, small/medium, angular, sparse; dark brown, small, angular, sparse

44. Brick (local)
Surface: 10 YR 8/3 very pale brown
Fabric: 7.5 YR 8/4 pink **[34]**
Inclusions: purple, large/medium, angular, common; purple, medium, rounded, sparse; greyish-white, small/medium, angular, sparse; dark brown, small, angular, sparse

Appendix 4

Catalogue of finds

Key to the catalogue

The entries are divided into six separate parts:

- Description of the fragment
- Measurements (H = height; L = length; D = diameter)
- Description of surface colour
- Fabric (only of amphorae) and description of fabric colour
- Provenance
- Date

AMPHORAE
Corinthian A

1. Handle and part of rim
H: 6.2 cm
Surface: 7.5 YR 8/6 reddish-yellow
Fabric: 1 (N7 dark grey)
Provenance: Marina di Caronía, *contrada* Pantano
Date: late sixth/early fifth century BC

North Sicilian MGS II /'Pseudo-Chian'

2. Rim
H: 6.8 cm; D. rim: 16.2 cm
Surface: pinkish beige wash (7.5 YR 7/4 pink)
Fabric: 4 (5 YR 6/6 reddish-yellow)
Provenance: Marina di Caronía, *contrada* Pantano
Date: fifth/fourth century BC

Locrian MGS II

3. Rim
H: 4.8 cm; D. rim: *c.* 14.5 cm
Surface: 10YR 8/4 very pale brown
Fabric: 3 (10YR 7/4 very pale brown)
Provenance: Marina di Caronía, *contrada* Pantano (surface survey)
Date: fifth/early fourth century BC

4. Rim
H: 4.7 cm; D. rim: *c.* 17.0 cm
Surface: 10YR 8/4 very pale brown
Fabric: 3 (10YR 7/4 very pale brown)
Provenance: Marina di Caronía, *contrada* Fiumara (surface survey)
Date: late fifth/early fourth century BC

Campanian MGS III

5. Rim
H: 3.2 cm; D. rim: *c.* 17.0 cm
Surface: 10YR 8/4 very pale brown
Fabric: 5b (2.5YR 5/8 light red)
Provenance: Marina di Caronía, *contrada* Pantano (surface survey)
Date: second half of the fourth century BC

Locrian MGS III

6. Rim
H: 3.3 cm; D. rim: *c.* 10.0 cm
Surface: 10 YR 8/4 very pale brown
Fabric: 3 (10 YR 8/3 very pale brown)
Provenance: Marina di Caronía, *contrada* Pantano
Date: second half of the fourth century BC?

7. Toe
H: 9.0 cm; D. toe: 2.4 cm
Surface: 10 YR 7/4 very pale brown
Fabric: 3 (10 YR 8/3 very pale brown)
Provenance: Marina di Caronía, *contrada* Pantano
Date: second half of the fourth century BC?

Local MGS III

8. Rim
H: 3.6 cm; D. rim: 14.0 cm
Surface: 5YR 6/6 reddish-yellow with traces of wash (5YR 5/2 reddish-grey)
Fabric: 36 (5YR 6/6 reddish-yellow)
Provenance: Caronía (surface survey)
Date: late fourth/early third century BC

Locrian amphora with *echinus*-shaped rim

9. Rim
H: 3.8 cm; D. rim: *c.* 16.5 cm
Surface: 10 YR 8/4 very pale brown
Fabric: 3 (10 YR 8/3 very pale brown)
Provenance: Marina di Caronía, *contrada* Pantano (surface survey)
Date: second half of the fourth century BC?

Campanian MGS V

10. Rim
H: 7.0 cm; D. rim: 14.5 cm
Surface: 10YR 8/4 very pale brown
Fabric: 4b (2.5YR 5/8 light red)
Provenance: Marina di Caronía, *contrada* Pantano
Date: *c.* 320/260 BC

11. Rim
H: 6.1 cm; D. rim: 17.0 cm
Surface: 10 YR 8/3 very pale brown
Fabric: 4a (7.5 YR 7/4 pink)
Provenance: Caronía, *contrada* Sotto S. Francesco (cistern)
Date: late fourth/first half of the third century BC

12. Rim
H: 2.8 cm; D. rim: *c.* 13.0 cm
Surface: 10YR 8/4 very pale brown
Fabric: 4a (10YR 8/3 very pale brown with pink core)
Provenance: Caronía (surface survey)
Date: *c.* 320/200 BC

13. Small hollow toe (not illustrated)
H: 2.8 cm; D. toe: 2.9 cm
Surface: 10YR 8/4 very pale brown
Fabric: 4b (2.5YR 5/8 light red)
Provenance: Caronía, *contrada* Sotto S. Francesco
Date: *c.* 320/260 BC

Local/North Sicilian MGS V

14. Rim
H: 2.4 cm; D. rim: *c.* 15.0 cm
Surface: 10 YR 8/3 very pale brown
Fabric: 5 (7.5 YR 7/4 pink)
Provenance: Marina di Caronía, *contrada* Pantano
Date: late fourth/first half of the third century BC

Ramón 7.1.2.1

15. Rim
H: 4.2 cm; D. rim: *c.* 13.0 cm
Surface: 2.5 Y 8/2 pale yellow
Fabric: 10 (2.5 Y 8/2 pale yellow with core 2.5 YR 7/4 light reddish-brown)
Provenance: Marina di Caronía, *contrada* Pantano
Date: third century BC

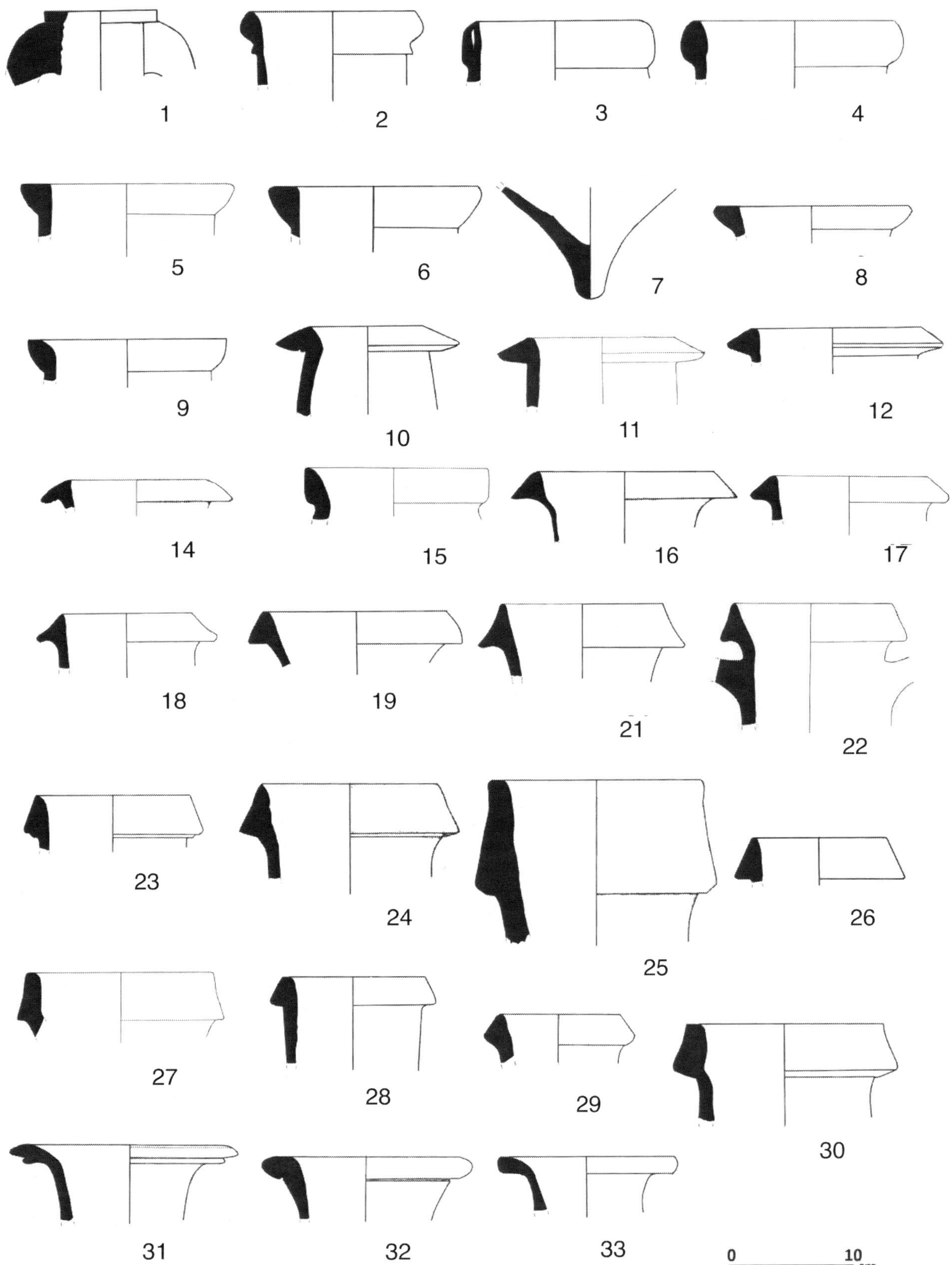

Fig. A4.1 Catalogue of finds nos 1–33 (amphorae)

Local/North Sicilian MGS VI / late Greco-Italic

16. Rim
H: 6.1 cm; D. rim: *c.* 11.5 cm
Surface: 7.5 YR 7/4 pink
Fabric: 6 (5 YR 6/4 light reddish-brown)
Provenance: Caronía, *contrada* Sotto S. Francesco
Date: 200/130 BC

17. Rim
H: 4.8 cm; D. rim: 12.5 cm
Surface: 10YR 8/2 very pale brown (wash)
Fabric: 6 (2.5 YR 6/6 light red with streaks of buff)
Provenance: Caronía (surface survey)
Date: *c.* 200/130 BC

Campanian MGS VI

18. Rim
H. 4.2 cm; D. rim: 15.0 cm
Surface: 10YR 8/4 very pale brown with rough black flakes
Fabric: 8 (10YR 8/3 very pale brown with pink core)
Provenance: Caronía, *contrada* Sotto S. Francesco
Date: *c.* 200/130 BC

19. Rim
H: 4.7 cm; D. rim: 16.1 cm
Surface: 7.5YR 8/6 reddish-yellow; glistening black and gold flakes
Fabric: 8 (2.5YR 5/8 red)
Provenance: Marina di Caronía, *contrada* Pantano
Date: *c.* 200/130 BC

20. Fragment of handle with part of stamp: A[….; possibly ΑΝΔΡΩΝ or ΑΝΔΡΩΝΟΣ (Fig. A4.1a)
H: 3.9 cm
Surface: wash (10 YR 7/6 yellow)
Fabric: 4a (5 YR 5/6 yellowish-red)
Provenance: Caronía, *contrada* Sotto S. Francesco (cistern)
Date: late fourth/first half of the third century BC

Campanian Dressel 1

21. Rim of Dressel 1A
H. 6.1 cm; D. rim: 12.0 cm
Surface: 7.5YR 8/6 reddish-yellow; glistening black and gold flakes on the surface
Fabric: 7 (2.5YR 5/8 red)
Provenance: Marina di Caronía, *contrada* Pantano
Date: *c.* 130/50 BC

22. Neck of Dressel 1A with rim and parts of handles

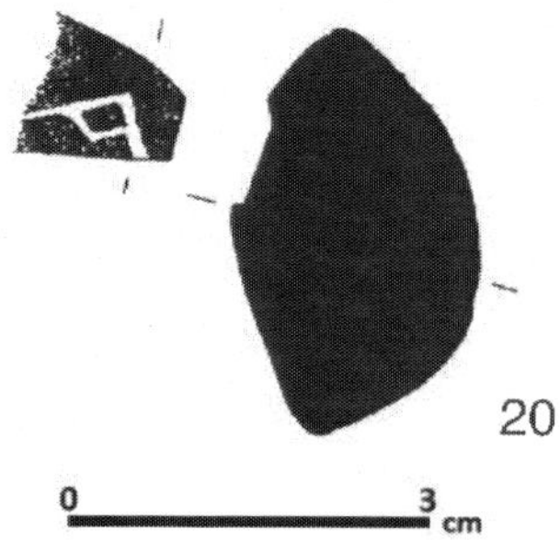

Fig. A4.1a Catalogue of finds no. 20 (stamped amphora handle)

H: 10.3 cm; D. rim: *c.* 14.0 cm
Surface: 7.5YR 8/6 reddish-yellow; glistening black and gold flakes on the surface
Fabric: 7 (2.5YR 5/8 red)
Provenance: Marina di Caronía, *contrada* Pantano (surface survey)
Date: *c.* 130/50 BC

23. Rim of Dressel 1A
H: 4.5 cm; D. rim: 14.2 cm
Surface: 5 YR 5/6 yellowish-red
Fabric: 7 (5 YR 5/6 yellowish-red)
Provenance: Marina di Caronía, *contrada* Pantano
Date: *c.* 130/50 BC

24. Rim of Dressel 1A
H: 8.0 cm; D. rim: *c.* 14.5 cm
Surface: 7.5 YR 6/6 reddish-yellow
Fabric: 7 (5 YR 6/6 reddish-yellow)
Provenance: Marina di Caronía, *contrada* Pantano
Date: first century BC

25. Rim of Dressel 1C
H: 12.8 cm; D. rim: *c.* 16.0 cm
Surface: 7.5 YR 7/6 reddish-yellow
Fabric: 7 (2.5 YR 5/8 red)
Provenance: Marina di Caronía, *contrada* Pantano
Date: first century BC

(North?) Sicilian Dressel 1 A

26. Rim
H: 3.7 cm; D. rim: *c.* 13.0 cm
Surface: buff wash
Fabric: 6 (2.5 YR 5/6 red, very badly mixed, with stripes of 10 YR 8/4 very pale brown)
Provenance: Marina di Caronía, *contrada* Pantano
Date: late second/early first century BC

Local Dressel 1

27. Rim of Dressel 1A
H: 5.1 cm; D. rim: *c.* 15.0 cm
Surface: buff wash
Fabric: 34 (5 YR 5/6 yellowish-red)
Provenance: Marina di Caronía, *contrada* Pantano
Date: first century BC

28. Rim of Dressel 1A
H: 7.0 cm; D. rim: 12.8 cm
Surface: 5 YR 7/6 reddish-yellow
Fabric: 34 (5 YR 5/6 yellowish-red)
Provenance: Marina di Caronía, *contrada* Pantano
Date: late second/early first century BC

29. Rim of Dressel 1A
H: 4.1 cm; D. rim: *c.* 13.0 cm
Surface: 10 YR 7/4 very pale brown
Fabric: 34 (2.5 YR 5/4 reddish brown)
Provenance: Marina di Caronía, *contrada* Pantano
Date: second century BC

30. Rim of Dressel 1B
H: 8.0 cm; D. rim: 14.5 cm
Surface: 7.5 YR 6/6 reddish-yellow
Fabric: 35 (5 YR 6/6 reddish-yellow)
Provenance: Marina di Caronía, *contrada* Pantano
Date: first century BC

Maña C/Ramón 7.4.2.1–7.4.3.3

31. Rim
H: 6.2 cm; D. rim: *c.* 16.5 cm
Surface: 7.5 YR 8/3 pink
Fabric: 10 (2.5 YR 5/8 red)
Provenance: Marina di Caronía, *contrada* Pantano
Date: late second century BC/early first century AD

Ramón 7.5.2.1

32. Rim
H: 5.1 cm; D. rim: 16.2 cm
Surface: 2.5 Y 8/3 pale yellow
Fabric: 11 (2.5 YR 5/8 red)
Provenance: Caronía, *contrada* Sotto San Francesco
Date: second/first century BC

Ramón 7.6.1.1

33. Rim
H: 4.4 cm; D. rim: *c.* 13.8 cm
Surface: 7.5 YR 7/6 reddish-yellow, single very large white calcite chunks (5 mm) visible
Fabric: 12 (5 YR 6/6 reddish-yellow)
Provenance: Marina di Caronía, *contrada* Pantano
Date: first century BC

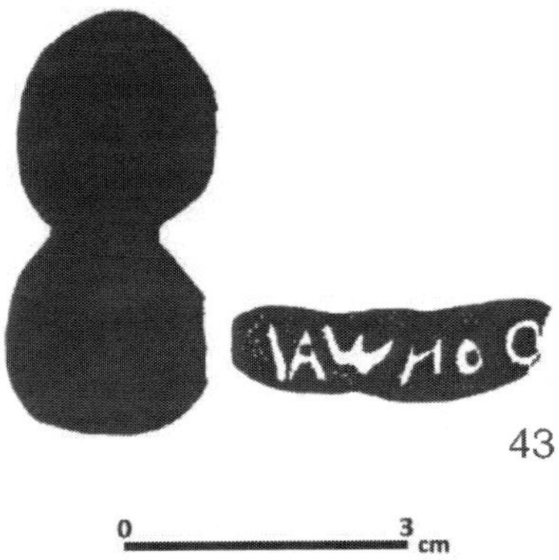

Fig. A4.2a Detail of stamped handle no. 43

Undefined late Punic

34. Rim
H: 4.2 cm; D. rim: *c.* 16.0 cm
Surface: 2.5 Y 8/3 pale yellow
Fabric: 10 (2.5 YR 5/8 red)
Provenance: Marina di Caronía, *contrada* Pantano (surface survey)
Date: second/first century BC

35. Handle
L: 4.5 cm
Surface: 10 R 5/8 red
Fabric: 10 (10 R 6/8 light red)
Provenance: Marina di Caronía, *contrada* Pantano
Date: first century BC/early first century AD

36. Hollow toe
H: 7.4 cm; D. toe: 4.4 cm
Surface: 10 YR 7/6 yellow
Fabric: 10 (5 YR 6/6 reddish-yellow)
Provenance: Marina di Caronía, *contrada* Pantano
Date: second/first century BC

North Sicilian tubular amphora

37. Ringed hollow toe
H. 13.1 cm; D. toe: 3.0 cm
Surface: gley 2 6/1 bluish-grey
Fabric: 8 (2.5 YR 5/8 red)
Provenance: Marina di Caronía, *contrada* Pantano
Date: first century BC (cf. Bonanno 2009, 47, tav. 9g)

Dressel 26

38. Rim and neck
H: 7.4 cm; D. rim: *c.* 15.0 cm
Surface: 10 YR 7/4 very pale brown
Fabric: 13 (10 YR 7/4 very pale brown)
Provenance: Marina di Caronía, *contrada* Pantano
Date: first century BC/early first century AD

Rhodian

39. Rim
H: 4.8 cm; D. rim: *c.* 10.0 cm
Surface: 10 YR 8/3 very pale brown
Fabric: 14 (7.5 YR 6/4 light brown)
Provenance: Marina di Caronía, *contrada* Pantano
Date: second/first century BC

40. Rim with part of handle
H: 5.9 cm; D. rim: *c.* 8.0 cm
Surface: 10 YR 8/3 very pale brown
Fabric: 14 (5YR 6/6 reddish-yellow)
Provenance: Marina di Caronía, *contrada* Pantano
Date: second/first century BC

Koan

41. Rim and bifid handle
H. 7.7 cm; D. rim: 11.0 cm
Surface: 5Y 8/3 – 8/4 pale yellow
Fabric: 18 (5Y 8/3 – 8/4 pale yellow with pink core (7.5 YR 8/4) (cf. Bezeczky 2013, pl. 60, 50)
Provenance: Marina di Caronía, *contrada* Pantano
Date: second/first century BC

42. Rim with handle
H: 5.4 cm; D. rim: *c.* 9.5 cm
Surface: buff wash (5 Y 8/2 pale yellow)
Fabric: 15 (10 YR 7/3 very pale brown)
Provenance: Marina di Caronía, *contrada* Pantano
Date: second/first century BC

43. Handle with retrograde stamp: IACΩNOC
L: 6.9 cm
Surface: white wash (2.5 Y 8/2 pale yellow)
Fabric: 15 (5 YR 6/4 light reddish-brown)
Provenance: Marina di Caronía, *contrada* Pantano
Date: late second century BC

44. Toe
H: 5.8 cm; D. toe: 2.0 cm
Surface: buff wash
Fabric: 15
Provenance: Marina di Caronía, *contrada* Pantano
Date: second/first century BC

Knidian

45. Handle
L: 9.2 cm
Surface: 5 YR 6/6 reddish-yellow
Fabric: 16 (5 YR 6/6 reddish-yellow)
Provenance: Caronía, *contrada* Sotto S. Francesco
Date: first century BC

Lamboglia 2

46. Rim
H: 5.9 cm; D. rim: *c.* 15.0 cm
Surface: 10 YR 8/3 very pale brown
Fabric: 17 (5 YR 6/6 reddish-yellow)
Provenance: Marina di Caronía, *contrada* Pantano
Date: late second century BC/last quarter of first century BC

47. Rim
H: 3.7 cm; D. rim: *c.* 16.0 cm
Surface: 7.5 YR 7/6 reddish-yellow
Fabric: 17 (7.5 YR 7/4 reddish-yellow)
Provenance: Marina di Caronía, *contrada* Pantano
Date: late second century BC/last quarter of first century BC

48. Rim
H: 4.5 cm; D. rim: *c.* 17.0 cm
Surface: 10 YR 7/6 yellow
Fabric: 17 (10 YR 7/6 yellow)
Provenance: Marina di Caronía, *contrada* Pantano
Date: late second century BC/early first century AD

49. Handle and part of body
L: 11.4 cm
Surface: 10 YR 7/2 light grey
Fabric: 17 (7.5 YR 7/4 pink)
Provenance: Caronía, *contrada* Sotto S. Francesco
Date: late second century BC/last quarter of first century BC

Campanian Dressel 2/4

50. Rim
H: 4.3 cm; D. rim: 13.0 cm
Surface: 10 YR 7/6 yellow
Fabric: 7 (2.5 YR 5/6 red)
Provenance: Marina di Caronía, *contrada* Pantano
Date: first/early second century AD

51. Handle
L: 8.7 cm
Surface: 10 YR 8/4 very pale brown
Fabric: 7 (2.5 YR 5/6 red)
Provenance: Marina di Caronía, *contrada* Pantano
Date: first/early second centuryAD

52. Toe.
H: 6.8 cm; D. toe: 4.8 cm

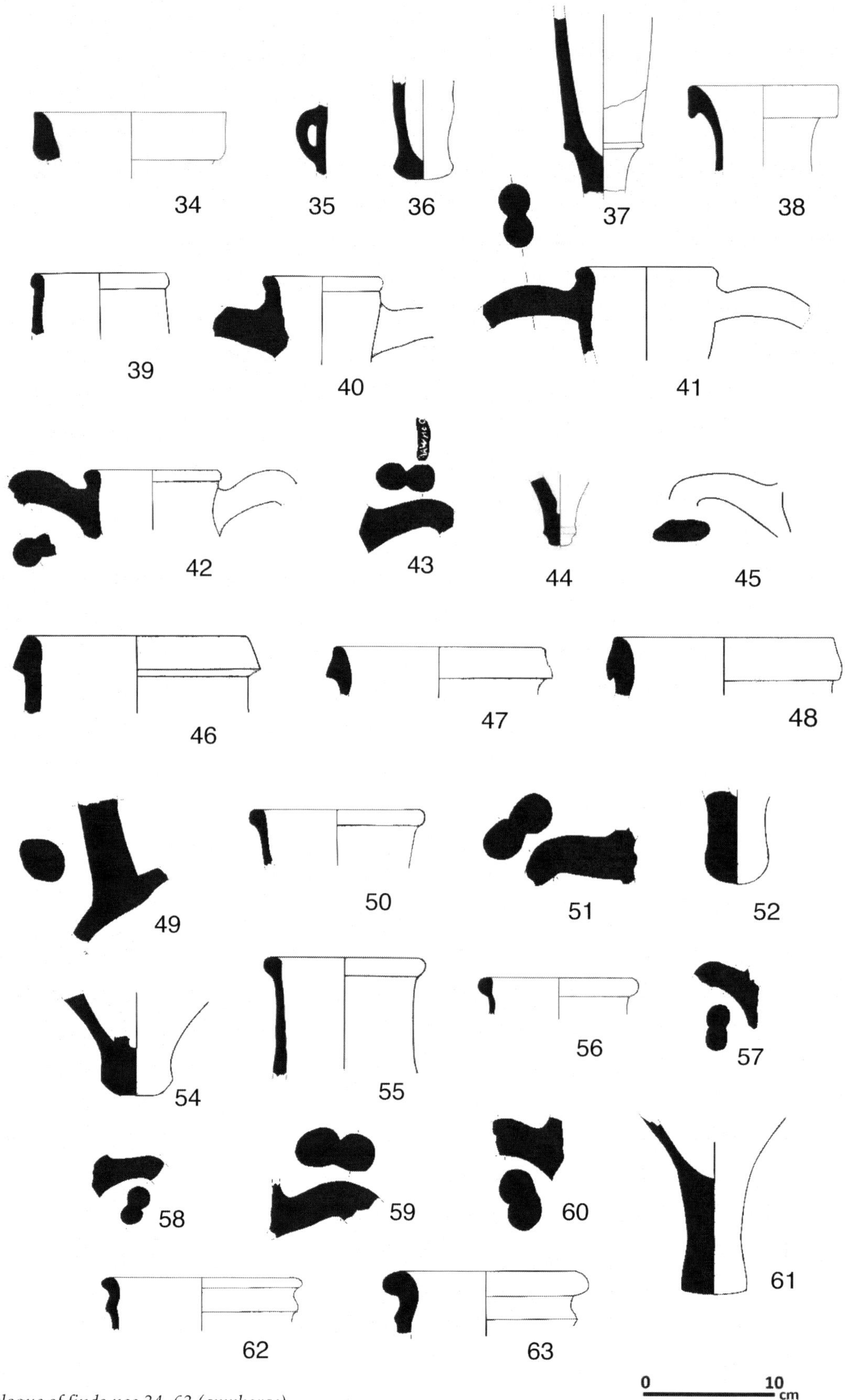

Fig. A4.2 Catalogue of finds nos 34–63 (amphorae)

Surface: 2.5 Y 7/4 pale yellow
Fabric: 7 (10 YR 7/4 very pale brown)
Provenance: Marina di Caronía, *contrada* Pantano
Date: first century AD

Central Italian/Campanian Dressel 2/4

53. Handle (not illustrated)
L: 8.5 cm
Surface: 7.5 YR 8/2 pinkish-white
Fabric: 19 (10 YR 6/4 light yellowish: cf. Bezeczky 2013, 131, Italian Fabric B, pl. 78, 323–34 and 326)
Provenance: Marina di Caronía, *contrada* Pantano
Date: late first century BC/first century AD

54. Toe
H: 7.7 cm; D. toe: 5.2 cm
Surface: 7.5 YR 8/2 pinkish-white
Fabric: 19 (10 YR 6/4 light yellowish-brown) (cf. Bezeczky 2013, 131, Italian Fabric B, pl. 78, 323–34 and 326)
Provenance: Marina di Caronía, *contrada* Pantano
Date: late first century BC/first century AD

Local Dressel 2/4

55. Rim with neck
H: 9.5 cm; D. rim: *c.* 11.0 cm
Surface: 5 YR 6/6 reddish-yellow
Fabric: 36 (5 YR 6/6 reddish-yellow)
Provenance: Marina di Caronía, *contrada* Pantano
Date: probably first century AD

56. Rim
H: 3.2 cm; D. rim: *c.* 16.0 cm
Surface: 5 YR 6/6 reddish-yellow
Fabric: 37 (2.5 YR 6/4 light reddish-brown, core 7.5 YR 4/1 dark grey)
Provenance: Marina di Caronía, *contrada* Pantano
Date: probably first century AD

57. Bifid handle
L: 5.1 cm
Surface: wash (5YR 5/2 reddish-grey)
Fabric: 37 (5YR 5/4-5/6 reddish-brown to yellowish-red), core 2.5 YR 5/8 red
Provenance: Marina di Caronía, *contrada* Pantano
Date: first/early second century AD

58. Bifid handle
L: 4.9 cm
Surface: pinkish-grey (5YR 6/2)
Fabric: 37 (5YR 5/4-5/6 yellowish-red to 2.5 YR 5/8 red)
Provenance: Marina di Caronía, *contrada* Pantano
Date: first/early second century AD

59. Bifid handle
L. 8.6 cm
Surface: 2.5YR 6/6 light red
Fabric: 37 (2.5 YR 5/6 reddish-brown)
Provenance: Marina di Caronía, *contrada* Pantano
Date: first/early second century AD

60. Bifid handle
L: 5.1 cm
Surface: 2.5 YR 6/6 light red
Fabric: 36 (2.5 YR 5/6 – 5/8 red)
Provenance: Marina di Caronía, *contrada* Pantano
Date: probably first century AD

61. Toe
H: 14.4 cm; D. toe: 5.2 cm
Surface: 2.5 YR 6/8 light red
Fabric: 37 (2.5 YR 5/6 red)
Provenance: Marina di Caronía, *contrada* Pantano
Date: first/early third century AD

Local Dressel 21/22

62. Rim
H: 3.9 cm; D. rim: 15.2 cm
Surface: wash (10 YR 8/4 very pale brown)
Fabric: 39 (2.5 YR 5/8 red)
Provenance: Marina di Caronía, *contrada* Pantano
Date: end of the first century BC (?)/first century AD

63. Rim
H. 4.5 cm; D. rim: *c.* 15.0 cm
Surface: wash (10 YR 8/3 very pale brown)
Fabric: 40 (2.5 YR 5/8 red)
Provenance: Marina di Caronía, *contrada* Pantano
Date: end of the first century BC (?)/first century AD

64. Rim
H: 3.4 cm; D. rim: *c.* 16.5 cm
Surface: wash (5 YR 7/3 pink)
Fabric: 39 (2.5 YR 5/6 red)
Provenance: Marina di Caronía, *contrada* Pantano
Date: end of the first century BC (?)/first century AD

65. Rim
H: 3.8 cm; D. rim: 15.0 cm
Surface: 2.5 YR 5/6 red
Fabric: 39 (2.5 YR 4/8 red)
Provenance: Marina di Caronía, *contrada* Pantano
Date: end of the first century BC (?)/first century AD

66. Rim
H: 5.8 cm; D. rim: 15.0 cm
Surface: 5 YR 7/4 pink
Fabric: 40 (5 YR 6/6 reddish-yellow)
Provenance: Marina di Caronía, *contrada* Pantano
Date: end of the first century BC (?)/first century AD

67. Small rim
H: 5.2 rim; D. rim: *c.* 14.5 cm
Surface: wash (2.5 Y 7/11 pale yellow)
Fabric: 40 (7.5 YR 4/3 brown)
Provenance: Marina di Caronía, *contrada* Pantano
Date: end of the first century BC (?)/first century AD

68. Rim
H: 4.0 cm; D. rim: 16.0 cm
Surface: 2.5 YR 5/6 red
Fabric: 40 (2.5 YR 5/6 red)
Provenance: Marina di Caronía, *contrada* Pantano
Date: end of the first century BC (?)/first century AD

69. Rim and part of neck
H: 9.1 cm; D. rim: 12.1 cm
Surface: 5 YR 8/3 pink
Fabric: 40 (5 YR 6/3 light reddish-brown)
Provenance: Marina di Caronía, *contrada* Pantano
Date: end of the first century BC (?)/first century AD

70. Rim
H: 4.7 cm; D. rim: *c.* 22.0 cm
Surface: wash (10 YR 7/2 light grey)
Fabric: 40 (2.5 YR 6/6 light red)
Provenance: Marina di Caronía, *contrada* Pantano
Date: end of the first century BC (?)/first century AD

71. Rim
H: 4.9 cm; D. rim: 22.0 cm
Surface: 2.5 YR 8/2 pinkish-white
Fabric: 40 (2.5 YR 5/6 reddish-brown)
Provenance: Marina di Caronía, *contrada* Pantano
Date: end of the first century BC (?)/first century AD

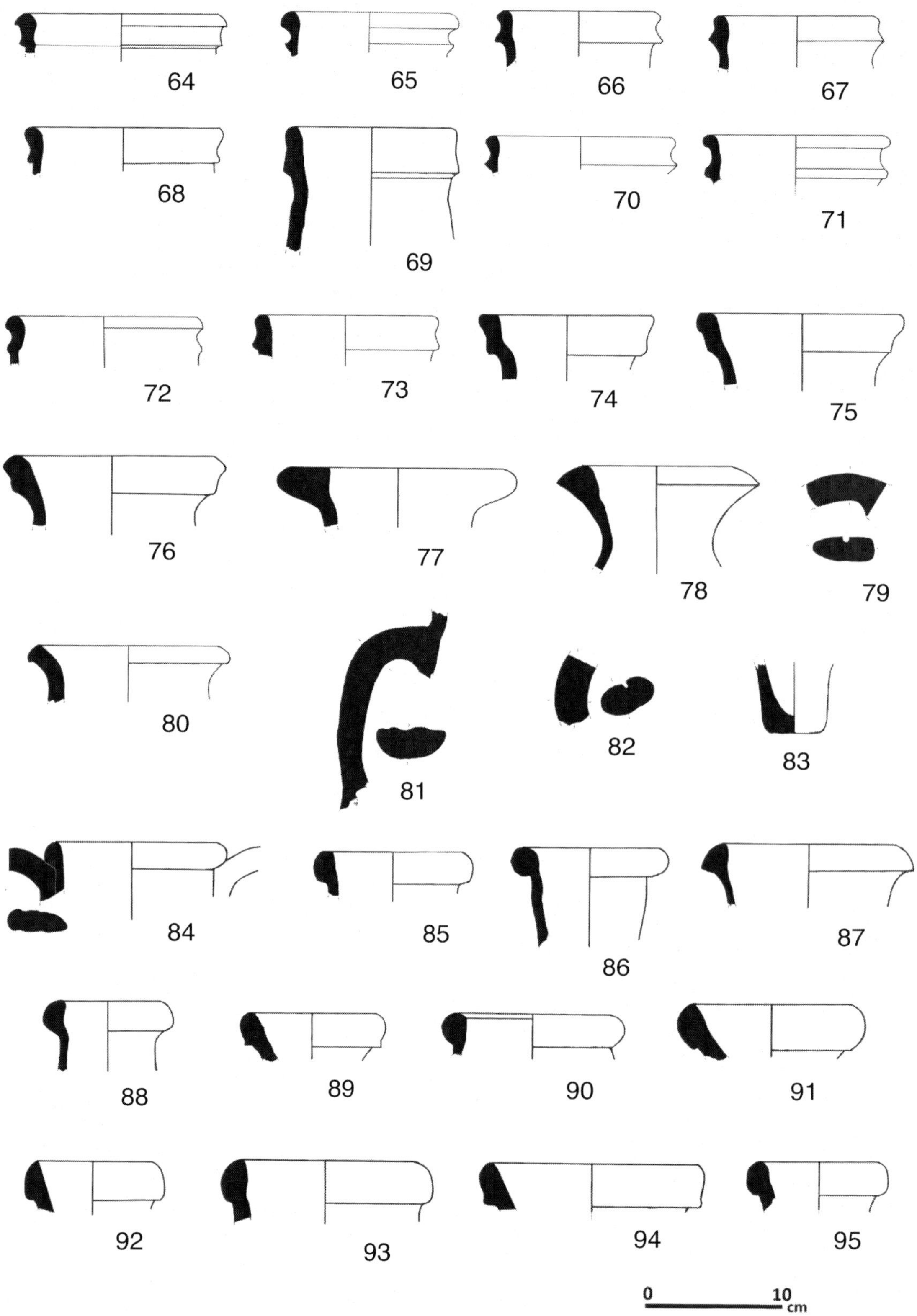

Fig. A4.3 Catalogue of finds nos 64–95 (amphorae)

72. Rim
H: 6.5 cm: D. rim: *c.* 14.0 cm
Surface: 10YR 5/2 greyish-brown
Fabric: 40 (2.5 YR 5/6 red)
Provenance: Caronía (surface survey)
Date: end of the first century BC/first century AD

73. Rim
H: 5.9 cm; D. rim: *c.* 15.0 cm
Surface: 2.5 YR 8/2 pinkish-white
Fabric: 40 (2.5 YR 5/6 reddish-brown)
Provenance: Caronía (surface survey)
Date: late first century BC/first century AD

Local Gauloise 2/3

74. Rim and part of neck
H: 5.0 cm; D. rim: *c.* 10.0 cm
Surface: 2.5 YR 6/6 light red
Fabric: 41 (2.5 YR 5/6 light red)
Provenance: Marina di Caronía, *contrada* Pantano
Date: first half of the first century AD

75. Rim and part of neck
H: 5.7 cm; D. rim: *c.* 16.0 cm
Surface: 5 YR 7/4 pink
Fabric: 41 (2.5 YR 5/6 red)
Provenance: Marina di Caronía, *contrada* Pantano
Date: first half of the first century AD

Local imitation Gaulish?

76. Rim with handle
H: 8.0 cm; D. rim: 16.0 cm
Surface: 5YR 6/6 reddish-yellow
Fabric: 41 (5 YR 6/8 reddish-yellow)
Provenance: Marina di Caronía, *contrada* Pantano
Date: first century AD?

Dressel 20

77. Rim
H: 4.7 cm; D. rim: *c.* 17.0 cm
Surface: 2.5 Y 7/4 pale yellow
Fabric: 20 (10 YR 6/4 light yellowish-brown)
Provenance: Marina di Caronía, *contrada* Pantano (surface survey)
Date: first/second century AD

78. Rim and neck
H: 8.1 cm; D. rim: *c.* 13.0 cm
Surface: 2.5 Y 7/4 pale yellow
Fabric: 20 (10 YR 6/4 light yellowish-brown)
Provenance: Marina di Caronía, *contrada* Pantano
Date: third century AD

Haltern 70

79. Handle with groove
L: 6.2 cm
Surface: 7.5 YR 8/6 reddish-yellow
Fabric: 20 (7.5 YR 6/6 reddish-yellow)
Provenance: Marina di Caronía, *contrada* Pantano
Date: first century AD

Dressel 7/11

80. Rim
H: 4.2 cm; D. rim: *c.* 14.0 cm
Surface: 10 YR 8/2 very pale brown
Fabric: 21 (10 YR 7/4 very pale brown)
Provenance: Marina di Caronía, *contrada* Pantano
Date: first/early second century AD

81. Handle
L: 16.1 cm
Surface: 10 YR 8/3 very pale brown
Fabric: 21 (10 YR 8/3 very pale brown)
Provenance: Marina di Caronía, *contrada* Pantano
Date: first/early second century AD

82. Handle
L: 5.2 cm
Surface: 10 YR 7/4 very pale brown
Fabric: 21 (10 YR 7/3 very pale brown)
Provenance: Marina di Caronía, *contrada* Pantano
Date: first/early second century AD

83. Hollow base
H: 5.6 cm; D. base: 6.7 cm
Surface: 10 YR 8/2 very pale brown
Fabric: 21 (10 YR 8/3 very pale brown)
Provenance: Marina di Caronía, *contrada* Pantano
Date: first century AD

Pélichet 47 / Gauloise 4

84. Rim with handle
H: 4.6 cm; D. rim: *c.* 14.0 cm
Surface: 7.5 YR 6/4 light brown
Fabric: 23 (7.5 YR 6/4 light brown)
Provenance: Caronía (surface survey)
Date: first/second century AD

85. Rim
H: 3.3 cm; D. rim: *c.* 12.5 cm
Surface: 7.5 YR 6/6 reddish-yellow
Fabric: 23 (7.5 YR 7/6 reddish-yellow)
Provenance: Marina di Caronía, *contrada* Pantano
Date: first/second century AD

86. Rim.
H: 7.1 cm; D. rim: *c.* 8.4 cm
Surface: 7.5 YR 6/4 light brown
Fabric: 23 (7.5 YR 6/4 light brown)
Provenance: Marina di Caronía, *contrada* Pantano
Date: first/second century AD

87. Rim
H: 4.7 cm; D. rim: *c.* 13.0 cm
Surface: 10 YR 7/6 yellow
Fabric: 23 (7.5 YR 7/6 reddish-yellow)
Provenance: Marina di Caronía, *contrada* Pantano
Date: first/second century AD

88. Rim
H: 5.2 cm; D. rim: *c.* 9.5 cm
Surface: 10 YR 6/6 brownish-yellow
Fabric: 23 (10 YR 5/8 yellowish-brown)
Provenance: Marina di Caronía, *contrada* Pantano
Date: first/second century AD

89. Rim
H: 3.9 cm; D. rim: *c.* 8.5 cm
Surface: 2.5 YR 6/6 light red
Fabric: 23 (2.5 YR 6/ light reddish-brown)
Provenance: Marina di Caronía, *contrada* Pantano
Date: third century AD

90. Rim
H: 3.4 cm; D. rim: 13.0
Surface: 5 YR 6/6 yellowish-red
Fabric: 23 (5 YR 5/8 yellowish-red)
Provenance: Marina di Caronía, *contrada* Pantano
Date: first/second century AD

91. Rim
H: 4.3 cm; D. rim: *c.* 12.5 cm
Surface: 7.5 YR 6/6
Fabric: 23 (7.5 YR 6/4 light brown – 2.5 YR 6/6 light red)
Provenance: Marina di Caronía, *contrada* Pantano
Date: first/second century AD

92. Rim
H: 3.9 cm; D. rim: 10.0 cm
Surface: 7.5 YR 5/8 dark brown
Fabric: 23 (7.5 YR 5/6 dark brown)
Provenance: Marina di Caronía, *contrada* Pantano
Date: third century AD

93. Rim.
H: 4.4 cm; D. rim: *c.* 14.0 cm
Surface: 10 YR 7/4 very pale yellow
Fabric: 23 (10 YR 7/4 very pale

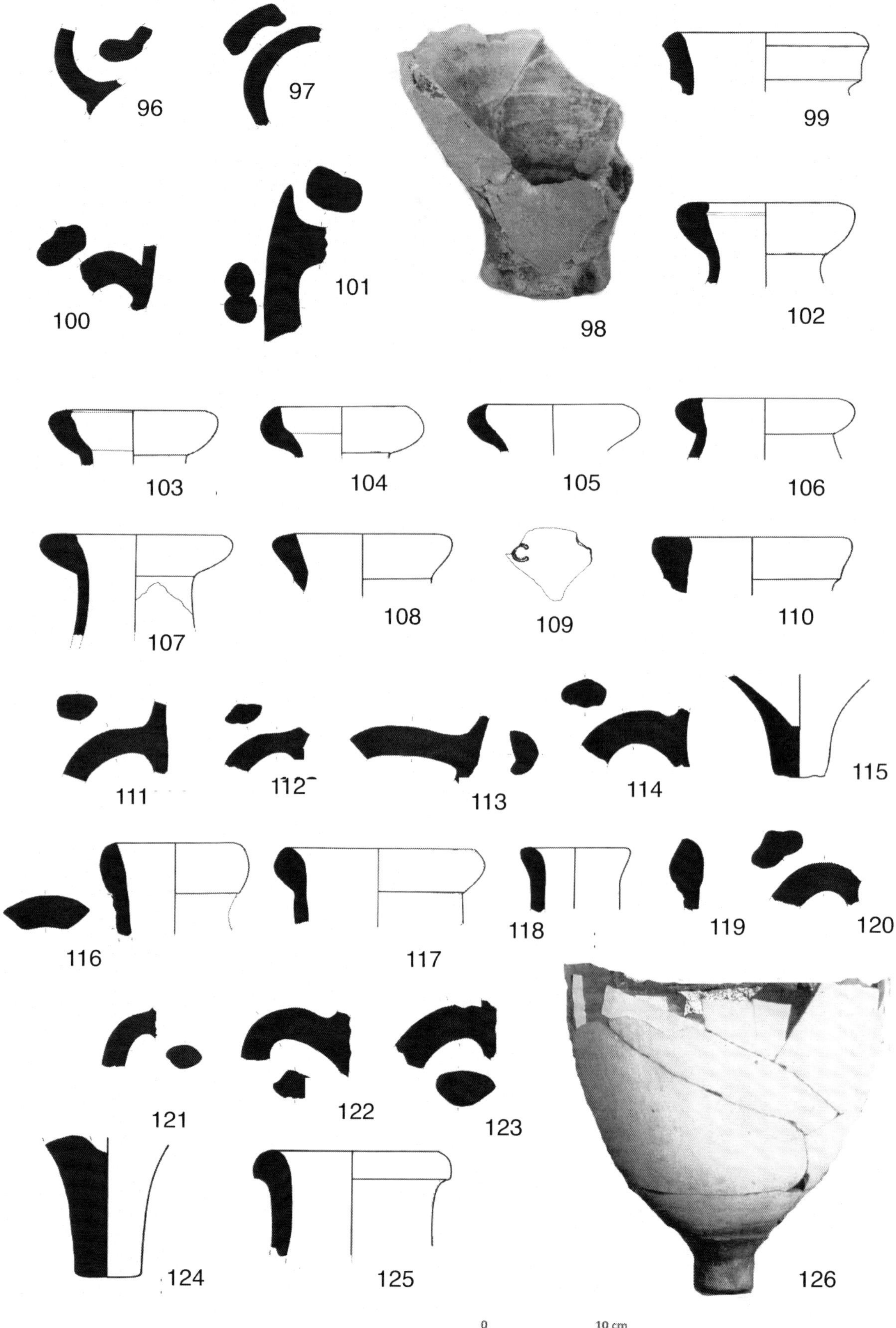

Fig. A4.4 Catalogue of finds nos 96–126 (amphorae)

yellow)
Provenance: Marina di Caronía, *contrada* Pantano
Date: first / second century AD

94. Rim
H: 3.2 cm; D. rim: 14.0 cm
Surface: 7.5 YR 6 / 8 reddish-yellow
Fabric: 23 (5 YR 5 / 6 yellowish-red)
Provenance: Marina di Caronía, *contrada* Pantano
Date: second / third century AD

95. Rim
H: 3.4 cm; D. rim: *c.* 10.0 cm
Surface: 10 YR 7 / 3 very pale brown
Fabric: 23 (5 YR 7 / 4 pink)
Provenance: Marina di Caronía, *contrada* Pantano
Date: third century AD

96. Handle
L: 6.8 cm
Surface: 5 YR 7 / 8 reddish-yellow
Fabric: 23 (7.5 YR 6 / 6 reddish-yellow)
Provenance: Marina di Caronía, *contrada* Pantano
Date: first / third century AD

97. Handle
L: 8.4 cm
Surface: 7.5 YR 5 / 6 dark brown
Fabric: 23 (5 YR 7 / 3 pink)
Provenance: Marina di Caronía, *contrada* Pantano
Date: first / third century AD

98. Base and lower part of body
H: 26.2 cm; D. base: 11.5 cm
Surface: 7.5 YR 7 / 6 reddish-yellow
Fabric: 23 (7.5 YR 7 / 8 reddish-yellow)
Provenance: Marina di Caronía, *contrada* Pantano
Date: third century AD

Tripolitanian 1

99. Rim
H: 4.9 cm; D. rim: 16.4 cm
Surface: 10 R 7 / 4 pale red
Fabric: 24 (10 R 6 / 6 light red)
Provenance: Marina di Caronía, *contrada* Pantano
Date: first / early second century AD

Richborough 527

100. Handle
L: 6.2 cm
Surface: 2.5 Y 8 / 2 pale yellow
Fabric: 25 (2.5 Y 8 / 2 pale yellow, very coarse)
Provenance: Caronía, *contrada* Sotto S. Francesco
Date: first century AD

Shöne-Mau 13/Agora G198/ Pompeii 13

101. Handle
L: 12.6 cm
Surface: 7.5 YR 7 / 6 reddish-yellow, with flakes of golden mica
Fabric: 26 (7.5 YR 7 / 4 pink)
Provenance: Marina di Caronía, *contrada* Pantano
Date: first century AD

Africana I

102. Rim
H: 6.4 cm; D. rim: *c.* 13.0 cm
Surface: 7.5 YR 7 / 6 reddish-yellow
Fabric: 27 (5 YR 6 / 6 reddish-yellow)
Provenance: Marina di Caronía, *contrada* Pantano
Date: mid- second / fourth century AD

103. Rim
H: 4.4; D. rim: *c.* 12.0
Surface: 5 YR 7 / 6 reddish-yellow
Fabric: 27 (2.5 YR 6 / 8 light red)
Provenance: Marina di Caronía, *contrada* Pantano
Date: third / fourth century AD

104. Rim
H: 4.3 cm; D. rim: *c.* 14.0 cm
Surface: 5 YR 7 / 6 reddish-yellow
Fabric: 27 (2.5 YR 6 / 8 light red)
Provenance: Marina di Caronía, *contrada* Pantano
Date: mid-second / fourth century AD

105. Rim
H: 8.1 cm; D. rim: 15.0 cm
Surface: 2.5 Y 7 / 1 light grey
Fabric: 27 (light red – pink 2.5YR 6 / 8, no dark core).
Provenance: Marina di Caronía, *contrada* Pantano
Date: fourth century AD

106. Rim
H: 5.5 cm; D. rim: 15.0 cm
Surface: 5YR 7 / 6 reddish-yellow
Fabric: 27 (2.5YR 6 / 8 light red with purple-brown core)
Provenance: Marina di Caronía, *contrada* Pantano
Date: third / fourth century AD

107. Rim
H: 8.1 cm; D. rim: 14.2 cm
Surface: 2 gley 8 / 1 bluish grey
Fabric: 27 (2.5 YR 6 / 8 light red)
Provenance: Marina di Caronía, *contrada* Pantano
Date: third / fourth century AD

108. Rim
H: 4.4 cm; D. rim: 13.0 cm
Surface: 2 gley 8 / 1 light bluish-grey
Fabric: 27 (2.5 YR 6 / 8 light red)
Provenance: Marina di Caronía, *contrada* Pantano
Date: third / fourth century AD

109. Body sherd of probably Africana 1 with a 'C' stamped in the clay before firing
L: 6.1 cm
Surface: 10 YR 6 / 3 pale brown
Fabric: 27 (2.5 YR 6 / 8 light red)
Provenance: Marina di Caronía, *contrada* Pantano
Date: late second / fourth century AD

110. Rim
H: 4.3 cm; D. rim: 13.0 cm
Surface: 2.5 YR 7 / 6 light red
Fabric: 27 (2.5 YR 7 / 6 light red)
Provenance: Marina di Caronía, *contrada* Pantano
Date: third century AD

111. Handle
L: 9.1 cm
Surface: 7.5 YR 7 / 2 pinkish-grey
Fabric: 27 (5 YR 7 / 6 reddish-yellow)
Provenance: Marina di Caronía, *contrada* Pantano
Date: late second / fourth century AD

112. Handle
L: 7.0 cm
Surface: 5 YR 6 / 6 reddish-yellow
Fabric: 27 (5 YR 6 / 6 reddish-yellow)
Provenance: Marina di Caronía, *contrada* Pantano
Date: late second / fourth century AD

113. Handle
L: 11.6 cm
Surface; 10 YR 8 / 2 very pale brown
Fabric: 27 (5 YR 6 / 8 reddish-yellow)
Provenance: Marina di Caronía, *contrada* Pantano
Date: late second / fourth century AD

114. Handle
L: 8.8 cm
Surface: 10 YR 6 / 2 light brownish-grey
Fabric: 27 (2.5 YR 6 / 4 light reddish-brown)
Provenance: Marina di Caronía, *contrada* Pantano

Date: *c.* 180 / fourth century AD

115. Toe
H: 8.1 cm; D. toe: 4.1 cm
Surface: 5 YR 6 / 6 reddish-yellow
Fabric: 27 (2.5 YR 6 / 6 light red)
Provenance: Marina di Caronía, *contrada* Pantano
Date: late second / fourth century AD

Africana 2

116. Rim with handle
H: 7.5 cm; D. rim: *c.* 9.5 cm
Surface: 7.5 YR 7 / 4 pink
Fabric: 27 (2.5 YR 6 / 8 light red)
Provenance: Marina di Caronía, *contrada* Pantano
Date: mid-second / fourth century AD

117. Rim
H: 6.0 cm; D. rim: 15.0 cm
Surface: 10 R 6 / 1 reddish grey
Fabric: 27 (10 R 5 / 8 red)
Provenance: Marina di Caronía, *contrada* Pantano
Date: third / fourth century AD

118. Rim
H: 5.2 cm; D. rim: 8.6 cm
Surface: 10 R 5 / 6 red
Fabric: 27 (10 R 4 / 6 red)
Provenance: Marina di Caronía, *contrada* Pantano
Date: third / fourth century AD

119. Rim
H: 6.0 cm; D. rim: ?
Surface: 10 R 7 / 6 light red
Fabric: 27 (10 R 7 / 6 light red)
Provenance: Marina di Caronía, *contrada* Pantano
Date: third / fourth century AD

120. Handle
L: 8.2 cm
Surface: 7.5 YR 8 / 3 pink
Fabric: 27 (5 YR 7 / 4 pink)
Provenance: Marina di Caronía, *contrada* Pantano
Date: third / fourth century AD

121. Handle
L: 9.2 cm
Surface: 7.5 YR 7 / 4 pink
Fabric: 27 (5 YR 6 / 8 reddish-yellow)
Provenance: Marina di Caronía, *contrada* Pantano
Date: late second / fourth century AD

122. Handle
L: 9.0 cm
Surface: 7.5 YR 6 / 6 reddish-yellow
Fabric: 27 (7.5 YR 6 / 6 reddish-yellow)
Provenance: Marina di Caronía, *contrada* Pantano
Date: late second / fourth century AD

123. Handle
L: 9.0 cm
Surface: 7.5 YR 6 / 8 reddish-yellow
Fabric: 27 (7.5 YR 6 / 6 reddish-yellow)
Provenance: Marina di Caronía, *contrada* Pantano
Date: late second / fourth century AD

124. Toe
H: 11.2 cm; D. toe: 4.2 cm
Surface: 2.5 YR 8 / 2 pinkish-white
Fabric: 27 (10 R 5 / 8 red)
Provenance: Marina di Caronía, *contrada* Pantano
Date: late second / fourth century AD

Keay 25Q/Africana 3

125. Rim
H: 8.6 cm; D. rim: 15.0 cm
Surface: 2.5 YR 8 / 1 white
Fabric: 27 (2.5 YR 5 / 6 red)
Provenance: Marina di Caronía, *contrada* Pantano
Date: fourth century AD

Keay 27

126. Lower part of body and toe
H: 34.1 cm; D. toe: 5.6 cm
Surface: 10 YR 6 / 3 pale brown
Fabric: 38 (gley 2 4 / 1 dark bluish-grey)
Provenance: Marina di Caronía, *contrada* Pantano
Date: second half of the fourth century AD

Keay 13A

127. Rim
H: 3.3 cm; D. rim: *c.* 11.0 cm
Surface: 10 YR 8 / 4 very pale brown
Fabric: 28 (2.5 YR 6 / 6 light red)
Provenance: Marina di Caronía, *contrada* Pantano
Date: fourth century AD

Tripolitana 2/3

128. Rim
H: 7.2 cm; D. rim: *c.* 13.0 cm
Surface: 7.5 YR 5 / 1 grey (5 YR 7 / 6 reddish-yellow on interior)
Fabric: 29 (10 R 5 / 8 red)
Provenance: Marina di Caronía, *contrada* Pantano
Date: third / fourth century AD

129. Rim
H: 6.2 cm; D. rim: 15.0 cm
Surface: 2 gley 6 / 1 bluish-grey
Fabric: 29 (2.5 YR 6 / 6 light red)
Provenance: Marina di Caronía, *contrada* Pantano
Date: third / fourth century AD

130. Rim
H: 6.1 cm; D. rim: 16.2 cm
Surface: 7.5 YR 5 / 1 grey
Fabric: 29 (10 R 5 / 8 red)
Provenance: Marina di Caronía, *contrada* Pantano
Date: third / fourth century AD

131. Rim
H: 4.4 cm; D. rim: *c.* 16.0 cm
Surface: 7.5 YR 5 / 1 grey
Fabric: 29 (10 R 5 / 8 red)
Provenance: Marina di Caronía, *contrada* Pantano (surface survey)
Date: third / fourth century AD

Keay 1B/Dressel 30

132. Hollow toe
H: 6.7 cm; D. toe: 4.2 cm
Surface: 10 YR 5 / 3 brown–2.5 YR 6 / 8 light red
Fabric: 30 (7.5 YR 5 / 3 brown–2.5 YR 5 / 6 red)
Provenance: Marina di Caronía, *contrada* Pantano
Date: third century AD

133. Hollow toe
H: 6.2 cm; D. toe: 5.5 cm
Surface: 10 YR 6 / 1 grey
Fabric: 30 (10 YR 4 / 1 dark grey)
Provenance: Marina di Caronía, *contrada* Pantano
Date: third century AD

Almagro 51

134. Rim with handle
H: 4.0 cm; D. rim: *c.* 11.0 cm
Surface: 2.5 YR 6 / 6 light red
Fabric: 32 (2.5 YR 5 / 6 red)
Provenance: Marina di Caronía, *contrada* Pantano
Date: third / fourth century AD

135. Hollow toe
H: 8.0 cm; D. toe: 4.8 cm
Surface: 2.5 YR 7 / 6 light red
Fabric: 32 (2.5 YR 6 / 4 light reddish-brown)
Provenance: Marina di Caronía, *contrada* Pantano
Date: third / fourth century AD

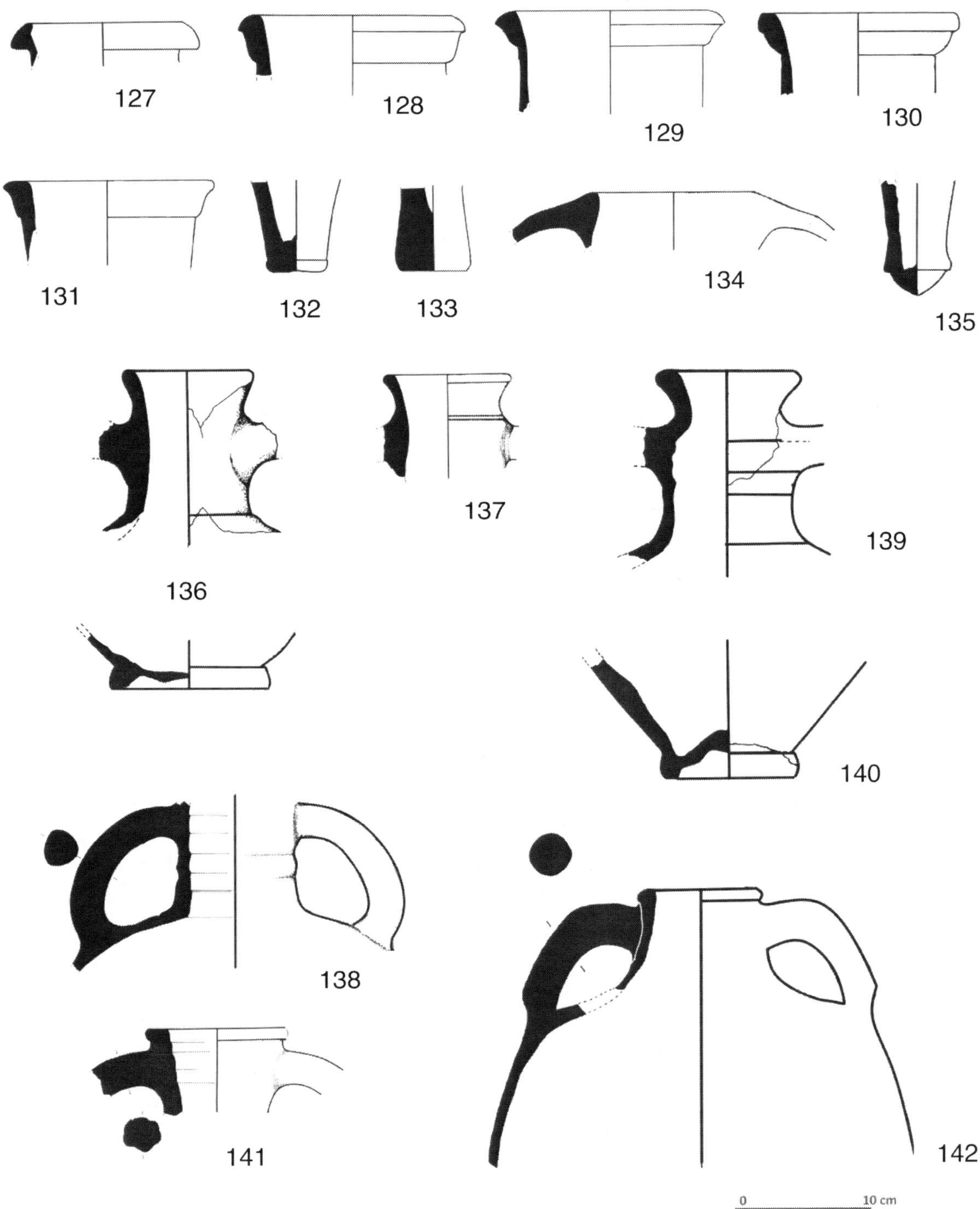

Fig. A4.5 Catalogue of finds nos 127–42 (amphorae)

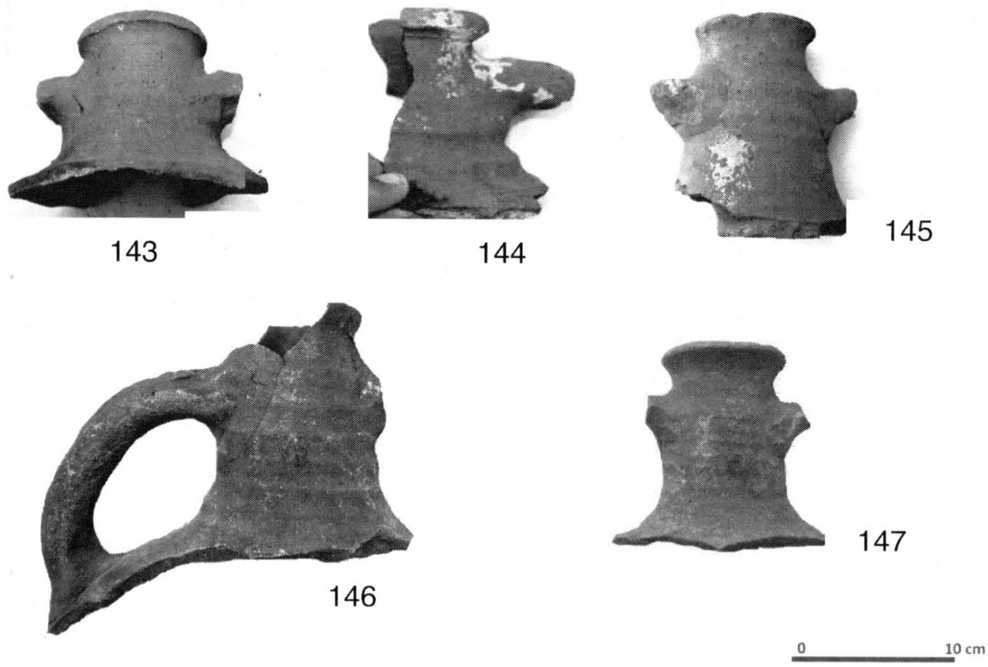

Fig.A4.6 Catalogue of finds nos 143–7 (amphorae)

Local Termini Imerese 151/354

136. Rim
H: 11.5 cm; D. rim: 7.9 cm
Surface: 5YR 7/6 reddish-yellow; surface very soft and powdery
Fabric: 42 (2.5 YR 5/6 red)
Provenance: Marina di Caronía, *contrada* Pantano
Date: late third/fourth century AD

137. Rim
H: 7.4 cm; D. rim: 9.4 cm
Surface: reddish-yellow 5YR 7/8
Fabric: 42 (reddish-yellow 5YR 6/8)
Provenance: Marina di Caronía, *contrada* Pantano
Date: late third/fourth century AD

138. Neck with handle
H: 11.5 cm; D. neck: 6.4 cm
Surface: 2.5 YR 6/4 light reddish-brown
Fabric: 42 (2.5 YR 6/8 light red)
Provenance: Marina di Caronía, *contrada* Pantano
Date: late third/fourth century AD

139. Neck with handle and part of body
H: 14.2 cm; D. neck: *c.* 6.0 cm
Surface: 5 YR 7/6 reddish-yellow
Fabric: 42 (2.5 YR 6/8 light red)
Provenance: Marina di Caronía, *contrada* Pantano
Date: late third/fourth centuryAD

140. Base
H: 7.0 cm; D. base: 9.4 cm
Surface: 5 YR 7/8 reddish-yellow
Fabric: 42 (5YR 6/6 reddish-yellow)
Provenance: Marina di Caronía, *contrada* Pantano
Date: late third/fourth century AD

141. Rim with handle
H: 6.6 cm; D. rim: 10.6 cm
Surface: 10YR 8/3 very pale brown
Fabric: 42 (5YR 6/6 reddish-yellow)
Provenance: Marina di Caronía, *contrada* Pantano
Date: late third/fourth century AD

142. Rim, handle and part of body
H: 22.5 cm; D. rim: 7.0 cm
Surface: wash (10 YR 8/3 very pale brown) rough, many large inclusions, powdery feel
Fabric: 42 (5YR 8/3 pink)
Provenance: Marina di Caronía, *contrada* Pantano
Date: late third/fourth century AD

143. Neck with rim and handles
H: 7.7 cm; D. rim: 7.0 cm
Surface: 5YR 5/4 reddish-brown
Fabric: 42 (5YR 4/1 dark grey)
Provenance: Marina di Caronía, *contrada* Chiappe, kiln dump (surface survey)
Date: fifth/early sixth century AD

144. Rim, neck with handle
H: 5.4 cm; D. rim: *c.* 8.0 cm
Surface: 5YR 5/4 reddish-brown
Fabric: 42 (5YR 6/6 reddish-yellow)
Provenance: Marina di Caronía, *contrada* Chiappe (surface survey)
Date: early/mid-fifth/early sixth century AD

145. Neck with rim and parts of handles
H: *c.* 10.0 cm; D. rim: 8.0 cm
Surface: 5YR 5/4 reddish-brown
Fabric: 42 (5YR 5/4 reddish-brown)
Provenance: Marina di Caronía, *contrada* Chiappe, kiln (surface survey)
Date: fourth century AD

146. Neck with rim and handle
W: 18.0 cm; D. rim: 6.8 cm
Surface: 10 R 5/8 red
Fabric: 42 (5 YR 6/8 reddish-yellow)
Provenance: Marina di Caronía, *contrada* Chiappe, kiln (surface survey)
Date: late fourth/first half of fifth century AD

147. Rim, neck, and parts of handles
H: 12.1 cm; D. rim: 7.9
Surface: 5YR 6/4 light reddish-brown
Fabric: 42 (2.5YR 6/6 light red)
Provenance: Marina di Caronía, *contrada* Chiappe, kiln (surface find)
Date: late fourth/first half of the fifth century AD

FINE WARES

Sicilian red-figure ware

148a and b. Lid of *lekanis* with part of a female head with *sakkos*, painted in black and white
H: 1.3 cm; D. lid: *c.* 14.0 cm
Fabric: 7.5 YR 8/6 reddish-yellow
Provenance: Caronía (cistern)
Date: late fourth/early third century BC

149. Sherd with probable palmettes and floral motif
L: 4.8 cm
Surface: 2.5 YR 6/6 light red with gloss gley 2 2.5/1 bluish-black with bluish sheen
Fabric: 2.5 YR 6/8 light red
Provenance: Caronía, *contrada* Sotto S. Francesco (cistern)
Date: late fourth/early third century BC

150. Neck of *olpe* decorated with short dark-brown vertical stripes; under a painted frieze of vine-leaves in whitish-cream colour
H: 4.8 cm
Surface: dark brown to brownish-red
Fabric: 5 YR 7/6 reddish-yellow
Provenance: Caronía, *contrada* Sotto S. Francesco (cistern)
Date: late fourth/early third century BC

Regional black-gloss

151. Handle and rim of *skyphos*
H: 3.6 cm
Surface: handle and upper part of the rim on the exterior is painted with a blackish colour (gley 2 3/1, very dark bluish-grey)
Fabric: 5 YR 6/6 reddish-yellow
Provenance: Caronía (cistern)
Date: late fourth/third century BC

152. Base of bowl
H: 3.1 cm; D. base: 8.0 cm
Surface: 5 YR 7/4 pink. The paint is unevenly dark brown to light brown, on the interior red-brown. Decorated with concentric circles both on the exterior and the interior. Under the base, an 'A' is painted in the same brown colour.
Fabric: 5 YR 7/4 pink
Provenance: Caronía (cistern)
Date: third century BC

153. Base of cup stamped with flowers and palmettes
H. 1.5 cm; D. base: *c.* 7.0 cm
Surface: traces of black glaze (gley 2/ 2.5), extremely badly preserved, almost completely worn away
Fabric: 5 YR 5/6 yellowish-red
Provenance: Marina di Caronía, *contrada* Pantano
Date: third/early second century BC

154. Hollow conical base of cup/*skyphos* with two grooves on the exterior; black-gloss on the interior, very matt, but well preserved
H. 2.4 cm; D. base: 5.5 cm
Surface: 2.5 YR 5/4 reddish-brown
Fabric: 2.5 YR 6/8 light red
Provenance: Marina di Caronía, *contrada* Pantano
Date: first half third century BC
Cf. Caflisch 1991, 99–103 ('offene Gefässe mit profiliertem Fuss'), nos 415–42, Abb. 12–13

155. Wide rim of cup
H: 2.8 cm
Surface: hard gloss, shiny (7.5 YR 2.5/1 black)
Fabric: 2.5 YR 6/6 light red
Provenance: Caronía, *contrada* Sotto S. Francesco
Date: third century BC

156. Base of *skyphos* Morel 4373 a2
H: 1.5 cm; D. base: *c.* 5.5 cm
Surface: transparently shiny gloss (2.5 Y 2.5/1 black)
Fabric: 5 YR 5/6 yellowish-red
Provenance: Caronía, *contrada* Sotto S. Francesco (cistern)
Date: end of fourth/early third century BC

157. Rim of cup with incised wave-band decoration
H: 3.0 cm; D. rim: ?
Surface: 2.5 YR 3/1 dark reddish-grey
Fabric: 2.5 YR 6/6 light red
Provenance: Caronía, *contrada* Sotto S. Francesco
Date: end of the fourth/first half of the third century BC
Cf. Caflisch 1991, 94–8, nos. 386–414, Abb. 11–12 (offene Gefässe mit verdickter Lippe – Bacino-Gruppe)

158. Rim of *Salznapf*
H: 2.6 cm; D. rim: 6.6 cm
Surface: worn, hard, matt gloss (10 YR 3/1 very dark grey)
Fabric: 7.5 YR 6/6 reddish-yellow
Provenance: Marina di Caronía, *contrada* Pantano
Date: *c.* 300 BC
Cf. Caflisch 1991, 122, nos 566–7, Abb. 17

159. Body sherd of cup with painted ivy leaves and berries in black
H: 6.0 cm
Surface: 10 R 4/8 red
Fabric: 7.5 YR 8/4 pink
Provenance: Marina di Caronía, *contrada* Pantano
Date: fourth century BC

160. Base of cup/*skyphos*
H: 2.2 cm; D. base: 5.4 cm
Surface: 2.5 Y 5/2 greyish-brown on exterior, painted reddish-orange to brownish-red in interior
Fabric: 5 YR 5/6 yellowish-red badly fired in the centre
Provenance: Caronía, *contrada* Sotto S. Francesco (cistern)
Date: probably third century BC

161. Rim of bowl
H: 3.7 cm; D. rim: *c.* 19.0 cm
Surface: 2.5 Y/1 black
Fabric: 5 YR 5/6 yellowish-red
Provenance: Caronía, *contrada* Sotto S. Francesco
Date: third century BC

162. Base of bowl with two concentric painted circles on floor
H: 2.4 cm; D. base: 5.9 cm
Surface: 5 YR 4/1 dark grey
Fabric: 5 YR 6/6 reddish-yellow
Provenance: Caronía, *contrada* Sotto S. Francesco (cistern)
Date: third century BC

163. Base of black-gloss cup
H: 1.7 cm; D. base: 8.0 cm
Surface: black gloss on the interior; on the exterior black gloss worn, bad quality
Fabric: 5 YR 6/6 reddish-brown.
Provenance: Marina di Caronía, *contrada* Pantano
Date: third century BC

164. Rim of cup
H: 2.2 cm; D. rim: 6.4 cm
Surface: grey 1 2/5 black
Fabric: 5 YR 5/6 yellowish-red
Provenance: Caronía, *contrada* Sotto S. Francesco
Date: third century BC

165. Rim of bowl
L: 3.2 cm
Surface: 1 gley 1 2.5/1
Fabric: 2.5 Y 8/2 pale yellow
Provenance: Caronía, *contrada* Sotto S. Francesco (cistern)
Date: third century BC

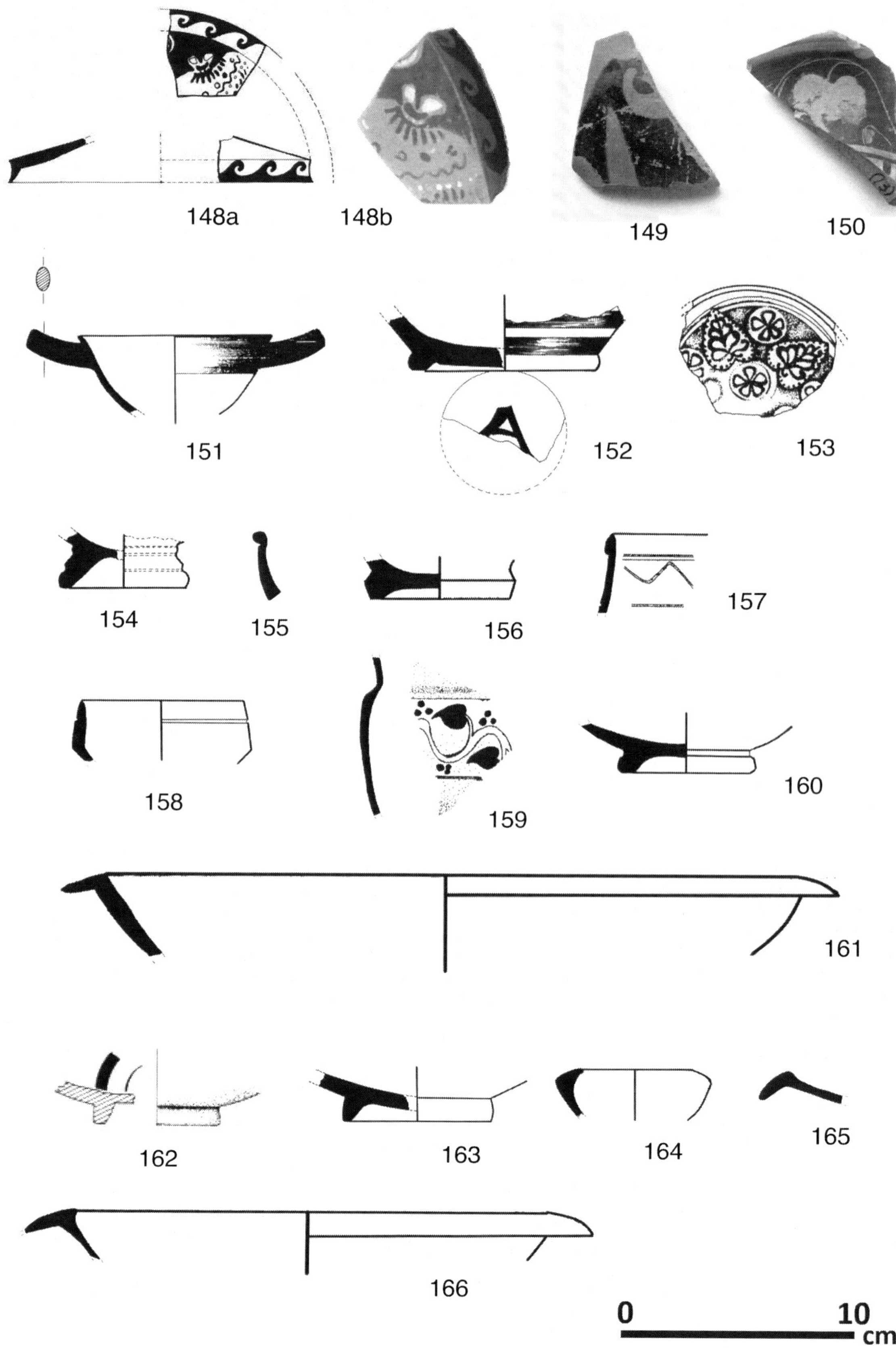

Fig. A4.7 Catalogue of finds nos 148–66 (fine wares)

166. Rim of bowl
H: 1.7 cm; D.: *c.* 19.0 cm
Surface: metallic, bluish, oily gloss (10 YR 2/1 black)
Fabric: 2.5 YR 6/6 light red
Provenance: Caronía, *contrada* Sotto S. Francesco (cistern)
Date: end of fourth/first half of the third century BC
Cf. Morel 1981, type 1534; Caflisch 1991, 115, no. 517, Abb. 16.

167. Raised ring-base and lower body of bowl with a rosette stamp in the centre of the cup surrounded by a circle; half a flower visible with five petals
H: 3.5 cm; D. base: 5.4 cm
Surface: gley 1 2.5/ black
Fabric: 5YR 6/6 reddish-yellow
Provenance: Marina di Caronía, *contrada* Pantano
Date: third century BC

168. Ring-base with profiled foot of *skyphos*
H: 1.8 cm; D. base: 8.0 cm
Surface: interior gley 1 2.5/ black; exterior reddish-yellow
Fabric: bluish-grey
Provenance: Marina di Caronía, *contrada* Pantano
Date: third century BC

Regional Campana A

169. Base of bowl of Lamboglia form 36
H: 3.4 cm; D. base: *c.* 6.0 cm
Surface: hard, worn gloss, matt but slightly shining (7.5 YR 2.5/1 black)
Fabric: 5 YR 6/6 reddish-yellow
Provenance: Marina di Caronía, *contrada* Pantano
Date: second/first half of the first century BC

170. Base of platter/bowl
H: 2.3 cm; D.: *c.* 7.0 cm
Surface: gloss 10 YR 3/1 very dark grey
Fabric: 5 YR 5/6 yellowish-red
Provenance: Caronía, *contrada* Sotto S. Francesco
Date: late second/first half of the first century BC

171. Rim of platter
L: 4.8 cm
Surface: 2 gley 2.5/1 bluish-black
Fabric: 7.5 YR 6/8 reddish-yellow
Provenance: Marina di Caronía, *contrada* Pantano
Date: late second/first half of first century BC

Campana B

172. Base of bowl/platter
L: 3.9 cm
Surface: gloss with metallic sheen (5 Y 2.5/1 black)
Fabric: 7.5 YR 6/4 light brown
Provenance: Marina di Caronía, *contrada* Pantano
Date: late second/early first century BC

Campana C

173. Ring base with groove of platter (similar to Morel 2284 d1)
H: 1.5 cm; D. base: 10.5 cm
Surface: 2.5 Y N4/ dark grey, black-gloss on the interior; the gloss is quite lucid and well preserved. In the floor concentric circles with rouletting
Fabric: 7.5 YR 6/4 light brown.
Provenance: Marina di Caronía, *contrada* Pantano
Date: second half of the second century BC

174. Hanging lip of carinated platter
H: 2.0 cm; D. rim: *c.* 31.0 cm
Surface: gley 2 3/1 very dark bluish grey
Fabric: gley 2 4/1 dark bluish grey
Provenance: Marina di Caronía, *contrada* Pantano
Date: second half of the second/last quarter of the first century BC

175. Lower part of large bowl with groove in the ring-base; two bands of rouletting (form similar to Morel 1314d 1, but larger)
H: 4.2 cm; D. base: 14.2 cm
Surface: gley 2 3/1 very dark bluish grey
Fabric: gley 2 4/1 very dark bluish grey
Provenance: Marina di Caronía, *contrada* Pantano
Date: late second century BC

Regional black-gloss

176. Base and lower part of bowl
H: 4.2 cm; D. base: 6.0 cm
Surface: 2.5 YR 2.5/1 reddish black
Fabric: 10 YR 7/4 very pale brown
Provenance: Caronía, *contrada* Sotto S. Francesco
Date: second/first century BC

Republican red-gloss

177. Rim of bowl
H: 4.0 cm; D. rim: 14.4 cm
Surface: 10 R 5/6 red
Fabric: 2.5 YR 4/8 red
Provenance: Marina di Caronía, *contrada* Pantano
Date: first two thirds of first century BC

178. Profiled base of cup
H: 2.2 cm; D. base: 6.5 cm
Surface: 2.5 YR 5/6 red
Fabric: 5 YR 6/6 reddish-yellow
Provenance: Marina di Caronía, *contrada* Pantano
Date: first two thirds of first century BC

179. Profiled base of cup
H: 2.6 cm; D. base: 5.1cm
Surface: 2.5 YR 5/6 red
Fabric: 5 YR 7/6 reddish-yellow
Provenance: Marina di Caronía, *contrada* Pantano
Date: first two thirds of first century BC

Local red-gloss jugs

180. Rim
H: 4.8 cm; D. rim: 14.5 cm
Surface: 7.5 YR 6/8 reddish-yellow
Fabric: 2.5 YR 6/8 light red
Provenance: Marina di Caronía, *contrada* Pantano
Date: first century BC/early first century AD

Megarian bowls

181. Body-sherd with flower
L: 2.5 cm
Surface: 2.5 YR 5/6 red
Fabric: 5 YR 6/6 reddish-yellow
Provenance: Marina di Caronía, *contrada* Pantano
Date: first century BC

Eastern *terra sigillata* A

182. Base of cup
H: 2.4 cm; D. base: 7.5 cm
Surface: 10 R 4/8 red
Fabric: 2.5 Y 8/6 pale yellow
Provenance: Marina di Caronía, *contrada* Pantano
Date: first two thirds of the first century BC

183. Rim of bowl/platter
H: 3.0 cm
Surface: 10 R 4/6 red
Fabric: 10 YR 7/4 very pale brown
Provenance: Marina di Caronía, *contrada* Pantano
Date: first two thirds of the first century BC

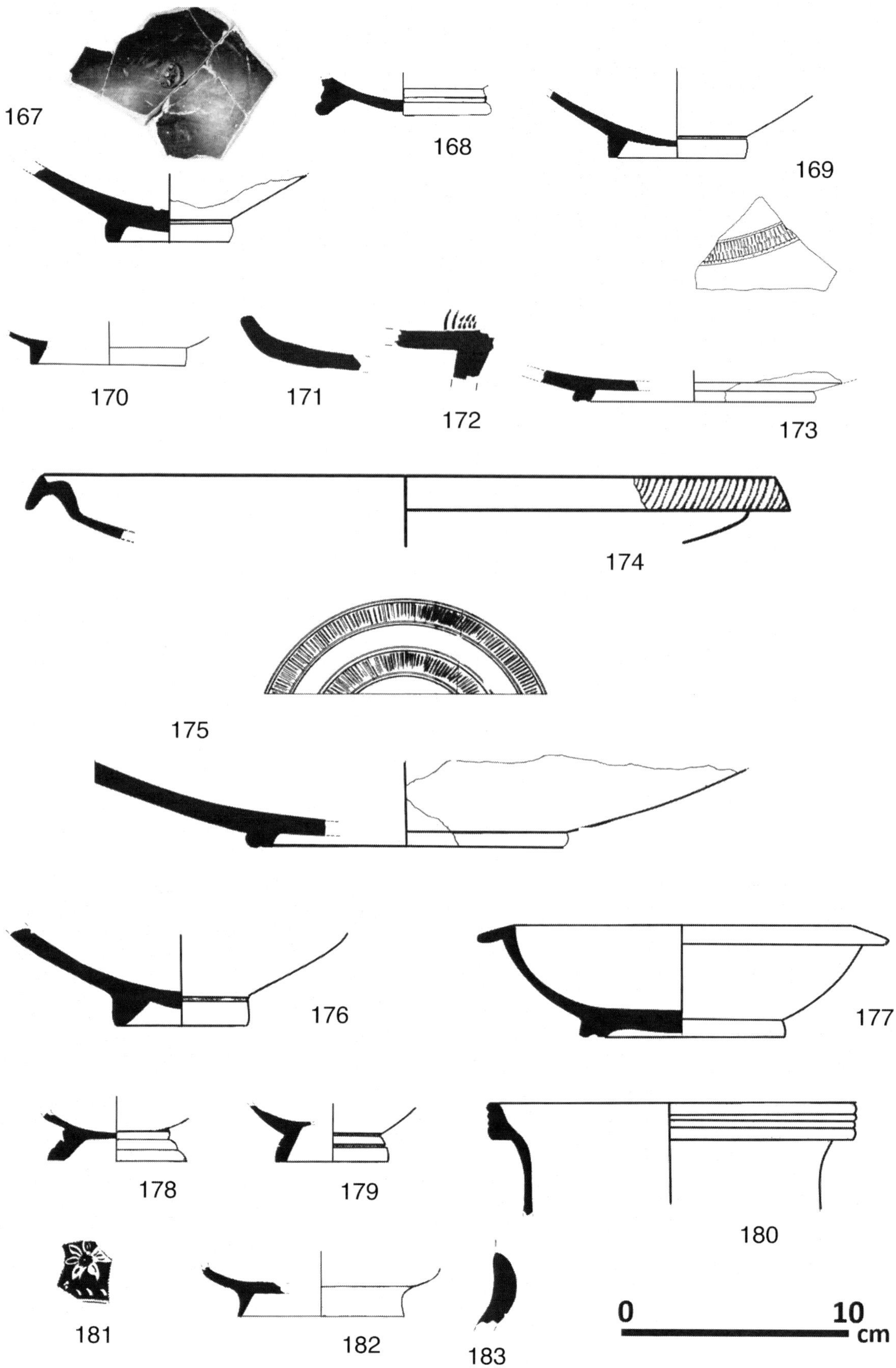

Fig. A4.8 Catalogue of finds nos 167–83 (fine wares)

Thin-walled ware

184. Handle of cup
H: 4.4 cm
Surface: 2.5 Y 8/6 pale yellow
Fabric: 2.5 Y 8/6 pale yellow
Provenance: Marina di Caronía, *contrada* Pantano
Date: first century BC/early first century AD

185. Cup
H: 5.8 cm; D. rim: 7.2 cm
Surface: 7.5YR 3/2 dark brown
Fabric: 10 YR 8/4 very pale brown
Provenance: Marina di Caronía, *contrada* Pantano
Date: first century BC/early first century AD

Pergamene (?) appliqué ware

186. Fragment of cup with moulded decoration of ivy leaves and berries
H: 2.6 cm
Surface: 10 R 4/8 red
Fabric: 10 YR 8/3 very pale brown
Provenance: Marina di Caronía, *contrada* Pantano
Date: late first century BC/first century AD

Italian *terra sigillata*

187a and b. Raised ring-base of bowl; *in planta pedis* stamp on the inside, LRPIS (Lucius Rasinius Pisanus)
H: 1.7 cm; D. base: 6.7 cm
Surface: 2.5YR 4/8 red
Fabric: 5YR 7/4 pink
Provenance: Caronía Marina, *contrada* Pantano
Date: AD 50/120

188. Sherd with moulded floral decoration
H: 4.5 cm
Surface: 10 R 4/6 red
Fabric: 10 R 6/8 light red
Provenance: Marina di Caronía, *contrada* Pantano
Date: late first century BC/early first century AD

189. Rim of platter
H: 3.6 cm; D.: *c.* 27.0 cm
Surface: 2.5 YR 4/8 red
Fabric: 2.5 YR 5/6 red
Provenance: Caronía, *contrada* Sotto S. Francesco
Date: first century AD

190. Rim of large platter, Ettlinger et al. 1990, form 20.4.1
H: 3.3 cm; D. rim: 38.0 cm
Surface: 2.5YR 4/8 red
Fabric: 5YR 7/4 pink
Provenance: Marina di Caronía, *contrada* Pantano
Date: mid-first century AD

191. Rim of platter with appliqué mask, Ettlinger et al. 1990, form 20.4.1
H: 4.8 cm
Surface: 2.5 YR 4/8 red
Fabric: 5 YR 5/6 yellowish-red
Provenance: Caronía, *contrada* Sotto S. Francesco
Date: mid-first century AD

192. Base of platter with band of rouletting
L: 4.8 cm; D. base: 17.5 cm
Surface: 2.5 YR 4/6 red
Fabric: 2.5 YR 5/6 red
Provenance: Marina di Caronía, *contrada* Pantano
Date: first century AD

193. Fragment of cup with moulded decoration
H: 4.6 cm
Surface: 10 R 4/6 red
Fabric: 2.5 YR 6/6 light red
Provenance: Marina di Caronía, *contrada* Pantano
Date: late first century BC/first century AD

194. Ring-base of cup; *in planta pedis* stamp. Probably Ettlinger et al. 1990, form 34.1.1
H: 2.5 cm; D. base: 6.0 cm.
Surface: 10 R 5/6 red
Fabric: 10 R 6/6 light red
Provenance: Marina di Caronía, *contrada* Pantano
Date: *c.* AD 30/70

South Gaulish *terra sigillata*

195a and b. Base of cup; *in planta pedis* stamp inside a circle with the letters ARDACI. Form similar to Ettlinger et al. 1990, type 32.1.1.
H: 1.5 cm; D. base: 6.0 cm
Surface: 10 R 6/8 red
Fabric: 10 R 4/8 red
Provenance: Marina di Caronía, *contrada* Pantano
Date: *c.* AD 15/50.

'Tripolitanian' *terra sigillata*

196. Rim and part of body of cup
H: 3.6 cm; D. rim: 7.0 cm
Surface: 10 R 5/8 red
Fabric: 2.5 YR 5/8 red
Provenance: Marina di Caronía, *contrada* Pantano
Date: late first century BC/first century AD

Moulded ware (Sicilian?)

197. Fragment of vessel with moulded kneeling figure, possibly Aphrodite
H: 6.2 cm
Surface: 10 YR 8/6 yellow with traces of black slip
Fabric: 10 YR 8/3 very pale brown
Provenance: Marina di Caronía, *contrada* Pantano
Date: first century BC/early first century AD

African Red Slip

198. Rim of bowl, Hayes form 8A
H: 4.3 cm; D. rim: 20.2 cm
Surface: 2.5 YR 6/8 light red
Fabric: 10 R 6/6 light red
Provenance: Marina di Caronía, *contrada* Pantano
Date: late first century/mid-second century AD

199. Bowl, Hayes form 3C
H: 4.4 cm; D. rim: 21.5 cm
Surface: 2.5 YR 5/8 red
Fabric: 2.5 YR 5/8 red
Provenance: Marina di Caronía, *contrada* Pantano
Date: first half of the second century AD

200. Rim of bowl similar to Hayes form 78
H: 1.0 cm; D. rim: *c.* 16.0 cm
Surface: 2.5 5/8 red
Fabric: 2.5 YR 5/6 red
Provenance: Marina di Caronía, *contrada* Pantano
Date: fifth century AD?

201. Rim of bowl
H: 4.2 cm; D. rim: 18.5 cm
Surface: 2.5 YR 6/6 light red
Fabric: 2.5 YR 6/6 light red
Provenance: Marina di Caronía, *contrada* Pantano
Date: second/fourth century AD

202. Rim of flat-based dish, type Hayes 58 A
H: 2.5 cm; D. rim: *c.* 20.0 cm
Surface: 2.5 YR 6/8 light red
Fabric: 2.5 YR 6/8 light red
Provenance: Marina di Caronía, *contrada* Pantano
Date: *c.* AD 290–300/375

203. Rim of dish, Hayes form 27
H: 3.0 cm; D. rim: 22.0 cm
Surface: 2.5 YR 5/8 red
Fabric: 2.5 YR 5/8 red
Provenance: Marina di Caronía, *contrada* Pantano
Date: *c.* AD 160/220

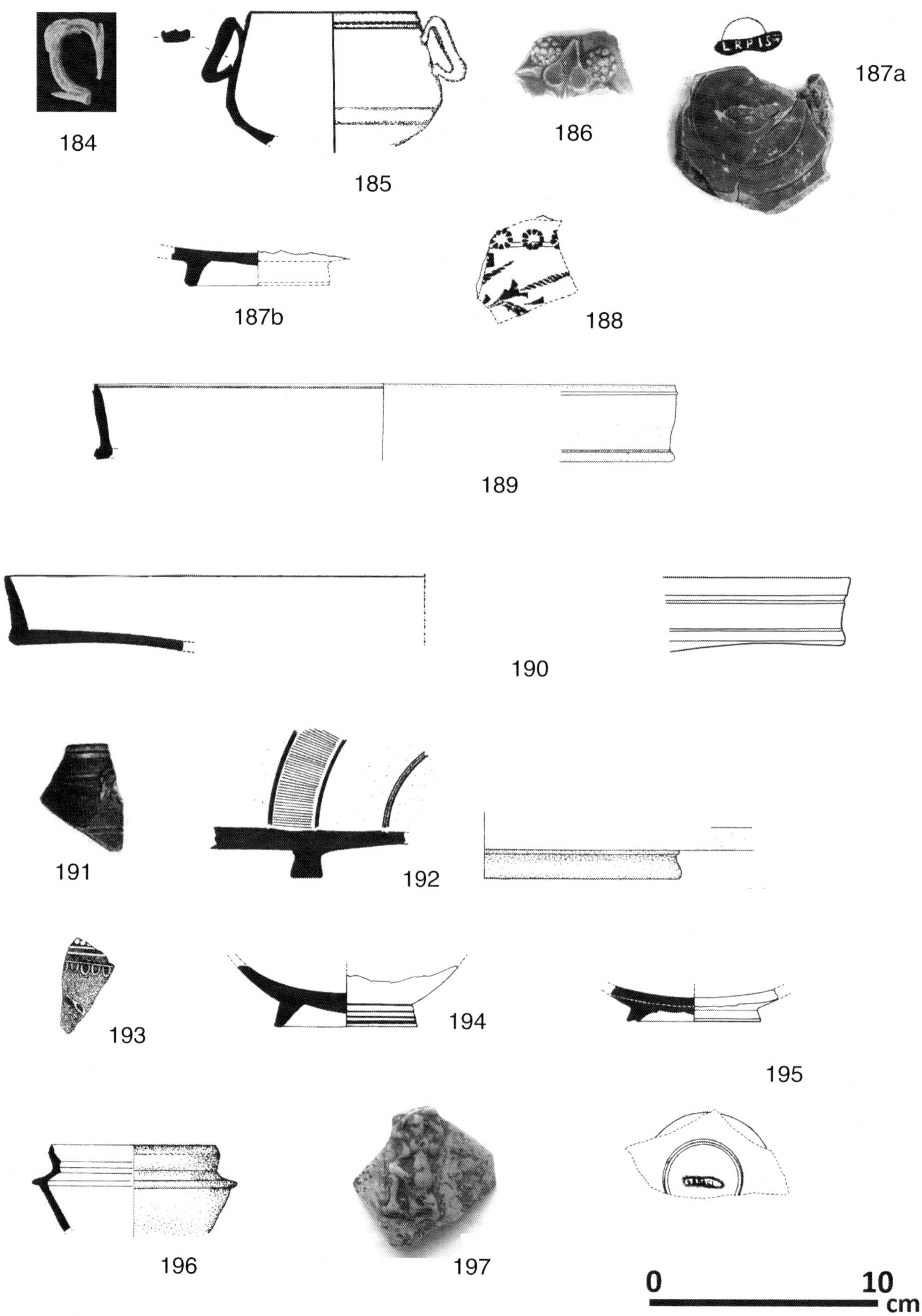

Fig. A4.9 Catalogue of finds nos 184–97 (fine wares)

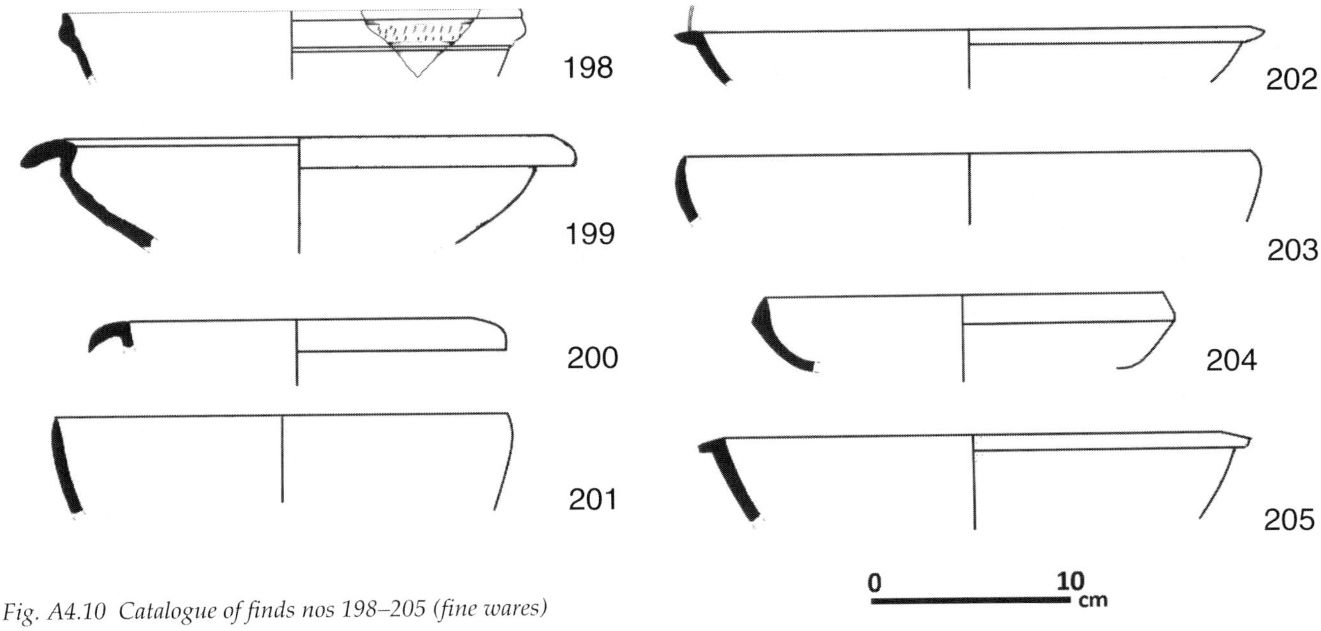

Fig. A4.10 Catalogue of finds nos 198–205 (fine wares)

204. Rim of bowl, Hayes form 58
H: 3.0 cm; D. rim: 18.0 cm
Surface: 2.5 YR 6/8 light red
Fabric: 2.5 YR 6/8 light red
Provenance: Marina di Caronía, *contrada* Pantano
Date: *c.* AD 290/375

205. Rim of flat-based dish, Hayes form 61
H: 4.0 cm; D. rim: *c.* 18.0 cm
Surface: 2.5 YR 5/8 red
Fabric: 2.5 YR 5/8 red
Provenance: Marina di Caronía, *contrada* Pantano
Date: AD 325/400

Corinthian bowls

206. Base with part of moulded scene with figures
H: 3.0 cm; D. base: 4.6 cm
Surface: 10 R 6/6 light red with traces of red slip
Fabric: 10 R 6/6 light red
Provenance: Marina di Caronía, *contrada* Pantano
Date: third century AD

207. Fragment with part of a moulded scene with figures
H: 2.0 cm
Surface: 10 YR 8/3 very pale brown
Fabric: 10 YR 8/3 very pale brown
Provenance: Marina di Caronía, *contrada* Pantano
Date: third century AD

LAMPS
Sicilian Hellenistic lamps

208. Squat globular lamp on raised ring-base
H: 4.0 cm; D base: 5.5 cm
Surface: black gloss on interior and exterior
Fabric: 5YR 7/6 reddish-yellow
Provenance: Caronía, *contrada* Sotto S. Francesco (cistern)
Date: third century BC

209. Side-wall and rim
L: 6.3 cm; D. base: 5.1 cm
Surface: high-quality black gloss (2.5 YR 2.5/0) with metallic sheen
Fabric: 5 YR 7/6 reddish-yellow
Provenance: Caronía, *contrada* Sotto S. Francesco (cistern)
Date: probably first century BC

210. Side-wall
L: 4.5 cm
Surface: traces of black gloss
Fabric: 7.5 YR 6/8 reddish-yellow
Provenance: Marina di Caronía, *contrada* Pantano
Date: second half of first century BC

211. Nozzle
L: 6.0 cm
Surface: black gloss on the inside, well preserved; on the exterior mostly worn away, but where preserved the black gloss has large brown patches
Fabric: 5 YR 5/8 yellowish-red
Provenance: Marina di Caronía, *contrada* Pantano
Date: end second/early first century BC

212. Nozzle (not illustrated)
L: 5.5 cm
Surface: black gloss both on exterior and interior, well preserved
Surface: gley 2 2.5/1 bluish-black
Fabric: 2.5 YR 6/8 light red
Provenance: Marina di Caronía, *contrada* Pantano
Date: second half of the first century BC

Sicilian Corinth XVI lamps

213. Nozzle (not illustrated)
L: 4.8 cm
Surface: 10 R 5/8 red
Fabric: 5 YR 5/6 yellowish-red
Provenance: Marina di Caronía, *contrada* Pantano
Date: first century BC/first half first century AD

Central Italian *Warzenlampen*

214. Shoulder and part of discus (not illustrated)
L: 6.0 cm
Surface: gloss (10R 5/8 red)
Fabric: 7.5 YR 7/4 pink
Provenance: Marina di Caronía, *contrada* Pantano
Date: first century BC

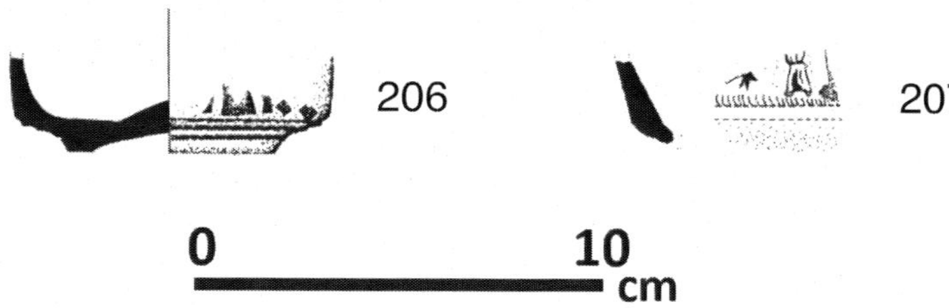

Fig. A4.11 Catalogue of finds nos 206–7 (fine wares)

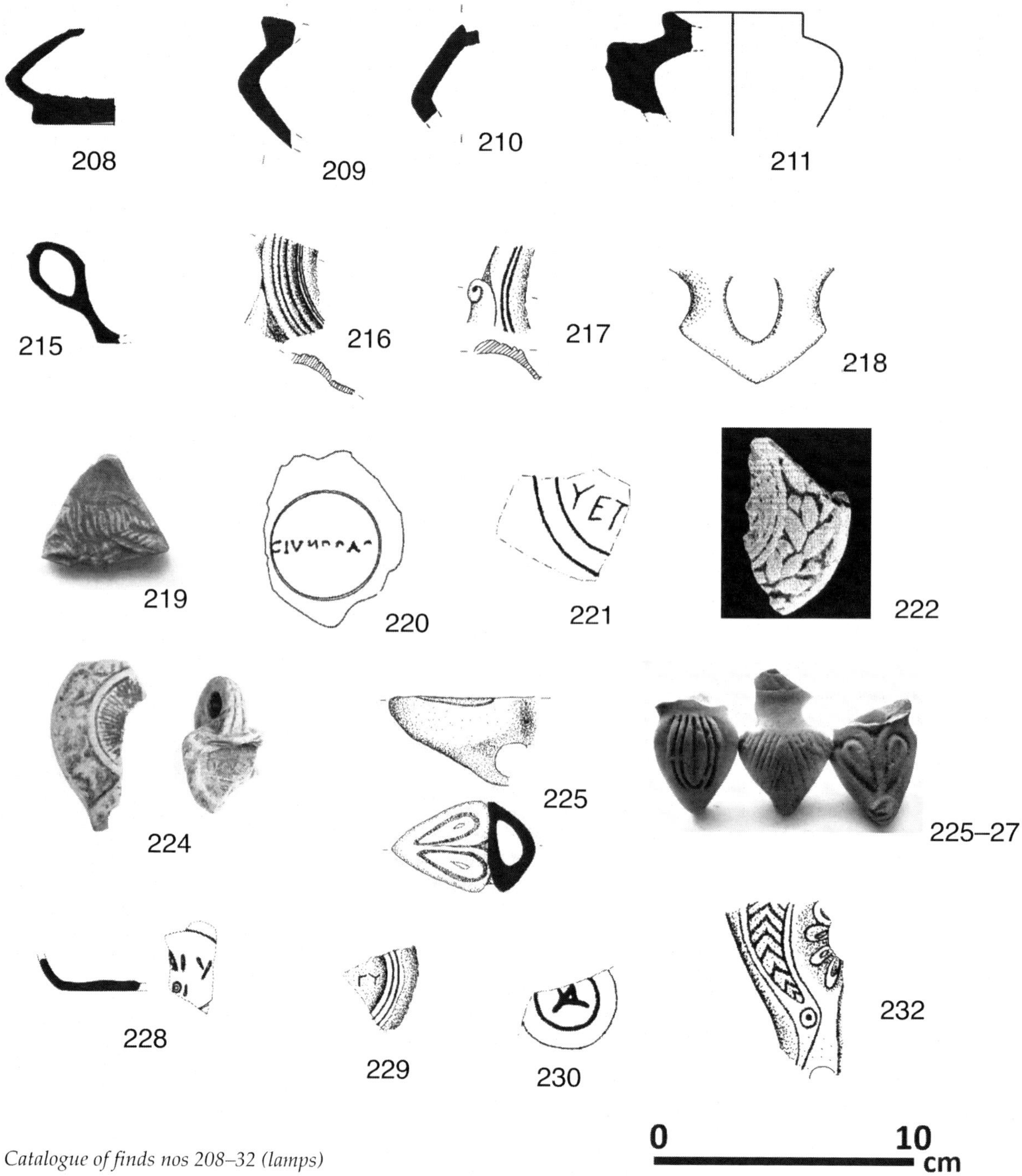

Fig. A4.12 Catalogue of finds nos 208–32 (lamps)

215. Handle and part of base
L: 2.8 cm
Surface: 10 R 4/8 red
Fabric: 2.5 YR 7/6 light red
Provenance: Marina di Caronía, *contrada* Pantano
Date: first century BC

Central Italian volute lamps

216. Part of shoulder and disc
L: 4.0 cm
Surface: 10 YR 7/4 very pale brown
Fabric: 10 YR 7/4 very pale brown
Provenance: Caronía, *contrada* Sotto S. Francesco
Date: first century AD

217. Fragment with volute, part of shoulder and disc
L: 3.4 cm
Surface: red gloss 2.5 YR 4/8 red – 2.5 YR 6/8 light red
Fabric: 7.5 YR 7/6 reddish-yellow
Provenance: Marina di Caronía, *contrada* Pantano
Date: *c.* 50 BC/AD 50

218. Triangular nozzle, type Bailey A
L: 3.7 cm
Surface: 5 YR 5/1 grey
Fabric: overfired, 5 YR 5/1 grey
Provenance: Caronía, *contrada* Sotto S. Francesco
Date: first century AD

North African/Italian fat lamps

219. Fragment of discus with running mammal
H: 3.6 cm
Surface: 7.5 YR 5/8 dark brown
Fabric: 7.5 YR 7/6 reddish-yellow
Provenance: Marina di Caronía, *contrada* Pantano
Date: second century AD

220. Base of lamp. On exterior of base circle with stamp inside: CIVNDRAC
L: 6.4 cm; D. base: 4.8
Surface: 7.5 YR 8/4 pink, traces of red wash
Fabric: 7.5 YR 8/4 pink
Provenance: Marina di Caronía, *contrada* Pantano
Date: AD 100/150

221. Base with letters YET incised before firing
L: 3.4 cm
Surface: 5 YR 4/6 yellowish-red
Fabric: 5 YR 5/6 yellowish-red
Provenance: Marina di Caronía, *contrada* Pantano
Date: late second/third century AD

222. Shoulder decorated with a wreath of olive leaves, and part of discus
L: 5.8 cm
Surface: 10 YR 8/3 very pale brown
Fabric: 10 YR 7/4 very pale brown
Provenance: Marina di Caronía, *contrada* Pantano
Date: late second/third century AD

223. Shoulder and part of discus (not illustrated)
L: 4.4 cm
Surface: 10 YR 8/3 very pale brown
Fabric: 2.5 YR 7/4 light reddish-brown
Provenance: Marina di Caronía, *contrada* Pantano
Date: second/third century AD

224. Shoulder decorated with vines, and part of sloping disc with rays
L: 6.8 cm
Surface: 10 YR 6/4 light yellowish-brown
Fabric: 10 YR 7/4 very pale brown
Provenance: Marina di Caronía, *contrada* Pantano
Date: second half of the second/beginning of the third century AD

Sicilian Proclus Agyrios lamps

225. Heart-shaped heat-shield and part of handle
L: 5.5 cm
Surface: 7.5 YR 6/6 reddish-yellow
Fabric: 7.5 YR 6/6 reddish-yellow
Provenance: Marina di Caronía, *contrada* Pantano
Date: late first/first half of the second century AD

226. Heat-shield and handle
L: 5.8 cm
Surface: 5 YR 6/6 redddish-yellow
Fabric: gley 2 5/1 bluish-grey
Provenance: Marina di Caronía, *contrada* Pantano
Date: late first/first half of the second century AD

227. Heat-shield and handle
L: 6.0 cm
Surface: 7.5 YR 6/6 reddish-yellow
Fabric: 7.5 YR 5/8 dark brown
Provenance: Marina di Caronía *contrada* Pantano
Date: late first/first half of the second century AD

228. Base with the letters AΓϒ/PI incised before firing
L: 4.0 cm
Surface: 2.5 YR 4/3 reddish-brown
Fabric: 2.5 YR 4/6 red
Provenance: Marina di Caronía, *contrada* Pantano
Date: late first/first half of the second century AD

229. Base with letters ..]Γϒ incised before firing
L: 2.8 cm
Surface: 5 YR 6/6 reddish-yellow
Fabric: 5 YR 6/8 reddish-yellow
Provenance: Marina di Caronía, *contrada* Pantano
Date: late first /first half of the second century AD

230. Base with the letter A incised
L: 3.1 cm
Surface: 5 YR 6/8 reddish-yellow
Fabric: 5 YR 6/8 reddish-yellow
Provenance: Marina di Caronía, *contrada* Pantano
Date: late first /first half of the second century AD

North African globular fat lamps

231. Handle with part of shoulder decorated with rows of dots and part of discus (not illustrated)
L: 6.6 cm
Surface: 10 YR 8/4 very pale brown
Fabric: 10 YR 8/4 very pale brown
Provenance: Marina di Caronía, *contrada* Pantano
Date: third/first half of the fourth century AD

North African lamps

232. Part of shoulder, disc and side-walls. Discus decorated with flower
L: 5.5 cm
Surface: 2.5 YR 6/8 light red
Fabric: 2.5 YR 6/8 light red
Provenance: Marina di Caronía, *contrada* Pantano
Date: second half of the fourth century AD

Notes

Notes to Chapter One

1. Fazello 1558, 1.9.4.
2. Cluverius 1619, 291–3.
3. Adamesteanu 1962, 191–2, tav. XCIII.
4. Scibona 1987, 10–11.
5. Bonanno 1997–98, 429–30, fig. 5.
6. Bonanno 1993–94; 1997–98.
7. Lentini et al. 2002.
8. Bonsignore and Trifirò 2009, 63 (12 coins); Lentini et al. 2002, 101–02, figs 35–6 (4 coins); Carroccio and Collura 2016 (6 coins). The dominant presence of coins minted by Morgantina was the main argument for identifying Serra Orlando as Morgantina in the 1950s (Erim 1958).
9. Scibona 1971b.
10. See Chapter 2, p. 33.
11. I have deliberately chosen the terms 'settlement' and 'settle' instead of 'colony' and 'colonisation' when dealing with places in Sicily founded by Greeks/Sikels in Archaic and Classical times. I am here adhering to the view that the term 'colony' is misleading, and not well suited to describe this kind of foundation, in contrast to Roman colonies, where 'colony' and 'colonisation' are appropriate, partly because the Romans themselves used the term (*colonia*), but above all because they were urban centres planned, settled and governed by Rome, whereas Greek settlements very soon became independent of their original founders (Lindhagen 2015).
12. Herodotus 6.22–23. On the origins of Kale Akte and the foundation by Ducetius, see Lindhagen forthcoming a.
13. For a head in Daedalic style from the end of the seventh century BC, Bonanno 2009, 57, no. 173, tav. XVII, fig. 21; and for an Ionian cup B1 (?) of *c.* 620/550 BC from *contrada* Pantano, Collura 2019a, 106, no. 1.
14. Scibona 1987, 11; Collura 2016, 233–4, fig. 1; 242–3, fig. 7. For an early attempt to understand the ancient topography of Kale Akte, Fiore 1971c.
15. Scibona 1987, 11. For the location of *contrada* di Noto, see p. 4, Fig. 1.4, no. 5. For surface finds of pottery of sixth- and fifth-century date, and contrasting views on the nature of Archic/Classical settlement at Kale Akte at this period, see now Collura 2019a, 5, 89–117, 128, 203, n. 23 and 223, n. 55.
16. The coastline has not changed dramatically since antiquity. The excavations at Marina di Caronia in 2003–05 showed that the coastline was only a few metres closer than it is now (Sudano 2009, 18).
17. Scibona 1987; Lindhagen 2006, 84, 136–7 and 162; Collura 2016, 311–37.
18. The suggestion by Prestianni Giallombardo that only the 'fair coast' overall should be preferred is based on the supposedly 'generic' nature of oracular responses, and the fact that they often indicated 'territories' rather than exact places to settle (Prestianni Giallombardo 2006, 140). It does not seem probable, however, that the settlers would have travelled all the way from Asia Minor to Sicily if a precise location had not already been suggested by the Zancleans.
19. For example Scibona 1987; Lentini et al. 2002; Bonanno 2009; Prestianni Giallombardo 2006.
20. Most recently in Strassler 2009, 435.
21. The earliest building known at Marina di Caronia (near the railway station) is still unexcavated; it probably dates to *c.* 400 BC, judging by the finds made in the section which cuts through a slope, in which the walls of the ancient building can also be seen (cf. Collura 2016, 201–02).
22. For finds from the Bronze Age from the hill-slopes of Caronia and in *contrada* Fiumara (for its location, see Fig. 1.4 on p. 4), Collura 2016, 50–1.
23. Collura (2016, 291) does not consider the possibility of a Sikel settlement at the hill of Caronia, and regards Pizzo Cilona as originally an autonomous settlement which was only later converted to a *phrourion* by the *polis* of Kale Akte.
24. Bonanno 1997–98, 433. For the location of *contrada* San Todaro, see map on p. 4, Fig. 1.4.
25. The site of Paliké has remains of a regular street–grid (Pope 2006).
26. Diodorus Siculus 11.78.5; Fischer-Hansen et al. 2004, 178. The urban site at Mineo clearly continued into Hellenistic times, something which suggests that this is indeed the Menai founded by Ducetius. It is mentioned as having been moved to a plain, but this must be a later misunderstanding of the original text. A Sikel settlement not founded on a hill during this period of continual conflict and insecurity is unimaginable.
27. Bell 2000; Walsh 2006, 237, n. 11.
28. Diodorus Siculus 11.88.6; Pope 2014.
29. On the whole site, Maniscalco 2008 (17–21 on the hilltop); latest work in Maniscalco and McConnell 2015 and Maniscalco 2015.
30. Diodorus Siculus,11.89.8; Maniscalco and McConnell 2003, 376; Pope 2006.
31. Adamesteanu 1962, 33.
32. Diodorus Siculus 11.92.1–4.
33. Diodorus Siculus 12.8.2; 12.29.1.
34. Prestianni Giallombardo 2006.
35. Several scholars are of the opinion that the foundation of Kale Akte was supported by Syracuse: Holm 1870–98, vol. 1, 485–6; Rizzo 1970; Asheri 1992; Prestianni Giallombardo 2006. Those like Adamesteanu 1962 and Meister 1992, who thought that the foundation of the settlement took place without the consent of Syracuse, have read the text as 'having broken the agreement',

without taking into consideration the alternative possibility.

36. Diodorus Siculus 12.8.3–4. It has been claimed that Ducetius enjoyed ties with the Syracusan aristocracy, such as intermarriage, which would explain why the Sikel chief was punished relatively mildly, and allowed to return from exile to found a new settlement (Maniscalco and McConnell 2003, 176, n. 177).
37. Adamesteanu 1962.
38. Ibid, 195–6. Recently Arena (2016, 363) has also followed this view, regarding the northern Sikels as being independent of Syracusan influence.
39. See note 35 above.
40. Rizzo 1970; Asheri 1992.
41. Rizzo 1970, 160.
42. It is probably not correct to depict Ducetius as a Greek tyrant; in the sources he is simply called ἡγεμών, 'leader'. He was rather acting in the same political landscape of the fifth century as both Greek tyrants as well as democratic *poleis*, who all acted as οἰκισταί (Jackman 2006, 41).
43. Diodorus Siculus 12.29.1–3; Rizzo 1970, 170–1.
44. It is not known whether the Archonides of Herbita who founded Halaesa is identical with the *dynastes* of Herbita, who collaborated with Ducetius in the foundation of Kale Akte. It has been argued by Agostiniani (1988-89, 191–2) that the name Ducetius might be related to the Latin word *dux*, 'leader', but this seems far-fetched.
45. Diodorus Siculus 12.29.1.
46. Diodorus Siculus 12.29
47. Head of Athena/octopus, ΑΛΟΝΤΙΝΩΝ; Corinthian helmet/octopus, ΑΛΟΝΤΙΝΩΝ; head of female/antropomorphic bull, ΑΛΟΝΤΙΝΩΝ (Facella 2010, 46). Carroccio (2004, 53) dates the first issues of bronze coins to 280/70 BC: female head with wreath/charging bull (also Hoover 2012, nos 213, 215–16). Later coins from the late third century BC onwards: a man with Phrygian helmet/antropomorphic bull with water coming out of the mouth; bearded Heracles/club, bow and quiver (Frey-Kupper 2013, 367, dated 211/150 BC); young Dionysus/ ΑΛΟΝΤΙΝΩΝ within laurel wreath; bearded Heracles/eagle with prey; Apollo/ man-faced bull; Hermes/*petasos* (Hoover 2012, nos 214, 217–21).
48. Wilson 1990, 171.
49. This is probably on the high side; Lipara and Tyndaris, which, as a *municipium* and a *colonia* respectively, were more important, would have had only around 1,500–1,800 inhabitants (so Wilson 1990, 171).
50. The majority of these sources are collected in Scibona 1987.
51. We have, for example, the historian of Hannibal, Silenos, who was born at Kale Akte (Athenaeus 12.542; Cornelius Nepos, *Hann.* 13.3), and who obviously seems to have been drawn to the Punic cultural sphere rather than the Greek. For an overview of the archaeology of the Nebrodi area, see Collura 2019a.
52. Herbita was possibly situated at Monte Alburchia in the Valle del Salso between Gangi and Nicosia (Wilson 1990, 149; for references to the discussion on Herbita's whereabouts, ibid. 378, n. 19). For a different view, arguing for a location closer to the coast: Collura 2016, 57.
53. De Angelis 2001, 172.
54. Caccamo Caltabiano 1999, 304, tav. 94, 1. On Halaesa, see in general Facella 2006; Scibona and Tigano 2008; and most recently Collura 2019a, 125–36.
55. Bernabò Brea 1975, 20–1; Calciati 1983, 63.
56. Bonanno and Arcifa 2009, 601; no tombs found in the cemeteries date earlier than the fourth century BC (ibid., 616). On Haluntium in general, see most recently Collura 2019a, 150–4.
57. A *capanna* from the Bronze Age was found at Piazza San Teodoro, and also fragments of *hydriai* of the sixth century BC (Bonanno and Arcifa 2009, 600). As suggested by Bernabò Brea (1958, 183; Facella 2006, 46), a clue to the prehistoric past might be found in a local myth, recorded by Dionysius of Halicarnassus (1.51.2). He mentions that Haluntium was founded by the Acarnanian Patron at the time that the Trojans were fleeing from their destroyed city. An ancient past is also suggested for nearby Agathyrnum, which according to myth was founded by Agathyrnos, son of the god of the winds, Aiolos (Diodorus Siculus 5.8.1–3).
58. Scibona 1982, 149.
59. Bonanno and Arcifa 2009.
60. *Tetras* with Zeus wearing a laurel wreath and the legend ΖΕΥΣ ΕΛΕΥΘΕΡΙΟΣ/winged lightning bolt and ear of grain, legend ΑΛΟΝΤΙΝΩΝ (Castrizio 2000, 70, 103; Calciati 1986 [volume II], 444, n. 9).
61. Most scholars have agreed that Apollonia is to be located at Monte Vecchio near San Fratello (Salinas 1880, 197–8; Freeman 1891, 144; Bernabò Brea 1975, 15; Wilson 1985a, 299. *Contra*: Manni 1981, 145, who opted for Pollina, merely because of the correspondence between the ancient and modern names.
62. Bernabò Brea 1958, 183; Facella 2006, 46; Collura 2019a, 144–50.
63. Bonanno 2008.
64. Diodorus Siculus 16.72.2–5.
65. Wilson 1990, 149; Collura 2019a, 170–2.
66. Diodorus Siculus, 14.78.6. On Tyndaris see most recently Leone and Spigo 2008; Collura 2019a, 154–61.
67. Most of the rural settlements identified in the Halaesa survey are located on the slopes of the Halaisos valley (Burgio 2008, tav. 1). For Herbita, Naselli 1949 and 1951; Boehringer 1981; Pontorno 1966; Collura 2019a, 168–70; and see note 52 above.
68. Numbers taken from Collura 2016, 305–6.
69. Collura 2016, 296–9.
70. Tigano 2012, 370
71. Burgio 2008.
72. Hansen 1995, 45–81; De Angelis 2001, 156.
73. Collura 2016, 413–34; also ibid., 59, 61 and 291–2.
74. Manganaro 2009; Arena 2016.
75. Diodorus Siculus 19.6.1–2.
76. Diodorus Siculus 20.56.4.
77. Collura 2016, 99–102.
78. Caccamo Caltabiano 1999, 305. An *epimeletes* is known

to have been installed at Kephaloidion in 312 BC (Diodorus Siculus 20.56.3, in Karlsson 1992, 17, n. 36).

79. Polybius 1.8.1; Plutarch, *Pyrr.* 23.1; Prestianni Giallombardo 1998, 71; Facella 2006, 177.
80. Karlsson 1992, 18, n. 37.
81. Diodorus Siculus 23.4.
82. Polybius 1.25.1–4.
83. Burgio 2008, 251.
84. This very important piece of evidence for Sicilian agriculture was found at Tusa (Halaesa) in the sixteenth century. It has unfortunately been lost, but the text was copied in various manuscripts. These have not yet received extensive study. For rural organisation based on this evidence, see Prestianni-Giallombardo 1998 and more recently Burgio 2008, 46–52.
85. This is the most likely dating, preferred by most scholars today (for an overview of the different attempts, Burgio 2008, 46, n. 90).
86. Burgio 2008, 47.
87. The only archaeological find from here is a hand-mill: Fiore 1991, 125, fig. 3.
88. Prestianni Giallombardo 1998, 69.
89. Burgio 2008, 241.
90. Collura 2016, 305–6.
91. Ibid.
92. Wilson 1990, 23–7.
93. Caccamo Caltabiano 1999, 308–9, tav. XCV.II.
94. Mannino 1986–87, 125–7.
95. Ibid., 127; Carroccio 2004, 56; Crawford 1985, 113–15 with pl. 38, top left; Frey-Kupper 2013, 189. Interest has been focused on the largest and earliest issue in bronze, depicting Athena's head on the obverse, and an owl standing on a fallen amphora on the reverse. The iconography closely imitates what had been thought to be Athenian silver *tetradrachms* of the third century BC, and Mannino (1986–87, 127) follows the suggested date of these *stephanephoroi* to the beginning of the second century BC. She argued that because of special, privileged, commercial contacts with Athens, Kale Akte would have adopted this issue as a symbol of its *filia* to Athens. It is now known, however, that the New Style silver coinage at Athens on which the earliest issue at Kale Akte is modelled did not start production until 164 BC (and so Kale Akte's coinage must be later than that date), but since Athenian tetradrachms of this type did not generally circulate in Sicily, it is unclear how and why Kale Akte chose to model its earliest coinage on this Athenian issue (Hoover 2012, 148). In this context a funerary inscription of the second or first century BC at Athens of a Kalaktinian named Aischylos, son of Apollodoros: Αἰσχύλος Ἀπολλόδωρου Σἰκελός από Καλές Ακτής (Mannino 1986–87, 126) is of interest. We have no evidence whatsoever that Kale Akte would have had any particular commercial or other link to Athens, and it may therefore be a mere coincidence that a certain Aischylos from Kale Akte died there. On the dating of the smaller coin-type, with head of Dionysus on the obverse, and bunch of grapes on the reverse, chosen by several cities including Kale Akte, see Frey-Kupper 2013, 242–4 (late second century BC).
96. Gàbrici 1927, 121–2; Calciati 1983; Scibona 1987, 9.
97. Lentini et al. 2002, 100–01.
98. Wilson 1990, 149–50.
99. Bonanno 2008.
100. Calciati 1983, 137; Cicero, *Verr.* 2.5.33.86.
101. Bonanno 2008, 63; 82.
102. Stone 1983, 11–13.
103. Stone 1983, 14, fig. 1; 20, n. 80.
104. Stone 1983, 20.
105. Diodorus Siculus 16.7.1; Stone 1983, 15.
106. Carettoni 1959, 349; 296, 301, 302–4, 296–316; Facella 2006, 259, nn. 191–3.
107. Bonanno 1993–94, 970; Bonanno 1997–98, 438; see below.
108. The excavators speak about a gradual abandonment, but it seems clear that there was only sporadic settlement after the Late Republican period. Most of the abandoned rooms excavated clearly contain Late Republican contexts (Bonanno 2008).
109. Scibona 1971a, 5–11, no. 1; *AE* 1973.266; Prag and Tigano 2017, 35–7, no. 8.
110. Calciati 1983, 147.
111. Burgio 2008, 241; 245.
112. Ibid.
113. Scibona 1982. It has been dated to second/early first century BC.
114. Wilson 1990, 223, n. 153.
115. Burgio 2008, 227–45.
116. Wilson 1990, 37, n. 37.
117. *CIL* X.7458 (Halaesa); 7463 (Haluntium).
118. Wilson 1990, 42.
119. Bernabò Brea 1975, 12.
120. Wilson 1990, 157, with n. 60 (for the bibliography on Agathyrnum and its identification with Capo d' Orlando; Spigo 1995; and for coin-finds, Puglisi 2008.
121. Cicero, *Verr.* 2.3.170.
122. Wilson 1990, 150.
123. Dr. Carmela Bonanno, pers. comm.
124. Bonanno 2008, 67; 82.
125. Leone and Spigo 2008, 109–10.
126. Ibid.
127. Facella 2006; Wilson 1990, *passim*.
128. Burgio 2008, 248.
129. Leone and Spigo 2008, 111; Maurici 2010, 121; Bernabò Brea 1996.
130. Leone and Spigo 2008, 110.
131. No traces were found of late Imperial settlement on the lower-lying slopes of the hill in the excavations between 1993 and 1999.
132. See note 129.
133. Scibona and Tigano 2008, 67.
134. Maurici 2010, 115.
135. Maurici 2010, 136.
136. Ibid., 114.
137. Fiore 1991, 56, no. 8 on map.
138. Wilson 1990, 197, fig. 163, n. 57.
139. Collura 2016, 305–6. Mosaics, said to be *magnifici*, are reported from Portale, 2 km west of Marina di Caronia,

presumably the site of a well-appointed villa: Fiore 1971c, 58 and location map on 57, no. 8.
140. Uggeri 1997–98, 334.
141. Jordanes, *Getica*, 308; Cassiodorus, *Var.* 10.2.
142. Burgio 2008, 256–7.
143. Carroccio and Collura 2016, 387–8, no. 19; 390.
144. Bonanno 2009, 26, n. 17.
145. Collura 2016, 263–7.
146. Krönig 1977, 119; cf. also the review discussion of this book by Scibona 1978.
147. Krönig 1977, 21 thought that *in essa* was a mistake for *presso* ('near'), but this is unnecessary.

Notes to Chapter Two

1. Uggeri 1997–98, 301–02.
2. Verbrugghe 1976; Uggeri 1997–98; 2004.
3. Uggeri 1997–98, 310–11.
4. Buttrey 1989, 79–80, nos 96–106 (Alaesa), 107–11 (Aluntium), 112 (Amestratus), 113–16 (Calacte).
5. Collura 2016, 413–34.
6. Pipitò 1996, 205–07, figs 8–11. A document from 1579 discusses the construction of this bridge at length, among other things its three arches (*Notamento circa il ponte del fiume di Caronia*, Archivio di Stato di Palermo, Deputazione del Regno, vol. 261, 39–41; Fiore 1991, 98–9). The arches constitute the only feature reminiscent of Roman architecture; but there is no doubt that the whole of the visible structure dates to the late sixteenth century, with construction in full swing in 1586 (Maurici and Minnella 2006, 35–6 and 73 with fig. 10 and pls. XXXIX–XLI). For a different view, Krönig 1977, 13; Uggeri 2004, 136 ('elementi riferibili all'epoca romana'); Collura 2016, 285–7 ('età altoimperiale').
7. The pavement is visible in Collura 2016, 286, fig. 21.
8. Cicero, *Verr.* 2.3.43.103.
9. Pais 1893, 123.
10. Uggeri 1997–98, 328; 2004, 132–8 (for all these roads).
11. Collura 2016, 413–34. See also ibid., 59, 61; 291–2.
12. Tigano 2012, 370.
13. Ibid.
14. Bejor 1982, 758.
15. Cicero, *Verr.* 2.3.43.101.
16. Cicero, *Verr.* 2.3.83.192.
17. *SEG* XIX.390.
18. Manganaro 1964–65; Manni 1966. The inscription records the Sicilian cities in a logical order for an itinerary until the portion where the lines are missing. After what presumably is Assorum, a line with the letter M follows, beneath which comes the initial K. Underneath this either two or three lines are missing. The next readable city is Halaesa, and the list ends with Thermae and Lipara. Manganaro interprets the initial K as standing for Kalè Akté, believing that the order in which the names appear on the list is identical that of a visit taken by the *theoroi*, Kale Akte being a logical next stop after Assorum and then a smaller town in the interior, beginning with the letter M. Manni, on the other hand, found it inconceivable that the *theoroi* would first have travelled eastwards to Haluntium after Kale Akte and then back westwards again to Halaesa and Thermae without stopping at Cephaloedium. He thought rather that the initial K stood for the more important city of Cephaloedium (in Greek Kephaloidion), and that Halaesa would have been the last stop of the journey. Later, Thermae and Lipari were added to the list, since they were now accessible after the Roman occupation of these sites in 252 BC (Manni 1966, 173–4). This would explain the apparent disorder in the itinerary.
19. Manni 1966, 125.
20. Facella 2006, 192–5.
21. Manganaro 2009; Arena 2016. Kale Akte also issued coins with Apollo and lyre in the late second century BC.
22. Uggeri 1997–98, 308; 313–15.
23. Ibid., 309.
24. Ibid., 315.
25. Fiore 1974; 1980; Scibona 1971a.
26. Scibona suggests that the road essentially followed the same course as the modern road towards Capizzi (Scibona 1971a, 24, n. 12).
27. Scibona 1987, 11; Collura 2016, 17, 43, 212–13, 251, 255, 272 and 293.
28. Morley 2002, 64–5.
29. Cicero, *Verr.* 2. 3.43.101 mentions how the inhabitants of Kale Akte were forced by Verres to transport their tithes of grain to Amestratus for delivery to the Roman governor, instead of the other way round, which had always previously been the case. See also below.
30. Lentini et al. 2002, especially 84 and 89–94.
31. Diodorus Siculus 14.16.3. It was probably situated in the area between the port of modern Castel di Tusa and the mouth of the Tusa river.
32. Cicero, *Verr.* 2.5.33.86.
33. Wilson (1990, 402, n. 127) suggested that Kale Akte (Marina di Caronía) served also as the harbour of Haluntium, certainly a possibility since the former was bigger than the much smaller *scalo* at Torrenova Marina below S. Marco d'Alunzio.
34. Scramuzza 1937, 293.
35. Wilson 1990, 157, n. 60.
36. This route is mentioned by ancient authors: Philostratus, *VA* 5.11; Strabo 2.4.3; Pliny, *NH* 6.206.
37. A typical example of a ship on a long-distance route, unloading and loading in several different ports along the way, is the first-century BC vessel at the site of La Cavalière (Charlin et al. 1978, 89–93). It was a small-sized ship, starting in North Africa, loaded with Punic amphorae of unknown contents (fish products perhaps), and moving past the north Sicilian coast. Here the ship may have made a stop to load Campana C pottery, produced in Sicily. No doubt some of the African products were also offloaded there. Continuing northwards, first Adriatic wine, and then Campanian wine and Campana A and B pottery, were bought. Part of the wine stock was traded against salted pork in Liguria. Further on, in the Antibes area, more of the remaining wine was sold, and the ship continued west towards Spain, when it sank off the French coast.

38. Horden and Purcell 2000, 118, 140, 365 and 565.
39. Barley: Tusa 1997, 180; Leighton 1999, 57. Wheat: Malone and Stoddart 2000.
40. Carcopino 1914; Scramuzza 1937, 237–9; Rickman 1980, 37–8.
41. Cicero, *Verr*. 2.2.3.144.
42. Cicero, *Verr*. 2.2.3.163.
43. John Serrati claims that Halaesa and Centuripae were situated between the Syracusan and Carthaginian domains in 264 BC, and therefore did not pay a tithe to Syracuse (Serrati 2000, 115–33; 126). This is clearly false, since we know that Halaesa had surrendered to Hieron II in 269 BC. See Karlsson 1992, 18.
44. Cicero, *Verr*. 2.3.73.170.
45. Cicero, *Verr*. 2.3.73.170. We do not know if this was a tithe or a larger part of the total harvest. If it is correct that it was a tithe, the city would have been able to feed 20,000 inhabitants. This number is obviously exaggerated; the assumed area of Halaesa would only contain 2,500 – 3,000 inhabitants at most, using the figures of Wilson, who reckons around 100 persons per hectare as a normal figure in Roman provincial cities (Wilson 1990, 171).
46. *CIL* X.7458. For *civitas stipendiaria* and *municipium*, see Manganaro 1964–65.
47. Pinzone 1990.
48. Scramuzza 1937, 268–9.
49. Scramuzza 1937, 319, following Carcopino 1906, whose calculations are controversial and far from trustworthy.
50. Cicero, *Verr*. 2.3.39.89: *Amestratinos, homines tenues*: 'the people of Amestratus – poor people'.
51. Wilson (1990, 194) emphasises the extra costs for transporting surplus grain from the interior to the harbours. Morley (2002, 65) stresses also the importance of good communications.
52. Cicero, *Verr*. 2.3.82.192; Wilson 1990, 13.
53. Hodos 2000, 47–8.
54. Courtot 1989, 83: 'La vigne, colonisatrice par excellence des terres peu fertiles, des sols minces, sablonneux ou cailloteux'.
55. Horden and Purcell 2000, 214.
56. Prestianni Giallombardo (2003) departs from the usual suggestion that coins reflect in their choice of featured deity the most important cults of the city. Wilson (1990, 23) takes for granted the connection between coins featuring bunch of grapes and viticulture.
57. Calciati 1986, 445–7; Hoover 2012, no. 513 (Entella). For elsewhere: ibid., nos 201, 207 (Halaesa), 221 (Haluntium, on obv. alongside the head of Dionysus), 241–2 (Entella), 396 (Enna), 615, 632 (Katane), 1597, 1602–3 (Tauromenium, but the second and third with Hera on obv., the third with Apollo), 1630 (Tyndaris) and 1794 (Lipara, with grapes on the obv. and a dolphin on the rev.). Monte Iato: Frey-Kupper 2013, 242, Abb. 47.3 (late second century).
58. Vandermersch 1994, 38–41.
59. For the *Eugeneum* of Taormina, Pliny, *NH* 14.25. For the sources for the viticulture of Naxos, see Vandermersch 1994, 41. For the coins, see note 57; that with the bunch of grapes in a subordinate position above Apollo's lyre is Hoover 2012, no. 1585 (rev.).
60. Young head of Dionysus facing to the right, wreathed with ivy; bunch of grapes behind / ΑΛΟΝΤΙΝΩΝ in laurel wreath (Calciati 1983, 69, no. 11= Hoover 2012, no. 221).
61. Pliny, *NH* 14.80.
62. Head of Silenus crowned with ivy, facing right / bunch of grapes (Calciati 1987, 96, no. 7 = Hoover 2012, no. 615), of which there are many issues.
63. Pesavento Mattioli 2001, 10–11, fig. 2.5. See also Chapter 4, p. 86.
64. Silius Italicus, *Pun*. 14.204.
65. Vandermersch 1994, 49.
66. Head of Dionysus to the right, wreathed with ivy / bunch of grapes (Calciati 1983 [volume I], 82, no. 24).
67. Bonanno 1997–98, 38.
68. Vandermersch 1994, 41.
69. Peña 1999, 155. For recent discussions, see especially Franco and Capelli 2014a and b.
70. Franco and Capelli 2014b, 551–2.
71. Barrels: Wilson 1990, 194. Amphorae: Ollà 2001.
72. Hellenistic production: Bonanno 1997–98, 442. Late Roman: Franco and Capelli 2014b, 553–4.
73. *IG* XIV.352.
74. Part of the *Tabulae Halaesinae* concerns legal rights revolving around an olive grove (*elaiokomion*) consisting of two lots (Prestianni Giallombardi 1998, 68). From it we understand that hides were often tanned in the vicinity of oak groves or forests because of the important ingredient that oak produced, tannin, which was used in the tanning process in combination with urine. The resultant waste liquid was also an excellent fertiliser for olive trees (Prestianni Giallombardo 1998, 77–78).
75. Holm 1870–98, no. 531; Wilson 1990, 22.
76. Silius Italicus, *Pun*. 14.232–237. Captain Smyth, RN, on a British naval reconnaissance to Sicily in the early nineteenth century, mentions these forests, 'the largest in Sicily . . . nearly fifty miles in circumference', as the prinicipal asset of Caronía ('which possesses but one good street and a population of about two thousand people', most of them employed in forestry work). He mentions oak, elm, pine and ash of excellent quality, but laments that some of the finest trees were burnt to make charcoal (Smyth 1824, 96–7).
77. The grove of Apollo at Halaesa (*IG* XIV.352, col. 2, 54 and 63) was one of many in Sicily. According to Scramuzza, such sacred groves were rich in timber. For the ancient sources on other Sicilian sacred groves, see Scramuzza 1937, 277).
78. Scramuzza (ibid., 276–7) calls the area 'the very basis of Sicilian shipping'.
79. Ibid., 277.
80. Cicero, *Verr*. 2.5.33.86.
81. Cicero, *Verr*. 2.5.51.133.
82. Scibona 1971a, 5–11, tav. II.
83. *Edict. Diocl*. 12, 10; and 12, 12.

84. Scramuzza 1937, 309.
85. Bonanno 2009, 43, 57–8, tav. XVIII–XIX, figs 23–5 and 27–8; Collura 2016, 147–8, nos 199–201; 171, figs 199–201.
86. Braudel 1972, 45–6; 206; Horden and Purcell 2000, 81.
87. Diodorus Siculus 34–35.2.27.
88. Malone and Stoddart 2000; Wilson 2000c, 290.
89. Cicero, *Verr.* 2.2.2.5.
90. Horden and Purcell 2000, 85.
91. Strabo 6.2.6.
92. Morley 2002, 144.
93. That mixed farming was the most common strategy in Sicily in general in the Imperial period is also suggested by Wilson (1990, 195).
94. Malone and Stoddart 2000, 471–2; Wilson 2000c, 290. Sources on products from sheep: Ar. *Vesp.* 838 (dairy products); Athenaeus, 14.658a–b; 1.4d; 27d; 27f; 7.311c (cheese).
95. Wool as a Sicilian export good is mentioned by Strabo (6.2.3.), and in the fourth century AD as among Sicily's *negotia utilia* in the *Expositio Totius Mundi et Gentium* 65.
96. Prestianni Giallombardo 1998, 77–8.
97. Scramuzza 1937, 281.
98. Cicero, *Verr.* 2.1.10.28; and 2.2.7.20.
99. Cicero, *Verr.* 2.1.10.27–28; and 2.2.7.20.
100. *Expositio, in fine.*
101. Diodorus Siculus 4.84.1. (Scramuzza 1937, 282); Varro, *De Re Rustica* 2.4.3: 'Who of our people cultivates a farm without keeping swine?'.
102. Malone and Stoddart 2000; Wilson 2000c, 290.
103. Solinus, *Coll.* 5.12; Scribonius Largus, *Comp. Med.* 163.
104. Wilson 2000b, 364; 2000c, 290.
105. *Edict. Diocl.* 8, 24.
106. Silius Italicus, *Pun.* 14.251.
107. Athenaeus 7. 315d. On the importance of fish and fish-products in the Roman world, see now Marzano 2013 (also Marzano 2018) and Botte and Leitch 2014.
108. *P. London* 214137.
109. Athenaeus 5.209a.
110. Scramuzza 1937; Purpura 1982, n. 6. Tyndaris: Athenaeus 7.302; Cefalù: Archestratus cited in Athenaeus 7.302.
111. Purpura 1982; 1985. For a recent overview of Sicilian fish-salting installations, Botte 2018.
112. Wilson 1990, 229.
113. There is a huge variety in the terminology of fish-products (*salsamenta*) in antiquity: for example, 167 *tituli picti* on Baetican amphorae alone document *garum, lympha*(*tum*?), *cordyla, liquamen, laccat*(*atum*?), *muria* and *saxitanus*, in descending order of frequency. Even a town as far inland such as Sagalassos in Asia Minor received a variety of scombrids (including tuna [*Thunnus* sp.], Atlantic bonito [*Sarda sarda*] and Spanish mackerel [*Scomber japonicus*]) as well as other sea-fish such as seabream and mullet. For full details, see van Neer et al. 2010. Analysis of the nature of Sicilian fish-products (whether in basins or amphorae) has yet to begin, with the notable exception of a recent find at Milazzo, where tuna and bluefish were documented: Ollà 2015; 2018 (for a discussion of such evidence in amphorae, Grainger 2013, 16–19 with Table 2). On the terms *garum, liquamen, muria* and *allec*, see Grainger 2014 and 2018.
114. Athenaeus 14.252–3; 7.302a.
115. Collura 2016, 224, no. 76.
116. See Chapter 4, pp. 87–8.
117. In *Il libro del re Ruggero*, 25, 53.
118. Desse-Berset and Desse 2000, 74.
119. Other fish attested along the northern coast of Sicily include crab, crayfish (the best were said to be those in in the Aeolian islands), scallops (Tyndaris) and sprats (Lipari): Scramuzza 1937, 283–5. All might have been present in and around Kale Akte.

Notes to Chapter Three

1. Bonanno 1993–94; 1997–98; Lentini et al. 2002, especially 86–9; Collura 2016, 72–83; 2019a, 137–44.
2. One stamp with the letters of the *polis* was first published by Scibona (1971b), and others are known from Marina di Caronia (Bonanno 2009, tav. XIX, fig. 30) and in the hinterland: see further Chapter 4, note 145.
3. See Chapter 2, p. 33.
4. Fiore 1991, figs 32–3 and 36.
5. Carettoni 1961, 313.
6. Collura 2016, 29; 97–102, figs 80–94.
7. Bonanno 1995, 47, fig. 13.
8. Lentini et al. 2002, 86–9; Collura 2016, 82–4, figs 31–40.
9. A similar technique can be discerned in walls at Halaesa; it is reminiscent of Punic and (later) Roman *opus africanum*, but the sections of ashlars are here replaced by sections of brickwork, which (unlike the ashlars) are keyed into the stonework on either side.
10. Bonanno 1997–98, 432.
11. Collura 2016, 37.
12. Ibid.
13. Ibid., 36–7. The medieval wall, which we know surrounded the top of the hill, is known in parts, and enclosed in any case only the uppermost part of the plateau (Collura 2016, 259, fig. 12). There is nothing to suggest that the ancient city wall would underlie the medieval one, except for its southern stretch.
14. Maniscalco and McConnell 2003, 154.
15. The new, large-scale, urban layout of Morgantina of Greek type from *c.* 450 BC is no longer attributed to Ducetius, but possibly to settlers from Kamarina and of Sikel origin (Bell 2000; Walsh 2006, 237, n. 11).
16. He speaks about Ducetius establishing 'many settlers' there (Diodorus Siculus 12.28.1).
17. Bonanno 1994–95, 960.
18. Collura 2016, 122, fig. 136.
19. In comparison, the vastly larger Morgantina has only two *plateiai.*
20. Collura 2016, 121–2.
21. Bonanno 1994–95, 961–2 and 969.
22. Collura 2016, 106 and 109, figs 111–13.
23. Bonanno 2008.
24. Ibid., 19.
25. Bonanno 1993–94, 962.

26. Ibid., 961–2. For the use of bricks in Hellenistic Caronía, Collura 2019b.
27. Bonanno 1997–98, 432.
28. Scibona 1987, 11.
29. Burgio 2008, 242–5, fig. 181.
30. Fiore 1971b, 37–8. Fiore (1976, 47) also suggests that the aqueduct was intended to reach the small settlement of Solusapre in the hinterland, but it seems unlikely that such a minor rural settlement was provided with an aqueduct.
31. Burgio 2008, n. 123.
32. Between Piazza S. Francesco and the beginning of via Ducezio: Collura 2016, 36, 116.
33. Inscription: Arena 2016 (it measures 12.7 x 14 cm and is 3.5 cm thick); statue: Collura 2016, 147, no. 194; 170, fig. 194; sundial: ibid., 373–8.
34. The statue is indicated by Scibona (1987, 10) as coming from the area of the modern cemetery, but Bernabò Brea (1975, 21) indicates that the northern slope below Caronia was the find-spot. This would also be more logical, since one imagines that it was originally placed in the *agora* of the town.
35. Cicero, *Verr.* 2.4.22.49.
36. Collura 2016, chapter 5.
37. Scibona 1987, 11; Collura 2016, 233–4 and 238.
38. Facella 2006, 318–22.
39. Ibid., 321.
40. Pecoraino 1989, 68 and 280, cat. no. 25; Lentini et al. 2002, 82, fig. 7.
41. Scibona and Tigano 2008, 31.
42. Facella 2006, 328.
43. Calciati 1983.
44. See Chapter 2, pp. 35–6, for a discussion of the motif in connection with the economy of the Sicilian cities.
45. Facella 2006, 334.
46. Ibid., 333–4.
47. Athenaeus 12.542; Cornelius Nepos, *Hann.* 13.3.
48. Carroccio 2004, 216–20.
49. Facella 2006, 185–6 and 327–8.
50. Facella 2006, 327.
51. See discussion in Chapter 4, p. 103.
52. The extramural, prostyle and tetrastyle Hellenistic temple at San Marco d'Alunzio is called the 'Tempio di Eracle' only because coins with the image of Heracles are common finds in the town. There is no proof of such an identification (Bernabò Brea 1975, 13).
53. Facella 2006, 332–3; Scibona and Tigano 2008, 30–1.
54. Collura 2016, 94; 135; 139, no. 58; 140, n. 101; and 347.
55. Karlsson 1995, *passim*.
56. A fragment of *terra sigillata* was found inside one of the walls (Bonanno 1997–98, 438).
57. A similar situation can be seen at Tindari, where new houses obliterated old cisterns in the third quarter of the first century BC (Stone 1983, 200; Bernabò Brea and Cavalier 1965b).
58. Stone 1983.
59. Bonanno 1993–94, 969. Another lead sling-bolt was found during a field survey of the north slope of the hill (F. Collura, pers. comm.).
60. Stone 1983, 14.
61. Dio 49.12.5; Dio 48.17.6; Strabo 6.2.4; Diodorus Siculus 16.7.1; Stone 1983, 13–16; see his fig. 1 for Sicilian sites with signs of destruction in the 30s BC.
62. Dio 48.48.6.
63. Pliny, *NH* 2.94.
64. Bonanno 1993–94, 969.
65. See note 34.
66. The column fragment is today found at the altar of the church. I thank Salvatore Serio for this information.
67. The use of marble columns in construction is unlikely to have been introduced to Sicily before the late Trajanic period (Wilson 1990, 241). Fluted columns, although a few are known of first-century date in Italy, are at their most plentiful during the second century, especially in the Eastern Mediterranean, but a few examples continued also to be used in the West in the period AD 250/350: see H. Snell at https://www.academia.edu/9088563/Spirally-fluted_columns_origins_context_and_architectural_fantasy (viewed March 30th 2020).
68. For the cistern in *proprietà* Barna, Bonanno 2009, 73–7, who dates it to the first century BC on the basis of some late Republican red-slip wares found in the fill; but these were part of the abandonment deposits and cannot be used to date the structure, and in any case brick-faced concrete does not appear even in Rome before *c.* 40 BC. In Sicily it is not likely to be earlier than the second half of the first century AD (*pace* Venuti 2019, who thinks the Naumachia reservoir at Taormina might be as early as the late first century BC; by contrast Campagna and La Torre 2008, 143, date it later, perhaps AD 50/100). Torre 2019, 216, dates this cistern to 'I–II sec. d.C.'. The same chronological argument applies to the second cistern, still visible in *contrada* Palme, which Scibona 1987 also dated to the first century BC. For a fuller account, Scibona 2011, 72–3, where no date is offered; it is said to measure 15 m x 10 m (which sound like 'rounded' numbers and therefore approximate); cf. also the discussion by Wilson, 1990, 102 with nn. 283–6 on 371; his measurements are 14 m x 8.30 m. A date in the second century AD for this cistern (along with others in Sicily of the double-'aisled' type) seems likely.
69. Lentini et al. 2002, 94; Lindhagen 2006, 20.
70. Bonanno 1997–98, 435; Collura 2016, 38 and 136.
71. Cluverius 1619, 291–3.
72. Collura 2016, 225. Smyth (1824, 96) makes no mention of a harbour.
73. Collura 2016, 228.
74. Ibid., 206–8, figs 39–42.
75. Ibid., 207 and 212, fig. 49.
76. Bonanno 2009, 12; Collura 2016, 199, figs 20–2.
77. Bonanno 1997–98, 429 and 431–2, fig. 6. Cf. also Scibona 2011, 69–71, describing seven brick-built *a fossa* graves in *contrada* Palme, immediately south of the bridge over the railway line in ex-proprietà Lipari: he suggests a date for them in the late fourth century AD or later.
78. Lentini et al. 2002, 89–94.
79. Bonanno and Sudano 2006; Bonanno 2009. The excav-

ations were supervised in the field for the most part by Fabrizio Sudano and Tiziana Fisichella.
80. Bonanno and Sudano 2006; Bonanno 2009.
81. For the sake of clarity and in order to avoid confusion, I have chosen to employ the same letters to identify buildings as those used in Bonanno 2009. I am indebted to Carmela Bonanno for information concerning the discoveries from the campaign of 2003–05, and for showing me the site at the end of the 2004 season.
82. Sudano 2009, 16, dates the earliest phase to prior to 300 BC ('sicuramente antecedente al IV sec. a. C.'), but only one find in this context can be dated to the period earlier than the fourth century BC (*c.* 410 BC).
83. Bonanno and Sudano 2006, 437–8.
84. Collura 2016, 61.
85. Sudano 2009, 20.
86. Ibid., 16–18, fig. A.
87. Ibid., 18. The dating of this flood varies in different accounts. In the latest and most substantial publication, Building 1, which was built above it, is presumed to have been constructed in the late fourth or beginning of the third century BC (Bonanno and Sudano 2009, 18). This conclusion can certainly be disputed, however, since a coin from the mint of Kale Akte was found on the bed of sea pebbles, constituting a *terminus post quem* for Building 1 sometime in the second century BC.
88. Sudano 2009, 18.
89. Ibid., 18–19, fig. B.
90. Ibid., 20, fig. 9.
91. Ibid., 19.
92. This coin is identical with cat. no. 59, fig. 36 in Lentini et al. 2002, 102–03.
93. Lentini et al. 2002, 102, cat. no. 57, fig. 34; Särström 1940, 106–08, pls 29–30.
94. Bonanno and Sudano 2009, 18.
95. Bonanno 2009, 73–7. See note 68 above.
96. Ibid., 73. It was subsequently reused for several different purposes, including for burial. This interesting cistern was reported by Scibona (1987, 11) as part of the *proprietà eredi* Carolina Aversa, but is now part of *proprietà* Barna.
97. Bonanno 2009, 20 and 22, fig. 12 (U/S 155).
98. Sudano 2009, 21–2, fig. 13.
99. Bonanno 2009, 73–4, n. 5.
100. Sudano 2009, 24.
101. Ibid., 19.
102. Bonanno and Sudano's dating of the building is to be questioned: they separate the southern annex of the building from the rest, and date it to the 'Byzantine period', basing their arguments on the single find of a complete amphora there. However, this amphora is a typical example of the Termini Imerese 151/354 type which can be dated to the fourth century AD (Bonanno 2009, 26 and 40, tav. XIV, no. 73, tav. XVI.73 = in this book, p. 95, Fig. 4.28b); for a parallel of that date from nearby Lipari, see Messina 2000, 27.
103. Sudano 2009, 24, fig. 22.
104. Appendix 4, cat. no. 126. The fabric consists of iron-rich, silty clay, rich also in quartz and calcite (Appendix 2, sample 10, p. 171 with Fig. A2.11).
105. Bonanno and Sudano 2006, 443, n. 47; Bonanno 2009, 32, n. 42. For late Roman contexts in general at Marina di Caronía, Bonanno 2007.
106. Libanius, *Or.* 18.292; Ammianus Marcellinus 26.10.15–19; Jerome, *Chron.* 244; Di Vita 1982, 134–9; Wilson 2018. Earthquakes in antiquity: Guidoboni 1994; possible such damage now in Halaesa: Scibona 2009, 25–6.
107. Guidoboni et al. 2000, 60; cf. also Wilson 2018, 454.
108. Wilson 1990, e.g. on 337.
109. Bonanno 2009, 26 and 40 (see the full discussion in note 102 above).
110. Strangely enough, this consideration was made for the southern-most rooms in Building 1, but not for those in Building 2 (Bonanno 2009, 20).
111. Bonanno 2009, 81.
112. These walls were excavated in 1999–2000, and were subsequently almost completely destroyed by the landowner; they were therefore never studied in their original state by the geologists or excavators. Collura (2016, 198, n. 22) is also sceptical about the conclusion of this limited geological inspection.
113. Collura 2016, 275–308.
114. Wilson 1990, 330–1; 334, fig. 284; and 333.
115. Burgio 2008, 256–7.
116. Bonanno 2009, 26.
117. Collura 2016, 243, fig. 7.
118. Ibid., 242. See also note 77 above.
119. *CIL* X.7469; Bivona 1970, 57–8, no. 41; Fiore 1971a.

Notes to Chapter Four

1. See, for example, Belvedere et al. 1993.
2. In addition to the amphorae published in Bernabò Brea and Cavalier 1965a, Tav. 41, 52–3 and Campagna 2000, see also Cavalier 1985 and Messina 2000.
3. Denaro 1995; Malfitana et al. 2008.
4. Wilson 1990, 262: 'In Sicily the systematic study of amphorae from land excavations is still in its infancy, and no clear picture can therefore yet emerge of the fluctuating pattern of foodstuff imports…'.
5. Lindhagen 2006, 45; see (for example) Spagnolo 2002; Polizzi 1997.
6. Wilson 1990.
7. From the first (and still important) classification of Roman amphorae by Heinrich Dressel in 1890, until the corpus of stamps by Callender in 1965, the study of amphorae made almost no progress, the only exception being the work of Virginia Grace, pioneer in the study of Greek amphorae. It was only in the early 1970s, when a series of congresses was organised by the École Française in Rome, and the important publications from the *Terme del Nuotatore* at Ostia by Clementina Panella and others, that the study of amphorae and Roman amphorae in particular became an important source for ancient economic history for the first time (*Ostia* I–IV). However, it was only in the 1980s that attention began to be paid to amphora fabrics, and analyses were conducted to localise areas of production, a field in which David Peacock was the pioneer (Peacock 1971;

Peacock and Williams 1986).

8. E.g. Malfitana et al. 2008; 2013. Malfitana and Franco 2011; 2013; Franco and Capelli 2014b.
9. Sites where amphora studies have been prominent include Naxos, Termini Imerese, Segesta and Messina. However, fabric descriptions are often vague, lacking detail and thin-sections, or photographs of fabrics for comparison.
10. This is witnessed by the many shipwrecks found in the Mediterranean: Peacock (1982, 158), points out that very few contained only pottery, and questions the idea that pots would have been important as traded merchandise in their own right. An exception to this rule are Attic painted vases, which might have been valuable enough to constitute a business of their own (Boardman 1999).
11. Morel 1989, 523–7.
12. *Meligunìs Lipára* volumes I–XII.
13. Stone 2014.
14. Caflisch 1991.
15. Cavalier 1985, 89–90.
16. Lipari: Cavalier 1985, 25–31, figs 2–4; 60–2, 73–4, 78–9, fig. 20, nos 94–5; fig. 22, no. 109. Himera: Vassallo 2003, 331–9 (seventh/early fifth century BC); Tindari: Leone and Spigo 2008, 258.
17. Koehler 1981; 1992.
18. Collura 2016, 331, 335, tav. IV, no. 1, 8–9; 336, tav. V, e, m. The finds, along with other late Archaic/early Classical pottery, were made in dumped spoil heaps found not far from the excavation area in *contrada* Pantano (see note 39 below).
19. Koehler 1981, 454, n. 23, pl. 98g; Sourisseau 2006, 139, fig. 5, no. 4c.
20. Koehler 1981, 456.
21. Cavalier 1985, 38: Leone and Spigo 2008, 258.
22. Collura 2016, 201–02, fig. 29.
23. Spigo 1987, 1, n. 5.
24. Adamesteanu 1962; Scibona 1987, 10.
25. Collura 2016, 311; 314–16; 318–22, tav. I–III. My thanks go to Francesco Collura and Salvatore Serio for showing me these fragments.
26. Collura 2016, 319, tav. II, no. 30.
27. Bonanno and Sudano 2006, 437, n. 9.
28. Parallels are found in tombs on other Sikel sites, for example at Morgantina (Lyons 1996, 140, no. 4-25, pl. 11; pl. 17).
29. Collura 2016, 318, tav. I, no. 3.
30. Collura 2016, 318, tav. I, no. 23; 321, no. 23.
31. Vandermersch 1994, 65–9; Will 1982 for the older term, 'Greco-Italic' (= MGS IV–VI). The shape and fabrics of the MGS II–VI from the Bonanno excavations at Marina di Caronía are not known: all were treated as one category, and none were illustrated, in Bonanno 2009. The number of MGS fragments given (only 12) is likely to reflect a tiny fraction of the true number of fragments present (Bonanno 2009, 33–4, tav. XXV, graph 3).
32. Albanese Procelli 1996, 118–20; Cavalier 1985, 90.
33. Vandermersch 1994, 68.
34. Campagna 2000, 445–6.
35. Porticello: Jones, Eiseman and Ridgway 1987, 49–50; Parker 1992a, 332–4, no. 879. Marzamemi H: Parker 1976–77, 630.
36. Albanese Procelli 1996, 117; Cavalier 1985, 39 and 81.
37. Collura 2016, 330–3, fig. 11; 335, tav. I, nos. 5–7; 336, tav. II, g–l; 337.
38. The find was made in Bonanno's excavations at Marina di Caronía, and came from the same fifth-century BC context as the Corinthian A handle discussed above.
39. Several finds out of context, which were discovered in a dump in *contrada* Pantano. It seems probable that they come from construction work in the 1980s and 1990s in the south-western part of Marina di Caronía, in the border area between *contrade* Nunziatella and Pantano. Another find comes from the same context as the Corinthian A amphora from the early fifth century BC, and thus chronologically fits well with the type (cf. the parallel in *Himera* V, tav. XI, no. 12). I am indebted to Dr Carmela Bonanno for showing me the fragment.
40. I follow here the definition of imitations by Roman Beat Caflisch in *Studia Ietina 4*, who differentiates between colonial and regional imitations. The 'colonial' products were made in a Greek settlement, imitating mainland Greek types, whereas the 'regional' wares were often much freer imitations of Greek models and come from Hellenised centres of non-Greek origin (Caflisch 1991, 21).
41. Caflisch 1991, 57, n. 112; Vassallo 1999, 200.
42. Vassallo 1999, 201–02, fig. 198.
43. Ibid.
44. Trendall 1967, 583–664.
45. Spigo 2000, 111.
46. Trendall 1989, 30.
47. Bernabò Brea and Cavalier 1965a, 231.
48. Personal information from Dr Shelley Stone.
49. The finds from San Marco d'Alunzio are exhibited in the town's museum. For the rich finds from Troina, see Militello 1961, 322–404.
50. For a survey of the most important find-spots of red-figure Sicilian pottery, Spigo 1987, 19, n. 65; for finds in western Sicily, cf. Tullio 1997–98, tomb 148 containing a Sicilian red-figure *olpe* (tav. CLXXXIII, fig. 1); and Giglio 1997–98, tav. CLXXXVIII, fig. 2. Entella: De Cesare 2003. Segesta: De Cesare 2003, 267, n. 46 (and 258, nn. 43–6 on the distribution of the work of the NYN painter in western Sicily).
51. Collura 2016, 244, fig. II (also 154, no. 12).
52. Trendall 1989, 163.
53. De Cesare 2003, 258.
54. Messina, Tindari, Himera, Polizzi Generosa, Montagna dei Cavalli, Entella and possibly Segesta (De Cesare 2003, 258, nn. 43–6).
55. Trendall 1989, no. 286
56. Bonanno 1995, 47, fig. 13; Collura 2016, 244–5, figs III a–b and IV.
57. The type is found at Tindari (Spigo 1987, 20, n. 5) and at Polizzi Generosa near Cefalù, where Pagenstecher *lekythoi* are very common (Tullio 1997, 269; 272–4). For a hypothetical Sicilian production of this type and its distribution, see Spigo 1987, 2.

58. Collura 2016, 318–19; 321–2, tav. I–II, nos 14 and 43.
59. Bailey 1975, 296.
60. The type is Ramón 10.1.2.1: Collura 2016, 314, 317, 330, 334–5 and 336; tav. Va–d; 337, nos 2–4.
61. Ramón 1995, 131–3.
62. Alaimo et al. 1998.
63. Collura 2016, 282, fig. 12.
64. Cavalier 1985, 37; Leone and Spigo 2008, 260, fabric M1.
65. An example from the *tomba del kottabos* at San Marco d'Alunzio (*c.* 320/280 BC) (Scibona 1981), as well as an unidentified amphora from Halaesa (Carettoni 1959, 316, fig. 23e) seem to be of the MGS III type. Apollonia: Bonanno 2008, 40, tav. 2a; Solunto: Polizzi 1997, 95–103; Capo d'Orlando: Bonanno 2004, 86–7, t. 8. Vandermersch (1994, 73) considers the amphora from the *tomba del kottabos* an MGS IV, but Campagna (2000, 447, n. 38) disputes this on morphological grounds. Tindari: Leone and Spigo 2008, 259–60. More than one third of the amphorae here were MGS III or MGS IV amphorae (*anfore ad orlo di echino*).
66. Vandermersch 1994, 70; Campagna 2000, 447–8.
67. Campagna 2000, 449.
68. A complete neck was found in the earliest known domestic context of Kale Akte near the *case popolari*, in *contrada* Sotto San Francesco (Collura 2016, 138, no. 28; photo on 155, no. 28).
69. Vandermersch 1994, 73–80.
70. MGS IV amphorae from the Filicudi F wreck were lined with resin, and the type is commonly associated with wine-drinking vessels (Vandermersch 1994, 75–6).
71. Vandermersch 1994, 75.
72. Cavalier 1985, 82. More than 200 fragments were found here.
73. Vandermersch 1994, 78–80.
74. Tchernia 1986, 51.
75. Olcese 2004; 2005–06; 2010.
76. Olcese 2004; Campagna 2000, 459 (impasto F1).
77. See, for example, Blanck 1979.
78. See the distribution map of stamps from Ischia / the Bay of Naples in Olcese 2010, 92–166; also Olcese 2005–06.
79. The fabric is considered very similar to the local Ischian one, and the same as that bearing the well-known stamp TR.LOISIO (Olcese 2004, 177).
80. Olcese 2004, 182.
81. Vandermersch 1994, 75.
82. Burgio 2008, 241.
83. Hesnard et al. 1989, 38–43.
84. Bonanno 2009, 48, cat. no. 27, fig. 2, tav. III.
85. My warmest thanks go to Dr. Malcolm Bell and Dr. Carmela Bonanno for giving me access to the depots of the museum at Aidone.
86. See the index of stamps in Vandermersch 1994, 166, 169 and 174.
87. Belvedere et al. 1993, 218, fabric A9.
88. Campagna 2000, 452 and 459 (impasto F1); Leone and Spigo 2008, 262.
89. Ramón 1995, 205.
90. Arthur 1990.
91. Ramón 1995, 630, fig. 264, map 73; Arthur 1990, 32.
92. Denaro 1995, 185, fig. 1.
93. Campagna 2000, 457.
94. Tigano 1993–94, 1066–7, tav. CXII, fig. 6. But Milazzo was a producer of its own fish-products, as demonstrated by the excavation of fish-tanks there; discoveries included a dump of fish residues, mainly of tuna and bluefish: Ollà 2015; 2018.
95. Van der Werff 1977–78, 182.
96. Empereur and Hesnard 1987, 39.
97. I thank Dr. Malcolm Bell for this information.
98. Cavaliere 2000, 67–72.
99. Curtis 1991, 100.
100. The fragments belong to the Maña B, C and D types, roughly corresponding to Ramón's types 6.1.1.1, 7.1.2.1, 5.2.3.1 and 5.2.3.2, and dating mainly from the late fourth to the third centuries BC. With these fragments were also found Italic Republican wine containers such as the Greco-Italic and Dressel 1 types, but in smaller numbers (Purpura 1982, 52, fig. 11).
101. Purpura 1982, 53.
102. Scramuzza 1937; Purpura 1982.
103. Appendix 2, sample 9, p. 171 with Fig. A2.10.
104. Morel 1980, 88.
105. Morel 1981, 126; Bernabò Brea and Cavalier 1965a, 225, fig. 29; 244, n. 4, tav. CCX,1c.
106. Blanck 1979.
107. Olcese 2004.
108. Morel 1980, 92.
109. Stone 2014, 128.
110. Morel 1980, 88; Caflisch 1991, 106.
111. Bonanno 2008, 39, n. 5; 43, tav. 4e and 4f.
112. Bonanno 2009, 30, cat. nos 2–3, tav. I. Form 1514 has been found also in the *chora* of Halaesa (Burgio 2008, 87, no. 3, fig. 150).
113. Finds of Morel type 3210 and 2630 have been made in the *chora* of Halaesa (Burgio 2008, 87, 5, fig. 150; 154, no. 1).
114. Bonanno 2009, 30, cat. nos 13–17, tav. II.
115. Ibid., 31, cat. no. 21, tav. II.
116. Ibid., 2009, 31, cat. nos 18–20, tav. II; Collura 2016, 180–1, tav. 2–3.
117. Caflisch 1991, nos 415–42; Morel type 3133a1 from Lipari (Morel 1981, 250, pl. 87).
118. Bonanno 2009, 31, cat. no. 23, tav. II.
119. Collura 2016, 157, no. 46; 162, no. 98.
120. Compare Caflisch 1991, Abb. 22, 713; Taf. 13, 713 and 770. A cup with a rosette from the necropolis of Morgantina is dated to the third century BC (inv. no. 59–2231, deposit IK 2) (personal information from Dr Shelley Stone). Another shallow bowl with a stamped rosette on the floor can be dated to the first half of the second century BC, but the decoration clearly belongs mainly to the third century (Stone 2014, 200–01).
121. Bonanno and Sudano 2006, 439, n. 18; Collura 2016, 143, nos 121, 129 and 131; 146, no. 170; 149, no. 226; 168, no. 170; Bernabò Brea and Cavalier 1965a, tav. k–l. Palmette stamps in the form of a cross are also common in western Sicily.
122. Monte Iato: Caflisch 1991; Lipari: Bernabò Brea and

Cavalier 1965a, 312.
123. Carettoni 1959, 337, fig. 39 (centre); Caflisch 1991, 118, no. 536, Taf. 10, Abb. 16; Bernabò Brea and Cavalier 1965a, tav. 1, nos 14 and 25.
124. Scibona 1981, 320, fig. 9 and 323, fig. 12.
125. Burgio 2008, 127, no. 8, fig. 101, cf. Caflisch 1991, 168–9, zP10, tav. 11. 532, *c.* 300 BC; Burgio 2008, 60, no. 3, compare Caflisch 1991, 168, zP7. Fig. 11, 694, third century BC.
126. Stone 2014, 229–70.
127. Collura 2016, 180, tav. 2, no. 13.
128. Collura 2016, 145, no. 148; 166, no. 148.
129. Find from surface survey at Caronía: Collura 2016, 144; 165, no. 144.
130. Stone 2014, 267–8, pls 122–3, nos 590–600, especially no. 600.
131. Stone 2014, 459, pl. 142.
132. Stone 2014, 271–2.
133. Collura 2016, 145, no. 150; 166, no. 150; Stone 2014, 92, pls 4 and 73; 271, pl. 140.
134. Collura 2016, 246, fig. VIII a–b. A similar type without gloss is ibid., 248, fig. XIX.
135. Bonanno 1993–94, 983, tav. 97, fig. 1.
136. Bernabò Brea and Cavalier 1965a. The absence of profile drawings of these lamps makes the determination of any exact parallel impossible.
137. Käch 2006, 44, nos 132–3 (260/220 BC). At Monte Iato, 1,994 fragments were found.
138. Bernabò Brea and Cavalier 1965a.
139. Observation from the study of Hellenistic amphora material in the depot of the Archaeological Museum of Aidone in 2003.
140. Collura 2016, 291.
141. Krönig 1977, 123–4.
142. *IG* XIV.2393.340; *IG* XIV.2395.7.
143. Tigano 2009, 32, fig. 58; Carettoni 1961, 312.
144. Scibona 1971b, 22; the inscription is 13.4 cm long and 4 cm high.
145. Bonanno 2009, 44–5, tav. XIX, fig. 30. Others are known from *contrada* Sampieri in the hinterland of Caronia; there is more than one die. See now in full, Collura 2019a, 257–64.
146. In addition to the structures recorded in Bonanno 1993–94; 1997–98 and Lentini et al. 2002, remains of walls built in the identical technique were recorded during a short survey in February 2000 in *contrada* Telegrafo, *proprietà* Di Fede, on the north slope of the hill, towards *contrada* San Todaro (*Piano dei Pupiddi*). See further Collura 2019b.
147. Carettoni 1961, 288–9, figs 23 and 25; 291, fig. 28.
148. Bonanno 1993–94, tav. 93, fig. 1.
149. Sjöqvist 1960, 131; Stillwell 1967, 247; Wilson 1979, 18, n. 39.
150. Carettoni 1961, 313–18.
151. Fiore 1991, 147. The heights of the terracotta heads in Fig. 4.14 are as follows: (a) 5.3 cm; (b) 7.7 cm; (c) 8.1 cm; (d) 8.2 cm.
152. Collura 2016, 139, no. 56; 140 and 159, no. 68; 158, no. 51; and 160, no. 70. Parallels for the slave appliqué: Stone 2014, pl. 125, 618–19.
153. Parker 1992a, 117, no. 233.
154. Morel 1980. For the massive export of Campanian and central Italian wines towards (especially) Gaul, see Tchernia 2016, 277–95.
155. It is not certain if the stamp belongs specifically to the Ischia production (it may be related to stamps ANΔP or ANΔPΩ from there), but these amphorae were made somewhere in the Bay of Naples region (Olcese 2010, 92–3). Distribution of this stamp in Sicily (Palazzolo Acreide, Licata, Selinunte) as well as in southern Italy, southern France and eastern Spain: Olcese 2010, 94. For the dating, Olcese 2010, 93 and Panella 2010, 31–2. The Originally I dated this stamp to the first half of the third century BC, and suggested that it belonged to an MGS V amphora (Lindhagen 2006, 54), in the belief that Greek stamps on the 'ancient' Greco-Italic MGS V amphorae disappeared when MGS VI started production. It is now known, however, that Greek stamps did continue alongside Latin ones in the second half of the third century. A fragmentary stamp with an A (surface find without context), in the same fabric as that of the ANΔPΩNOΣ stamp, can only be dated approximately to the third century BC (p. 183, no. 20).
156. A rim of MGS VI is reported from Marina di Caronía, with a fabric described as orange with only a few, small, white inclusions (Bonanno 2009, 34, cat. no. 28).
157. Peacock and Williams 1986, 87 and 90.
158. Riley 1979, 135; Peacock and Williams 1986, 90.
159. Peacock 1971.
160. Zevi 1966. It has long been well known that these containers, produced mainly in the famous grape-growing territories of Fondi, Caecuba, Falernum and Pompeii, held wine, as is also attested by the many *tituli picti* (Tchernia 1986, 45). Kilns have been found at Fondi and Sinuessa, in the area of *ager Falernus*: it was at Fundi (Fondi) that Pliny tells us these famous *grands crus* were produced (*NH* 14. 61 and 65; 17.31).
161. Peacock and Williams 1986, 86.
162. Ollà 2001, 47.
163. Rasocolmo C, 150/75 BC? (Dressel 1A), Vulcano, *c.* 100/80 BC (Dressel 1B); Scialandro A and B, mid/late second century BC (varieties of Dressel 1A); Cala Mindola, *c.* 100/25 BC (Dressel 1B and C) (Parker 1992a, nos 1229, 1048–49 and 150).
164. Illustrated also by the finds from the 2003–05 excavations: Bonanno 2009, tav. XXV, graph 3.
165. Bonanno 2009, 34. Dressel 1A: cat. nos 34–6, 39–40, 44–5, tav. III, tav. XXV, graph 3; Dressel 1B: cat nos 37–8, 41 and 43, tav. XXV, graph 3; Dressel 1C: cat. nos 33 and 42, tav. XXV, graph 3. The dominance of Dressel 1 amphorae is also attested at Tindari (Leone and Spigo 2008, 73).
166. Bonanno 2008, 34.
167. For finds of Campanian Dressel 1 at Carthage, Martin-Kilcher 1993, 274–5.
168. Tchernia 1969; Baldacci 1972; Peacock and Williams 1986, 82; Manacorda and Pallecchi 2012.
169. Empereur and Hesnard 1987, 34.

170. Bonanno 2008, 45, 8e, n. 56. A rim from Marina di Caronía may possibly be of the Brindisi type from Apani (compare Lentini et al. 2002, 99, fig. 29, no. 40 with Palazzo 2013, 23, fig. 87).
171. Caflisch 1991, 196.
172. Campana B is found at Syracuse, Agrigento, Heraclea Minoa, Solunto and Monte Iato (Caflisch 1991, 197). It is doubtful whether any finds from Morgantina can be attributed to this category (personal information from Dr. Shelley Stone).
173. Caflisch 1991, 180.
174. Capo Graziano A (Parker 1992a, no. 233).
175. Bonanno and Sudano 2006, 439, n. 19; for Campana 'B-ish' ware, Caflisch 1991, 197 ('B-oïd').
176. Käch 2006, 612.
177. Bailey 1980, 338–9, Q 713, pl. 133.
178. See pp. 71–2 (regional MGS V).
179. Bonanno 2008, 47.
180. Cabella et al. 2008.
181. Lamboglia 1952, 139.
182. Bernabò Brea and Cavalier 1965a, 249, n. 4.
183. Stone 1984, 99–100.
184. Wilson 1988, 240, n. 154, and 257–8. Campana C ends by *c.* 25 BC at Morgantina and most other sites (personal information from Dr Shelley Stone).
185. Morel 1981, 45.
186. Curcio and Pelagatti 1970, 469.
187. Stone 1984, 262.
188. It is reported in considerable quantity at Lipari, Panarea and Tindari. Curcio and Pelagatti (1970, 467–9) considered these finds as belonging to Campana A ware produced at Ischia, but this seems unlikely in view of the plentiful evidence that we have now of a north Sicilian production.
189. Stone 1984, 125; Curcio and Pelagatti 1970, 467–9; Benoît 1961, 75; Bernabò Brea and Cavalier 1965a, 249, n. 4; Caflisch 1991, 236–7.
190. The diagnostic fragments which can be included in the category of Campana A shapes were *c.* 20 (around 55% of Campana ware) compared to 15 (40%) for Campana C, all from Marina di Caronía.
191. Stone 1984, 271; Carettoni 1959, 301.
192. The open forms include Morel types 1300 and 1400; Bonanno and Sudano 2006, 439.
193. Bonanno 2009, 30, cat. nos 4–7; Bonanno 2008, 39–50.
194. Morel form 2255: Bonanno 2009, 30, cat. nos 8–10.
195. Perhaps Morel form 2574a1: cf. Caflisch 1991, no. 881, Taf. 7, Abb. 28.
196. Bonanno 1997–98, 445, n. 27.
197. Stone 1984, 99–100.
198. Bonanno and Sudano 2006, 439.
199. Carettoni 1959, 301–45.
200. Morel forms 2352 and 1440: Bonanno 2008, 30, cat. no. 11.
201. Morel forms 2266a and 1252a1: Bonanno 2008, 42–3, tav. 3a, 5a, 3c and 5b.
202. Black-gloss vessels at Morgantina with a fabric similar to this are considered by Stone to be locally made, possibly a forerunner to Campana C production (personal information from Dr. Shelley Stone).
203. Wilson 1990, 253.
204. Personal information from Dr. Shelley Stone. The mould has a ring foot and a hemispherical body. The interior has three friezes incuse, of which the uppermost depicts isolated beads between reels, the central frieze *boukrania* alternating with lozenge-shaped leaves, and the lowest vertical leaves.
205. Wilson 1990, 253; Caflisch 1991, 228.
206. Only one fragment is recorded in Bonanno 2009, cat. no. 143, fig. 12bis.
207. Bailey 1980, 315 (Q677), also found at Tindari, Palermo, Himera and Solunto, but outside the north coast only at Marsala and Agrigento. Other Bailey types represented at Caronía include Bailey Q101, Q445, Q450 and Q706.
208. Collura 2016, 147, no. 192; 170, fig. 192.
209. Types Q678–9 in Bailey 1980, 315–16.
210. Collura 2016, 152, n. 134, T12–14.
211. Appendix 2, sample 6, Fig. A2.7.
212. Bonanno 2009, 49, cat. no. 43, tav. IV.
213. Stone 2014, 169–70.
214. Wilson 1988, 244; Stone 2014, 169–92.
215. About 25 fragments are reported from the Bonanno excavations (Bonanno 2009, 31, tav. XXVI, graph 5).
216. Bonanno 1993–94, 970, n. 25.
217. Lamboglia 1951; Biondi 2002. Morgantina has huge amounts of 'Republican red-gloss pottery' (personal information from Dr Shelley Stone).
218. Bonanno 1993–94, 973.
219. They were also very common in the Bonanno excavations (Bonanno 2009, 31, cat. no. 140, tav. X).
220. Bonanno 1993–94, 981.
221. Lentini et al. 2002, 87, fig. 15.
222. Collura 2016, 146, no. 184; 169, no. 184.
223. Maña 1951; van der Werff 1977–78.
224. Ramón 1995.
225. Empereur and Hesnard 1987, 38.
226. Van der Werff 1977–78, 173, fig. 16, 1–3.
227. Pliny, *NH* 14.8.1.
228. See the survey of Late Hellenistic Punic amphora shapes in Ramón 1995, 501, fig. 140; Curtis 1991, 41–3, fig. 1.
229. Van der Werff 1977–78, 193, 195 and 197.
230. Van der Werff 1977–78, 178–80.
231. Just a few fragments of 'anfore neo-puniche' are reported by Bonanno (2008a, 35, tav. XXV, graph 4), but this rather reflects the fact that the material has not yet been studied in detail; the real number must be much higher. None is illustrated in the publication.
232. Ramón 1995, 633–5, figs 267–9, maps 79–83.
233. Ramón 1995, 215–16. Maña C is also Ramón type 7.4.2.1–7.4.3.3.
234. Ramón 1995, 218.
235. Ramón 1995, 639, fig. 273, map 92.
236. Hesnard 1980, 150.
237. One find from Carthage had a Punic graffito on the inside of the rim (Martin-Kilcher 1993, 285, n. 88).
238. Martin-Kilcher 1993, 285.

239. Ramón 1995, 536, fig. 173, no. 224; van der Werff 1977–78, 190, fig. 6, no. 034-209.
240. Carettoni 1959, 303, no. 4, n. 3: [ΕΠΙ ΑΡΙΣΤΑ]ΝΑΚΤΟΣ ΥΑΚΙΝΘΙΟΥ ('in the priesthood of Aristanax, in the month of Hyakinthios'); ΘΕΟΦΙΛΟΥ ('[product of] Theophilos'), second half of the second century BC; ibid., 323–4, no. 5, n. 1: ΕΠΙ ΠΕΙΣΙ[ΣΤΡΑΤΟΥ] ΑΓΡΙΑΝΙΟΥ ('in the priesthood of Peisistratos, in the month of Agrianios'); [ΕΠΙ ΑΡΙ]ΣΤΟΔΑΜΟΥ ΠΕΔΑΓΕΙΤΝΟΥ ('in the priesthood of Aristodamos, in the month of Pedageitnos'), anchor-shaped stamp; ibid., 333, no. 12, n. 3: ΑΓΑΘΟΚΛΕΥΣ ('[product] of Agathokles'), who was active between 220 and 180 BC; ibid., 334, no. 19, n. 3: ΕΠΙ ΘΕΡΣΑΝΔΡΟΥ ('in the priesthood of Thersander'), second half of the second century BC; ΤΙΜΟΥΣ ('[product] of Timos'), widespread in both Sicily and Italy.
241. Denaro 1995, 185, fig. 1.
242. Bonanno 1997–98, 405, n. 4.
243. The period from *c.* 210 to 175 BC is the peak of Rhodian imports at Lilybaeum (Vandermersch 1994, 120).
244. Tchernia 1986, 105.
245. Bonanno 1997–98, 447; Collura 2016, 22, n. 40.
246. One of the stamps is published in Bonanno 2009, 33, cat. no. 26, fig. 1, tav. III. I thank Fabrizio Sudano for this information. Cf. Finkielsztejn (2001, 135) in Garozzo 2003, 594, n. 390.
247. Collura 2016, 22, tav. I, nos 8–10.
248. Bonanno 2008, 53.
249. Bezeczky 2013, 59, pls 60 and 50.
250. Appendix 2, sample 13, pp. 171–2 with Fig. A2.15.
251. Tchernia 1986, 105.
252. For instance, they are found at Pompeii (Empereur and Hesnard 1987, 22).
253. Bonanno 1997–98, 405, n. 4.
254. Empereur and Hesnard 1987, 22.
255. A Rhodian stamp of this producer is known at Erice (Garozzo 2003, 631; 2011, 270–2).
256. Grace 1934, 56.
257. Peacock and Williams 1986, 99.
258. Riley 1979, 156–7; Peacock and Williams 1986, 100–01; Martin-Kilcher 1994, II, 428. Riley describes the fabric as cream or buff (7.5 YR 7/4–6/4–10 YR 8/3–7/3), sometimes with dull red or red grits and with moderate amounts of mica.
259. Lindhagen 2009, 86.
260. Peacock and Williams 1986, 99.
261. Lindhagen 2009. XRF-analyses have been undertaken on stamped amphorae from both the Italian and Dalmatian coasts in addition to finds from the presumed kiln-site at Vis/Issa. The analyses have shown that fragments from both sides of the Adriatic are identical to each other as well as to finds from Vis (Lindhagen forthcoming c). Royal 2012 puts the Dalmatian production in the context of the intense eastern Adriatic trading activity, based on shipwreck evidence. Forti (2011, 234), Menchelli (2011, 239) and Manacorda (2011, 268) all seem to accept the possibility of a central Dalmatian production, but regard it as one among many. Carre et al. (2014, 427), who catalogue the production sites along the Adriatic coast of Italy, accept the possibility of a production of Greco-Italic amphorae at Issa, but oddly dismiss a connection there with wine. Panella (2010) rules out a central Dalmatian production altogether. Cf. now Pilar Eberle and Le Queré 2017 (33, n. 22), who maintain that Panella 2010 and Carre et al. 2014 'clearly have overstated their argument when they argue that there was no production of amphorae in Dalmatia'. Forti (2011, 236) admits similarities between amphora materials at Picenum and those of Dalmatia. See also Lindhagen 2013 for the close links between the freedmen active in the wine-trade at Narona and Delos, and Sondi and Slovenec 2003 for chemical analysis of Lamboglia 2 from the eastern Adriatic coast.
262. Cipriano and Carre 1989, 96. See also note 271.
263. Peacock and Williams 1986, 9.
264. Empereur and Hesnard 1987, 33–4.
265. Calle et al. 2014.
266. Formenti, Hesnard and Tchernia 1978.
267. Denaro 1995, 189.
268. Agatharchides of Knidos wrote in the second century BC about the wine from Issa that 'tasted better than any other' (Agatharchides, in Athenaeus 1.52).
269. Kirigin et al. 2006, 193.
270. Lindhagen 2009, 85.
271. Stamps have been found at Syracuse, Morgantina, Erice, Marsala, Segesta, Palermo and Agrigento (for the last five places, Garozzo 2011, 525–39).
272. Capo Graziano H (off Filicudi), Ognina, Triscina B, Marzamemi G, Punta Scario C, Lipari and Plemmyrio outside Syracuse: Denaro 1995, 186, fig. 2.
273. Bonanno 2008, 47, tav. 9d.
274. Cambi 1989, 321–2.
275. *CIL* III.14265; Cambi 1989, 321.
276. Peacock and Williams 1986, 100.
277. Denaro 1995, 186, fig. 2; 189–91.
278. Martin-Kilcher 1994, II, 428; . . . 'hellbeigem, fast weisslichem feinem Ton mit grossen roten Einschlüssen . . .'.
279. Lindhagen 2009, 85. The same error has been made at Tindari, where a Lamboglia 2 rim has been identified as a Dressel 6 because of the square rim (Ollà 2008, 280, tav. 1. AR/2).
280. Lindhagen 2009. It is, however, present at both Carthage and Berenice (Riley 1979, 151–7; Martin-Kilcher 1993).
281. Lindhagen 2009, 96–7, fig. 5.
282. The Dressel 6B amphora carried olive oil from Istria in the northern Adriatic. The finds from the villa of Laecanius Bassus on the island of Brioni near Pula in Istria (Bezeczky 1998) show without doubt that the type was used as an olive-oil container. The oil seems not to have been distributed to Sicily or the central Mediterranean, probably because of a regional production of oil in Sicily itself, and because substantial quantities of imported Baetican oil, which did reach Sicily, prevented Istrian competition. It is also true that the Dressel 6B amphorae in general seem to have been aimed principally at the markets of northern Italy as well as

north of the Alps for the legions stationed there (Cipriano and Mazzochin 2000, 150–91). This is also indicated by the fact that very few shipwrecks carrying Dressel 6B have been identified in the Adriatic, compared with the enormous quantity of Lamboglia 2 cargoes. Only one small-scale shipwreck with Dressel 6 on board is known from the central Dalmatian coast (Cambi 1989, 323 and 336).

283. Muscolino 2006.
284. Collura 2016, 132; 142, nos 101–2 (photos on 162).
285. Appendix 2, samples 7 and 8, p. 171 with Figs A2.8–9.
286. Ibid., sample 8, Fig. A2.9.
287. Ibid., p. 176, for changing manufacturing traditions over time. It must be stressed that the Dressel 2/4 amphorae made at Caronía might have been produced for a period as long as 150 years.
288. Ollà 2001, 47–8, fig. 2; 54, no. 2; Pesavento Mattioli 2001, 10–11, fig 2.5; Giorgetti and Gonzalez Muro 2011, 111–12, fig. 14; Ollà 2008, 281, tav. 1, AR/5 (example of reduced size). The export to Pompeii of Taormina wine in Dressel 2/4 containers, but also in other types (mainly Schöne 11/Pompeii 2020/Dressel 26, but also other varieties), is documented on a substantial scale (more than 150 identified containers), principally through *tituli picti* naming the contents: Peña 2007a.
289. Bonanno 2008, 47, tav. 10a.
290. Sangineto 2002, 213.
291. Sangineto 2002, 214, n. 61; also n. 62 for Dressel 2/4 amphorae, produced in Bruttium, being found also in Campania and Tuscany.
292. Another is published in Bonanno 2009, 35, cat. no. 32, tav. III.
293. Ollà 2001, 48, figs 5–6.
294. One find has been made at Tindari: it is uncertain whether it is of local or Gaulish origin (Ollà 2008, 280).
295. Peacock and Williams 1986, 96; Domergue 1973, 112–15; van der Werff 1986, 114; Bernal et al. 2003, 312. Alcamo Marina: Giorgetti 2006. For thin-section analysis of these amphorae, Capelli and Piazza 2006.
296. Domergue 1973, 112–15; van der Werff 1986, 114.
297. Bernal et al. 2003, 312.
298. Curtis 1984, 58–9; Bernal et al. 2003; Domergue (1973, 115) considers that these amphorae most likely contained salted fish and/or *garum*.
299. Domergue 1973, 113.
300. Types 8.2.1.1 and 9.1.1.1: Ramón 1995, 225–7.
301. Albrecht and Loeschcke 1942, 105.
302. Zevi 1966, 222, n. 47.
303. Lindhagen 2006, 66–7.
304. Botte 2009, 162; 2018, 383.
305. See above, p. 78, fig. 4.17; also p. 82.
306. Ramón type 9.1.1.1: Ramón 1995, 226–7; 586, fig. 223, nos 826–9.
307. Purpura 1985, 68–9, fig. 18. Finds have been made also of wine containers including Greco-Italic and Dressel 1, but it is not impossible that they contained wine used in the process of making '*oeno-garum*', a type of *garum* mixed with wine (Curtis 1991, 8, n. 12; 165, n. 25).
308. Callender 1965, 13. The shipwreck of Grado in the Adriatic, dating to the first half or the middle of the second century AD, carried exclusively fish products in several different types of containers, many of them obviously reused. One Dressel 21/22 amphora was part of the cargo, but unfortunately no remains of its contents were preserved (Auriemma 2000, 46).
309. Karivieri and Forsell 2008; Lindhagen forthcoming b.
310. Curtis 1988; Auriemma 2000, 45.
311. Giorgetti 2006. See also Ollà 2015 for a fish-salting installation at Milazzo, where Dressel 21/22 were also produced. The types there, however, have different rims than those from Caronía, judging from the published photographs.
312. Denaro 1995, 197.
313. Belvedere et al. 1993, 219.
314. On the large quantity from Monte Iato, which in shape and also in fabric looks similar but not identical with that at Caronía, Palaczyk 2014.
315. A certain Ceionius Fructuarius ('rich in fruits'), is known from a funerary inscription found in Naples, and it has been suggested that he was the same man as this Ceionius Maximus, since the name *Fructuarius* occurs on *tituli picti* of Campanian Dressel 21/22 amphorae recording fruit as the contents (Botte 2009). It seems however, in the light of the new discoveries, that this suggestion can now be ruled out.
316. Lo Cascio 1990, 33–9.
317. Rizzo 1993, 219–20.
318. Solunto: Parker 1992a, no. 1052, Scoglio della Formica A, second century BC, containing mostly Punic (Maña C) amphorae. The two Dressel 21/22 amphorae were included by Tusa as perhaps coming from this wreck, but this is not certain. Panarea (wreck II): Tusa 2010, 269.
319. Sangineto 2002, 213–14.
320. Athenaeus 5.209.
321. Silius Italicus, *Pun*. 14.251.
322. Locally-produced Dressel 2/4, incidentally, account for another third of that total. The fragments reported in Bonanno 2009 (35, tav. XXV, graph 3), approximately 12, is only a small fraction of the total of Dressel 21/22 amphorae found in her excavations.
323. Bonanno 2008, 45, tav. 8d.
324. See colour Pl. 12; also Lindhagen forthcoming b.
325. Appendix 2, samples 4 and 11–12, Figs A2.5 and 12–14.
326. Ibid., sample 12, p. 171 with Figs 2.13–14.
327. Belvedere et al. 1993, 219.
328. Wilson 1988, 287.
329. In *contrada* Lineri: Collura 2016, 288–9. The bricks produced here measure 50 x 35 cm or 35 x 20 x 8/11 cm (rectangular) and 50 x 50 x 8/9 cm (square).
330. In *contrada* Sugherita: Collura 2016, 43, 13, 208, 225 and 252.
331. Zevi 1966, 216.
332. *Ostia* III, 502; Tchernia 1986, 236–8.
333. Arthur 1982; Panella 1989, 141–3.
334. Peña 1999, 155.
335. The 2003–05 excavations yielded nearly 40 fragments in addition to those recorded in 1999–2001 (Bonanno 2009, 34–5, tav. XXV, graph 3).

336. Bezeczky 2013, 131; pl. 78, 323–4 and 326.
337. Appendix 2, sample 2, p. 170 with Fig. A2.3. The golden mica on the surface was, however, not discernible in the small thin-section made of a sample.
338. Stone 2014, 214–15.
339. See pp. 18–19 above. The Bonanno excavations reported about 50 fragments (Bonanno 2008, 32, cat. nos 145–6, 148, figs 13–15; cat. nos 153–4, tav. XXIV, graph 1; tav. XXVI, graph 5).
340. Mandruzzato 1988, 424.
341. Hedinger 1999.
342. Stone 2014, 209–28.
343. For a study of undecorated *terra sigillata* in Sicily, Polito 2000.
344. Leone and Spigo 2008, 169–77.
345. Cascella and Collura 2016, 393–412.
346. Plates or platters of forms 18–21 are especially common, as well as hemispherical cups (Forms 33–34): Ettlinger et al. 1990. Also common are cups in a range of other shapes in forms 7, 17, 23 and 46. Cf. Cascella and Collura 2016, 399–401; Collura 2016, 224, no. 79. For the stamps, Oxé, Comfort and Kenrick 2000, *passim*; for a discussion and a list of stamps found just in Sicily, Malfitana 2004a.
347. Ettlinger et al. 1990, forms 10–12 (Goudineau 6 and 15), all typical early Arretine products, while forms Goudineau 12 and 27 have been found in the upper town: Bonanno 1993–94, 967, n. 19.
348. Ettlinger et al. 1990, forms 18 and 20.
349. Mandruzzato 1988, 424–9 and 433–6. The type is Ettlinger et al. 1990, form 34/Goudineau 38. Also represented are fragments of form 23.2 / Goudineau 40 (mid-first century AD), and one of form 29, Tiberian/Flavian.
350. Bonanno and Sudano 2006, 440, n. 28; Bonanno 2009, 32, cat. no. 153; for the stamp, Oxé, Comfort and Kenrick 2000, no. 1213.
351. Bonanno and Sudano 2006, 440; Bonanno 2009, 32 and 56, cat. no. 154 (who records it as C ENT(1) FIRM(I), not realizing that an S is ligatured with the E; she mistakenly confuses it with Firmus, a Po-plain potter); Oxé, Comfort and Kenrick 2000, no. 1869.4 (and no. 1328.1 for Optatus [1]).
352. Wilson 1990, 253, n. 82; Burgio 2008, no. 32, platter with stamp, LR]ASI PIS; another stamp, LRPIS, was a chance surface find made by the author in April 2004.
353. Bonanno and Sudano 2006, 440, n. 28; Bonanno 2009, 32, cat. no. 153.
354. The potter Ateius is well represented at Monte Iato: some of his production has been attributed to Pisa. Bettina Hedinger (1999) points out the excellent geographical position of Pisa to take advantage of exports to Sicily.
355. P. MESSENIVS MENOPILVS (in a square), central Italian, *c.* 40/1 BC; CISSV/RASINI (in a square), Rasinius (owner), Cissus (slave maker), *c.* 20 BC and later (Carettoni 1959, 333, no. 10; 334, no. 17). Campania was suggested by Wilson (1988, 246, n. 180) as a possible location for Cissus; Oxé, Comfort and Kenrick 2000, no. 1642, however, leave the question open.
356. PHILO, probably *Philositus Titi* from Arezzo (Bonanno and Arcifa 2009, 609, n. 20; Oxé, Comfort and Kenrick 2000, 1452); CAE, Augustan period (Bonanno and Arcifa 2009, 609, n. 20; Malfitana et al. 2008, 313).
357. Kenrick 1985, 283–302.
358. Soricelli 2004, with Sicilian distribution on 303, with references (23% of stamped ware at Lipari, and *c.* 15% at Catania, but only 4% at Syracuse and barely more at Solunto). For the few examples of this ware at Morgantina, Stone 2014, 223–7.
359. Hedinger 1999, 243.
360. Tindari: Leone and Spigo 2008, 332. For volute lamps, Bailey 1980, 126–222 (his Types A–D).
361. Four are reported from the Marina di Caronía excavations of Bonanno (2009, 33, tav. XXVII, graph 7), and others from the 1993 work in *contrada* Sotto San Francesco in the upper town (Bonanno 1993–94, 970).
362. First half of the first century AD: Bonanno 1997–98, 48–9, figs 16–17. For parallels, Bailey 1980, Q1025 and Q1050. The decoratve ornament is in the form of the female genitalia.
363. Type Broneer XXI: Carettoni 1959, 312–13, no. 5, fig. 19c; Bailey 1980, Q1024, pls 32 and 35.
364. Bailey 1980, 133, Q766.
365. Bailey 1980, 191, Q972, pl. 23.
366. Bailey 1980, 23–34 (also known as *Leibundgut* XVI–XVII).
367. Bernabò Brea and Cavalier 1965a, tav. 229.3.
368. Bonanno 2009, 46, tav. 21, E24.1.
369. Bailey 1980, 293–313 (Type O). The more common type (Type P: ibid., 314–18) is not widespread before AD 79: they are late Flavian to Antonine.
370. Borgard 2000, 255–344.
371. Borgard et al. 2005; Pesavento Mattioli 2001, 10; Pliny, *NH* 35.184.
372. Denaro 1995, 193–5.
373. Denaro 1995, 186, fig. 2.
374. Bonanno 2009, tav. XXV, graph 3
375. See Chapter 2, p. 38.
376. Mayet 1980, 203–04; Wilson 1988, 257.
377. Mayet 1980, 204; 222, fig. 7.
378. *A pareti sottili insabbiate*: Bonanno 1993–94, 972, fig. 7, tav. XCVI.
379. Bonanno and Sudano 2006, 440.
380. Oxé, Comfort and Kenrick 2000, 213, no. 748. It is possible that a circular stamp from Monte Iato is of the same type (Hedinger 1999, 187, S263, Abb. 22).
381. Rotroff 1997, 408, no. 1647, pl. 131; see also Kenrick 1985, fig. 10, no. 86.2.
382. Stone 2014, 273–4, n. 202.
383. Wilson (2000a, 536) convincingly argues that ΑΓΥΡΙΟ is likely to indicate the workshop location rather than merely referring to the town of origin of the producer (for the latter view, see Branciforti 1992, 105). In some cases, ΑΓΥ is placed prior to the name Proklos, implying that the lamp was produced at Agyrion by Proklos (because if the label was intended only to indicate where Proklos hailed from, it would always have been placed after the name). For a different view,

that the lamps were made in Catania, Manganaro 2003.
384. Wilson 1990, 260; Deneauve 1969, no. 644; Wilson 2000a, 536, n. 56; Branciforti 1992, 105. The type (cf. Bailey 1988, 209–210, Q1861–7) has also been found at Agira, Assoro, Aidone, Catania, Centuripe, Troina, Tindari, Taormina, Syracuse, Halaesa, Sabucina Bassa, Piano Camera (near Gela), Piano del Conte, Butera, Chiaramente Gulfi, Solunto, Segesta, Palermo, Termini Imerese and Sciacca (Wilson 2000a, 551, n. 56, fig. 322).
385. Bailey 1988, 208; Panvini and Zavettieri 1993–94, 854–6.
386. Bonacasa Carra and Panvini 2002, 253–4, no. 45, fig. 31; 256, no. 56, fig. 38c.
387. Bonanno and Sudano 2006, 439–40, fig. 4; Bonanno 2009, 33, cat. nos 165–6, fig. 17, tav. XXVII, graph 7; Collura 2016, 149–50, nos 230, 232 and 236; 174, nos 230, 232 and 236.
388. Several exact parallels from the necropolis of Sambuco and from a rural building north-east of Gela: Bonacasa Carra 1993–94, tav. LXIII, fig. 2; tav. LXVI, fig. 2; Panvini and Cammineci 1993–94, 835, n. 33, tav. LV, fig. 2.
389. Carettoni 1961, 283–4, no. 4, fig. 20.
390. Branciforti 1992, 105.
391. Peacock and Williams 1986, 115–16. Previously thought to have reached Rome by *c.* 50 BC, Haltern 70 amphora are now seen to be not earlier than *c.* 30 BC, i.e. they are a new production in early Augustan times: Rizzo and Moreno Mégias 2019, 28.
392. Denaro 1995, 192, fig. 5.
393. Parker 1992a, 235.
394. Peacock and Williams 1986, 136.
395. See, for example, Martin-Kilcher 1994, volume II.
396. Ollà 2008; find-spots in Wilson 1988, 267, nn. 276–8 (one is Castagna: Wilson 1985b, 24, fig. 19.4).
397. The same is true for the material from the Bonanno excavations, with only one or two fragments reported (Bonanno 2009, 35, tav. XXV, graph 3). Dressel 20 amphorae continued to be made until *c.* 260/70, but the Baetican oil industry did not cease then: oil was now transported in Dressel 23 containers, production sites for which have recently been found by fieldwork in the Genil valley, a tributary of the Guadalquivir, and continued into the fifth century (Bourgeon 2017). It reached elsewhere in Spain then (far outnumbering, for example, African and eastern oil amphorae in fifth-century deposits at Tarragona), but it is not known if (and it seems unlikely that) Baetican oil reached the central Mediterranean in any appreciable quantity then.
398. Cambi 1989, *passim*.
399. Cambi 1989, 388.
400. Martin-Kilcher 1994, 393–409.
401. Denaro 1995.
402. Parker 1992a, 312.
403. Martin-Kilcher 1993, 282–3.
404. In addition, four or five fragments have been recovered from the excavations of Bonanno (2009, 34, tav. XXV, graph 3).
405. It corresponds to fabric 26 from Augst (Martin-Kilcher 1994, 3, 620). It is also attested at Carthage.
406. For the sources on the contents of Gaulish amphorae, *Ostia* III, 547–51; Widemann et al. 1979.
407. *Ostia* III, 201.
408. Laubenheimer 1985.
409. Peacock and Williams 1986, 143; Martin-Kilcher 1994, 360.
410. Denaro 1995, 191: from Cattolica Eraclea, Favignana (Marsala), Panarea and Segesta. For the example from Castagna (Cattolica Eraclea on Denaro's map), Wilson 1985b, 22 and fig. 19.2; 1988, 266.
411. Wilson 1988, 266, n. 272. See also Malfitana et al. 2013, 425 and 455, fig. 3, who conclude that only small quantities arrived in the island.
412. The numbers of 'Gaulish' amphorae from the 2003–05 excavations (about 14 fragments) also suggest a not inconsiderable presence of this type (Bonanno 2009, 35, tav. XXV, graph 3).
413. Martin-Kilcher 1994, 621 (TG 31).
414. Ibid., 620–1 (TG 27).
415. Denaro 1995, 186, fig. 2.
416. Wilson 1988, 249, n. 193.
417. Wilson 1990, 253; Parker 1992a, no. 784.
418. Bonanno and Sudano 2006, 440, fig. 5 (the shape is Dragendorff 29b). Ardacius specialized in Dragendorff 27 cups (for this shape in Italian *sigillata*, Ettlinger et al. 1990, Form 32).
419. Bonanno 2009, 32, tav. XXVI, graph 5.
420. See, for example, Wilson 1990, 264.
421. *Ostia* III, 562 and 568–71.
422. Revilla Calvo 2001.
423. The finer of the two fabrics described by Peacock and Williams 1986, 167. One fragment of the coarser fabric came from the 2003–05 excavations.
424. Five fragments were found in the Bonanno excavations (2009, 36, cat. nos 48–9, tav. IV, tav. XXV, graph 4).
425. Hayes 1972, 6–7 and 288. For a comprehensive account of African red slip pottery all over Sicily, see now the magisterial two-volume survey edited by Malfitana and Bonifay (2016).
426. Carettoni 1959.
427. For African Red Slip in Sicily, see note 425 above and also Vitale in Bonacasa Carra and Vitale 1997–98, 407–13 and 424–47.
428. Bonanno 1993–94, 963, n. 16.
429. Hayes 1972, 33–4, no. 18.
430. Ibid., 21–5.
431. Ibid., 234, fig. 40.
432. Bonanno and Sudano 2006, 443; Bonanno 2008, 32.
433. Cascella and Collura 2016, 396, fig. 2.
434. Robinson 1959, 43; Reynolds 2005, 564–5 (for an origin in Cilicia).
435. On this ware Lund 2005; in Sicily, Wilson 1988, 242–3; for a distribution map of it in Sicily, Malfitana 2004b, 248, fig. 5.
436. Stone 1984, 196, n. 198; Carettoni 1961, 318, n. 5; 316, fig. 23F; Morel 1976, 492, nn. 70–1.
437. About five sherds of eastern *terra sigillata* A are reported from Bonanno's excavations (Bonanno and Sudano 2006, 440; Bonanno 2009, 32, tav. XXVI, graph 5).

438. Cascella and Collura 2016, 397, fig. 4.
439. Arthur 1989. In the preliminary publication of the finds made in 2002, I also used the label Keay 52, but I have chosen here to call them, more correctly, Termini 151/354 containers.
440. *Ostia* I, tav. 26, figs 455–6.
441. Keay 1984, 268.
442. Pacetti 1998, 35.
443. See, for example, Carignani et al. 1986, 284, fig. 7.
444. Arthur 1989; Pacetti 1998, 187–9.
445. Gargallo di Castel Lentini 1970, 315.
446. Ollà 2001, 49–53 and 56–8, nos 13–24; Wilson 2000b, 362, fig. 20D–E; Rizzo et al. 2014 (Agrigento); Branciforti 2006, 94–101 and 143–5; Amari 2008 (kilns at S. Venera al Pozzo near Acireale).
447. Ollà 2004; Tigano 2009; Bonanno 2009; Rizzo 1993.
448. Belvedere et al. 1993, 223–5.
449. Ollà 2004, 113.
450. See for example Reynolds 1995, 69; Peña 1999, 79; Whitehouse et al. 1985, 190–200.
451. Tchernia 1986, 236–8.
452. Panella 1989, 139–78. For the flat-bottomed Sant'Alessio type amphora, Muscolino 2005–06.
453. Ollà 2001, 58, no. 22. Its shape is closer to that of Termini 151/354 amphora than it is to a Keay 52 one.
454. Panella 1993, 647–8.
455. If we can believe SHA, *Aur*. 48.76.
456. Pacetti 1998.
457. Peña 1999, 18.
458. *Expositio* 65.14–15.
459. See the distribution map in Reynolds 1995, fig. 165.
460. It depends on which date is the correct one for the city walls: Cambi 1989, 333–5.
461. McCann 1994, 36. Both examples from the wreck were reused as water-raisers, as indicated by the small hole beneath the handle. A fabric very similar to that from Caronía was identified in the Termini 151/354 amphorae from the late Roman shipwreck at Skerki bank, north-west of Sicily. Even if those examples cannot in themselves confirm a Sicilian wine export to North Africa, the presence of a complete amphora of the same type, reused in a child's cremation burial at Carthage, proves that these containers did reach Africa (McCann 1994, 35, n. 62). Earlier Sicilian wine-carriers (Middle Roman 1) certainly reached North Africa: e.g. Fig. 4.28d is from El Djem.
462. It is, however, doubtful whether any Sicilian wine arrived at Carthage after the Vandal occupation (Reynolds 1995, 118), because of constant Vandal raiding of Sicilian shores during the mid-fifth century.
463. Scibona 1987.
464. My thanks to Francesco Collura for showing me the site. A few specimens from the kiln-site are depicted in Collura 2016, 253–4, figs 1–3 and 6–7. For the Crypta Balbi amphora type, Arena et al. 2001, 217–18, I.8.19.
465. Scibona and Tigano 2008, 53, D–E, G–H.
466. These are mainly quartz, quartzite, limestone, sandstone, feldspar, mica and occasionally amphiboles, siltite, argillite and calcareous fossils, clinopyroxene, tourmaline and titanite. See Appendix 2, especially pp. 170, 174 (fig. A2.2, thin-section 1) and 176; Cabella et al. 2009.
467. According to Bonanno, this is a 'Byzantine' amphora (no exact type is given) of the sixth or seventh century AD (Bonanno 2009, 40, cat. no. 73, tav. XIV, 5; tav. XVI, fig. 8). The shape is, however, clearly a typical Termini 151/354, and has a rather long neck, with the handles attached to the middle of it (in favour of a fourth-century dating), in contrast to types from the fifth/sixth centuries and later, which usually have short necks, and handles attached immediately below the rim. Bonanno claims that MRA 1 and Keay 52 amphorae are also present in the destruction deposits at Marina di Caronía without providing illustrations. All the 500+ fragments that I have seen from the Lentini excavations are of type Termini 151/354. It is easy to confuse classifications when dealing with small fragments: for example, fifth-century variants have a triangular rim, similar to that on Keay 52 amphorae, but a short neck, unlike the Keay 52 containers, which have a tall neck.
468. Belvedere et al. 1993, 237.
469. Pacetti 1998, 200–01. Fifth-century finds include those from the Temple of Cybele on the Palatine and the Basilica Hilariana on the Caelian.
470. Messina 2000, 113–14.
471. Slej 2008, 225 and 248, no. V-201, pl. 184. A find from Marseille (Fouilles de la Bourse) might have been made at Calacte, on the basis of shape (Sciallano and Sibella 1991, 106: 'amphore Agora M 302/Keay LII'), but fabric analysis is necessary to confirm this.
472. Appendix 2, samples 1 and 5 (p. 170), Figs A2.2 and 6.
473. Peña 1999, 78; Casalini and Crespi 2010, 103, fig. 1; 10–12, fig. 3; 105, fig. 2.1–3.
474. Franco and Capelli 2014a, 352. It is worth underlining that these finds all have fabrics that were considered as products of the kilns of Marína di Caronía, and therefore in all probability provide evidence for close contact between Calacte and these sites.
475. On amphora production at Naxos, Ollà 2001.
476. Pacetti 1998, 197.
477. See notes 463–4 above.
478. Rizzo 1993, 224; Rizzo et al. 2014, 216; Spigo et al. 2006, 453–9.
479. Peña 1999, 78; Pacetti 1998, 199.
480. Arena et al. 2001, 292.
481. Bonanno 2009, 41: they make up only 3.75% of total finds, consisting of approximately 30 fragments. For this ware, Fiertler 2003; Santoro Bianchi et al. 2003; and Tusa et al. 2009, 91–106 and 227–36. On regular imports of North African cookware, beginning in the first quarter of the second century, Malfitana et al. 2013.
482. E.g. Capo Graziano M; the Plemmirio wreck; Capo Ognina (*c*. 250/300 AD): Kapitän 1972, 243–52.
483. Africana 1 amphorae are not usually lined with resin, and so probably contained olive oil (Auriemma 2000, 31; Panella 1993, 631, n. 70). Martin-Kilcher (1994, II, 448) also considers the type to be an oil-carrier.
484. Auriemma 2000, 27–31.

485. *Ostia* III, 576–7.
486. Peña 1999, 23–4.
487. About 26 fragments are reported from the excavations of Bonanno (2009, 35, cat. nos 54–6, tav. IV; tav. XXV, graph 4).
488. Keay 1984, 447.
489. Callender 1965, 135.
490. The type, also known as the 'Ostia IV.142–160', was present in only low numbers in the 2003–05 excavations (Bonanno 2009, 36, tav. XXV, graph 4).
491. For the class (Keay's type Q), see Keay 1984, 197.
492. Burgio 2008, 92, UT 40.1–2, fig. 150.
493. Cf. Keay's fabric 1: Keay 1984, 447.
494. Ibid., 188.
495. Ibid., 193.
496. Ibid., 212.
497. Ibid., 140.
498. Ibid., 142. For the contents, see *Ostia* III, 533.
499. Keay 1984, 450 (his fabric 3).
500. Ibid., 142.
501. Especially the type in Tigano 2009, 180, fig. 16, sep. 47; and 182.
502. Appendix 2, sample 10, p. 171 with Fig. A2.11.
503. The material from the Bonanno excavations seems to confirm that much lower numbers of Africana 2 are present by comparison with those of Africana 1, although the real number of the former is likely to have been much higher than the five fragments reported (Bonanno 2009, 35–6, tav. XXV, graph 4).
504. Riley 1979; *Ostia* III, 584.
505. Giglio Porto, Italy (Parker 1992a, no. 453): Africana 2A, with a pitch lining inside, contained many shells. Cap Blanc, Spain (Parker no. 176): Africana 2B–D contained fish bones and scales. Cap de Garde, Algeria (Parker no. 185): lead labels on eight Africana 2D amphorae referred to the contents as fish-sauce.
506. Martin-Kilcher 1994, II, 449.
507. Martin-Kilcher 1994, II, 448; *Ostia* III, 588 (olive oil?); contrast Lequément 1975 (fish-sauce).
508. Denaro 1995, 202; Parker 1992a, nos 401 and 755.
509. Denaro 1995, 194, fig. 6; 202; and 206, fig. 13.
510. Bonanno 2009, 32, n. 41.
511. Ibid., 32–3, cat. nos 161–2, tav. XIII (Hayes stamped motives of types D1 and D2).
512. Bonanno and Sudano 2006, 443, n. 47; Bonanno 2009, 32, n. 42.
513. Bonanno 1997–98, 428–9, n. 7 (Hayes' stamped decoration type A).
514. At Conventazzo, Hayes forms 67, 80, 91c, 99a and 103 were found (Kislinger et al. 2004, 126–8); at Tindari Hayes forms 80A, 91 and 99 have been recovered from contexts of the late fifth and sixth centuries AD (Leone and Spigo 2008, 199–200).
515. Another fragment with a stamp of the same producer was also found in the 2003–05 campaign (Bonanno and Sudano 2006, 440).
516. Bernabò Brea and Cavalier 1965a, 346–7, date the lamps to AD 50/150 (Lipari). The stamp is very common in the *sub divo* necropolis of *contrada* Lannari, east of Caltanissetta: Panvini and Zavettieri 1993–94, 853, 855, 857, 860 and 865. At the antiquarium of the Roman villa at Patti Marina, 70 km east of Caronía, three examples are displayed (unpublished), and two are known from Tindari (Leone and Spigo 2008, 245).
517. Bailey 1988, 188, Q1705, pl. 14.
518. Deneauve 1969, 180, pl. LXXVI, 828; probably Flavian/Antonine or even later.
519. Bailey 1980, 71–80.
520. Bailey 1988, 188, Q1708, pl. 14; figs 56 and 150 (last quarter of the second or early third century AD).
521. Deneauve 1969, pl. XXXIV, 920–5 (Deneauve type VIIB); also attested at the Sambuco necropolis (Panvini and Zavettieri 1993–94, 856, n. 13).
522. Carettoni 1961, 283. A lamp with the same stamp is known at Cotta in Marocco (Ponsich 1961, no. 344).
523. Bailey 1988, 188–9, Q1709; also attested at the Sambuco necropolis (Panvini and Zavettieri 1993–94, 864, n. 26).
524. Deneauve 1969, pls CVI–CIX.
525. Bonanno and Sudano 2006, 440.
526. Carettoni 1961, 283.
527. Bailey 1988, 181.
528. Vitale in Bonacasa Carra and Vitale 1997–98, 403–05 and 418–20.
529. Type 1: Bonanno and Sudano 2006, 443; Bonanno 2009, 33, cat. nos 170–1, tav. XXVII, graph 7; Collura 2016, 151, no. 252; 175, no. 252.
530. Käch 2006, 212, no. 1128.
531. Bonanno 1995, 47.
532. About 13% of the total number of finds from the 2003–05 excavations, approximately a hundred fragments (Bonanno 2009, 41, tav. XXVII, graph 8). These are only preliminary figures, and only a small part of the actual total found.
533. *Ostia* III, 563 and 566.
534. Parker 1992a, no. 246.
535. Denaro 1995, 194, fig. 6; 202.
536. *Ostia* III, 564 and 568–74.
537. The number from the Bonanno excavations is also quite significant (about 23 fragments: Bonanno 2009, 36, cat. nos 53 and 57–9, tav. IV and XXV, graph 4).
538. Panella (*Ostia* III, 604–05) and Manacorda (1977) considered it an oil container.
539. *Ostia* III, 602–03; Peacock and Williams 1986, 172.
540. Denaro 1995, 194, fig. 6.
541. Only two fragments are reported by Bonanno (2009, 35, cat. no. 60, tav. V, tav. XXV, graph 4), but again this must be due to the highly preliminary character of this publication.
542. Malfitana 2007; Malfitana et al. 2008; Hayes 1972, 412 (and in Kenrick 1985, 338).
543. Malfitana 2007 lists 17 fragments, including one of unknown Sicilian provenance and one in Malta; the others he records are at Messina (3), Milazzo (3), Lipari (2), Syracuse (5) and one each at Ramacca (CT) and Mazzarone (RG). See also Ollà 2004, 110, fig. 1..
544. Malfitana et al. 2008, 26; Kenrick 1985, 338.
545. Bonanno and Sudano 2006, 443; Bonanno 2009, 32, tav. XXVI, graph 5.

546. Peacock and Williams 1986, 130–1; Carandini and Panella 1981.
547. Parker 1989, 650–3 (in Wilson 1990, 267–8, n. 142).
548. Peacock and Williams 1986, 131.
549. Carbè 2008.
550. Carettoni 1959; id. 1961.
551. Carroccio and Collura 2016, 385–7, tav. 1, no. 16.
552. Carbè 2008, 70, nos 73–111; ibid., 69–70, nos 49–53 and 62–8 (Apollonia); Bonsignore and Trifirò 2009, 68, nos 23–9 (Kale Akte).
553. Gàbrici 1927, 121–2; Calciati 1983; Scibona 1987, 9; Carbè 2008, 68, nos 6–18.
554. Mannino 1986–87, 125–7; Caccamo Caltabiano 1999, 295–311.
555. Late third-century BC chronology: Carroccio 2004, *passim* but especially 292 with references; cf. also Caccamo Caltabiano et al. 2004, 58. Early second-century date: Mannino 1986–87, 127 (and note 95 of Ch. 1 above). Late second century BC: Frey-Kupper 2013, 242–4.
556. Frey-Kupper 2013, with discussion in Wilson 2015, especially 556–7. A chronology in the late second century is also supported by Hoover 2012, 148–9.
557. Except for the coins from the mint of Kale Akte, there is only one coin that certainly dates to the first century BC from Marina di Caronía.
558. Bonacic-Mandinic 2014, 203–04, n. 6; 206, n. 15; 215–16, no. 5.
559. The same situation is reflected by the very large quantities of numismatic material from Monte Iato (Frey-Kupper 2013).
560. Scibona and Tigano 2008, 124.

Notes to Chapter Five

1. Braudel's *conjonctures* is difficult to translate; 'trends' or 'rhythms' probably come closest, as 'conjunctures' in English does not work in this context. *Conjonctures* refer essentially to a 'history of the rhythms and forces at work in economic systems, scientific and technological developments, political institutions, conceptual changes, states, societies, civilisations and forms of warfare' (Hughes-Warrington 2014, 22). The Annales school as an inspiration to archaeology: Bintliff 1991. For the settlement history of Kale Akte from a Braudelian perspective, Lindhagen 2012.
2. I have defined these terms as follows: local = produced at Kale Akte or its territory; regional = produced in Sicily (including Lipari) and/or in southern Bruttium; extra-regional = outside this area. Origin has been determined on the basis of general research on pottery, including studies of morphology, *tituli picti*, epigraphic and literary sources, kiln sites and the thin-section analyses discussed in Appendix 2. In this chapter, I use Kale Akte and Calacte interchangeably, the former to refer to the Classical and Hellenistic periods, the latter (its Roman name) to allude to the settlement at Caronía, and especially Marina di Caronía, in imperial times.
3. For Halaesa's coin issues from the late fourth and then the second century BC depicting bunches of grapes (Hoover 2012, nos 182 and 207), and the connection between such motifs and viticulture, see p. 36.
4. Amphorae were the principal containers for foodstuffs in the Mediterranean throughout the period here under consideration. The abundant evidence of the pottery industry from innumerable sites around the Mediterranean, and the use of amphorae well into the Medieval period, make the hypothesis of a sudden change from ceramic containers to wooden barrels unlikely. Tchernia (1986, 290–9) hypothesised that wine amphorae were partly substituted by barrels in the second century AD, but this was necessarily an *argumentum e silentio,* since the wine amphorae of the second and third centuries AD were much less known at the time he was writing. For his latest views on Roman trade, Tchernia 2016. Possible use of skins for local movement of wine is discussed by Lawall 2005, 193.
5. Campagna 2000, 449–50.
6. A similar situation can be postulated for Campania (De Sena and Ikäheimo 2003, 309).
7. See Bekker-Nielsen 2005 for the importance of fish products in the ancient diet. Wine had many functions; it was used for medicinal purposes as well as serving as an important ingredient in cooking; bad wine was used for the slaking of lime kilns and the extinguishing of fires (Peña 1999, 10).
8. Albanese Procelli 1996, 123.
9. For mean capacity of amphorae, see Peña 1999, 197.
10. Trade between Athens and the fish-producing areas in the Black Sea and southern Spain is attested by several ancient authors (Curtis 1991, 126–9).
11. Pliny, *NH* 9.169; Juvenal, *Sat.* 5.93–106; Scramuzza 1937, 352; Curtis 1991, 100, n. 250. Curtis, however, notes that no author mentions salted fish specifically.
12. For discussion on the content of Punic amphorae, see Chapter 4 above, p. 72.
13. Martin-Kilcher 1994, III, 448.
14. Many examples of this amphora type were found at the large *garum* factories at Setùbal, south of Lisbon (Martin-Kilcher 1994, II, 431, n. 552).
15. Wilson 1990, 256.
16. See the survey of Archaic amphorae in Sicily by Albanese Procelli 1996.
17. See Chapter 4, pp. 67–8.
18. Albanese Procelli 1996, 104–10.
19. The MGS II container, which started production in the fifth century BC, dominated markets completely during that century and the next, judging from the finds from the necropolises of Lipari, and other sites on the south Tyrrhenian Sea, such as Messina and Roccagloriosa.
20. Himera (Vassallo 2003); Monte Polizzo (Mühlenbock 2008).
21. Corinthian B amphorae from Kerkyra have been reported from Messina (Spagnolo 2002, 45), Lipari, Roccagloriosa, Solunto, Entella and Gela (Barone et al. 2004), and are also present at Morgantina.
22. At Morgantina, far more Western Greek amphorae were discovered than those of Corinthian B from Kerkyra. The vast majority of amphorae found at Lipari

from the sixth to the third centuries BC were of regional origin, i.e. from Sicily or southern Italy. In fact the proportion of amphorae of regional origin may be even higher, since the Corinthian B category probably also comprises a regional version of that type. A primarily regional trade can also be concluded from the data yielded by a study of Punic amphorae at Solunto.

23. Albanese Procelli 1996, 122, n. 75.
24. Alaimo et al. 2002; Alaimo et al. 2003; Toti 2002.
25. They amount only to a small percentage of amphorae from the Rifriscolaro necropolis at Camarina (Albanese Procelli 1996, 122; Sourisseau 2006). Among the Archaic and Classical amphorae from Messina published by Spagnolo, there are no Punic examples (Spagnolo 2002, 45).
26. For example, at Morgantina and at Monte Polizzo (Mühlenbock 2008). This is especially noteworthy at Monte Polizzo, since that site was in close proximity to the principal Punic settlements in Sicily.
27. Spigo 2000. By this period almost all red-figure and black-gloss pottery at Lipari was Sicilian, except for just a few imports from Magna Graecia. Significantly, not even at Morgantina, where huge amounts of material have been excavated, has Apulian red-figure pottery been detected (pers. comm. Shelley Stone).
28. Bailey 1975, 296.
29. Polizzi 1997, 95.
30. Corretti and Capelli 2003.
31 Arthur 1990, 287–8.
32. Denaro 1995, 187, fig. 1.
33. This is in accordance with Morel's assumption that Campana A pottery was not exported outside the Campanian region before the second century BC.
34. Such is the conclusion provided by work at Monte Iato and Lipari, as well as at San Marco d'Alunzio and elsewhere on the north coast, where little black-gloss from outside the region was ever imported.
35. Caflisch 1991, 107.
36. See Chapter 4, p. 83.
37. See Chapter 4, ibid.
38. Belvedere et al. 1993.
39. *Meligunìs Lipàra* I–XII.
40. Caflisch 1991; Stone 2014.
41. Denaro 1995, 188–9, fig. 3.
42. Lamboglia 1952, 156.
43. See Chapter 4, p. 80.
44. See Chapter 4, ibid.
45. De Sena and Ikäheimo 2003, 309.
46. Denaro 1995, 194, fig. 6; and 202.
47. Peña 1999, 153.
48. Tchernia 1986, 261.
49. Parker 1992a. Since then, of course, a huge amount of fresh underwater excavation and survey has added to his data of 1,189 Mediterranean wreck-sites (up to AD 1500), e.g. a survey of east Mediterranean wrecks yielded a further 457. See now especially J. Strauss at oxrep.classics.ac.uk/databases/shipwrecks_database/. For an excellent overview of the shipwreck evidence in an overall assessment of trade, see now Rice 2016. Recently explored Sicilian shipwrecks await a detailed overview, but some of the key new finds (as well as long-known wrecks) are presented in Tusa 2010 (and for a full publication of one underwater excavation, that of Scauri off Pantelleria, see Tusa et al. 2009).
50. I am aware that it is difficult to count the frequency of a particular type within each cargo, when figures of the percentage of individual amphora shapes present in each cargo are missing. However, in many cases the amphora categories shown in Fig. 5.14 were among the principal cargoes on board.
51. Capo Graziano C, Spanish Dressel 2/4; Panarea (Alberti), probably imported from Pompeii or its region (Parker 1992a, nos 235 and 784).
52. Denaro 1995, 189 and 191.
53. In the index of the amphora types from Mediterranean shipwrecks, only six cargoes have been identified which carried Tripolitanian amphorae, whereas as many as 35 cargoes contained Africana 2, and 16 are known with Africana 1 amphorae on board, usually as the main cargo (Parker 1992a, 514 and 518).
54. Cargoes with amphorae listed under the heading 'cylindrical' total 35 (Parker 1992a, 515).
55. See Chapter 4, pp. 87–8 and Appendix 2, pp. 170–6.
56. See Chapter 4, p. 88.
57. See Chapter 4, pp. 95–7. The Kapitän 1 and 2 containers are the most common eastern imports to the Sicilian east coast during the Severan period (Malfitana, Franco and Di Mauro 2013, 425).

Notes to Chapter Six

1. Temin 2001; 2013. For a somewhat critical attitude to Temin's ideas, Tchernia 2016, 72–96. For a thoughtful discussion of the whole debate, in the context of the Hellenistic market and 'non-market' exchange, see Archibald 2005, especially 10–22.
2. Rostovtzeff 1957.
3. Love 1991, 212; Finley 1973.
4. Love 1991, 212–13.
5. For example, the flourishing trade under the Roman Empire was explained as reflecting provisions from the estates of the senatorial class for their residences in Rome: Whittaker 1983; Tchernia 1986; Manacorda 1989.
6. Paterson 1998, 156.
7. Cohen 2002, 5, with bibliography.
8. Polanyi, Arensberg and Pearson 1957, 68; Polanyi 1944, 63–4; Lowry 1987, 2; Humphreys 1978, 152; Cohen 1992, 4.
9. Polanyi 1977, 35–6.
10. Peter Temin characterises the system in this way: 'A system in which people aim toward a rough balance between the goods and services they receive and those they give to others. The reciprocal obligations are determined by social obligations and tradition, and they change only slowly' (Temin 2001, 170).
11. Polanyi 1977, 35–6.
12. Pryor 1977.
13. Temin 2001, 171.
14. Horden and Purcell 2000, 376; Paterson 1998. Temin

illustrates this using the example of seventeenth- and eighteenth-century England and Holland, which are considered by everyone as market economies based on agriculture. Yet a substantial part of the marketed output was allocated by 'centric transfers' in the form of taxes (Temin 2001, 172).

15. Temin 2001. For a critical discussion of the primitivist position, disagreeing with Polanyi's ideas, Schaps 1998.
16. Although there is a tendency towards greater state control of the economy in late antiquity, everything suggests continuity, and most work on this period presupposes the existence of markets. This is most evidently attested by the price edict of Diocletian, which clearly attempted to control flexible market prices (Temin 2001, 173).
17. Harris (2002, 68) mentions Adam Smith, Karl Marx, Herbert Spencer and Emile Durkheim; also Weber 1947, 225 (in Harris 2002, 71). It must be stressed that specialisation of labour alone is not sufficient to consider an economy a market one (Harris 2002, 72–3).
18. Harris 2002, 69, 88–99.
19. Harris 2002, 71; Weber 1947, 225.
20. *Amphoreaphoros* or *-poios*: *IG* II^2.1554.28–31; *heduoinoi*: Xenophon, *Vect.* 5.3; *luchnopoles*: Aristophanes, *Eq.* 739; *oinopoles*: Theophrastus, *Char.* 30.5; *tarichopoles*: *IG* II^2.1557.68–71; Theophrastus, *Char.* 6.9.; *arguramoibos*: Plato, *Plt.* 289e; *trapezites*: Demosthenes 21.215; 45.63; 36 *passim*; Demosthenes 49 *passim*; Dinarchus 1.43; Theophrastus, *Char.* 21.12. (in Harris 2002, 88–97).
21. Harris 2002, 71.
22. Harris 2002, 71.
23. Plato, *Resp.* 370a–c (in Harris 2002, 71–2). He argues that man is not self-sufficient; he needs many different things. That is the condition for the birth of the *polis*, where an increasing demand for different types of craftsmen is a consequence, and exchange becomes essential in order to make people's lives better.
24. Vandermersch 1994, 93–4.
25. See Chapter 2, p. 37.
26. Bekker-Nielsen 2005, 31.
27. Morris 2002.
28. Several sources attest individual acts of commercial enterprise in the Archaic period: Solon, *Fragments* 12.41–6; Plutarch, *Sol.* 2.3–3.1; Herodotus 4.152; Strabo 17.1.33. Bravo 1974, 123, considers a business letter from Berezan in the Black Sea, dating to *c.* 500 BC, which attests the existence of agents in trade and a successful attempt to confiscate the cargo of a ship (in Meijer and van Nijf 1992, 30–2). See also the sources listed in Osborne 1996.
29. Aristotle, *Pol.* 1257a31–6, b3–5; 1258b 1–4.
30. Cohen 1992, 5.
31. Xenophon, *Oec.* 1.15
32. Morris 2002, 33.
33. See, for example, Osborne 1996.
34. Temin 2001, 177; Cato, *Agr.* 144–8.
35. Temin 2001, 175.
36. Purcell 1985, 7, n. 27; Frederiksen 1984, 232 (in Olcese 2004, 179).
37. Livy 21.63.
38. Manacorda 1989; Lindhagen 2009.
39. Goldsberry 1980, 132–3; Consolo Langher 2000.
40. See Chapter 1, p. 20.
41. Narotzky 1997, 58.
42. Ibid.; Aristotle, *Pol.* 1.9; *Nik.* 5.5.
43. Temin 2001.
44. In recent years this discussion has been held mainly in connection with the medieval economies of Britain and Scandinavia.
45. Kim 2002. For 'substantivist' studies of Greek coinage, viewing it as mainly having symbolic value, see von Reden 1995 and Kurke 1999.
46. Schaps 2004, 111–15.
47. Lentini et al. 2002; Carettoni 1959, 1961. Halaesa coinage: Hoover 2012, 51–5. The huge degree of monetarisation in the fourth century BC in Sicily is well illustrated by the abundant finds of coins from Morgantina (Buttrey 1989).
48. Temin 2001, 181–5.
49. Cohen 1992.
50. Reger 2003, 342; Cohen 1992, 34. Demosthenes is our most important source on maritime loans in the Classical period: see, e.g., Demosthenes, *Against Aphobus* I.9–11; *Against Apaturius* 4–5; *Against Lacritus* 10–13; *Against Zenothemis* 4–6; *Against Phormio* 6–9 (sources collected in Meijer and van Nijf 1992, 46–51).
51. All Greek colonies were situated by the coast. The absence of Sikel coastal sites is obvious from the map in Albanese Procelli 1996.
52. Polanyi et al. 1957.
53. Malkin 2011.
54. Gras 1993, 106 (in Horden and Purcell 2000, 397).
55. Collura 2016, 311–44.
56. For a discussion of a typical 'gateway community', see Lindhagen 2016.
57. Horden and Purcell 2000, 392–3; the theory of 'gateway settlement' derives from Polanyi et al. 1957. The small river at Caronía, which cannot have been navigable even in antiquity, constituted a route into the interior, and must be seen as having been one of the very few existing river valleys to give easier access to the massive Nebrodi mountain chain.
58. Horden and Purcell 2000, 396.
59. Albanese Procelli 1996, 126.
60. The demand for wine increases at Sikel settlements in the late sixth and the beginning of the fifth century BC, as attested by tomb finds (Albanese Procelli 1997, 15).
61. Hodos 2000, 47; Albanese Procelli 1997, 15.
62. Hodos 2000, *passim*.
63. Sahlins (1972) thinks reciprocity was only practised within restricted social groups, even in prehistoric times.
64. Horden and Purcell 2000, 392–3.
65. Harris 2002, 76.
66. The publication of black-gloss wares from Monte Iato clearly shows large-scale imports of Greek 'colonial' and Aegean fine wares (Caflisch 1991, 19–74).
67. An inland Sikel site where amphorae of practically

all the types known in Sicily were imported in the Archaic period – Corinthian A, Corinthian A′, Attic SOS, *à la brosse*, Chian, Samian, Miletian, eastern Greek, 'Corinthian B' and Pseudo-Chian/MGS II. The important scale of these imports is underlined by the fact that there were fifty examples of the MGS II type (Albanese-Procelli 1996, 95–120).

68. Monte Iato was situated further inland, and goods would have travelled a longer distance through more hands in order to reach the town (Caflisch 1991, 20).
69. Murray 1993, chapter 13; Boardman 1999. Cf. the centre-periphery model (Rowlands et al. 1987).
70. See Chapter 2, pp. 37–9.
71. Wilson underlines how the shelving slopes of the Nebrodi towards the north coast would have facilitated the transport of timber to the sea (Wilson 1990, 194).
72. Vandermersch 1994, 95.
73. There is no evidence for *ateliers* in antiquity which produced only one product (Vandermersch 1994, 97).
74. Vandermersch 1994, 117.
75. See Chapter 4, p. 75.
76. A production of amphorae in some way controlled by the *polis* as late as the first century AD can be inferred from the discovery at Naxos of a locally produced Dressel 2/4 amphora with the stamp ΔΑ(μόσιον) (Garozzo 2001, 43).
77. For example, the stamps MESS/MAM, ΝΑΞΙΟΣ (for the latter, Garozzo 2011, 429–36).
78. The first Latin stamps on Campanian MGS VI amphorae contain many names of important Roman *gentes* involved in the wine business, such as the Antestii, the Baebii, the Iuventii, the Valerii, etc. (Manacorda 1989, 444).
79. The Caronía material and that from Lipari (in the necropolis at *contrada* Portinenti, 11 out of the 15 MGS V amphorae present are Campanian: Campagna 2000) show clearly that the Campanian MGS V amphora is more common on the north coast than any other version of MGS V amphorae. All stamped Greco-Italic handles from Morgantina in the museum of Aidone examined by the author are of the same Campanian fabric as the finds from Caronía. Among them was the stamp ΕΛΩ, interpreted by Vandermersch (1994, 115) as a toponym of the Sicilian city of Heloros south of Syracuse. Since the stamp is evidently Campanian, it must represent an abbreviated Ischian or Campanian name.
80. Manacorda 1989.
81. Whittaker has underlined the importance of the *vicus* in large-scale production (Whittaker 1990, 114).
82. Vandermersch 1994, 106.
83. See Chapter 1, p. 23.
84. See Chapter 5, pp. 108–09, figs 5.3–4.
85. Of the approximately 300 Greco-Italic stamps listed by Vandermersch, only eighteen can be considered Sicilian, whereas as many as 165 are stamps considered by Olcese as probably Campanian (Olcese 2004, 177–8 and 182–3). For a record of stamps on MGS amphorae in western Sicily, Garozzo 2011.
86. Corinthian B, MGS IV, Gela (Manfria): Vandermersch 1994, 75; MGS V/VI, Naxos, Kamarina: Vandermersch 1994, 86; MGS II, Messina: Barone et al. 2004.
87. In the list of Greco-Italic stamps provided by Vandermersch (1994, 161–80), only two stamps of certain Sicilian origin, a Mamertine one (from Pergamon) and a Gela-produced stamp (Carthage), have been found outside Sicily.
88. Sicilian pottery of the fourth and third centuries BC hardly travelled outside the island, and then, it seems, only in small quantities (Vandermersch 1994, 154). For most of the fourth century BC, red-figured and black-gloss pottery had been supplied to the western Mediterranean outside Sicily by Athens, and from the late fourth/third centuries BC, the *ateliers des petites éstampilles* of Etruria, Latium and Campania took over this role (Vandermersch 2001).
89. From the start, Archaic western Greek wine production must have been primarily an answer to the demands of wine-consuming western colonies, but increasingly in the fifth and fourth centuries BC, it went also to indigenous settlements. The importance of wine in the economy of a *polis* is shown by Locri's issues of silver coins featuring a bunch of grapes, and by the bronze issues of Kale Akte, Halaesa and other north-east Sicilian centres in the Late Republican period (Vandermersch 1994, 41). Gras (1988, 297) claimed that the most powerful Archaic city states would probably have had an agricultural surplus destined for export. The largest exporters of wine in the Archaic and Classical periods in the western Mediterranean, apart from Locri and Sybaris, were Corinthian Kerkyra (Corfu) and cities in Sicily such as Messana (cf. Spagnolo 2002). The depiction of bunches of grapes on the *symmachia* issues of Halaesa by the middle of the fourth century shows clearly that it was important to signal the importance of that town's wine production.
90. The attraction of Sicilians to the *symposion* and wine-related games such as *kottabos* (for example, the *tomba del kottabos* at San Marco d'Alunzio: Scibona 1981) from the late fifth century BC is well attested, and is indicated also by the growing popularity of the cult of Dionysus during the fourth century BC, and by the *andron* becoming a standard part of domestic architecture, as for example at Gela and Morgantina.
91. Vandermersch 1994, 104. The settlement project of Ducetius at Kale Akte must have included 'democratic' land allotments to the settlers. The founding of Halaesa is the most evident case of 'democratic movements' in the area, where mercenaries were invited to settle, and the equal distribution of land was the main attraction.
92. Cornell 1995, 385.
93. Woolf considers local demand as the most important factor behind surplus production for export (Woolf 1998, 201).
94. Vandermersch 1994; see above.
95. For the early large-scale wine-export from Campania, Chapter 4, pp. 71–2. Campanian stamps are found all over the Mediterranean (from Spain to Greece), but few

of those which are certainly Sicilian have been found outside Sicily. The dominance of Campanian Greco-Italic containers is confirmed by finds from Lipari and elsewhere in Sicily, as well as those from Caronía.

96. Fentress 2001, 260.
97. Vandermersch 2001, 167–8. These villas can clearly also be connected with the mass production of the Campana A *ancienne* of Ischia and the *atelier des petites éstampilles*. The shift from the production of red-figured Etrurian and Campanian wares to the *atelier à petites éstampilles* has been described as a passage from one world to another (Vandermersch 2001, 181).
98. Morley 2002, 122 and 124.
99. Carandini 1985, 197 (in Morley 2002, 126).
100. This is evident, for example, from the Halaesa survey (Burgio 2008).
101. Wilson 1990, 233: '. . . the countryside of imperial Sicily was dotted with plentiful farms, villas and larger nuclei, probably already in the first century, and certainly by the beginning of the second century'. On Lipari (Termini Imerese 151 / 354 amphorae), see especially Messina 2000, 115.
102. Peacock and Williams 1986, 35–7.
103. Purpura 1982; 1985.
104. Curtis 1991, 148.
105. Curtis 1991, 158.
106. Fish-product amphorae are found everywhere at Pompeii, in shops and *tabernae*, and in both rich and poor houses. The prices given in the Edict of Diocletian (AD 301) shows that these products were not more expensive than other commodities (Curtis 1991, 173–4). In addition, the sheer number of amphorae carrying fish products found throughout the Mediterranean and the Roman Empire suggests a very widespread diffusion through all socio-economic levels.
107. Manacorda 1989; Tchernia 1986. Paterson (1998, 156–7), on the other hand accuses these authors of not acknowledging the existence of a free market.
108. For the importance of, and specialisation in, olive-growing in Spain and North Africa, see Mattingly 1988.
109. Gibbins 2001, 327 and 330; also Hitchner 2002.
110. Mattingly 1988, 54–5.
111. Morley (2002, 57) considers changes in the economy of the provinces as a consequence of the demands of the city of Rome.
112. Morley 2002, 81–2.
113. Paterson 1998, 165.
114. The view that agriculture in Italy declined in the first century AD due to provincial competition can be traced back to Rostovtzeff (1957, 199–203). It has been criticised as being too modernistic with regard to the Roman economy. Morley has put forward a more modern interpretation of this 'crisis of the villa', which implies that viticulture on a large scale became too costly and too risky an investment when provincial wines from Gaul and Spain began to arrive on the market. Morley therefore views the disappearance of Italian wines not as an agricultural crisis, but as a deliberate reduction in the scale of production (Morley 2002, 141–2). See Tchernia 2016, 297–316 on the economic crisis in imperial Italy and provincial competition.
115. Horden and Purcell 2000, 606. 'Redistribution' was a term coined by Polanyi, who so labelled his second general stage of economic development, implying the 'centric transfers' (see note 119) of goods organised by a central state (Polanyi 1977, 35–6 and 40–1).
116. Horden and Purcell 2000, 368–9.
117. See Chapter 4, pp. 79–80.
118. Paterson 1998, 164; Foraboschi 1994.
119. Arthur 1989, 139. A 'centric transfer' refers to a state-directed transfer of goods to a few, important key-sites or centres, in contrast with the widespread distribution of goods which is characteristic of a 'market'.
120. Since Greek wine amphorae are found on all Punic sites from the Classical period onwards, and Punic ones are also present on most Greek sites, it seems obvious that they are the result of a commercial exchange between Greek cities on the one hand, and Punic settlements on the other (see Chapter 4, pp. 70, 72, 79 and 81–2).
121. Issa, Narona and elsewhere in the Adriatic were well situated for export to the eastern Mediterranean, and Lamboglia 2 containers, as Tchernia argues, seem to have been aimed partly for there, whereas Campanian wine was less dominant in the East than in the West (Tchernia 1986, 68–74). The central Adriatic was not well situated for exports to Rome, and so it cannot be argued that the wine export from there was mainly in response to Rome's demands; but for the rich finds of such amphorae in Rome, Cafini and d'Alessandro 2010.
122. Osborne 1996.
123. Consolo Langher 1997, 250–1.
124. Vandermersch 1994, 141–2, n. 190.
125. Carandini and Panella 1981; Tchernia 1986, 197–299, 321–49; Panella 1989; 1992; Panella and Tchernia 1994 (in Peña 1999, 11, n. 90).
126. *CIL* VI.9677 = *ILS* 7278 (in Peña 1999, 28–9). Another trader in fish products has been recorded from Rome, a *negotians salsamentarius et vinarius maurarius* (*CIL* VI.9676, in Peña 1999, 29).
127. Bekker Nielsen 2005.
128. Peña 1999, 29, n. 269 with bibliography: Evans 1981, 519–29; Morel 1963; Pucci 1983, 109–12; Tomber 1993, 142–5.
129. Peña 1999, 36, n. 332 with bibliography: Tortorella 1981; Parker 1992a; Pontacolone and Incitta 1991. For pottery as cargo in general, see Rhodes 1989, 46 and 50; Parker 1992b, 90 and 96; Olcese 1993, 52–6; Millett 1993.
130. Aubert 1994, 213–14 in Peña 1999, 36 and 55, n. 331. *CIL* XIII.2033 (Lyon) appears to record a *n[egotiat]or vina[arius et art]is cret[ariae*, a 'wine and pottery merchant'.
131. Peña 1999, 36.
132. Prestianni Giallombardo 1998, 71.
133. Consolo Langher 2000, 273, especially n. 18 for the sources. For taxation on agricultural products already under the Deinominids, Carcopino 1914, 54–5; Schenk von Stauffenberg 1933, 80; for the age of Dionysius and Agathocles, Rostovtzeff 1957, 351; Berve 1959, 46 and

54. In the Classical period, taxation was common in most Greek city-states, not only in the Athenian Empire. That this would also have been so in the Sicilian Empire of Dionysius I seems clear from some passages in Pseudo-Aristotle (Thomsen 1964, 38–42).

134. Consolo Langher 2000, 273–5.
135. Consolo Langher 2000, 273; Scramuzza 1937, 272; Nicolet 1994, 225.
136. See Chapter 4, p. 70.
137. Consolo Langher 2000, 273.
138. Cicero, *Verr.* 2.3.7.18.
139. See Chapter 1, p. 20.
140. For the grain *annona*, see above and Chapter 1, p. 23. For state-directed trade during the Roman period, Tchernia 2016, chapter 4.
141. Peña 1999, 8. For staple provisions and food supplies to Rome, Tchernia 2016, 189–99 and 202–10.
142. Wickham 1988, 191; Mattingly 1988, 53–4.
143. Mattingly 1988, 53.
144. Rickman 1980, 17.
145. Ibid., 126.
146. Wickham 1988, 191.
147. It has been argued that Campana C pottery was commercialised outside Sicily, but this is very doubtful, considering the many similar productions of 'grey-ware' existed elsewhere in the Mediterranean area at this time (information from Dr. Shelley Stone).
148. The fact that the Romans brought Sicilian vines such as *Eugeneum*, *Aminaeum* and *Murgantinum* to Campania is clear evidence that there was a strong interest in growing these highly-prized vines, and trading the produce from them in Italy rather than just in Sicily.
149. Morley 2002, 57.
150. Wickham 1988, 191–3.
151. This traffic was interrupted by the large *garum* exports from Baetica to Rome in the first century AD, which followed in the wake of Baetican oil.
152. It is interesting to note that wine production at Kale Akte was apparently important also in late Hellenistic times, judging from the coins with Dionysus and a cluster of grapes (colour Pl. 15), but only a very small surplus for export then (the second and first centuries BC) can be identified in the ceramic record.
153. Soraci 2011, 151.
154. Ibid., 195.
155. Ibid., 202.
156. Ibid., 176–7.
157. Ibid., 186.
158. Ibid., 196.
159. We know that at least a certain amount of the grain, known as the *frumentum in cellam* or *aestimatum*, was ear-marked especially for the governor and his staff (Scramuzza 1937, 268).
160. Cicero, *Verr.* 2.4.27.62 (Scramuzza 1937, 273).
161. At Ostia African oil amphorae are already more numerous than Spanish by the Flavian period (Mattingly 1988, 55).
162. For *tituli picti* on Dressel 20 amphorae, see Peña 1999, 21–2.
163. Peña 1999, 21.
164. Ibid., 23; SHA, *Sev.* 18.3.
165. This can be deduced from the continuation of the *mensae oleariae*, which distributed State oil, until at least this period (Peña 1999, 28).
166. A dedication to a *procurator ad oleam* is recorded from AD 175, but State involvement can be presumed already from the 140s AD (Peña 1999, 21). On the impact of African oil on the Mediterranean market in the middle and late Empire, as seen from a Spanish perspective, see especially Reynolds 2010, 137–47.
167. Mattingly (1988, 56) reached the conclusion that oil had a 'good free-market potential', as was emphasised by the fact that there was a continuity of trade in African oil also after the fall of the Roman Empire, until as late as the beginning of the Islamic period.
168. Wilson 1990, 266.
169. Fentress et al. 2004, 160.
170. Vallat 1991, 14.
171. See above, p. 135, with n. 135.
172. Peña (1999, 155) bases this argument on finds of Middle Roman 1 and Palatine East 1 amphorae, of probable north-eastern Sicilian production, on the Palatine.
173. Peña 1999, 16 and 18.
174. Cassiodorus, *Var.* 10.2. (in Wilson 1990, 336, n. 56).
175. *Codex Theodosianus* XI.2, 1–2.
176. Pacetti 1998, 190.
177. Bücher 1901, 371; Morley 2002, 18–20. Alternative models have presented other concepts such as the 'service city', 'la cité organisatrice' and the 'processor city' as best illustrating the economic mechanisms of the ancient city. For the 'service city', Engels 1990; for 'la cité organisatrice', Leveau 1983. These have been greeted with some scepticism by Whittaker and Paterson, and the latter considers the consumption city model the best adapted to answer questions concerning the Roman economy (Whittaker 1990; Paterson 1998).
178. Weber 1976, 337–52.
179. Finley 1973.
180. Morley 2002, 15.
181. Morley 2002, 9. For recent discussions on the city of Rome and its role in Roman trade and production, Tchernia 2016.
182. See Chapter 1, pp. 17 and 19.
183. Consolo Langher 1997, 236.
184. Already in the reign of Dionysius I, the power of Syracuse had managed to bring together all Greek and Sikel cities on the island under its sway, forming a loosely knit empire or *arché* of *poleis*. This development would have affected Kale Akte and the eastern part of the north coast with the foundation of the settlement at Tyndaris after the successful war against the Carthaginians in 396 BC. The new foundation had the character of a military colony (Consolo Langher 1997, 118, n. 23), and the submission of Soluntum, Thermae, Cephaloedium and Lipari leaves no room for doubt that Dionysius now wanted to control the whole Tyrrhenian coast, not only of Sicily but of the toe of Italy opposite: for the Syracusan *epikrateia* of Dionysius

extended also into Bruttium, with the Greek colonies Locri, Caulonia and Hipponion coming under his control (Consolo Langher 1997, 234). With a very important wine production at Locri in mind (see Chapter 4, pp. 67–8 and 70–1), this Syracusan expansion had an economic as well as a political and military dimension. Cities such as Metapontion, Velia, Hipponion, and Terina now minted coins identical to those issued by Agathocles. North Africa was also an important area of interest, which is shown by the African War of 310–307 BC; it is probable that Syracuse had commercial interests there too, although the archaeological evidence for it is still not abundant. The Adriatic was also a further sphere of Syracusan interest: Sicilian pottery has been found as far north as Spina.

185. The empires of the early Hellenistic period have many aspects in common, especially militarism, colonisation and taxation. There is a trend towards higher population levels and intensification of agriculture in the Hellenistic kingdoms in general. During the fourth century BC a trend towards the creation of larger states or empires becomes clear. In Sicily it existed perhaps earlier than anywhere else in the Greek world.
186. The control of Apollonia by the tyrant of Engyon is another indication of increasing interest in the north Sicilian coast, already in the 340s BC (see Chapter 1, pp. 16–17).
187. Hopkins 1980, a model now regarded with some scepticism.
188. Billows 2003, 196 and 199.
189. Harris 1979, 56.
190. Locri, one of the earliest wine-suppliers of Kale Akte, was the main producer of wine on the western Greek wine market in the sixth century, together with Sybaris. Amphorae from Locri constitute the single largest group at Messina in the sixth century BC, comprising one third of the total; amphorae from Sybaris account for almost as much (*c.* 28 %: Spagnolo 2002). Sybaris was destroyed in 510 BC.
191. Olcese 2004, 179; Vandermersch 2001, 186.
192. It continued to be exported in large quantities in the eastern Mediterranean.
193. *CIL* X.7459 (in Wilson 1990, 28, n. 88).
194. Tchernia 1986.
195. See Chapter 4, pp. 77–8 and 83–5.
196. Wilson 1990, 35.
197. Peña 1999, 155; Sangineto 2002, 213–14; Tchernia 2016, 297–316.
198. Wilson 2012, 291; Tchernia 2016.
199. Hopkins 1980, 221–2.
200. Ibid., 222 and 224.
201. Diodorus Siculus 16.191; Livy 7.27.2.
202. Loseby 2012, 345.
203. Ibid., 345.
204. Ibid., 347.
205. Rome's population contracted significantly, from somewhere around half a million in the middle of the fifth century AD, to a much lower figure in the sixth century. According to Procopius, the city was left deserted after the Gothic siege in 546 (Procopius, *De Bell.* VII.22.19). Although obviously a wild exaggeration, it probably reflects a strong decrease in population (in Wickham 1988, 193).

Notes to Appendix 1

1. The excavation was supervised together with Dr. Kristian Göransson, to whom I extend my warmest thanks, during most of the campaign of 1999/2000, and part of that of 2001. In the latter excavation season, I was responsible for the overall direction together with Dr. Rossella Pace of the University of Cosenza, to whom I am also greatly indebted. An extensive report was published on this work: see Lentini et al. 2002.
2. Ikäheimo 2003.
3. Thanks are due to Francesco Collura for giving me the opportunity to study this material.
4. Bonanno 2009.
5. Ibid., 29.
6. Ibid., Tav. I–XIV. A little over a quarter of the finds illustrated there (28 pieces) represent amphorae.
7. Riley 1979, 101.
8. Orton 1975; 1980. For a thoughtful discussion of many of the key issues in assessing amphora assemblages, especially in the context of hellenistic material, see Lawall 2005.
9. Riley 1979.
10. Orton 1993. It was observed during the work of quantifying the fragments that most handles were broken in two (seldom more) fragments, and rims and bases generally into not more than four.
11. Exceptions are the publications of finds from Termini Imerese (Belvedere et al. 1993) and from Messina (Bacci and Tigano 1999–2002).
12. See for example Lentini 2001, 13–39; Garozzo 2001, 41–6; Ollà 2001, 47–60; Williams 2001, 61–2.
13. Peacock and Williams 1986, 12.
14. Peña 2007b; cf. also Lawall 2005, 193.
15. Peña 2007b, 63.
16. Ibid.
17. Pliny, *NH* 14.66; Peña 2007b, 64–5.
18. Ibid., 69–70.
19. Ibid., 72.
20. Lawall 2011, 37.
21. Bonanno 2009, 41–3.
22. *Meligunìs Lipára* I–XII.
23. Morgantina: Stone 2014; Monte Iato: Caflisch 1991.
24. Vitale in Bonacasa Carra and Vitale 1997–98. For the lamps, see Bernabò Brea and Cavalier 1965a, for the Roman ones, especially Tav. 228–31; *Meligunìs Lipára* VII, 140–1, Tav. 101–18. Many lamps are also published in *Meligunìs Lipára* XI.
25. Bailey 1975; 1980; 1988.

Notes to Appendix 2

1. Peacock and Williams 1986.
2. Peacock 1977; 1982; Whitbread 1995.
3. Lindahl et al. 2006.
4. Ibid.

Bibliography

Abbreviations

AE	*L'Année Épigraphique*
AEA	*Archivo Español de Arqueología*
AJA	*American Journal of Archaeology*
ANRW	*Aufstieg und Niedergang der römischen Welt*
ArchStMess	*Archivio Storico Messinese*
ASNP	*Annali della Scuola Normale Superiore di Pisa*
BABesch	*Bulletin Antieke Beschaving*
BAR	*British Archaeological Reports*
BdA	*Bollettino d'Arte*
BTCGI	*Bibliografia topografica della colonizzazione greca in Italia e nelle isole tirreniche*
CIL	*Corpus Inscriptionum Latinarum*
CronA	*Cronache di Archeologia*
IG	*Inscriptiones Graecae*
JRA	*Journal of Roman Archaeology*
JRS	*Journal of Roman Studies*
MEFRA	*Melanges de l'École française de Rome. Antiquité*
NSc	*Notizie degli scavi di antichità*
OpRom	*Opuscula romana*
PBSR	*Papers of the British School at Rome*
QuadMess	*Quaderni dell'Istituto di Archeologia della Facoltà di Lettere e Filosofia della Università di Messina*
RCRFActa	*Rei Cretariae Romanae Fautorum Acta*
RM	*Mitteilungen des Deutschen Archäologischen Instituts. Römische Abteilung*
SEG	*Supplementum Epigraphicum Graecum*
SicA	*Sicilia Archeologica*

Bibliography

ADAMESTEANU, D. 1962 'L'ellenizzazione della Sicilia ed il momento di Ducezio', *Kokalos* 8, 190–6

AGOSTINIANI, L. 1988–89 'I modi del contatto linguistico tra Greci e indigeni nella Sicilia antica', *Kokalos* 34–5, 167–206

ALAIMO, R., GRECO, C. and MONTANA, G. 1998 'Le officine ceramiche di Solunto: evidenza archeologica ed indagini archeometriche preliminari', in E. Acquaro and B. Fabbri (eds), *Produzione e circolazione della ceramica fenicia e punica nel Mediterraneo: il contributo delle analisi archeometriche* (Ravenna: Consiglio Nazionale di Ricerca), 7–26

ALAIMO, R., ILIOPOULOS, I. and MONTANA, G. 2002 'Analisi petrografica degli impasti delle anfore fenicie e puniche', in M. L. Famà (ed.), *Mozia. Gli scavi della "Zona A" dell'abitato* (Bari: Edipuglia), 355–63

ALAIMO, R., MONTANA, G. and ILIOPOULOS, I. 2003 'Le anfore puniche di Solunto. Discriminazione tra produzioni locali ed importazioni mediante analisi al microscopio polarizzatore', in *Quarte giornate internazionali di studi sull'area elima, Erice 1 – 4 dicembre 2000. Atti del convegno* (Pisa: Scuola Normale Superiore di Pisa), 1–9

ALBANESE PROCELLI, R. M. 1996 'Appunti sulla distribuzione delle anfore commerciali nella Sicilia arcaica', *Kokalos* 42, 91–137

ALBANESE PROCELLI, R. M. 1997 'Échanges dans la Sicile archaïque: amphores commerciales, intermédiaires, et redistribution en milieu indigène', *Revue archéologique* 89, 3–25

ALBRECHT, C. and LOESCHCKE, S. 1942 *Das Römerlager in Oberaden und das Uferkastell in Beckinghausen an der Lippe. Band II, 2. Die Römische und die Belgische Keramik, die Gegenstände aus Metall* (Dortmund: W. Ruhfus)

AMARI, S. 2008 'A Late Roman amphorae production in eastern Sicily', in O. Menozzi, M. L. Di Marzio and D. Fossataro (eds), *SOMA 2005. Proceedings of the IX Symposium on Mediterranean Archaeology, Chieti (Italy), 24–26 February 2005* [BAR International Series 1739] (Oxford: Archaeopress), 473–9

ARCHIBALD, Z. 2005 'Markets and exchange: the structure and scale of economic behaviour in the Hellenistic Age', in Archibald et al. 2005, 1–26

ARCHIBALD, Z., DAVIES, J. K., GABRIELSEN, V. and OLIVER, G. (eds) 2001 *Hellenistic economies* (London: Routledge)

ARCHIBALD, Z., DAVIES, J. K. and GABRIELSEN, V. (eds) 2005 *Making, moving and managing. The new world of ancient economies, 323–31 BC* (Oxford: Oxbow Books)

ARENA, E. 2016 'Il decreto onorifico tardo-ellenistico da Caronia (*SEG* LIX, 1102): per una nuova edizione', in Collura 2016, 351–67

ARENA, M. S., DELOGU, P., PAROLI, L.,RICCI, M., SAGUI, L. and VENDITELLI, L. (eds) 2001 *Roma dall'Antichità al Medioevo. Archeologia e storia nel Museo Nazionale Romano Crypta Balbi* (Milan: Electa).

ARTHUR, P. 1982 'Roman amphorae and the Ager Falernus under the Empire', *PBSR* 50, 22–33

ARTHUR, P. 1989 'Some observations on the economy of Bruttium under the later Roman Empire', *JRA* 2, 133–42

ARTHUR, P. 1990 'Amphorae', in M. Gualtieri and H. Fracchia (eds), *Roccagloriosa 1. L'abitato. Scavo e ricognizione topografica, 1976–86* (Naples: Centre Jean Bérard), 278–89

ASHERI, D. 1992 'Sicily, 478–431 B.C', in D. M. Lewis, J. Boardman, J. K. Davies and M. Ostwald (eds), *Cambridge Ancient History, V. The Fifth Century B.C.*, 2nd edition (Cambridge: Cambridge University Press), 147–70

AUBERT, J. J. 1994 *Business managers in ancient Rome. A social and economic study of* institores, *200 B.C.–A.D. 250* [Columbia studies in the classical tradition 21] (Leiden and New York: Brill)

AURIEMMA, R. 2000 'Le anfore del relitto di Grado e il loro contenuto', *MEFRA* 112, 27–51

BACCI, G. M. and TIGANO, G. (eds) 1999–2002 *Da Zancle a Messina. Un percorso archeologico attraverso gli scavi*, volumes 1–3 (Messina: Sicania)

BAILEY, D. M. 1975 *A catalogue of the lamps in the British Museum 1. Greek, Hellenistic and early Roman pottery lamps* (London: British Museum Publications)

BAILEY, D. M. 1980 *A catalogue of the lamps in the British Museum 2. Roman lamps made in Italy* (London: British Museum Publications)

BAILEY, D. M. 1988 *A catalogue of the lamps in the British Museum 3. Roman provincial lamps* (London: British Museum Publications)

BALDACCI, P. 1972 *Recherches sur les amphores romaines: colloque sur l'utilisation en histoire économique des données fournies par les amphores romaines* [Collection de l'École française de Rome 10] (Rome: École française de Rome)

BARONE, G., CRUPI, V., GALLI, S., LONGO, F., MAJOLINO, D., MAZZOLENI, P. and SPAGNOLO, G. 2004 'Archaeometric analyses on "Corinthian B" transport amphorae found at Gela (Sicily, Italy)', *Archaeometry* 46, 553–68

BEJOR, G. 1982 'Città di Sicilia nei decreti da Entella', *ASNP*³ 12, 815–40

BEKKER-NIELSEN, T. 2005 'Fish as a source of food in antiquity', in T. Bekker-Nielsen (ed.), *Ancient fishing and fish processing in the Black Sea region* (Aarhus and Oakville CT: Aarhus University Press), 21–30

BELL, M. 2000 'Camarina e Morgantina al congresso di Gela', in *Un ponte fra l'Italia e la Grecia. Atti del simposio in onore di Antonino di Vita* (Padova: Bottega d'Erasmo), 291–7

BELVEDERE, O., BURGIO, A., MACALUSO, R. and RIZZO, M. S. 1993 *Termini Imerese: ricerche di topografia e di archeologia urbana* (Palermo: Istituto di Archeologia)

BENOÎT, F. 1961 *Fouilles sous-marines: l'épave du Grand Congloué à Marseille* (Paris: CNRS)

BERNABÒ BREA, L. 1958 *La Sicilia prima dei greci* (Milan: Il Saggiatore)

BERNABÒ BREA, L. 1975 'Che cosa conosciamo dei centri indigeni della Sicilia che hanno coniato monete prima dell'età di Timoleonte?', in *Le emissioni dei centri siculi fino all'epoca di Timoleonte e i loro rapporti con la monetazione delle colonie greche di Sicilia. Atti del IV Convegno del centro internazionale di studi numismatici* (Rome: Istituto italiano di numismatica), 3–51

BERNABÒ BREA, L. 1996 'Note sul terremoto del 365 d.C. a Lipari e nella Sicilia nord-orientale', in G. Giarrizzo (ed.), *La Sicilia dei terremoti. Lunga durata e dinamiche sociali* (Catania: G. Maimone), 87–98

BERNABÒ BREA, L. and CAVALIER, M. 1965a *Meligunìs Lipára, II. La necropoli greca e romana nella contrada Diana* (Palermo: S. F. Flaccovio)

BERNABÒ BREA, L. and CAVALIER, M. 1965b 'Tindari – Area urbana. L'insula IV e le strade che la circondano', *BdA* ser. v, 50, 205–09

BERNABÒ BREA, L. and CAVALIER, M. 2000 *Meligunìs Lipára X. Scoperte e scavi archeologiche nell'area urbana e suburbana di Lipari* (Palermo: Regione Siciliana and Rome: L'Erma di Breschneider)

BERNABÒ BREA, M. A., CULTRARO, M., GRAS, M., MARTINELLI, M. C., POUZADOUX, C. and SPIGO, U. (eds) 2018 *À Madeleine Cavalier* [Collection du Centre Jean Bérard 49] (Naples: Centre Jean Bérard)

BERNAL, D., ARÉVALO, A. and LORENZO, L. 2003 'Imitations of Italic amphorae for fish sauce in Baetica. New evidence from the salt-fish factory of Baelo Claudia (Hispania)', *RCRFActa* 38, 305–13

BERVE, H. 1959 *König Hieron II* [Bayerische Akademie der Wissenschaften. Philosophisch-Historische Klasse. Abhandlungen. Neue Folge 47] (Munich: Verlag der Bayerischen Akademie der Wissenschaften)

BEZECZKY, T. 1998. *The Laecanius amphora stamps and the villas of Brijuni* [Österreichischen Akademie der Wissenschaften. Philosophisch-Historische Klasse. Denkschriften 261] (Vienna: Verlag der Österreich-ischen Akademie der Wissenschaften)

BEZECZKY, T. 2013 *The amphorae of Roman Ephesus* [Forschungen in Ephesos, Band 15/1] (Vienna: Verlag der Österreichischen Akademie der Wissenschaften)

BILLOWS, R. 2003 'Cities', in Erskine 2003, 196–215

BINTLIFF, J. (ed.) 1991 *The Annales school and archaeology* (London: Leicester University Press)

BIONDI, G. 2002 'Nuovi materiali di età ellenistica e romana dell'area del Calvenio', in G. Rizza (ed.), *Scavi e ricerche a Centuripe* [Studi e materiali di archeologia mediterranea 1] (Catania: Consiglio Nazionale di Ricerche), 169–87

BIVONA, L. 1970 *Iscrizioni latine lapidarie del Museo di Palermo* (Palermo: S. F. Flaccovio)

BLANCK, H. 1979 'Der Schiffsfund von der Secca di Capistello bei Lipari', *RM* 85, 91–111

BOARDMAN, J. 1999 *The Greeks overseas: their early colonies and trade*, 4th edition (London: Thames and Hudson)

BOEHRINGER, C. 1981 'Herbita', *Numismatica e antichità classiche. Quaderni Ticinesi*, 10, 95–114

BONACASA CARRA, R. M. 1993–94 'Il complesso ipogeico di corso Gramsci a Marsala', *Kokalos* 39–40, 1457–67

BONACASA CARRA, R. M. and VITALE, E. 1997–98 'Ceramiche di produzione locale e ceramiche d'importazione nella Sicilia tardoantica', *Kokalos* 43–4, 397–452

BONACASA CARRA, R. M. and PANVINI, R. 2002 *La Sicilia centro-meridionale tra il II ed il VI sec. d.C. Catalogo della mostra* (Caltanissetta: Salvatore Sciascia Editore)

BONACIC-MANDINIC, M. 2014 'The coin finds from the Vlaška njiva Necropolis at Vis (Nalazi novca s nekropole Vlaška njiva u Visu)', *Vjesnik za arheologiju i historiju dalmatinsku* (Journal of Dalmatian Archeology and History, Split) 107, 201–40

BONANNO, C. 1993–94 'Scavi e ricerche a Caronia e a S. Marco d´Alunzio', *Kokalos* 39–40, 953–85

BONANNO, C. 1995 'Ricerche archeologiche a Caronia – Kalè Akté', in *Giornate di archeologia – architettura – storia. Da Tindari per Agatirno ad Alesa. Capo d'Orlando, 5 agosto 1995* (Capo d'Orlando: Archeoclub d'Italia, sede comprensoriale di Capo d'Orlando)

BONANNO, C. 1997–98 'Scavi e indagini nel territorio di Caronia e San Marco d'Alunzio', *Kokalos* 43–4, 423–51

BONANNO, C. 2004 'La necropoli', in Spigo 2004, 79–90

BONANNO, C. 2007 'L'insediamento in località Pantano di Caronia Marina (Messina): contesti tardo antichi e bizantini', in M. Bonifay and J.-C. Tréglia (eds), *LRCW2. Late Roman coarse wares, cooking wares and amphorae in the Mediterranean. Archaeology and archaeometry 2* [BAR International Series 1662] (Oxford: Archaeopress), 353–63

BONANNO, C. (ed.) 2008 *Apollonia. Indagini archeologiche sul Monte San Fratello 2003–2005* (Rome: L'Erma di Bretschneider)

BONANNO, C. (ed.) 2009 *Kalè Akté. Scavi in contrada Pantano di Caronia Marina 2003–2005* (Rome: L'Erma di Bretschneider)

BONANNO, C. and ARCIFA, L. 2009 'Nuovi scavi a S. Marco d'Alunzio (1997–1998)', *Kokalos* 47–8, 599–624

BONANNO, C. and SUDANO, F. 2006 'Kale Akte. L'insediamento in contrada Pantano a Caronia Marina', in Malfitana et al. 2006, 435–49

BONETTO, J., BUKOWIECKI, E., and VOLPE, R. (eds) 2019 *Alle origini del laterizio romano. Nascita e diffusione del mattone cotto nel Mediterraneo tra IV e I secolo a.C. Atti del II convegno internazionale "laterizio", Padova 26–28 aprile 2016* (Rome: Quasar)

BONSIGNORE, A. and TRIFIRÒ, D. 2009 'Le monete', in Bonanno 2009, 63–72

BORGARD, P. 2000 'L'atelier de potier du vallon de Portinenti (Lipari). Note préliminaire sur la production amphorique (Ier s. avant J.-C. – IIIe s. après J.-C.)', in Bernabò Brea and Cavalier 2000, 273–303

BORGARD, P., BRUN, J.-P. and PICON, M. (eds) 2005 *L'alun de Méditerranée* (Naples and Aix-en-Provence: Centre Jean Bérard)

BOTTE, E. 2009 *Salaisons et sauces de poissons en Italie du sud et en Sicile durant l'antiquité* [Collection du Centre Jean Bérard 31] (Naples: Centre Jean Bérard)

BOTTE, E. 2018 'Fish processing in Italy and Sicily during antiquity', *Journal of Maritime Archaeology* 13, 377–87

BOTTE, E. and LEITCH, V. (eds) 2014 *Fish & ships. Production and commerce of* salsamenta *during Antiquity/Production et commerce de* salsamenta *durant l'Aniquité. Actes de l'atelier doctoral, Rome 18–22 juin 2012* [Bibliothèque d'Archéologie Mediterranéenne et Africaine 17], Aix-en-Provence: Publications du Centre Camille Jullian

BOURGEON, O. 2017 'Baetican olive-oil trade under the Late Empire: new data on the production of Late Roman amphorae (Dressel 23) in the lower Genil valley', *JRA* 30, 517–29

BRANCIFORTI, M. G. 1992 'Lucerne degli ΑΓΥΡΙΝΑΙΟΙ nei Musei di Catania e di Siracusa', *CronA* 31, 93–105

BRANCIFORTI, M. G. (ed.) 2006 *L'area archeologica di Santa Venera al Pozzo* – Acium (Palermo: Regione Siciliana)

BRAUDEL, F. 1972 *The Mediterranean and the Mediterranean world in the age of Philip II*, volume 1 (London: Collins, and New York: Harper and Row)

BRAVO, B. 1974 'Une lettre sur plomb de Berezan: colonisation et modes de contact dans le Pont', *Dialogues d'histoire ancienne* 1, 111–87

BURGIO, A. 2008 *Il paesaggio agrario nella Sicilia ellenistico-romana. Alesa e il suo territorio* [Studi e materiali 12] (Rome: L'Erma di Bretschneider)

BUTTREY, T. V. 1989 *The coins* [Morgantina studies 2] (Princeton NJ: Princeton University Press)

BÜCHER, K. 1901 *Industrial evolution*, translated by S. M. Wickett (New York: H. Holt)

CABELLA, R., CAPELLI, C. and PIAZZA, M. 2008 'Analisi in sezione sottile di ceramiche da S. Fratello', in Bonanno 2008, 55–6

CABELLA, R., CAPELLI, C. and PIAZZA, M. 2009 'Analisi petrografiche in sezioni sottili da Caronia e Furnari Tonnarella', in Bonanno 2009, 59–61

CACCAMO CALTABIANO, M. 1999 'Identità e peculiarità dell'esperienza monetale siciliana', in *Magna Grecia e Sicilia. Stato degli studi e prospettive di ricerca. Atti dell'incontro di studi* (Messina: DiScAM), 295–311

CACCAMO CALTABIANO, M., CAMPAGNA, L. and PINZONE, A. (eds) 2004 *Nuove prospettive della ricerca sulla Sicilia del III sec. a.C. Archeologia, numismatica, storia* [Pelorias 11] (Messina: DiScAM)

CAFINI, M.-L. and D'ALESSANDRO, L. 2010 'Anfore adriatiche a Roma', *RCRFActa* 41, 93–100

CAFLISCH, R. B. 1991 *Die Firniskeramik vom Monte Iato. Funde 1971–1982* [Studia Ietina 4] (Zürich: E. Rentsch)

CALCIATI, R. 1983–87 *Corpus nummorum Siculorum. La monetazione di bronzo*, volumes 1–3 (Milan: Editori G.M.)

CALLENDER, M. H. 1965 *Roman amphorae with index of stamps* (London: Oxford University Press)

CAMBI, N. 1989 'Anfore romane in Dalmazia', in *Amphores romaines et histoire économique. Dix ans de recherche. Actes du colloque de Sienne, 22 – 24 mai 1986* [Collection de l'École française de Rome 114] (Rome) 311–37

CAMPAGNA, L. 2000 'Le anfore della necropoli in contrada Portinenti (proprietà Leone)', in Bernabò Brea and Cavalier 2000, 443–78

CAMPAGNA, L. and LA TORRE, G. F. 2008 'Ricerche sui monumenti e sulla topografia di Tauromenion: una stoa ellenistica nell'area della Naumachia', *Sicilia Antiqua* 5, 115–46

CAPELLI, C. and PIAZZA, M. 2006 'Analisi minero-petrografiche su anfore Dressel 21-22 da Alcamo Marina', in Giorgetti 2006, 171–3

CARANDINI, A. (ed.) 1985 *Settefinestre. Una villa schiavistica nell'Etruria romana* (Modena: Panini)

CARANDINI, A. and PANELLA, C. 1981 'The trading connections of Rome and Central Italy in the late second and third centuries. The evidence of the Terme del Nuotatore excavations, Ostia', in A. King (ed.), *The*

Roman West in the third century. Contributions from archaeology and history, 2 volumes [BAR International Series 109] (Oxford: British Archaeological Reports), 487–503

CARBÈ, A. 2008 'Le monete', in Bonanno 2008, 63–73

CARCOPINO, J. 1906 'La Sicile agricole au dernier siècle de la République romaine', *Vierteljahrschrift für Sozial- und Wirtschaftsgeschichte* 4, 128–85

CARCOPINO, J. 1914 *La loi de Hiéron et les Romains* (Paris: Fontemoing)

CARETTONI, G. 1959 'Scavi di Halaesa (Prima relazione)', *NSc* 1959, 239–349

CARETTONI, G. 1961 'Scavi di Halaesa (Seconda relazione)', *NSc* 1961, 266–321

CARIGNANI, A., CIOTOLA, A. and PACETTI, F. 1986 'Roma. Il contesto del tempio della Magna Mater sul Palatino', in A. Giardina (ed.), *Società romana e impero tardoantico, 3. Le merci, gli insediamenti* (Rome: Laterza), 27–43

CARRE, M.-B., MONSIEUR, P. and PESAVENTO MATTIOLI, S. 2014 'Transport amphorae Lamboglia 2 and Dressel 6A: Italy and / or Dalmatia?', *JRA* 27, 417–28

CARROCCIO, B. 2004 *Dal basileus Agatocle a Roma. Le monetazioni siciliane d'età ellenistica (cronologia–iconografia–metrologia)* [Pelorias 10] (Messina: DiScAM)

CARROCCIO, B. and COLLURA, F. 2016 'Ritrovamenti monetali di epoca greca nel territorio di Caronia, antica Kalè Akté–Calacte', in Collura 2016, 379–92

CARTLEDGE, P., COHEN, E. and FOXHALL, L. (eds) 2002 *Money, labour and land. Approaches to the economies of ancient Greece* (London: Routledge)

CASALINI, M. and CRESPI, M. 2010 'Anfore tardoantiche di piccoli dimensioni a fondo piatto dalle pendici nord-orientali del Palatino', *RCRFActa* 41, 101–11

CASCELLA, S. and COLLURA, F. 2016 'Sigillata italica dalla collina di Caronia', in Collura 2016, 393–412

CASTRIZIO, D. 2000 *La monetazione mercenariale in Sicilia: strategie economiche e territoriali fra Dione e Timoleonte* (Soveria Mannelli: Rubbettino)

CAVALIER, M. 1985 *Les amphores du VIe au IVe siècle dans les fouilles de Lipari* [Cahiers du Centre Jean Bérard 11] (Naples: Centre Jean Bérard)

CAVALIERE, P. 2000 'Anfore puniche utilizzate come contenitori di pesce. Un'esempio olbiese', *MEFRA* 112, 67–72

CHARLIN, G., GASSEND, J.M. and LEQUÉMENT, R. 1978 'L'épave antique de la baie de Cavalière (Le Lavandou, Var)', *Archaeonautica* 2, 9–93

CIPRIANO, M. T. and CARRE, M.-B. 1989 'Production et typologie des amphores sur la côte adriatique de l'Italie', in *Amphores romaines et histoire économique. Dix ans de recherche. Actes du colloque* [Collection de l'École française de Rome 114] (Rome: École française de Rome), 67–104

CIPRIANO, S. and MAZZOCHIN, S. 2000 'Considerazioni su alcune anfore Dressel 6B bollate. I casi di vari PACCI e PACCI, APICI e APIC, P. Q. SCAPULAE, P. SEPULLIP. F. e SEPULLIUM', *Aquileia Nostra* 71, 149–92

CLUVERIVS, P. 1619 *Sicilia antiqua: cum minoribus insulis ei adjacentibus, item Sardinia et Corsica* (Lugduni Batavorum)

COHEN, E. 1992 *Athenian economy and society: a banking perspective* (Princeton NJ: Princeton University Press)

COHEN, E. 2002 'Introduction', in Cartledge et al. 2002, 1–7

COLLURA, F. (ed.) 2016 *Studia Calactina I. Ricerche su una città greco-romana di Sicilia: Kalè Akté – Calacte* [BAR International Series 2813] (Oxford: British Archaeological Reports)

COLLURA, F. 2019a *I Nebrodi nell'antichità. Città, culture, paesaggio* (Oxford: Archaeopress)

COLLURA, F. (ed.) 2019b 'L'impiego del laterizio di tradizione siceliota nei centri della Sicilia settentrionale in età ellenistica. Il caso di *Kalè Akté*', in Bonetto, Bukowiecki and Volpe 2019, 261–70

CONSOLO LANGHER, S. N. 1997 *Un imperialismo tra democrazia e tirannide. Siracusa nei secoli V e IV a.C.* [Supplementi a *Kókalos* 12] (Rome: Giorgio Bretschneider)

CONSOLO LANGHER, S. N. 2000 *Agatocle. Da capoparte a monarca fondatore di un regno tra Cartagine e i Diadochi* [Pelorias 6] (Messina: DiScAM)

CORNELL, T. J. 1995 *The beginnings of Rome. Italy and Rome from the Bronze Age to the Punic wars (c. 1000 – 264 B.C.)* (London: Routledge)

CORRETTI, A. and CAPELLI, C. 2003 'Entella. Il granaio ellenistico (SAS 3). Le anfore', in *Atti delle quarte giornate internazionali di studi sull'area elima, Erice 1–4 dicembre 2000* (Pisa: Scuola Normale Superiore), 287–351

COURTOT, R. 1989 *Campagnes et villes dans les huertas valenciennes* (Paris: Éditions du Centre National de la Recherche Scientifique)

CRAWFORD, M. H. 1985 *Coinage and money under the Roman Republic. Italy and the Mediterranean economy* (London: Methuen)

CURCIO, G. and PELAGATTI, P. 1970 'Akrai (Siracusa). Ricerche nel territorio', *NSc* 1970, 436–523

CURTIS, R. I. 1984 'The salted fish industry of Pompeii', *Archaeology* 37.6, 58–9 and 74–5

CURTIS, R. I. 1988 'A. Umbricius Scaurus of Pompeii', in R. I. Curtis (ed.), *Studia Pompeiana and Classica in honor of Wilhelmina F. Jashemski* (New Rochelle NY: A. D. Caratzas), 19–49

CURTIS, R. I. 1991 Garum *and* salsamenta. *Production and commerce in* materia medica (Leiden: E. J. Brill)

DE ANGELIS, F. 2001 'Archaeology in Sicily, 1996–2000', *Archaeological Reports* 47, 145–201

DE CESARE, M. 2003 'La ceramica figurata italiota e siceliota ad Entella', in *Quarte giornate internazionali di studi sull'area elima, Erice 1 – 4 dicembre 2000. Atti del convegno* (Pisa: Scuola normale superiore), 253–69

DENARO, M. 1995 'La distribuzione delle anfore ellenistico-romane in Sicilia (III sec. a.C.–III sec. d.C.)', *Kokalos* 41, 183–205

DENEAUVE, J. 1969 *Lampes de Carthage* (Paris: Centre national de la recherche scientifique)

DE SENA, E. C. and IKÄHEIMO, J. P. 2003 'The supply of

amphora-borne commodities and domestic pottery in Pompeii, 150 BC–AD 79: preliminary evidence from the House of the Vestals', *European Journal of Archaeology* 6, 301–21

DESSE-BERSET, N. and DESSE, J. 2000 '*Salsamenta, garum* et autres préparations de poissons. Ce qu'en disent les os', *MEFRA* 112, 73–97

DI VITA, A. 1982 'Evidenza dei terremoti del 306–310 e del 365 in monumenti e scavi di Tunisia, Sicilia, Roma e Cirenaica', *Africa* 7–8, 127–39

DOMERGUE, C. 1973 *Belo, 1. La stratigraphie* (Madrid: Casa de Velázquez)

EISEMAN, C. J. and RIDGWAY, B. S. 1987 *The Porticello shipwreck: a Mediterranean merchant vessel of 415–385 B.C.* (College Station TX: Texas A & M University Press)

EMPEREUR, J.-Y. and HESNARD, A. 1987 'Les amphores hellénistiques', in P. Lévêque and J.-P. Morel (eds), *Céramiques hellénistiques et romaines*, volume 2 (Paris: Belles Lettres), 9–71

ENGELS, D. 1990 *Roman Corinth. An alternative model for the classical city* (Chicago: University of Chicago Press)

ERIM, K. 1958 'Morgantina', *AJA* 62, 79–90

ERSKINE, A (ed.) 2003 *A companion to the Hellenistic world* (Oxford and Malden MA: Blackwell)

ETTLINGER, E., HEDINGER, B., HOFFMAN, B., KENRICK, P. M., PUCCI, G., ROTH-RUBI, K., SCHNEIDER, G., VON SCHNURBEIN, S., WELLS, C. and ZABEHLICKY-SCHEFFENEGGER, S. 1990 *Conspectus formarum terrae sigillatae italico modo confectae* (Bonn: Rudolf Habelt)

EVANS, A. K. B. 1981 'Pottery and history', in A. C. Anderson (ed.), *Roman pottery research in Britain and North-West Europe. Papers presented to Graham Webster* [BAR International Series 123] (Oxford: British Archaeological Reports), 517–35

FACELLA, A. 2006. *Alesa Arconidea. Ricerche su un'antica città della Sicilia tirrenica* (Pisa: Edizioni della Normale)

FACELLA, A. 2010 'San Marco d'Alunzio', in *BTCGI* 18, 44–57

FAZELLO, F. T. 1558. *De rebus Siculis decades duae, nunc primum in lucem editae* (Panormi)

FENTRESS, E. 2001 'Villas, wine and kilns. The landscape of Jerba in the late hellenistic period', *JRA* 14, 249–68

FENTRESS, E., FONTANA, S., HITCHNER, R. B. and PERKINS, P. 2004 'Accounting for ARS: fineware and sites in Sicily and Africa', in S. Alcock and J. F. Cherry (eds), *Side-by-side survey. Comparative regional studies in the Mediterranean world* (Oxford: Oxbow Books), 147–62

FIERTLER, G. 2003 'La *Pantellerian ware* dal quartiere ellenistico-romano di Agrigento. Aspetti della problematica e proposta per una tipologia', in G. Fiorentini, M. Caltabiano and A. Calderone (eds), *Archeologia del Mediterraneo. Studi in onore di Ernesto De Miro* (Rome: L'Erma di Bretschneider), 321–37

FINKIELSZTEJN, G. 2001 *Chronologie détaillée et révisée des éponymes amphoriques rhodiens, de 270 à 108 av. J.-C. environ. Premier bilan* (Oxford: Archaeopress)

FINLEY, M. 1973 *The ancient economy* (Berkeley and London: University of California Press)

FIORE, P. 1971a 'Il cippo di Quinto Cecilio Calactense e la zona archeologica dell'antica Calacta', *SicA* 13, 50–3

FIORE, P. 1971b 'Acquedotto sacro a Demetra', *SicA* 14, 37–9

FIORE, P. 1971c 'Contributo all'individuazione della zona archeologica dell'antica Calacta', *SicA* 16, 54–61

FIORE, P. 1974 'Il diverticulum Calacte–Solusapre e la viabilità antica nella zona delle Caronie', *SicA* 26, 41–9

FIORE, P. 1976 'Sull'antico acquedotto calactino', *SicA* 31, 43–8

FIORE, P. 1980 'Alla ricerca di Solusapre', *SicA* 44, 31–8

FIORE, P. 1991 *Ducezio, Caronia, Calacta. Venticinque secoli di storia* (Palermo: Flaccovio).

FISCHER-HANSEN, T., HEINE NIELSEN, T. and AMPOLO, C. 2004 'Sikelia', in T. Fischer-Hansen (ed.), *An inventory of archaic and classical* poleis (Oxford: Oxford University Press), 172–248

FORABOSCHI, D. 1994 'Economie plurali ed interdipendenze', in *L'Italie d'Auguste à Dioclétien. Actes du colloque international, Rome 25–28 mars 1992* [Collection de l'École française de Rome 198] (Rome: École française de Rome), 215–18

FORMENTI, F., HESNARD, A. and TCHERNIA, A. 1978 'Une amphore Lamboglia 2 contenant du vin dans l'épave de la Madrague de Giens', *Archaeonautica* 2, 95–100

FORTI, S. 2011 'Le anfore romane del porto romano di Ancona: problemi e prospettive di ricerca', *Ocnus* 19, 231–8

FRANCO, C. and CAPELLI, C. 2014a 'Sicilian flat-bottomed amphorae (1st–5th c.). New data on typo-chronology and from a distribution and from an integrated petrographic and archaeological study', in D. Malfitana and G. Cacciaguerra (eds), *Archeologia classica in Sicilia e nel Mediterraneo. Didattica e ricerca nell'esperienza mista CNR e università* (Catania: Officina della stampa), 341–62

FRANCO, C. and CAPELLI, C. 2014b 'New archaeological and archaeometric data on Sicilian wine amphorae in the Roman period (1st to 6th century AD). Typology, origin and distribution in selected western Mediterranean contexts', *RCRFActa* 43, 547–55

FREDERIKSEN, M., 1984 *Campania* (Rome: British School at Rome)

FREEMAN, E. A. 1891 *The history of Sicily from the earliest times*, volume 1 (Oxford: Clarendon Press)

FREY-KUPPER, S. 2013 *Die antiken Fundmünzen vom Monte Iato 1971–1990. Ein Beitrag zur Geldgeschichte Westsiziliens*, 2 volumes [Studia Ietina 10] (Prahins: Éditions du Zèbre)

GÀBRICI, E. 1927 *La monetazione di bronzo nella Sicilia antica* (Palermo: Scuola Tipografia "Boccone del Povero")

GARGALLO DI CASTEL LENTINI, P. 1970 'The ports of ancient Syracuse', *Archaeology* 23, 312–17

GARNSEY, P., HOPKINS, K. and WHITTAKER, C. R. (eds) 1983 *Trade in the ancient economy* (London: Chatto & Windus)

GAROZZO, B. 2001 'Segesta. Bolli su anfore e laterizi rinvenuti nelle campagne 1995–1997 con aggiornamenti per gli anni 1990–1993', *ASNP* ser. iv, 6, 502–10

GAROZZO, B. 2003 'Nuovi dati sull'*instrumentum domesticum* bollato – anfore e laterizi – dal palermitano', in *Quarte giornate internazionali di studi sull'area elima, Erice 1 – 4 dicembre 2000. Atti del convegno* (Pisa: Scuola Normale Superiore), 557–683

GAROZZO, B. 2011 *Bolli su anfore e laterizi in Sicilia (Agrigento, Palermo, Trapani)* (Pisa: Scuola Normale Superiore)

GIBBINS, D. 2001 'Shipwrecks and hellenistic trade', in Archibald et al. 2001, 273–312

GIGLIO, R. 1997–98 'Attività di ricerca archeologica nella provincia di Trapani', *Kokalos* 43–4, 793–869

GIORGETTI, D. (ed.) 2006 *Le fornaci romane di Alcamo. Rassegna ricerche e scavi 2003/2005* (Rome: Aracne)

GIORGETTI, D. and GONZALEZ MURO, X. (eds) 2011 *Le fornaci romane di Alcamo. Rassegna di studi e ricerche 2006/2008. Catalogo dei materiali* (Imola: La Mandragora Editrice)

GOLDSBERRY, M. A. S. 1980 *Sicily and its cities in Hellenistic and Roman times* (Ann Arbor: UMI Dissertation Services)

GRACE, V. 1934 'The stamped amphora handles found in 1931–1932', *Hesperia* 3, 197–310

GRAINGER, S. 2013 'Roman fish sauce: fish bones residues and the practicalities of supply', *Archaeofauna* 22, 13–28

GRAINGER, S. 2014 '*Garum, liquamen*, and *muria*: a new approach to the problem of definition', in Botte and Leitch 2014, 37–46

GRAINGER, S. 2018 '*Garum* and *liquamen*, what's in a name?', *Journal of Maritime Archaeology* 13, 247–61

GRAS, M. 1988 'L'apport des amphores à la connaissance des commerces archaïques en mer Tyrrhénienne', *Pact* 20, 291–9

GRAS, M. 1993 'Pour une Méditerranée des emporia', in A. Bresson and P. Rouillard (eds), *L'emporion* [Publications du Centre Pierre Paris 26] (Paris: Centre Pierre Paris), 103–11

GUIDOBONI, E. 1994 *Catalogue of ancient earthquakes in the Mediterranean area up to the 10th century* (Rome: Istituto Nazionale di Geofisica)

GUIDOBONI, E., MUGGIA, A. and VALENSISE, G. 2000 'Aims and methods in territorial archaeology: possible clues to a strong fourth-century AD earthquake in the Straits of Messina (southern Italy)', in W. J. McGuire, D. R. Griffiths, P. L. Hanock and I. S. Stewart (eds), *The archaeology of geological catastrophes* [Geological Society London, Special Publications 171] (London: Geological Society), 45–70

HANSEN, M. H. 1995 'Kome: a study in how the Greeks designated and classified settlements which were not *poleis*', in M. H. Hansen and K. Raaflaub (eds), *Studies in the ancient Greek polis* [Papers from the Copenhagen Polis Centre 2] (Stuttgart: Franz Steiner Verlag), 45–81

HARRIS, W. V. 1979 *War and imperialism in Republican Rome, 327–70 B.C.* (Oxford: Clarendon Press)

HARRIS, E. M. 2002 'Workshop, marketplace and household. The nature of technical specialization in classical Athens and its influence on economy and society', in Cartledge et al. 2002, 67–99

HAYES, J. W. 1972 *Late Roman pottery* (London: British School at Rome)

HEDINGER, B. 1999 *Die frühe Terra sigillata vom Monte Iato, Sizilien (Ausgrabungen 1971–1988) und frühkaiserzeitliche Fundkomplexe aus dem Peristylhaus 1* [Studia Ietina 8] (Lausanne: Payot)

HESNARD, A. 1980 'Un dépôt augustéen d'amphores à la Longarina, Ostie', *Memoirs of the American Academy in Rome* 36, 141–56

HESNARD, A., RICQ, M., ARTHUR, P., PICON, M. and TCHERNIA, A. 1989 'Aires de production des Gréco-Italiques et des Dr 1', in *Amphores romaines et histoire économique. Dix ans de recherche. Actes du colloque de Sienne* [Collection de l'École française de Rome 114] (Rome: École française de Rome), 21–65

HITCHNER, R. B. 2002 'Olive production in the Roman economy: the case for intensive growth in the Roman Empire', in Scheidel and von Reden 2002, 71–83

HODOS, T. 2000 'Wine wares in protohistoric eastern Sicily', in Smith and Serrati 2000, 41–54

HOLM, A. 1870–98 *Geschichte Siciliens im Alterthum*, volumes 1–3 (Leipzig: W. Engelmann)

HOPKINS, K. 1980 'Taxes and trade in the Roman Empire, 200 B.C.–A.D. 400', *JRS* 70, 101–25

HOOVER, O. D. 2012 *Handbook of coins of Sicily (including Lipara). Civic, royal, Siculo-Punic and Romano-Sicilian issues. Sixth to first centuries BC* [Handbook of Greek Coinage Series 2] (Lancaster PA and London: Classical Numismatic Group)

HORDEN, P. and PURCELL, N. 2000 *The corrupting sea. A study of Mediterranean history* (Oxford and Malden, MA: Blackwell)

HUGHES-WARRINGTON, M. 2014, *Fifty key thinkers on history* [Routledge Key Guides] (London: Routledge)

HUMPHREYS, S. C. 1978 *Anthropology and the Greeks* (London: Routledge and Kegan Paul)

IKÄHEIMO, J. P. 2003 'The ploughsoil assemblage of zone 4a at Ficana (Monte Cugno)', *OpRom* 28, 34–45

JACKMAN, T. 2006 'Ducetius and fifth century Sicilian tyranny', in S. Lewis (ed.), *Ancient tyranny* (Edinburgh: Edinburgh University Press), 33–48

KÄCH, D. 2006 *Die Öllampen vom Monte Iato: Grabungskampagnen 1971–1992* [Studia Ietina 9] (Lausanne: Payot)

KAPITÄN, G. 1972 'Le anfore del relitto romano di Capo Ognina (Siracusa)', in *Recherches sur les amphores romaines* [Collection École française de Rome 10] (Rome: École française de Rome), 243–52

KARIVIERI, A. and FORSELL, R. 2008 'New results from the campaigns of 2003–2006 in the Casa di Caecilius Iucundus (V, 1, 22–27)', in P. G. Guzzo and M. P. Guidobaldi (eds), *Nuove ricerche archeologiche nell'area vesuviana (scavi 2003–2006). Atti del convegno internazionale, Roma, 1–3 febbraio 2007* [Studi della Soprintendenza archeologica di Pompei 25] (Rome: L'Erma di Bretschneider), 103–08

KARLSSON, L. 1992 *Fortification towers and masonry techniques in the hegemony of Syracuse, 405–211 B.C.* [Skrifter utgivna av Svenska Institutet i Rom 49] (Stockholm: Svenska Institutet i Rom)

KARLSSON, L. 1995 'The symbols of freedom and democracy on the bronze coinage of Timoleon', in T. Fischer-Hansen (ed.), *Ancient Sicily* [Acta Hyperborea 6] (Copenhagen: Museum Tusculanum Press), 149–69

KEAY, S. J. 1984 *Late Roman amphorae in the western Mediterranean. A typology and economic study. The Catalan evidence*, 2 volumes [BAR International series 196] (Oxford: British Archaeological Reports)

KENRICK, P. M. 1985 *Excavations at Sidi Khrebish, Benghazi (Berenice). Volume 3.1, The fine pottery* (Tripoli: Department of Antiquities)

KIM, H. S. 2002 'Small change and the moneyed economy', in Cartledge et al. 2002, 44–51

KISLINGER, E., METAXAS, S., OTT, I., ANSORGE, C., NEUBAUER, W., MENCARELLI, B., NIGST, P., SCHARRER-LIŠKA, G. and SEREN, S. 2004 'Conventazzo (Torrenova/ME): Archäologie und Geschichte (FWF-Projekt P14997)', *Anzeiger der Philosophisch-historischen Klasse der Österreichischen Akademie der Wissenschaften* 139, 101–71

KOEHLER, C. G. 1981 'Corinthian developments in the study of trade in the fifth century', *Hesperia* 50, 449–58

KOEHLER, C. G. 1992 'A brief typology and chronology of Corinthian transport amphoras' (a translation of part of a book in Russian published in Saratov by V. I. Kats and S. I. Monakhov) http://projects.chass.utoronto.ca/amphoras/corab92.htm

KRÖNIG, W. 1977 *Il Castello di Caronia in Sicilia: un complesso normanno del XII secolo* (Rome: Edizioni dell' Elefante)

KURKE, L. 1999 *Coins, bodies, games and gold. The politics of meaning in Archaic Greece* (Princeton: Princeton University Press)

LAMBOGLIA, N. 1951 'Ceramica 'presigillata' a Ventimiglia, a Minorca e in Sicilia', *AEA* 24, 35–41

LAMBOGLIA, N. 1952 *Per una classificazione preliminare della ceramica campana* (Bordighera: Istituto Internazionale di Studi Liguri)

LAUBENHEIMER, F. 1985 *La production des amphores en Gaule Narbonnaise* (Paris: Les Belles Lettres)

LAWALL, M. 2005 'Amphoras and Hellenistic economies: addressing the (over)-emphasis on stamped amphora handles', in Archibald et al. 2005, 188–232

LAWALL, M. 2011 'Greek amphorae in the archaeological record', in M. Lawall and J. Lund (eds), *Pottery in the archaeological record. Greece and beyond. Acts of the international colloquium held at the Danish and Canadian Institutes in Athens, June 20–22 2008* (Aarhus: Aarhus University Press), 38–50

LEIGHTON, R. 1999 *Sicily before History. An archaeological survey from the palaeolithic to the Iron Age* (London: Duckworth)

LENTINI, M. C. 2001 'Naxos di Sicilia dall'età ellenistica all'età bizantina', in Lentini 2001, 13–39

LENTINI, M. C. (ed.) 2001 *Naxos di Sicilia in età romana e bizantina ed evidenze dai Peloritani* (Bari: Edipuglia)

LENTINI, M.C., GÖRANSSON, K. and LINDHAGEN, A. 2002 'Excavations at Sicilian Caronia, ancient Kale Akte, 1999–2001. With a contribution by Paola Pelagatti', *OpRom* 27, 79–108

LEONE, R. and SPIGO, U. (eds) 2008 *Tyndaris 1. Ricerche nel settore occidentale. Campagne di scavo 1993–2004* (Palermo: Regione Siciliana)

LEVEAU, P. 1983 'La ville antique, "ville de consommation"? Parasitisme et économie antique', *Études rurales* 89–91, 275–83

LÉVÊQUE, P., MOREL, J.-P. and BRUNEAU, P. (eds) 1980 *Céramiques hellénistiques et romaines*, volume 1 (Paris: Belles Lettres)

LINDAHL, A., FERROW, E., FUGLESANG, D. and SKÖLD, P. 2006 'The San Giovenale pottery: production and raw material', in A. Gibson (ed.), *Prehistoric pottery: some recent research* [BAR International Series 1509] (Oxford: Archaeopress), 89–10

LINDHAGEN, A. 2006 *Caleacte. Production and exchange in a north Sicilian town, c. 500 BC–500 AD*, PhD dissertation (Lund: Lund University)

LINDHAGEN, A. 2009 'The Lamboglia 2 and Dressel 6A amphorae: a central Dalmatian origin?', *JRA* 21, 83–108

LINDHAGEN, A. 2012 'Change and continuity. Long-term processes of urbanization and ruralisation at Kale Akte (Sicily)', in N. M. Burström, and F. Fahlander (eds), *Matters of scale. Processes and courses of events in the past and the present* [Stockholm Studies in Archaeology 56] (Stockholm: Department of Archaeology and Classical Studies), 129–45

LINDHAGEN, A. 2013 'The freedmen milieus at Delos and Narona. New perspectives on the Lamboglia 2 wine-trade', in A.-L. Schallin (ed.), *Perspectives on ancient Greece. Papers in celebration of the 60th Anniversary of the Swedish Institute at Athens* (Stockholm: Svenska Institutet i Athen), 231–50

LINDHAGEN, A. 2015 Review of M. Lombardo and F. Frisone (eds), *Colonie di colonie: le fondazioni sub-coloniali greche tra colonizazzione e colonialismo. Atti del convegno*, in *BABesch* 90, 241–3

LINDHAGEN, A. 2016 'Narona in Dalmatia. The rise and fall of a gateway community', in K. Höghammar, B. Alroth and A. Lindhagen (eds), *Ancient ports. The geography of connections. Proceedings of an international conference at the Department of Archaeology and Ancient History, Uppsala University, 23–25 September 2010* [Acta Universitatis Upsaliensis. Boreas Uppsala Studies in Ancient Mediterranean and Near Eastern Civilizations 34] (Uppsala: Uppsala Universitet), 226–51

LINDHAGEN, A. forthcoming a 'Kale Akte – "the Fair Promontory". New research and interpretations on the urban history and foundation by Ducetius', *CLARA. Classical Art and Archaeology* (Oslo: University of Oslo), forthcoming

LINDHAGEN, A. forthcoming b 'Amphorae from two tabernae (V,1, 24a and 25) in the House of Caecilius Iucundus at Pompeii', to be published on the homepage of the Swedish Pompeii Project:

www.pom-pejiprojektet.se

LINDHAGEN, A. forthcoming c 'A central Dalmatian origin of the Adriatic wine amphorae? New evidence from xrf-analysis', in *Proceedings of the 3rd IARPotHP conference at Split. Exploring the neighbourhood. The role of ceramics in understanding place in the Hellenistic world, Kastela, May 2017*, forthcoming

LO CASCIO, P. 1990 'Solanto: nuove scoperte archeologiche', *SicA* 73, 33–9

LOSEBY, S. T. 2012 'Post-Roman economies', in Scheidel 2012, 334–60

LOVE, J. R. 1991 *Antiquity and capitalism: Max Weber and the sociological foundations of Roman civilisation* (London: Routledge)

LOWRY, S. T. 1987 *The archaeology of economic ideas: the classical Greek tradition* (Durham NC: Duke University Press)

LUND, J. 2005 'An economy of consumption: the eastern sigillata industry in the Late Hellenistic period', in Archibald et al. 2005, 233–52

LYONS, C. L. 1996 *The archaic cemeteries* [Morgantina Studies 5] (Princeton NJ: Princeton University Press)

MALFITANA, D. 2004a 'Italian sigillata imported in Sicily: the evidence of stamps', in Poblome et al. 2004, 309–36

MALFITANA, D. 2004b 'Anfore e ceramiche fini da mensa orientali nella Sicilia tardo-ellenistica e romana: merci e genti tra Oriente ed Occidente', in J. Eiring and J. Lund (eds), *Transport amphorae and trade in the Eastern Mediterranean. Acts of the International Colloquium at the Danish Institute at Athens, September 2–2, 2002* [Monographs of the Danish Institute at Athens 5] (Athens: Danish Institute at Athens), 239–50

MALFITANA, D. 2007 *La ceramica "corinzia" decorata a matrice. Tipologia, cronologia ed iconografia di una produzione ceramica greca di età imperiale* [*RCRFActa* Supplementum 10] (Bonn: Habelt Verlag)

MALFITANA, D. and BONIFAY, M. (eds) 2016 *La ceramica africana nella Sicilia romana/La céramique africaine dans la Sicile romaine*, 2 vols (Catania: Istituto per i Beni Archeologici e Monumentali, C.N.R.)

MALFITANA, D., BOTTE, E., FRANCO, C., MORGANO, M. G. and PLAZO, A. L. 2008 'Roman Sicily Project («RSP»): ceramics and trade. A multidisciplinary approach to the study of material culture assemblages. First overview: the transport amphorae evidence', *Facta, a journal of Roman material culture studies* 2, 127–92

MALFITANA, D. and FRANCO, C. 2011 'Contesti archeologici, cultura materiale ed economie dal territorio di Priolo e dall'*hinterland* in età romana e tardo-romana. Dati ed evidenze dal «Roman Sicily Project: Ceramics and Trade»', in D. Malfitana and G. Cacciaguerra (eds), *Priolo romana, tardo romana e medievale. Documenti, paesaggi, cultura materiale. Volume 1* (Catania: Istituto Beni Archeologici e Monumentali), 111–42

MALFITANA, D., FRANCO, C. and DI MAURO, A. 2013 'Economy and trade of Sicily during Severan period. Highlights between archaeology and history', in E. C. Sena (ed.), *The Roman Empire during the Severan dynasty. Case studies in architecture, economy and literature* (Piscataway NJ: Gorgias Press), 415–62

MALFITANA, D. and FRANCO, C. 2013 "*Fructuosissima atque opportunissima provincia*' (Cicerone, *In Verrem* II.3.226): il sistema 'Sicilia' ed il ruolo economico delle città nella Sicilia romana. Il contributo dell' evidenza ceramica', in S. Keay (ed.), *Rome, Portus and the Mediterranean* [Archaeological Monographs of the British School at Rome 21] (London: British School at Rome), 177–204

MALFITANA, D., POBLOME, J. and LUND, J. (eds) 2006 *Old pottery in a new century. Innovating perspectives on Roman pottery studies. Atti del convegno internazionale di studi, Catania, 22–24 aprile 2004* (Catania: Istituto Beni Archeologici e Monumentali)

MALKIN, I. 2011 *A small Greek world. Networks in the ancient Mediterranean* (Oxford: Oxford University Press)

MALONE, C. and STODDART, S. 2000 'A house in the Sicilian hills', *Antiquity* 74, 471–2

MANACORDA, D. 1977 'Le anfore', in *Ostia IV* [Studi Miscellanei 23], 117–254

MANACORDA, D. 1989 'Le anfore dell'Italia repubblicana. Aspetti economici e sociali', in *Amphores romaines et histoire économique. Dix ans de recherche. Actes du colloque de Sienne, 22–24 mai 1986* [Collection École française de Rome 114] (Rome: École française de Rome), 443–6

MANACORDA, D. 2011 'Conclusioni', in *Ocnus* 19, 267–9

MANACORDA, D. and PALLECCHI, S. 2012 *Le fornaci romane di Giancola (Brindisi)* (Bari: Edipuglia)

MAÑÀ, J. M. 1951 'Sobre tipologia de las ánforas púnicas', *Crónica del VI Congreso Arquelógico del sudeste. Alcoy 1950* (Cartagena: Papeleria Española), 203–10

MANDRUZZATO, A. 1988 'La sigillata italica in Sicilia. Importazione, distribuzione, produzione locale', *ANRW* II, 11.1, 414–49

MANGANARO, G. 1964–65 'Città di Sicilia e santuari panellenici nel III e II sec. a.C.', *Siculorum Gymnasium* 17–18, 40–69

MANGANARO, G. 2003 'Agyrios capostipite di una famiglia di lucernari nella Catania del II sec. d.C.', in *Epigraphica. Atti delle Giornate di Studi di Roma e di Atene in memoria di Margherita Guarducci (1902–1999)* [Opuscula Epigraphica 10] (Rome: Edizioni Quasar), 135–40

MANGANARO, G. 2009 'Un frammento iscritto erratico dall'area di Caronia (Kaleakté)', *Zeitschrift für Papyrologie und Epigraphik* 170, 87–98

MANISCALCO, L. (ed.) 2008 *Il santuario dei Palici. Un centro di culto nella Valle del Margi* (Palermo: Regione Siciliana)

MANISCALCO, L. 2015 'Il santuario dei Palici alla luce delle ultime indagini', *Kokalos* 52, 161–76

MANISCALCO, L. and McCONNELL, B. 2003 'The sanctuary of the divine Palikoi (Rocchicella di Mineo, Sicily). Fieldwork from 1995 to 2001', *AJA* 107, 145–80

MANISCALCO, L. and McCONNELL, B. E. 2015 'Recent

discoveries at the Sanctuary of the Divine Palikoi', in Militello and Öniz 2015, 517–21

MANNI, E. 1966 'Note siciliote', *Kokalos* 12, 171–87

MANNI, E. 1981 *Geografia fisica e politica della Sicilia antica* (Rome: Giorgio Bretschneider)

MANNINO, K. 1986–87 'La monetazione di Kalacte', *QuadMess* 2, 125–43

MARTIN-KILCHER, S. 1993 'Amphoren der späten Republik und der frühen Kaiserzeit in Karthago', *RM* 100, 269–320

MARTIN-KILCHER, S. 1987–94 *Die römischen Amphoren aus Augst und Kaiseraugst: ein Beitrag zur römischen Handels- und Kulturgeschichte,* volumes 1–3 [Forschungen in Augst 7] (Augst: Amt für Museen und Archäologie des Kantons Basel-Landschaft)

MARZANO, A. 2013 *Harvesting the sea: the exploitation of marine resources in the Roman Mediterranean* (Oxford: Oxford University Press)

MARZANO, A. 2018 'Fish and fishing in the Roman world', *Journal of Maritime Archaeology* 13, 437–47

MATTINGLY, H. 1940 *Coins of the Roman Empire in the British Museum IV. Antoninus Pius to Commodus* (London: Trustees of the British Museum)

MATTINGLY, D. 1988 'Oil for export? A comparison of Libyan, Spanish and Tunisian olive oil production in the Roman empire', *JRA* 1, 33–56

MAURICI, F. 2010 'Le città della Sicilia bizantina: un problema aperto', in M. Congiu, S. Modeo and M. Arnone (eds), *La Sicilia bizantina: storia, città e territorio* (Caltanissetta: Salvatore Sciascia Editore), 113–46

MAURICI, F. and MINNELLA, M. 2006 *Antichi ponti di Sicilia* (Palermo: L'EPOS Società Editrice)

MAYET, F. 1980 'Les céramiques à parois fines: état de la question', in Lévêque et al. 1980, 201–30

McCANN, A. M. 1994 *Deep water archaeology. A Late-Roman ship from Carthage and an ancient trade route near Skerki bank off northwest Sicily* (Ann Arbor MI: Journal of Roman Archaeology)

MEIJER, F. and VAN NIJF, O. 1992 *Trade, transport and society in the ancient world: a sourcebook* (London: Routledge)

MEISTER, K. 1992 'La rottura degli equilibri. Dal contrasto con Siracusa all'ultima lotta con Cartagine', in L. Braccesi and E. De Miro (eds), *Agrigento e la Sicilia greca. Atti della settimana di studio, 2–8 maggio 1988* (Rome: L'Erma di Bretschneider), 114–20

MENCHELLI, S. 2011 'Anfore vinarie adriatiche: il Piceno e gli altri contesti produttivi regionali', *Ocnus* 19, 239–44

MESSINA, E. 2000 'Alcune anfore tardoromane di Lipari', in U. Spigo and M. C. Martinelli (eds), *Nuovi studi di archeologia eoliana* [Quaderni del Museo archeologico regionale eoliano 3] (Palermo: Regione Siciliana), 113–24

MILITELLO, E. 1961 'Troina. Scavi effettuati dall'Istituto di archeologia dell'Università di Catania negli anni 1958 e 1960', *NSc* 15, 322–404

MILITELLO, P. M. and ÖNIZ, H. (eds) 2015 *SOMA 2011. Proceedings of the 15th Symposium on Mediterranean archaeology, held at the University of Catania 3–5 March 2011* [BAR International Series 2695] (Oxford: Archaeopress)

MILLETT, M. 1993 'Samian from the sea: Cava Culip shipwreck IV', *JRA* 6, 415–19

MOREL, J.-P. 1963 'Recherches archéologiques et topographiques dans la region d'Assoro', *MEFRA* 75, 263–301

MOREL, J.-P. 1976 'Céramiques d'Italie et céramiques hellénistiques', in P. Zanker (ed.), *Hellenismus in Mittelitalien. Kolloquium in Göttingen vom 5. bis 9. Juni 1974* (Göttingen: Vandenhoeck und Ruprecht), 471–97

MOREL, J.-P. 1980 'La céramique campanienne, aquis et problèmes', in Lévêque, et al. 1980, 85–122

MOREL, J.-P. 1981 *La céramique campanienne: les formes* [Bibliothèque des Écoles françaises d'Athènes et de Rome 244] (Rome: École française de Rome)

MOREL, J.-P. 1989 'Les amphores et les autres céramiques (sur quelques problèmes amphoriques)', in *Amphores romaines et histoire économique. Dix ans de recherche. Actes du colloque de Sienne, 22–24 mai 1986* [Collection École française de Rome 114] (Rome: École française de Rome), 523–7

MORLEY, N. 2002 *Metropolis and hinterland: the city of Rome and the Italian economy, 200 B.C.–A.D. 200* (Cambridge: Cambridge University Press)

MORRIS, I. 2002 'Hard surfaces', in Cartledge et. al 2002, 8–43

MURRAY, O. 1993 *Early Greece* (London: Fontana Press, and New York: Harper Press)

MUSCOLINO, F. 2005–06 'A deposit of early-imperial amphorae from the harbour area of Naxos, Sicily', *Skyllis* 7, 104–14

MUSCOLINO, F. 2006 'Kalathoi iberici da Taormina. Aggiornamento sulla diffusione della ceramica iberica dipinta in Sicilia', *AEA* 79, 217–24

MÜHLENBOCK, C. 2008 *Fragments from a mountain society: tradition, innovation and interaction at archaic Monte Polizzo, Sicily*, PhD dissertation (Göteborg)

NAROTZKY, S. 1997 *New directions in economic anthropology* (London: Pluto Press)

NASELLI, S. 1949 *Engio e Gangi: nella storia, nella leggenda, nell'arte* (Palermo: Kefa-Lo Giudice)

NASELLI, S. 1951 *L'inesplorato Monte Albura o Alburchia nei rinvenimenti archeologici, nella leggenda e nella storia* (Castelbuono: Tipografia Le Madonie)

NICOLET, C. 1994 'Dîmes de Sicile, d'Asie et d'ailleurs', in *Le ravitaillement en blé de Rome et des centres urbains des débuts de la République jusqu'au Haut-Empire. Actes du colloque international organisé par le Centre Jean Bérard Naples, 14–16 février 1991* (Naples: Centre Jean Bérard), 215–27

OLCESE, G. 1993 *Le ceramiche comuni di Albintimilium. Indagine archeologica e archeometrica sui materiali dell'area del cardine* [Università di Siena. Quaderni del Dipartimento di archeologia e storia delle arti 35] (Florence: All'Insegna del Giglio)

OLCESE, G. 2004 'Anfore greco-italiche antiche. Alcune osservazioni sull'origine e sulla circolazione alla luce di recenti ricerche archeologiche ed archeometriche', in E. De Sena and H. Dessales (eds), *Metodi e approcci archeologici. L'industria e il commercio nell'Italia antica. Archaeological methods and approaches. Industry and commerce in ancient Italy* (Oxford: Archaeopress), 173–92

OLCESE, G. 2005–06 'The production and circulation of Greco-Italic amphorae of Campania. The data of the archaeological and archaeometric research', *Skyllis* 7, 60–75

OLCESE, G. 2010 *Le anfore greco italiche di Ischia. Archeologia e archeometria: artigianato ed economia nel Golfo di Napoli* (Rome: Quasar)

OLLÀ, A. 2001 'La produzione di anfore vinarie a Naxos (III a.C.–V d.C.)', in Lentini 2001, 47–60

OLLÀ, A. 2004 'Ceramica da Bagnoli–S. Gregorio: importazioni e produzioni locali', in Spigo 2004, 109–32

OLLÀ, A. 2008 'Anfore romane', in Leone and Spigo 2008, 279–87

OLLÀ, A. 2015. 'A manufacturing plant for fish salting in the first period of the Roman imperial age in Milazzo (ME)', in Militello and Öniz 2015, 603–8

OLLÀ, A. 2018. 'Impianti di *salsamenta* e di salse di pesce a Milazzo', in Bernabò Brea et al. 2018, 421–30

ORTON, C. R. 1975 'Quantitative pottery studies: some progress, problems and prospects', *Science and archaeology* 16, 30–5

ORTON, C. R. 1980 *Mathematics in archaeology* (London: Collins)

ORTON, C. R. 1993 'How many pots make five? – an historical review of pottery quantification', *Archaeometry* 35, 169–84

OSBORNE, R. 1996 'Pots, trade and the archaic Greek economy', *Antiquity* 70, 31–44

Ostia I = Carandini, A. et al. 1968 *Le Terme del nuotatore: scavo dell'ambiente IV* [Studi miscellanei 13] (Rome: De Luca)

Ostia II = Berti, F. et al. 1970 *Le Terme del nuotatore: scavo dell'ambiente I* [Studi miscellanei 16] (Rome: De Luca)

Ostia III = Carandini, A. et al. 1973 *Le Terme del nuotatore: scavo degli ambienti III, VI, VII* [Studi miscellanei 21] (Rome: De Luca).

Ostia IV = Anselmi, L. et al. 1977 *Le Terme del nuotatore: scavo dell'ambiente XVI e dell'area XXV* [Studi miscellanei 23] (Rome: De Luca)

OXÉ, A., COMFORT, H. and KENRICK, P. 2000 *Corpus vasorum Arretinorum. A catalogue of the signatures, shapes and chronology of Italian sigillata*, 2nd edition (Bonn: Rudolf Habelt)

PACETTI, F. 1998 'La questione delle Keay LII nell'ambito della produzione anforica in Italia', in L. Saguì (ed.), *Ceramica in Italia: VI–VII secolo. Atti del convegno in onore di John W. Hayes* (Florence: All'Insegna del Giglio), 185–208

PAIS, E. 1893 'Emendazioni diodorei', *Studi di filologia classica* 1, 113–26

PALACZYK, M. 2014 'Können Transportamphoren etwas über "social identity" aussagen? Fallbeispiel der Amphoren Dressel 21–22 vom Monte Iato', *RCRF Acta* 43, 581–8

PALAZZO, P. 2013 *Le anfore di Apani (Brindisi)* (Rome: Scienze e lettere)

PANELLA, C. 1989 'Gli scambi nel Mediterraneo occidentale dal IV al VII secolo dal punto di vista di alcune merci', in C. Abadie-Reynal et al., *Hommes et richesses dans l'empire byzantin, 1. IVe – VIIe siècle* (Paris: P. Lethielleux), 129–41

PANELLA, C. 1992 'Mercato di Roma e anfore galliche nella prima età imperiale', in F. Laubenheimer (ed.), *Les amphores en Gaule. Production et circulation. Table ronde internationale, Metz 4–6 octobre 1990* [Centre de recherches d'histoire ancienne 116] (Paris: Les Belles Lettres), 185–206

PANELLA, C. 1993 'Merci e scambi nel Mediterraneo tardoantico', in *Storia di Roma* 3. *L'età tardoantica, 2. I luoghi e le culture* (Turin: Giulio Einaudi editore), 613–97

PANELLA, C. 2010 'Roma, il suburbio e l'Italia in età medio- e tardo-repubblicana: cultura materiale, territori, economie', *Facta, a journal of Roman material culture studies* 4, 11–123

PANELLA, C. and TCHERNIA, A. 1994 'Produits agricoles transportés en amphores. L'huile et surtout le vin', in *L'Italie d'Auguste à Dioclétien. Actes du colloque international, Rome 25–28 mars 1992* [Collection de l'École française de Rome 198] (Rome: École française de Rome), 145–65

PANVINI, R. and CAMMINECI, A. 1993–94 'Il complesso rurale di contrada Piano Camera', *Kokalos* 39–40, 825–39

PANVINI, R. and ZAVETTIERI, G. 1993–94 'La necropoli *sub divo* di contrada Lannari', *Kokalos* 39–40, 851–66

PARKER, A. J. 1976–77 'Sicilia e Malta nel commercio marittimo dell'antichità', *Kokalos* 22–3, 622–31

PARKER, A. J. 1989 'Amphores Almagro 50 de l'épave de Randello, Sicilie', in *Amphores romaines et histoire économique. Dix ans de recherche. Actes du colloque de Sienne, 22–24 mai 1986* [Collection École française de Rome 114] (Rome: École française de Rome), 650–3

PARKER, A. J. 1992a *Ancient shipwrecks of the Mediterranean and the Roman provinces* [BAR International Series 580] (Oxford: British Archaeological Reports)

PARKER, A. J. 1992b 'Cargoes, containers and stowage. The ancient Mediterranean', *International Journal of Nautical Archaeology* 21, 89–100

PATERSON, J. 1998 'Trade and traders in the Roman world. Scale, structure, and organisation', in H. Parkins and C. Smith (eds), *Trade, traders and the ancient city* (London: Routledge), 149–67

PEACOCK, D. P. S. 1971 'Roman amphorae in pre-Roman Britain', in D. Hill and M. Jesson (eds), *The Iron Age and its hill-forts. Papers presented to Sir Mortimer Wheeler on the occasion of his eightieth year at a conference held by the Southampton University Archaeological Society 5th–7th March, 1971* (Southampton: University of Southampton, Department of Archaeology), 161–88

PEACOCK, D. P. S. 1977 'Roman amphorae: typology, fabric

and origin', in *Méthodes classiques et méthodes formelles dans l'étude des amphores. Actes du Colloque de Rome, 27–29 mars 1974* [Collection de l'École française de Rome 32] (Rome: École française de Rome), 261–78

PEACOCK, D. P. S. 1982 *Pottery in the Roman world. An ethnoarchaeological approach* (London: Longman)

PEACOCK, D. P. S. and WILLIAMS, D. F. 1986 *Amphorae and the Roman economy. An introductory guide* (London: Longman)

PECORAINO, M. (ed.) 1989 *La Sicilia di Jean Houel all'Ermitage* (Palermo: Sicilcassa)

PEÑA, J. T. 1999 *The urban economy during the early dominate: pottery evidence from the Palatine Hill* [BAR International Series 784] (Oxford: Archaeopress)

PEÑA, J. T. 2007a 'Two groups of *tituli picti* from Pompeii and environs: Sicilian wine, not flour, and hand-picked olives', *JRA* 20, 233–54

PEÑA, J. T. 2007b *Roman pottery in the archaeological record* (Cambridge: Cambridge University Press)

PESAVENTO MATTIOLI, S. 2001 'Nuovi dati sull'economia di Padova in epoca romana', *Bollettino del museo civico di Padova* 90, 7–18

PILAR EBERLE, L. and LE QUERÉ, E. 2017 'Land traders, trading agriculturalists? Land in the economy of the Italian diaspora in the Greek East', *JRS* 107, 27–59

PINZONE, A. 1990 'La *cura annonae* di Pompeo e l'introduzione dello *stipendium* in Sicilia', *Messana* n.s. 3, 169–200 [= Pinzone 1999, 173–206]

PINZONE, A. 1999 *Provincia Sicilia. Ricerche di storia della Sicilia romana da Gaio Flaminio a Gregorio Magno* [Testi e Studi di Storia Antica 7] (Catania: Edizioni del Prisma)

PIPITÒ, G. 1996 'I ponti della Via Valeria in Sicilia', *Rivista di Topografia Antica* 6, 197–210

POBLOME, J., TALLOEN, P., BRULET, R. and WAELKENS, M. (eds) 2004 *Early Italian sigillata. The chronological framework and trade patterns* [BABesch Supplement 10] (Leuven, Paris and Dudley, MA: Peeters)

POLANYI, K. 1944 *The great transformation* (New York: Rinehart and Co.)

POLANYI, K., ARENSBERG, C. M. and PEARSON, H. 1957 *Trade and market in the early empires: economies in history and theory* (London: Collier-Macmillan Ltd)

POLANYI, K. 1977 *The livelihood of man*, edited by H. W. Pearson (New York: Academic Press)

POLITO, A. 2000 'La circolazione della sigillata italica liscia in Sicilia', *QuadMess* 7, 65–99

POLIZZI, C. 1997 'Materiali dalla necropoli punica di Solunto: studi preliminari. Anfore greche da trasporto', in *Archeologia e territorio* (Palermo: Palumbo), 95–103

PONSICH, M. 1961 *Les lampes romaines en terre cuite de la Maurétanie Tingitane* [Services des antiquités du Maroc 15] (Rabat: Service des Antiquités du Maroc)

PONTACOLONE, L. and INCITTA, M. 1991 'Un relitto con carico di merci africane di età imperiale alle Trincere (Tarquinia)', in A. Mastino (ed.), *L'Africa romana. Atti dell'VIII Convegno di studio. Cagliari, 14–16 dicembre 1990* (Sassari: Galizzi), 543–70

PONTORNO, S. 1966 *Il sito di Erbita rilevato coi dati della Cosmographia e delle Verrine* (Nicosia: Tipografia Lacagnina)

POPE, S. 2006 *The fourth century settlement at Palike, Sicily*, PhD dissertation, Brown University

POPE, S. 2014 'Developments in Greek fortifications in Sicily in the fourth century BC', in M. Tsipopoulou (ed.), *Meditations on the diversity of the built environment in the Aegean Basin and beyond. Proceedings of a colloquium in memory of Frederick E. Winter* [Publications of The Canadian Institute in Greece 8], Athens: The Canadian Institute in Greece

PRAG, J. and TIGANO, G. 2017. *Alesa Archonidea: il lapidarium* [Introduzioni all'archeologia di Halaesa 8], Palermo: Regione Sicilia

PRESTIANNI GIALLOMBARDO, A. M. 1998 'Società ed economia in Alesa arconidea', in A. M. Prestianni-Giallombardo (ed.), *Colloquio alesino. Atti del colloquio tenutosi il 7 maggio 1995 in S. Maria delle Palate (Tusa)* [Testi e studi di storia antica 6] (Catania: Edizioni del Prisma), 59–80

PRESTIANNI GIALLOMBARDO, A. M. 2003 'Divinità e culti in Halaesa Archonidea. Tra identità etnica ed interazione culturale', in *Quarte giornate internazionali di studi sull'area elima, Erice 1 – 4 dicembre 2000. Atti del convegno* (Pisa: Scuola Normale Superiore), 1059–1103

PRESTIANNI GIALLOMBARDO, A. M. 2006 'Ducezio, l'oracolo e la fondazione di Kale Akte,' in *Diodoro Siculo e la Sicilia indigena. Atti del convegno di studi* (Palermo: Regione Siciliana), 135–49

PRYOR, F. L. 1977 *The origins of the economy: a comparative study of distribution in primitive and peasant economies* [Studies in social discontinuity] (New York: Academic Press)

PUCCI, G. 1983 'Pottery and trade in the Roman period', in Garnsey et al. 1983, 105–17

PUGLISI, M. 2008 'Coin finds from Capo d'Orlando (Messina, Sicily)', *Schweizer Münzblätter* 232, 99–102

PURCELL, N. 1985 'Wine and wealth in ancient Italy', *JRS* 75, 1–19

PURPURA, G. 1982 'Pesca e stabilimenti antichi per la lavorazione del pesce in Sicilia: I – S. Vito (Trapani), Cala Minnola (Levanzo)', *SicA* 48, 45–60

PURPURA, G. 1985 'Pesca e stabilimenti antichi per la lavorazione del pesce in Sicilia: II – Isola delle femmine (Palermo), Punta Molinazzo (Punta Rais), Tonnara del Cofano (Trapani), S. Nicola (Favignana)', *SicA* 57–8, 59–86

RAMÓN, J. 1995 *Las ánforas fenicio-púnicas del Mediterráneo central y occidental* [Col·lecció Instrumenta 2] (Barcelona: Universitat de Barcelona)

REGER, G. 2003 'The economy', in Erskine 2003, 331–53

REVILLA CALVO, V. 2001 'Las ánforas tunecinas y tripolitanas de los siglos II y III d. C.: tipologias y circulacion', in J. M. Blazquez Martinez and J. Remesal Rodriguez (eds), *Estudios sobre el Monte Testaccio (Roma). II* [Corpus International des timbres amphoriques 8, Instrumenta 10] (Barcelona: Universidad de Barcelona), 367–90

REYNOLDS, P. 1995 *Trade in the western Mediterranean, AD 400–700. The ceramic evidence* [BAR International Series 604] (Oxford: Tempus Reparatum)

REYNOLDS, P. 2005 'Levantine amphorae from Cilicia to Gaza: a typology and analysis of regional production trends from the 1st to 7th centuries', *LRCW I. Late Roman coarse wares, cooking wares and amphorae in the Mediterranean: archaeology and archaeometry* [BAR International Series 1340] (Oxford: Archaeopress), 563–612

REYNOLDS, P. 2010 *Hispania and the Roman Mediterranean, AD 100–700. Ceramics and trade* (London: Duckworth)

RHODES, M. 1989 'Roman pottery lost en route from the kiln site to the user. A gazetteer', *Journal of Roman Pottery Studies* 2, 44–58

RICE, C. 2016 'Shipwreck cargoes in the western Mediterranean and the organization of Roman maritime trade', *JRA* 29, 165–92

RICKMAN, G. 1980 *The corn supply of ancient Rome* (Oxford: Clarendon Press)

RILEY, J. A. 1979 'The coarse pottery from Berenice', in G. Barker, A. Bonanno, J. A. Riley and J. Lloyd, *Excavations at Sidi Khrebish, Benghazi (Berenice). Volume 2* [Libya Antiqua Supplement 5] (Tripoli: Socialist People's Libyan Arab Jamahiriya, Secretariat of Education, Department of Antiquities), 91–467

RIZZO, F. P. 1970 *La repubblica di Siracusa nel momento di Ducezio* (Palermo: U. Maneredi Editore)

RIZZO, G. and MORENO MEGÍAS, V. 2019 'Roma e le prime importazioni di alimenti ispanici trasportati in anfora', *JRA* 32, 23–38

RIZZO, M. S. 1993 'Anfore', in Belvedere et al. 1993, 217–25

RIZZO, M. S., ZAMBITO, L., GIANNICI, F., GIARRUSSO, R., and MULONE, A. 2014 'Anfore di tipo siciliano dal territorio di Agrigento,' in N. Poulou-Papadimitriou, E. Nodarou, and V. Kilikoglou (eds), *LRCW 4. Late Roman coarse wares, cooking wares and amphorae in the Mediterranean: archaeology and archaeometry. The Mediterranean: a market without frontiers* [BAR International Series 2616] (Oxford: Archaeopress), 213–23

ROBINSON, H. S. 1959 *The Athenian agora V. Pottery of the Roman period* (Princeton NJ: The American School of Classical Studies at Athens)

ROSTOVTZEFF, M. I. 1957 *The social and economic history of the Roman Empire*, 2nd edition revised by P. M. Fraser (Oxford: Clarendon Press)

ROTROFF, S. I. 1997 *The Athenian agora. Results of excavations conducted by the American School of Classical Studies at Athens 29. Hellenistic pottery: Athenian and imported wheelmade table ware and related material* (Princeton NJ: The American School of Classical Studies at Athens)

ROWLANDS, M., LARSEN, M. and KRISTIANSEN, K. (eds) 1987 *Centre and periphery in the ancient world* [New directions in archaeology] (Cambridge: Cambridge University Press)

ROYAL, J. G. 2012 'Illyrian Coastal Exploration Program (2007–2009). The Roman and Late Roman finds and their contexts", *AJA* 116, 405–60

SAHLINS, M. 1972 *Stone age economics* (Chicago: Aldine-Atherton)

SALINAS, A. 1876 *Le monete delle città antiche di Sicilia* (Palermo: Stabilimento tipografico di Francesco Lao)

SALINAS, A. 1880 'Escursioni archeologiche a S. Marco, S. Fratello, Patti e Tindari', *NSc* 1880, 191–4

SANGINETO, A. B. 2002 'Trasformazioni o crisi nei *Bruttii* fra il II a. C. ed il VII d. C.?', in E. Lo Cascio, and A. Storchi Marino (eds), *Modalità insediative e strutture agrarie nell'Italia meridionale in età romana* (Bari: Edipuglia), 203–46

SANTORO BIANCHI, S., GUIDUCCI, G. and TUSA, S. (eds) 2003 Pantellerian ware. *Archeologia subacquea e ceramiche da fuoco a Pantelleria* (Palermo, Regione Siciliana and Dario Flaccovio Editore)

SÄRSTRÖM, M. 1940 *A study in the coinage of the Mamertines* (Lund: Gleerup)

SCHAPS, D. M. 1998 Review of Tandy 1997 in *Bryn Mawr Classical Review* https://bmcr.brynmawr.edu/1997/97.11.07.html

SCHAPS, D. M. 2004 *The invention of coinage and the monetization of ancient Greece* (Ann Arbor: University of Michigan Press)

SCHEIDEL, W. (ed.), 2012 *The Cambridge companion to the Roman economy* (Cambridge: Cambridge University Press)

SCHEIDEL, W. and VON REDEN, S. (eds) 2002 *The ancient economy* (New York: Routledge)

SCHENK VON STAUFFENBERG, A. 1933 *König Hieron der Zweite von Syrakus* (Stuttgart: Kohlhammer)

SCIALLANO, M. and SIBELLA, P. 1991 *Amphores. Comment les identifier?* (Aix-en-Provence: Edisud)

SCIBONA, G. 1971a 'Epigraphica Halaesina', *Kokalos* 17, 6–20

SCIBONA, G. 1971b 'Nota a I.G. XIV 2395.7 (Instrumentum publicum Calactinum)', *Kokalos* 17, 21–5

SCIBONA, G. 1978 'Archeologia classica e architettura normanna. Il castello di Caronia, di Wolfgang Krönig', *ArchStMess* 36, 431–40

SCIBONA, G. 1981 'Un 'kottabos' dalla terra dei Siculi', *ArchStMess* 39, 313–32

SCIBONA, G. 1982 'San Marco d'Alunzio (Messina): campagna di scavi 1979', *Beni Culturali Ambientali Sicilia* 3, 149

SCIBONA, G. 1987 'Caronia', in *BTCGI* 5, 6–9

SCIBONA, G. 2009 'L'agorà (scavi 1970–2004)', in Scibona and Tigano 2009, 9–43

SCIBONA, G. 2011 'Ricerche di topografia nel territorio dell'antica Καλὲ Ακτέ', in *Da Halaesa ad Agathyrnum. Studi in memoria di Giacomo Scibona* (Sant'Agata di Militello: Edizioni del Rotary Club Sant'Agata di Militello), 69–86

SCIBONA, G. and TIGANO, G. 2008 *Alesa Archonidea. Guida all'antiquarium* [Introduzione all'archeologia di Halaesa 1] (Palermo: Regione Siciliana)

SCIBONA, G. and TIGANO, G. (eds) 2009 *Alaisa–Halaesa. Scavi e ricerche (1970–2007)* (Messina: Sicania)

SCRAMUZZA, V. M. 1937 'Roman Sicily', in T. Frank (ed.),

An economic survey of ancient Rome 3 (Baltimore: The Johns Hopkins Press), 225–377

SERRATI, J. 2000 'Garrisons and grain', in Smith and Serrati 2000, 115–33

SJÖQVIST, E. 1960 'Excavations at Morgantina (Serra Orlando). Preliminary report 4, 1959', *AJA* 64, 125–35

SLEJ, K. 2008 'Transport amphorae', in M. Cullhed and K. Slej, *The Temple of Castor and Pollux. The finds and trenches* [Occasional papers of the Nordic Institutes] (Rome: L'Erma di Bretschneider), 201–70

SMITH, C. and SERRATI, J (eds) 2000 *Sicily from Aeneas to Augustus. New approaches in archaeology and history* (Edinburgh: Edinburgh University Press)

SMYTH, W. H. 1824 *Memoir descriptive of the resources, inhabitants, and hydrography, of Sicily and its islands, interspersed with antiquarian and other notices* (London: John Murray)

SONDI, I. and SLOVENEC, D. 2003 'The mineralogical characteristics of the *Lamboglia 2* Roman-age amphorae from the Central Adriatic (Croatia)', *Archaeometry* 45, 251–62

SORACI, C. 2011 *Sicilia frumentaria. Il grano siciliano e l'annona di Roma* [Saggi di storia antica 32] (Rome: L'Erma di Bretschneider)

SORICELLI, G. 2004 'La produzione di terra sigillata in Campania', in Poblome et al. 2004, 299–307

SOURISSEAU, J.-C. 2006 'Les amphores commerciales de la nécropole de Rifriscolaro, Camarine. Remarques préliminaries sur les productions corinthiennes de type A', in P. Pelagatti, G. Di Stefano and L. de Lachenal (eds), *Camarina 2600 anni dopo la fondazione. Nuovi studi sulla città e sul territorio. Atti del convegno internazionale, Ragusa, 7 dicembre 2002, 7–9 aprile 2003* (Ragusa: Centro Studi Feliciano Rossitto, and Rome: Istituto Poligrafico dello Stato), 129–47

SPAGNOLO, G. 2002 'Le anfore da trasporto arcaiche e classiche nell'occidente greco: nuove acquisizioni da recenti rinvenimenti a Messina', in Bacci and Tigano 1999–2002, volume 2.2, 31–46

SPIGO, U. 1987 'La ceramica siceliota a figure rosse – variazioni sul tema', *BdA*, ser. vi, 44–5, 1–24

SPIGO, U. 1995 'Il complesso termale di età imperiale romana della contrada Bagnoli–S. Gregorio. Scavi 1987–1994', in *Giornate di archeologia – architettura – storia, Da Tindari per Agatirno ad Alesa* (Capo d'Orlando; Archeoclub d'Italia, sede comprensoriale di Capo d'Orlando))

SPIGO, U. 2000 'Rapporti della pittura vascolare siceliota con la ceramica attica dello stile di Kerc per un approccio al problema', in B. Sabattini (ed.), *La céramique attique du IVe siècle en Méditerranée occidentale* (Naples: Centre Jean Bérard), 111–20

SPIGO, U. (ed.) 2004 *Archeologia a Capo d'Orlando. Studi per l'Antiquarium* (Milazzo: Rebus)

SPIGO, U., OLLÀ, A. and CAPELLI, C. 2006 'La ceramica di produzione locale dalle terme di Bagnoli–S.Gregorio a Capo d'Orlando', in Malfitana et al. 2006, 451–64

STILLWELL, R. 1967 'Excavations at Morgantina (Serra Orlando). Preliminary report 9, 1966', *AJA* 71, 245–50

STONE, S. C. 1984 *Roman pottery from Morgantina in Sicily*. PhD dissertation, Princeton University (Ann Arbor: University Microfilms)

STONE, S. C. 1983 'Sextus Pompey, Octavian and Sicily', *AJA* 87, 11–22

STONE, S. C. 2014 *The Hellenistic and Roman fine pottery* [Morgantina studies 6] (Princeton NJ: Princeton University Press)

STRASSLER, R. B. 2009 *The landmark Herodotus: the histories* (New York: Pantheon Books)

SUDANO, F. 2009 'La campagna di scavi 2003–2005 e le fasi dell'insediamento', in Bonanno 2009, 15–28

TCHERNIA, A. 1969 'Informations archéologiques: directions de recherches archéoloqiques sous marines', *Gallia* 27, 465–99

TCHERNIA, A. 1986 *Le vin de l'Italie romaine: essai d'histoire économique d'après les amphores* [Bibliothèque des écoles françaises d'Athènes et de Rome 261] (Rome: École française de Rome)

TCHERNIA, A. 2016 *The Romans and trade* (Oxford: Oxford University Press)

TEMIN, P. 2001 'A market economy in the early Roman Empire', *JRS* 91, 169–81

TEMIN, P. 2013 *The Roman market economy* (Princeton NJ: Princeton University Press)

THOMSEN, R. 1964 *Eisphora. A study of direct taxation in ancient Athens* [Humanitas 3] (Copenhagen: Gyldendal)

TIGANO, G. 1993–94 'Archeologia a Milazzo. Nuove acquisizioni', *Kokalos* 39–40, 1059–85

TIGANO, G. 2009 'La necropoli settentrionale: scavi in proprietà Purpura (1990–1993; 2007)', in Scibona and Tigano 2009, 153–84

TIGANO, G. 2012 'L'attività della Soprintendenza di Messina nel settore dei beni archeologici tra la fine del 2010 e il primo semestre del 2012', *ArchStMess* 93, 335–70

TOMBER, R. 1993 'Quantitative approaches to the investigation of long-distance exchange', *JRA* 6, 142–66

TORRE, R. 2019 'L'uso del laterizio e delle decorazioni fittili nell'architettura domestica siciliana in età tardo ellenistica', in Bonetto, Bukowiecki and Volpe 2019, 213–52

TORTORELLA, S. 1981 'Ceramica di produzione africana e rinvenimenti archeologici sottomarini della media e tarda età imperiale. Analisi dei dati e dei contributi reciproci', *MEFRA* 93, 355–72

TRENDALL, A. D. 1967 *The red-figured vases of Lucania, Campania and Sicily* (Oxford: Clarendon Press)

TRENDALL, A. D. 1989 *Red figure vases of South Italy and Sicily: a handbook* (London: Thames and Hudson)

TULLIO, A. 1997–98 'La necropoli ellenistica di Polizzi Generosa (contrada S. Pietro). Scavi 1993–1996', *Kokalos* 43–4, 721–30

TULLIO, A. 1997 'La necropoli di Polizzi Generosa (Contrada S. Pietro) a cinque anni dalla scoperta (1992–1996)' in *Archeologia e territorio* (Palermo: Palumbo), 267–74

TUSA, S. 1997 'Origine della società agro-pastorale,' in S. Tusa (ed.), *Prima Sicilia. Alle origini della società siciliana* (Palermo: Regione Siciliana), 171–91

TUSA, S. 2010 *Archeologia e storia nei mari di Sicilia* (Udine: Magnus Edizioni)

TUSA, S., ZANGARA, S. and LA ROCCA, R. (eds) 2009 *Il relitto tardo-antico di Scauri a Pantelleria* (Palermo: Regione Siciliana)

UGGERI, G. 1997–98 'Itinerarie e strade, rotte, porti e scali della Sicilia tardoantica', *Kokalos* 43–4, 299–364

UGGERI, G. 2004 *La viabilità della Sicilia in età romana* (Galatina: Mario Congedo Editore)

VALLAT, J.-P. 1991 'Survey archaeology and rural history – a difficult but productive relationship', in G. Barker and J. Lloyd (eds), *Roman landscapes. Archaeological survey in the Mediterranean region* [Archaeological Monographs of the British School at Rome 2] (London: British School at Rome), 10–17

VANDERMERSCH, C. 1994 *Vins et amphores de grande Grèce et de Sicile, IVe–IIIe s. avant J.-C.* [Études Centre Jean Bérard 1] (Naples: Centre Jean Bérard)

VANDERMERSCH, C. 2001 'Aux sources du vin romain dans le Latium et la Campanie à l'époque médio-républicaine', *Ostraka* 10, 157–206

VAN DER WERFF, J. H. 1977–78 'Amphores de tradition punique à Uzita', *BABesch* 52–3, 171–200

VAN DER WERFF, J. H. 1986 'The amphora wall in the House of the Porch, Ostia. Excavations in the House of the Porch (V.ii.4–5) at Ostia', *BABesch* 61, 96–137

VAN NEER, W., ERVYNCK, A. and MONSIEUR, P. 2010 'Fish bones and amphorae: evidence for the production and consumption of salted fish products outside the Mediterranean region', *JRA* 23, 161–95

VASSALLO, S. (ed.) 1999 *Colle Madore: un caso di ellenizzazione in terra sicana* (Palermo: Regione Siciliana)

VASSALLO, S. 2003 'Himera, necropoli di Pestavecchia. Un primo bilancio sulle anfore da trasporto', *Kokalos* 45, 329–79

VENUTI, M. 2019 'L'introduzione dell'opus latericium a Taormina: i casi della cd. Naumachia e del Teatro', in Bonetto, Bukowiecki and Volpe 2019, 253–60

VERBRUGGHE, G. P. 1976 *Sicilia* [Itinera Romana 2] (Bern: Kümmerly und Frey)

VON REDEN, S. 1995 *Exchange in ancient Greece* (London: Duckworth)

WALSH, J. 2006 *Ethnicity, daily life, and trade: domestic assemblages from fifth-century BCE Morgantina (Sicily)*, PhD dissertation, University of Virginia

WEBER, M. 1947 *The theory of social and economic organization*, translated by A. M. Henderson and T. Parsons (New York: The Free Press)

WEBER, M. 1976 *The agrarian sociology of ancient civilizations*, translated by R. I. Frank (London: NLB)

WHITBREAD, I. K. 1995 *Greek transport amphorae. A petrological and archaeological study* [Fitch Laboratory Occasional Paper 4] (London: British School at Athens)

WHITEHOUSE, D., COSTANTINI, L. and GUIDOBALDI, F. 1985 'The Schola Praeconum 2', *PBSR* 53, 163–210

WHITTAKER, C. R. 1983 'Late Roman trade and traders', in Garnsey et al. 1983, 163–80

WHITTAKER, C. R. 1990 'The consumer city revisited. The *vicus* and the city', *JRA* 3, 110–18

WICKHAM, C. 1988 'Marx, Sherlock Holmes and late Roman commerce', *JRS* 78, 183–93

WIDEMANN, F. et al. 1979 'Analytical and typological study of Gallo-Roman workshops producing amphorae in the area of Narbonne', in *Proceedings of the 18th international symposium on archaeometry and archaeological prospection 1978* (Cologne: Rheinland Verlag, and Bonn: R. Habelt Verlag), 317–41

WILL, E. L. 1982 'Greco-Italic amphoras', *Hesperia* 51, 338–56

WILLIAMS, D. 2001 'A petrological note on Roman pottery from Naxos, Sicily', in Lentini 2001, 61–2

WILSON, A. I. 2012 'A forum on trade', in Scheidel 2012, 287–318

WILSON, R. J. A. 1979 'Brick and tile in Roman Sicily', in A. McWhirr (ed.), *Roman brick and tile* [BAR International Series 68] (Oxford: British Archaeological Reports), 11–43

WILSON, R. J. A. 1985a Review of E. Manni, *Geografia fisica e politica della Sicilia antica* (1981), in *JRS* 75, 296–9

WILSON, R. J. A. 1985b 'Un insediamento agricolo romano a Castagna (comune di Cattolica Eraclea, AG)', *SicA* 57–8, 11–35

WILSON, R. J. A. 1988 'Trade and industry in Sicily', *ANRW* II, 11.1 (Berlin and New York: Walter de Gruyter), 207–305

WILSON, R. J. A. 1990 *Sicily under the Roman Empire. The archaeology of a Roman province, 36 BC – AD 535* (Warminster: Aris and Phillips)

WILSON, R. J. A. 2000a 'Iscrizioni su manufatti siciliani in età ellenistico-romana', in M. I. Gulletta (ed.), *Sicilia epigrafica. Atti del Convegno di studi, Erice, 15–18 ottobre 1998* [Annali della Scuola Normale Superiore di Pisa, Quaderni 1999, 1–2] (Pisa: Scuola Normale Superiore), 531–56

WILSON, R. J. A. 2000b 'Rural settlement in Hellenistic and Roman Sicily – excavations at Campanaio (AG) 1994–1998', *PBSR* 68, 337–69

WILSON, R. J. A. 2000c 'Campanaio – an agricultural settlement in Roman Sicily', *Antiquity* 74, 289–90

WILSON, R. J. A. 2015 'The coinage of Iaitas in the context of western Sicily', *JRA* 28, 554–8

WILSON, R. J. A. 2018 'Archaeology and earthquakes in Late Roman Sicily. Unpacking the myth of the *terrae motus per totum orbem* of AD 365', in Bernabò Brea et al. 2018, 445–66

WOOLF, G. 1998 *Becoming Roman: the origins of provincial civilization in Gaul* (Cambridge: Cambridge University Press)

ZEVI, F. 1966 'Appunti sulle anfore romane, 1. La tavola tipologica del Dressel', *Archeologia Classica* 18, 208–47

List of Illustrations

Colour plates (between pp. 118 and 119)

Plate 1. View from the south of the Norman castle at Caronía, presumed site of the acropolis of Kale Akte

Plate 2. Caronía at sunset

Plate 3. Caronía, the site of Kale Akte, perched on its rocky hill-top 302 m high, as seen from the west. The remains of the so-called Ponte Romano, of late sixteenth-century date, crosses the Fiume di Caronía in the foreground.

Plate 4. Marina di Caronía, aerial view looking north-west

Plate 5. Marina di Caronía, aerial view showing the position of the ancient settlement (excavation site arrowed) (red); cisterns (blue); the site of the necropolis; and an area of scattered suburban activity (yellow)

Plate 6. Caronía, aerial photograph of the modern town, with overlays showing the approximate extent of the ancient town of Kale Akte, the suggested street layout and the site of the *agora* (all in red) and of the necropolis (in yellow)

Plate 7. Halaesa, site of the ancient city from the south-east, with the line of the defensive walls in the immediate foreground and the remains of the *stoa* bordering the *agora* at the centre (under the red roof). The island of Alicudi in the Isole Eolie is visible in the distance.

Plate 8. San Marco d'Alunzio, the so-called Temple of Hercules, a small Hellenistic temple (the steps and west wall on the left are original) turned into the church of S. Marco in the high Middle Ages

Plate 9. San Marco d'Alunzio, 548 m high, from the north. The summit was crowned by a castle built in 1061, but less remains of it than of its counterpart at Caronía

Plate 10. Caronía, sherds of red-figure Sicilian pottery from a cistern deposit, excavated in 1999; last quarter of the fourth century BC

Plate 11. Caronía, surface find, black-gloss imitation of a medallion bowl, with painted rosette; third century BC

Plate 12. Pompeii, House of Caecilius Iucundus, example of a Dressel 21/22 amphora, of North Sicilian production, found in a shop attached to this property; late first century BC/first century AD

Plate 13. Marina di Caronía, Roman cistern, showing the central dividing wall in a double-aisled structure; probably second century AD. Its location is indicated by the southern-most blue circle on colour Plate 5

Plate 14. Marina di Caronía, Roman cistern, the other face of the same structure illustrated in plate 13, showing the use of brick-faced concrete for the walls; the beginning of the barrel-vaulted roof is also visible.

Plate 15. Coin from the mint of Kale Akte depicting a bunch of grapes; late second century BC

Plate 16. A tuna-fish vendor, detail of a red-figure bell krater made in Sicily in the early fourth century BC, found in 1864 in a necropolis at Lipari (Cefalù, Museo Mandralisca)

Plate 17. Amphora and brick fabrics:

1. MGS II (northern Sicily), fabric catalogue no. 2
2. MGS II, MGS III (Locri, Calabria), fabric catalogue no. 3
3. MGS V (Ischia, Campania), fabric catalogue no. 4a
4. MGS V (Ischia, Campania), fabric catalogue no.4b
5. MGS V–VI (northern Sicily), fabric catalogue no. 5
6. Ramón 7.1.2.1 (north-west Sicily?), fabric catalogue no. 9
7. Ramón 7.4.2.1-7.4.3.3/Maña C (Tunisia), fabric catalogue no. 10
8. Ramón 7.5.2.1 (Tunisia), fabric catalogue no. 11
9. Rhodian (Rhodes), fabric catalogue no. 14
10. Koan (Kos), fabric catalogue no. 15
11. Koan 2 (Kos), fabric catalogue no. 18
12. Knidian (Knidos), fabric catalogue no. 16
13. Lamboglia 2 (Vis, Dalmatia), fabric catalogue no. 17
14. Dressel 2/4 (central Italy), fabric catalogue no. 19
15. Baetican Dressel 20; Haltern 70 (Guadalquivir Valley, Andalucia) fabric catalogue no. 20
16. Baetican Dressel 7/11 (Cadiz, Andalucia), fabric catalogue no. 21
17. Pélichet 47/Gauloise 4 (Narbonne, southern France), fabric catalogue no. 23
18. Richborough 527 (Lipari), fabric catalogue no. 25
19. Schöne-Mau 13/Agora G198 (Cilicia/south-east Turkey?), fabric catalogue no. 26
20. Tripolitanian 2/3 (western Libya), fabric catalogue no. 29
21. MGS III (local), fabric catalogue no. 33
22. MGS V–VI (local/northern Sicily), fabric catalogue no. 6

23. MGS V–VI (local / northern Sicily)
24. Dressel 1A (local), fabric catalogue no. 34
25. Dressel 1B (local), fabric catalogue no. 35
26. Dressel 2/4 (local, coarse), fabric catalogue no. 37
27. Dressel 2/4 (local, fine), fabric catalogue no. 36
28. Dressel 21/22 (local/north-western Sicily), fabric catalogue no. 39
29. Dressel 21/22 (local/north-western Sicily), fabric catalogue no. 39
30. Dressel 21/22 (local/ north-western Sicily), fabric catalogue no. 40
31. Gauloise 2/3 (local), fabric catalogue no. 41
32. Termini Imerese 151/354 (local), fabric catalogue no. 42
33. Brick (local), fabric catalogue no. 43
34. Brick (local), fabric catalogue no. 44

Figures

1.1. The hill-town Caronía, ancient Kale Akte, seen from the west
1.2 Map of ancient Sicily
1.3. The north coast of Sicily as seen from a satellite, indicating the locations of ancient towns
1.4. Caronía and Marina di Caronía, map of rural settlements and archaeological discoveries
1.5. Marina di Caronía, view looking north-westwards
1.6. Caronía (left of centre, on the hill) and Marina di Caronía, together with the adjacent coastline, seen from the north-east
1.7. A view of the coast looking eastwards towards Caronía (centre)
1.8. The plateau of *contrada* San Todaro, presumed site for the intended Ionian settlement in 494 BC
1.9. The plateau of *contrada* San Todaro, as seen from the site of the ancient harbour
1.10. Halaesa, the archaeological site, view from the south
1.11. The town of San Marco d'Alunzio (ancient Haluntium), view from the west
1.12. The hill of Monte Vecchio di San Fratello, site of ancient Apollonia, seen from the north
1.13. Monte Vecchio (at the centre of the photograph), location of ancient Apollonia, view from the west
1.14 Pizzo Cilona, view from the north-east
1.15 Pizzo Cilona, aerial view showing the location of the principal archaeological features
1.16. Halaesa, an inscription dedicated 'to all the gods', from the *agora*; the Kalaktinoi are named in line 5
1.17, Torrenova (foreground) and Capo d'Orlando (ancient Agathyrnum), view from the west
1.18. Caronía, the Norman castle and presumed site of the acropolis of Kale Akte, view from the south

2.1. Part of the so-called Roman bridge ('Ponte romano'), crossing the Torrente Caronía to the west of Caronia, looking south
2.2. A detail of the 'Ponte romano'
2.3. The valley of the Halaisos, looking south from Halaesa
2.4. Tabula Peutingeriana, detail showing Sicily, with Kale Akte included as Calacte near the centre of the north coast
2.5. Loom weights: (a) with swastika and (b) with circle decoration, both from the *phrourion* at Pizzo Cilona, fifth century BC; (c) with an image of Medusa, from Caronía, surface find during field survey
2.6. Sheep grazing in *contrade* Mastrostefano and Impallaccionata on the edge of the Nebrodi forests
2.7. Spirited horses of the San Fratello breed
2.8. Mules in a field near Pizzo Cilona, south of Caronía

3.1 Caronía, plan showing the location of the archaeological excavations in *contrada* Sotto San Francesco between 1992 and 2005. *Contrada* Telegrafo lies on the north side of the hill in the area of 'Scavo 1992' (top left).
3.2 Detail of a terrace wall with a supporting pillar of locally-made bricks, found during excavations in *contrada* Telegrafo, 1992–93
3.3 Terrace wall of stonework with a middle section (left) made of brickwork (probably in the first century BC), found during excavations in *contrada* Sotto San Francesco, 1999
3.4 Part of a courtyard paved with locally made bricks, *contrada* Telegrafo, 1992–93
3.5 Honorary inscription in Greek from the east slope of Caronía (late third / early second century BC)
3.6 Sundial of limestone, a surface find from the east slope of Caronía (perhaps late first century BC or early first century AD?)
3.7 Terracotta foot, perhaps from a life-size statue, a surface find at Caronía
3.8 Headless statue of a *togatus*, marble, from Caronía (Tindari, Antiquarium)
3.9 Headless marble statue from Caronía, possibly of Apollo, now lost, known from an eighteenth-century drawing by Jean Houel
3.10 The hill of Caronía, as seen from the settlement of Marina di Caronía below (at the excavation site in *contrada* Pantano). The house in the foreground is the site of the cistern of the later first or second century AD (*proprietà* Barna).
3.11 Fragment of a Roman marble column with spiral fluting, now kept near the altar in the Church of the Annunziata at Marina di Caronía (second century AD or later)
3.12 The drained marshland in *contrada* Pantano, now filled with stones, probably the site of the ancient harbour basin
3.13 Plan of the structures at *contrada* Pantano (*proprietà* Barna) at Marina di Caronía at the close of the first excavation campaign, February 2000
3.14 Marina di Caronía, *contrada* Pantano, schematic plan of Buildings 1 and 2, phases 2a and 2b
3.15 The northern part of Building 1, seen from the west, excavations of 2003–05
3.16 The southern part of Building 1, seen from the northwest, excavations of 2003–04

3.17 View of Building 1 during the excavations of 1999–2000, seen from the north
3.18 View of Building 1 during the excavations of 1999–2000, seen from the south
3.19 Building 2 (Phase 2) seen from the west, with room Δ at the centre and room M and Λ to the right, during excavations in 2004. The south wall of Building 2 with its entrance was destroyed prior to the start of these excavations, and so is not visible. The Phase-3 water drain marked by the row of square bricks can be seen at top left.
3.20 Building 2 viewed from the west, during excavation in 2001
3.21 Bone spoon from Building 2 (first century BC or first century AD)
3.22 Stylus and possible eraser (?) from Building 2, found in 2001 (first century BC or first century AD)
3.23 Roof-tile collapse and a fallen brick pillar (left) in Room B of Building 1, 2004
3.24 The entrance to Building 2, later blocked, excavated in 1999–2000
3.25 Schematic plan of Buildings 1 (H–Φ) and 2 (Δ, Λ and M) as well as newly-built structures (T, Σ, Ξ and Y). The plan shows buildings in use during Phase 3, destroyed in the mid-fourth century, except for Ξ which probably belongs to Phase 4
3.26 Remains of parts of four storage-buildings from three different phases, as excavated in 2004; north is at the top. On the extreme right is the west wall of Building 1 (Phase 2a, second century BC), with the portico added later (Phase 2b, probably late first century BC or early first century AD). The three walls in the centre of the photograph are, from bottom upwards, T, S and A, of which the first two belong to successive periods in Phase 3, and the last to Phase 4 (fifth century AD). The wall in the uppermost part of the photograph belongs to phase 1 (end of fifth / early fourth century BC).
3.27 Copper alloy tool for mending fishing nets, from the excavations
3.28 Funerary monument of Q. Caecilius, probably from *contrada* S. Anna at Marina di Caronía, late first century BC or first century AD (Palermo, Museo Archeologico Regionale)

4.1 Amphora types 1: (a) Corinthian A; (b) Corinthian B; both mid-fifth century BC
4.2 Fragment of an Attic black-figured column-*krater*, surface find, *contrada* Pantano; *c.* 500 BC
4.3 Fragment of the neck of an Attic black-figured column *krater*, surface find, *contrada* Pantano; *c.* 500 BC
4.4 Fragment of the base of a Corinthian *kotyle*, surface find, *contrada* Pantano; *c.* 500 BC
4.5 Amphora types 2: (a) MGS II; (b) MGS III; (c) MGS IV (d) MGS V; (e) MGS VI
4.6 Sicilian red-figured *lekythos* with a female head wearing a *sakkos* (a hair covering made of cloth), from the south necropolis of Kale Akte in *contrada* Trappeto at Caronía; late fourth century BC (private collection)
4.7 Pagenstecher *lekythos* with a painted bird, from the south necropolis in *contrada* Trappeto; late fourth / early third century BC (private collection)
4.8 Fragments of Gnathian ware, found during surface survey at Caronía; third century BC
4.9 Black-gloss medallion bowl, moulded figure depicting Nike sitting on a pile of shields, and writing on another of them; *c.* 275 / 175 BC
4.10 Moulded appliqué from a black-gloss vessel, head possibly of Herakles, found during surface survey at Caronía; third century BC
4.11 Brick-stamp from Caronía with an abbreviated reference to the *polis* of Kale Akte; *c.* third / first century BC
4.12 Sherd of locally-produced pottery with the stamp Δ, standing for *demosion* ('of the people'); *c.* third / first century BC
4.13 a–b Terracotta mould for the head of a male figurine (a), and a modern impression taken from it (b), from the cistern in *contrada* Sotto San Francesco, Caronía, excavated in 1999; first century BC
4.14 a–d Heads of female terracotta figurines, found during surface survey at Caronía; third / second century BC
4.15 Terracotta head of a silenus, local production, found during surface survey at Caronía
4.16 Fragmentary handle of a Campanian MGS VI amphora stamped ΑΝΔΡΩΝΟ[Σ in retrograde, found unstratified at Marina di Caronía; third century BC
4.17 Amphora types 3: (a) Dressel 1A; (b) Dressel 1B; (c) van der Werff 1 / Ramón 7.4.3.3 / Maña C2B; (d) van der Werff 2 / Ramón 7.5 / Maña C2C; (e) Rhodian
4.18 Late Hellenistic mould-made oil-lamp, found during surface survey at Caronía; late second / first century BC
4.19 Fragmentary oil-lamp of type Corinth XVI, found during surface survey at Caronía
4.20 Fragmentary oil-lamp made in a Sicilian workshop, found during surface survey at Caronía; late first century BC
4.21 Rim of a *louterion* with mould-made scenes of running hounds and floral decoration; excavated in *contrada* Sotto San Francesco, 1999
4.22 Stamp of a Rhodian amphora, of the producer Marsyas, in the Rhodian month of Panamos, found during surface survey at Caronía; *c.* 170 / 160 BC
4.23 Stamp of a Rhodian amphora, produced in the Rhodian month of Pedageitnos, found during surface survey at Caronía; late third / second century BC
4.24 Amphora types 4: (a) Lamboglia 2; (b) Dressel 6A; (c) Dressel 2/4; (d) Gauloise 2; (e) Gauloise 3
4.25 A fragment of Iberian *kalathos*, found during surface survey at Caronía; first century BC
4.26 Amphora types 5: (a) Dressel 21/22; (b) Richborough 527, type 1; (c) Richborough 527, type 2; (d) Haltern 70; (e) Dressel 20
4.27 Amphora types 6: (a) Dressel 7/11; (b) Tripolitanian 1; (c) Schöne-Mau 13 / Agora G198 / Pompeii 13
4.28 Amphora types 7: (a) Gauloise 4; (b) Termini Imerese 151/354 (from Marina di Caronía); (c) Keay 52; (d) Middle Roman 1
4.29 Drawing of the neck of a Termini 151/354 amphora

from the kiln in *contrada* Chiappe at Marina di Caronía; *c.* fifth/early sixth century AD
4.30 A local amphora of type Crypta Balbi 2, from the necropolis at Halaesa; fourth/fifth century
4.31 Ceramic amphora stoppers found in excavations at *contrada* Pantano (the central one cut from a lamp stamped CIVNDRAC); late third/fourth century AD
4.32 An amphora of Termini 151/354 type from the Boni excavations of the Temple of Castor and Pollux at the Forum Romanum, Rome, of identical fabric to that of Fig. 4.29
4.33 Amphora types 8: (a) Africana 1; (b) Keay 25/Africana 3; (c) Keay 27; (d) Africana 2; (e) Tripolitanian 2; (f) Tripolitanian 3
4.34 Amphora types 9: (a) Keay 1B/Dressel 30; (b) Almagro 50; (c) Almagro 51
4.35 Bronze coin from the mint of Syracuse with (a) the head of Poseidon on the obverse and (b) his trident on the reverse, surface find in *contrada* Telegrafo at Caronía; issued by Hieron II, 263/212 BC
4.36 The coin series minted by Kale Akte, as recorded by Antonino Salinas in 1876
4.37 Bronze coin from the mint of Kale Akte with (a) head of Athena on the obverse and (b) an owl sitting on an amphora on the reverse; late second century BC (Coin Cabinet, Museum of Cultural History, University of Oslo)
4.38 Bronze coin from the mint of Kale Akte with the head of Dionysus on the obverse; late second century BC (private collection)
4.39 Bronze coin from the mint of Kale Akte showing (a) the head of Apollo on the obverse and (b) his lyre on the reverse; late second century BC (private collection)
4.40 Bronze coin from the mint of Kale Akte showing (a) the head of Hermes on the obverse and (b) his *caduceus* on the reverse; late second century BC (private collection)
4.41 *Antoninianus* minted by Quintillus, AD 270, from the excavations in *contrada* Pantano, 1999/2000

5.1 Imported foodstuffs transported in amphorae which have been found at Caronía and Marina di Caronía, separated according to content. The numbers (and in Figs 5.2–6) are based on the estimated minimum number of vessels (amphorae) present
5.2 Foodstuffs transported in amphorae found at Caronía (all types of contents), both locally made and imported
5.3 Wine amphorae at Caronía, showing the likely sources of each type
5.4 Estimated amounts of commodities at Caronía for Period E (here AD 200–500), in litres
5.5 Olive oil amphorae at Caronía, showing the likely sources
5.6 Amphorae at Caronía carrying fish and fish products, showing the likely sources
5.7 Sources of fine wares found at Caronía. The numbers (and on Fig. 5.8) represent the percentages of total finds.
5.8 Sources of lamps found at Caronía
5.9 Map illustrating the sources of imported goods, Period A (*c.* 500–320 BC). This and the following maps (Figs 5.10–13) are based on the estimated minimum number of finds.
5.10 Map illustrating the sources of imported goods, Period B (*c.* 320–200 BC)
5.11 Map illustrating the sources of imported goods, Period C (*c.* 200–30 BC)
5.12 Map illustrating the sources of imported goods, Period D (*c.* 30 BC–AD 100)
5.13 Map illustrating the sources of imported goods, Period E (*c.* AD 100–500)
5.14 Number of shipwrecks in Sicilian waters with principal cargoes of a specific amphora type
5.15 Most common amphora types at Caronía and Marina di Caronía based on the number of finds

6.1 Map showing the catchment area of Rome's supplies, based on the cost of transport. It shows clearly that the north coast of Sicily was within the area of privileged access to Rome, closer, for example, than the inland parts of Etruria and Umbria in the heart of Italy

7.1 The bay of Caronía and the modern village of Marina di Caronía, site of the ancient maritime settlement of Kale Akte/Calacte, seen from the east in *contrada* Chiappe

A2.1 Micrograph in polarized light of sample 12 Dressel 21/22 local
A2.2 Micrograph in polarized light of sample 1 Termini Imerese 151/354 local
A2.3 Micrograph in polarized light of sample 2 Dressel 2/4 central Italy
A2.4 Micrograph in polarized light of sample 3 MGS VI Sicily
A2.5 Micrograph in polarized light of sample 4 Dressel 21/22 local?
A2.6 Micrograph in polarized light of sample 5 Termini Imerese 151/354 (from Rome but local)
A2.7 Micrograph in polarized light of sample 6 Dressel 1A local
A2.8 Micrograph in polarized light of sample 7 Dressel 2/4 local
A2.9 Micrograph in polarized light of sample 8 Dressel 2/4 local?
A2.10 Micrograph in polarized light of sample 9 MGS V Sicily
A2.11 Micrograph in polarized light of sample 10 Keay 27, from Tunisia
A2.12 Micrograph in polarized light of sample 11 Dressel 21/22 local?
A2.13 Micrograph in polarized light of sample 12 Dressel 21/22 local?
A2.14 Micrograph in parallel light of sample 12 Dressel 21/22 local?
A2.15 Micrograph in polarized light of sample 13 Koan amphora
A2.16 Micrograph in polarized light (magnified) of sample

4 Dressel21/22 local?
A2.17 Micrograph in polarized light (magnified) of sample 5 Termini Imerese 151/354 (from Rome but local)
A2.18 Micrograph in polarized light (magnified) of sample 7 Dressel 2/4 local
A2.19 Micrograph in polarized light (magnified) of sample 13 Koan amphora

A4.1 Catalogue of finds nos 1–33 (amphorae)
A4.1a Catalogue of finds no. 20 (stamped amphora handle)
A4.2 Catalogue of finds nos 34–63 (amphorae)
A4.2a Detail of stamp on item no. 43
A4.3 Catalogue of finds nos 64–95 (amphorae)
A4.4 Catalogue of finds nos 96–126 (amphorae)
A4.5 Catalogue of finds nos 127–42 (amphorae)
A4.6 Catalogue of finds nos 143–7 (amphorae)
A4.7 Catalogue of finds nos 148–66 (fine wares)
A4.8 Catalogue of finds nos 167–83 (fine wares)
A4.9 Catalogue of finds nos 184–97 (fine wares)
A4.10 Catalogue of finds nos 198–205 (fine wares)
A4.11 Catalogue of finds nos 206–7 (fine wares)
A4.12 Catalogue of finds nos 208–32 (lamps)

List of Tables

Table 2.1 Table showing cities minting coins which depict bunches of grapes among their motifs listed on the left, compared with archaeological evidence (column 1) and literary evidence (column 2) for wine production in antiquity, and places with notable grape and/or wine production today (column 3)

Table A1.1 Local and imported wine amphorae found at Caronía and Marina di Caronía
Table A1.2 Imported olive-oil amphorae found at Caronía and Marina di Caronía
Table A1.3 Local and imported fish-sauce amphorae found at Caronía and Marina di Caronía
Table A1.4 Locally produced amphorae (all types) found at Caronía and Marina di Caronía
Table A1.5 Non-local but Sicilian (or Calabrian) amphorae found at Caronía and Marina di Caronía
Table A1.6. Extra-regional (overseas) imported amphorae found at Caronía and Marina di Caronía

Table A2.1 Data derived from the microscopic analyses and the HCl test
Table A2.2 Scatter-plot diagram of grains greater than 0.1 mm
Table A2.3 Scatter-plot diagram of grains less than 0.1 mm and more than 0.01 mm
Table A2.4 Scatter-plot diagram of grains evaluated in a Principal Component Analysis (PCA)

Illustration credits

All photos and drawings are by the author unless otherwise credited

Colour Plates
3, 13, 14: photographs courtesy of R. J. A. Wilson
5–6: photographs Google Earth, with additions
12: photograph courtesy of the Swedish Pompeii Project
15: photograph courtesy of Francesco Collura

Black and white illustrations and line drawings
1.2: courtesy of R. J. A. Wilson
1.3: photograph Google Earth, with additions
1.1, 1.4, 1.8, 1.13, 1.15: photographs courtesy of F. Collura

2.1: photograph courtesy of the Soprintendenza per i Beni Culturali e Ambientali, Messina
2.4: photograph courtesy of R. J. A. Wilson
2.5a–c: photographs courtesy of F. Collura
2.7: photograph Wikipedia Commons

3.1: after Collura 2016, 71, Fig. 3
3.13: after Lentini et al. 2002, 90, fig. 18

3.2, 3.4, 3.8, 3.15, 3.16, 3.19, 3.23, 3.26, 3.28: photographs courtesy of the Soprintendenza per i Beni Culturali e Ambientali, Messina
3.5, 3.6, 3.7: photographs courtesy of Francesco Collura
3.9: after Pecoraino 1989, 68, plate illustrating cat. no. 25
3.14, 3.25: drawings by B. H. Eketuft Rygh (after Bonanno 2009, 17, Fig. B and 27, Fig. C–D)
3.27: drawing by C. Marano

4.1: after *Hesperia* 50 (1981), 455, fig 1d and 1 a
4.2–4: photographs courtesy of Salvatore Serio
4.5: after Vandermersch 1994, 66, 70, 74, 77 and 82 (in all cases Fig. A)
4.6–10, 4.12, 4.14 a–d, 4.15, 4.18–20, 4.22–23, 4.25, 4.35, 4.38–40: photographs courtesy of Francesco Collura
4.11: drawing by the author after Scibona 1971
4.17, 4.24, 4.26 (a, d and e), 4.27, 4.28 (a and c), 4.33 (a–b, d–f) and 4.34: University of Southampton, *Roman amphorae: a digital resource*, 2005/2014 (originator); York: Archaeology Data Service (distributor) (doi: 10.5284/1018074) https://archaeologydataservice.ac.uk/archives/view/amphora_ahrb_2005/index.cfm
4.26b and c: after Borgard 2000, 289, fig. 1
4.28b: after Bonanno 2009, Tav. XIV.5 (no. 73)
4.28d: after Wilson 1990, 264, Fig. 224b
4.29: drawing by Marina Prusac Lindhagen
4.31: photograph courtesy of the Soprintendenza per i Beni Culturali e Ambientali, Messina
4.32: drawing by K. Slej
4.33c: after Peacock and Williams 1986, 159, far right
4.36: after Salinas 1876, tav. XVI
4.37: photograph courtesy of H. Roland

6.1: after Morley 2002, 65

Index

Numbers in **bold** refer to pages with black-and-white or line illustrations (including tables) referring to the item indexed; numbers in *italics* refer to colour illustrations

Acireale 219 n. 446
Acium (Aci) 96
acropolis, of Kale Akte **26**, 75; *Col. Pl. 1*; of Apollonia 21
Adamesteanu, Dinu, archaeologist 1, 9, 203 n. 35
Adranon, deity, cult of 50
Adriatic 34, 84–5, 89, 92, 96, 102, 105, 136, 150, 206 n. 37, 215 n. 261, 215 n. 282, 216 n. 308, 225 n. 121, 227 n.184; wine production of, amphorae for 84, **85**, 89, **166**, 206 n. 37, 215 n. 261
Aegean 34, 83, 94, 102, 109–10, 114–15, 119, 121, 123, 129, 131, 134, **166**, 223 n. 66
Aeolian islands 5, 72, 208 n. 119
Africa Byzacena 37, 96, 99–100, 112
Africa Proconsularis 94, 96, 110–11, 120, 122, 124, 136
Africa Tripolitana 37, 99, 110, 119–20
Africana 1, amphorae 72, 99, **100**, 101–02, 111, 121–2, 137, 147, 161–2, **163**, 165, **166**, 219 n. 483, 222 n. 53
Africana 2, amphorae 99, **100**, 101, 103, 112, 121–2, 147, **164–6**, 222 n. 53, 220 n. 505
African red slip (ARS) pottery 27, 50, 63, 90, 94, 101, 113, 124, 134, 136, 197, **199**, 218 nn. 425 and 427; stamped decoration on 94–5, 101
Agathocles of Syracuse, tyrant 17, 19, 21, 45, 132, 135, 137, 139–40, 149, 225 n. 133, 227 n. 184
Agathyrnos, mythical founder of Agathynon 204 n. 57
Agathyrnon, Agathyrnum (Capo d'Orlando) 5, 13, 23, **24**, 25, 33–4, 95, 204 n. 57, 205 n. 120
agora 21, 38, 46–8, 50–1, 72, 127, 129, 209 n. 34; of Halaesa 12, **22**; *Col. Pl. 7*; of Kale Akte *Col. Pl. 6*
Agrigentum (Akragas, Agrigento) 38
Agrigento (Akragas, Agrigentum) 95, 120, 219 n. 446, 214 n. 172, 214 n. 207, 215 n. 271
Agrippa, M. Vipsanius 76
Agyrion (Agirio) 92, 217 n. 383; *see also* Agyrium
Agyrios, Proklos, lamp-producer 91–2, **200**, 201
Agyrium (Agirio) 30, 32; *see also* Agyrion
Aiolos, deity 204 n. 57
Aischylos, from Kale Akte, funerary inscription of 205 n. 95
Akragas (Agrigentum, Agrigento) 8–9, 12; *see also* Agrigento
Alcamo, Alcamo Marina 86–9, 216 n. 95
Alexandria, in Egypt 34, 39, 88
Algeria 102, 220 n. 505; *see also* Mauretania
Alicudi, island *Col. Pl. 7*
Al-Idrisi, geographer 27–8, 41
allec (fish-sauce) 41, 112, 208 n. 113
Almagro 50/51, amphorae **102**, 103, 112, **166**
alum, from Lipari 91, 112
Amestratum, Amestratus (Mistretta) 12, 15–16, 22, 165, 206 n. 4 and 29
Aminaeum, *Aminaei*, wine 96, 99, 226 n. 148
amphora, amphorae, *passim* but *see especially* **65–103**, **106–24**, **160–92**; stamps on 71–2, **77**, 81, **83**, 84, 87–8, 100
Anaxilaos of Rhegion, tyrant 3
Ancona 105
annona 23, 32–3, 92, 99, 102, 135–8, 143, 147–50, 226 n. 140
Antonine period 99, 101, 217 n. 369, 220 n. 518
Antoninus Pius, Emperor 92
apoikia 42, 44
Apollo, deity, cult of 32, **48–9**; coinage depicting, 36–7, 103, **105**, 204 n. 47, 206 n. 21, 207 nn. 57 and 59; grove of, at Halaesa 207 n. 77; oracle of, at Delphi 8, 33; sanctuary at Kale Akte 12
Apollonia (Monte Vecchio, San Fratello) 10–11, **14–16**, 17, 19–21, 25, 31–4, 38–9, 42–43, 45, 48, 71–3, 78–80, 83–4, 86, 88, 91, 139, 144, 149, 204 n. 61, 212 n. 65, 227 n. 186, coins from 103–04, 221 n. 552
Apulia, Apulian 68, 73, 78–9, 84, 86, 110, 120, 137, **166**, 222 n. 27
aqueduct, of Kale Akte 46, 209 n. 30
Arab (Islamic) period 27–8, 226 n. 167
Archagathos, Jewish slave 12
Archaic period 3–5, 11, 15, 19, 42, 65, 67–8, 70, 114–16, 127–30, 133–4, 137, 140, 144, 149–50, 203 n. 11, 211 n. 18, 221 n. 16, 222 n. 25, 223 n. 28, 224 n. 67, 224 n. 89
Archonides of Halaesa 8–10, 12–13, 29, 134, 139, 204 n. 44
Aristotle, philosopher 127
Artemis, deity, cult of 48
Asia Minor 3, 29, 80, 91, 94, 103, 138, 203 n. 18, 208 n. 113
Assoro (Assoros) 218 n. 384; *see also* Assorum
Assorum (Assoro) 30, 32, 206 n. 18; *see also* Assoro
atelier des petites éstampilles 73, 224 n. 88, 225 n. 97
Athena, deity, cult of 37, 49; coinage depicting 103, **104**, 204 n. 47, 205 n. 95
Athenaeus, historian 39, 41, 88
Athens, in Greece 38, 49, 66–7, 88, 126–8, 134, 205 n. 95, 221 n. 10, 224 n. 88
Attic, pottery **67**, 68, 70, 72, 79, 113–16, 129, 134, 211 n. 10; black-figured **67**; SOS amphorae 224 n. 67
Augst (Augusta Raurica), in Switzerland 93–4, 101, 218 n. 405
Augustus, Emperor 12, 21, 23–4, 35, 105
Augustan period 12, 22, 24, 37, 79–80, 84–6, 89–91, 93, 99, 108–09, 112–13, 118, 122, 133, 140–41, 149, 217 n. 356, 218 n. 391

barley 19, 207 n. 39
black-gloss pottery 48, **67**, 70, 72–3, **74–5**, 79–80, 113–17, 123, 145, 193, **194**, 195, **196**, 214 n. 202, 222 nn. 27 and 34, 223 n. 66; *Col. Pl. 11*; stamped decoration on 67, 73
Black Sea 221 n. 10
Braudel, Fernand, historian 29, 106, 125, 221 n. 1
brick, bricks 42–4, **44**, 45, **46**, 48, 56, **58**, 59–61, 63, 75–6, 89, 130, 160, 208 n. 9, 209 nn. 26, 68 and 77, 216 n. 329;

brick-faced concrete *Col. Pl. 14*;
brick-stamps 3, **75**
bridge ('Ponte Romano') **30–1**,206 n. 6; *Col. Pl. 3*
Brindisi 110;
amphorae from 78, 84, 118, **163, 166**, 214 n. 170
Bronze Age 5, 15, 17, 34–5, 130, 144, 203 n. 22, 204 n. 57
Bruttium (*see also* Calabria) 116, 138, 141, 216 n. 291, 221 n. 2, 227 n. 84
Bücher, Karl 125, 138
Butera 218 n. 384
Byzantine period 23, 25–8, 37, 53, 63, 113, 143, 210 n. 102, 219 n. 467;
coins 105
Byzantium 148

cabotage 144–5, 149, 151
Cadiz, in Spain 39
Caecilius Iucundus, amphora from the house of *Col. Pl. 12*
Caecilius of Kale Akte, rhetorician 12
Caecilius, Quintus, funerary monument of **64**
Caecuba 78, 213 n. 160
Calabria (Bruttium), Calabrian 37, 67, 71–3, 86, 88, 108, 116;
wines of 95–6, 108, 114
Calacte, *statio* 25, 27, **33**, 51–2, 64, 75–6, 99, 105–06, 108–13, 119, 123–4, 137, 143, **145**, 146–7, 149–51, 161, 219 n. 471 and 474, 221 n. 2
Campana A, pottery 72, 79–80, 90, 117–18, 124, 206 n. 37, 214 nn. 188 and 190, 222 n. 33, 225 n. 97
Campana B, pottery 79–80, 113, 123, 133, 195, **196**, 214 n. 172
Campana C, pottery 57, 79–80, 90, 113, 118, 124, 133, 195, **196**, 206 n. 37, 214 nn. 184, 190 and 202, 226 n.147
Campanaio 39, 95, 120
Camarina (Kamarina) 70–1, 103, 114, 222 n. 25
Campania, Campanian 66, 68–9, 73, 79, 81, 83, 90–1, 99, 108, 131–2, 136, 139–42, 221 n. 6;
pottery production of 117–18, 124, 217 n. 355, 222 n. 33, 225 n. 97;
wine of, amphora production for 70–2, **77–8**, 86–9, 108–09, 116–18, 121–4, 147, 161, **163**, 164, **166**, 224 nn. 78, 79, 85, 88, 95, 225 n. 121, 226 n. 148, 206 n. 37, 213 n. 154, 213 n. 167, 216 n. 291
Capitium (Kapition; *see also* Capizzi) 27, 30, 32, 39
Capizzi (Capitium, Kapition) 27, 206 n. 26
Capo d'Orlando (Agathyrnum) 13, **24**, 120, 205 n. 120, 212 n. 65
Capo Graziano, shipwreck 79
Capo Graziano A, shipwreck 214 n. 174
Capo Graziano C, shipwreck 92, 222 n. 51
Capo Graziano M, shipwreck 101, 219 n. 482
Capo Graziano H, shipwreck 215 n. 272
Capo Ognina, shipwreck 101, 215 n. 272, 219 n. 482
Capo Peloro 1, 21
Capo Plaia, shipwreck 102
Carthage 15, 17, 20, 34, 72, 78, 85, 91, 93, 96, 101, 122, 138–41, 143, 213 n. 167, 214 n. 237, 215 n. 280, 218 n. 405, 219 nn. 461–2, 224 n. 87
Carthaginian, Carthaginians 15, 19–20, 28, 128, 142, 148, 207 n. 43, 226 n. 184
Castel di Tusa 17, 34, 206 n. 31
Castor and Pollux, temple of, in Rome 98, **99**
Catalonia, see also *Hispania Tarraconensis* 89
Catania (*see also* Catina, Katane) 30–1, 36–7, 217 n. 358, 218 nn. 383–4;
plain of 31
Catina (*see also* Catania, Katane) 25, 29–30, 32, 95
Cato, M. Porcius, the Elder, author 127, 132
cattle 30, 38
Caulonia 227 n. 184
Cefalù (Kephaloidion, Cephaloedium) 3, 13, 25, 44, 68, 92, 208 n. 110, 211 n. 57
Centuripae (Centuripe) 20, 38, 207 n. 43
Centuripe (Centuripae) 69, 81, 113, 218 n. 384
Cephaloedium (Cefalù, Kephaloidion) 13, 20, 39, 41, 44, 226 n. 184, 206 n. 18
Ceres, deity, cult of, at Halaesa 49
Cetaria 39
cheese 38, 208 n. 94
chora 35, 128, 131, 144, 212 nn. 112–13
Chian, pseudo-Chian, amphorae (*see also* MGS II) 224 n. 67
Cicero, M. Tullius, rhetorician 12, 23–4, 30, 32, 35, 38–9, 47, 51, 137, 206 n. 29, 207 n. 50
cistern, cisterns, at Caronia 43, 45, 50;
at Marina di Caronía **51**, 52, 60, 209 n. 68; *Col. Pls 5* and *13–14*
city walls, of Haluntium 15;
of Halaesa 20–1; *Col. Pl. 7*;
of Kale Akte 6, 208 n. 13;
of Salona 96, 219 n. 460
civitas 64, 131
civitas decumana 12, 20
civitas stipendiaria 12, 23, 35, 207 n. 46
Classical period 3–5, 11, 13, 19–20, 37, 42, 45, 48, 51, 65–6, 70, 103, 106, 113–17, 125–31, 134–5, 137, 140, 149, 160, 167, 203 nn. 11 and 15, 211, n. 18, 221 n. 2, 222 n. 25, 223 n. 50, 224 n. 89, 225 n. 120, 226 n. 133
Cleomenes, of Syracuse 38
coins, coinage 3, 11–12, 15, 19, 21–2, **36**, 37–8, 42, 48–50, 56, 59, 63–64, 74, 76, 84, 92, **103–05**, 127, 130, 160, 223 n. 45, 227 n. 184, 209 n. 52;
from Capo d'Orlando 205 n. 120;
from Morgantina 223 n. 47;
of Athens 205 n. 95;
of Halaesa 221 n. 3, 223 n. 47;
of Haluntium 204 n. 47;
of Kale Akte 203 n. 8, 205 n. 95, 206 n. 21, 210 n. 87, 221 n. 557, 226 n. 152, 210 n. 92; *Col. Pl. 15*;
with bunch of grapes 207 nn. 56–7, 224 n. 89
Colle Madore 68, 114
colonisation 13, 34, 45;
Greek 110, 129, 137, 148
colony, colonial 17, 129, 147, 211 n. 40, 223 n. 66;
Greek 203 n. 11, 223 n. 51, 224 n. 89;
Hellenistic 227 n. 185;
of Narona 84;
of Tyndaris 204 n. 49, 226–7 n. 184;
Roman 203 n. 11
column-krater, Attic **67**
columns, of brick 59, 160;
of marble 42, 48, **51–2**, 209 nn. 66–7
Commodus, Emperor 136
conjonctures 146, 148, 150, 221 n. 1
Constantinian period 101
Constantinople 27, 29, 136, 143, 150
contrada Arìa 19
contrada Chiappe **145**, amphora kiln at 27, 63, 96–7
contrada di Noto 3, 52–3, 203 n. 15
contrada Fiumara 19, 203 n. 22
contrada Lineri 216 n. 329
contrada l'Urmo 19
contrada Palme 52, 209 nn. 68 and 77
contrada Pantano 3, 27, 41, **51–5**, 66, **67**, 68, 70, 75, 77, 83–4, 90, **98**, 96–101, **105**, 129, 146, 149, 160, 203 n. 13, 211 nn. 18 and 39
contrada Samperi 34, 213 n. 145
contrada Sant'Anna **64**
contrada San Todaro 6, **8–9**, 43, 48, 65, 76, 203 n. 24, 213 n. 146

contrada Sotto San Francesco 3, **42–5**, **76**, 77, 81, **82**, 83, 94, 160, 212 n. 68, 217 n. 361
contrada Sugherita 26, 52, 216 n. 330
contrada Telegrafo 3, **43–6**, 69, 81, 83, 94, **103**, 213 n. 146
contrada Trapiessi 1, 67
contrada Trappeto **69**
cooking ware, cook-ware (*see also* kitchen-ware) 99, 219 n. 481
Corinth, in Greece 8–10, 12, 110, 113–14, 129, 137, 140
Corinth XVI, lamp-type 110, 113
Corinthian, Corinthians 8–12, **66–7**, 80, **81**, 102, 110, 114, 122, 129, 224 n. 89;
bowls 197, **199**;
lamps 67;
pottery **67**, 116
Corinthian A and A′ amphorae 66–7, 114, 116, **121**, 122, **163**, **166**, 211 nn. 38–9, 224 n. 67
Corinthian B, amphorae **66**, 114, 116–17, 122, 221–2 nn. 21–2, 224 nn. 67 and 86
Crypta Balbi 2, amphorae 96–**7**, 219 n. 464
Cumae 69

Dalmatia, Dalmatian 84–5, 92, 96, 105, 109, 118, 136–7, 141, 147, 215 n. 261, 216 n. 282
Damophilos of Enna 38
decuma (*see also* tithe) 148, 150
deer, red, roe and fallow 39
Delos, in Greece, island 141, 215 n. 261
Delphi, in Greece 32, oracle of 8, 10, 33
Demeter, deity, cult of 35, 49
Dio of Halaesa 39
Diocletian, Emperor 38;
price edict of 39, 96, 223 n. 16, 225 n. 106
Diodorus Siculus, historian 6–10, 12, 16, 19, 34, 38, 45
Dionysius of Halicarnassus, historian 204 n. 57
Dionysius I of Syracuse, tyrant 7, 13, 16, 67, 135, 139, 225–6 nn. 133 and 184
Dionysus, deity, coins depicting, 19, 22, **36–7**, 74, 84, 103, **104**, 204 n. 47, 205 n. 95, 207 nn. 57, 60 and 66, 226 n. 152;
cult of 49, 224 n. 90
donkey 39
Dressel 1, amphorae 71, 77, **78**, 81, 83–4, 86, 88–9, 108–09, **121–2**, 123, 146, 161–2, **163–4**, **166**, 177, **181**, 182, 212 n. 100, 213 nn. 163, 165 and 167, 216 n. 307; *Col. Pl. 17.24–5*
thin-section analysis of **169, 174–5**
Dressel 2/4, amphorae 27, 37, 83, **85**, 86, 88–9, 96, 106, **108**, 109, 119, **121–22**, 146, 161, **163–4**, 165, **166**, 178, **184**, 18–6, 216 nn. 287–88, 291 and 322, 222 n. 51, 224 n. 76; *Col. Pl. 17.14* and *26–7*
thin-section analysis of **169, 175**
Dressel 6A, amphorae 84–**5**, 109, 215–16 nn. 279 and 282
Dressel 6B, amphorae 85, 215 n. 282
Dressel 7/11, amphorae 92, **93**, 112, 123, **164**, **166**, 178, **186**, 187, *Col. Pl. 17.16*
Dressel 20, amphorae **87**, 92–3, 99, 122, 137, **163, 166**, 178, **186**, 187, 218 n. 397, 226 n. 162; *Col. Pl. 17.15*
Dressel 21/22, amphorae 27, 79, 86–7, 88, 111–12, 118–19, **122–4**, 146, 161, **163–4**, 165, 179, 185, **186**, 216 nn. 308, 311, 315, 318 and 322; *Col. Pl. 17.28–30*;
from Pompeii *Col. Pl. 12*;
thin-section analysis of **169, 174–5**
Dressel 23, amphorae 218 n. 397
Dressel 26, amphorae 82–3, 118, **163**, **166**, 177, 183, **184,** 216 n. 288
Dressel 30 (Keay 1B), amphorae **102**, 109, 121, **163, 166**
Ducetius, Sikel leader 1, 3, 6–13, 29, 34, 42, 44–5, 48, 55, 67, 110, 128–30, 134, 148–9, 203 nn. 12 and 26, 204 nn. 36, 42 and 44, 208 nn. 15–16, 224 n. 91

earthquake, earthquakes 43;
at Tyndaris 25;
of the late first century 50, 60, 86, 149;
of the AD 360s 63, 105, 146, 150, 210 n. 106;
Egadi islands 41
Egypt, Egyptian 27, 29, 34–5, 38–9, 136, 141
emporion 5, 128
Engyon (Troina?) 16–17, 30–1;
tyrant of 227 n. 186
Enna (Henna) 30, 32, 35–6, 38;
coinage of 207 n. 57
Entella 68, 88, 114, 116, 211 nn. 50 and 54, 221 n. 21;
coinage of **36–7**, 207 n. 57
Erice (Eryx) 72, 84, 92, 116, 215 nn. 255 and 271
Erythrai, in Asia Minor, coin of 103
Etna group (of pot-painters) 69
Etruria 34, 71, 77–9, 141, **142**, 224 n. 88, 225 n. 97
Etruscan 13, 176;
wine 114
Eugeneum, wine 207 n. 59, 226 n. 148
Eupolemos, citizen of Kale Akte 12
export, *passim* but *see especially* Chapters 4 and 5

Favignana 218 n. 410
Fazello, Tommaso, historian 1
Filicudi, island 79, 92, 215 n. 272
Filicudi A, shipwreck 77
Filicudi F, shipwreck 71, 212 n. 70
Finley, Moses, historian 125, 138
fish, fishing, fish-products 27–8, 34, 39, **41**, **64**, 70, 72, 79, 81–2, 87–8, 96, 99, 100–01, 103, 106, 109–110, **111**, 112, 115–21, 123–4, 126–7, 132–5, 139, 143, 146–8, 160, 162, **164**, 165, 206 n. 37, 208 nn. 107, 111, 113, 119, 212 n. 94, 216 nn. 298, 308 and 311, 220 nn. 505 and 507, 221 nn. 7 and 10–11, 225 nn. 106 and 126
fish-sauce (*see also garum* and fish-products) 41, 72, 79, 81, 88, 92, 100–02, 106, 109, 111–12, 118–19, 120–1, 123, 132, 141, 143, 146, 162, **164**, 165, 220 nn. 505 and 507
forest, forests 13, 20, 35, 37–40, 128, 130–1, 144, 207 nn. 74 and 76
forum 46–7, 49, 51, 76;
of Halaesa **22**; *Col. Pl. 7*
Forum Romanum, Rome 98, **99**, 168
France, French 35, 37, 88, 93, 122, 206 n. 37, 213 n. 155
Furnari, amphora production at 120

Galen, physician 96
Gallia Narbonensis, province 34, 93
garum (*see also* fish-sauce, *muria*, *allec*) 34, 41, 112, 118, 123, 165, 208 n. 113, 216 nn. 298 and 307;
oeno-garum 216 n. 307, 221 n. 14, 226 n. 151
gateway community 128–30, 134, 223 nn. 56–7
Gaul, Gaulish 34, 78, 86, 88, 91, 93–4, 98–9, 109, 113, 119, 121–3, 138, 141, 147, 161–2, **166**, 213 n. 154, 216 n. 294, 218 nn. 406 and 412, 225 n. 114
Gauloise 2/3, amphorae **85**, 86, 93, 109, **163–4**, **166**
Gauloise 4 (Pélichet 47), amphorae 86, 93, **95**, 102, 106, 109, 122, **163**, **166**
Gela 68, 70–2, 114, 131, 218 nn. 384 and 388, 221 n. 21, 224 nn. 86–7 and 90
Gelon, tyrant 38, 135
glass 160
Gnathian ware, pottery 73, **74**, 116
goat, goats 39
Gothic Wars 143, 146, 227 n. 205

Grado, shipwreck 99, 165, 216 n. 308
grain 17, 20–1, 23, 27, 110, 132, 134–9, 141, 143–5, 147–9, 206 n. 29, 207 n. 51, 226 nn. 140 and 159
grapes 102, 126–7, 130, 213 n. 160;
bunch of grapes, **36**, 37, 74, 84, 103–04, 205 n. 95, 207 nn. 56–7, 59–60, 62, 66, 221 n. 3, 224 n. 89, 226 n. 152; *Col. Pl. 15*
Greco-Italic amphorae (*see also* MGS IV, V and VI amphorae) 71–2, 77–8, 83–4, 86, 89, **121–2**, 123, 146, 163, 211 n. 31, 212 n. 100, 213 n. 155, 215 n. 261, 216 n. 307, 224 nn. 79, 85 and 87, 225 n. 95
Greece 66, 102, 108, 116, 134, 142, 224 n. 95
Greek, Greeks 3, 11, 13, 15–17, 19–20, 29, 33–5, 37–9, 42, 44–5, 47–8, 66–8, 70–5, 80–1, 89, 102, 109–11, 113–15, 117, 119, 125–35, 137, 140, 142, 145, 148–50, 203 n. 11, 204 nn. 42 and 51, 206 n. 18, 208 n. 15, 210 n. 7, 211 n. 40, 213 n. 155, 221 n. 22, 223 nn. 45, 51 and 66, 224 n. 67, 225 n. 120, 226–7 nn. 133, 183, 184;
western 224 n. 89, 227 n. 190
Gregory the Great, Pope 12, 150
Guido, geographer 13
gymnasia 37

Hadrian, Emperor 92
Halaesa (Halaisa) 1, 9–13, **14**, 15–17, 19–21, **22**, 23–7, 30–9, 42–6, 48–50, 53, 71–3, 75–6, 80, 83, 86, 89–90, 92, 94–6, **97**, 100–01, 103–05, 117–18, 127, 130–1, 139, 141, 143–4, 149, 204 nn. 44, 54 and 67, 205 nn. 84 and 117, 206 n. 18, 207 nn. 45 and 74, 208 n. 9, 218 n. 384, 224 n. 90, 225 n. 100, 212 n. 65;
agora of *Col. Pl. 7*;
chora of 212 nn. 112–13;
coinage of 207 n. 57, 221 n. 3, 223 n. 47, 224 n. 89;
earthquake damage at 210 n. 106
Halaisa (Halaesa) 13
Halaisos, river and river valley 10, 17, 30–1, **32**, 204 n. 67
Haltern 70, amphorae **87**, 92, **163, 166**, 218 n. 391
Haluntium (Halontion, San Marco d'Alunzio) 5, 10–11, **14–15**, 16–17, 19–21, 23–4, 30, 33–4, 36–8, 42–3, 46, 49, 104, 139, 149, 204 nn. 56–7, 206 n. 18; *Col. Pls 8–9*;
coinage of 207 n. 57;
harbour of 206 n. 33
harbour, harbours (see also port) 13, 25–9, 32, 34–5, 38–9, 42, 58–62, 64–65, 67, 70, 94–5, 99, 103–04, 111, 128–30, 137, 139, 141, 144–5, 149, 207 n. 51;
of Acquedolci 16;
of Cefalú 25;
of Halaesa 17, 21;
of Haluntium 206 n. 33;
of Kale Akte 3–6, **9**, 10–11, 16, 23, 26–7, 42, 44–5, 51–2, **53**, 55, 59–61, 63–4, 108, 124, 149–50, 209 n. 72; *Col. Pl. 5*;
of Solunto 52
Hasebroek, Johannes, economic historian 125
Hellenisation 8, 10, 13, 16, 148, 211 n. 40
Hellenistic ruler (?), head depicting **76**
Hellenistic period 3, 5, 7, 11, 15, 19–21, 23–7, 37, 39, 41–2, 44, 46–8, 51, 54, 64–6, 68, 70–1, 73, 75–7, 80–1, 83–4, 89, 103–04, 106–07, 113, 116–19, 123, 125–8, 130–1, 134–7, 139–40, 145–9, 160, 163, 165, 167, 203 n. 26, 207 n. 72, 209 nn. 26 and 52, 213 n. 139, 214 n. 228, 221 n. 2, 222 n. 1, 226 n. 152, 227 nn. 185 and 8
Henna (Enna), coinage of 49
Heraclea Minoa 85, 95, 120, 214 n. 172
Heracles, deity, cult of 49;
appliqué head of (?) 74, **75**
coinage depicting 103, **104**, 204 n. 47, 209 n. 52;
temple of *Col. Pl. 8*
Herakleia 38
Herbita (Monte Alburchia) 8, 10, 12–13, 15–17, 19, **21–2**, 23, 29–36, 38–9, 139, 204 nn. 44, 52 and 67
Hermes, deity, coinage depicting 22, 37, 103, **105**, 204 n. 47;
cult of 49
Herodotus, historian 3
Himera 3, 13, 38, 52, 66–8, 70, 114, 116, 128, 211 nn. 16, 39 and 54, 214 n. 207, 221 n. 20
Hieron II, of Syracuse, king 20, 35, 88, 127, 135, 140, 207 n. 43;
coinage of **103**
Hippias, son of Philoxenos, from Kale Akte 12
Hipponion 227 n. 184
Hispania, Hispania Baetica, province (see also Spain) 83, 89, 110, **166**;
Hispania Tarraconensis (*see also* Catalonia) 89;
wine, oil and fish-sauce of 92–3
histoire événementielle 29, 106
honey, Iberian 85
horse, horses 39, **40**
Iberian 103;
honey 85;
kalathoi 85, **86**
Imperial cult, at Halaesa 50
Imperial period 5, 11, 15, 21, 23–7, 34, 36–8, 48, 51, 53–4, 57, 65–6, 75, 79, 86, 88–9, 93–6, 98, 100–02, 105–06, 118–20, 123–5, 130–6, 145–9, 165, 167, 205 n. 131, 206 n. 6, 208 n. 93, 221 n. 2, 225 n. 101 and 114
imports, *passim* but *see especially* Chapters 4 and 5
inscription, inscriptions 65, 84;
from Athens 205 n. 95;
from Caronía 12, 19, 46, **47**, 209 n. 33;
from Delphi 32, 206 n. 18;
from Halaesa 12, 20, **22**, 23, 37–8, 141;
from S. Gregorio (Agathyrnum) 24
Iaitas (Monte Iato) 36–7; *see also* Monte Iato
Iato K 480, cup 68
Ibn-Qalaqi, Kadì poet 41
Ionia, Ionian, Ionians 3–4, 6, 8, 128;
cup 203 n. 13
Ionian-Massaliote, amphorae 114
Iron Age 5, 15, 34, 129–30
Ischia 71–2, 79, 124, 136, 140;
wine-, amphora- and pottery production of 212 nn. 78–9, 213 n. 55, 214 n. 188, 224 n. 79, 225 n. 97
Isola delle Femmine 41
Issa (Vis, in Croatia), island 84, 105, 109, 136, 147;
wine and amphora production of 215 nn. 261 and 268, 225 n. 121
Italy, Italian 4, 22–3, 29, 32, 34–5, 37, 63, 66–71, 73, 77, 79–82, 84–6, 88–91, 94–6, 99, 101–03, 106, 108–09, 112–19, 121–4, 127, 131–3, 136, 141, **142**, 143, 145–50, 168, **169**, 209 n. 67, 213 nn. 154–5, 215 nn. 240, 261 and 282, 217 n. 355, 218 n. 418, 220 n. 505, 222 n. 22, 225 n. 114, 226 nn. 148 and 184
itineraries 13, 32, **33**, 206 n. 18
Itinerarium Antonini 12, 24, 33

Jerome, Saint 63
Jordanes, historian 27
Julian the Apostate, Emperor 63

Kanus, M. Papius, wine-producer 84
Kapitän 1 and 2 amphorae 110, **121**, 123, 222 n. 157
Kapition (Capizzi) 32, 165
Katane (*see also* Catania, Catina),

coinage of 36, 49, 103, 207 n. 57
Keay 1B (Dressel 30), amphorae **102**, 109, 121, **163**, **166**, 190, **191**
Keay 13A, amphorae 100, **163**, **166**, 190, **191**
Keay 25, amphorae **100**, **163**, **166**, **188**, 190, 220 n. 491
Keay 27, amphorae **100**, **166**, **188**, 190, thin-section analysis of **169**, **174–5**
Keay 52, amphorae **95**, 96, 219 nn. 439, 453, 467 and 471
Kephaloidion (Cefalù, Cephaloedium) 4, 205 n. 78, 206 n. 18;
coinage of 49
kerdos 150
Kerkyra (Corfù), in Greece, wine from 66, 114, 117, 221 nn. 21–2, 224 n. 89
kiln, kilns 63, 65, 78, 88, 130, 118, 170, 221 n. 2;
at Marina di Caronía 75, 89, 95–7, 99, 219 nn. 464 and 474;
at S. Venera al Pozzo 219 n. 446;
lime kilns 221 n. 7
of the *ager Falernus* 213 n. 160;
of Vis / Issa 215 n. 261
kitchen-ware, see also cooking ware, cook-ware 99, 102, 160, 167
Klüver, Phillip (Cluverius), historian 1
Knidos, Knidian, wine amphorae of 84, 109, **163, 166**, 178, 183, **184**
Kore, cult of, see also Persephone 49;
coinage depicting 103
Kos, Koan, wine amphorae of 83–4, 109, 118, **163**, 165, **166**, 178, 183, **184**;
thin-section of 168**, 169, 175**
kottabos, tomba del, at Haluntium 212 n. 65, 224 n. 90

Laevinus, M. Valerius, consul 29
Lamboglia 2, amphorae 83–4, **85**, 109, 121, **122**, 134, 147, **163**, **166**, 215 nn. 261 and 279, 216 n. 282, 225 n. 121
Latium 71, 77–9, 224 n. 88
Lepcis Magna, in Libya 98
lex Claudia 127
lex frumentaria (Terentiae et Cassiae) 35
lex Hieronica 20, 135
Libya, Libyan 34, 82, 90, 94, **166**
Lilybaeum (Marsala) 1, 29, 33–4, 82, 134, 215 n. 243
Lipara (Lipari), city 13, 50, 64, 204 n. 49, 206 n. 18;
coinage of 36, 207 n. 57
Lipari, island(s) 25, 34, 36–7, 41, 65–74, 76, 80, 84–6, 90–1, 94–5, 97, 101–02, 108, 112–14, 116–20, 132, 134, 145, 164–**5**, 167, 206 n. 18, 208 n. 119, 211 n. 16, 212 nn. 117 and 122, 214 n. 188, 215 n. 272, 217 n. 358, 220 nn. 516 and 543, 221 nn. 2, 19 and 21–2, 222 nn. 27 and 34, 224 n. 79, 225 nn. 95 and 101, 226 n. 184;
red-figure krater from *Col. Pl. 16*
livestock (see also cattle) 30, 38, 130
Locri, Locrian, in Calabria **165**, 224 n. 89, 227 n. 184;
amphorae from 67, **68**, 70–1, 180, **181**;
coinage of 224 n. 89;
export of wine 224 n. 89, 227 nn. 184 and 190
longue durée 29, 65, 106, 130, 133, 144, 149–50
loom-weights 38, **39**, 160
louterion, louteria 81, **82**
Lucania, *see* Calabria, Bruttium
Lucullus, Lucius, general 47
Lusitania, Lusitanian, province **166**

Madrague de Giens, shipwreck 84
Mamertine, Mamertines 20, 31, 135, 139, 224 n. 87;
coinage of 103
Mamertinum, wine 131
Mare Nostrum 29
Marina di Caronia 1, **3–7**, 11, 13, 21, 23–7, 42, 50–5, 59, 61, 63–5; Chapter 4, *passim*; 113, 115, 117, 123, 128–9, 131, 143–4, **145**, 146, 148, 160–1, **163–5**, 166, **167**, 203 nn. 16 and 21, 205 n. 139, 206 n. 33, 208 n. 2, 210 n. 105, 211 nn. 31 and 38–9, 213 n. 156, 214 nn. 170 and 190, 217 n. 361, 219 nn. 467 and 474, 221 nn. 557 and 2; *Col. Pls 4–5 and 13–14*
Marina di Torrenova **24**, 34, 101, 206 n. 33
market, markets 58, 106–09, 111–13, 117–19, 121–51, 215 n. 282, 221 n. 19, 222 n. 1, 223 nn. 14 and 16–17, 225 nn. 107, 114 and 119, 226 nn. 166–7, 227 n. 190
Marsala (Lilybaeum) 1, 68, 72, 82, 84–5, 214 n. 207, 215 n. 271, 218 n. 410
Marx, Karl, philosopher 125, 138, 223 n. 17
Mauretania, Mauretanian 102, 109, 121, **166**; *see also* Algeria
meat 38–9
medallion ware 73, **75**;
imitation of *Col. Pl. 11*
Medieval period 208 n. 13, 221 n. 4, 223 n. 44
Medusa **39**
Megarian bowls 80, 147, 195, **196**
Menai (Mineo) 7–8, 10, 42, 45, 48, 203 n. 26
Menainon, coinage of 49
Messana (Messina, *see also* Zancle) 20, 25, 29, 33–5, 38, 83, 103, 131, 134–5, 224 n. 89
Messina (Messana, *see also* Zancle) 29, 33–5, 38, 102, 128, 211 nn. 9 and 54, 220 n. 543, 221 nn. 19 and 21, 222 n. 25, 224 n. 86, 227 nn. 190 and 11;
Straits of 19, 25, 63, 73, 85, 95
mercenary, mercenaries 13, 15, 44, 139, 224 n. 91
Metapontion 227, n. 184
MGS amphorae, stamps on 224 n. 85
MGS II, amphorae 66–7, **68**, 70, 108, 114, 116, 146, **163, 165**, 180, **181**, 211 n. 31, 221 n. 19, 224 nn. 67 and 86
MGS III, amphorae **68**, 70–1, 74, 114, 146, **163, 165,** 180, **181**, 211 n. 31, 212 n. 65
MGS IV, amphorae **68**, 71, 211 n. 31, 212 nn. 65 and 70, 224 n. 86
MGS V, amphorae **68**, 71–2, 74, 79, 108, 116–17, 121–3, 146–7, **163–6,** 180, **181**, 211 n. 31, 213 n. 155, 214 n. 178, 224 nn. 79 and 86; *Col. Pl. 17.3–4*;
thin-section analysis of **169, 174–5**
MGS VI, amphorae **68**, 72, **77**, 79, 108, **121**, 122–3, 146, **163**, **165–6**, 180, **181**, 182, 211 n. 31, 213 nn. 155–6, 224 nn. 78 and 86; *Col. Pl. 17.5*;
thin-section analysis of **169, 174–5**
middle ground 128
Milazzo (Mylai) 3, 13, 70, 72, 102, 128, 208 n. 113, 212 n. 94;
fish-salting plant at 216 n. 311
Miletians 3–4, 6, 129, 134
Miletos, in Asia Minor 3;
amphorae from 224 n. 67
milk 38
Mistretta (Amestratum) 16, 31
Mithradates of Pontus, king 47
Montagna dei Cavalli 211 n. 54
Montagna di Ramacca 114, 134
Monte Alburchia (Herbita?) 17, 204 n. 52
Monte Erice 84
Monte Iato (Iaitas) 21, 36, 66, 68, 73–4, 79–80, 84, 88, 90, 92, 95, 104, 114, 116, 118, 129, 134, 167, 207 n. 57, 212 n. 122, 213 n. 137, 214 n. 172, 216 n. 314, 217 nn. 354 and 380, 221 n. 559, 222 n. 34, 223 n. 66, 224 n. 68, 227 n. 23
Monte Pellegrino 84
Monte Polizzo 221 n. 20, 222 n. 26
Monte Trefinaidi 31
Monte Testaccio, Rome 123, 133
Monte Vecchio (Apollonia) **14–16**, 21–2, 204 n. 61
Morgantina 3, n. 8, 6–7, 19, 30, 66, 68,

71–4, 76, 79–81, 84, 90–1, 95, 114, 118, 167, 211 n. 28;
amphorae from 221, nn. 21–2, 224 n. 79;
amphora stamps from 215 n. 271;
coins from 223 n. 47;
domestic architecture at 224 n. 90;
lamps from 227 n. 23;
pottery from 212 n. 120, 214 nn. 172, 184, 202 and 217, 217 n. 358, 222 nn. 26–7;
urban layout of 208 nn. 15 and 19
moulded ware 197, **198**
Mount Etna 30, 36–8, 68, 71–2, 96, 99, 139
mule, mules **40**, 128
municipium 23–4, 35
Murgantinum, wine 129, 226 n. 148
muria (fish-sauce) 41, 112, 208 n. 113
Mylai (Milazzo) 3, 13, 128

Naples, in Italy 140, 216 n. 315;
Bay of 71, 79, 90, 164, 212 n. 78, 213 n. 155
Narona (Vid, near Metkovic), in Croatia 84, 109, 147, 215 n. 261, 225 n. 121
Naulochus, battle of 21, 60, 76
Naxios, wine amphora stamp 131
Naxos (Giardini Naxos), Sicily 36, 52, 70–1, 78, 86, 95–6, 98, 114, 119–20, 131, 163;
amphorae 211 n. 9, 219 n. 475, 224 nn. 76 and 86;
coinage of 19;
wine of 207 n. 59
Nebrodi mountain chain, forest 9–10, 13, 16, 23, 25, 29–32, 37–9, **40**, 46, 48–50, 68, 71–2, 75, 84, 91, 94, 103, 107, 128–9, 131–2, 136, 139, 146, 148–9, 204 n. 51, 223 n. 57, 224 n. 71
necropolis, necropolises 3–4, 19, 48, 52–3, 64–6, **69**, 72, 74, 92, **97**, 120;
of Kale Akte 3–4, 64; *Col. Pl. 17.5–6*;
of Morgantina 212 n. 120
Nike (Victoria), deity 73, **75**
Norman period 27–8;
castle at Caronìa, **26**, 75; *Col. Pl. 1*;
castle at San Marco d'Alunzio *Col. Pl. 8*
North Africa, North African 27, 29, 34, 61, 70, 72, 81, 91–2, 94, 96, 98–102, 106, 110–13, 115–21, 124–5, 133, 136–7, 139, 141–3, 145, 147–8, 162, 206 n. 37, 219 n. 461, 227 n. 184;
cookware of 219 n. 481;
olive-growing in 225 n. 108

Octavian, future Emperor 21, 23, 35, 50, 59, 84, 149
oikos 126–7, 129
oil-lamps, lamps 19, 37, 48, 56, 60, 67, 70, 74, 79–80, **81**, 90–2, **98**, 101–02, 106, 113, **114**, 115–21, 123–4, 126, 133, 135–6, 160, 167, 199, **200**, 201, 220 nn. 516 and 522;
Corinth XVI **81,** 199, **200**;
fat lamps 91–2, 101;
from Lipari 213 n. 136, 227 n. 24;
Hellenistic 74, 80, **81**, 199, **200**;
North African 92, 101, **200**, 201, 220 nn. 516 and 522;
Proklos Agyrios lamps 91–2, **200**, 201, 217 n. 383; stamps on 92, **98**, 101;
volute lamps 90–1, **200**, 201, 217 n. 360;
Vogelkopf 91;
Warzenlampen 79, 199
oleiculture 37
olives, olive trees 19–20, 127, 137, 207 n. 74
olive oil 34, 36–7, 65–6, 78, 82, 84, 92, 94, 96, 99–102, 106, 109, **110**, 111–12, 116, 118, 120, 123, 126, 132–8, 141, 145, 147–8, 162, **163**, 165;
from Istria 215 n. 282;
from North Africa 219 n. 483, 225 n. 108;
from Spain 225 n. 108
oppidum, oppida 23–4, 104
opus africanum 208 n. 9
opus signinum 55
opus testaceum 56
Ostia 34, 37, 89, 93, 95, 99, 101, 121, 134;
amphorae at 210 n. 7, 226 n.161
Ostrogothic kingdom 150

Paestum 68–9
Pagenstecher *lekythoi* **69**, 211 n. 57
Palermo (Panhormus) 72, 88, 92, 214 n. 207, 215 n. 271, 218 n. 384
Palestine 95
Paliké (Rocchicella) 7–8, 10–11, 42, 45, 48, 203 n. 25
Panarea, shipwreck 71, 88, 94, 214 n. 188, 216 n. 318, 218 n. 410, 222 n. 51
Panhormus (Palermo) 26, 34, 44
Pantelleria 222 n. 49
Pantellerian ware 99
pastoralism 29, 38
Patron, mythical founder 204 n. 57
Patti Marina, Roman villa at 220 n. 516
Pergamon, in Asia Minor 91, 224 n. 87
Pergamene appliqué ware 91, 147
Persephone, deity, cult of 49
Phoenicians 13
phrourion 5, 19, 30–1, **39**, 203 n. 23
Piazza Armerina, villa of 63
pig, *see* swine
piracy, pirates 12–13, 19, **22**, 29, 38
Pisa, *terra sigillata* from 89–90, 217 n. 354
Pizzo Cilona 5, **18**, 19, 70, 128, 203 n. 23
plateia 45, 208 n. 19
Pliny the Elder, historian 12, 23–4, 82, 213 n. 160
Polanyi, Karl, sociologist 125–6, 128, 130, 223 n. 15, 225 n. 115
polis, poleis 3, 6–7, 10, 12, 19–21, 24–5, 27, 72, 74, **75**, 86, 103–04, 114–15, 130–1, 134, 138–40, 144, 146, 148–50, 223 n. 23, 224 nn. 76 and 89;
of Kale Akte 203 n. 23, 208 n. 2;
Pompeii 77, 87–8, **93**, 94, 215 n. 252, 225 n. 106;
wine export of 213 n. 160, 216 n. 288, 222 n. 51
Pompey, Sextus, general 21, 23, 50, 59–60, 84, 103, 149
Ponte Romano **30**, **31**, 206 n. 6; *Col. Pl. 3*
pork 39, 206 n. 37
port, ports (*see also* harbour) 122, 128, 133–4, 137, 139, 146–7, 149, 160, 167, 206 n. 37;
of Halaesa 206 n. 31
Porticello, shipwreck 67
port of trade 128
Portus 134
Poseidon, deity, coinage depicting **103**
Procopius, historian 227 n. 205
Proklos, lamp-maker, *see* Agyrios
Ptolemy, geographer 12, 33
Punic 13, 111–12, 115, 123, 134, 204 n. 51, 208 n. 9, 222 n. 26
Punic amphorae 72, 78, **79**, 81–2, 87, 110–12, 115–17, 136, 146–7, 165, 206 n. 37, 214 nn. 228, 231 and 237, 216 n. 318, 221 n. 12, 222 nn. 22 and 25, 225 n. 120
Punic Wars, First 20–1, 23, 71, 118, 132, 149;
Second 12, 21, 23, 77, 118, 128, 140, 149–50
Puteoli (Pozzuoli) 34, 77, 80, 91
Pythian games 32

Quintillus, Emperor, coin of **105**

Ramón 7.1.2.1, amphorae **164, 166**, 177, 180, **181**, 212 n. 101; *Col. Pl. 17.6*
Ramón 7.4.2.1–7.4.3.3, amphorae **164**, **166**, 177, **181**, 182; *Col. Pl. 17.7*
Ramón 7.5.2.1, amphorae **164**, **166**, 177, **181**, 182; *Col. Pl. 17.8*

Ramón 7.6.1.1, amphorae **164**, **166**, 177, **181**, 182
Ramón 10.1.2.1 amphorae 212 n. 260
red-figured pottery, Sicilian 67–8, **69**, 71, 193, **194**, 222 n. 27, 224 n. 88, 225 n. 97; *Col. Pls 10 and 16*
Republican period 10–11, 22, 24–5, 30, 36, 65, 75, 77–8, 81–2, 84, 108, 118, 122, 130, 132, 135–8, 140–1, 143, 146, 148–9, 167, 205 n. 108, 209 n. 68, 212 n. 100, 224 n. 89
Republican red-gloss, pottery 81, 195, **196**, 214 n. 217
reuse, of amphorae 164–5, 167, 216 n. 308, 219 n. 468;
  of cistern 210 n. 96
Rhegion (Reggio Calabria) 3
Rhodes, Rhodian, wine amphorae of **78, 83**, 84, 109, 118, **163, 166**, 177, 183, **184**, 215 nn. 243 and 255
Rhône, river 86, 94, 96
Richborough 527, amphorae **87**, 91, 112, 164, **165**
road, roads 3, 25, 29–34, 128, 131, 146, 206 nn. 10 and 26
Roccagloriosa (Calabria) 72, 116, 221 nn. 19 and 21
Roman, Romans 3, 5, 11–13, 15, 17, 19–27, 29–31, 33–5, 37–9, 41–2, 46, 48–53, 56, 73, 75–6, 82, 84, 86–7, 89–90, 92, 95–6, 106, 108–09, 113, 116, 118–21, 124, 146–50, 162, 164, 167;
  coinage 103–05;
  late Roman 25, 63–4, 110
Rome 12, 15, 17, 20–1, 23, 27, 29, 31–2, 34–6, 38, 50, 73, 85–6, 88–9, 92–4, 96–8, **99**, 100, 102–04, 106, 112, 120, 122–3, 125, 132–41, **142**, 143–50, 168, **169**, **174–5**, 203 n. 11, 209 n. 68, 218 n. 391, 222 n. 5, 225 n. 126, 226 nn. 141, 151 and 180, 227 n. 205;
  response to demands of 225 nn. 111 and 121
roof-tile **60**, 61, 63, 75, 88–9, 130, 160
Rostovtzeff, Mikhail, historian 125, 225 n. 114
rural, ruralisation **4**, 19–20, 23, 25–7, 39, 218 n. 388;
  settlements 204 n. 67, 209 n. 30

Sagalassos, in Turkey 208, n. 113
Salso, river, river valley 31, 204 n. 52
salted fish 27, 39, 41, 87–8, 111–12, 119, 121, 126, 136, 149, 216 n. 298, 221 n. 11
Samian, Samians 3–4, 6, 8, 129, 134 (*see also* Samos)
Samos, in Greece 3
Sanfratellani, horse-breed **39**
San Fratello **15**, 39, 204 n. 61
San Giovenale, survey of 176
San Marco d'Alunzio (*see also* Haluntium) 5, **14–15**, 23–4, 68, 71, 73–4, 90, 101, 222 n. 34; *Col. Pl. 9*;
  temple at *Col. Pl. 8*
San Vito lo Capo 41, 72
Sant'Agata di Militello 34
Sardinia 70, 72
Schöne-Mau 13 / Pompeii 13, amphorae **93**, 94–5, **163, 166**, **188**, 189, 216 n. 288
Scipio, C. Asiaticus, *denarius* of 103
Scipio, L. Cornelius, governor 141
Secca di Capistello, shipwreck 71–3
Segesta 38, 68, 88, 118, 211 nn. 9, 50 and 54, 215 n. 271, 218 nn. 384 and 410
Septimius Severus, Emperor 99, 137
settlement, settlements 3–11, 13, 15–17, 19–21, 23–8, 65–8, 70–1, 73, 75, 86, 88, 90, 94, 99, 101, 103, 105, 107, 110–11, 114, 124, 139, 141–51, 160–1, 165
Severan period 222 n. 57
sheep 38–39, **40**, 208 n. 94
ships, shipping 3, 5–6, 21, 34–5, 38, 122, 127, 134–7, 141, 144–5, 147–9, 206 n. 37, 223 n. 28;
  building of 38, 130, 207 n. 78
shipwrecks 67, 71–2, 77–80, 84–6, 88, 92–4, 99, 100–03, **121**, 122–4, 133, 145, 165, 211 n. 10, 215 n. 261, 216 nn. 282 and 308, 219 n. 461, 222 nn. 49 and 53
Sikel, Sikels 1, 3–13, 15–17, 19, 30–1, 33, 42, 44–5, 48, 67, 115, 128–30, 134, 139, 148–9, 208 n. 15, 211 n. 28, 204 nn. 36 and 38;
  and wine drinking 223 n. 60;
  cities of 226 n. 184;
  coastal sites of 223 n. 51;
  imported amphorae at sites of 223–4 n. 67;
  settlements of 203 nn. 11, 23 and 26
Sikel-Greek 45
Sikelia 36
Silenos of Kale Akte 12, 49, 204 n. 51
silenus 19, 49, 76;
  coin depicting 207 n. 62
Silius Italicus, poet 41, 88
Simeto river 31
Solunto, Soluntum 21, 39, 41, 52, 70–1, 73, 76, 79, 88, 90, 115, 119, 216 n. 318, 218 n. 384, 221 n. 21, 222 n. 22, 226, n. 184;
  pottery at 217 n. 358
Solusapre 33, 209 n. 30
Soprintendenza, of Messina 1, 42, 53–4, 160
Soprintendenza, of Syracuse 53
Spain, Spanish 34–5, 37, 70, 78, 82, 85–7, 89, 91–3, 100, 109, 112, 115, 119–20, 122–3, 133–4, 136, 141–2, 164–5, 206 n. 37, 213 n. 155, 218 n. 397, 220 n. 505, 221 n. 10, 224 n. 95;
  mackerel from 208 n. 113
  oil export from 226 nn. 161 and 166;
  olive growing in 225 n. 108;
  wines from 222 n. 50, 225 n. 114
spatula, spatulae 160
Spina 227 n. 184
state 106, 125–43, 226 nn. 133, 140 and 165–6, 227 n. 185;
  state control 223 n. 16, 225 nn. 115 and 119
statio 50–1, 63–4, 105
statue, statues **46–9**, 209 nn. 33–4
statuette 49
stenopos, stenopoi 44–5, 50
Sthenius of Thermae 51
Strabo, geographer 25
street 25, 44–6, 48;
  street-grid 7, 10, 42, 45, 203 n. 25;
  of Kale Akte *Col. Pl. 6*
sundial 46, **47**, 209 n. 33
swine (pig) 29, 208 n. 101
Sybaris, wine of 224 n. 89, 227 n. 190
symposion 19, 224 n. 90
Syracusae (Syracuse) 31 (*see also* Syracuse)
Syracuse, Syracusans 8–13, 15–17, 19–21, 23, 25, 31, 33, 38, 44, 48, 67, 70, 79, 84, 91, 95, **103**, 113, 118, 120, 204 nn. 36 and 38, 214 n. 172, 215 nn. 271–2, 217 n. 358, 218 n. 384, 220 n. 543, 224 n. 79;
  empire of 207 n. 43, 226 n. 184;
  kingdom of 35, 127, 134–5, 138–41, 143;
  mint of 3;
  role in foundation of Kale Akte 203 n. 35
Syria, Syrian 95, 113, 119

taberna 58, 61, 225 n. 106
Tabula Peutingeriana, map 12, **33**
Tabulae Halaesinae 20, 38, 207 n. 74
Taormina (*see also* Tauromenion, Tauromenium) 85, 92, 218 n. 384;
  Naumachia at 209 n. 68;
  wine of 207 n. 59, 216 n. 288
Tauromenion (Taormina, Tauromenium) 21, 71;
  coinage of 103, 207 n. 57
Tauromenium, wine 131 (*see also* Taormina, wine of)
tax, taxation 17, 23–4, 126–7, 129, 135, 137–9, 141, 145, 147–9, 223 n. 14, 225–6 n. 133,

227 n. 185
Terina 227 n. 184
Termini Imerese 151/354, amphorae 63, 86, 88–9, **95–7,** 98, **99**, 108, 111, 120–1, 146, 161–2, **163–4**;
thin-section of **169, 175**, 210 n. 102, 218 n. 439, 219 nn. 453, 461 and 467, 225 n. 101
Termini Imerese (Thermae Himeraeae) 72, 87–9, 95–7, 99, 110, 114, 116, 118–20, 123, 211 n. 9, 218 n. 384, 227 n. 11 (*see also* Termini Imerese 151/354, amphorae)
terracotta figurines **76–7**, 160, 213 n. 151
terra sigillata, pottery 22, 66, 141, 119, 209 n. 56, 217 n. 343;
Eastern 81, 95, 119, 147, 195, **196**, 218 n. 437;
Italian 50, 59, 89–90, 106, 113, 123–4, 197, **198**;
Sicilian 91;
South Gaulish 94, 119, 123, 147, 197, **198**;
stamps on 90–1, 94;
'Tripolitanian' (Campanian) 147, 197, **198**
Terrasini A, shipwreck 92
Tetricus, usurper, coins of 105
Theodosius II, Emperor 96
theoroi, from Delphi 32–3, 206 n. 18
Thermae Himeraeae (Termini Imerese) 21, 64, 206 n. 18, 226 n. 184
thermopolium 58, 61
thin-section analysis, of amphorae 65, 72, 79, 81, 83, 86, 88–9, 97–8, 100, 146, 163–5, **168–76**
thin-walled ware 91, 197, **198**
timber 20, 34, 38, 75, 128, 130, 207 n. 77, 224 n. 71
Timoleon 16;
symmachia of 15
Tindari (Tyndaris) 3, 25, **47**, 52, 66, 70–2, 76, 81, 85–6, 90, 92, 94–5, 101, 118, 209 n. 57, 211 nn. 16, 54 and 57;
amphorae at 212 n. 65, 213 n. 16, 215 n. 279, 216 n. 294;
pottery at 214 nn. 188 and 207, 217 n. 360, 218 n. 384, 220 nn. 514 and 516
tithe (*see also decuma*) 135–9, 141, 206 n. 29, 207 nn. 43 and 45
tituli picti 87, 93, 102, 109, 164, 208 n. 113, 213 n. 160, 216 nn. 288 and 315, 221 n. 2, 226 n. 162
tomb, tombs 27, 48, 53, 64, 92, 204 n. 56, 211 nn. 28 and 50, 212 n. 65, 223 n. 60, 224 n. 90
tonnara 88;
at Caronìa 41
Tonnara del Cofano 72
Torrente di Caronìa, river 20, **30**, 31, 89; *Col. Pl. 3*
Torrente Furiano 12
trading-post, at Kale Akte 4, 13, 42, 128, 144, 146, 148
transhumance 30, 38
trazzera, trazzere 27, 30–1, 39
Tripolitanian amphorae 222 n. 53
Tripolitanian 1, amphorae 83, **93**, 94, 102, **163, 166**
Tripolitanian 2/3, amphorae **100**, 102, 147, 161, **163, 166**
Tripolitanian *sigillata* 90, 147
Troina (Engyon?) 16, 68, 94, 211 n. 49, 218 n. 384
Trojans 204 n. 57
tuna, tuna-fish 27–8, 39, **41**, 87–8, 111–12, 119, 121, 136, 208 n. 113, 212 n. 94;
vendor of *Col. Pl. 16*
Tunisia, Tunisian 72, 82, 88, 94, 99, 100–01, 103, 124, 132, 136–7, 141, 161–2, 164–5, **166**, 168, **169**
tunny (*see also* tuna, tuna-fish) 41, 149
Tusa 13, 17, 72, 205 n. 84
Tusa, river 206 n. 31
Tyndaris (Tindari) 3, 13, 16, 20–1, 25, 49, 80, 139, 204 nn. 49 and 66;
coinage of, 50, 207 n. 57;
fish of 208 nn. 110 and 119;
foundation of 226 n. 184
Tyrrhenian Sea 68, 71, 74, 77, 89, 114, 116, 118, 122, 125, 130, 138–42, 221 n. 19, 226 n. 184

Umbria 141, **142**
urban, urbanisation 1, 3, 6–7, 11, 13, 15–17, 19–21, 23–7, 203 nn. 11 and 26, 208 n. 15

Valentinian and Gratian, Emperors, edict of 138
Valentinian III, Emperor 64
Vandal, Vandals 64, 99, 150, 219 n. 462
Verres, Caius, governor 12, 21, 35, 38–9, 137, 206 n. 29
via Pompeia 33
via Selinuntina 33
via Valeria 12, 24, 29–30, 33, 51, 62
Victoria (Nike), deity 73
vicus, of Marína di Caronía (*see also* Calacte, *statio*) 25–6, 97, 99, 131, 146, 150, 224 n. 81
villa, villas 27, 51, 146, 215 n. 282, 225 nn. 101 and 114;
at Capo d'Orlando 24;
at Halaesa 26;
at Patti Marina 220 n. 516;
at Piazza Armerina 63;
near Caronía 206 n. 139;
of Campania 225 n. 97
Vis, in Croatia (Issa), island 84, 105, 215 n. 261
viticulture 28, 35–6, 131, 141, 225 n. 114;
and coinage 207 nn. 56 and 59, 221 n. 3

Weber, Max, sociologist 125–6, 138
wheat 19, 23, 72, 207 n. 39
wine, wines 20, 27, 61, 64–7, 70–2, 74, 77–9, 81–6, 88–9, 92–6, 98–9, 102, 105–07, **108**, 109–11, 114, 116, 118–21, 123–4, 126–7, 130–43, 145–50, 162, **163**, 164–5, 212 n. 100, 213 n. 160, 216 n. 307, 219 n. 461, 221 n. 4;
Adriatic 206 n. 37, 215 n. 261;
demand for 223 n. 60, 224 n. 89;
export of Campanian and Italian 206 n. 37, 213 nn. 154 and 160, 224 nn. 78–9 and 95, 225 nn. 114, 121 and 130;
from Taormina 216 n. 288;
from Issa (Vis) 215 nn. 261 and 268;
of Kale Akte 226 n. 152;
production of Locri 227 nn. 184 and 190;
use of 221 n. 7;
western Greek production 224 n. 89, 227 nn. 184 and 190;
wine-related games 224 n. 90
wool 38, 130, 208 n. 95

Xenophon, historian 127
Xerxes of Persia, Great King 38

Zancle (Messina, Messana), Zancleans 3–4, 6, 13, 128, 149, 203 n. 18
Zeus, deity, cult of 50;
coins depicting 204 n. 60;
oracle of at Dodona 8;
Zeus Eleutherios, cult of 50;
Zeus Meilichios, cult of 49